The International Survey of Family Law

2014 Edition

The International Survey of Family Law

Published on behalf of the International Society of Family Law

2014 Edition

General Editor
Bill Atkin
Faculty of Law
Victoria University of Wellington
PO Box 600
Wellington
New Zealand

Associate Editor (Africa)
Fareda Banda
Reader in the Laws of Africa
School of Oriental and African Studies
London

Family Law

Published by Family Law
a publishing imprint of
Jordan Publishing Limited
21 St Thomas Street
Bristol BS1 6JS

British Library Cataloguing-in-Publication Data

A catalogue record for this book is available from the British Library.

ISBN 978 1 84661 991 5

Typeset by Letterpart Limited, Caterham on the Hill, Surrey CR3 5XL

Printed in Great Britain by Hobbs the Printers Limited, Totton, Hampshire SO40 3WX

CONTENTS

THE INTERNATIONAL SOCIETY OF FAMILY LAW – MEMBERS

ASSOCIATION INTERNATIONALE DE DROIT DE LA FAMILLE
INTERNATIONALE GESELLSCHAFT FÜR FAMILIENRECHT

Website: www.law2.byu.edu/ISFL

Officers and Council Members 2012-2016

PRESIDENT
Professor Patrick Parkinson
Faculty of Law
University of Sydney
SYDNEY 2006
AUSTRALIA
Tel: +61 2 9351 0309
Fax: +61 2 9351 0200
E-mail: patrickp@law.usyd.edu.au

EDITOR OF THE INTERNATIONAL SURVEY
Professor Bill Atkin
Faculty of Law
Victoria University of Wellington
PO Box 600
Wellington
NEW ZEALAND
Tel: +64 04 463 6343
Fax: +64 04 463 6366
E-mail: bill.atkin@vuw.ac.nz

TREASURER
Professor Adriaan van der Linden
Beetslaan 2
3818 VH Aersfoort
THE NETHERLANDS
Tel: +31 33 461 90 97
Fax: +31 33 465 94 29
E-mail: a.vanderlinden@law.uu.nl

SECRETARY-GENERAL
Professor Marsha Garrison
Brooklyn Law School
250 Joralemon Street
Brooklyn, NY 11201
USA
Tel: +1 718 780 7947
Fax: +1 718 780 0375
E-mail: marsha.garrison@brooklaw.edu

EDITOR OF THE NEWSLETTER
Professor Margaret F Brinig
Fritz Duda Family Professor of Law
University of Notre Dame
Box 780, 3157 Eck Hall of Law
Notre Dame, IN 46556
USA
Tel: +1 574 631 2303
Fax: +1 574 631 3595
Email: mbrinig@nd.edu

Immediate past president

Professor Dr Bea Verschraegen LLM, MEM
Abteilung für Rechtsvergleichung
Universität Wien – Juridicum
Schottenbastei 10-16
A-1010 Wien
AUSTRIA
Tel: +43 1 4277 35102
Fax: +43 1 4277 9351
E-mail: bea.verschraegen@univie.ac.at

Vice presidents

Professor Olga Dyuzheva
Law Faculty
Moscow State University (Lomonosov)
Moscow 119991
RUSSIA
Tel: +7 495 939 5153
Fax: +7 495 939 5195
E-mail: odyuzheva@gmail.com

Professor Hugues Fulchiron
Faculté de Droit
Université Jean Moulin
Lyon 3, 15 quai Claude-Bernard
F-69007 Lyon
FRANCE
Tel: +33 4 72 41 05 54
Fax: +33 4 78 78 71 31
E-mail: hugues.fulchiron@online.fr

Professor Dominique Goubau
Faculté de droit de l'Université Laval
Québec QUE
G1V 0A6
CANADA
Tel: +1 418 656 2131 (#2384)
Fax: +1 418 656 7230
E-mail: Dominique.goubau@fd.ulaval.ca

Professor Giselle Groeninga
Rua Professor Artur Ramos 241 #93
São Paulo SP 01454-030
BRAZIL
Tel: +55 11 30315320
Fax: +55 11 30315320
E-mail: giselle@groeninga.com.br

Professor Satoshi Minimakata
Faculty of Law
Niigata University
8050 Ikarashi-ninocho
Nishi-ku
Niigata
JAPAN 950-2181
Tel: +25 262 6522 or 6478
Fax: +25 262 5435
E-mail: satoshi@jura.niigata-u.ac.jp

Professor June D Sinclair
PO Box 651479
Benmore 2010
SOUTH AFRICA
Tel: +27 82 900 8690
E-mail: june.sinclair@up.ac.za

Executive council

Professor Penelope Agallopoulou
University of Piraeus
4 Kyprou Str
154 52 P Psychico
Athens
GREECE
Tel/Fax: +30 210 67 75 404
E-mail: agal@otenet.gr

Professor Dr MV Antokolskaia
VU University Amsterdam
Faculty of Law
De Boelelaan 1105
1081 HV Amsterdam
THE NETHERLANDS
Tel: +31 20 5986294
Fax: +31 20 5986280
E-mail: m.v.antokolskaia@rechten.vu.nl

Associate Professor Datin Noor Aziah Mohd Awal
Faculty of Law
Universiti Kebangsaan Malaysia
43600 Bangi
Selangor
MALAYSIA
Tel: +60 3 89215921
Fax: +60 3 89215117
E-mail: naha@pkrisc.cc.ukm.my

Peter Barth
Federal Ministry of Justice
Museumstraße 7
1070 Wien
AUSTRIA
Tel: +43 1 52152 2069
Fax: +43 1 52152 2829
E-Mail: peter.barth@bmj.gv.at

Dr Ursula Cristina Bassett
Faculty of Law
Pontificia Universidad Católica Argentina
Santa María de los Buenos Aires
Alicia Moreau de Justo 1400
Buenos Aires
ARGENTINA
Tel: +54 005411 43490200
E-mail: ubassett@uca.edu.ar

Professor Dr Nina Dethloff LLM
Institut für Deutsches, Europäisches und Internationales Familienrecht
Universität Bonn
Adenauerallee 8a
D 53113 Bonn
GERMANY
Tel: +49 228 739290
Fax: +49 228 733909
E-mail: dethloff@uni-bonn.de

Dr Piotr Fiedorczyk
Faculty of Law
University of Bialystok
15-213 Bialystok
Ul Mickiewicza 1
POLAND
Tel: + 48 85 7457146
E-mail: fiedorczyk@tlen.pl

Professor Sanford N Katz
Boston College Law School
885 Centre Street
Newton Centre, Mass 02459
USA
Tel: +1 617 552 437
Fax: +1 617 552 2615
E-mail: sanford.katz@bc.edu

Professor Olga A Khazova
Institute of State and Law
Russian Academy of Sciences
Znamenka Str 10
119992 Moscow
RUSSIA
Tel: +7 495 691 1709
Fax: +7 495 691 8574
E-mail: o.khazova@gmail.com

Associate Professor Zdeńka Králíčková
Faculty of Law
Masaryk Univerzity
Veveří 70
611 80 Brno
CZECH REPUBLIC
Tel:+420 723 727 060
Fax:+420 549 49 7926
E-mail: zdenka.kralickova@law.muni.cz

Professor Nigel Lowe
Cardiff Law School
University of Wales
PO Box 427
Cardiff CF10 3XJ
UK
Tel: +44 029 20 874365
Fax: +44 029 20 874097
E-mail: lowe@cardiff.ac.uk

Professor Dr Miquel Martin-Casals
Facultat de Dret
Universitat de Girona
Campus de Montilivi 17071
Girona
SPAIN
Tel: +34 972 41 81 39
Fax: +34 972 41 81 46
E-mail: martin@elaw.udg.edu

Professor Marie-Therese Meulders
29, Chaussee de la verte voie
1300 Wavre
BELGIUM
Tel: +32 10 24 78 92
Fax: +32 10 22 91 60
E-mail: meulders@cfap.ucl.ac.be

Professor Jo Miles
Trinity College
Cambridge
CB2 1TQ
UK
Tel: +44 1223 339922
Fax: +44 1223 338564 [FAO Jo Miles]
E-mail: jkm33@cam.ac.uk

Professor Linda Nielsen
Copenhagen University
Faculty of Law
Studiegården, Studiestræde 6
1455 Copenhagen K
DENMARK
Tel: +45 35 32 31 23
Fax: +45 35 32 32 06
E-mail: Linda.Nielsen@jur.ku.dk

Professor Avv Maria Donata Panforti
Dipartimento di Scienze del linguaggio e della cultura
Largo Sant'Eufemia 19
I-41100 Modena
ITALY
Tel: +39 059 205 5916
Fax: +39 059 205 5933
E-mail: panforti.mariadonata@unimore.it

Professor JA Robinson
Faculty of Law
Room 8, Old Main Building
Potchefstroom Campus of the North West University
Potchefstroom 2520
SOUTH AFRICA
Tel: +27 18 299 1940
Fax: +27 18 299 1933

Professor Carol Rogerson
Faculty of Law
University of Toronto
78 Queen's Park
Toronto M5S 2C5
CANADA
Tel: +1 416 978 2648
Fax: +1 416 978 3715

Professor Anna Singer
Uppsala University
Faculty of Law
PO Box 512
SE-751 20 Uppsala
SWEDEN
Tel: +46 18 471 20 35
Fax: +46 18 15 27 14
E-mail: anna.singer@jur.uu.se

Professor dr juris Tone Sverdrup
Department of Private Law
Faculty of Law, University of Oslo
PO Box 6706 St Olavs plass
NO-0130 Oslo
NORWAY
Tel: +47 22859781
Fax: +47 22859620
E-mail: tone.sverdrup@jus.uio.no

Professor Hazel Thompson-Ahye
Eugene Dupuch Law School
Farrington Road
PO Box SS-6394
Nassau, NP
THE BAHAMAS
Tel: +242-326-8507/8
Fax: +242-326-8504
E-mail: thomahye2000@yahoo.com

Professor Paul Vlaardingerbroek
Faculty of Law
Tilburg University
PO Box 90153
5000 LE Tilburg
NETHERLANDS
Tel: +31-013-466-2032/2281
Fax: +31-013-466-2323
E-mail: p.vlaardingerbroek@uvt.nl

Professor Lynn D Wardle
Bruce C Hafen Professor of Law
518 J Reuben Clark Law School
Brigham Young University
Provo, UT 84602
USA
Tel: +1 801 422 2617
Fax: +1 801 422 0391
E-mail: Wardlel@law.byu.edu

Professor Dr Jinsu Yune
School of Law, Seoul National University
599 Gwanak-ro, Gwanak-gu
Seoul, 151-743
Republic of Korea
Tel: +82 2 880 7599
Fax:+82 2 885 7584
E-mail: jsyune@snu.ac.kr

Professor Barbara Bennett Woodhouse
LQC Lamar Chair in Law
Co-Director of the Barton Child Law and Policy Clinic
Emory University
Gambrell Hall
1301 Clifton Road
Atlanta, GA
USA
Tel: +1 404 727 4934
Fax: +1 404 727 6820
E-mail: barbara.woodhouse@emory.edu

THE INTERNATIONAL SOCIETY OF FAMILY LAW – OVERVIEW

A THE HISTORY OF THE SOCIETY

On the initiative of Professor Zeev Falk, the Society was launched at the University of Birmingham, UK, in April 1973. The Society's first international conference was held in West Berlin in April 1975 on the theme *The Child and the Law*. There were over 200 participants, including representatives of governments and international organisations. The second international conference was held in Montreal in June 1977 on the subject *Violence in the Family*. There were over 300 participants from over 20 countries. A third world conference on the theme *Family Living in a Changing Society* was held in Uppsala, Sweden in June 1979. There were over 270 participants from 26 countries. The fourth world conference was held in June 1982 at Harvard Law School, USA. There were over 180 participants from 23 countries. The fifth world conference was held in July 1985 in Brussels, Belgium on the theme *The Family, The State and Individual Security*, under the patronage of Her Majesty Queen Fabiola of Belgium, the Director-General of UNESCO, the Secretary-General of the Council of Europe and the President of the Commission of the European Communities. The sixth world conference on *Issues of the Ageing in Modern Society* was held in 1988 in Tokyo, Japan, under the patronage of HIH Takahito Mikasa. There were over 450 participants. The seventh world conference was held in May 1991 in Croatia on the theme, *Parenthood: The Legal Significance of Motherhood and Fatherhood in a Changing Society*. There were 187 participants from 37 countries. The eighth world conference took place in Cardiff, Wales in June/July 1994 on the theme *Families Across Frontiers*. The ninth world conference of the Society was held in July 1997 in Durban, South Africa on the theme *Changing Family Forms: World Themes and African Issues*. The Society's tenth world conference was held in July 2000 in Queensland, Australia on the theme *Family Law: Processes, Practices and Pressures*. The eleventh world conference was held in August 2002 in Copenhagen and Oslo on the theme *Family Life and Human Rights*. The Society's twelfth world conference was held in Salt Lake City, Utah in July 2005 on the theme *Family Law: Balancing Interests and Pursuing Priorities*. The Society's thirteenth world conference was held in Vienna in September 2008. The Society has also increasingly held regional conferences including those in Lyon, France (1995); Quebec City, Canada (1996); Seoul, South Korea (1996); Prague, Czech Republic (1998); Albuquerque, New Mexico, USA (June 1999); Oxford, UK (August 1999); and Kingston, Ontario (2001). In 2003, regional conferences took place in Oregon, USA; Tossa de Mar, Spain; and Lyon, France and, in July 2004, in Beijing, China, on the theme 'Divorce and its Consequences'. In 2005, a regional conference took place in Amsterdam (the Netherlands) and dealt with the centennial anniversary of the establishment of legislation on child protection and the juvenile courts. In 2007 there were regional conferences in Chester (England), entitled 'Family Justice: For Whom and How?' and Vancouver (Canada), entitled 'Making Family Law: Facts, Values and Practicalities'. In 2009 there were conferences in Tel Aviv (Israel), Porto (Portugal) and Sao Paolo (Brazil), and in 2010 Kansas City (USA), Tsukuba University (Japan), the University of Ulster (Northern Ireland) and the Caribbean. There has since been a world conference in Lyon (France) in July 2011 and regional conferences in Iowa City in June 2012, Israel in December 2012, Brooklyn in New York in June 2013, Seoul, South Korea in October 2013, and Israel in January 2014. The next world conference will be in Recife, Brazil from 6 to 9 August 2014.

B ITS NATURE AND OBJECTIVES

The following principles were adopted at the first Annual General Meeting of the Society held in the Kongresshalle of West Berlin on the afternoon of Saturday 12 April 1975.

(1) The Society's objectives are the study and discussion of problems of family law. To this end the Society sponsors and promotes:

   (a) International co-operation in research on family law subjects of worldwide interest.
   (b) Periodic international conferences on family law subjects of worldwide interest.
   (c) Collection and dissemination of information in the field of family law by the publication of a survey concerning developments in family law throughout the world, and by publication of relevant materials in family law, including papers presented at conferences of the Society.
   (d) Co-operation with other international, regional or national associations having the same or similar objectives.
   (e) Interdisciplinary contact and research.
   (f) The advancement of legal education in family law by all practical means including furtherance of exchanges of teachers, students, judges and practising lawyers.
   (g) Other objectives in furtherance of or connected with the above objectives.

C MEMBERSHIP AND DUES

In 2011 the Society had approximately 630 members.

(a) Membership:

- Ordinary Membership, which is open to any member of the legal or a related profession. The Council may defer or decline any application for membership.
- Institutional Membership, which is open to interested organisations at the discretion of, and on terms approved by, the Council.
- Student Membership, which is open to interested students of law and related disciplines at the discretion of, and on terms approved by, the Council.
- Honorary Membership, which may be offered to distinguished persons by decision of the Executive Council.

(b) Each member shall pay such annual dues as may be established from time to time by the Council. At present, dues for ordinary membership are €50 (or equivalent) for one year, €120 (or equivalent) for 3 years and €180 (or equivalent) for 5 years, plus €12.50 (or equivalent) if cheque is in another currency.

D DIRECTORY OF MEMBERS

A Directory of Members of the Society is available to all members.

E BOOKS

The proceedings of the first world conference were published as *The Child and the Law* (F Bates, ed, Oceana, 1976); the proceedings of the second as *Family Violence* (J Eekelaar and S Katz, eds, Butterworths, Canada, 1978); the proceedings of the third as *Marriage and Cohabitation* (J Eekelaar and S Katz, eds, Butterworths, Canada, 1980); the fourth, *The Resolution of Family Conflict* (J Eekelaar and S Katz, eds, Butterworths, Canada, 1984); the fifth, *Family, State and Individual Economic Security (Vols I & II)* (MT Meulders-Klein and J Eekelaar, eds, Story Scientia and Kluwer, 1988); the sixth, *An Ageing World: Dilemmas and Challenges for Law and Social Policy* (J Eekelaar and D Pearl, eds, Clarendon Press, 1989); the seventh *Parenthood in Modern Society* (J Eekelaar and P Sarcevic, eds, Martinus Nijhoff, 1993); the eighth *Families Across Frontiers* (N Lowe and G Douglas, eds, Martinus Nijhoff, 1996) and the ninth *The Changing Family: Family Forms and Family Law* (J Eekelaar and T Nhlapo, eds, Hart Publishing, 1998). The proceedings of the tenth world conference in Australia were published as *Family Law, Processes, Practices and Pressures* (J Dewar and S Parker, eds, Hart Publishing, 2003). The proceedings of the eleventh world conference in Denmark and Norway were published as *Family Life and Human Rights* (P Lødrup and E Modvar, eds, Gyldendal Akademisk, 2004). The proceedings of the twelfth world conference held in Salt Lake City, Utah have been published as *Family Law: Balancing Interests and Pursuing Priorities* (L Wardle and C Williams, eds, Wm S Hein & Co, 2007). The proceedings of the thirteenth world conference held in Vienna in 2008 have been published as *Family Finances* (B Verschraegen, ed, Jan Sramek Verlag, 2009) and those of the world conference held in Lyon in 2011 in Hugues Fulchiron (ed) *Les solidarités entre générations/Solidarity between generations* (Bruylant, Brussels, 2013). These proceedings are commercially marketed but are available to Society members at reduced prices.

F THE SOCIETY'S PUBLICATIONS

The Society regularly publishes a newsletter, *The Family Letter*, which appears twice a year and which is circulated to the members of the Society and reports on its activities and other matters of interest. *The International Survey of Family Law* provides information on current developments in family law throughout the world and is received free of charge by members of the Society. The editor is currently Bill Atkin, Faculty of Law, Victoria University of Wellington, PO Box 600, Wellington, New Zealand 6140. The Survey is circulated to members or may be obtained on application to the Editor.

PREFACE

We sometimes ask what the purpose of family law is. Is it to control how we live? Is it to empower people? Is it to facilitate people as they sort out their personal lives? Is it to lay down sensible ground rules for personal relationships? Is it to reflect local culture and values? Is it to protect the vulnerable? Is it something else or a combination of a variety of things?

As I read the wonderful contributions that people make to the *International Survey*, I appreciate how significant family law is for much of our existence. I also realise how my own preconceptions about the purpose and shape of family law, largely established by the country where I live, are challenged by what is happening elsewhere in the world. I hope that others find the same as they read this edition of the Survey.

Many of the chapters are about children. Children are often especially vulnerable. So, we read about such children in Lesotho, alternative care in Mozambique, adoption in Solomon Islands, and child poverty in New Zealand. Issues relating to parental responsibility and joint custody arise in Germany, Italy and Switzerland. Pre-birth debates on matters such as abortion and surrogacy are occurring in Ireland and India. Empirical research on post-divorce relief in China is brought to our attention. Non-traditional families, such as unmarried couples, same-sex marriages and same-sex parenting, arise in the chapters on Brazil, Canada, England and Wales, France, the Netherlands, Puerto Rico, and the United States. Customary polygamy in Papua New Guinea and among the indigenous Mapuches of Chile is explored, plus the law of adultery in South Korea and male headship in Iran. Issues to do with transgender persons appear in Australia, Hong Kong and Japan. Property and financial topics are found by reading Australia, Kenya, Iran and Armenia, and Poland. The question of the impact of high level legislation on family law has become important: the 2013 Constitution in Zimbabwe and 2010 one in Kenya, and the inclusion of family law in the Civil Code in the Czech Republic and Macedonia.

We have a bumper edition this year. This is the result of the level of interest by people wishing to write for the Survey. After I added up, the number came to 46 when co-authors were all included. It does mean a lot of work. So, as always, generous thanks are owed to the publishers, including their fine editor, Cheryl Prophett, those who translate the abstracts into French – Dominique Goubau as well as the team at the Centre for Family Law, Lyon – Angela

Funnell, my administrative assistant who offers willing and expeditious help, referees for the small number of chapters that have to be reviewed, and all the authors. I also make special mention of my outstanding research assistant, Sean Brennan. It has been great working with him: he will make a fantastic contribution as a lawyer in the years ahead.

Bill Atkin
General Editor
Wellington, New Zealand
June 2014

INTERNATIONAL SOCIETY OF FAMILY LAW
SUBSCRIPTION FORM

☐ I prefer to communicate in ☐ English ☐ French

☐ Please charge my credit card ☐ **MASTERCARD or EUROCARD** ☐ **VISA or JCB**

☐ Subscription for 1 year €50

☐ Subscription for 3 years €120

☐ Subscription for 5 years €180

Name of Card Holder: ____________________

Card no. |_|_|_|_| |_|_|_|_| |_|_|_|_| |_|_|_|_|

CVC-code (three figures at the back of your card behind the 16 figures): |_|_|_|

Expiry date: ____/____

Address of Card Holder: ____________________

____

☐ I pay by *postgiro* to ***63.18.019*** €180[1] for 5 years, €120 for 3 years or €50 for one year, ***plus €12.50*** **if cheque in another currency** (from)

The International Society of Family Law,
Beetslaan 2
3818 VH Amersfoort
The Netherlands

(We have a bank account at the Postbank, Amsterdam, The Netherlands. The IBAN code is: NL22 PSTB 0006 3180 19; BIC: PSTBNL21)

☐ Payment enclosed *by cheque* to the amount of €180[1] for 5 years, €120 for 3 years or €50 for one year, ***plus €12.50*** **if cheque in another currency**.

Date: ____________________ Signature: ____________________

☐ *New member, or*

☐ *(Change of) name/address:* ____________________

____

Tel: ____________________

Fax: ____________________

E-mail: ____________________

Comments: ____________________

____

To be sent to the treasurer of the ISFL:
Dr Adriaan van der Linden, International Society of Family Law
Beetslaan 2, 3818 VH Amersfoort
THE NETHERLANDS (or by fax: +31-33-4659429;
E-mail address: a.p.vanderlinden@uu.nl)
Website ISFL: http://www.law2.byu.edu/ISFL

[1] Or its *counter*value in US dollars.

ASSOCIATION INTERNATIONALE DE DROIT DE LA FAMILLE FORMULAIRE DE COTISATION

☐ Je désire de communiquer ☐ en français ☐ en anglais

☐ Je vous prie de charger ma carte de crédit: ☐ **MASTERCARD/EUROCARD** ☐ **VISA/JCB**

☐ Souscription pour une année €50

☐ Souscription pour trois années €120

☐ Souscription pour cinq années €180

Le nom du possesseur de la carte de crédit: ____________________

Carte no |_|_|_|_| |_|_|_|_| |_|_|_|_| |_|_|_|_|

CVC-code (trois numéros sur l'arrière-coté de votre carte) |_|_|_|

Date d'expiration: ____ / ____

L'adresse du possesseur de la carte de crédit: ____________________

____

☐ Je payerai par postgiro à ***63.18.019*** €180[1] pour 5 ans ou €120 pour 3 ans ou €50 pour 1 an, ***plus €12.50*** **surcharge si paiement est un autre cours,**

(du) International Society of Family Law
Beetslaan 2
3818 VH Amersfoort
Les Pays-Bas
(Nous avons un crédit au Postbank, Amsterdam, les Pays-Bas. Le *code IBAN* est: *NL22 PSTB 0006 3180 19; BIC: PSTBNL21*)

☐ Paiement est inclus avec un chèque de €180[1] pour 5 ans ou €120 pour 3 ans ou €50 pour 1 an, ***plus €12.50*** **surcharge si paiement est un autre cours**.

La date: ____________ Souscription: ____________

☐ *Nouveau membre, ou*

☐ *(Changement de) nom/adresse:* ____________________

____

Tel: ____________________

Fax: ____________________

E-mail: ____________________

Remarques: ____________________

____

Veuillez envoyer ce formulaire au trésorier de l'Association:
Dr Adriaan van der Linden, International Society of Family Law
Beetslaan 2, 3818 VH Amersfoort
LES PAYS BAS (ou par fax: +31-33-4659429;
E-mail address: a.p.vanderlinden@uu.nl)
Website ISFL: http://www.law2.byu.edu/ISFL

[1] Ou la *contre*valeur en US dollars.

AUSTRALIA

GENDER IDENTITY DYSPHORIA UPDATE AND DEVELOPMENTS IN PROPERTY SETTLEMENT LAW

*Lisa Young**

Résumé

Ce chapitre fait d'abord le point sur la question du traitement des enfants atteints de dysphorie de genre, thème qui a déjà été analysé dans la contribution australienne dans l'édition 2013. Depuis, il a été jugé qu'il n'est pas nécessaire pour le tribunal d'autoriser le «traitement de niveau 1», qui implique un traitement par médication et réversible, mais qu'il faut plutôt passer par le «traitement de niveau 2». Le niveau 2 est irréversible et nécessite l'évaluation de la capacité de l'enfant à consentir au traitement. Ensuite, le chapitre explore la jurisprudence en matière de partage des biens matrimoniaux et s'intéresse particulièrement aux affaires qui impliquent d'importantes fortunes. Une question qui a divisé les tribunaux est celle de l'impact que peuvent avoir les «compétences particulières» d'une partie sur le résultat du partage.

I INTRODUCTION

As noted at the end of the Australian chapter in the 2013 edition of the *International Survey*,[1] aside from the extension of the law to cover de facto couples, there has been little recent legislative appetite to change the basic approach to resolving family law property disputes in Australia. However, recent case-law is raising questions about whether there needs to be some refining of the very general provisions in the Family Law Act 1975 (Cth) (FLA).

Australia has a separate property regime, with the family courts having the power to alter the property interests of married and de facto (including same-sex) partners. Under FLA, s 79(1)[2] a court 'may make such order as it considers appropriate'. The next relevant subsection says the 'court shall not

* Associate Professor, School of Law, Murdoch University, Western Australia. I would like to thank Professor Robyn Carroll for her comments on a draft of this chapter.

1 Lisa Young 'New Frontiers for Family Law' in B Atkin (ed) *The International Survey of Family Law 2013 Edition* (Jordan Publishing Ltd, Bristol, 2013) at 81–82.

2 The provisions referred to relate to married persons; for the substantially similar de facto provisions see FLA, Pt VIII AB.

make an order under this section unless it is satisfied that, in all the circumstances, it is just and equitable to make the order': s 79(2). Section 79(4) then sets out a list of mandatory considerations when making (or not making) an order altering property interests, that relevantly includes:

- direct and indirect, financial and non-financial, contributions of the parties to the acquisition, conservation or improvement of property; and
- contributions made to the welfare of the family (meaning the parties and their children) including any homemaker and parent contributions.

Thus, it can be seen the legislation provides little in the way of prescription as to how matters should be determined or relative contributions weighed. As is to be expected, the case-law has therefore developed a range of principles that give more shape to the exercise of this broad discretion. One example was the Full Court adoption of a four-step approach to resolving property disputes: *Hickey v Hickey*.[3] However, the High Court decision in *Stanford v Stanford*[4] has created uncertainty as to whether the process required is in fact different, and the extent to which that might (or should) affect outcomes.

Another area where the Full Court has developed jurisprudence influencing the exercise of discretion is so-called 'big money cases'. If a partner can show they have exercised some sort of special skill (or made a special contribution) then they can expect a weighting on their contribution; this rule is routinely applied in favour of 'breadwinner' spouses who have accumulated very significant assets during the relationship. This principle, which has no direct statutory basis, has also come under recent judicial scrutiny.

In this chapter, both of these developments in property settlement law are considered in detail and some comment is made on the question of whether, as in the area of child-related proceedings in Australia,[5] it is time for greater legislative direction. However, before turning to those issues, it is timely to report on the outcome of the Full Court appeal in *Re Jamie*.[6] Last year's Australian chapter in the 2013 edition of the *International Survey* considered the question of whether treatment of children for gender identity dysphoria (GID)[7] should require family court approval, as a 'special medical procedure'. It was noted that an appeal was pending in the case of *Re Jamie* which would directly challenge the accepted legal position that parental authority did not

---

3 [2003] FLC 93-143.

4 [2012] HCA 52; [2012] FLC 93-495.

5 The FLA has considerably more prescription when it comes to resolving parenting disputes: FLA, Pt VII. This is discussed in more detail in Lisa Young 'Reflections on the Shared Parenting Experience' in B Atkin (ed) *The International Survey of Family Law 2012 Edition* (Jordans Publishing Ltd, Bristol, 2012).

6 [2013] FamCAFC 110.

7 There are good reasons for not adopting a title that pathologises the situation these children find themselves in, however, as the Full Court adopted this terminology it has been used here.

extend to cover such treatment. Last year's chapter can be consulted for the detailed background to the case.[8] However, a brief introduction is provided.

II SPECIAL MEDICAL PROCEDURES AND GENDER IDENTITY DYSPHORIA: AN UPDATE

Over 20 years ago, the Australian High Court held in *Re Marion* that the sterilisation of intellectually disabled girls is a 'special medical procedure' outside the scope of parental authority.[9] The High Court's reasoning was based on the following factors: (i) the non-therapeutic nature of the treatment, (ii) the procedure involved major, invasive and irreversible surgery, (iii) there was a significant risk of parents making a wrong decision either as to the child's capacity to consent or whether it was in the child's best interests to have the surgery, and (iv) the particularly grave consequences of a wrong decision. As discussed in detail in the 2013 Australian chapter of the *International Survey*,[10] the Family Court of Australia has subsequently held that the treatment of children for GID similarly requires court approval. It was argued in that chapter that the considerations which led the High Court to require court approval in the case of the sterilisation of intellectually disabled girls do not apply in the case of GID. Most particularly, whereas sterilisation in this situation involves a non-therapeutic treatment, and has the grave risk of parental interests conflicting with those of the child, the same cannot be said in either regard of GID. The question of whether treatment of children for GID is a special medical procedure has recently been considered by the Full Family Court in *Re Jamie*.

The Full Court has decided that court authorisation is required in respect of what is known as Stage 2 treatment, which is irreversible, to determine whether the child in question is '*Gillick*' competent.[11] Stage 1 treatment, which involves reversible drug treatment, can now proceed without court approval. Thus, Australia will remain the only country in the world that requires parents to meet the considerable expense of court proceedings when wishing their child to undertake Stage 2 treatment.[12]

How then did the Full Court reach this decision? The unanimous decision of Bryant CJ, Finn and Strickland JJ[13] was the subject of three separate judgments.

---

8 Young, above n 1, at 71ff.

9 *Department of Health & Community Services v JWB & SMB* [1992] HCA 15; (1992) 175 CLR 218; (1994) FLC 92-448 (*Re Marion*).

10 Lisa Young 'New Frontiers for Family Law' in B Atkin (ed) *The International Survey of Family Law 2013 Edition* (Jordans Publishing Ltd, Bristol, 2013) at 71ff.

11 Australia has followed the House of Lords decision in *Gillick v West Norfolk AHA* [1986] AC 112 to the effect that mature minors can have the capacity to consent (in this case to a medical procedure) according to the circumstances of a case.

12 J Hewitt, C Paul, P Kasiannan, S Grover, L Newman and G Warne, 'Hormone Treatment of Gender Identity Dysphoria in a Cohort of Children and Adolescents' (2012) 196 Med J Aust 578.

13 Delivered on 31 July 2013.

However, it is Bryant CJ's judgment which sets out the Court's reasoning in detail. Bryant CJ begins by characterising GID as a bodily malfunction or disease, a requirement for the application of the special medical procedure test as set out in *Re Marion*. Though recognising this is an uncomfortable conclusion for those who argue transsexualism is merely an example of 'diversity in human sexual formation, rather than ... a psychiatric condition',[14] her Honour held this must be the case based on the weight of medical opinion as expressed in DSM-IV and DSM-V, which both identify GID as a psychological condition.[15] As part of this discussion, Bryant CJ rejected the submission of the Australian Human Rights Commission (AHRC) (which was invited to intervene in *Re Jamie*) that Stage 2 should continue to be treated as a special medical procedure[16] because, unlike other psychological disorders, Stage 2 treatment sought not to address the underlying psychological issue but rather to alter permanently a healthy body to accord with the state of mind.[17]

Her Honour then turned to a detailed consideration of *Re Marion*,[18] concluding the majority decision in that case was confined to cases of sterilisation of minors incapable of consenting to the treatment.[19] The question therefore was, said her Honour, whether *Re Alex: Hormonal Treatment for Gender Identity Dysphoria*,[20] the Family Court decision of Nicholson CJ which extended the principle to GID, should be followed. Her Honour considered *Re Alex* technically distinguishable on its facts.[21] More importantly, however, as her Honour pointed out, in *Re Alex* the case was argued on the basis that the two stages of treatment should be considered as a single treatment plan, thus not allowing Nicholson CJ to distinguish between them. Bryant CJ said she 'could not be certain ... his Honour would have come to the same conclusion had he considered only stage one'.[22] This reasoning (that is, the fact the stages could be considered separately in *Re Jamie*) supported her divergence from the outcome in *Re Alex*.

As to the evidence itself and how it related to the test as set out in *Re Marion* and as applied in *Re Alex*, her Honour found that stage one treatment was therapeutic[23] and was not 'invasive, permanent and irreversible';[24] hence the finding that court authorisation was not required for Stage 1 treatment. There was, however, in her Honour's view a 'relevant distinction'[25] where Stage 2

---

14 [2013] FamCAFC 110 at [68].
15 Ibid at [69].
16 Ibid at [83]–[85].
17 Ibid at [66].
18 *Department of Health & Community Services v JWB & SMB* [1992] HCA 15; (1992) 175 CLR 218; (1994) FLC 92-448.
19 [2013] FamCAFC 110 at [74].
20 [2004] FamCA 297; (2004) FLC 93-175.
21 Because the applicant in that case was not a parent, but the government department that was acting as legal guardian: [2013] FamCAFC 110 at [77].
22 Ibid at [86].
23 Ibid at [98].
24 Ibid at [88].
25 Ibid at [111].

treatment was concerned, namely that the treatment was irreversible. Her Honour accepted that a *Gillick* competent child could consent to such a treatment.[26] However, the key issue in her Honour's mind was who should decide if a child was *Gillick* competent. After considering relevant articles from the Convention on the Rights of the Child,[27] Bryant CJ concluded '[w]ith some reluctance',[28] that she was bound by the High Court majority's statement in *Re Marion* to the effect that court oversight was required 'because of the significant risk of making the wrong decision as to a child's capacity to consent, and secondly because the consequences of a wrong decision are particularly grave'.[29] Thus, an application will be required to determine the *Gillick* competence of children for Stage 2 treatment. Her Honour also said that if any dispute arose between the various parties (parents, child and doctors) regarding the treatment then court oversight is required; though, as Finn J pointed out, in the normal course of events any dispute about such an issue could only be resolved by a court.[30]

Finn and Strickland JJ agreed with her Honour, both adding however that the question of 'proportionality' must be accounted for; namely the 'therapeutic benefits of the treatment would have to be weighed or balanced against the risks involved and the consequences which arise out of the treatment being irreversible'.[31]

There are a number of ways in which this decision is perplexing. The first is the question of the applicability of *Re Marion*. Despite Bryant CJ being explicit that in *Re Marion* the High Court 'was dealing exclusively with the question of sterilisation' of intellectually disabled minors,[32] all Justices considered themselves bound by that section of the High Court's judgment which discusses the significant and grave risks of making a mistake as to a child's capacity to consent or the best interests of the child, where irreversible treatment is being considered. Bryant CJ says that it is the 'nature' of Stage 2 GID treatment that renders authorisation necessary,[33] though it is not clear whether her Honour means something other than the risk factors mentioned above. None of their Honours seems to consider the possibility that *each* of the requirements set out by the High Court is mandatory – that is, court consent is *only* required for a non-therapeutic, irreversible procedure, with the relevant risks referred to above.[34] This is despite the High Court in *Re Marion* having specifically stated

---

26 Ibid at [134]–[135].

27 Arts 5 and 12.

28 [2013] FamCAFC 110 at [137].

29 Ibid.

30 Under FLA, s 67ZC which is the provision which gives the family courts jurisdiction in such matters as these.

31 [2013] FamCAFC 110 at [182] and [195].

32 Ibid at [74].

33 Ibid at [137].

34 Notwithstanding that the Chief Justice (in discussing the issue of whether GID is a medical condition or disorder) seems to make clear that the High Court was only discussing medical conditions requiring treatment; ibid at [97]. Further, her Honour recites Nicholson CJ's summary of the ratio in *Re Marion*, where his Honour clearly states that, for the rule to apply,

that the very reason sterilisation requires court consent is *because* of this constellation of factors; one of which is the non-therapeutic nature of the treatment.[35] There is no discussion by the High Court of therapeutic treatments and the High Court specifically says that it is not referring to therapeutically required sterilisation. The Full Family Court, however, has taken the view that *Re Marion can* apply to therapeutic treatments – despite Bryant CJ saying at one point that the *sole* fact of Stage 1 treatment being for therapeutic purposes took it beyond the ambit of *Re Marion*.[36]

And why is the capacity to consent significant when both parents and child agree? These cases are not like *Re Marion*, where there was little real question of the child being able to consent to the procedure. If a child does not have capacity to consent to a *therapeutic* treatment, then the parent does and can take the decision. If the child has capacity, then they take the decision. If child and parents disagree, then they go to court. How can it matter legally whether or not the decision as to the child's competence is correct, where all agree about undertaking a therapeutic procedure? Finally, it is difficult to understand why Finn and Strickland JJ believe that judges are better placed than doctors and parents to weigh the therapeutic benefits of the treatment against the risks of its irreversible nature. The statement is telling though. It indicates that, for these judges at least (and perhaps for the AHRC), something more lies at the heart of the decision; that there is something about the *nature* of this particular procedure that causes these judges to want an oversight role.

This decision leaves parents and doctors in an unfortunate situation. Regardless of unanimous agreement on the need for therapeutic treatment, the Full Court has held that *every* case where Stage 2 treatment for GID is proposed must go to court to decide the child's *Gillick* competency. Moreover, it is not clear what other therapeutic treatments might be caught by this principle.

It is submitted that the Full Court has not grappled with what lay at the heart of the *Re Marion* decision – concern about parents having non-therapeutic treatments performed on their children in circumstances where there was a danger of the parents' and child's interests conflicting.[37] Bryant CJ spelled out that there was no question in the case of GID of such a conflict of interest;[38] that is precisely because the treatment is therapeutic, a very different situation from removing a healthy uterus from an intellectually disabled young woman.

---

the procedure had to be non-therapeutic, in addition to the other requirements: ibid at [22]. So too does the AHRC argue that *Re Marion* is confined to non-therapeutic treatments: ibid at [42]. It is at [137] that her Honour links the need for court authorisation of *Gillick* competence to the decision in *Re Marion*, without considering the rest of the requirements for *Re Marion* to apply.

35 *Department of Health & Community Services v JWB & SMB* [1992] HCA 15; (1992) 175 CLR 218; (1994) FLC 92-448 at [48]-[49].

36 [2013] FamCAFC 110 at [98].

37 See the discussion of this point in Lisa Young 'New Frontiers for Family Law' in B Atkin (ed) *The International Survey of Family Law 2013 Edition* (Jordan Publishing Ltd, Bristol, 2013) at 72ff.

38 [2013] FamCAFC 110 at [107].

This decision leaves parents, children and doctors in a very difficult position and it is submitted that a better position is for Court authorisation to be reserved for the very limited category of cases that fit all elements of the High Court's formula, like non-therapeutic sterilisations and saviour sibling organ donations.

III THE PROCESS FOR RESOLVING PROPERTY DISPUTES

As mentioned in the Introduction, the Full Family Court of Australia had laid down a four-step process when deciding property alteration applications under FLA, s 79:[39]

> 'Firstly, the Court should make findings as to the identity and value of the property, liabilities and financial resources of the parties at the date of the hearing. Secondly, the Court should identify and assess the contributions of the parties ... and determine the contribution based entitlements of the parties expressed as a percentage of the net value of the property of the parties. Thirdly, the Court should identify and assess the [future needs factors] ... so far as they are relevant and determine the adjustment (if any) that should be made to the contribution based entitlements of the parties established at step two. Fourthly, the Court should consider the effect of those findings and determination and resolve what order is just and equitable in all the circumstances of the case ...'

In *Stanford v Stanford*[40] the High Court was considering a case which involved an application for property orders in circumstances where the parties' marital relationship had not broken down, but the elderly couple were physically separated after the wife went into care. The applicant was the wife's daughter as case guardian, and the case was continued after the wife's death; an order altering the parties' property interests was made in the wife's favour at first instance and upheld on appeal to the Full Court.[41] In this decision the High Court considered the role of s 79(2) – the 'just and equitable' requirement. A number of statements in the High Court decision call into question whether s 79(2) is the final consideration (ie determined after contributions and future needs are considered), or whether in fact it is to be considered first up (ie the starting position is the legal and equitable ownership of property and an independent case needs to be made for some alteration thereof, before contributions and future needs are considered). And what does this mean for the last quarter century of jurisprudence on the operation of s 79?

Initially, many judges and commentators read *Stanford* to require a reconsideration of the four-step process in *Hickey*.[42] However, the Full Family

---

39 *Hickey v Hickey* [2003] FLC 93-143 at [39].
40 [2012] HCA 52; [2012] FLC 93-495.
41 [2012] FamCAFC 1.
42 See the cases cited in P Parkinson, 'Family Property Law and the Three Fundamental Propositions in *Stanford v Stanford*' (2013) 3 Fam L Rev 80 at 87 (and indeed this is the view of Parkinson).

Court is not so convinced. In *Bevan & Bevan*[43] the Full Family Court pointed out that their longstanding jurisprudence recognised that the *Hickey* approach, while to be preferred in many cases, is not prescribed and is simply a means to an end, 'an approach that illuminated the path to the ultimate result'.[44] The Full Court said it has always stressed the overriding limit on the court that it can only make an order if it is just and equitable to do so.[45] Further, the Full Court's view is that the vast majority of cases fall into a category recognised by the High Court as obviously requiring a property alteration order; thus they concluded *Stanford* will have no impact on most cases.[46] Judges should, however, be careful not to adopt a reasoning that 'elevate[s] the four step process to the status of a statutory edict'.[47] The Full Court summarised three 'fundamental propositions' laid down in *Stanford* (original emphasis):[48]

> '1. Determination of a just and equitable outcome of an application for property settlement begins with the identification of existing property interests (as determined by common law and equity);
> 2. The discretion conferred by the statute must be exercised in accordance with legal principles and must not proceed on an assumption that the parties' interests in the property are or should be different from those determined by common law and equity;
> 3. A determination that a party has a right to a division of property fixed by reference *only* to the matters in s 79(4), and without separate consideration of s 79(2), would erroneously conflate what are distinct statutory requirements.'

The first proposition is, according to the Full Court, 'nothing new'.[49] The Full Court was not convinced much would be gained in future property proceedings by judges complicating cases by first ascertaining parties' equitable interests in marital property,[50] as the outcome of any order would be determined not by those interests, but rather by reference to ss 79(4) and 75(2).[51] Nor did the Full Court see the second proposition as adding anything new to the jurisprudence.[52] The third proposition is perhaps more significant, as it establishes that testing whether it is 'just and equitable' to make an order must now be (at least in part) a preliminary question. However, the Full Court indicated this discretionary decision could not be reached without consideration of s 79(4) (indeed the plain words of s 79(4) demand that).[53] This of course

43 [2013] FamCAFC 116.
44 Reflecting the words of the Full Court in *Norman & Norman* [2010] FamCAFC 66 at [60].
45 [2013] FamCAFC 116 at [59]–[64].
46 Ibid at [69]–[70].
47 Ibid at [72].
48 Ibid at [73].
49 Ibid at [74].
50 Contrast the views expressed in P Parkinson, 'Family Property Law and the Three Fundamental Propositions in Stanford v Stanford' (2013) 3 Fam L Rev 80 at 87ff.
51 [2013] FamCAFC 116 at [77].
52 Ibid at [80].
53 Note that Kent J in *Berrell & Berrell (No 3)* [2013] FamCA 1012 at [227]–[228] has challenged whether this is a proper interpretation of what the Full Court found, on the basis that such an interpretation is inconsistent with what the High Court actually did in *Stanford* –

leads to the problem identified by the High Court of conflating the two distinct tasks – determining if *an* order should be made, and determining what *that* order should be; but as the Full Court points out, conflation is only a problem in the very few cases where justice and equity may require no alteration of property interests (cases such as *Stanford* and *Bevan*).[54] The plurality (Bryant CJ and Thackray J) went on to say:[55]

> 'We do not consider it helpful, and indeed it is misleading, to describe this separate enquiry as a "threshold" issue. We say this for two reasons. First, as was emphasised in *Stanford*, the initial enquiry is to determine the existing legal and equitable interests of the parties. Secondly, although s 79(2) is cast in the negative and amounts to a prohibition against making any order unless it is just and equitable to do so, the corollary is that if the court does make an order, such order itself must be just and equitable ... The just and equitable requirement is therefore not a threshold issue, but rather one permeating the entire process.'

In the end, therefore, the Full Court said it was appropriate for judges to separate out the two stages of the process, though a failure to do so may not result in an appellable error if it is possible to discern that in reaching their ultimate conclusion a judge has considered both issues separately.[56]

As to the outcome in *Bevan* itself, their Honours were of the view that it was an unusual case, and the trial Judge had, in fact, conflated the two considerations; the appeal was therefore upheld.[57] In *Bevan* the parties had separated long before trial in circumstances where the husband left the country telling the wife she could keep all the Australian assets and treat them as her own, which she did. When the husband later applied for a share of what then remained of the Australian assets, the trial judge was adamant that the representations of the husband were irrelevant.[58] However, in the Full Court it was found that the peculiar facts of this case, and the way the parties had treated their property in the years before the trial, were relevant to the preliminary question of whether it was now just and equitable to alter the parties' interests in the Australian property[59] and ultimately decided that the parties' interests in the property should not be altered.

---

that is, the High Court determined it was not just and equitable to make an order *without* considering the factors set out in s 79(4). This is perhaps an oversimplification of the High Court and Full Court's reasoning. No doubt in *Stanford* and *Bevan*, were it not for the other factors, it would have been clear that, based on contributions alone, an order would have been just and equitable. In many cases, a cursory consideration of the state of affairs (including the fact of separation and various competing contributions) will indicate that some form of order altering interests is appropriate; it is in determining the precise orders that s 79(4) will be considered in detail. As to the outcome, the facts of *Berrell* were quite different to *Bevan* and Kent J found that this case fell into that more normal category of cases where it was just and equitable to make an order altering the property interests of the parties.

54 Ibid at [85].

55 Ibid at [86].

56 Ibid at [89].

57 See *Bevan & Bevan* [2014] FamCAFC 19 where, after hearing further submissions, the Full Court decided it was not appropriate to make any property settlement order in this case.

58 At [50]–[53] in the first instance decision, recited in [2013] FamCAFC 116 at [47].

59 Ibid at [124].

This is a particularly interesting outcome. Australian family law has long grappled with the vexing question of how to deal with informal and unenforceable agreements entered into in good faith by parties on separation, only to be followed some years later by an application by one party for property settlement. It is clear that a non-binding agreement cannot oust the jurisdiction of the court under s 79; but where the agreement was fair at the time and one of the spouses has acted to their detriment in reliance on it, that spouse might naturally later argue that the court should not usurp the agreement. Not surprisingly the case-law was clear in confirming that such agreements could be overridden[60] though there were examples where the agreement was given effect to.[61] The just and equitable requirement under s 79(2), as interpreted in *Stanford*, provides a coherent way of addressing the relevance of any such agreement.

Parkinson has argued that *Stanford* should fundamentally affect decision-making under s 79, calling it a 'shot across the bows to the Family Court in relation to its whole approach to family property'.[62] Parkinson sees *Stanford* as a stimulus for the court to reconsider its approach to the exercise of s 79 discretion more generally and he discusses what *Stanford* might mean in respect of a range of different aspects of property settlement law; in Parkinson's view *Stanford* invites, and the jurisprudence in this area would benefit from, more sophisticated and principled reasoning concluding: '[t]he gravitational pull of equality exercises a powerful force in the absence of principled reasoning'.[63] Conversely, while the Full Family Court explicitly left some issues for later consideration (as they were not raised in *Bevan*), their assessment of the impact of *Stanford* is that it is somewhat more benign and of most relevance to atypical cases.

The very reason Australian family law has a statutory power to alter property interests in the FLA, which has recently been extended to apply to de facto spouses, is to overcome the harsh and unfair outcomes (predominantly) women would face if the normal rules of property ownership – including in relation to equitable interests – applied. Parkinson suggests that once it is determined that it is just and equitable to alter the parties' interests, and ss 79(4) and 75(2) are considered, the court should make an 'appropriate' order – the order should not be 'tested against some broader measure of justice and equity'.[64] The Full Court in *Bevan*, on the other hand, firmly connects the question of whether it is just and equitable to make the particular order, to the consideration of the s 79(4) factors,[65] which are expressly designed to ensure that non-financial contributions to the accumulation of property are not undervalued, or indeed

---

60 *Woodcock & Woodcock* (1997) FLC 92-739; *Woodland and Todd* (2005) FLC 93-217.
61 See for example *Faraone* (1988) FLC 91-956.
62 P Parkinson, 'Family Property Law and the Three Fundamental Propositions in Stanford v Stanford' (2013) 3 Fam L Rev 80 at 91.
63 [2013] FamCAFC 116 at [80].
64 Above n 62 at 87.
65 Ibid at [84]; though see n 53.

ignored. The wording of s 79(2) is consistent with the Full Court's proposition that it must be just and equitable to make *an* order, and to make *the* order in question.

In moving to the next topic – big money cases – it is timely to ponder just how strong the 'gravitational pull of equality' in Australian property settlement law really is.

IV BIG MONEY CASES – WHERE TO NOW?[66]

The foundations of the Australian 'special skill' principle were laid by the High Court in *Mallet v Mallet*[67] and cemented by the Full Family Court of Australia in *Ferraro v Ferraro*,[68] a case which exemplifies the factual scenario which attracts this principle: a long marriage, few assets at the outset and a fortune having been accumulated during marriage as the result of a business enterprise run predominantly by one of the parties. These cases are not about inheritances, sudden windfalls or parents who come into a marriage with significant assets (the Paul McCartney scenario). Were it not for the size of the asset pool generated,[69] these cases would otherwise see an assessment of 50/50 based on the parties' respective contributions as breadwinner and homemaker. The basis of different treatment is that the breadwinners in these cases are seen to have exercised a special skill (more recently referred to as 'special contribution') that is assumed to have resulted in the fortune, thus increasing their relative contribution above the more 'normal' contributions of their spouse. While it has been said primary caregivers can attract the operation of this principle,[70] as the discussion in recent cases evidences, in practice that is not how the principle is applied. Moreover, to attract the operation of the principle, a fortune of many millions is required.[71]

Until the 2002 case of *Figgins*,[72] this approach was unchallenged judicially, though there has been ongoing academic critique.[73] While *Figgins* was actually

---

66 This section of the chapter is based on L Young and L Wreck '*Smith v Fields*: The Future of 'Special Skill", which was first published in the February 2014 edition of *Brief* the official journal of the Law Society of Western Australia.

67 [1984] HCA 21; (1984) 156 CLR 605.

68 (1993) FLC 92-335.

69 See for example the case of *Stay v Stay* (1997) FLC 92-751 where the value of the asset pool was held to be too low to attract the operation of this principle.

70 See for example *Ferraro*, above n 68 at 79,572.

71 See the case at n 69; more recent case law suggests an asset pool in excess of $10m would be required.

72 (2002) FLC 93-122.

73 L Young 'Sissinghurst, Sackville-West and "Special Skill"' (1997) 11 AJFL 268; L Young 'A Special Rule for "Special Skill": Is it Really Common Sense?' (2001) 7 Current Family Law 189; P Parkinson 'Quantifying the Homemaker Contribution in Family Property Law' (2003) 31 Federal Law Review 1; R Ingleby 'Cry "Figgins" and Let Loose the Dogs of War' (2002) 8 Current Family Law 192; A Dickey '"Special Contributions" to Property and the Case of *Figgins*' (2003) 77 Australian Law Journal 575; L Young 'Rich Women and Divorce: Looking for a "Common Sense" Approach' (2004) 22 Australian Canadian Studies 95.

an inheritance case, the Full Family Court made obiter comment on, and questioned, the special skill principle, saying it would be desirable for it to be 'reconsidered in an appropriate case',[74] noting there was no legislative basis for the approach and recognising it invited invidious comparisons of different spheres of endeavour in a marriage.[75] Referring to UK authority,[76] the majority in *Figgins* evidenced a preference for a partnership model of marriage, which would preclude a weighting in these cases just because one party's endeavours were 'productive of money in large quantities'.[77] *Figgins* thus highlighted a judicial difference of opinion in the appellate court on this matter, and while some later decisions referred to the critique in *Figgins*,[78] as Ryan J noted in *Atkins & Atkins*[79] in 2007, the Full Court had not at that stage authoritatively rejected special skill and the 'argument [was] ... still available'.[80]

However, there has been something of a recent judicial revolt over this principle in a number of first instance decisions and as a result a few appeals have proceeded to the Full Court. In *Smith & Fields* Murphy J at first instance openly challenged the special skill approach.[81] The facts were typical: a very long marriage with three children, few assets at the outset and a fortune from a family construction business in the order of $32–40m, with the husband the main contributor to the business.

Murphy J reminded us that this principle has no basis in statute.[82] His Honour highlighted that while the judges in *Mallet* rejected a presumption of equality of contribution as a starting point, some of the judgments provide a foundation

---

74 (2002) FLC 93-122 at [57].

75 Ibid.

76 *White v White* [2000] UKHL 54; [2001] 1 AC 596; [2001] 1 All ER 1.

77 (2002) FLC 93-122 at [133]-[134].

78 A differently constituted Full Court in *Hill & Hill* [2005] FamCA 42 (Kay, Holden and Boland JJ) referred to the relevant critique in *Figgins*. However, this was not the basis on which they upheld an appeal of a first instance decision that credited the husband with a 75% contribution towards the $10.6m fortune amassed during the 17-year marriage. In the same year, in the unreported decision of *D & D* [2005] FamCA 1462 at &&[271] O'Ryan J agreed with the submission made to him '[t]hat the notion of special contribution has all been a terrible mistake' saying it is a 'false doctrine' designed as 'a polite way of getting around the drift toward equality'(referred to in *Atkins & Atkins* [2007] FamCA 656 at [204]–[206] and in *Smith & Fields* at [27]). In *Atkins & Atkins* [2007] FamCA 656 Ryan J referred to *Hill* and to O'Ryan J's comments and concluded that the Full Court had not been as strong in rejecting special skill as O'Ryan J, and the net result of the case-law is that the special skills argument remains open.

79 [2007] FamCA 656.

80 Ibid at [206]. See also *Kane & Kane* (2011) FamCA 480 where Austin J considers the authorities concluding that the principle is still of application. As to the uncertainty, see Watts J in *Newman & Newman* [2013] FamCA 37 who says (after noting recent decisions including *Smith v Fields*): 'insofar as there is a special contribution case, this is not one of them' at [118].

81 [2012] FamCA 510.

82 [2012] FamCA 510 at [18]–[19]. Collier J in *Rebane & Rebane* [2012] FamCA 970 cites some of Murphy J's comments with approval at [121]–[122].

for the notion of 'partnership' in assessing contribution under s 79.[83] Recognising some judges may find the lack of guidance in the legislation difficult his Honour contended that:[84]

> 'while some assistance may be rendered from using expressions such as "special skills" or "special" or "extraordinary" contribution, in my view, the use of such expressions is apt to mislead and to obscure, rather than to illuminate, the task at hand. The real danger lies in the promulgation of a notion that, by establishing "special contribution" or "special skills" – whatever the expression, or the indicia comprising any such expression might be said to be – a result of a particular type, or a particular range should follow. That is an improper fetter on an extraordinarily wide discretion. It smacks of a presumption antithetical to what the section requires.'

In Murphy J's view the provisions are clear and judges cannot avoid the requirement to exercise their discretion under s 79 in assessing contributions, however uncomfortable.[85] Thus, when counsel for the husband tendered a table of 'big money' cases with outcomes,[86] saying there was a consistency of results that could not be ignored,[87] his Honour stated that 'care must be exercised' in order to do 'individual justice by reference to individual circumstances'.[88]

Murphy J also recognised the irony of past case-law, maintaining that a finding of special skill is *not* dependent on the size of the asset pool,[89] however, those same cases only identifying special skills where the assets were extremely large.[90] In challenging the notion of special skills, his Honour said 'the terms of s 79 suggest no such thing' and 'doing so risks giving insufficient or "token" weight to the "sphere" comprising contributions to the welfare of the family or other indirect contributions and doing so is contrary to authority'.[91] He went on to cite Deane J in *Mallet* who referred to 'a practical union of both lives and property'[92] in a long marriage; as Murphy J noted, 'one party is more able to make contributions within their role by reason of the contributions made by the other within their role.'[93] His Honour refused to draw a distinction between contributions on the basis that the contributions of one party were described as 'special' and he noted there was no clear definition of what 'special skill' may mean or is intended to connote.[94] Rather, Murphy J saw the exercise of discretion as being shaped by: the nature, form, characteristics and origins of

---

83 *Smith & Fields* [2012] FamCA 510 at [10].
84 Ibid at [26].
85 Ibid at [27].
86 Ibid at [87].
87 Ibid at [87].
88 Ibid at [88].
89 *JEL v DDF* [2000] FamCA 1353 at [133].
90 [2012] FamCA 510 at [17].
91 Ibid at [78].
92 [1984] HCA 21 at [5].
93 [2012] FamCA 510 at [77].
94 Ibid at [88].

the property; the nature and form of the matrimonial partnership; and the nature, form characteristics and extent of the contributions.[95]

Having said this, his Honour concluded somewhat confusingly by saying (emphasis added):[96]

> 'what remains is the exercise of discretion – to do what is just and equitable – as between these particular parties, not because one or the other has "special skills" or because there is a "matrimonial partnership", but because the identification and comparison of contributions and the *"general counsel of experience" pulls toward a particular result.*'

Murphy J did not ultimately find the contributions of the spouses in this case to be equal, though he did not accept the husband's submissions which sought to limit or ignore the wife's contributions to the business.[97] His Honour recognised that when the couple were starting up their business the wife was 'overwhelmingly responsible' for homemaking and parenting and that she received 'very little, if any, assistance from a marriage partner who had little time at home to do other than sleep'.[98] However, Murphy J nonetheless found the husband's contribution to the business to have been greater than the wife's, particularly after separation. His Honour noted the business continued to do well in adverse economic conditions,[99] highlighting the husband's 'ingenuity and stewardship of the business', which was extremely successful in a difficult industry and which benefited from the husband's input into the designs of the homes sold.[100] Despite his comment referred to above in relation to the table of outcomes, in assessing the husband's contribution at 60%, Murphy J said that, while caution had to be exercised, the outcomes of appellate cases with similar facts *could not be ignored*.[101]

Although Murphy J rejected an argument of special skills/contributions, in its result his Honour's decision is little different from those where the argument has succeeded, though perhaps at the more generous end to the wife. The 'general counsel of experience' still pulled this decision-maker towards seeing the husband's skill in generating money as a greater contribution than the wife's contributions to their family. While his Honour chose different terminology, in taking account of prior appellate outcomes he was in effect adopting the basis of those decisions, which was special skill. His Honour gives scant consideration to what abandoning special skill, and embracing *Figgins*, practically means in such cases (indeed he did not discuss *Figgins*). It is a telling outcome, as it brings home the intuitive attraction of this principle.

---

95 Ibid at [28]–[29]. Note the similar wording used by the Full Court in *Dickons & Dickons* [2012] FamCAFC 154 at [21].
96 [2012] FamCA 510 at [30].
97 Ibid at [55]-[56].
98 Ibid at [52].
99 Ibid at [75].
100 Ibid at [77] and [83].
101 Ibid at [89].

Six months later Brewster FM delivered his judgment in *Hoffman & Hoffman*.[102] His Honour argued he was free to abandon superior authorities in this area,[103] referring to his earlier comments in *Palmer & Palmer*[104] where he had presaged the demise of special skill. While his Honour found there may have been elements of luck involved, he considered Mr Hoffman did not 'sit on his hands'; that is, he played a role in the building of the assets. However, his Honour was clear in rejecting the approach in both *Mallet* and *Ferraro*, preferring (and adopting) the reasoning of Thorpe LJ in the UK case of *Lambert*,[105] which case he predicted would win the future favour of our Full Court.[106] In relation to *Mallet* (where this approach finds its roots), his Honour made the following points. The case was decided when s 79 was differently worded, there still being a statutory link between homemaker contributions and the accumulation of assets at that time.[107] Further, the discussion in *Mallet* assumes there is a meaningful way financial contributions can be compared with non-financial contributions when in fact this is like comparing 'apples and carrots';[108] his Honour saw this judicial analysis as 'bristling' with problems.[109] Thus, *Mallet* should be confined to its bare ratio: 'when one is confronted with a long marriage, there is no "starting point" of equality and that, if anything, the starting point is the legal and equitable interests of the parties'.[110] As for *Ferraro*, his Honour pointed to the incongruence between what the Full Court said in that case and what it did; while purporting to endorse the recognition of the value of homemaker contributions it failed to value the contributions of Mrs Ferraro, who was an outstanding homemaker.[111] His Honour saw the principle of special skill as 'infected by gender bias' and due to the 'zeitgeist' of the era in which the judges grew up:[112]

> 'when the ghost of *Mallet* stands in the path of a just and equitable outcome, clanking its gender biased chains, the proper course for a judge is to pass through it undeterred.'[113]

His Honour accordingly divided the assets of just under $10m equally between the parties, noting that even if he were wrong on the issue of the applicability of *Ferraro*, the size of the asset pool was too small to warrant recognition of special skill.[114]

---

102 [2012] FMCAfam 1061.
103 Ibid at [36].
104 [2010] FMCAfam 999.
105 [2002] EWCA Civ 1685.
106 [2012] FMCAfam 1061 at [37]–[38].
107 Ibid at [55].
108 Ibid at [42].
109 Ibid at [44].
110 Ibid at [56].
111 On this point see further L Young 'Sissinghurst, Sackville-West and "Special Skill"' (1997) 11 AJFL 268.
112 [2012] FMCAfam 1061 at [46].
113 Ibid at [57].
114 Not a position his Honour warmly embraced given he believes no basis exists for distinguishing cases based solely on the size of the asset pool; however, he considered the case-law endorsed such an approach.

Two earlier cases also deserve mention. In *SL & EHL*,[115] Warnick J also took issue with special skills but addressed more broadly the question of the nature of the exercise under s 79. His Honour concluded it is appropriate for the court to state explicitly the values that underpin decision-making; 'unless the role of values' in this exercise is recognised 'the chain of authority is mysterious':[116]

> 'Mallet is recognised as confirming the proposition that "… the wife's contribution as homemaker should be recognized in a substantial and not merely in a token way" …
>
> In my respectful view, this is a "value", the source of which is unidentified save that, as a prelude to a similar statement, Gibbs CJ said that it was implicit in many of the sections contained in Part VIII of the Family Law Act, that the parties to a marriage are equal in status …'

Why his Honour considers recognition of the fact that provision of unpaid labour in raising children is a substantial contribution (even if just financially) is the expression of a 'value' of 'unidentified' source is unclear. But this just illustrates the difficult terrain s 79 presents for judges. His Honour discusses his view of the role of values and the impact of changing values in a genuine attempt to consider more deeply how s 79 should be applied. Perhaps unsurprisingly, his Honour asks more questions than he considers it appropriate to answer, concluding the parties' contributions in this case (where the assets were conservatively only $8m and thus again arguably below the special skills threshold) were equal.

In *Bulleen & Bulleen*,[117] which squarely fits the 'big money' case profile, Cronin J drew on the partnership approach in *Figgins* eschewing the husband's special skills argument; his Honour found that, aside from an initial contribution and inheritance on the part of the husband which did warrant an adjustment, the parties' contributions were otherwise equal in a marriage of 47 years that netted a fortune of $150m.

Thus, it can be seen that, despite appellate authority, family court judges at first instance have become increasingly less inclined to apply a doctrine of special skills; one must assume they expected appeals to follow. While the special skill principle obviously makes legal sense to some,[118] as these recent decisions indicate there are strong arguments to be made against its adoption. It is timely

---

[115] [2005] FamCA 132. See Young J's comments in *Sebastian & Sebastian (No 5)* [2013] FamCA 191 at [163] endorsing aspects of the decisions in *Bulleen & Bulleen* [2010] FamCA 187 and *SL & EHL*.

[116] [2005] FamCA 132 at [247].

[117] [2010] FamCA 187. For discussion of this case, see R Ingleby 'Hans Christian Anderson, Bulleen and the Emperor's New Clothes' (2010) 24 AJFL 272.

[118] See for example the case made in the paper cited at n 124 below.

to summarise briefly some key arguments against Australia's special skill principle,[119] a number of which have not been addressed in the appellate judicial discussion to date:

1. Big money cases were initially said to recognise 'special skill'. The legislation says nothing of skill, and talents or skills that make much less money are not rewarded as a special contribution, no matter how 'special' they might be.
2. If these cases *are* about 'special contributions' as opposed to skills (a device later decisions adopted to avoid the problematic use of the term 'skill'), why do counsel/the court continually revert to discussions of skill?[120]
3. If these decisions are *not* about the *skill* of making money (which the court has previously maintained), what is special about the *contribution* of earnings? Money derived from labour outside the home is not a 'special contribution' to a marriage – it is a common one. The rationale *must* therefore be that the *amount* of money earned makes the contribution 'special';[121] no matter how diligent, hard-working and clever an average breadwinner is, no special contribution is recognised where the assets accumulated as a result are in the 'normal' range.[122] Where, and how, then does one draw the line?
4. If contributions are identified as 'special' by virtue of the 'value' of their product, why are homemakers not judged by the same yardstick, for example, the quality of their offspring?
5. If the value of the assets accumulated during marriage triggers the rule, then the Court *must* assume it can determine causality, partialling out other factors that may have contributed to this success (be they luck or otherwise).[123]
6. If these breadwinners had been unsuccessful despite making their best efforts, the homemaker spouse would have shared *equally* in the losses of the relationship. What is the rationale for sharing losses but not profits? This reverts to causation – the profit is assumed (retrospectively) to have been guaranteed by the skill of the breadwinner.
7. Until the requisite threshold of wealth is passed, the parties' property is essentially joint. That is, if Mr and Mrs Ferraro had separated earlier with more modest assets, the Court would – without doubt – have concluded

---

119 See for example L Young 'Sissinghurst, Sackville-West and "Special Skill"' (1997) 11 AJFL 268 and L Young 'A Special Rule for "Special Skill": Is it Really "Common Sense"?' (2001) Current Family Law 189.

120 See for example *Atkins & Atkins* [2007] FamCA 656 at [204]; see also the trial judge in *Hill & Hill* who adopts the term 'contribution' but then refers to the husband's 'expertise, astuteness and business acumen' at [53] as the key factors; and see the Full Court in that case at [60].

121 Though the Full Court has rejected this analysis: *JEL and DDF* [2000] FamCA 1353 at [152].

122 This is reflected by the Full Court's decision in *Stay v Stay* [1997] FLC 92-751.

123 See the discussion of this point in L Young 'Sissinghurst, Sackville-West and "Special Skill"' (1997) 11 AJFL,268 and L Young 'Rich Women and Divorce: Looking for a "Common Sense" approach' (2004) 22 Australian Canadian Studies 95.

the contributions were equal. The assets these husbands used to generate the wealth were therefore not theirs alone; they had the benefit of using, as they wished, the shares of their wives. The wives were silent partners *who shared all of the risks*. Why is the contribution of that half share of assets to the creation of wealth not recognised as a *significant* financial contribution (in addition to the women's other contributions)?

8. The alternative to 'special skills' is not, as some judges assume,[124] a presumption of joint contribution. The High Court in *Mallet* was clear that the mere fact there is often a finding of joint contribution is not the same as applying a presumption of equality. The effect of *Ferraro* is to treat 'normal' and 'big money' cases differently, such that *Mallet* only applies to the latter category; it implicitly endorses an assumption of equality of contribution where the asset pool is small or medium-sized, but not where it is very large. This is the very opposite of the point of *Mallet*.

As many judges are now accepting, the special skills approach defies logical explanation and results in the different treatment of mega-wealthy 'breadwinners' in a gender discriminatory way. Both members of the couple contribute labour – the product of one spouse's labour may be mostly money (all of which is accounted for as benefitting the family, however much that might be) and the product of the other partner's labour will be a range of diverse outcomes usually other than money, but again benefitting the family. Section 79 accommodates the fact that contributions can be directed at different aims – i e to earning money or to other things of benefit to the family – but both are still to be assessed and valued. *Contributions are about inputs, not outputs*. Section 43 – which applies generally to matters under the FLA – directs the court to have regard to the need to protect and preserve the 'union' of marriage and the family it gives rise to, particularly where the raising of children is concerned. Section 79 then exhorts the court to recognise and value the variety of different contributions spouses make to that union.

Big money cases highlight the inherent difficulty in applying s 79 and should lead to more general consideration of its proper application, as in *SL & EHL*. However, the Full Court does not need to go this far in its decision on *Smith & Fields*; if it considers the basis for the different treatment of these cases and finds no justification, then no special principle should apply and a spouse could not make an argument for increased contribution on the basis of the high dollar value of the product of their labour. *Bulleen* exemplifies this approach. In that case Cronin J makes the crucial point that it is the *disparity* in contributions that warrants differing percentage allocations of contributions:

> 'This marriage was a partnership and each performed their respective roles admirably. It would be totally inappropriate to retrospectively endeavour to

[124] See for example Hon Justice P Guest 'Special Contributions in Big Money Cases – "Never Mind the Law, Feel the Politics"', Anglo-Australian Colloquium, Oxford Centre for Family Law and Policy, July 2004, at [71] available at www.familycourt.gov.au/wps/wcm/resources/file/eba9aa49cfe89ff/guest072004.pdf (accessed 14 October 2013).

allocate non-financial contributions by some monetary worth. That is not to say however, that their respective contributions as distinct from their roles, was not different and cannot be identified ...'[125]

'In a marriage of the duration of over 40 years where the parties treated their respective roles as important, to distinguish those roles retrospectively and arbitrarily would be wrong. This was a classic partnership of two people who contributed differently but with one goal. They saw themselves as equals contributing to the best of their abilities. That is the way the community would expect those roles to be viewed. That does not mean that there cannot be contributions outside of the partnership roles which are identifiable and make a discernible difference to the parties' wealth.'[126]

Thus, the fact of initial contributions and an inheritance shifted the weighting slightly in the husband's favour; however the mere fact that the husband's endeavours produced great wealth did not. This reflects the approach commonly adopted for couples of lesser wealth and shows the alternative to special skills is *not* just assumed equality of contribution. Further, it may be that the way a couple manages their life is different to the traditional partnership model and this may affect the question of contribution, as the Full Court noted in *Dickons & Dickons*:[127]

'That task [applying s 79] is also undertaken by reference to the nature and form of the particular marriage partnership manifested by the particular circumstances of this particular marriage. Is it, for example, a relationship, as Deane J put it in *Mallet* at 640–641 "...where the parties have adopted the attitude that their marriage constituted a practical union of both lives and property ..." or is it, for example, a union where parties lived very separate domestic and financial lives?'[128]

While the Full Court decision in *Smith & Fields* (which bench includes the Chief Judge) was still pending at the time of writing, a differently constituted Full Court has, in the meantime, handed down a decision on this issue in *Kane & Kane*.[129] One has to wonder, reading the decision of the plurality in *Kane*, whether their Honours were mindful of the pending decision in *Smith & Fields* and preferred to leave that court to decide the fate of the special skills doctrine. *Kane* involved a very long marriage, four children and assets in excess of $4m. The husband argued a special contribution on the basis of making a particularly successful share purchase that the wife had opposed.[130] The trial judge accepted special 'skills' could be attributed extra weight according to existing case-law[131] and found the husband's contribution to be 66.67% in respect of that particular asset,[132] which formed a significant portion of the overall assets. The shares had been bought with the funds realised from the sale

125 [2010] FamCA 187 at [25]–[26].
126 Ibid at [164].
127 [2012] FamCAFC 154.
128 Ibid at [21].
129 (2013) FamCAFC 205.
130 Ibid at [56].
131 Ibid at [60].
132 Ibid at [66].

of the parties' home and the wife had resisted such a large investment in one company. Nonetheless the husband proceeded and (unlike some other investments he had made) the return was significant. The trial Judge's approach resulted in the husband receiving 63.55% of the total assets.

The plurality (May and Johnston JJ), in upholding the wife's appeal and remitting the matter for rehearing, did not go so far as to reject the special skills principle, though they considered the incorrect weighting of contributions in this case in favour of the husband reflected precisely the concerns raised with the rule by Murphy J in *Smith & Fields*. Faulks DCJ, in a separate judgment, went a step further, endorsing and adopting Murphy J's reasoning,[133] and going on to say:[134]

> 'To the extent that the trial judge believed himself to be obliged by authority to determine the division of the property of the parties by reference to some doctrine acknowledging "special skills" in my opinion, for the reasons set out above, he was mistaken. The Act does not require and in my opinion the authorities do not mandate, any such doctrine and if judgments of the Full Court of this Court might be thought to have espoused such a principle in my opinion, they should no longer be regarded as binding.'

His Honour went on to point out some of the difficulties with the special skills principle, including the assumption of causation in these cases (between effort and product) and the troubling issue of sharing losses but not profits.

So, while it appears *Kane* has not definitively sounded the death knell of special skills, a ground swell of judicial concern is pointing in that ultimate direction.

V CONCLUSION

It is no compliment to the legal system that the approach to big money cases has been so unclear for over a decade, to the very great cost of the litigants involved. Moreover, while these cases may be exceptional, they have much to say about how Australian family law values non-financial familial contributions and are raising important questions about how s 79 is applied more generally. The role of s 79(2) considered in *Stanford* is another example of unnecessary legislative uncertainty.[135] It might therefore be argued it is time for a legislative reconsideration of s 79 so that the significant issues of policy, and process, being raised in modern property decisions can be explicitly addressed.[136]

However, it should not be assumed that legislative reform will create greater certainty. It can hardly be said that the greater legislative prescription

---

133 Ibid at [5].
134 Ibid at [7].
135 Note the controversy over what *Stanford* means highlighted in n 53.
136 There are other confounding issues that could be addressed; one obvious one is the relevance of domestic violence to property proceedings: see *Kennon v Kennon* (1997) 22 Fam LR 1.

introduced into Pt VII of the FLA dealing with children has been a resounding success; the complexity, vague language and reliance on a starting point of 50/50 shared care for all cases where there is joint guardianship[137] are all bones of contention. No doubt many think we need to start again with that Part of the FLA. Recent reforms to child support laws to address perceived problems have also resulted in an extremely complex system that is now being criticised because the users of the system cannot understand it; this may result in yet another review. Striking the right legislative balance between simplicity (and leaving it to the court to fill in the gaps) and confounding complexity (in the hope of better guiding the exercise of discretion) is obviously harder than it might appear.

There is a lot that is good about s 79 and over time the Full Court has, in many regards, developed mature and principled positions that reflect the core principles that underlie that section – this is no doubt why it has endured with relatively little amendment. While the development of sound principles which guide the exercise of discretion under s 79 is slow and depends upon the right cases going on appeal, judicial debate over points of principle has more to commend it than much of the debate in our legislatures. For that reason, any reform to property settlement laws under the FLA should be targeted and minimal and seek to preserve, and align with, the core purpose of those provisions. Unlike the new Pt VII relating to children, there is no objects section in Pt VIII, and this might be a welcome addition. It is important to remember that 'achievement of [economic justice for the homemaker spouse on the breakdown of marriage] was the objective of the introduction ... of statutory schemes giving the courts wide discretionary powers to redistribute assets between husband and wife, overriding existing legal or equitable rights, in accordance with considerations of past contributions to the marriage partnership (both financial and non-financial) and future needs'.[138]

No doubt this is the end of the road in relation to court authorisation for treatment of GID in children. While it is an important point worthy of further consideration, it is hard to imagine that parents will be able to justify the expense of a High Court challenge or that law firms will be prepared to go so far on a pro bono basis, particularly with the spectre of a costs order if unsuccessful. Of course, later Full Courts are not bound by *Re Jamie*, but appeals even to the Full Court level are unlikely. At least parents are now able to postpone court intervention till later in the process and can address, with the guidance of medical professionals, the pressing problems that arise for these children around the time of puberty.

---

137 Known as 'equal shared parental responsibility' in the FLA.

138 HA Finlay, R Bailey-Harris, M Otlowksi *Family Law in Australia* (5th edn, Butterworths, Sydney, 1997) at [6.2].

BRAZIL

SAME-SEX FAMILIES IN BRAZIL: AN OVERVIEW AFTER THE TRIAL OF ADI 4277 AND ADPF 132 BY THE SUPREME COURT

Marianna Chaves[*]

Résumé

En 2011, la Cour suprême du Brésil a estimé que les couples de même sexe sont des entités familiales et qu'ils doivent bénéficier de tous les droits et obligations découlant de l'union stable entre un homme et une femme, mariage y compris. La décision de la Cour suprême est un véritable changement de paradigme. Bien que celle-ci s'impose à tous, il existe encore des juges qui contestent cette décision. Le Brésil est un pays de droit écrit. Par conséquent, il est essentiel que la décision de la Cour suprême soit intégrée à la législation par modification de la Constitution, par une réforme du Code civil ou par la promulgation d'une loi spéciale.

I INTRODUCTION

It is not a novelty and not even a controversy the fact that homosexual individuals form relationships and have existed as families for a long time in their various forms and degrees of visibility. The diversity of the family, as well as that of human sexuality, is something that precedes any effort for regulation or even definition.

Same-sex unions have existed since ancient times, but from the moment that the Catholic Church consecrated the concept of family, giving it merely procreative finality, homosexual relations became a target of prejudice and social rejection. The most harmful consequence of exclusion from the legal framework is the absolute invisibility to which these emotional bonds are often condemned.

* PhD candidate in Civil Law from the University of Coimbra; Master in Law from Lisbon University; Secretary of International Relations of IBDFAM – Brazilian Institute of Family Law; Vice-President of the Committee of Sexual Diversity and LGBT Rights of OAB-PB (Brazilian Bar Association – Paraiba Section); Consultant Member of the Special Committee of Sexual Diversity of the Brazilian Bar Association; Legal Consultant.

These unions and families did not need public acceptance or legal recognition to be formed, although their existence was less protected because of this omission. But the emancipatory struggle, the blossoming of human rights and the laicisation of the states are forging the construction of new societies worldwide, recognising that marriage between people, regardless of their sexual orientation, is a union of affections and as such can be identified. Gradually the so-called civilised world is waking up, turning into reality what has been proclaimed by the French Revolution: the right to liberty and equality, with the issuing of assured rules of civil rights for individuals and gay couples.

Brazil, following the steps of the most progressive countries, recognised same-sex unions as a family and granted the same juridical treatment as that of the stable union between man and woman. Interestingly, even though it is part of the Roman-Germanic system,[1] Brazil ended up behaving in this matter as a common law country, since the solutions were being built by the jurisprudence that has been crystallising over more than a decade all over the country.

The popular demand, the inexorable omission by the legislative branch, allied to the inexcusable duty of the Brazilian Supreme Court to manifest itself in relation to homosexual unions, led to the recognition of the so-called 'homo-affective' family in Brazil. There was no lack of criticism about the path taken.

A unique fact about the Brazilian situation is that projects of law on the regulation of homosexual unions never got to be voted in a plenary session, going from one parliamentary committee to another until they were shelved indefinitely. The legislative power peremptorily accuses the judiciary of judicial activism, of affront to the principle of separation of powers, but no one dares talk about the bills that have been proposed in the legislative houses since 1995 and never come to be voted on. It is not mentioned that almost 3 years have passed since the trial of ADI 4277 and ADPF 132 without any movement by the legislature to regulate lesbian, gay, bisexual and transgender (LGBT) rights especially when in the last voting session the former President of the Brazilian Supreme Court, Justice Cezar Peluso, textually urged the legislature to act on the matter.[2]

---

1 Of which one of the characteristic features resides in the fact that the law is organised in large codifications (resulting in prestige for the written law).

2 In the words of Justice Cezar Peluso: 'The legislative power, from today, from this trial needs to expose and regulate situations in which the application of the Court's decision will be also justified from a constitutional point of view. There is therefore a call implied in the Court's decision in relation to the Legislative Power, so it assumes this task, which so far it seems it has not yet felt very prone to exercise, of regulating for this equivalence.'

II RIGHT TO DIVERSITY AND FREE SEXUAL ORIENTATION

In the structuring of the individuality of a person, sexuality constitutes a fundamental measure of the constitution of subjectivity and an essential mainstay for the capacity of free development of personality. Therefore, it can be said that the issues concerning sexual orientation are related closely with the protection of human dignity.

The relation established between the protection of human dignity and sexual orientation is immediate. The appreciation of the constitutive features of a person's individuality is legally prescribed by the Brazilian Constitution.[3] The recognition of the dignity of the human being is indeed a core element of sociality. It marks the concept of the Democratic State of Law, which provides citizens with something beyond abstaining from unfounded interference in their personal lives: the positive promotion of their freedoms.[4] Even to consider the possibility of prejudice, contempt or disrespect for a person because of their sexual orientation would confer undignified treatment on the human being.

The above-mentioned idea was enshrined by the Brazilian Supreme Court when it ruled that sexuality is a personality property and fundamental right, sexual orientation being a direct emanation from the principle of human dignity and thus a 'powerful factor of affirmation and personal elevation'.[5]

In addition, it was stated in the trial in the Supreme Court that dignity is closely linked to freedom and this autonomy must extend to all perspectives of every individual's lives, encompassing the sentimental and sexual freedom and communion with others. As Justice Carmen Lucia said: 'what is undignified leads to socially imposed suffering. And the suffering that is hosted by the State is undemocratic. And ours is a democratic constitution.'[6]

Moreover, in the trial of ADI 4277 and ADPF we were reminded that the Brazilian Constitution explicitly prohibits any form of prejudice – included therein prejudice based on gender or sexual orientation. Furthermore, the Constitution purposely did not regulate the effective use of human sexuality, which is why one can surmise that such usage constitutes a freedom of choice

---

3 In the same sense, Paulo Vecchiatti states that it must highlighted that fundamental rights are thus considered (fundamental) precisely because of the assumption that without them human beings cannot have a dignified life. In other words, fundamental rights are exteriorisations of the principle of human dignity, as being intended to ensure a decent life for all citizens. Thus, although some fundamental rights have different gradations of human dignity in their content they all represent the externalisation of an aspect of human dignity that the constituents wanted to protect. Paulo Roberto Iotti Vecchiatti *Manual da Homoafetividade*: da possibilidade jurídica do casamento civil, da união estável e da adoção por homossexuais (São Paulo: Editora Método, 2008) 155–156.

4 Cf Jorge Reis Novais *Contributo para uma Teoria do Estado de Direito*: do Estado de Direito Liberal ao Estado Social e Democrático de Direito (Coimbra: Almedina, 1987) 210.

5 See Justice Ayres Britto, p 20.

6 See Justice Carmen Lúcia, p 6.

for each individual, resulting in individual liberties, which materializes in the right to intimacy and the right to privacy.[7]

Thus, in this area the free exercise of sexuality must be understood as a genuine right of personality, something already carried or 'catapulted' into the inviolable sphere of autonomy of the will of the people, inasmuch as it is practised and experienced as 'an element of spiritual and psychophysical composure of the human being in search of his existential fulfilment'.[8]

The principle of freedom concerns not only the creation, maintenance and termination of family arrangements, but also its permanent constitution and reinvention. Once family was disconnected from its traditionalist functions, the idea is unreasonable that it is the State's interest to regulate duties that profoundly restrict freedom, intimacy and private life of individuals, when there is no impact on the public interest.[9]

III THE HOMO-AFFECTIVE UNION AS A FAMILY

Given the absence of legislation that expressly regulates same-sex unions until recently, the Brazilian judiciary committed all sorts of injustices, since a large share of citizens were left in the margin of the law. When a lawsuit related to homosexual relationships was proposed, in the face of the legislative gap, the tendency was the rejection of the complaint because of the failure to state a cause of action. Consequently, the suit was immediately extinguished by the legal impossibility of the claim.

The Brazilian Magna Charta of 1988 was emphatic in prohibiting discrimination of any kind. However, it turned out that it explicitly protected just the family formed by a woman and man, heterosexual marriage and the single-parent family, forgetting that heterosexuality is not the only form of expression of human feeling. The Civil Code followed the same line of reasoning.

---

7 On this matter Justice Carlos Ayres Britto said that 'it cannot be otherwise, because there is nothing more intimate and more private for individuals than the practice of their own sexuality. The normative silence of our highest law implies logically, as to this practice, the free use of human sexuality in the legal and fundamental categories of intimacy and privacy of individuals. The initial part of the Art. 10 and § 1 of Art. 5 of the Constitution states: "intimacy, private life, honour and image of persons are inviolable" and "the provisions defining the fundamental rights and guarantees have immediate applicability". It follows that the sexual freedom of the human being just would cease to fit within the incidence of these last constitutional provisions (item X and § 1 of Art. 5), if there was also a constitutional enunciation in a different way. Something that does not exist'. See Justice Ayres Britto, p 22.

8 See Justice Ayres Britto, p 18.

9 As we have already stated elsewhere. In this regard, cf Marianna Chaves *Homoafetividade e direito*: proteção constitucional, uniões, casamento e parentalidade (Curitiba: Juruá, 2nd edn, 2012) 80–81.

There seems to be no obstacle of an ontological character to prevent the extension of the specific characteristics of affectio maritalis to same-sex couples. There is no basis that justifies attributing the decision to unite their lives affectively only to heterosexual couples.[10]

In this sense, the paradigm shift began with the justice of the state of Rio Grande do Sul in 2000. The partner's right to the marriage portion was secured, seeing homosexual relationships as affective bonds, to be inserted into the context of family law. Using subsidies from the legislation that regulates stable unions, the 7th Civil Chamber of the Court of Rio Grande do Sul determined that there should be equal division of the net assets accumulated during the existence of the relationship. The presumption of mutual collaboration led to the recognition of the condominium status.[11]

In this long and arduous process of recognition of a homo-affective union as a family entity, the Maria da Penha Act of 2006 (Law no 11.340/2006) represented a major milestone as it explicitly includes homosexual unions in the concept of family. Article 2 states that 'every woman, regardless of class, race, ethnicity, sexual orientation, income, culture, educational level, age and religion, is guaranteed the fundamental rights inherent to the human person'.

The sole paragraph of art 5 of the Act explicitly mentions that personal relationships and situations that represent family and domestic violence are independent of sexual orientation of the people involved. So, as legal protection is assured to events that occur within the domestic environment, it is understood that homosexual unions are family entities. Domestic violence, as the terminology itself says, is violence that occurs within a family. Thus, the Maria da Penha Act extended the concept of family to homo-affective unions.[12]

It can be concluded, therefore, that the Maria da Penha Act, considered an innovative framework, introduced a new concept of family into the Brazilian legal system, which includes same-sex unions. It is noteworthy that, under the principle of equality, the relations between two men should also be considered a family entity for the purposes of the protection of the Act.

A jurisprudential construction has existed since the beginning of the twenty-first century to grant the family character to homosexual unions in Brazil. Even so, it was necessary for the Federal Supreme Court to rule on the

---

10 In the same sense, see Ana Carla Harmatiuk Matos *União entre pessoas do mesmo sexo: aspectos jurídicos e sociais* (Belo Horizonte: Del Rey, 2004) 65.

11 10 years ago, Maria Berenice Dias said about the sentence: 'The pioneering decision, without hypocrisy, envisioned a true family entity. In the face of legal omission, by analogy, the legislation of the Family Law was applied. The lack of regulation spotted in the trial shows the indifference of the state to regulate the unions between persons of the same sex who deserve to have in Brazil, as in most countries of the world, appropriate regulation.' Maria Berenice Dias *Conversando sobre homoafetividade* (Porto Alegre: Livraria do Advogado Editora, 2004) 44–45.

12 As stated by Maria Berenice Dias *A Lei Maria da Penha na Justiça* (São Paulo: Editora Revista dos Tribunais, 2007) 35.

matter to finally succeed in extirpating any haze of doubts about whether same-sex relationships constitute genuine family entities or not.

At the trial of ADI 4277 jointly with ADPF 132 one of the arguments used by the justices of the Supreme Court was that the art 226[13] of the Constitution should not be considered numerus clausus or an exhaustive roll, but only an exemplary list of family entities, as doctrine had already advocated for many years.

As stated by Paulo Lôbo,[14] the heading of art 226 brought the most profound transformation relating to the effectiveness of the constitutional protection to the family. There is no mention of a certain type of family, as occurred with the previous Constitutions. By eliminating the expression 'constituted by marriage' (art 175 of the Constitution 1967–1969), without replacing it with another, the constitutional legislator put 'family' under constitutional protection, meaning any family.

IV STABLE UNION AND MARRIAGE

As already indicated, on 5 May 2011, Brazil experienced an historic moment in the joint trial of ADPF 132 and ADI 4277, which represented a paradigm shift and progress in family law. The Supreme Court held that the homo-affective union is a family entity and deriving from it are all the rights and obligations emanating from the stable union between a man and woman.[15] It is important to emphasise that this position had already been expressed for over a decade by judges of first degree and state courts throughout Brazil.

Thus, with the identification of the legal requirements for the configuration of a stable union recognised in public and with continuing and lasting coexistence for the purpose of family formation, homosexual couples 'form stable unions suitable for the enjoyment of all rights and obligations arising from the exercise of the same sentiment: love'.[16] Thus, homo-affective unions were treated like stable unions composed of people of the opposite sex.

---

[13] Article 226. The family, foundation of society, has special protection of the State.
§ 1 – Marriage is civil and its celebration is free.
§ 2 – The religious marriage has civil effects, in accordance with law.
§ 3 – For purposes of protection of the state, the stable union between man and woman is recognised as a family entity, and the law should facilitate its conversion into marriage.
§ 4 –The community formed by any parent and her or his offspring is also considered as a family entity.

[14] Paulo Luiz Netto Lôbo 'Entidades familiares constitucionalizadas: para além do *numerus clausus*' in Rodrigo da Cunha Pereira (ed) *Família e cidadania:* o novo CCB e a *vacatio legis* – Anais do III Congresso Brasileiro de Direito de Família (Belo Horizonte: Del Rey/IBDFAM, 2002) 89–107 at 94.

[15] Cf Marianna Chaves 'O STF e as uniões homoafetivas' (13–20 May 2010) 13(14) *A Semana – Política, Economia e Comportamento* 22.

[16] As stated by Enézio de Deus Silva Júnior 'Amor e Família Homossexual: o fim da invisibilidade

What about marriage? As an effect of the decision, there was a doctrinal and jurisprudential uproar about the possibility of the conversion of homo-affective stable unions into marriage.

There was no need for any hermeneutic exercise, but only some brief and logical reasoning: if the Supreme Court recognised a same-sex union as a stable union and the Brazilian Constitution itself states that the law should facilitate its conversion into marriage, no other understanding would be possible: stable unions, whether hetero or homo-affective, can be converted into a marriage in accordance with art 1.726 of the Brazilian Civil Code.[17]

Notwithstanding the decision of the Supreme Court (that has binding effect and erga omnes force), here and there we encounter decisions in which the application for conversion of a homo-affective stable union into marriage has been denied. This fact brings to light the necessity of editing the existing rules, considering that Brazil is a country where the written law is highly prestigious, often interpreted literally and away from the spirit of the system. There are cases where prosecutors and magistrates of first degree, although in isolated occurrences, insist on questioning the decision of the Supreme Court. It is important that the decision of the Supreme Court be embedded in legislation in an ostensible and literal way, stating that same-sex unions and marriage are legal, either through constitutional amendment, reform of the Civil Code or enactment of the Sexual Diversity Statute.[18]

Besides the argument put forward by the Supreme Court – equalisation of the homo-affective union with the stable union – and its derivative consequence in the field of civil marriage by conversion, it is also necessary to legislatively enshrine the possibility of direct same-sex marriage. It is a viable alternative in accordance with the doctrine and jurisprudence of the Superior Court of Justice, which accepted the special appeal of two women who were trying to marry directly.

It has been argued, already for some time in Brazil, that the proposal of non-existent marriage held by part of the traditional doctrine was a mere doctrinal creation without any legal support for that idea in the country. There was not and still there is no legal provision stating that a marriage between two persons of the same sex is non-existent, as there was in Portugal, for instance, until 2010. Gender equality does not constitute any of the matrimonial impediments in art 1.521 of the Brazilian Civil Code, neither the explicit nor

---

através da decisão do STF' (2011) available at http://por-leitores.jusbrasil.com.br/noticias/2676091/amor-e-familia-homossexual-o-fim-da-invisibilidade-atraves-da-decisao-do-stf (accessed 7 December 2013).

[17] Article 1.726. The stable union can be converted into marriage, upon request of the partners to the judge and entry in the Civil Register.

[18] A draft bill has been prepared by the Sexual Diversity of the Brazilian Bar Association to be presented to the Commission on Human Rights and Legislative Participation of the Senate, which aims to establish a microsystem with the imposition of affirmative rules regarding the LGBT population, as happened with the Statute of Children and Adolescents, the Elderly Statute and the Statute of Racial Equality.

the implicit prohibitions. And even if it were held that the expression 'male and female' present in arts 1.514, 1.517 and 1.565 of the Civil Code constitute an 'implied prohibition', the magistrate could always use the diffuse control of constitutionality and may decide not to apply to the case a rule that he deems unconstitutional. Moreover, there are no implicit bans in the Brazilian system. As the Constitution provides, no one is obliged to do or refrain from doing something except by virtue of law. Therefore direct same-sex marriage is not forbidden, so even if not explicitly stated it is allowed since the emergence of the Civil Code of 2002 and there is no legal basis preventing homosexuals from having access to civil marriage as currently regulated in the Brazilian legal system.

Corroborating this understanding, the 4th Chamber of the Superior Court of Justice ruled that direct same-sex marriage is indeed possible in Brazil. This is a precedent, a very important leading case on the matter. Unfortunately, it does not override the need for legislation that addresses the topic, given the subsequent sentences contesting the absolutely irremovable possibility of converting the stable union into a same-sex marriage, enacted after the trial at the Supreme Court.

As the argument of direct same-sex marriage is a recent doctrinal and jurisprudential construction, without binding effect, a law that guarantees the possibility proves to be opportune in order to remove any doubt. Although there is a resolution of the National Council of Justice (no 175, 14 May 2013), that prohibits the competent authorities from refusing the application, celebration of civil marriage or conversion of same-sex stable union into marriage, the resolution has been questioned by the legislature, which aims to halt the effects of it through two drafts of a legislative decree restraining normative acts of executive power.

V SAME-SEX ADOPTION

Subsequent to the trial of ADI 4277 and ADPF 132 by the Supreme Court in May 2010, adoption by same-sex couples can be easily equalised within the current context of the Brazilian system. The unvarnished reading of the rules relating to the issue easily leads us to the conclusion that there are no legal obstacles of any kind for a homosexual couple to apply for joint adoption of a child or adolescent.

Article 42, § 2 of the Statute of Children and Adolescents establishes as a requirement for joint adoption that applicants are united by marriage or live in a stable union demonstrating family stability. The homo-affective union was equated to a stable union for all purposes. Therefore, any legal impediment that could be envisioned through a more restrictive interpretation no longer has any room in today's Brazilian legal system.[19]

---

[19] Cf Marianna Chaves 'Algumas Notas sobre as Uniões Homoafetivas no Ordenamento

VI CONCLUSION

On behalf of the principles of human dignity, equality and freedom, equal rights should be granted to homosexuals, for example, the right to enter into civil marriage, the right to parenthood, the right to exercise their sexual orientation without fear of rejection, social exclusion or suppression of rights. This idea is embodied in the certainty that family, safeguarded in several constitutions around the world, is focused on the development of human beings that integrate it. The family entity is not tutored for itself other than as a means for personal fulfilment of its components.

It can be said that, although today there is some legal certainty in relation to the recognition of LGBT rights, there is still a huge disparity, an abysmal gap between legal recognition and legislative recognition in Brazil.

The trial of the Supreme Court is a true representation of a paradigm shift, of the enshrining of equality, pluralism, diversity, freedom and all the islands that form the protected continent of human dignity. Fundamental rights, personality rights were finally assured to LGBT families.

However, it is still necessary to advance in this field. As previously mentioned, Brazil is a state of Roman-Germanic origin, where the written law has crucial importance. This fact proves to be so true that, even with a trial held by the Supreme Court with binding effect and erga omnes efficacy, there are members of the judiciary who still challenge the decision. The legislative power rages about a supposed judicial activism. Therefore, it is imperative that laws be edited, to ensure legislatively what has already been secured in the courts, although this fact seems to have a more symbolic than practical effect. After all, the legislative omission is yet another form of oppression and intolerance.

Brasileiro após o Julgamento da ADPF 132 e da ADI 4277 pelo STF' 13(66) (2010) *Revista Síntese de Direito de Família* (São Paulo: Síntese) 7–15 at 14.

CANADA

UNMARRIED COHABITATION IN QUEBEC – LIBERTÉ OU ÉGALITÉ?

*Martha Bailey**

Résumé

Le niveau de conjugalité hors mariage est plus élevé au Québec que dans n'importe quelle autre province canadienne et il se rapproche de celui des trois territoires peu peuplés qui s'étendent dans la partie nordique du Canada. Le statut juridique des conjoints de fait au Québec est également distinct en ce que, contrairement aux autres provinces, le Québec ne les soumet ni à une obligation alimentaire ni à un quelconque partage de biens. La constitutionnalité de cette exclusion a été récemment contestée, mais en vain, devant la Cour suprême du Canada. Ce chapitre s'intéresse également à la situation d'un groupe hassidique ultra orthodoxe du nom de Lev Tahor. Les services de protection de la jeunesse du Québec sont récemment intervenus et les procédures judiciaires concernant les enfants de cette communauté sont toujours pendantes, mais entre-temps les enfants ont été déplacés vers d'autres parties du Canada et, pour certains, aussi loin qu'au Guatemala. Tenter de ramener ces enfants au Canada n'a pas été une mince affaire.

I INTRODUCTION

For the past half-century, Quebec has been known as a 'distinct society' within Canada, an epithet that acknowledges the province's unique history, language, culture and laws.[1] Canada is a bilingual (English and French) country – almost a third of Canada's 34 million residents speak French, and for 22% of the population French is the mother tongue. But most of Canada's francophones live in Quebec, and the large majority of Quebeckers speak French.[2] And Quebec is Canada's one mixed-law jurisdiction. The common law tradition that

* Martha Bailey, LLB, (University of Toronto), LLM, (Queen's University), DPhil (Oxford University), is a Professor of Law at Queen's University and can be reached at baileym@queensu.ca.

1 Canada *Royal Commission on Bilingualism and Biculturalism* (Ottawa, 1963); Robert Sheppard 'Quebec Nationalism, a Long History' (CBC News) 23 November 2006, available at www.cbc.ca/news2/background/parliament39/quebecnation-history.html.

2 Canada, Office of the Commissioner of Official Languages, 'Quick Facts about Canada's Francophonie' available at www.ocol-clo.gc.ca/html/quick_facts_faits_bref_franco_e.php.

applies in the rest of Canada is limited to public law matters in Quebec. For private law matters, Quebec has a codified civil law.[3]

Quebec has also been a distinct society in regard to both family life and family law. Civil marriage was opened up to same-sex couples across Canada in 2005.[4] But prior to this exercise of federal power over marriage, Quebec enthusiastically endorsed same-sex marriage. Although unable to act on this issue because provinces do not have legislative competence in regard to the essential validity of marriage, in 2002 Quebec legislators unanimously passed a broad 'civil union' law that permits same-sex and opposite-sex couples who register to obtain the same legal rights and obligations as married couples in matters within provincial legislative jurisdiction.[5] This was a full 3 years before the federal government, less enthusiastically and not unanimously, enacted legislation to open up civil marriage to same-sex couples.

II LIMITED STATUTORY COVERAGE FOR UNMARRIED COHABITATION

Another distinctive aspect of family life in Quebec relates to unmarried cohabitation. Quebec's rate of unmarried cohabitation is higher than in the other provinces and similar to that of Canada's three sparsely populated territories that span the northern part of the country. For Canada as a whole, the 2011 Census revealed that 16.7% of all families involve unmarried cohabitation, 67% married couples, and 16.3% single parents.[6] For Quebec, 31.5% of families include unmarried cohabitants, 51.9% married couples and 16.6% single parents.[7]

The legal framework for unmarried couples in Quebec is also distinctive. In Quebec, as in the rest of Canada, the rights and obligations relating to children are not affected by the marital status of the parents. And Quebec, like the rest of Canada, treats unmarried couples as spouses for various public law purposes and in regard to dealings between couples and third parties. So in matters such as social assistance, pensions and insurance, unmarried couples are treated as

---

3 For a helpful review of mixed law jurisdictions, see William Tetley 'Nationalism in a Mixed Jurisdiction and the Importance of Language' (2003) 78 Tul L Rev 175.

4 Civil Marriage Act, SC 2005, c 33.

5 An Act Instituting Civil Unions and Establishing New Rules of Filiation, SQ 2002, c 6 (in force 8 June 2002).

6 Statistics Canada (Minister of *Portrait of Families and Living Arrangements in Canada: Families, households and marital status, 2011 Census of Population* Industry: Ottawa, 2012) 6. It should be noted that Statistics Canada uses the term 'common-law couples' and judges and others have also used the term 'common-law marriage' when referring to unmarried cohabitation (see eg *Egan v Canada* [1993] 3 FC 401). I use the term 'unmarried cohabitation' to make clear that I am *not* referring to legal marriages that have been contracted in an irregular way.

7 Statistics Canada *Portrait of Families and Living Arrangements in Canada: Families, households and marital status, 2011 Census of Population* (Minister of Industry: Ottawa, 2012) 6.

spouses.[8] But Quebec differs in regard to the mutual rights and obligations of unmarried couples. All other provinces and territories extend the spousal support rights and obligations to unmarried couples who have cohabited for a certain period.[9] Three provinces and two territories have also extended marital property rights to unmarried couples.[10] Quebec has not included unmarried couples in either the spousal support or marital property regime.

Quebec's approach to unmarried cohabitation is not based on bias or disapprobation but on respect for autonomy of the parties. The government has explicitly declined to impose the mutual rights and obligations of marriage on those who do not signal their consent by entering into a marriage or a civil union. Since the late 1970s Quebec legislators have repeatedly considered extending mutual rights and obligations to unmarried couples, each time rejecting the extension in order to preserve the freedom of parties from a government-imposed regime.[11]

---

8 Individual and Family Assistance Act, RSQ, c A-13.1.1; An Act respecting the Québec Pension Plan; An Act respecting the Government and Public Employees Retirement Plan, RSQ, c R-10; An Act respecting the Civil Service Superannuation Plan, RSQ, c R-12; Supplemental Pension Plans Act; An Act respecting the conditions of employment and the pension plan of the Members of the National Assembly, RSQ, c C-52.1; An Act respecting the Pension Plan of Certain Teachers, RSQ, c R-9.1; An Act respecting the Pension Plan of Peace Officers in Correctional Services, RSQ, c R-9.2; An Act respecting the Pension Plan of Elected Municipal Officers, RSQ, c R-9.3; An Act respecting the Teachers Pension Plan, RSQ, c R-11; Automobile Insurance Act, RSQ, c A-25; An Act respecting insurance; RSQ, c A-32.

9 The requisite period of cohabitation and relevant statute for each province and territory are: Alberta (3 yrs cohabitation or less if child or agreement), Adult Interdependent Relationships Act, SA 2002, c A-4.5, s 3, Family Law Act, SA 2005, c F-4.5, s 57; British Columbia (2 yrs cohabitation or less if child), Family Law Act, SBC 2011, c 25, s 3; Manitoba (3 yrs cohabitation or 1 yr if child), Family Maintenance Act, CCSM c F20, ss 1, 4; New Brunswick,(3 yrs cohabitation or less if child), Family Services Act, SNB 1980, c F-2.2, s 112; Newfoundland (2 yrs cohabitation or 1 yr if child), Family Law Act, RSNL 1990, c F-2, ss 35, 36; Northwest Territories (2 yrs cohabitation or less if child), Family Law Act, SNWT 1997, c 18, ss 1, 16; Nova Scotia (2 yrs cohabitation), Maintenance and Custody Act, RS NS 1989, c 160, ss 2(aa), 3; Nunavut (2 yrs cohabitation or less if child) Family Law Act, SNWT (Nu) 1997, ss 1, 15; Ontario (3 yrs cohabitation or less if child), Family Law Act, RSO 1990, c F.3, ss 29, 30; Prince Edward Island (3 yrs cohabitation or less if child), Family Law Act, RSPEI 1988, c F-2.1, ss 29, 30; Saskatchewan (2 yrs cohabitation or less if child), Family Maintenance Act, SS 1997, c F-6.2, ss 2, 5; Yukon (gone through a form of marriage + cohabitation of some permanence, no set period), Family Property and Support Act, RSY 2002, c 83, s 37.

10 British Columbia (2 yrs cohabitation), Family Law Act, SBC 2011, c 25, s 3; Manitoba (3 yrs cohabitation), Family Property Act, CCSM, c F25, s 1, 2.1; Northwest Territories (2 yrs cohabitation or less if child), Family Law Act, SNWT 1997, s 18, ss 1, 36; Nunavut (2 yrs cohabitation or less if child), Family Law Act, SNWT (Nu), ss 1, 36; Saskatchewan (2 yrs cohabitation), Family Property Act, SS 1997, c F-6.3, ss 2, 21.

11 *Quebec (Attorney General) v A*, 2013 SCC 5 ('*A*'), paras 105–109, online at http://scc-csc.lexum.com/scc-csc/scc-csc/en/10536/1/document.do. Then Quebec Minister of Justice Serge Ménard explained to the National Assembly of Quebec that the province did not previously include unmarried couples within its scheme of marital rights and obligations out of respect for the autonomy of those who do not wish to submit themselves to the legal regime of marriage: Quebec, Debates of the National Assembly, 18 June 1998.

III THE SUPREME COURT

In 2013, the Supreme Court of Canada (SCC) handed down its decision on the constitutionality of Quebec's exclusion of unmarried couples from the spousal support and property rules applicable to those who are married or who have entered into a civil union.[12] It should be noted that in Quebec, as in the rest of Canada, unmarried couples are free to enter into contracts that provide for support or property division in the event of dissolution of the relationship. So there are three methods of obtaining marital support and property rights and obligations. In the absence of some signal that the couple agrees to take on marital rights and obligations – by entering into a marriage, civil union or contract – the default rule is that no such rights and obligations exist.

The case involves a couple, called 'A' and 'B' in the Supreme Court decision, who met in A's home country in 1992. A, just 17 years old at the time, was living with her parents and attending school. B was 32 years old and a successful business owner. In early 1995, the couple decided to settle in B's home province of Quebec. Over the next few years A gave birth to their three children. She did not work outside the home. B supported A and the children. The couple never married, apparently because of B's resistance to the institution of marriage. B suggested that he might someday marry in order to give official status to a long-term relationship. In the event, the parties separated in 2002 after living together for 7 years.

The issues of child custody and child support are not affected by the marital status of the parents and were not at issue in the appeal to the Supreme Court.[13] The Quebec Superior Court awarded joint custody of the three children. B was ordered to pay A the sum of $34,260.24 a month in child support and certain specific expenses, including the children's tuition fees, expenses related to their extracurricular activities, the salaries of two nannies and a cook. B was also ordered to pay all costs relating to the residence of A and the children, including school and municipal taxes, home insurance premiums, and general maintenance and renovation costs. B remained the owner of that residence.[14]

A's claims for spousal support, a lump sum, the right to claim a compensatory allowance and partition of the family patrimony and the legal matrimonial

---

12 *A*, paras 105–109.

13 Justice LeBel summarised Quebec's law in *A* at para 104: 'The legislature also eliminated the distinctions between legitimate, natural, adulterine and incestuous children. It thus established the principle that children are equal regardless of the circumstances of their birth and the nature of their filiation. Article 522 CCQ [Civil Code of Quebec] now codifies the principle that all children whose filiation is established have the same rights and obligations. The rules on parental authority (arts 597 CCQ et seq), the obligation of support (art 585 CCQ) and intestate succession (art 655 CCQ) therefore apply to all children. In addition, art 604 CCQ provides that, "[i]n the case of difficulties relating to the exercise of parental authority, the person having parental authority may refer the matter to the court, which will decide in the interest of the child after fostering the conciliation of the parties".'

14 *A* at para 7.

regime of partnership of acquests were at issue. A challenged the constitutionality of Quebec's exclusion of unmarried couples from the family law regime pursuant to s 15 of the Charter, which enshrines the guarantee of equality.[15] Section 15 guarantees that 'every individual is equal before and under the law and has the right to the equal protection and equal benefit of the law without discrimination' on the basis of grounds enumerated in the provision, which include sex, as well as analogous grounds, which include marital status.[16]

A's challenge to the constitutionality of Quebec's family property rules came just a decade after the decision of the Supreme Court in *Nova Scotia (Attorney General) v Walsh*.[17] In *Walsh*, the Supreme Court held that exclusion of unmarried couples from Nova Scotia's family property statutes was *not* discriminatory within the meaning of s 15 of the Charter. The majority stated that those who marry can be said to freely accept the rights and obligations of marriage, and that the decision not to marry should be respected. The Court also pointed out that alternative choices and remedies are available to persons who are unwilling or unable to marry. In order for A to succeed in her challenge to the family property rules, she would have had to persuade the Supreme Court to reverse or somehow distinguish the *Walsh* decision.

More promising was the possibility of a successful challenge to the exclusion of unmarried couples from the spousal support regime. The concurring opinion of Gonthier J in the *Walsh* case supported A's argument on the support issue. Justice Gonthier expressed the view that family property division is aimed at dividing assets according to the regime chosen by parties, either explicitly or implicitly by getting married. In contrast, stated Gonthier J, the purpose of support laws, which generally apply to both marriage and cohabitation, is to meet the needs of spouses and children. Family property schemes are contractual in nature, while support laws are not contractual but rather responsive to situations of dependency. Justice Gonthier wrote:[18]

> 'The division of matrimonial assets and spousal support have different objectives. One aims to divide assets according to a property regime chosen by the parties, either directly by contract or indirectly by the fact of marriage, while the other seeks to fulfil a social objective: meeting the needs of spouses and their children. This Court also recognized ... that one of the objectives of spousal support is to alleviate the burden on the public purse by shifting the obligation to provide support for needy persons to those spouses who have the capacity to support them. The support obligation responds to social concerns with respect to situations of dependency that may occur in common law relationships.'

Following this reasoning, the Supreme Court could have upheld A's challenge to Quebec's exclusionary spousal support rules in order to address the situation of dependency of dependency and to meet the needs of the dependent spouse and

---

15 The Constitution Act 1982, being Sch B to the Canada Act 1982 (UK), 1982, c 11.
16 *Miron v Trudel* [1995] 2 SCR 418.
17 2002 SCC 83 ('Walsh').
18 *Walsh* at para 204.

the children. The respect for autonomy that underpinned the *Walsh* decision did not apply in regard to the spousal support issue.

In the event, the Supreme Court dismissed all of A's challenges and upheld not just the family property rules, but the spousal support rules as well. Justice LeBel, writing for a four-judge plurality, rejected the distinction between the family property regime and the spousal support regime as 'inappropriate'. He wrote that such a distinction ignores the nature of the economic partnership established by Quebec for marriages and civil unions. Because the obligation of support is tied to the other incidents of marriage and of civil union, such as the obligation to contribute to household expenses and rights, it cannot be separated from the family law regime as a whole and applied without reference to the other parts of the broader regime.[19]

Justice Lebel wrote that the Quebec family law regime was not discriminatory. As in the *Walsh* case, great emphasis was placed on the importance of respecting the autonomy of parties and not imposing family law rights and obligations on couples without their mutual consent. He wrote:[20]

> 'In Quebec family law, these rights and obligations are always available to everyone, but imposed on no one. Their application depends on an express mutual will of the spouses to bind themselves. This express, and not deemed, consent is the source of the obligation of support and of that of partition of spouses' patrimonial interests. As we have seen, this consent is given in Quebec law by contracting marriage or a civil union, or entering into a cohabitation agreement. Participation in the protective regimes provided for by law depends necessarily on mutual consent. In this regard, the conclusion of a cohabitation agreement enables *de facto* spouses to create for themselves the legal relationship they consider necessary without having to modify the form of conjugality they have chosen for their life together.'

The other five judges found that Quebec's family law regime discriminated on the basis of marital status. Chief Justice McLachlin ruled that the discrimination in regard to both property and support was justified under s 1 of the Charter. Section 1 of the Charter provides that:

> 'The *Canadian Charter of Rights and Freedoms* guarantees the rights and freedoms set out in it subject only to such reasonable limits prescribed by law as can be demonstrably justified in a free and democratic society.'

Justice Abella said that neither the property nor the spousal support exclusion could be justified and would have ruled both unconstitutional. She would have preferred an opt-out scheme that would give couples the freedom to contract out of the regime if they chose to do so, while protecting vulnerable cohabiting spouses by automatically extending spousal support and property division entitlements to them. Justice Abella reasoned that the benefits of ensuring that the vulnerable spouse is protected outweigh concerns about impinging on the

---

[19] *A* at paras 229 and 230.
[20] *A* at para 257.

parties' freedom of choice and autonomy. The remaining three judges took the view that the exclusion from property division was justified under s 1 of the Charter but that the exclusion from spousal support was not justified. So with the four judges who ruled that there was no discrimination plus the vote of McLachlin CJ, there was a majority ruling that Quebec's rules on property and support do not violate the Charter.

The division in the Supreme Court may reflect the broader division in Canadian society on the issues raised. There has been considerable support among some academics and women's groups for imposing the incidents of marriage on those who do not choose it. The Women's Legal Education and Action Fund, one of the intervenors in *A*, supported A's position, contending that spousal relationships are marked by gender inequality, that the Supreme Court should take that inequality into account in determining whether the impugned statutory provisions are discriminatory, and advocating that the family property and spousal support laws be applied to unmarried cohabitants.[21] Often it is the party with more economic resources who does not want marriage, or at least does not want marriage in the absence of a marriage contract that opts out of default family property and spousal support obligations.[22] The powerlessness of the less wealthy to force the other party to agree to marriage has given rise to concerns when the wealthier party gets all the benefits of marriage and family without taking on all the responsibilities. If the needs of the dependent party are not adequately addressed through property division or support provision, this may be problematic not just for the dependent party but also for the children of the union. As noted above, the marital status of parents does not affect obligations in respect to children. However, child support may not fully address the costs to the custodial parent of rearing children or the problem of a child alternating between a relatively wealthy parent and a relatively poor parent.[23]

IV LEV TAHOR, CHILD ABUSE, AND ESCAPE FROM THE JURISDICTION

Another case from Quebec that was ongoing at the time of writing involves the ultra-Orthodox Hasidic group called Lev Tahor ('Pure Heart').[24] This group was founded by Rabbi Shlomo Helbrans in Israel in the 1980s. Helbrans, an anti-Zionist, decided to relocate to New York with his followers in the early 1990s. While living in New York, Helbrans was convicted of conspiracy to kidnap a boy who had been sent to him for religious training.[25] Five years after

---

21 *A* at para 49.

22 *Hartshorne v Hartshorne*, 2004 SCC 22.

23 Robert Leckey 'Developments in Family Law: The 2012–2013 Term' (2014) 64 *Supreme Court Law Review* (2d) 241.

24 For helpful background on Lev Tahor, see Shay Fogelman 'Lev Tahor: Pure as the driven snow, or hearts of darkness?' *Haaretz*, 9 March 2012 and 'When you're on the path of truth, you don't care what others say' *Haaretz*, 16 March 2012.

25 Craig Wolff 'Rabbi Agrees to Guilty Plea in Boy's Kidnapping' *New York Times*, 8 March 1994.

this conviction, he was deported to Israel.[26] Helbrans was then granted asylum in Canada, and he and his followers settled in the town of St-Agathe-des-Monts in Quebec by 2001.

Beginning in 2012, Quebec's child welfare services began investigating Lev Tahor. This investigation culminated in proceedings commenced on 14 November 2013 in respect of 14 children in which the authorities raised concerns of forced marriage of children under the age of 16, failure to provide adequate education for the children, inappropriate discipline of child by use of force and neglect of the parents in the physical care of the children.[27]

It should be noted that the investigation of Lev Tahor took place at a time when the province was debating a Charter of Values proposed by the governing Parti Québécois. Among the most controversial aspects of the proposed Charter of Values is its prohibition of public sector employees from wearing or displaying 'conspicuous' religious symbols, such as religious headgear. The many critics of the proposed Charter point to the parochial intolerance that it seems to embody. Former Supreme Court of Canada judge Louise Arbour, for example, has said that the restriction violates freedom of religion and that its proponents have not demonstrated the necessity for such a violation.[28]

While religious animus may have had no role in the investigation of the Lev Tahor community, debates about the Charter of Values may have given rise to concerns in the community or bolstered pre-existing narratives of religious persecution within the group. Lev Tahor members wear highly conspicuous religious garb, including burqa-like coverings for the women. There have long been conflicts between closed religious sects wanting to raise their children in a manner consistent with their values and governments seeking to protect the vulnerable. Determining when to overrule decisions of parents on questions of child-rearing in such circumstances is challenging. The US Supreme Court cautioned in *Wisconsin v Yoder*:[29]

> 'We must not forget that, in the Middle Ages, important values of the civilization of the Western World were preserved by members of religious orders who isolated themselves from all worldly influences against great obstacles. There can be no assumption that today's majority is 'right,' and the Amish and others like them are 'wrong.' A way of life that is odd or even erratic but interferes with no rights or interests of others is not to be condemned because it is different.'

The hearing in Quebec was scheduled for 19 November 2013. The children who were the subject of the scheduled proceeding and most of their parents and other Lev Tahor members left Quebec on 18 November. The parents who remained in Quebec attended the hearing, where they indicated that they would

---

26 'Rabbi Is Deported 5 Years After Conviction, Lawyer Says' *New York Times*, 12 May 2000.

27 *Chatham-Kent Children's Services v AH*, 2014 ONCJ 50 at paras 5–6.

28 Tu Thanh Ha 'Former Supreme Court justices offer conflicting views of Quebec's secular charter' *Globe & Mail*, 7 February 2014.

29 *Wisconsin v Yoder,* 406 US 205 (1972) at 223–224.

not present the children to the court because they were concerned that the children would be removed from them. The judge determined that the Quebec court had jurisdiction based on the domicile of the families in Quebec. When the matter came on for a full hearing on 27 November 2013, none of the parents or children attended, but counsel for the parents and the children were present. The judge ordered that the children be placed in foster care for 30 days, that they receive medical examinations and any psychological help if needed, and that contact between the parents and children be determined by the child welfare authority.[30] The allegations of abuse and neglect have not yet been tested in Quebec and the allegations cannot be resolved until the children are returned.

After leaving Quebec, the group took up residence in Chatham, Ontario. The local child welfare authorities, the Chatham-Kent Children's Services (CKCS), received notice of the Quebec proceedings, and applied for an order authorising them to deliver the children to the child protection authorities in the Province of Quebec. Unfortunately, Ontario's child welfare statute has no provision regarding recognition and enforcement of extra-provincial child welfare orders.[31] Courts have responded to this lacuna by invoking the recognition provisions of Ontario's custody statute and broadly interpreting child welfare orders as 'custody' orders within the meaning of that statute.[32] This was the approach taken by the Ontario court hearing the application of CKCS for return of the children. The court ruled that it had jurisdiction under the child custody statute, that the children were habitually resident in Quebec at the time proceedings were commenced there, and that the order of the Quebec court that the children be placed in foster care in Quebec should be recognised. The court noted that the policy reasons for the legislative scheme for recognition of extra-provincial custody order were:[33]

> 'to avoid multiplicity of proceedings between jurisdictions involving custody of children, and discourage the abduction of children in the face of lawful orders made by the jurisdiction where the children were habitually resident. To do otherwise would simply encourage jurisdictional chaos as others try to escape the lawful processes where children habitually reside.'

The court made an exception from its order of return for one of the 14 children who was herself a parent of one of the other children. The court further ordered that the CKCS take control of the children as necessary pending their return to Quebec, and that the children not be removed from the Chatham-Kent area.[34] The court stayed its ruling to give the respondents an opportunity to appeal.

Pending the appeal of the order to return the 14 children to Quebec, the group fled without giving notice to the CKCS or their own lawyers. Six of the 14

---

30 *Chatham-Kent Children's Services v AH*, 2014 ONCJ 50 at paras 9–14.

31 Child and Family Services Act, RSO 1990, c C.11.

32 Children's Law Reform Act, RSO 1990, c C.12, s 40.

33 *Chatham-Kent Children's Services v AH*, 2014 ONCJ 50 at para 71.

34 *Chatham-Kent Children's Services v AH*, 2014 ONCJ 50 at para 77.

children were apprehended in Trinidad and Tobago, on their way to join other members of Lev Tahor in Guatemala. Two others were apprehended at the Calgary airport. The eight apprehended children were taken into the care of the CKCS. The appeal of the order to return the children to Quebec was adjourned to April 2014.[35]

Attempts by Canada to have the children returned from Guatemala have been stymied so far. The Convention on the Civil Aspects of International Child Abduction provides for immediate return of children who have been wrongfully removed or retained in violation of the rights of custody of a person or institution. Arguably, the Ontario court seized with the case of the CKCS had rights of custody within the meaning of the Abduction Convention at the time the children were removed from Canada. The Abduction Convention has been in force in Canada since 1983 and in Guatemala since 2002.[36] However, Guatemala acceded to the Abduction Convention, and Canada has not yet accepted its accession. Article 38 of the Abduction Convention provides that an 'accession will have effect only as regards the relations between the acceding State and such Contracting States as will have declared their acceptance of the accession'. Therefore, the Abduction Convention does not apply as between Canada and Guatemala and cannot be used to obtain and order of return in respect of the remaining six children.

The 1996 Hague Convention on Jurisdiction, Applicable Law, Recognition, Enforcement and Co-operation in Respect of Parental Responsibility and Measures for the Protection of Children provides important tools to supplement the operation of the Abduction Convention. The Abduction Convention provides for immediate return of children who have been wrongfully removed or retained, but does not establish rules of jurisdiction or enforcement of custody and access rights and does not provide for provisional orders to ensure safe returns. The 1996 Convention fills this gap and it explicitly applies to child welfare proceedings and measures to protect children who have been displaced by war or natural disasters. The 1996 Convention covers a broader range of issues than the Abduction Convention and deals with both private and public law matters. Like the Abduction Convention, it establishes measures for co-operation among contracting states. These measures of co-operation include providing assistance in locating a child who may be in need of protection, providing a social report on the situation of the child, and facilitating agreed solutions for the protection of the child or the property of the child on the request of another contracting state.

The 1996 Convention provides the legal framework for dealing with the problems raised in the Lev Tahor case. Unfortunately, neither Canada nor Guatemala is a party to the 1996 Convention. So not only do Canadian provinces lack clear-cut statutory frameworks relating to jurisdiction,

---

35 *Chatham-Kent Children's Services v AH*, 2014 ONSC 1697.

36 Hague Conference on Private International Law, Convention on the Civil Aspects of International Child Abduction, Status Table, online at www.hcch.net/index_en.php?act=conventions.status&cid=24.

applicable law and recognition in interprovincial child welfare cases, but Canada has failed as yet to sign on to the 1996 Convention that addresses these issues in an international context. The breadth of the 1996 Convention creates challenges in implementation. In Canada, both the federal and provincial governments have legislative powers in respect of issues that fall under the scope of the 1996 Convention. Most of these issues are within provincial legislative competence as matters of 'property and civil rights within the provinces'.[37] However, pursuant to its exclusive jurisdiction over divorce,[38] the federal Parliament has enacted laws relating to custody and access that apply when the parties are seeking or have obtained a divorce under Canada's Divorce Act.[39] Within each province, responsibility for issues covered by the 1996 Convention rests with more than one ministry, and are dealt with in multiple statutes, regulations and procedures. But these challenges are no greater than those faced by many countries that have signed on to the 1996 Convention. It is hoped that the wide publicity of the Lev Tahor case will spur the government to proceed with ratification and implementation of the 1996 Convention.

As things stand, neither the Abduction Convention nor the 1996 Convention is available to effect return of the six children. The Guatemalan and Canadian authorities are trying to work out a solution, but it is not clear how the case will be resolved. The Guatemalan Ministry of Foreign Affairs spokesperson was quoted as saying: 'Until that abuse is proven in Guatemala, Canada cannot proceed to take them back.'[40] Back in Canada, the appeal of the order of return of the children to Quebec is scheduled for early April and presumably will proceed. Going forward, it is hoped that the government of Canada and provincial legislatures will now have a clearer understanding of the perils of 'jurisdictional chaos' in child welfare proceedings and newly resolve to ratify and implement the 1996 Convention and to enact statutory provisions for jurisdiction, applicable law and recognition in interprovincial child welfare cases.

---

37 The Constitution Act, 1982, being Sch B to the Canada Act 1982 (UK), 1982, c 11, s 92, s 92(12).

38 The Constitution Act, 1982, being Sch B to the Canada Act 1982 (UK), 1982, c 11, s 91(26).

39 RSC 1985, c 3 (2nd Supp).

40 Karla Zabludovsky 'Members of a Jewish Sect Lev Tahor Flee Canada for Guatemala' *Newsweek*, 31 March 2014.

CHILE

THE MAPUCHES AND CHILEAN FAMILY LAW

*Ursula Pohl**

Résumé

Ce texte explore quelques-unes des tensions qui existent entre le droit chilien d'origine occidentale et la culture autochtone des Mapuches. Le droit de la famille et des successions s'applique à tous les Chiliens, incluant les Mapuches. Il en résulte une certaine négation des us et coutumes mapuches. Par exemple, les Mapuches connaissaient la polygamie mais celle-ci est interdite depuis 1884. Pourtant, la polygamie existe toujours. Cela se reflète également dans l'augmentation des enfants illégitimes, même récemment: 54% en 2003 et 65% en 2011. Quoi qu'il en soit, le mélange des cultures a eu pour résultat que tous les Chiliens accordent une valeur fondamentale à la famille; les racines de cet attachement sont à trouver dans la structure familiale traditionnelle des Mapuches.

One can understand Chile only if one also occupies oneself with the culture and the customs of the aboriginals. 75% of the Chileans are Mestizos. That means that they are a mixture of white and red. The combination of ethnic groups led inevitably to a combination of the culture. The Araukanes who were later called Mapuches[1] arrived in the territory in about 1350. This was later claimed by the Spanish conquerors, and it became the Republic of Chile in the nineteenth century.[2] They lived widely scattered in autonomous bands and the tribe (tribu) was their highest organisation.[3] A system of laws in the Western sense was only established under the Spanish crown.[4] These laid the foundation for a Spanish–American legal system (Derecho de las Indias).[5] When this legal system was drafted, the missions led by the Jesuits, Franciscans and Capuchins were of the greatest importance.[6]

When America was conquered two diametrically opposed cultures clashed. On the one hand there was the so-called Western culture, its basic assumptions originating in the Bible, namely that the Jewish–Christian God created man on

* Dr jur. Practising lawyer.

1 Omar Lobos *Los Mapuches* (Buenos Aires: 2008) 7.

2 Díaz del Río Eduardo *Los Araucanos y el Derecho* (Santiago de Chile: 2006) 9.

3 Díaz del Río Eduardo *Los Araucanos y el Derecho* (Santiago de Chile: 2006) 9.

4 Díaz del Río Eduardo *Los Araucanos y el Derecho* (Santiago de Chile: 2006) 9.

5 Díaz del Río Eduardo *Los Araucanos y el Derecho* (Santiago de Chile: 2006) 9.

6 Díaz del Río Eduardo *Los Araucanos y el Derecho* (Santiago de Chile: 2006) 9.

the sixth day and gave him dominion over the earth and the animals living on the earth – they also being creatures of the same God.[7] In this manner the culture of the Western man is legitimised from the very beginning to think of himself as lord of the world and nature.[8]

In the culture of the Mapuches, by contrast, man is one additional element in the entire creation. The God who protects them, Nguenechén, is also mankind's God, but not the God of the rest of creation. The religiosity of the Mapuches – above all – aimed at the maintenance of the balance in nature as well as the existence of all powers. Their religiosity is also aimed at the coexistence of all powers. Man is responsible for its maintenance.[9] The centre of this society and the only permanent institution was the family. The family was quite numerous and expansive. All male descendants of the father and chiefs of the family lived together.[10] The Mapuches had abundant resources at their disposal and their relationship to nature and the natural biological order, which reigned at the heart of the extended family, made the existence of rulers, fiefdoms and kingdoms superfluous.[11] The society of the Mapuches is therefore to be classified as one of the acephalic groups. Such tribal societies are designated as egalitarian, since they lack any permanent specialised political and bureaucratic authority.[12] The official opinion in Spain assumed that so-called civilisations had the authority to place backward peoples under subjection.[13] This caused the war against las Indias to become perfectly legitimate. It lasted for three hundred years, following the occupation of Chile by the Spaniards. After the first two centuries a phase of relative quiet ensued, after which the warlike quarrels resumed with new vigour. In 1879, in the so-called conquest of the desert (conquista del desierto), the final subjection of the Indios came to an end. Bengoa called the military action in the summer of 1869 wars of annihilation against the Mapuches.[14]

In the tradition of the Mapuches polygamy existed, ie one man could have more than one woman. Under this practice, carried out by the aboriginals, they found themselves in glaring contradiction to the legal codes at the time of the conquest, as well as after the foundation of the Republic of Chile. The marriage law of 1884 had in art 102 a provision under which marriage was described as one man and one woman united together in a final and indissoluble way. Polygamous relationships were therefore illegal.[15]

---

[7] Lobos *Los Mapuches* (Buenos Aires: 2008) 12.

[8] Lobos *Los Mapuches* (Buenos Aires: 2008) 12.

[9] Díaz del Río *Los Araucanos y el Derecho* (Santiago de Chile: 2006) 12.

[10] José Bengoa *Historia del Pueblo Mapuche, Siglos XIX y XX* (Santiago de Chile: 2000) 30.

[11] José Bengoa *Historia del Pueblo Mapuche, Siglos XIX y XX* (Santiago de Chile: 2000) 30.

[12] Bundeszentrale für politische Bildung, Afrika, available at www.bpb.de/themen/17KiXT,2,0, Vorkoloniale-politische p 3, last accessed 15 August 2011.

[13] Díaz del Río *Los Araucanos y el Derecho* (Santiago de Chile: 2006) 18.

[14] Bengoa *Historia del Pueblo Mapuche, Siglos XIX y XX* (Santiago de Chile: 2000) 43.

[15] Ursula Pohl *Familienrecht in Chile, Rechtsreform und gesellschaftlicher Wandel* (Baden-Baden, 2013) 211.

Already before the official foundation of the state of Chile on 1 January 1818, at the time of the process of independence between 1810 and 1818, the Chileans functioned as lawgivers toward the aboriginals. On 1 July a first decree was promulgated by which the araukani nomads were to be settled by receiving land. They were to be settled in a permanent locality. At this moment they became Mapuches, ie mapu – land and che – human. This means humans who work the land.[16] It is true that this work was exclusively the task of women. The men looked upon work as dishonourable. They could only identify with hunting and fighting in wars.[17] In the same decree of 1 July 1813 the Mapuches were guaranteed the same civil rights as the rest of the Chileans.[18]

After 1813 there was a constant stream of decrees and laws which pertained to the aboriginals. Often they contained laws which again curtailed their guaranteed rights, for example decree 109 of 14 March 1853 which allowed the Mapuches to sell their land only if an official functionary was present who, for example, determined the price for the land.[19] Apart from such exceptional discriminatory special rules, as for the rest, the paragraphs of the civil law of the Republic of Chile of 1857 were to be binding on all Chilean inhabitants. Family law and inheritance law were therefore binding on the Mapuches, as they were on all other Chileans.

The colonial period was characterised by common-law marriages in which a couple often lived in the legal family household; the family consisting of mother and child was regarded as universally valid as a family model. Regarding the polygamous way of life, the customs of the Mapuches were not in any way different from those of the conquerors. From the beginning of the Republic of Chile this was at least the claim of the ruling class, which changed as it searched for a link to the civilised world. One now saw relationships not legitimised through marriage and the single mother as products of a social group that had missed the boat.[20] According to Montecino Aguirre the ruling class in Chile still held on in the twentieth century, as appearances go, to the Christian Western family model, but furtively they retained illegitimate relationships. This became the cause of the multitude of illegitimate children.[21] Thus, in 2003 there were already 54% children born out of wedlock in Chile. In 2011 there were 65%.[22] The understanding of the family held by the minority of Mapuches who live in Chile is different from the Chilean majority consisting of 75% Mestizos and 20% Whites,[23] insofar as polygamy had always been practised by the aboriginals while the upper classes forming the majority of Whites and Mestizos elevated monogamy to be exemplary, beginning in the nineteenth

---

16 Díaz del Río *Los Araucanos y el Derecho* (Santiago de Chile: 2006) 47.

17 Díaz del Río *Los Araucanos y el Derecho* (Santiago de Chile: 2006) 11.

18 Decree of 1 July 1813, § 1.

19 Decree No 109 from 14 March 1853, art 5.

20 Sonia Montecino Aguirre *Madres y Huachos* (Santiago de Chile: 2007) 54.

21 Sonia Montecino Aguirre *Madres y Huachos* (Santiago de Chile: 2007) 55.

22 Statistica.com/statistik/daten/studie/200794/umfrage/anteil-der-nichtehelich ge (accessed 23 January 2012).

23 Auswärtiges Amt Berlin.

century. However, this by no means meant the demise of 'underground' liaisons, while the middle and lower classes held on to the family centred on the mother with an absent father.[24]

Ramón Curivil explained on Radio Mapuche that for the aboriginals there was no difference whether one had two religions or two wives. This proved that there was not much of a change in the consciousness of the minority. It shows a penetrating weakness of the Christian inspired family law. In its place came the social customs and social rules of the aboriginals. The use of existing rules of law pertaining to the polygamous way of life resembled that of the Conquistadores. The result was a multitude of illegitimate children who did not have an easy time in Chilean society, as they were regarded as illegitimate bastards.[25] The mixing of cultures did, among other factors, lead to the result that all Chileans assign a high value to the family. They give it a central place in their lives. The family had a central significance among the aboriginals. This fact that pertains now to all Chileans also has at least a root in the family structure of the Mapuches.

Although the majority of Chileans identify with their families, 60% believe that the family is in crisis; that is to say, the present condition of the family is a source of problems.[26]

Marriage which is anchored in law, between a man and a woman, is valid as a concept for all Chileans. However, there exists simultaneously – even still today – in the south of Chile the practice in Mapuche families where a man lives together with two women and their respective children. Of course according to the law, he can be married to only one of them. Besides, there are, in the entire country, sufficient men belonging to the majority of the population, who live together with their wives and children in an unmarried state, even though they are legally married to somebody else. If that were not so, Chile would not have had, in the year 2011, a quota of 65% illegitimate children. From this one could conclude that the concepts of family for the Mapuches and the majority of Chileans differ in theory, but in practice they do not diverge very much at all.

The legal status of children born out of wedlock was legally adjusted only in 1998 to that of children born in wedlock.[27] Divorce was also made possible only in 2005, when the divorce law of 1884 was abolished.[28] It took 10 years for that law, which had already been drafted in 1995, to be passed. This fact could be attributed, among other factors, to the great influence of the clergy in Chilean society. A contradiction is apparent in the fact that, in spite of that, an enormously high number of illegitimate children had materialised. The number of marriages dropped by 40% between 1994 and 2009; but simultaneously the

---

24 Montecino Aguirre *Madres y Huachos* (Santiago de Chile: 2007) 55.

25 Montecino Aguirre *Madres y Huachos* (Santiago de Chile: 2007) 54.

26 S Valdés and E Valdés *Familia y Vida Privada* (Santiago de Chile: 2005) 168.

27 Law No 19.585 of 26 October 1998.

28 Law No 19.947 of 17 May 2005.

number of so-called factual families increased.[29] A legal foundation for these is still, as always, lacking. All reforms of family law were set in motion only after the reintroduction of democracy in 1989. Neither the socialist government of Allende from 1970–1973 nor the military junta under Pinochet from 1973–1989 had any interest in changing family law.

---

29 See www.cepchile.cl//dms/lang_1/buscar.html?textobuscar=/LCox_Sem_Divorcio-en-chile.p.&tipologica=or&pagina=1 (accessed 20 April 2011).

CHINA

EMPIRICAL RESEARCH ON JUDICIAL PRACTICE OF THE POST-DIVORCE RELIEF SYSTEM – TARGETED ON SAMPLED CASES HANDLED IN A GRASS-ROOTS PEOPLE'S COURT IN CHONGQING IN 2010–2012

Wei Chen, Lei Shi and Wenjun He[*]

Résumé

A fin d'examiner la pratique judiciaire du système de secours post-divorce en Chine, nous avons isolé des cas de divorce sur lesquelsla cour populaire de Chongqing a statué entre 2010 et 2012. En utilisant les statistiques de notre enquête, nous avons recherché les carences du système de secours post-divorce. Nous avons trouvé les raisons de ces lacunes. Sur la base de cette analyse, nous présentons des suggestions sur la façon d'améliorer le système actuel: renforcer la formation des juges en ce qui concerne la théorie du genre ; mettre en place des juridictions dédiées aux matières familiales ; améliorer le régime de la charge de la preuve dans les cas concernant les dommages relatifs au divorce ; recadrer le principe pour déterminer les « difficultés de vie » dans les cas d'aide financière post-divorce ; et, enfin, élargir le champ d'application de la compensation économique post-divorce.

I OVERVIEW OF THE SURVEY OF CHINA'S JUDICIAL PRACTICE OF THE POST-DIVORCE RELIEF

The authors introduce the overview of the survey on three levels, i e the survey background, survey targets and survey methods.

(a) Survey background

In China, with the continuous development of the social economy, people's living standards continue to improve. People's ideas of marriage and family are changing. The statutory conditions for divorce have been loosened. Thus, from

* Civil and Commercial Law, Southwest University of Political Science and Law, Chongqing, 401120.

economic, conceptual, and legal perspectives, it is easier for parties in a dead marriage where affection no longer exists to exit through divorce. The Marriage Law 1980 stipulates that the legal principle to grant a divorce is that 'spousal affection no longer exists'. In the Marriage Law Amendment 2001, the statutory facts to confirm 'spousal affection no longer exists' were added so as to judge more easily. The statistics issued by the Ministry of Civil Affairs showed that the crude divorce rate in China steadily increased for 8 years; 3,104,000 couples divorced in 2012.[1] According to the statistics from Civil Affairs Bureau of Chongqing, 293,000 couples married and 105,000 couples divorced in Chongqing in 2012. The ratio of marriages to divorces is 35.8%. From 2003 to 2011, the divorce rate went up steadily.[2] Divorce freedom is fully protected in law, while the negative effects of divorce on parties and society should not be neglected. In particular, problems caused by the post-divorce relief system are worth studying. This survey aims at the judicial practice of the post-divorce relief system and tries to analyse its achievements and shortcomings so as to provide first-hand empirical data for the government decisions and improve the post-divorce relief system.

(b) Survey targets

This survey targets the local people's court in the main city zone of Chongqing. Since we are investigating the recent 3 years' judicial practice, we sampled 120 cases each year from 2010 to 2012, including divorce judgments and divorces by mediation in court, a 3-year total of 360 cases.

(c) Survey methods

We use the following methods in this survey, i e case file analysis, classification statistics and individual interviews.

First, we read each of the 360 cases we sampled and recorded data.

Secondly, we categorised information in each case and carried out classification statistics in the following aspects: the parties' gender, age and profession; length of their marriage; their grounds to petition for divorce; how the case closed; claims for divorce damages, financial assistance and economic compensation after divorce and their results.

Thirdly, we interviewed the judges hearing these cases and analysed their shortcomings and difficulties with a view to finding solutions. The content of these interviews covered how to determine domestic violence, how to apply

---

1 See *Statistical Communiqué of the People's Republic of China on the 2012 National Social Service Development released by Ministry of Civil Affairs*, www.mca.gov.cn/article/zwgk/mzyw/201306/20130600474640.shtml (accessed 4 March 2014).

2 Tao, Kun 'Divorce to marriage ratio in Chongqing reaches 35.8%, marriages of 30-50 years old at high risk of marital breakdown' *Chongqing Times*, 22 August 2013, http://cq.qq.com/a/20130822/002648.htm, (accessed 4 March 2014).

divorce damages, financial assistance and economic compensation after divorce, and the relevant divorce proceedings.

II STATISTICS OF JUDICIAL PRACTICE OF THE POST-DIVORCE RELIEF SYSTEM IN CHINA

In the investigation, we collected information in the following six aspects, including: parties' basic information such as gender, age, profession etc; the petitioner's grounds for divorce request; how the case is closed; claims for divorce damages; claims for divorce financial assistance; claims for divorce economic compensation.

(a) The basic information of divorce cases' parties

(i) Parties' gender

Table 1-1 Parties' gender in the Surveyed Cases in 2010-2012

item	male	female
petitioner	117	243
percentage	32%	68%
defendant	243	117
defendant	68%	32%

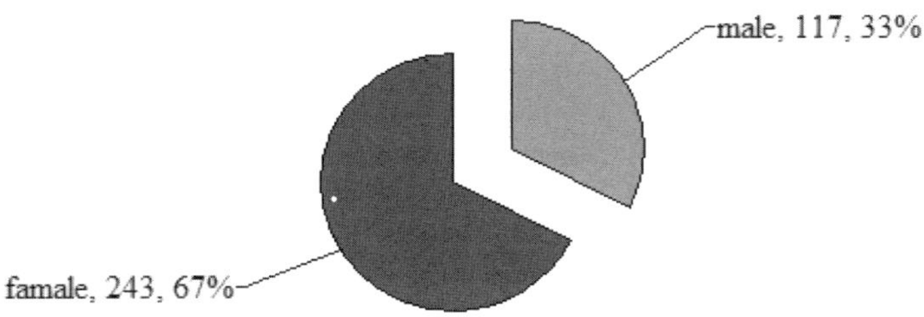

Chart 1-1a Petitioners' gender ratio in the surveyed cases in 2010–2012

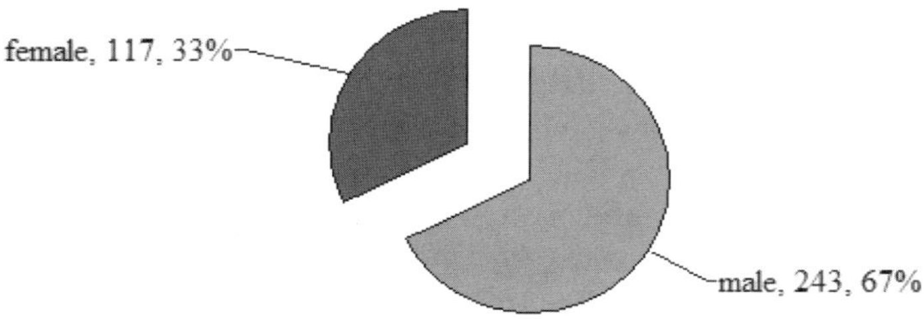

Chart 1-1b Defendants' gender ratio in the surveyed cases in 2010–2012

Charts 1-1a and b show clearly that the female petitioners reach 243, accounting for 68%. However, the male petitioners reach 117, accounting for 32% (see Chart 1-1a). Women as defendants are 117, accounting for 32%, while men as defendants are 243, accounting for 68% (see Chart 1-1b). So, the female petitioners, as a major group, represent seven-tenths of all the divorce petitioners.

(ii) Parties' age

Table 1-2 Parties' age in the surveyed cases in 2010–2012

Items	Age				
	20–30	31–40	41–50	51–60	Over 61
Petitioner	100	138	76	28	18
Percentage	27.8%	38.3%	21.1%	7.8%	5%
Defendant	73	127	109	35	16
Percentage	20.2%	35.3%	30.3%	9.7%	4.4%

In the surveyed cases, the age range of the petitioners is from 20 years old to 78 years old. From the petitioners' age distribution, the top three groups are 31–40 years old, 20–30 years old, and 41–50 years old, separately accounting for 38.3%, 27.8%, and 21.2%. These groups are followed by 51–60 years old and over 61 years old, respectively, 7.8% and 5% (see Chart 1-2a). From the perspective of defendants' age, the top three groups are 31–40 years old, 41–50 years old and 20–30 years old, each accounting for 35.3%, 30.3%, and 20.2%. The next two groups are 51–60 years old and over 61 years old, respectively, 9.7% and 4.4% (see Chart 1-2b).

The statistical data above shows that the petitioners' age is mainly distributed in three groups, ie from 20 to 50 years old.

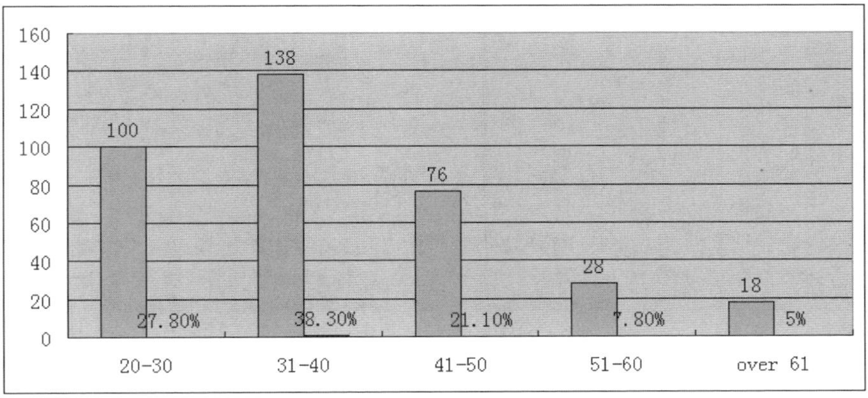

Chart 1-2a Petitioners' age in the surveyed cases in 2010–2012

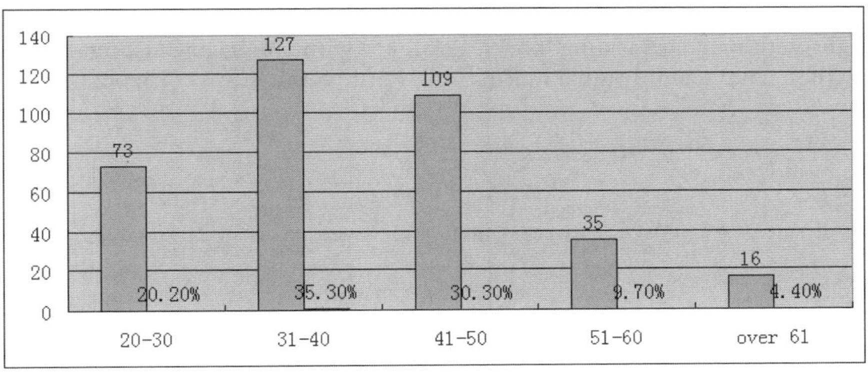

Chart 1-2b Defendants' age in the surveyed cases in 2010–2012

(iii) Length of marriage

Table 1-3: Length of marriage in the surveyed cases in 2010–2012

Length of marriage	1–5 yrs	6–10 yrs	11–20 yrs	over 21 yrs
Number of cases	143	83	85	49
Percentage	39.7%	23.1%	23.6%	13.6%

The data in Table 1-3 shows that 143 cases fall into the first group in which parties' marriage lasts for 1–5 years, accounting for 39.7%; 6–10 years marriage group has 83 cases, accounting for 23.1%; 23.6% of these cases fall into the 11–20 years marriage group, 85 in total. In 49 cases, parties married for over 21 years, accounting for 13.6% (see Chart 1-3a).

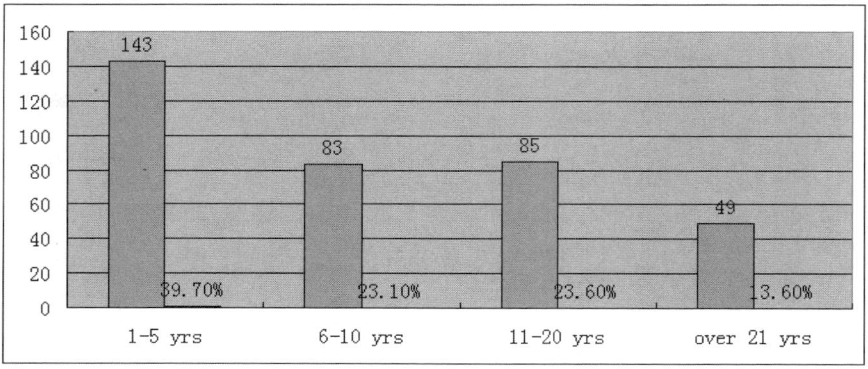

Chart 1-3a: Length of marriage in the surveyed cases in 2010–2012

It demonstrates that in the first group, ie during the early marriage, the first 5 years, the divorce rate is higher, accounting for four-tenths. Then the divorce rate falls with marriage lasting longer. For those with a marriage lasting over 21 years, they have a more stable marital relationship and a lower divorce rate.

(iv) Divorcees' professions

Table 1-4 Divorcees' careers in the surveyed cases in 2010–2012

Items	Career						
	unem-ployed	civil servant	employee in a company	peas-ant	self-employed	re-tired	others
petitioner	83	17	93	33	29	19	19
percentage	28.3%	5.8%	31.7%	11.3%	10%	6.5%	6.5%
defendant	75	11	80	19	21	13	11
percentage	32.6%	4.5%	34.5%	8.3%	9.1%	5.7%	4.5%

In the divorce case files sampled, some parties did not fill in the blank for career. Only 293 cases have recorded petitioners' careers; 230 cases have information on defendants' careers. In occupational distribution of petitioners in these cases, the top three careers are employee in a company, unemployed and peasant, respectively, 25.8%, 23.1%, and 9.2% (see Chart 1-4a). From the perspective of defendants' professions, the top three positions are held by employee in a company, unemployed and self-employed. Their proportions are 22.2%, 20.8% and 5.8% respectively (see Chart 1-4b).

The statistical data demonstrates that the first two professions of petitioners and defendants are employee in a company and unemployed. These two groups almost account for half of all the cases. They are the main portion of divorcees.

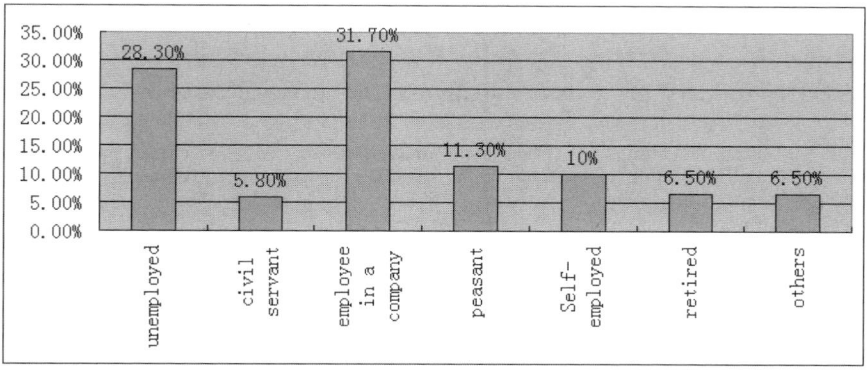

Chart 1-4a Petitioners' careers in the surveyed cases in 2010–2012

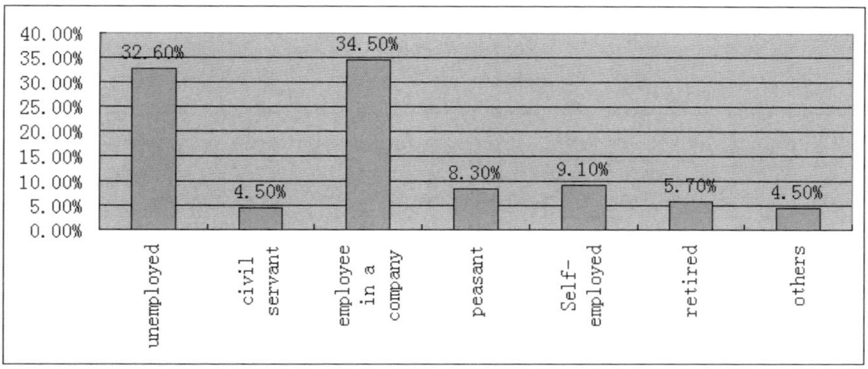

Chart 1-4b Defendants' careers in the surveyed cases in 2010–2012

Besides, in the divorce cases investigated, 303 petitioners were in their first marriage, accounting for 84.2%; 47 petitioners were remarried, accounting for 15.8%; 276 defendants were in their first marriage, accounting for 76.7%; 58 defendants were remarried, accounting for 16.1%. As regards the number of divorce requests, 278 cases were the first request for a divorce, accounting for 77.2%. Petitioners in 82 cases petition for a divorce for the second time or more, accounting for 22.8%. So, in the sampled cases, most parties were in their first marriage, accounting for over eight-tenths. About 80% petitioners request a divorce for the first time.

(b) Petitioners' grounds for divorce

Table 2-1 Petitioners' grounds for divorce in the surveyed cases in 2010–2012

Grounds Year	cohabitation with the third one	domestic violence	lack of mutual affection	addiction of gambling & drugs etc and no correction	2 yrs separation due to discord	imprisonment	others
2010	14	17	109	4	19	16	2
2011	4	22	97	26	17	8	1
2012	2	6	110	7	5	11	1
Total	20	45	316	37	41	35	4
percentage	5.6%	12.5%	87.8%	10.3%	11.4%	9.7%	1.1%

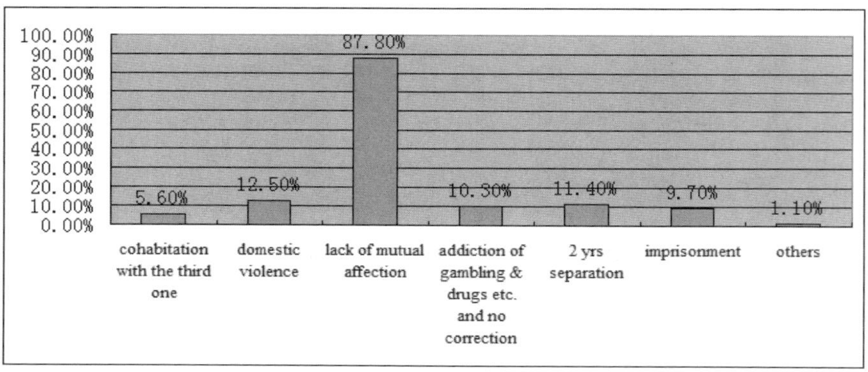

Chart 2-1a Petitioners' grounds for divorce in the surveyed cases in 2010–2012

The data illustrate that the top three grounds in divorce cases in 2010–2012 are lack of mutual affection, domestic violence and 2 years' separation due to lack of mutual affection, accounting respectively for 87.8%, 12.5% and 11.4% (see Chart 2-1a). In fact, in the surveyed cases, petitioners may request a divorce for several grounds. Therefore, the total percentage is over 100%.

From the grounds to petition for divorce, the most common ground is lack of mutual affection, almost accounting for 90%. Moreover, faulty grounds are used in almost half of the cases, such as domestic violence, imprisonment, cohabitation with the third person, addiction of gambling, drugs etc and no correction.

(c) How divorce cases closed

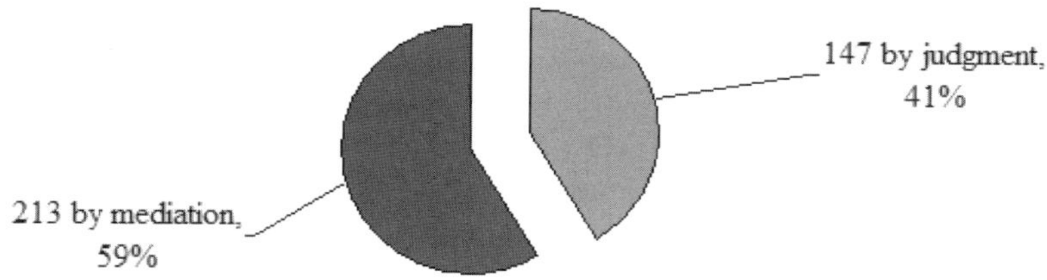

Chart 3-1 Closing methods of surveyed divorce cases in 2010–2012

As to the closing methods of these divorce cases investigated, 213 cases were closed by mediation, accounting for 59.2%; 147 cases were ended by judgment, accounting for 40.8% (among them, 70 cases dealt with the first request for divorce, 77 petitioners request a divorce more than once). So, mediation is the main way to handle divorce cases in court. Almost 60% of cases were closed by mediation. Furthermore, the court reluctantly supported petitioner's first divorce request.

(d) Claims for divorce damages

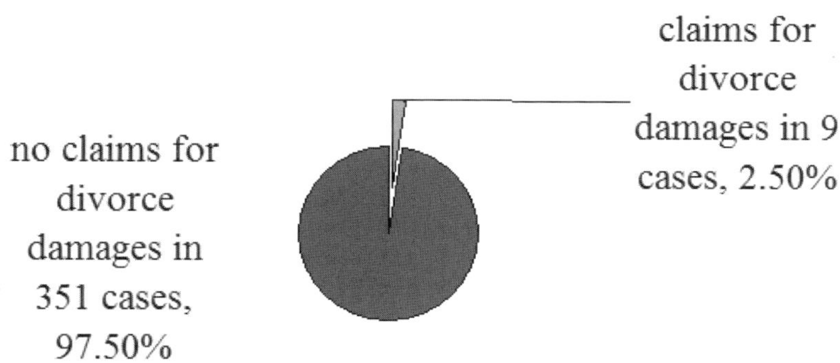

Chart 4-1a Claims for divorce damages in the survey cases in 2010–2012

Among the cases investigated, only nine petitioners claimed divorce damages based on the ground of cohabitation with the third party or domestic violence, accounting for 2.5% (See Chart 4-1a). However, 65 petitioners request a divorce on the ground of cohabitation with the third party or domestic violence, accounting for 18.1% (see Chart 2-1a). So, only nine petitioners, ie 13.8% of petitioners who request a divorce on statutory faulty ground and have the right to divorce damages, did claim divorce damages. On the other hand, even in these nine cases, the court rejected divorce damages claims based on insufficient evidence, lack of statutory grounds etc. Therefore, only five petitioners were awarded divorce damages. Among these five cases, two cases were closed by judgment. Petitioners in the two cases request divorce damages respectively for 200,000 RMB, 30,000 RMB. Based on the fault of the

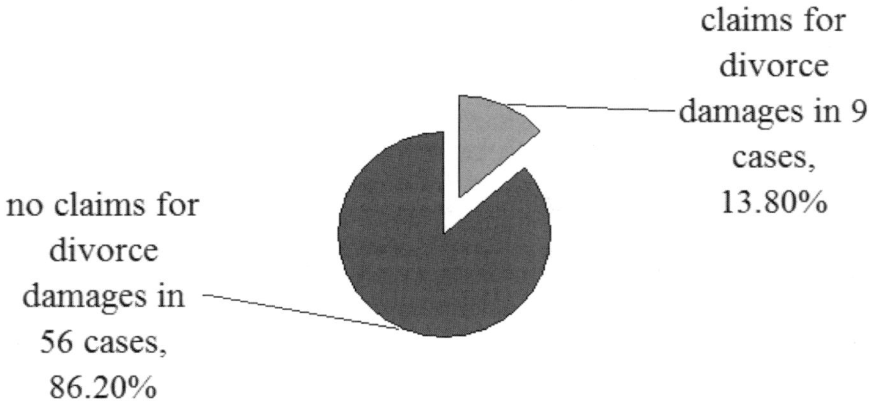

Chart 1-4b Claims for divorce damages in the survey cases with statutory grounds for divorce damages claim in 2010–2012

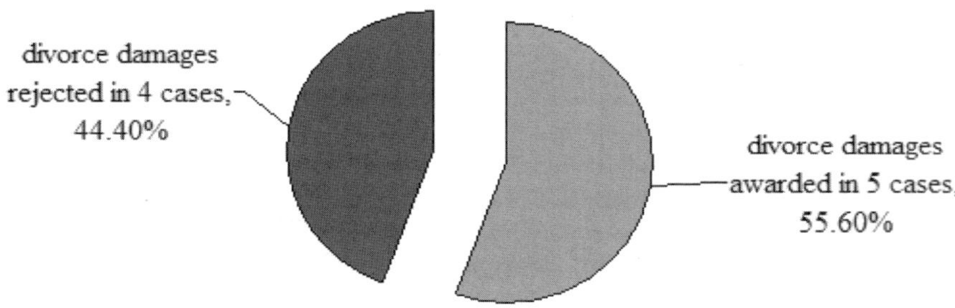

Chart 4-2 Results of divorce damages claims in the surveyed cases in 2010–2012

tortfeasor, consequences of the tort and actual losses etc, the court awarded to the petitioners respectively 30,000 RMB and 5,000 RMB. Another three cases were closed by mediation. Finally, petitioners in these cases got 6,000 RMB, 10,000 RMB and 8,000 RMB respectively as divorce damages.

The survey shows that only a few petitioners in these cases requested divorce damages and fewer were finally awarded divorce damages and in a low amount.

(e) Claims for divorce financial assistance

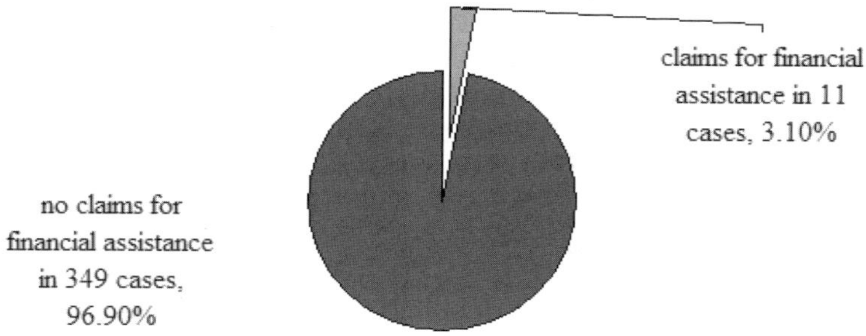

Chart 5-1 Claims for divorce financial assistance in the surveyed cases in 2010–2012

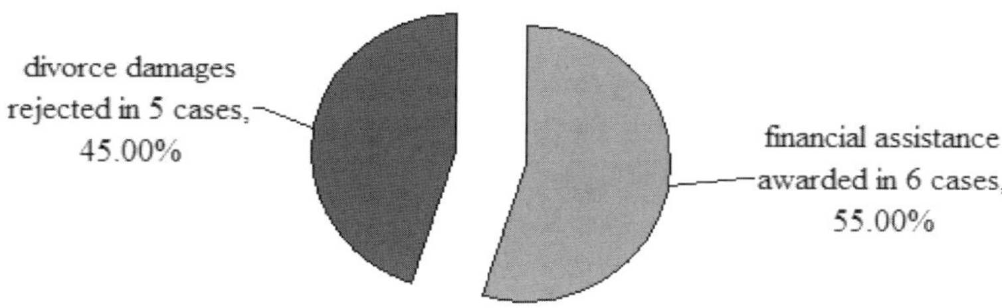

Chart 5-2 Results of financial assistance claims in the surveyed cases in 2010–2012

In the investigated cases, 11 petitioners requested financial assistance on the grounds of homework contribution, help for the other spouse's work, economic difficulties, accounting for 3.1%. In the 11 cases, there are three petitioners as a company employee, four as unemployed, three as a peasant and one as retired. On the other hand, there are five defendants as a company employee, four as unemployed and two as a peasant. Among the 11 cases, five petitioners' claims were rejected based on no factual or judicial grounds. Only one petitioner got a judgment supporting her claim. However, the amount of financial assistance is low. The petitioner requested 53,000 RMB as her financial assistance, while the court awarded her 6,000 RMB on the ground that 'the obligor has a low income and has no house to live after divorce', 'considering both parties' income etc'. The other five cases were ended by mediation. Each petitioner in the five cases got 48,000 RMB, 100,000 RMB, 1,000 RMB per month, 6,000 RMB and 5,000 RMB respectively.

Thus, few petitioners claimed financial assistance in divorce cases. Only 3.1% petitioners did so (see Chart 5-1). Among the 11 cases with financial assistance claims, only 55% petitioners got some financial assistance (see Chart 5-2).

(f) Claims for economic compensation

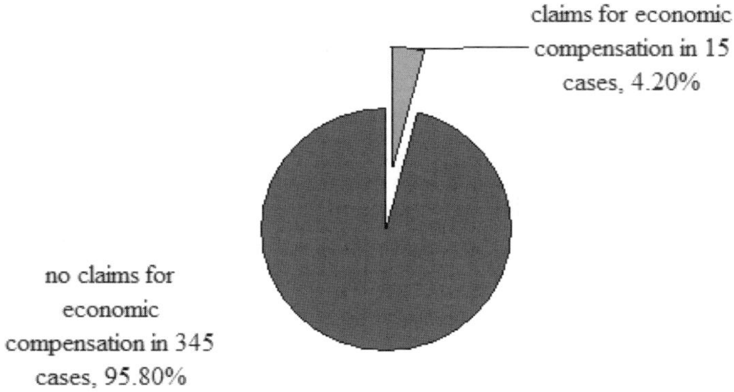

Chart 6-1 Economic compensation claims in the surveyed cases in 2010–2012

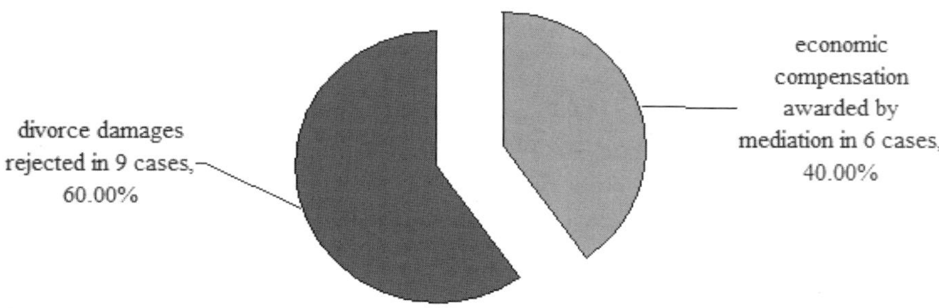

Chart 6-2 Results of economic compensation claims in the surveyed cases in 2010–2012

In the investigated cases, 15 petitioners claimed economic compensations on the grounds of child-raising, caring for the elders, helping with the other spouse's work etc, accounting for 4.2%. Unluckily, in these 15 cases, no one adopted a separate property system in their marriage. Therefore, the court did not support their claims. Only six petitioners get some compensation by mediation, respectively, 500 RMB per month (lasting for 2 years), 3,000 RMB, 12,000 RMB, 50,000 RMB, 72,000 RMB and 20,000 RMB. Thus, few petitioners requested economic compensation in divorce cases. Only 4.2% of petitioners did so (see Chart 6-1). Among these 15 cases, only 40% got some compensation after mediation (see Chart 6-2).

III INADEQUACIES OF POST-DIVORCE RELIEF SYSTEM AND ITS JUDICIAL PRACTICE IN CHINA

As mentioned earlier, in the surveyed divorce cases, female petitioners, which is the majority, represent 68% (see Chart 1-1a). The survey shows that the post-divorce relief system and its judicial practice in China have inadequacies, mainly in the following four areas: lack of gender awareness for some judges, difficulties in proving divorce damages, strict conditions to apply financial assistance after divorce and limited application of post-divorce economic compensation. The post-divorce relief system is occasionally applied so that the present law does not provide enough measures to protect the divorced women. Post-divorce relief system does not function as well as people expect.

(a) Lack of gender awareness of some judges

In a modern society in the 21st century, the trend in the reform of family law focuses on protecting the weak in a marriage or a family based on the goal of social law, ie protection of the weak and strengthening state supervision over personal behaviour based on the goal of protecting parties' legitimate interests.[3] However, the survey shows that due to lack of gender awareness, some judges paid more attention to parties' autonomy in mediation in divorce cases, but often neglected proper guidance in this process. Without legal information, some parties generally negotiated an agreement on divorce, property distribution and child-rearing etc, but drop claims for post-divorce relief even if they are legally entitled to it. Some petitioners are so anxious to divorce that they waive claims on joint property and child support etc. For instance, petitioner Zhang requested a divorce on the ground of the defendant's gambling and alcohol addiction and domestic violence. In her petition, she requested the defendant pay 500 RMB per month as child support. But because the defendant did not agree to divorce and she failed to produce convincing evidence to prove marital breakdown, she waived child support in order to reach a mediation agreement. Some judges did not inform the parties as stipulated at art 30 in the First Judicial Interpretation of the Marriage Law,[4] in order to avoid mediation failure, which is common in bitter controversies. Our investigation demonstrates that only three judges in 65 cases involving divorce damages did fulfil this notification. Thus, it is difficult to protect divorced women. As we

---

3 Wei Chen *Research on Legislation of China's Marriage and Family Law* (Beijing, China: Public Press, 2010) 34, 39.

4 Article 30 in the Interpretation No 1 of the Supreme People's Court on the Application of the Marriage Law of PRC stipulates that:
'When the people's court accepts a divorce case, it shall notify, in writing, the parties of the relevant rights and obligations as described in Article 46 of the Marriage Law. In the application of article 46 of the Marriage Law, it shall differentiate the following circumstances: ... In a divorce litigation where the innocent party is the defendant, if the defendant, during the first instance, fails to claim for compensation according to Article 46 of the Marriage Law, but he (she) claims for compensation in the second instance, the people's court shall conduct a mediation. If the mediation fails, the people's court shall inform the parties concerned to initiate a separate lawsuit within 1 year after the divorce.'

mentioned above, those who got divorce damages, financial assistance and economic compensation in 360 cases surveyed only account for 2.5%, 3.1% and 4.2% (see Chart 4-1a, Chart 5-1 and Chart 6-1).

(b) Difficulties in proving divorce damages

Article 46 in the Marriage Law stipulates that, where marital breakdown results from bigamy, cohabitation with a third party, domestic violence, or abuse or desertion of family members, the innocent party may claim divorce damages in divorce proceedings. However, our survey shows that only nine petitioned for divorce damages. Unluckily, four of them were rejected due to lack of statutory grounds. From the perspective of divorce grounds, 45 petitioners requested a divorce on the ground of domestic violence, accounting for 12.5%; 20 petitioners requested a divorce on the ground of cohabitation with a third party, accounting for 5.6% (see Chart 2-1a). Thus, few petitioners request divorce damages. Only nine did, accounting for 13.8%. Fewer petitioners got damages. Only five out of nine did (see Chart 4-2).

The reason mainly lies in difficulties in proof. The court refused petitioners' requests based on 'inadequacy of evidence'. Actually, domestic violence usually happened in a family, which is difficult to be found by the third party. Therefore, there are few witnesses giving testimony on domestic violence. Moreover, due to lack of awareness of collecting evidence, petitioners mainly accused their partners of domestic violence by oral evidence. That is why the court rarely confirmed domestic violence. The difficulties of proof also exist in those divorce cases on the ground of cohabitation with a third party. Even if there are witnesses in the neighbourhood, few of them are willing to be present in court due to the impact of 'acquaintance society'. Petitioners usually produced the third party's daily necessities in court as evidence to prove cohabitation with the third party. But this evidence does not have enough weight in court, and thus is inadmissible.

In conclusion, in divorce cases concerning damages claims, the present rules on divorce damages are rarely applied due to difficulties of proof. Therefore, the divorce damages system cannot realise its functions such as compensation, raising victims' spirits and preventing and punishing offences.

(c) Strict conditions applying to financial assistance after divorce

Article 42 in the Marriage Law Amendment[5] provides a financial assistance system after divorce. For those with living difficulties, the other party shall

[5] Article 42 in the Marriage Law stipulates that:
'If, at the time of divorce, one party has difficulty in supporting himself or herself, the other party shall render appropriate assistance with his or her own property such as his or her residential house. Specific arrangements shall be made by both parties through consultation. If they fail to reach an agreement, the People's Court shall make a judgment.'

render appropriate assistance. Article 27 in the First Judicial Interpretation of the Marriage Law[6] further stipulates where to apply financial assistance, ie the petitioner cannot keep their head above water with his or her own personal property and that granted to him or her on divorce, including without a place to live. The survey shows that the unemployed, accounting for about 20%, rank second only to company employees among parties in divorce cases (including petitioners and defendants) (see Charts 1-4a, 1-4b). However, only 11 petitioners claimed financial assistance, accounting for 3.1% (see Chart 5-1); five claims out of six cases closed by judgments were rejected due to lack of relevant facts and rules. For instance, in a divorce case of *Guo v Wang*, Guo (unemployed) claimed 100,000 RMB as financial assistance from Wang (company employee). But the court judged that 'the defendant refused and the petitioner had not enough evidence'. The claim was rejected.

So, the financial assistance system is rarely applied in judicial practice. The court seldom supported such claims, either. This resulted from strict conditions applying to the financial assistance system. The law adopts a strict standard to confirm whether one has living difficulties. This standard is only fit for a planned economy and the underdeveloped society at the beginning of reform and opening up of the economy. With the development of the social market economy and an improving social safety network, such a standard restricts the application of post-divorce financial assistance in judicial practice. The core of family policy is to protect the weak in a family.[7] It is not reasonable enough to adopt a strict standard of survival to confirm living difficulties in reality.[8] It means that the focus of the law is to ensure that the post-divorce living standard of a spouse will be not less than local basic living standards, instead of similar or equal to the living standard during the marriage.[9] The financial assistance system aims only to safeguard a citizen's right to survival without consideration of living standards during the marriage and of the woman's loss of her contribution to the family in this period.[10] Thus, it cannot fully protect divorced women's legitimate rights. As a scholar said, no matter how much we feel free to get a divorce, all the divorce consequences should not be allowed to be passed on to society, which in the end become a social burden.[11] We should

---

6 Article 27 in the First Judicial Interpretation of the Marriage Law provides that: 'The circumstance under which "either party has difficulties in life" as mentioned in Article 42 of the Marriage Law means that it cannot sustain the local basic living level by depending on the personal property and the property divided to him (her) at the time of divorce. A party who has no domicile after divorce conforms to the circumstance of having difficulties in life. At the time of divorce, one party may help the party who has difficulties in life by offering the dwelling right to or ownership of the house out of his (her) personal properties.'

7 Kai Wang 'Constitutional Guarantee of Matrimony and Family' (2013) 2 Law Review 3.

8 Dibo Wang 'On post-divorce support payment between ex-spouses' (2004) 6 Gansu Social Sciences 197.

9 Mei Jin *Modern Chinese Family Law in Transition* (Beijing, China: Law Press, 2010) 191.

10 Yinlan Xia *Theory on Freedom and Restriction of Divorce* (Beijing, China: China University of Political Science and Law Press, 2007) 250.

11 Mingxia Chen and Jihua Xu translated *Sociology of Divorce Law* (Beijing, China: Beijing University Press, 1991) 149.

not give up financial assistance for the weak in a marriage with the excuse that the social safety network is becoming more and more improved.

(d) Limited application of post-divorce economic compensation

Article 40 in the Marriage Law stipulates that post-divorce economic compensation can only be applied for where spouses made an agreement that the properties acquired during the marriage belong to the owner himself or herself rather than in common. Therefore, spouses adopting the joint property system are excluded. As mentioned earlier, only 15 petitioners requested economic compensation, accounting for 4.2%. In these 15 cases, only 40% of them got compensated (see Charts 6-1, 6-2). At present, women mainly take on domestic chores in China. This resulted from traditional gender roles in a family in China – 'men outside, women inside' (nan zhu wai, nyu zhu nei). Although, the influence of women's traditional roles has weakened since more and more women walk out of the home and devote themselves to their careers, their roles in a family have not changed totally.[12] The third survey of Chinese women's social status in 2010 showed that women's burden of housework is heavier. '72.7% of married people believe that, compared with husbands, wives bear more housework'; more than 72% of women bear the 'majority' and 'all' of domestic chores including cooking, washing dishes, laundry, house-cleaning, child-rearing etc. However, less than 16.0% of men bear such domestic chores. As regards 'helping children with their homework' and 'caring for elders', women account for 45.2% and 39.7% respectively, 28.2 and 22.9 percentage points higher compared with men.[13] Such traditional gender roles inherited from history lead to habituation and moralisation of gender roles. Thus, rights protection in a family is neglected by citizens.[14]

A scholar has argued that the joint property system is widely applied in China based on our tradition.[15] So, post-divorce economic compensation was applied rarely since the present rule puts the separate property system as a precondition to applying for economic compensation. It cannot achieve its predetermined value target. Where there are few joint properties at the time of divorce, this system cannot recognise the value of women's domestic chores. In fact, women's contributions to domestic chores were neglected because these contributions cannot be crystallised into tangible properties.[16] So, we hold that, where there are few joint properties, the spouse contributing a lot in a family cannot be compensated for that contribution. Rights and obligations between

---

12 Chongqing Women's Federation, and Chongqing Social Science Institute *Research on Women's Social Status in Chongqing (2000-2010)* (Beijing, China: China Women Press, 2013) 87.

13 Project Group of the 3rd Survey on the status of Chinese women 'Executive report of the 3rd Survey on the Status of Chinese women' (2011) 6 *Collection of Women's Studies* 5.

14 Geya Wang 'Divorce relief system: Practice and Rethink' (2011) 2 *Legal Forum* 30-33.

15 Junping He 'Post-divorce economic compensation should be applied when joint property system is adopted' in Wei Chen (ed) *Research on Family Law (2007)* (Beijing, China: Public Press, 2008) 79.

16 Yu Huang *Studies on the Feminist Approaches to the Family Law* (Beijing, China: Public Press, 2012) 255

husband and wife lose balance. One spouse bears obligations more while the other enjoys his or her rights more. For the women bearing more housework, it is unfair.[17]

IV PROPOSALS ON THE POST-DIVORCE RELIEF SYSTEM AND ITS JUDICIAL PRACTICE

Our survey investigated sampled divorce cases in the People's Court in 2010–2012. With the statistical data, we analysed the parties' information, divorce grounds, methods used to close divorce cases, and claims of divorce damages, post-divorce financial assistance and economic compensation. We found shortcomings in the judicial practice of this system and reasons for them. In the following part, we will make recommendations on improving the system.

(a) Strengthening training of judges in gender theory

First, we need to strengthen judges' training in gender theory. The *Chinese Women Development Program* (2011–2020) issued by the State Council of PRC in 2011 requires us 'to strengthen gender theory training. Incorporate gender theory into regular training courses for legislation, justice and enforcement departments; improve gender awareness of staff in these departments'. In China, almost half of the population of 130 million are women. As regards protecting women and other vulnerable people or being impartial in law enforcement, it is very critical that judicial officers have awareness of gender equality and exercise gender analysis in their judicial practice.[18] Only with gender awareness can judges apply gender theory in the hearing of divorce cases and better protect the divorced women's rights. For instance, if petitioners misunderstand the rules or do not know detailed regulations, judges should explain these rules or regulations to them and inform them of the right to divorce damages, post-divorce financial assistance and economic compensation, etc. It is a better way to protect the interests of the weak in a family (usually the women). The post-divorce relief system will fully perform its function too.

(b) Establishing family courts

We suggest establishing family courts in our society with reference to England's family courts,[19] Australian family law,[20] and family justice practice in Hong

---

[17] Wei Chen 'The legislative conception of the marital property regime in China' (2000) 1 *Chinese Legal Science* 89–92.

[18] Mingxia Chen 'Judicial practice and gender' in Lie Huang (ed) *Gender Equality and Legal Reform* (Beijing, China: China Social Science Press, 2009) 164, 169.

[19] Lei Shi 'The evolution of the modern family justice system in Great Britain and its enlightenment' (2012) 5 *Present day Law Science* 101.

[20] Wei Chen *Family Law Act 1975 of Australia (amended in 2008)* (Beijing, China: Public Press, 2009) 72–91.

Kong in China. First, we can promote specialisation of hearing divorce cases in national courts. On the basis of this, learning from the experiences of Jiawang District Court in Xuzhou City in Jiangsu Province,[21] and Family Courts in Guangdong Province,[22] family courts should be established for better protection of divorced women's rights. When hearing divorce cases, judges should stick to the following principles such as mediation before hearing, non-public hearing, promoting reconciliation or improving relationships between spouses, protection of the weak and declarations of family properties before litigation etc, so as to maximise opportunities to 'close the case and settle the dispute' (an jie shi liao). Moreover, we also suggest providing services for families involved in divorce litigation, i e family counselling and mediation for domestic disputes with reference to the Australian family justice experiences.[23] In this way, the hearing of divorce cases will be more specialised and the rights of divorced spouses and children can be better protected.

(c) Improving the burden of proof in cases concerning divorce damages

As regards difficulties in proving divorce damages, we suggest adopting the rule of preponderance of evidence as a supplement.[24] First, for producing evidence of domestic violence, we recommend adopting the rule of preponderance of evidence to allocate the burden of proof in divorce damages claims, which requires judges to balance which party has the 'obvious advantage' when evidence produced by the parties on the same fact conflicts. Therefore, it overcomes the parties' difficulties in producing evidence to some extent and makes up for shortcomings of the basic principle in litigation, i e 'whoever claims should bear the burden of proof'. As for cohabitation with a third party, admissible evidence should include the house rent bill, evidence of travelling and eating/sleeping together. Besides, testimony of children with sufficient competence, complaint records from residents committees, villagers committees or Women's Federation etc can also be adopted as evidence to prove a spouse's fault.

---

21 In 2012, Jiawang District Court in Xuzhou City in Jiangsu Province established a separate specialised family court based on analysis of family cases. It created '8 steps to mend a broken relationship'. To put it simply, the court will not clarify what is right from wrong in family disputes with a judgment, but target on mending a broken relationship and resisting antagonism in handling these disputes, so that the parties will be reasonable, calm and relaxed. The court will maximise opportunities to close the case and settle the dispute. Xijia Ru 'Family courts: judges resolve family disputes diplomatically' http://acwf.people.com.cn/n/2012/0829/c99013-18866483.html (accessed 8 February 2014).

22 Ling Tan, Wenlian Xie and Huiyi Yang etc 'Find new hearing model to promote families' harmony – Guangdong High People's Court survey on the pilot project of family courts' *People's Court Daily*, 16 June 2011, 8.

23 Wei Chen and Xianxin Cao 'On the latest developments of family dispute resolution mechanism in Australia and its inspiration' (2011) 8 *Hebei Law Science Journal* 39-46.

24 Wei Chen and Lei Shi 'Developments in China's Provisions for Postdivorce Relief in the 21st Century and Suggestions for Their Improvement' (2013) 54(5) *Journal of Divorce & Remarriage* 363 at 378.

Secondly, in order to realise the goal of 'finding objective truth, pursuing substantive justice', we suggest extending the court's power to investigate cases concerning domestic violence and cohabitation with a third party. In accordance with the Civil Procedure Law of the PRC[25] and some provisions of the Supreme People's Court on Evidence in Civil Procedures,[26] evidence of domestic violence and cohabitation with a third party should be produced by whoever claims. The court has no power to investigate in these cases. But, as some scholars have argued, the particularity of family disputes leads to the procedure dealing with them having a special value orientation different from ordinary civil procedures. Therefore, when hearing family disputes, courts should focus more on finding objective truth, which requires judges to take a proactive role with regard to truth-finding.[27] Divorce cases are a kind of family dispute. Judges should have more power to collect relevant evidence and realise substantive truth in family procedures.

(d) Reframing the standard to determine 'living difficulties' in post-divorce financial assistance

As to the strict conditions of post-divorce financial assistance, we recommend loosening these conditions replacing the present standard of local basic living levels to confirm financial difficulties with a more reasonable one. This new standard should be based on 'reasonable needs' with reference to the living standards during the marriage. Meanwhile, the financial difficulties of an ex-spouse after divorce should be considered rather than the difficulties only at the time of divorce. In this way, it can better realise the function of relieving the distress caused by divorce. Considerations for determining support for the weak spouse should include old age, illness, unemployment, child-raising, length of marriage, living standards during the marriage and contributions to the family etc. To put the living standards during the marriage into consideration does not mean that the weak should get enough support to live a life reaching the above-mentioned standard, but that this should be one of the factors considered when judges exercise their discretion.

(e) Expanding the scope of application of post-divorce economic compensation

The *Chinese Women Development Program* (2011–2020) issued by the State Council of PRC in 2011 requires us 'to protect the women's rights in marriages

---

25 Article 64 in the Civil Procedure Law of the PRC stipulates that 'litigants are obliged to present evidence for their assertions.'

26 Article 15 in Some Provisions of the Supreme People's Court on Evidence in Civil Procedures provides that:
'"evidence which the people's court deems necessary for the hearing" in Article 64 in the Civil Procedure Law refers to the following situations: (1) facts probably involving infringement of state interests, public interests or others' legitimate rights and interests …'

27 Dongqing Zhuo 'Proof of domestic violence in civil procedure' in Yinlan Xia and Yifei Long (eds) *Researches on Family Law* (Beijing, China: Social Sciences Academic Press, 2012) 267.

and families. When hearing divorce cases, judges should consider contributions the women made for their families during the marriage, women's life after divorce and their needs of raising children and fairly compensate their losses'. As to the limited application of post-divorce economic compensation, we suggest expanding the entitled spouses in this system to spouses adopting the default joint property system. In another words, not only are spouses adopting the separate property system entitled to post-divorce economic compensation, but also where there is no common property or few joint properties available for division when spouses adopt the joint property system, the judge should apply economic compensation to compensate the spouse contributing more to domestic chores during the marriage. Thus, the disadvantaged can get compensatory support so as to balance both parties' economic interests during the marriage. In this way, the law not only recognises contributions of domestic chores, but also considers the different situations of recipients. Fair compensation for contributions of domestic chores will be realised.[28]

As to the exact amount of compensation, namely, how to determine the value of housework, we suggest that judges should consider opportunity costs of the spouse doing housework, length of marriage, contributions made by the spouse doing housework, and the other spouse's benefit because of the contributions etc.

---

28 Wei Chen and Xianxin Cao, 'On compensation for the career opportunities lost by a spouse and the value of housework during the marriage', *Gansu Social Sciences*, 2010(4), p 33.

CZECH REPUBLIC

NEW FAMILY LAW IN THE CZECH REPUBLIC: BACK TO TRADITIONS AND TOWARDS MODERN TRENDS

*Zdeňka Králíčková**

Résumé

Comme dans de nombreux anciens pays communistes, on ne s'attendait pas en Tchéquie à des changements majeurs du droit familial sans passer par une recodification du Code civil. Au cours des dernières années, il y a eu plusieurs tentatives en ce sens, impliquant de nouvelles idées et de nouveaux auteurs. Tous ces projets ont en commun d'intégrer dans le Code civil le droit de la famille qui, depuis 1949, fait l'objet d'une législation particulière. Il aura fallu attendre jusqu'en 2012, après une longue «période transitoire», typique des amendements apportées aux codes en d'autres temps, pour que soit adopté le nouveau Code civil par le biais de la Loi No 89/2012 Coll. Le Code est entré en vigueur le 1er janvier 2014. On peut le qualifier de «compromis raisonnable» entre tradition et modernité. Le nouveau droit tchèque de la famille est en effet marqué du sceau de la continuité avec l'ancien droit car de nombreux changements, tant dans la loi que dans son application, avaient déjà été adoptés peu de temps après 1989 dans la foulée de réformes législatives et de décisions judiciaires, notamment celles de la Cour constitutionnelle et de la Cour européenne des droits de l'Homme.

I INTRODUCTION

The *International Survey of Family Law* has already several times published articles about the development of Czech family law. It was especially Professor Jiří Haderka who criticised, in his articles, the ideological foundations and the situation of Czech family law patterned upon the Soviet model after 1948 and its 'half-hearted reforms' carried out in a series of amendments to the previous Act on the Family from 1963 after the fall of the Communist regime in 1989.[1] As in many other post-Communist countries, radical changes to family law were not expected to take place in the Czech Republic without a recodification

* Associate Professor, Faculty of Law, Masaryk University, Brno, the Czech Republic.

1 See JF Haderka 'The Czech Republic – New Problems and Old Worries' in A Bainham (ed) *International Survey of Family Law 1996* (The Hague, Boston, London: Martinus Nijhoff, 1996) 181–197; JF Haderka 'A Half-Hearted Family Law Reform of 1998' in A Bainham (ed) *International Survey of Family Law, 2000 Edition* (Jordan Publishing Limited, 2000) 119–130.

of the Civil Code.[2] In the past years there were a number of attempts to create a New Civil Code involving a lot of new ideas and authors. Nevertheless, a common feature of all the Drafts was that Family Law, since 1949 a separate legal regulation, was to be integrated into the New Civil Code. Thus, the separateness of family law ideologically substantiated for a long time was supposed to disappear.[3] As late as 2012, after a long 'transitory' period typical of a great number of disparate amendments of the old codes that had been products of their times, a New Civil Code was adopted (Act No 89/2012 Coll).[4] It came into effect on 1 January 2014.

The main authors of the *Principles and Starting Points of the New Code of Private Law*[5] and the *Draft for the New Civil Code*,[6] Professors Karel Eliáš and Michaela Zuklínová, implemented Family Law into the second part of the New Civil Code. In accordance with the authors' intention the above-mentioned separateness of Family Law, lasting for more than 50 years, was thus eliminated and the law returned to the basics of the General Civil Code (ABGB, 1811).[7] The return to the tested European tradition cannot be, though, linked only with the systematic nature of the New Civil Code (NCC) but also especially with its content. The New Civil Code may be said to respect the traditional values of the European Christian-Jewish culture. However, individual institutes also include some important innovations that have been present in other European codes for a long time thanks to Human Rights Covenants, the case-law of the Constitutional Court of the Czech Republic and of the European Court of Human Rights and various academic activities originated especially in the Commission on European Family Law (CEFL).

II PRINCIPLES OF NEW CIVIL AND FAMILY LAW

Despite the fact that family law is dealt with in a separate part of the Civil Code, the second one, it is necessary to interpret and apply its rules in connection with the first one, ie the general part where the basic principles, values, starting points and interpretation and application rules can be found.

---

2 See Z Králíčková 'Czech Family Law: The Right Time for Re-Codification' in B Atkin (ed) *International Survey of Family Law, 2009 Edition* (Jordan Publishing Limited, 2009) 157–173.

3 From a general point of view see P Bělovskí 'Rodinné právo' (Family Law) in M Bobek, P Molek and V Šimíček (eds) *Komunistické právo v Československu. Kapitoly z dějin bezpráví* (*Communist Law in Czechoslovakia. Chapters in History of Injustice*) (Brno: Masarykova univerzita, 2009) 463 ff.

4 For details see 'Důvodová zpráva' (Explanatory Note) available on http://obcanskyzakonik.justice.cz/fileadmin/OZ_Duvodova_zprava_11042011.pdf (only in Czech).

5 See K Eliáš and M Zuklínová *Principles and Starting Points of the New Code of Private Law* (Praha: Linde, 2001).

6 See K Eliáš and M Zuklínová (main compilers) *Návrh občanského zákoníku* (*Draft for the Civil Code*) (Praha: Ministry of Justice, spring 2005).

7 For the theoretical questions and legal theory starting points, compare the study M Zuklínová 'Budoucí občanskí zákoník a rodinné právo' ('The Future Civil Code and the Family Law') in *Otázky rekodifikace soukromého práva* (*The Issues of Re-Codification of Private Law*) (Acta Universitatis Carolinae, Iuridica, 2003) No 1/2, 141 ff.

It states in the first place that 'the application of private law is independent of the application of public law' (NCC, s 1(1)). This principle is elaborated, for example, in the new civil law conception of the definition of residence based on factuality (NCC, s 80) and further in the new conception of parents deciding about the place of their child's residence due to their parental responsibility (NCC, s 858). The administrative record of persons is irrelevant.

Next, the New Civil Code puts emphasis on the application of the autonomy of the will. It provides for the principle that, unless expressly prohibited by the law, persons may agree upon rights and duties differently from the law; only agreements contravening 'good manners, public order or rights relating to the status of persons including right to protection of personality are prohibited' (NCC, s 1(2)). We may say that this formulation fully overrides the doctrine of the full force of family law except for status rules regulating the origin and termination of marriage, establishing and denying parenthood, etc. Autonomy of will is fully manifested in family law especially in marital property law (NCC, s 708), nevertheless with reasonable limits, for example if a special regime of things forming the usual equipment of the family household is at issue (NCC, s 698).

Quite an important provision is the one that expressly establishes the doctrine of the horizontal effect of constitutional law. By this, the New Civil Code respects the human rights dimension of civil or family law.[8] This had been considered by many family law experts to be the key value since the adoption of a number of international covenants, especially by the Council of Europe, such as the Convention for the Protection of Human Rights and Fundamental Freedoms.[9] The New Civil Code also establishes that each provision of private law may only be interpreted in compliance with the Charter of Fundamental Rights and Freedoms[10] and with the constitutional order, with the principles on which it is based, and with values which are protected by it. If an interpretation of an individual provision, by its very wording, diverges from this order it must be abandoned (NCC, s 2(1)).

Last but not least, it is also necessary to mention the establishing of a prohibition against abuse of the law (NCC, s 8) and a prohibition against the interpretation and application of a provision in contradiction to good manners (NCC, s 2(3)) and to the protection of honest conduct and good faith (NCC, s 7). The New Civil Code then expressly mentions a subsidiary option of applying analogies and principles of justice and principles on which it is based so that a good arrangement of rights and duties can be achieved with respect to

---

8 See Z Králíčková *Lidskoprávní dimenze českého rodinného práva* (*Human Rights Dimension of Czech Family Law*) (Brno: Masaryk University, 2009).

9 The Convention was adopted in 1950. Czechoslovakia did not accede to it until the fall of the Communist regime. It was published under No 209/1992 Coll.

10 See Constitutional Act No 23/1991 Coll; for details see E Wagnerova, V Šimíček, T Langášek, I Pospíšil et al *Listina základních práv a svobod. Komentář* (*Charter of Fundamental Rights and Freedoms. Commentary*) (Praha: Wolters Kluwer, 2012).

the customs of private life and with respect to both the state of jurisprudence and the established decision-making practice (NCC, s 10).

However, for family law there are especially important provisions establishing that private law protects the dignity and freedom of humans and their natural right to pursue their happiness and happiness of their families or close persons in such a way that does not groundlessly cause others any harm (NCC, s 3(1)). Further, it is important that the New Civil Code expressly states that private law is based on the following principles (NCC, s 3(2)):

(a) everyone has the right to protection of their life and health as well as freedom, reputation, dignity and privacy;
(b) family, parenthood and marriage enjoy special legal protection;
(c) no one may suffer groundless harm due to insufficient age, reason or dependent position; however, no one may groundlessly take advantage of their incapacity to the detriment of others; and
(d) a promise given is binding and contracts shall be performed.

No matter how redundant the provisions of the New Civil Code above mentioned may seem we hold the view that it was necessary to establish them. They create room for a new approach to family law and especially to its values. Prohibition of discrimination, protection of the weaker party, solidarity, etc are key concepts that will be important for the interpretation and application of the rules of the new family law.[11] We may say that for lawyers educated at the time of the rule of the Communist law the explicit establishment of these civilised values will be quite beneficial.

Besides general principles of private and family law, it is necessary to mention special principles governing key institutions of family law, for example the principle of dissolubility of marriage (NCC, s 755) which is a specific example of the general principle according to which 'nobody can be forced to stay in a union', and the non-consumer character of maintenance which the parents are obliged to provide to their children (NCC, ss 915, 917; for more details on this, see below).

III MARRIAGE, COHABITATION AND REGISTERED PARTNERSHIP

(a) General

The New Civil Code allows marriage to be solemnised only between a man and a woman. The Code establishes that marriage is a permanent union of a man and a woman originating in a manner prescribed by this law. The main purpose of marriage is establishing a family, a proper upbringing of children – even if

[11] On this see F Zoulík 'Soukromoprávní ochrana slabší smluvní strany' ('Private-Law Protection of the Weaker Party of a Contract') *Právní rozhledy*, 2002, No 3, 109 ff.

marriage may also be entered into by people who are not in the 'productive' age – and mutual support and help (NCC, s 655), which fully reflects the principle of solidarity. Despite the fact that marriage is characterized by the word 'permanency' divorce is a legitimate manner of terminating marriage.

No matter how the New Civil Code expressly protects the family established by marriage (cf NCC, s 3(2)(b)), it is necessary to mention that informal unions of a man and a woman, or anyone, also enjoy protection in connection with the Convention for the Protection of Human Rights and Freedoms as they are guaranteed by the right to respect for private and family life (Art 8 of the Convention, in connection with NCC, s 2(2) referring to the constitutional order itself). It should also be mentioned that if an unmarried man and an unmarried woman have a child they principally have parental responsibility by operation of law without being discriminated against in comparison with married parents of a child.

The Principles and Starting Points of the New Code of Private Law and many Drafts of the New Civil Code also regulated the registered partnership of persons of the same sex. Nevertheless, in the course of the legislative work, conservatism prevailed and, due to that, rules regulating the status union of persons of the same sex were taken out. Thus the special law regulating registered partnership[12] will continue to be effective. We should add that in many respects rights and duties of registered partners are similar to rights and duties of spouses (eg mutual maintenance duty) and in many aspects they are identical with the position of informal unions (eg lack of matrimonial community property, non-existence of common lease of flats ex lege, impossibility of jointly adopting a minor or becoming joint foster parents or guardians of minors, etc).

(b) Solemnisation of marriage

It is well known that for the Communist Family Law the typical obligatory form of marriage was civil marriage and there were cases of clergymen involved in church marriages being criminally prosecuted. Even though religious marriage was reintroduced into the Czech legal order shortly after 1989, many Drafts of the New Civil Code recognised only the civil one referring to the European standards. Nevertheless, in the course of the legislative process religious marriage was included in the New Civil Code.[13] Thus the engaged couple may be married in two manners, either civil or religious (NCC, s 657).

The marriage ceremony must be preceded in both forms by the pre-marriage proceedings before a register authority where especially the following issues are examined (NCC, s 673 ff):

---

12 See Act No 115/2006 Coll, on Registered Partnership.

13 Religious marriage may only be solemnised before registered churches with the so-called special authorisation under Act No 3/2002 Coll.

(a) the sex of the would-be spouses;[14]
(b) the age of the would-be spouses: principally it should be 18 or over;[15]
(c) legal obstacles for the marriage such as the existence of another marriage or registered partnership, family relationship in a direct line and between siblings, newly also the existence of guardianship or any other form of custody, and, finally, mental disorder and lack of legal capacity.

Marriage comes into origin at the moment when the would-be spouses publicly and solemnly declare in the presence of two witnesses that they enter together into marriage. The record in the register of marriages is only for registration purposes.

As for the surname after solemnisation of the marriage, the law makes it possible for the would-be spouses to declare at the wedding ceremony that:

(a) the surname of one of them will be their common surname;
(b) both of them will keep their own surnames;[16] or
(c) the surname of one of them will be their common surname, and the would-be spouse whose surname is not to be the common one will add his or her existing surname to their common surname in the second place (NCC, s 660).

If the requirements stipulated by the law for solemnization of marriage are breached the law sanctions them on the basis of seriousness of the issue:

(a) by the regime of apparent marriage *(matrimonium putativum)* which originates ex lege, for example when the church did not have special authorization; or
(b) by the regime of invalid marriage *(non matrimonium)* which must be decided by the court, for example in the case of bigamy or kinship.

---

[14] As for transsexuals, the law regulates change of sex in Section 29, NCC, establishing that the change of sex of a person occurs on the surgical operation disabling the reproduction functions and changing the sex organs. It is presumed that the day of the change of sex is the day recorded in the certificate issued by the provider of health services. The change of sex does not affect the personal state of a man/woman or their personal and property situation; marriage or registered partnership ceases to exist, though. Details are included in the Act No 373/2011 Coll., on Specific Health Services.

[15] Exceptions are laid down especially in NCC, s 672 establishing that marriage cannot be entered into by a minor who is not fully legally competent. In exceptional cases the court may allow a minor who is not fully legally competent and is over 16 to enter into marriage if there are serious reasons for that. Further, NCC, s 37 establishes that, if a minor who is not fully legally competent asks the court to award him or her competency, the court will do so if the minor has attained 16 years of age, if his or her ability to make a living and manage his or her affairs is attested, and if his or her legal representative agrees to that. In other cases the court agrees to the proposal if it is in the interests of the minor because of serious reasons.

[16] If the spouses keep their existing surnames they will also declare at the wedding ceremony which surname will be the surname of their mutual children according to NCC, s 661. Thus children cannot have so-called double surnames.

(c) Rights and duties of spouses

Rights and duties of spouses are traditional, especially personal ones. The law is based on equality of a man and a woman in the marriage, in the family and in society, drawing on previous legal regulations.[17] Spouses are obliged to respect each other, to live together, to be faithful, to respect mutually their dignity, to support each other, to maintain the family union, to create a healthy family environment, to jointly take care of their children (NCC, s 687), to represent each other (NCC, s 694), and to jointly manage the issues of the family (NCC, ss 693, 694). The law newly sets forth that either spouse has the right to be told by the other one about his or her income and the state of his or her property as well as about the existing and planned work, studies and similar activities. Further, either spouse is obliged, when choosing work, studies and similar activities, to take into consideration the interests of the family, of the other spouse and of the minors who have not attained full legal competency yet and who live with the spouses in the family household, and, potentially, also the interests of other members of the family (NCC, ss 688, 689).

As for the property aspects of marriage, the New Civil Code first of all paraphrases the previous regulations establishing that each spouse contributes to the needs of the family and the family household according to each's personal and property conditions, abilities and possibilities so that the standard of living of all members of the family can be the same. Providing property has the same importance as personal care of the family and its members (NCC, s 680). Besides the duty to contribute to the needs of the family the law also establishes a mutual maintenance duty for the spouses, to the extent of a right to the same standard of living (NCC, s 697).

There is an innovation in the institution of the usual equipment forming the common household (NCC, s 698). The law establishes that, regardless of the ownership of things that fulfil the necessary life needs of the family, a spouse needs consent of the other one when dealing with them; this does not apply if the thing is of negligible value. A spouse may claim invalidity of a legal act by which the other spouse dealt, without his or her consent, with a thing belonging to the usual equipment of the family household.

Another innovation is the regulation of a family enterprise (NCC, s 700), which is defined as an enterprise where the spouses work together, or at least with one of the spouses working with their relatives to the third degree, or persons related with the spouses by marriage up to the second degree, and the enterprise is owned by one of these persons. Those of them who permanently work for the family or the family enterprise are considered members of the family participating in the operation of the family enterprise. Members of the family participating in the operation of the family enterprise also participate in its profits and in things gained out of those profits as well as in the growth of the enterprise to the extent corresponding to the amount and kind of their work.

---

[17] See the Act No 121/1920 Coll, Constitutional Bill of Czechoslovakia, especially s 106(1).

This right may only be waived by a person with full legal capacity making a personal declaration (NCC, s 701). If the family enterprise is to be divided within the administration of the probate estate, a member participating in its operation has a pre-emptive right to it (NCC, s 704(1)).

The key institution of the marriage property law is community of property, which was introduced into the Czech legal order by the 1998 amendment to the previous Act on the family. In the first place the law regulates the legal regime of the property gains. which includes what one of the spouses has gained or what both spouses have gained in the course of their marriage except for (NCC, s 709):

(a) what serves the personal needs of one of the spouses;[18]
(b) what only one of the spouses has gained by gift, succession or bequest unless the donor or the testator in the will expressed a different intention;
(c) what one of the spouses has gained as compensation for a non-proprietary infringement of his or her natural rights;
(d) what one of the spouses has gained by legal dealings relating to his or her separate property; and
(e) what one of the spouses has gained as compensation for damage to or loss of separate property.

Community property includes profit from what is separate property of one of the spouses. It also includes an interest of a spouse in a company or a cooperative if that spouse has become a member the company or the cooperative in the course of the marriage (NCC, s 709).

Community property also includes debts assumed in the course of the marriage unless:

(a) the debts concern the separate property of one of the spouses – to the extent that they the profit from that property; or
(b) only one of the spouses has assumed them without the other spouse's consent and it was not within the fulfilment of everyday or common needs of the family (NCC, s 710).

The new law enables not only modifications of the legal regime of the acquired property but also the creation of the agreed regime (NCC, s 716) and establishing the regime of separated property (NCC, s 729). An innovation is to make arrangements for the case of termination of marriage due to divorce or death by making a contract of succession (NCC, s 718(2)). Both would-be spouses and spouses may do so at any time: before entering into marriage as

---

[18] Since 1998, the things one uses for the performance of one's job have not been excluded from the scope of the legal regime. For a different attitude, see K Boele-Woelki, F Ferrand, C González-Beilfuss, M Jänterä-Jareborg, N Lowe, D Martiny and W Pintens *Principles of European Family Law Regarding Property Relations Between Spouses* (Cambridge, Antwerp, Portland: Intersentia, 2013).

well as during the marriage. By this the lawmakers fully respect the principle of autonomy of will, which was completely curbed in the 1960s legal regulation. The parties to the contract are only required to keep the formality of a public deed. A record in the public list is optional (NCC, ss 698, 721).

Protection of an economically weaker spouse and third persons is expressly established in the New Civil Code in a separate provision which sets forth that a contract of marital property regime may not, due to its consequences, exclude the spouse's ability to maintain the family and may not affect, by its content or purpose, rights of a third person unless the third person agrees with it; the contract made without the third party's consent has no legal force for such a party (NCC, s 719). We consider it very important that the law further establishes that, if during the existence of community property a debt has arisen only for one of the spouses, the creditor may achieve satisfaction in the execution of the judgment recovering the debt also from what is in the community property (NCC, s 731). If a debt has arisen only for one of the spouses against the will of the other spouse who communicated his or her disagreement to the creditor without unnecessary delay after coming to know about the debt, their community property may be affected only up to the amount which would be the share of the debtor if the community property were cancelled and divided (pursuant to NCC, s 742). This also applies in the case of the spouse's duty to pay maintenance or if the debt comes from an illegal act of one of the spouses or in the case of the debt of one of the spouse having arisen before entering into marriage (Section 732, NCC).

The new provision protecting family housing is important, too, because the previous legal regulations belittled this issue. Of course, if the family dwelling is in the common property of the spouses, their position is equal and protection is provided by the regulation analysed above. If not, the situation of the economically weaker spouse is dealt with in the new Code by defining the so-called derived legal reason for housing. The law establishes that if the spouses' dwelling is a house or a flat in which one of the spouses has an exclusive right to live, and if it is a different right from the contractual one, by entering into marriage the other spouse obtains the right to housing (NCC, s 744). If one of the spouses has an exclusive contractual right to the house or the flat, especially the lease right, by entering into marriage both spouses obtain jointly the lease right ensuring the equality of rights and duties (NCC, s 745). Nevertheless, it may be contractually agreed in a different way (NCC, s745(2)), which is fully in harmony with the principle of autonomy of will.

The law also newly regulates the prohibition of the disposal of the family dwelling in a similar way as in the case of the rules relating to things forming the usual equipment of the household (NCC, s 698, see above). If at least one of the spouses has the right to dispose of the house or the flat in which the family household is situated and the house or the flat is necessary for the dwelling of the spouses and of the family, that spouse must refrain from and prevent anything that may endanger their dwelling or make it impossible. A spouse cannot, without consent of the other spouse, misappropriate such a house or flat, or create a right to the house, to part or the whole of a flat, the exercise of which is incompatible with the dwelling of the spouses or the family, unless he or she arranges a similar dwelling of the same standard for the other spouse or the family. If a spouse acts without consent of the other spouse contrary to this rule, the other spouse may claim invalidity of such legal conduct (NCC, s 747). If the spouses have a joint right to a house or a flat in which the family household of the spouses or of the family is situated the abovementioned prohibition applies similarly (cf NCC, s 748).

Last but not least, it is necessary to mention new civil law provisions against domestic violence.[19] The law sets forth that, if dwelling jointly in a house or a flat where the family household of the spouses is situated becomes for one of them intolerable due to physical or mental violence against that spouse or anyone else living in the family household of the spouses, the court may, at the motion of the affected spouse, restrict or exclude the right of the other spouse for a specified period to dwell in the house or the flat (NCC, s 751(1)). It is possible to proceed in the same manner in the case of divorced spouses as well as in the case when the spouses or ex-spouses live jointly elsewhere than in their family household (NCC, s 751(2)), and also in the case of persons other than spouses (NCC, s 3021). Restriction or exclusion of a spouse's right to live in the house or the flat is decided on by the court for the period of 6 months at most. The court will, on a motion, decide again if there are serious reasons for doing so (NCC, s 752).

(d) Dissolution of marriage

The New Civil Code sets forth that marriage is terminated only due to reasons established by the law (NCC, s 754). Drawing on the previous legal regulations these are death, declaring somebody dead (NCC, s 26), divorce (NCC, ss 755 ff), and, newly, a surgical change of sex where the marriage terminates on the day recorded in the certificate issued by the provider of health services (NCC, s 29).[20]

As for divorce, the new legal regulation, too, is based on irretrievable breakdown of marriage which was the only reason for divorce introduced in the Act on the Family as early as 1963. The New Civil Code sets forth that marriage may be dissolved if the joint life of the spouses is deeply, permanently and irretrievably broken down and its recovery cannot be expected (NCC,

---

[19] The New Civil Code thus complements the previous regulation established by a special law against domestic violence from 2006 by which an administrative ordering of sb (spouse) out of the joint dwelling (home ban) was introduced into the Act on Police (10 days), and the so-called court ordering of sb out of the family dwelling by injunction was introduced into the Civil Procedure Rules (one month, with the option of lengthening up to one year), and the so-called intervention centres were established. A special criminal law protection against domestic violence is from 2004. For details see Z Králíčková, E Žatecká, R Dávid and M Kornel *Právo proti domácímu násilí* (*Law Against Domestic Violence*) (Praha: CH Beck, 2011).

[20] See n 14 above.

s 755(1)). The court deciding about the divorce of marriage shall examine the fact of the breakdown of the marriage and reasons leading to it (NCC, s 756). This is called contested divorce.

However, if the spouses have agreed about the divorce, or the other spouse has joined the petition for divorce, the court does not examine reasons for the breakdown if it comes to the conclusion that the identical statements of the spouses about the breakdown of their marriage and about their intent to achieve divorce are true (NCC, s 757). This is called uncontested divorce[21] and the following requirements must be met:

(a) on the day of the commencement of the divorce proceedings the marriage has lasted for one year at least and the spouses have not lived together for more than 6 months;
(b) the spouses, who are parents of a minor without full legal capacity, have agreed on arrangements for the child for the period after the divorce and the court has approved their agreement; and
(c) the spouses have agreed on the arrangement of their property, their housing and, if the case may be, the maintenance for the period after the divorce; the contract must be in writing with officially authenticated signatures.

Like the previous law, amended in 1998, the new law establishes the so-called clause against harshness. The law sets forth that despite the breakdown of their living the marriage cannot be dissolved if it were against:

(a) the interest of a minor of the spouses due to special reasons; the court examines the child's interest in the existence of the marriage by inquiring of the custodian who is appointed by the court for the proceedings on the arrangement of the child's custody for the period of the divorce; and
(b) the interest of the spouse who was not predominantly involved in the breach of marital duties and who would suffer an especially serious harm by the divorce and there are extraordinary circumstances supporting the existence of marriage, unless the spouses have not lived together for 3 years at least (NCC, s 755(2)).

If the spouses have a minor, the court will not grant divorce until deciding on the custody of the child for the period after the divorce (NCC, s 755(3)). The court dealing with custody of the minor may decide on or approve the agreement of the spouses in the matter of entrusting the child into individual custody of one parent, alternating custody or joint custody (NCC, s 907). It is

---

[21] The new legal regulation does not know the so-called divorce on the basis of agreement, ie consensual divorce. Thus the Principles of European Family Law regarding Divorce were not taken into consideration (unlike the Principles of European Family Law Regarding Parental Responsibilities). For more see K Boele-Woelki, F Ferrand, C González-Beilfuss, M Jänterä-Jareborg, N Lowe, D Martiny and W Pintens *Principles of European Family Law Regarding Divorce and Maintenance Between Former Spouses* (Antwerp, Oxford: Intersentia, 2004).

necessary to emphasise that the parents of the child are both principally bearers of rights and duties resulting from parental responsibility (cf NCC, ss 865 ff) and the decision about after-divorce custody only determines whom the child will live with in the common household (besides the maintenance duty towards the child).

(e) Legal consequences of dissolution of marriage

Dissolution of marriage affects not only one's status but also one's property situation. If the marriage is terminated by death, or by declaring one of the spouses dead, the deceased's property passes to the spouse in the first inheritance class together with the testator's children (NCC, s 1635). If there are no children the property passes to the spouses in the second class together with the testator's parents and the so-called cohabiting persons (NCC, s 1636). However, in keeping with the previous law the surviving spouse is not the so-called forced heir who is entitled to an obligatory share (cf NCC, ss 1642 ff). Nevertheless, if there is a will, for example in favour of third persons, the New Civil Code establishes that the surviving spouse gains possessory title to movables that form the basic equipment of the family household (NCC, s 1667) and right to maintenance from the inheritance arises for him or her (NCC, s 1666). This arrangement is similar to that in the General Civil Code (ABGB, 1811). Special protection is ensured for the surviving spouse in relation to dwelling. The law regulates the transition of the joint lease of a flat ex lege (NCC, s 766) and the discretion of the court to create an easement of dwelling for the surviving spouse if he or she has custody of a minor – the easement being for a definite term and for payment corresponding to the usual rent (NCC, s 767(2)).

If the marriage was terminated by divorce it is necessary, first of all, to settle and adjust the community property of the spouses. As a rule, the law prescribes an agreement between the divorced spouses. If the agreement is not achieved, the court will decide on the basis of both quantitative and qualitative criteria such as the interests of unsupported children or the extent to which a spouse was involved in achieving and maintaining the property values falling within the community of property of the spouses (NCC, s 742). If within 3 years from the divorce no agreement is made or petition filed, a legal presumption will be applied (NCC, s 741).

As for the spouses' dwelling after the divorce, it depends on the legal basis of the marital dwelling. If the family dwelling was in the community of property of the spouses what has been said above in connection with its settlement and adjustment will be applied. If it was a joint lease of a flat by the spouses they may cancel it by rescinding the contract or having recourse to the court that will determine, when deciding about cancelling the joint lease, the manner of compensation for the loss of the right considering also the situation of the unsupported children and the opinion of the lessor among others (NCC, s 768(1)). If one of the spouses was an exclusive owner of the family dwelling the other spouse loses by divorce the so-called derived legal reason for housing and the court may decide about his or her moving out (NCC, s 769).

The maintenance duty between divorced spouses is regulated in the New Civil Code in a different manner from the previous law.[22] The basic presumption is dependence on maintenance, or incapacity to maintain oneself independently. But the law newly establishes that such incapacity to maintain oneself independently has to have its origin in the marriage or in connection with the marriage (cf NCC, s 760(1)). Another innovation is the list of factors that should be taken into consideration when deciding on adequate maintenance. The court will thus consider for how long the marriage lasted and for how long it has been dissolved and whether (NCC, s 76(2)):

(a) the divorced spouse has remained without a job even though not being prevented from finding a job due to serious reasons;
(b) the divorced spouse could have ensured maintenance by properly managing his or her property;
(c) the divorced spouse participated during the marriage in care of the family household;
(d) the divorced spouse has not committed a criminal act towards the ex-spouse or a close person; or
(e) whether there is another, similarly serious reason.

The right to maintenance for the period after the divorce terminates only when the beneficiary enters into a new marriage, or by death of the obligor or the beneficiary. If a substantial change of the situation occurs the court may decide about decreasing, increasing or abolishing the mutual duty of maintenance between the divorced spouses.

The New Civil Code, too, establishes an exceptional right to so-called 'punitive maintenance' to the extent of ensuring the same living standard. The spouse who did not cause the divorce or did not agree to the divorce and who suffered serious harm due to the divorce may file a motion to the court to determine a maintenance duty on the former spouse to such an extent that the ex-spouses can have the same living standard. The divorced spouse's right to maintenance may be considered justified only for a period adequate to the situation but for 3 years after the divorce at most (NCC, s 762).

---

22 On this, see Z Králíčková 'Legal Protection of Unmarried and Divorced Mothers in the Czech Republic' in B Verschraegen (ed) *Family Finances* (Vienna: Jan Sramek Verlag, 2009) 281–291.

IV KINSHIP AND PARENTHOOD

(a) General

The New Civil Code establishes that kinship is a relationship based on a blood tie or originated by adoption (NCC, s 771) which is seen as a status change (cf NCC, ss 794 ff).

The new legal regulation of blood parenthood may be characterised as a traditional one. It is grounded on the philosophy on which the General Civil Code (ABGB, 1811) was built. According to many authors it happened due to the natural law school having special importance for the origin of this code, especially from the human rights perspective.

As for adoption of a minor, the new legal regulation is in harmony with international standards established mainly by international covenants and the case-law of the European Court of Human Rights. A new thing in the New Civil Code is the adoption of a major, which continues in the tradition of the past legal regulations. As in most legal systems of the former Soviet Bloc, after 1949 the Czech legal order regulated only adoption of minor children. For political reasons, adoption of adults was abandoned as a 'bourgeois anachronism'. Thus the New Civil Code reintroduces it, in addition to the full adoption of minors.

(b) Motherhood

The old Roman law principle of mater semper certa est respecting the fact of birth has traditionally been considered in the Czech lands to be the basis for creating the status relationship of the mother and the child, even if expressis verbis it was not introduced in the legal order until 1998 by an amendment to the Act on the Family. The natural law idea of one mother and one father of the child fully corresponding to natural laws is respected by the lawmakers even today when Czech family law gains a human rights dimension but the medical science does not recognise any boundaries (see below). The child's mother is the woman who has given birth to the child (NCC, s 775). Despite being a relatively simple one, the new legal regulation of motherhood is quite apt. It is formulated as a mandatory rule from which it is not possible to divert one-sidedly (eg by giving up or abandoning a child, not expressing interest, etc) nor contractually (with or without payment).

The basis of the status condition of motherhood is the fact of birth, which includes assisted reproduction, too. The legal mother of the child is the woman who has given birth regardless of who was the donor of the egg. Legal motherhood is thus identical with biological motherhood and in the case of egg donation genetic motherhood is irrelevant.[23]

---

[23] The key regulation of artificial insemination, or assisted reproduction, can be found in the new Act No 373/2011 Coll, on Specific Health Services. This Act defines the basic concepts such as

As for surrogate motherhood, it is not regulated in the Czech legal order except for one note in connection with adoption among close relatives (on this, see section (d)(i) below).

Undoubtedly, motherhood is the basic status condition which is important for the whole legal order. The maternal status is crucial for humans. Therefore it is necessary – in compliance with international obligations, especially Art 7 of the Convention on the Rights of the Child – to register the child soon after the birth in connection with the mother thus making the child's status in connection with the parents certain. Public law regulations establish this duty as a rule especially for the medical staff assisting with the birth. Below, we give two examples when the child's rights give way to the mother's rights. We should note that these exceptions to the rule are not accepted without reservations by legal experts or the public in general.

A relatively new thing in the Czech legal order infringing protection of status rights of the child is the institution of hidden birth regulated by law.[24] A quite new Act establishes that a woman with permanent residency in the territory of the Czech Republic, if not a woman for whose husband there is an assumption of fatherhood, has a right to have her identity hidden in connection with a birth (Act on Health Services, s 37). Such a woman, if she wants to hide her identity in connection with a birth, submits to the provider of the respective health service a written application for hiding her identity where she also states she does not intend to take care of the child. The child has a mother but does not know her identity because it is hidden from him or her in the register of births. Rights of biological fathers are more or less omitted there.

Another new social phenomenon are the so-called baby-boxes which are not regulated or prohibited by any law in the Czech Republic. The founder of about 50 boxes for abandoning unwanted children, which enables mothers to give birth in fact anonymously, has since 2005 been a private fund.[25] If the identity

---

assisted reproduction, infertile couple, anonymous donor, mutual anonymity of the donor, the infertile couple and their child, etc, and especially the conditions for its realisation, ie the respective informed consent but also various restrictions, eg as far as age or kinship are concerned.

24 See Act No 372/2011 Coll, on Health Services. See also an older one, Act No 422/2004 Coll, so-called Act on Hidden Births. On the fierce critical comments see M Hrušáková and Z Králíčková *Anonymní a utajené mateřství v České republice – utopie nebo realita?* (*Anonymous and Secret Motherhood in the Czech Republic – Utopia, or Reality?*) *Právní rozhledy*, 2005, No 2, 53 ff.

25 For statistics see www.statim.cz. On the history, the contemporary state and unfortunately also the future of the boxes for abandoned children, see M Zuklínová 'Několik poznámek k právním otázkám okolo tzv. baby-schránek' ('Several Notes on the Legal Questions on the So-Called Baby-Boxes') *Právní rozhledy*, 2005, No 7, 250 ff. Compare further especially the conclusion, which is not very complimentary of the Czech Republic and its legislative practice. In this context see Committee on the Rights of the Child Reviews Report of the Czech Republic from 31st May 2011 available on www.ohchr.org/en/NewsEvents/Pages/DisplayNews.aspx?NewsID=11098&LangID=E.

of the mother whose child was abandoned in the baby-box has not been found out the child obtains the status of a foundling. Not every child is lucky enough to be adopted.

(c) Fatherhood

The new legal regulation for determining fatherhood (NCC, ss 776–793) is, too, based on three traditional legal assumptions drawing on probability: pater vero is est quem nuptiae demonstrant. We may say that this regulation of fatherhood does not differ much from the concept in other European legal regulations. However, the regulations establishing the legal assumptions of fatherhood were created at the time when legitimacy of a child was highly valued and when methods of assisted reproduction and paternal tests were still in their infancy.

The first assumption is then in favour of the mother's husband, if the child is born in wedlock or within 300 days after its termination (NCC, s 776). The second assumption respects the autonomy of will of the child's parents and is in favour of the man who has stated, together with the mother, that he is the father of her child (NCC, s 779). The third assumption is based on sexual intercourse in the so-called critical period: the father of an unmarried woman's child is considered to be the man who had sex with her within the period of 160 days prior to the birth and within the period not exceeding 300 days after the birth unless his fatherhood is excluded by serious reasons (NCC, s 783). The New Civil Code introduces some innovations that break the conservatism typical of this area of family law, namely:

(a) taking into account the fact that the Civil Code comes back to the rule of declaring someone missing (cf NCC, s 776(1)), which, within the context of the first assumption, has the same importance as the death of the mother's husband;
(b) enabling the so-called conversion of the first assumption into the second one (cf NCC, s 777(1)), ie if a child is born in the interim period lasting from the filing of the petition for divorce until the 300th day after the divorce it is possible to consider a man to be the child's father if he declares so and his statement is in conformity with the statement of the mother's husband, or the ex-husband, and with the statement of the child's mother;
(c) including the assumption of an unmarried mother's partner if he consented to artificial insemination (NCC, s 778);
(d) introducing new rules for making a consenting declaration about the second assumption if the issue in question is:
    (i) the declaration itself and its invalidity (NCC, s 782);
    (ii) declaring someone incompetent (NCC, s 780); and
    (iii) the declaration of a mother suffering from mental disorder, or if getting her consent is connected with serious difficulties (NCC, s 781);

(e) extending the denial period for the mother's husband if it is a denial of the first assumption from 6 months to 6 years since the birth of the child (see NCC, s 785);
(f) extending the denial period from 180–300 days to 160–300 days since the artificial insemination for both the husband and the partner of the mother (NCC, s 787);
(g) introducing the option of judicially pardoning one for missing the denial preclusive period if it is required by the child's interest and by the public order requirements (NCC, s 792);
(h) introducing the option for the court to start ex officio proceedings on denying fatherhood but only in the case of the second assumption in the situation when such a father cannot be the real father of the child and it is clearly required by the child's interest, and if the provisions guaranteeing the basic human rights are to be fulfilled (NCC, s 793).

Despite being included in the *Principles and Starting Points of the New Code of Private Law* as well as in the *Draft for the New Civil Code*, the child's denial right is not expressly regulated in the New Civil Code even if it has never been put into question by expert committees. Denial rights of putative fathers were completely omitted by the lawmakers. The number of persons actively legitimated for denying fatherhood is a traditional one – it is only the child's parents recorded in the Register of Births. We appreciate the fact that the New Civil Code does not establish an active legitimisation of the Attorney General's Office to deny fatherhood but we are aware of the fact that this loophole may lead to stalemate situations and, finally, it may be of no benefit to anyone. Another controversial drawback of the New Civil Code is the fact the court is not expressly empowered to start ex officio proceedings in the case of denial of the first assumption. As for the third assumption, conservatism prevailed even if the Constitutional Court and a lot of family law experts came to the conclusion that its traditional basis – the sexual intercourse within the critical period – has been antiquated by the revolutionary development of genetics.[26] Regarding rights of the putative father to establish legal fatherhood even against the will of the child's mother, they were introduced into the Act on the Family in 1998.

(d) Adoption

(i) Adoption of minors

Since 1949, adoption of minors has been understood – in relation to the concept mentioned above – as a benefit for both real and social orphans, unwanted or abandoned minor children. On the part of the adoptive parents, adoption is viewed as acceptance of a stranger's minor child as their own. Since 1963, the law regulated only full adoption of minor children. Besides, adoption of minors has been created as a status change, as an imitation of biological family ties: *adoptione natura imitatur*. Mainly due to the Czech Republic's accession to a number of international human rights conventions after 1989,

---

[26] Cf the Judgment of the Czech Constitutional Court of 28 February 2008, I ÚS 978/07.

the Czech legal order has broadened protection of the child's natural family, of the minor parents of the child, of the putative parents or parents without full legal capacity.[27] Let us add, that the main creators of the New Civil Code intended to adapt the new regulation of adoption of minors in the European Convention on the Adoption of Children (Revised).[28]

The new conception of adoption of minor children (NCC, ss 794 ff) primarily modifies the requirements of parental consent (NCC, ss 809 ff) and the option of consent withdrawal (NCC, s 817) or its expiry (NCC, s 816). The child's mother may give consent to the adoption after the expiry of 6 weeks from the delivery of child, ie after the *puerperium* (NCC, s 813). The child's father is allowed to give consent any time after the child's birth. The child's parents under 16 are not allowed to give consent to adoption (NCC, s 811(1)); any consent would be completely irrelevant. As an innovation, the law introduces the rule that the court may, while depriving the parents of their parental responsibility, also decide on the deprivation of the parental right to give consent to adoption (NCC, s 873).

As regards parents' non-interest, the law provides for a variety of situations, such as situations where a parent stays in an undisclosed location (NCC, s 818(1c)) or shows clearly no interest in the child thus permanently culpably breaching his or her parental duties (NCC, s 819). The law establishes a presumption of apparent non-interest, when non-interest lasts at least 3 months since any instruction, advice or assistance from the state authority (NCC, s 820). If there are close relatives of the child who are willing and able to provide care for the child personally, preserving family ties will always take precedence over adoption by a non-relative (NCC, s 822).

Regarding the adoptee, the child's participation rights guaranteed by international conventions have been strengthened. The law explicitly states that a child over 12 years old must always give consent to the adoption (cf NCC, s 806) and may revoke his or her consent to adoption (NCC, s 808). If, at the time during the adoption process, the child was of tender years the adoptive parents have a duty to inform the adoptee about adoption as soon as it is appropriate and no later than when the adoptee starts compulsory school attendance (NCC, s 836).

Another innovation is that the new law lifts a ban on adoption among close relatives. Close family ties used to be traditionally a disincentive for adoption. However, the lawmaker, being under quite a strong pressure, relinquished this natural, social and legal ban. The law then provides that adoption is excluded among persons who are relatives in the direct line and the siblings except for

---

[27] For details, see Z Králíčková 'Adoption in the Czech Republic: Reform in the Light of the Child Welfare Laws' in A Bainham (ed) *International Survey of Family Law, 2003 Edition* (Jordan Publishing Limited, 2003) 125–142.

[28] See Convention CETS No 058 from 1967, revised as CETS No 202 in 2008 – entry into force in 2011. For more see http://conventions.coe.int/Treaty/en/Treaties/Html/202.htm. However, the Czech Republic has not yet signed the revised version (11 November 2013).

kinship based on surrogate motherhood (NCC, s 804). It should be noted that medical law has never regulated surrogate motherhood.[29] The new Acts passed only recently do not deal with it, either.[30] However, surrogacy is a reality today. Private clinics, particularly, provide surrogacy without legal regulation. As mentioned above, the child's mother is a woman who delivered the child (NCC, s 755 for details see above, section IV(b)).

Discussions regarding same-sex adoption and adoption by de facto couples did not lead to any changes in the conception of the regulation of joint adoption. Only married couples may adopt a child jointly, although the Czech legal order regulates registered partnerships of persons of the same sex (see above, section III(a)). Besides adoption by a married couple, the law enables adoption by one of the spouses and exceptionally adoption by 'another person' (NCC, s 800).

The obligatory pre-adoption care was extended from 3 months to not less than 6 months (NCC, s 829). The new legal rule says that after the parents' consent to adoption and placing of the child to the pre-adoption care of the prospective adopters the exercise of parental responsibility of the child's parents is suspended by operation of law (NCC, s 825) and the court must appoint a guardian for the adoptee. The maintenance obligation of the child's parents or other persons is also suspended as the prospective adoptive parents are required to have the child with them at their own expense (NCC, s 829).

The new legislation also establishes the option of adoption and its circumstances to be kept secret from the child's original family. The option of secrecy applies for the child's parents and their consent to adoption, to (NCC, s 837). However, once the child reaches the age of majority and legal capacity, he or she is entitled to know the details of the adoption file (NCC, s 838). Regardless of this new rule, the traditional regulation on vital registers allows adoptees over 18 years old to inspect the registry books and collections of documents.[31] This is evidence that adoption has never been explicitly based on the principle of anonymity.

Another new feature of the new regulation is the possibility for the court to order surveillance on the success of the adoption for a necessary period, usually through the Child Protection Office NCC, s 839).

A key change concerns the consequences of adoption, ie the conversion of revocable adoption into an irrevocable one by operation of law if within 3 years after the adoption order becomes effective there is no petition for revocation of adoption (NCC, s 840(2)). An exception applies to situations when the

---

29 See J Haderka 'Surogační mateřství' ('Surrogate Motherhood') *Právny obzor*, 1986, No 10, 917 ff.

30 See Act No 372/2011 Coll, on Health Services, and Act No 373/2011 Coll, on Specific Health Services.

31 See Act No 301/2000 Coll, on Registers, Name and Surname.

adoption is in conflict with the law. However, the court may decide upon irrevocability of the adoption even before the expiry of 3-year period from the adoption order.

With regard to the surname of the adopted child, previously quite a rigid rule strictly ordered the change of the child's original surname to the adopters' surname. This was altered, too. The court may allow the adoptee to use both surnames together: the old one and the surname of the adopters (NCC, s 835(2)).

The new regulation, following tradition, allows so-called re-adoption: an adoption of an already adopted child (cf NCC, s 843).

(ii) Adoption of adults

As indicated above, the New Civil Code returns to the possibility of adopting an adult as it used to be regulated in the past (see ABGB, 1811, effective in Family Law matters till 1950).

The law distinguishes between two types of adoption of adult persons:

(a) adoption that is analogous to the full adoption of minors (NCC, s 847); and

(b) adoption that is not analogous to the full adoption of minors (NCC, s 848), ie not full adoption when the adoptee remains – especially with regard to property – connected with his or her family of origin (cf NCC, s 849).

(e) Parental responsibility

Parental responsibility is a key institution of Czech family law which was introduced into Act on the Family in 1998.[32] However, both the precursors of parental responsibility after the communist take-over in 1948 were built on the principle of equal rights and duties for fathers and mothers of a child, regardless of whether the child was born in or out of wedlock and regardless of the terms of personal rights and rights to property including rights of succession. This attitude of the legislature adopted in family codes was seen as a progressive step which led to the elimination of discrimination against children born outside marriage. Nevertheless, both old Acts on the Family were full of ideology and problematic issues.[33] The adoption of the Convention on the Rights of the Child and other conventions undoubtedly meant a turning

---

32 See J Haderka 'Rodičovská zodpovědnost a související otázky od účinnosti zákona č. 91/1998 Sb' ('Parental Responsibility and Connected issues since the Act No 91/1998 Coll Coming into Effect') *Právní praxe*, 1998, No 8, 482.

33 For details see P Bělovskí *Rodinné právo* (*Family Law*) above n 3.

point in this field.[34] Thanks to the case law of the Czech Constitutional Court, and in particular thanks to the case law of the European Court of Human Rights, a new perception of children's rights was introduced in the Czech Republic. The purpose of parental responsibility is (a) the protection of the child and his or her rights on the one hand and (b) giving the parents a free space for the realization of parenthood on the other hand. However, it should be in harmony with the best interests of the child and his or her welfare. We can say that the concept of parental responsibility reflects the legislature's efforts to anchor, to maintain and to protect the balance between the rights of children and their parents.

Let us add that the main creators of the New Civil Code, when writing the final version of the concept of parental responsibility (Section 865 NCC), reflected a major part of the Principles of European Family Law regarding parental responsibilities made by the Commission of European Family Law (CEFL).[35] Parental responsibility is now based not on the simple trichotomy like the current and originally proposed future concept of parental responsibility, but on following categories of rights and duties of parents, which are: (a) care; (b) protection of a child; (c) maintenance of personal relationships; (d) upbringing and education; (e) determination of the residence a child; (f) legal representation and (g) administration of property. This approach seems preferable as it takes into account the particular problem of 'open borders' and their negative consequences, ie the illegal transfer of children and the international child abductions, etc.

Parental responsibility arises from and belongs only to the legal parents of the child (as for the details see above, Part IV(b) and Part IV(c)). The parents must have in principle full legal capacity to do legal acts. If the parent is a minor the parental responsibility is vested in that parent but administration of parental responsibility of such a parent is suspended (Section 868, Sub-Section 1, NCC). There is only one exception; namely, such a parent is allowed to take personal care of the child. As for the parents limited in legal capacity due to a court order such a decision must take parental responsibility into consideration as well (Section 865, Sub-Section 2, and Section 868, Sub-Section 2, NCC).

The New Civil Code regulates rules for administration of parental responsibility in harmony with the best interests of the child and his or her welfare (Section 875, NCC) and special rules for the separated parents (Section 908, NCC) and the divorced ones (Section 906 and 907, NCC). The 'agreement and cooperation' of both parents are the key words in the New Civil Code. However, if the parents are not able to come to an agreement on the

---

34 See M Hrušáková *Dítě, rodina, stát* (*The Child, Family and the State*) (Brno: Masarykova univerzita, 1993).

35 Cf K Boele-Woelki, F Ferrand, C González-Beilfuss, M Jänterä-Jareborg, N Lowe, D Martiny and W Pintens *Principles of European Family Law Regarding Parental Responsibilities* (Antwerpen, Oxford: Intersentia, 2007).

personal care (custody) of the child the court takes a decision concerning (a) individual custody by one of the parents, (b) alternative custody, or (c) joint custody by both of them.

Parental responsibility is a dynamic phenomenon. That is why the law allows the court to change a judicial decision or court-approved agreement relating to changes in the child's family and the child's wishes and needs. So the child must get all the relevant information in a manner consistent with his or her age and intellectual maturity. The child must also be given room for expressing an opinion. The views of the child must be taken into consideration regardless of age or intellectual maturity. At the same time the court decision must be in the best interests of the child, which need not always correspond with the wishes of the child. However, the court must always take the child's opinion into consideration. In this context the right of everyone to fair trial should be emphasized. Thanks to the Czech Constitutional Court there is no model for judicial decision-making on child custody, on determining the intervals of visitation rights, or for family life in general.[36] Therefore, each case must be treated individually and in the light of the Convention for the Protection of Human Rights and Fundamental Freedoms that guarantees the right to respect to family life of everyone.

Parental responsibility terminates on the child's reaching maturity. Parental responsibility may also terminate by adoption of a minor child by another person (*adoptione natura imitatur*) or by death of a parent or a child. However, parental responsibility of one of the parents does not terminate when the child is placed into the individual custody of the other parent or to some form of substitute care: foster care (Section 958 NCC), institutional care (Section 971 NCC), etc. This issue must be considered in the light of its human rights dimension. The child is an integral part of his or her family of origin. Both parents have the right of exercising their parentage, not only theoretically but also practically. Therefore, the rights of parents to an essentially direct contact with the child must not be downplayed, fogged or circumvented.

Finally, we should mention the possibilities of intervention by the court in the administration of parental responsibility. There are three options:

---

[36] See the decision of the Czech Constitutional Court of 20 January, No II US 363/03: 'From the constitutional point of view it is not possible to give precedence to models of arrangement between separated parents and minor children used by public authorities over the interests of the child which are defined in Article 3 of the Convention on the Rights of the Child. However, these models, no matter how useful and usable they may be in many cases, cannot cover the situation of every minor. It is therefore up to the courts to take into account all the specific circumstances of the case and the consequent interests of the child that must always be primary in consideration of all the activities concerning children, whether undertaken by public or private social welfare institutions, courts or administrative authorities deciding the specific form of the most suitable arrangement of the relationship between parents and children. The fact that the parents are unable to make an agreement cannot change this rule.'

(a) suspension: if there is a serious obstacle for a parent to exercise parental responsibility and it is possible to assume that it is necessary for the interests of the child, the court may decide that the exercising of the parental responsibility is suspended for such a parent (Section 869, Sub-Section 1, NCC);
(b) limitation: if the parent does not exercise parental responsibility properly and if it is required by the interest of the child, the court will limit that parent's parental responsibility or the exercise of it while determining the extent of such a limitation (Section 870, NCC);
(c) deprivation: if a parent abuses parental responsibility or its exercise or neglects parental responsibility or its exercise in a serious way, the court will deprive that parent of parental responsibility (Section 781, Sub-Section 1, NCC). If a parent committed an intentional criminal act towards his or her child or made use of the child who is not criminally liable for committing a criminal act, or if a parent committed a criminal act as an accomplice, an abettor, a helper or an organizer of a criminal act committed by his or her child, the court will consider the circumstances deciding whether there are reasons for depriving such a parent of parental responsibility (Section 871, Sub-Section 2, NCC).

Legal experts appreciate a completely new provision that the previous legal regulations did not know at all, which caused many a problem in practice. The New Civil Code establishes that, before a judicial decision about limiting parental responsibility, the court will always consider whether it is necessary, with regard to the child's interest, to limit the right of the parent to have personal contact with the child. If a parent is deprived of parental responsibility the parent may have contact with the child only if the court decides to preserve this right for the parent in the interest of the child (Section 872, NCC).

(f) Maintenance duty towards children

The maintenance duty of parents towards children has not traditionally been part of parental responsibility. Both parents have a duty to maintain and support their child until he or she is able to make a living (Section 911, NCC), and it is supposed to be to the extent of the same standard of living (Section 915, NCC) including the option of making savings out of the maintenance (Section 917, NCC). Thus the New Civil Code fully respects the principle of solidarity and non-consumption aspect of maintenance as included for the first time into the Czech legal order by the 1998 amendment.[37]

To avoid the situation of a mere 'law in books' the lawmakers complemented the new legal regulation with other effective elements responding to two key problems confronted in the practice. The issue was:

---

37 For more see Z Králíčková 'Legal Protection of Unmarried and Divorced Mothers in the Czech Republic', above n 22.

(a) how to detect the income and property of the parents, especially when they get cash-in-hand pay for unreported work, when they are self-employed, etc.;
(b) how to enforce judgments ordering maintenance.

First, to make detection of income easier the lawmakers introduced a legal presumption of income of the liable parent (or grandparent) in order to 'improve' the minor child's position. The law provides that a parent must prove his or her income in court submitting documents necessary for the evaluation of his or her property situation and must enable the court to find out other facts, too, necessary for deciding the issue, by making the data protected by special acts accessible. If a parent fails to fulfil this duty, his or her average monthly earnings shall be presumed to amount to 25 times the minimum standard of living required for ensuring the maintenance and other fundamental personal needs of such a parent pursuant to a special act[38] (Section 916, NCC).

Regarding the enforcement of judgments, it is stated, as an innovation, that if a debtor fails to maintain and support a minor child an executor shall issue a writ of execution to suspend the debtor's driving licence. The executor will serve the writ on the driver and will deliver it to the registry of drivers. The debtor, ie the driver, is not allowed to drive until he or she pays the overdue maintenance (Section 71a).[39]

In addition, the criminal law traditionally considers failure to pay mandatory maintenance a criminal offence which may be punished in various ways including imprisonment (Section 196); recently, a new remedy has been introduced: preventing a person from driving for a certain period (Section 196a).[40]

V CONCLUSION

As mentioned above, the New Civil Code was adopted after a long period of legislative work and many twists and turns. It may be said to be 'a reasonable compromise' taking into account traditions and new phenomena, models and tendencies. After all, the family is considered to be a relatively conservative area of law which is interlinked with culture, religion, traditions and myths. The new Czech Family Law may then be characterized with the word 'continuity' with the previous legal regulation[41] because many changes of law or its application occurred shortly after 1989 as a consequence of amendments and the case law of the Constitutional Court and the European Court of Human Rights, among others. With the word 'discontinuity' we may characterize

38 See Act No 110/2006 Coll, on Living and Subsistence Level.
39 See Act No 120/2001 Coll, on Enforcement Officials and their Activities.
40 See Act No 40/2009 Coll, Criminal Code.
41 With regard to the current legislation on Czech Family Law, see M Hrušáková and L Westphalov *Family Law in the Czech Republic* (Alphen aan den Rijn: Kluwer Law International, 2011).

changes in civil law introduced into the New Civil Code, in particular, and also changes being brought about by the so-called accompanying legislation.[42]

42 See Act No 292/2013 Coll, on Special Civil Proceedings, and Act No 202/2012 Coll, on Mediation.

ENGLAND AND WALES

THE BATTLE FOR PARENTHOOD – LESBIAN MOTHERS AND BIOLOGICAL FATHERS

*Mary Welstead**

Résumé

De nombreux couples de lesbiennes vivent des conflits avec le père biologique de leurs enfants. Ces femmes aspirent à devenir des mères et choisissent généralement le don de sperme comme mode de procréation. Certains couples favorisent le don anonyme afin de pouvoir élever leur enfant au sein d'une famille sans homme. D'autres femmes privilégient ce qu'elles considèrent comme la voie la plus sécuritaire et font appel à un homme qu'elles connaissent, dans l'idée de créer une famille matricentrique autonome.

Les six cas analysés dans le présent texte démontrent que les pères biologiques qui sont connus des mères lesbiennes, préfèrent pourtant devenir de «véritables pères» plutôt que d'être écartés après la procréation. Chacun de ces cas révèle une absence totale de concordance dans l'intention des acteurs et dans leur perception du projet procréatif, ce qui engendre une situation chaotique pour les adultes comme pour les enfants.

Dans la gestion de ces conflits, les tribunaux ont tenté d'appliquer de nouvelles approches à ces familles lesbiennes qu'ils considèrent comme un monde familial complexe. Ce faisant, ils sont aux prises avec de nombreuses questions: l'impact des ententes sur les rôles parentaux conclues avant la conception ou la naissance, la pertinence du modèle familial hétérosexuel, le rôle du vocabulaire quand il s'agit de cerner la nature des formes nouvelles de relations familiales, la difficulté à définir le meilleur intérêt de l'enfant dans les situations où des adultes sont forcés de rester en relation, les différences entre les multiples ordonnances possibles dans le cadre de la Children Act 1989 et, finalement, les effets de la Human Fertilisation and Embryology Act 2008 (HFEA 2008).

La jurisprudence démontre que les tribunaux ont une attitude empathique à l'égard des demandes des femmes, au détriment de la volonté des pères biologiques qui voudraient maintenir des liens significatifs avec leurs enfants et au détriment du droit de ces derniers de bénéficier d'un modèle parental masculin. Cette tendance

* Mary Welstead CAP Fellow, Harvard Law School, Visiting Professor of Family Law, University of Buckingham.

s'explique peut-être par l'idée douteuse reflétée dans la HFEA 2008 selon laquelle les formes alternatives de familles sans pères répondent adéquatement aux besoins des enfants.

I INTRODUCTION

In *ML & AR v RW & SW*,[1] Hedley J recounted the distressing story of P, the 10-year-old daughter of a lesbian mother and a gay biological father, who had been conceived by artificial insemination. P's biological parents lived with their partners who regarded themselves as her psychological parents.[2] This young girl was traumatised as a consequence of the long-term conflict between her mothers and her fathers about her future and that of her younger sister, L. The contact facilitator described to the court:

> 'the reality of the way in which their agreement to have P has resulted in such misery for her. The misery is not because of the way in which she was created, it is because these adults and their failure to manage their own conflicting feelings, reactions and personal baggage have handed over the responsibility for coping with the mess to P. I have no doubt that this responsibility will also be handed on to L if there is not a resolution soon.'

Many lesbian couples and the biological fathers of their children have found themselves in an emotional tangle. The women long to become parents,[3] and until same-sex reproduction becomes a possibility, not an entirely speculative idea,[4] sperm donation is the most common method by which they acquire a family. Some couples prefer to use an anonymous sperm donor, which will leave them free to bring up their children without the involvement of biological fathers. Other couples take a different route and ask a man known to them, often a friend or relative, to become the biological father of their children, either by way of artificial insemination or by sexual intercourse. They feel that it is safer to conceive a child with a man whose social and medical background and personality are known to them. In some cases, the women want their children to have a male role model. However, as the six cases discussed in this chapter reveal, these women also want to create autonomous, nuclear, matricentric families with minimal, or no, involvement of the biological fathers.

---

1 [2011] EWHC 2455 (Fam).

2 See J Goldstein, A Freud and A Solnit *Beyond the Best Interests of the Child* (New York: The Free Press, 1973).

3 Lesbian parenthood by means of artificial insemination appears to have increased over the last 20 years, although it is difficult to estimate with any precision the extent of the increase. The 2011 census revealed that 8,000 same-sex families in the United Kingdom had dependent children living with them but it is silent about the means of procreation of these children. Some may have been adopted, a small number may have been born by way of surrogacy, and some will be the children of one of the partners from a prior heterosexual relationship. See also, K Almack 'Seeking Sperm: Accounts of Lesbian Couples' Reproductive Decision-Making and Understandings of the Needs of the Child' (2006) 20 Int J Law Policy and Family 1 (NB this article was written before the HFEA 2008 came into force).

4 Same-sex reproduction may not be such a long way away, see eg www.newscientist.com/article/mg19726413.000-editorial-getting-ready-for-samesex-reproduction.html.

Conflict inevitably ensues when the latter wish to become 'real fathers' to their children and not be regarded as sperm donors to be discarded once conception has been achieved.[5]

Black J (now LJ), in *Re D (contact and parental responsibility: lesbian mothers and known father)* (2006),[6] commented that the arrangements made between lesbian couples and men who are known to them 'presented more practical and emotional challenges than any of the adults had anticipated'.[7]

The judge's comment is a leitmotiv which runs throughout the case-law on disputes between biological fathers (and their partners) and their children's lesbian mothers (and their partners). These familial stories reveal a serious, if not a total, lack of concordance between the intentions of the participants in their procreative projects. Retrospective memories of their expectations and hopes, prior to or at the time of conception, become entangled with the emotions they experience once the longed for child becomes a reality.

In determining these disputes, the courts have grappled with:

- the role of agreements relating to the future parenting of a child;
- the relevance of the heterosexual family model to same-sex families;
- the absence of a vocabulary which adequately reflects the nature of the relationships in these families;
- the elusive nature, and possibly misplaced use, of the best interests of the child test when adult relationship stress is pleaded;
- the nature of the various orders relating to parenting under the Children Act 1989;
- the consequences for biological fathers of the Human Fertilisation and Embryology Act 2008 (HFEA 2008);
- the right to private and family life under Art 8 of the European Convention on Human Rights and Fundamental Freedoms 1950 (ECHR).

---

5 Although a biological father is the legal parent of his child he has no automatic rights to a parental relationship unless he is married to the mother of his child, or if not married to her, has been named on his child's birth certificate or signed an agreement with her. He may have no choice but to apply for a court order for parental responsibility, a residence order or a contact order in order to have a parental relationship with his child (Children Act 1989, ss 2, 4 and 8).

6 [2006] 1 FCR 556.

7 Ibid, para 3.

II THE SIX CASES

(a) *Re D (Contact and PR: Lesbian mothers and known father) (No 2)*(2006)

(i) The facts

In *Re D*,[8] A and C, a lesbian couple advertised for a man to father a child for them. B responded; he had sexual intercourse with A and a baby girl, D, was born in 2000. During the pregnancy, the three adults were unable to agree on B's future role in his child's life. B wanted to be treated in the same way as a non-resident parent after a heterosexual divorce or separation and share equally in the parenting of his child. The two women wanted him to have a role which would be complementary to theirs. He would be allowed to visit his daughter on a fairly infrequent basis and show a kind and loving interest in her.

After D's birth, emotions became heated. B wanted to see more of his daughter, and threatened to supplant C in her life. He also attempted to introduce himself to A's family and explain his relationship to the child. The two women saw B as a threat to their relationship. He felt that they regarded his role as obsolete once he had fulfilled his procreative function.

(ii) The decision in 2001

In 2001, B applied for parental responsibility and a contact order under the Children Act 1989.[9] Black J acknowledged the importance of B in his daughter's life. As she grew older, she would inevitably ask questions about the identity of her father and it would benefit her to have contact with him if it could be done without disturbance to A and C's relationship. Black J gave B a limited contact order of 2 hours per month.[10] A and C were given a joint residence order which, in effect, gave C parental responsibility for D alongside A. The judge thought that these arrangements would give D security in her primary home with A and C and allow the relationship between the two women to grow and strengthen.

(iii) The decision in 2006

By 2006, A and C had agreed to increase B's contact with his daughter to 7 hours, once a month, plus four additional visits each year at Christmas, Easter, and during the summer holidays. B was not content and applied once again for parental responsibility for his daughter. His application came before Black J. By this time, A and C had moved away from London and, not deterred by the

---

8 [2006] 1 FCR 556.

9 See ss 2, 4 and 8.

10 B had withdrawn his application for parental responsibility once he had realised that it was unlikely to succeed.

difficulties arising from their first efforts at procreation, had embarked on a further pregnancy with another man. A baby girl, E, was born in 2003.[11]

Dr Sturge, a consultant child psychiatrist, was asked to advise the court on, inter alia, the sociological and psychological impact on D, if B were to be given parental responsibility for her. Dr Sturge listed a number of important issues to be considered:

- societal reactions towards a lesbian family;
- given the biological reality that two women cannot procreate, D's origins could not be hidden from her;
- the lack of a vocabulary to describe the roles of those involved in same-sex families;
- the failure of law to deal explicitly with the nature of parenthood in same-sex families;[12]
- the psychological ability of a child to understand the complexity of her familial relationships (D had one biological mother, one biological father; a half-sister, a psychological mother and two psychological fathers – the fathers of her half-sister, E, who also wished to have contact with D);
- whether contact between a child and a biological father might undermine the lesbian family unit;
- the relative effects of any court order on B, his daughter, and the relationship between the two mothers.

Black J considered the rather opaque definition of parental responsibility in the Children Act 1989, which includes: 'all the rights, duties, powers, responsibilities and authority which by law a parent of a child has in relation to the child and his property'.[13] And she commented:[14]

> 'This is a wide definition and there is no doubt that parental responsibility can be an inaccessible concept at the best of times, not infrequently difficult for lawyers to grasp and often very challenging for those who are not lawyers.'

In deciding whether to give B parental responsibility, Black J accepted that the court must consider the best interests of the child.[15] Previous decisions, all essentially fact-based, had taken into account, inter alia, the father's degree of commitment and attachment to his child. None of them had involved a father's application in the context of a lesbian family. Society's attitudes to such a situation were still in the course of development, but changing rapidly:

---

11 Prior to E's conception, the women had entered into a written agreement with X, a gay man known to them who lived with Y, his gay partner. In spite of that agreement, legal proceedings relating to contact and parental responsibility were pending.

12 The Human Fertilisation and Embryology Act 2008, ss 42–55, has attempted to address this.

13 Section 3.

14 [2006] 1 FCR 556, para 19; see also the words of Butler-Sloss LJ in *Re RH (a minor)(parental responsibility)* [1998] 2 FCR 89.

15 The Children Act 1989, s 1.

> 'which is probably quicker than the pace of change in the views of society in general, where new ways of living have not yet wholly crystallised, and where language has not yet evolved to accommodate them.'

Black J was concerned at A and C's use of the term sperm donor to describe B. She found the expression unhelpful and totally inappropriate in the circumstances. It depersonalised and minimised B's relationship with his daughter. The judge suspected that:[16]

> 'Ms A and Ms C's use of such a term is a feature of their anxiety about establishing the status of their family without the complication of a third parent and in order to attempt to distinguish their situation from that of the divorced or separated heterosexual family.'

Black J acknowledged that B's commitment to his daughter and her contact with his family would benefit her. She would have the opportunity to view the world from another perspective. The court agreed to grant B parental responsibility on the basis that B had offered to limit its exercise with respect to D's education and medical treatment. Black J accepted that this would give him a parental status with little practical effect and that:[17]

> 'In this refined form, the concept of parental responsibility becomes even more difficult to grapple with. What is plain, however, and entirely understandable, is that its importance is in no way diminished because the order concerns itself with something that is both intangible and difficult to define precisely.'

Most importantly Black J stressed the reality:[18]

> 'that Mr B is D's father. Whatever new designs human beings have for the structure of their families, that aspect of nature cannot be overcome. It is to be hoped that as society accepts alternative arrangements more readily, as it seems likely will happen over the next few years, the impulse to hide or to marginalise a child's father so as not to call attention to an anomalous family will decline, although accommodating the emotional consequences of untraditional fatherhood and motherhood and of the sort of de facto, non-biological parenthood that is experienced by a step-parent or same sex partner will inevitably remain discomfiting.'

(iv) Comment

Black J, in the first of the six decisions, steered a middle road. Although sympathetic to the lesbian mothers' concerns, she balanced the rights of the father and daughter to have a relationship with each other against the purported risks to the mothers' relationship with each other. The former trumped the latter.

---

16 [2006] 1 FCR 556, para 53.
17 Ibid, para 21.
18 Ibid, para 89.

The judge drew attention to the nature of the nebulous concept of parental responsibility. In spite of its intangible nature, it is often considered to be the gold standard in the realm of parental orders in that it gives public recognition to the parental status of a successful applicant. The mothers were opposed to the grant of such an order for precisely this reason. Black J accepted that the grant of parental responsibility, with significant limitations, would be of little practical benefit to the father but it recognised an important and undeniable reality that lesbians cannot have children without men.

Black J suggested that societal attitudes were likely to change in the future and it would become less necessary for lesbian mothers to want to keep the identity of their children's fathers hidden. The remaining cases in this chapter imply that lesbian objections to the involvement of biological fathers in the lives of their children are not merely related to societal prejudice but more to a desire to have an autonomous paternal-free nuclear family. If this is correct, a change in societal attitudes will be unlikely to reduce the battles between biological fathers and lesbian mothers.

(b) *Re B (Role of Biological Father (sub nom TJ v CV, S and BA))* (2008)

(i) The facts

In *Re B*,[19] a lesbian couple, CV and S, who were civil partners, asked S's brother, TJ, to father a child with CV. Whether by sexual intercourse or artificial insemination, conception took place and, in 2005, CV gave birth to a boy, BA, who was, of course, TJ's nephew as well as his son. During the pregnancy, the relationship between TJ and the women broke down and by the time BA was born, TJ was completely estranged from them.

Following BA's birth, TJ had minimal, and always supervised, contact with his son. In retrospect, CV and S felt that asking TJ to become a biological father for their child was a dreadful mistake. They maintained that, prior to conception, nothing other than a rather distant avuncular role had been agreed for TJ. The latter claimed that there was a mutual understanding that he would have a real, albeit limited, parental role and insisted that he be allowed regular contact with BA. He viewed the potential relationship with his son as a chance, perhaps his only one, to be a father and was enthusiastic about such a role. He made an application for parental responsibility and a contact order.

(ii) The decision

Hedley J recognised that attitudes towards lesbian motherhood had changed.[20] He was, however, concerned that:[21]

---

19 [2008] 1 FLR 1015.

20 See *Re G (Residence Same-Sex Partner)* [2005] EWCA Civ 462.

21 [2008] 1 FLR 1015, para 5.

> 'The speed with which the law responds to social change is not uniform. Sometimes change is well advanced and accepted in society before there is legal recognition of it. At other times, Parliament or the courts react to the prompt of a minority and are in the vanguard of change. Sometimes legislation is actually passed to provoke change ... It cannot be assumed, therefore, that the majority of the population necessarily supports the provision of the Civil Partnership Act or the provisions of the Adoption and Children Act which will permit adoption by a same sex couple.'

As a consequence, Hedley J thought that judges could no longer necessarily reflect and apply broadly agreed societal norms in these complex family situations. They had the difficult task of devising and applying principles which should govern these new developments, in his view, a rather unfamiliar role for the judiciary.

He stressed the principle of the paramountcy of the welfare of the child as the basis for decisions relating to orders for contact and residence but acknowledged that the identification of welfare in this context was often unclear and very dependent on individual circumstances. In the case of BA, the factors to be taken into account included information about TJ and his role in his conception, and his need for a male role model. Hedley J thought BA's needs were being well taken care of by CV and S to whom he was securely attached. The limited contact he had had with his father had not disturbed that attachment.

Given this emphasis on BA's welfare, it is perhaps, surprising that Hedley J attempted to deconstruct the agreement between the three adults prior to the child's conception. He found that there had never been a meeting of minds between them:[22]

> 'The urgent, even desperate, desire of CV and S to conceive and have a child coupled with the possible fulfilment of TJ's dream of becoming a father, completely overbore the need for rational discussion and agreement over how things were to be managed in the future. In their quest for action each heard exactly what they wanted to hear and excluded everything that did not fit with their aspirations. It was a recipe for disaster and so it has transpired.'

One of the common problems which Hedley J specifically identified where artificial or unconventional means of creating a family were employed:[23]

> 'is that depths of emotions are engaged and feelings released that come as a surprise and a shock not only to others but in particular to the participants themselves. Just as we rightly ask as a society whether our capacity to manage the consequences of our technological skills ethically keeps pace with the advance of those skills, so we may have to recognise that our understanding of the psychological consequences of our technological skills is very incomplete.'

---

22 Ibid, para 18.
23 Ibid, para 15.

A further issue which was brought to Hedley J's attention was the actual way in which BA had been conceived. S had assumed that conception would be by artificial insemination and had maintained that she did not want to be present when this took place. CV insisted that artificial insemination was indeed what had taken place. However, TJ declared that normal sexual intercourse had taken place on a number of occasions over a short space of time. He also claimed that it had been a mutually enjoyable and emotional experience. Hedley J accepted that, from the child's point of view, the manner of conception was hardly relevant and declined to rule on what had taken place. However, he thought that it was easy enough to understand how and why it had become a major issue for the adults and had perhaps influenced the animosity and mistrust which had arisen.

Hedley J thought that there was a lack of a satisfactory nomenclature for the men who fathered children for lesbians:[24]

> 'Either the proposed word has contentious overtones (eg anything using "father") or it misleads somewhat (eg reference to "uncle") or it is simply unwieldy and unusable by a child (eg "male progenitor"). This problem has not been solved. Some have disposed of it by ignoring a male contribution altogether, some have focussed simply on the biological role of the male whilst others have insisted on a true (if limited) species of fatherhood.'

What was essential, he said, was to put aside the adults' fears and hopes, and to try to look at the situation through the eyes of BA. He would grow up in CV and S's home and his family life with them would seem normal until he went to school. There, he would be likely to face questions about his father. CV and S proposed to tell him that there was a kind man who helped his mother to create him. He would get to know his extended family and accept that TJ was one of his uncles. However, BA would inevitably discover the truth and it should not be hidden from him. For these reasons, Hedley J thought that it was in BA's interests to maintain some kind of relationship with TJ, whom he concluded was genuine in motivation even if clumsily heavy-handed in style.

In determining the issue of parental responsibility, Hedley J accepted that a parent's commitment, attachment and motivation were important factors but that the child's best interests came before them.[25] TJ had shown commitment and his motivation was not questionable. However, the judge held that parental responsibility was incompatible with the agreement at the time of conception that there would be a nuclear family, consisting of CV, S and a child fathered by TJ, which the latter would not undermine. CV and S felt that if TJ were to be given parental responsibility, he would, undoubtedly, seek to exercise it which would be a direct threat to that family.

---

24 Ibid, para 23.

25 However, as was pointed out in *Re H (Parental Responsibility)* [1998] 1 FLR 855, these applications remain subject to the overriding provisions of the Children Act 1989, s 1(1).

Hedley J did, however, give TJ a limited contact order. In doing so, he attempted to differentiate, in a rather incomprehensible manner, between TJ's dual roles of uncle and father. As an uncle TJ did not need a contact order; he and S had accepted that this relationship would have to be worked out in the ordinary course of the life of the extended family life which they shared. The limited contact order would allow irregular meetings between TJ and his son and keep open the door between them. It was not to give TJ any parental status or to permit the development of any sort of parental relationship which would threaten CV and S and their autonomy as a nuclear family but rather:[26]

> 'so that without artificiality he can picture TJ as someone significant but not ordinarily important in his life yet someone with whom (in time and if he so wishes) he can explore the implications of the kind man who enabled him to be and he can ask questions to satisfy his own natural curiosity.'

The contact order stated that TJ was to have contact with BA four times a year; one of the occasions could be at family gatherings, whilst the other three occasions would be for BA and TJ to meet alone on neutral territory for 2 hours during each school holiday. The contact at the family gathering, which might take place at Christmas or on a birthday, could be accompanied by a card and a modest present. A generous present might convey the wrong message. BA would have to know TJ merely by his first name until he became ready to ask questions about his origins, These arrangements, thought Hedley J, would allow the child to be able to 'accept and enjoy his conventional [sic] nuclear family as such on the one hand whilst being able to sate his natural curiosity on the other'.[27]

Finally, Hedley J accepted that the family needed a long break from any further litigation and made an order that no application could be made for any order, or variation of an order without the leave of the court.[28]

(iii) Comment

Hedley J's decision centred to a great extent on his view of the mismatch between societal attitudes to new forms of family life and the legal response to them. He implies throughout the judgment that the law has moved ahead of societal acceptance of lesbian families.

Given the subjective nature of the parents' pre-conceptual intentions, it is somewhat surprising that Hedley J viewed them as important. He acknowledged the way in which parental emotions change following the birth of a child but declined to take that into account.

The contact order, in the circumstances of the dual relationship between BA and his biological father and the existence of an extended family, who knew the

---

26 [2008] 1 FLR 1015, para 31.
27 Ibid, para 29.
28 See Children Act 1989, s 91(14).

circumstances of his birth, and to which the lesbian mothers, the father and the child all belonged, appears unrealistic and, probably, unsustainable. The order attempted to differentiate between the nature of the court-ordered contact, which would be enjoyed by the father and child, and the contact which would take place as a consequence of their uncle/nephew relationship. In the context of the former contact, he was forbidden to behave in a fatherly manner towards his son and give him presents, which would suggest the existence of an important relationship between them. In the context of the uncle/nephew relationship, the court accepted that it had no control. Emotional relationships do not readily lend themselves to such differentiation.

(c) *T v T (shared residence)* (2011)

(i) The facts

In *T v T*,[29] F, a gay man who was in a civil partnership, placed an advertisement in which he offered to become a father. M and L, a lesbian couple, who were also civil partners, responded. M was artificially inseminated with F's sperm and subsequently gave birth to two children. At the time of the Appeal Court hearing, G, the boy, was aged 10, and N, the girl, was aged 7. Both children lived primarily with M and L, but F played a significant part in their lives and had parental responsibility for them. The relationship between the two women and F and his partner deteriorated and M applied for an order to restrict F's parental responsibility and L applied for a joint residence order with M.

(ii) The County Court judgment

The recorder refused M and L's applications; instead, he gave L, who clearly played an important role in the children's lives, parental responsibility for G and N.[30] He also gave M and F a shared residence order which included a detailed schedule of the time the children were to spend with each of them. The time the children were ordered to spend with F and his partner, albeit significant, was not equal to that they were to spend with M and L.

(iii) The decision in the Appeal Court

The two women appealed and asked the Court of Appeal to set aside the shared residence order in favour of M and F and to substitute one in their favour. This they believed would reflect the reality of the children's lives. They were the children's primary carers and regarded themselves and the children as a close knit and autonomous nuclear family. In their view, the recorder's order marginalised L's role as a psychological mother to the two children. The women also maintained that the increase in contact set out in the schedule was too much. It failed to take into account the views of N, the younger child, who was worried about staying away from her primary home overnight. Furthermore, in

---

29 [2011] 1 FCR 267.

30 Children Act 1989, s 4ZA.

the light of the acrimonious relationship between the adults, the detailed arrangements were too complicated to manage.

For M and L, parental labels were important. They felt that the lack of a joint residence order in their favour would ultimately affect the children once they could understand what it meant. They were also worried that, although L had been given parental responsibility, it would not assist her should M die prematurely because F, armed with parental responsibility and a residence order, would be able to take the children to live with him.

Black LJ gave the main judgment and reiterated the view that these parental dispute cases are fact dependent and 'are shaped by the personalities, strengths and weaknesses of the individual human beings involved'.[31] In her attempt, yet again, to explain parental responsibility, Black LJ stated that the concept is a difficult one to grasp:[32]

> 'One might, perhaps, be forgiven for thinking that someone who has been granted parental responsibility has truly been recognised as a parent of the child. In this case, three people have parental responsibility, M, F and L, and have thereby been recognised as parents; it seems to me that that probably accords with how things look at the moment from the children's point of view.'

Parental responsibility differs from a residence order which determines with whom a child should live and can also be made in favour of more than one person.[33] If the people specified in the residence order do not live together, the order may define the amount of time the child is to spend with each one.[34] Shared residence orders, according to Black LJ, were not unusual and could be appropriate if they were in a child's best interests.[35]

Black LJ believed that Mostyn J's view, in *Re AR (a child: relocation)*,[36] that shared residence orders were now the rule rather than the exception went too far. She also accepted that it was not a prerequisite for such orders that the period of time spent with each adult should be equal or that it was necessary that there should be cooperation and goodwill between the adults. However, if there were a risk that the order might provide a battlefield for the parents to continue their personal war, obviously, it would not be in the children's best interests to make it.

---

31 *T v T (shared residence)* [2011] 1 FCR 267, para 22.
32 Ibid, para 23.
33 Children Act 1989, s 8(1).
34 Children Act 1989, s 11(4).
35 The former President of the Family Division, Sir Mark Potter, in *Re A (a child) (joint residence: parental responsibility)* [2008] 2 FLR 1593 explained: 'The making of a shared residence order is no longer the unusual order which once it was ... It is now recognised by the court that a shared residence order may be regarded as appropriate where it provides legal confirmation of the factual reality of a child's life or where, in a case where one party has the primary care of a child, it may be psychologically beneficial to the parents in emphasising the equality of their position and responsibilities ...'
36 [2010] 3 FCR 131.

In Black LJ's view, the recorder had taken into account the children's best interests in giving a shared residence order to M and F and not to L. He had taken into account the fact that the children genuinely regarded F as their parent and wanted to spend time with him. The children's interests did not require L to have a residence order; they already knew that she was part of their primary family. To give L the label here would have been for her and M's benefit rather than for that of the children. The women's fear that F's shared residence order to F would give him a licence to meddle inappropriately in the children's upbringing, was ill thought out.

Black LJ also rejected M and L's concerns about the increase in contact for F and complexity of the schedule. She thought that the recorder had taken into account all the relevant factors.

Finally, Black LJ considered L's concerns that, if M were to die unexpectedly, F would be able to move the children into his home. F had offered to agree to a tripartite residence order which would include L, an offer which her Ladyship thought it would be foolish to decline. It would, at least, ensure that the status quo could continue until any issues which needed to be resolved could be sorted out in an orderly fashion by the court. Black LJ emphasised that:[37]

> 'it cannot be anticipated that considerations relating to what may happen in the aftermath of an untimely death will regularly tip the balance in favour of a joint residence order in circumstances such as the present ones. In many cases, there will be a profusion of much more pressing factors that dictate another outcome.'

Black LJ's final words to M, L and F stressed the need for cooperation:[38]

> 'In parting with the case, I would invite the attention of all of the parties once again to what the recorder said to them at the end of his judgment. He told them that they must put aside their differences and that if the adults do not manage to resolve things by communicating with each other, the children inevitably suffer and the adults may also pay the price when the children are old enough to be aware of what has been going on. It is a great shame that that sound advice does not appear to have been heeded. It is a tremendous privilege to be involved in bringing up a child.
>
> Childhood is over all too quickly and, whilst I appreciate that both sides think that they are motivated only by concern for the children, it is still very sad to see it being allowed to slip away whilst energy is devoted to adult wrangles and to litigation. What is particularly unfair is that the legacy of a childhood tainted in that way is likely to remain with the children into their own adult lives.'

(iv) Comment

The decision in *T v T* illustrates the difference between parental responsibility and residence orders and the problems if parents do not possess both. The

---

37 *T v T (shared residence)* [2011] FCR 267, para 47.

38 Ibid, para 49.

women were not satisfied with having only parental responsibility for the children whose primary home was with them. They wanted a joint residence order to make the psychological mother feel less marginalised and to ensure that the status quo for the children continued were the biological mother to die.

Black LJ, as usual, showed a sensitive pragmatism in the judgment. She maintained that it would be inappropriate to give them a joint residence order, primarily, to satisfy their need for security. Such an order had to be for the benefit of the child and she would not normally have overruled the recorder and granted the women's appeal on this issue. However, she saw little point in not accepting the biological father's offer to share residence in a tripartite arrangement between him and the mothers which would make everyone happier and perhaps more cooperative in their dealings with the children.

Black LJ also recognised the need to spell out, in detail, contact arrangements when parents were at war with each other.

(d) *ML and AR v RW and SW* (2011)

(i) The facts

In *ML and AR v RW and SW*,[39] in 2001 RW and SW, a lesbian couple who lived in London, placed an advert seeking a biological father in the 'Pink Paper', a weekly gay newspaper. It read:[40]

> 'Somewhere over the rainbow we know that there is a gay man or couple who would like to start [a family] with a lesbian couple who are fun-loving, have a good sense of humour, are very attractive and financially secure. If you want to make our dream come true please contact us.'

ML and AR, a gay couple replied:[41]

> 'Somewhere over the rainbow are A and I. We have been together for many years and we have decided that we would love to be father and step-father. Like yourselves we are fairly secure. I am a fairly senior manager working at the head office of a major retail company based in Central London. My partner works for a restaurant chain as a manager. We currently live in Southampton, as it is only one and a quarter hours from London by train and we love our home. However, we are considering either moving back to London or establishing a second home there.'

Before embarking on conception, the two couples wrote to each other several times. SW stated that she would be the co-parent of any child born to RW and ML, and that she and RW would want HL and AR, whom she also described as father and 'stepfather', to be involved with the child or children. However, by

39 [2011] EWHC 2455.
40 Ibid, para 10.
41 Ibid, para 11.

the time conception took place, all four adults had failed to elaborate on what such involvement actually meant. They were more interested in RW becoming pregnant as soon as possible.

After the birth of the first child, a girl, P, ML and AR had regular contact with her. She stayed overnight with them and the men began to develop a relationship with her. ML was referred to as Daddy and AR as Addy. Father's Day cards and birthday cards were sent. In 2004, the couples were sufficiently happy with the situation that they decided to repeat the process. Artificial insemination took place and another daughter, L, was born to RW and ML. The two men moved house to live nearer to the children, apparently with the approval of RW and SW, and the couples shared a number of holidays.

In 2008, RW and SW became civil partners and the latter acquired parental responsibility for the children by agreement.[42] The relationship between the couples began to deteriorate. Regular arguments took place about contact between the children and ML and AR and the nature of the men's role in the children's lives. The older girl became very entangled in the disputes. She aligned herself with RW and SW and refused to have anything to do with ML and AR. The younger girl continued to see ML and AR but felt unable to talk about the visits to her older sister or to RW and SW.

After 3 years of serious conflict ML and AR applied for a residence order for both children. ML had already acquired parental responsibility at an earlier hearing. The men's application was vehemently opposed by RW and SW and they applied to limit ML's parental responsibility.

(ii) The decision

The applications came before Hedley J who drew attention to the significant emotional harm which the elder child had suffered, and the potential harm to her younger sister, as a consequence of the 3 years of conflict between the adults. He suggested that 'the four adults in this case regard the price paid by these two children as an acceptable price for the pursuit of their own adult disputes'.[43]

Hedley J accepted that, in these alternative family situations, the warring parties often had retrospective memories about their intentions prior to conception which were coloured by heightened emotions. He suggested that one way forward for such couples might be for them to make formal and precise agreements before they embarked on the creation of a family. He found, contrary to the claims of RW and SW that they never intended the men to play a major part in the children's lives, that the two women had acknowledged the men's parental role:[44]

---

42 Children Act 1989, s 4ZA.
43 [2011] EWHC 2455, para 3.
44 Ibid, para 17.

'albeit in a secondary capacity. That parenting role was to fulfil at least three purposes. The first was indeed to give a clear sense of identity to the child or children in due course. The second was to provide the male component of parenting which all must be taken to have acknowledged. Thirdly, there was a more general role of benign involvement which would have, but would certainly not be confined to, an avuncular aspect.'

He described how a visitor might have viewed the family in 2007 prior to the breakdown in the adults' relationship:[45]

'There is no doubt that one would have been aware of the complex structure of the family and the unusual nature of the relationships, of which, in fairness, all four adults were well aware. One could not have missed the fact that the principal parenting role was exercised by the respondents [RW and SW] who provided to these children the two parent family model, but it is equally clear that it would have been impossible to miss the parental, however secondary, role that was being exercised by the applicants [ML and AR]. The children entirely understood the nature of the relationships, even if they could not have articulated them and all the evidence suggests that they were comfortable with those relationships.'

The judge reiterated his belief that a new vocabulary was necessary which could reflect the true nature of the relationships in these new forms of family:[46]

'The best that I have achieved, and I confess to having found it helpful in thinking about this case, is to contemplate the concept of principal and secondary parenting. The reason why this case is not equivalent to a separated parent is that there was a clear agreement that the Respondents would do the principal parenting and that they would provide the two-parent care to these children. The Second Respondent clearly believes that her role in this regard has been brought into question, and it is certainly my view that her role in the concept of principal parenting, as one of the two principal parents, needs to be clearly affirmed and respected.'

Hedley J made an immediate detailed contact order for the younger child, including staying contact. He told the four adults that they were entitled to vary these arrangements by written agreement with each other. The success of this contact would be reviewed in a few months' time. He thought that a residence order would hinder any resolution of the adult's conflict. He encouraged all of them to acknowledge their respective parenting roles and take responsibility for finding a way forward for the children. They should take note of the children's pressing needs rather than their own wishes. He accepted, however, that this was unlikely to happen in the current maelstrom.

Hedley J emphasised that his decision was about trying to accommodate the needs of two children damaged by their experience of parenting and not one about resolving adult disputes.

---

45 Ibid, para 30.
46 Ibid, para 16.

(iii) Comment

Hedley J stressed the need for clear-cut agreements to be made by lesbian mothers and biological fathers, prior to embarking on conception, to avoid the problem of retrospective memories after the child's birth when emotions were high. This view must be questioned; should even the most formal and precise agreements entered into prior to a child's birth ever be of overriding importance in deciding a child's contact with his biological father? Agreements may be of some limited evidential importance in determining a father's commitment to the future parenting of his child. There may also be a case for accepting that a father may decide after the birth of a child that he would prefer not to play a part in his child's life. He could be given the same period of grace as that is given to parents who wish to give their child up for adoption or to surrogate mothers who agree to cede their parental rights to the commissioning parents.

The judge's emphasis on the need for a new vocabulary to describe the nature of the role of biological fathers and his use of the term 'secondary parents' must be questioned. They are parents and children have a right to a relationship with all of their parents, both psychological and biological, providing that it would not be harmful to them. New vocabulary has a tendency to demean and marginalise the role of biological fathers.

(e) *A v B and C (Lesbian co-parents: role of father)* (2012)

(i) The facts

The facts of *A v B and C*[47] were somewhat unusual in that the biological father, A, a gay man, was married to B, a lesbian woman. They were close friends from university days and had married for practical reasons with no intention of ever living together. B had done so in the hope that a marriage to A would disguise her relationship with C, her long-term partner. B's parents were Orthodox Middle Eastern Christians and were unable to accept their daughter's sexual orientation. Marriage to A would have a further advantage for B; she wanted to have a child whose parenting she would share with C. Unless she were married, she could not do so without incurring her parents' disapproval. Both the women believed that their longstanding and trusted friend, A, would be the perfect man to provide a child for them. Marriage to B also provided benefits for A; it would allow him to acquire automatically parental responsibility for any child he fathered with B and, with it, the possibility of playing a part in the child's life.

Prior to conception, the three friends discussed, often in a fraught manner, the parenting of any child who might be born to A and B. They were, however, unable to resolve their differing perceptions and hopes. In spite of this, artificial insemination took place, and in December 2008, B became pregnant. Throughout the pregnancy, A was supportive of both the women but particularly so of C who felt insecure and marginalised by B's family.

---

[47] *A v B and C* [2012] EWCA Civ 285.

In September 2009, when B gave birth to M, a baby boy, A was present at the hospital with his mother who had flown from America to see her new grandson. On the birth certificate, A was registered as M's father. The baby went to live with B and C in their home, cared for by a nanny. His two mothers continued in their high-powered careers. When the baby was christened, A attended along with B's family; the latter's presence meant that C had to be excluded. Regular visits were made by A to see his son but he was never allowed to take him home even though he lived close by.

Not surprisingly, the relationship between the three friends broke down. The mothers were very stressed, partly because of work and partly because C continued to feel insecure. She felt that her role in M's life was rather unstable even though she was clearly his psychological mother. She had no legal authority to make any decisions relating to him. She also felt that her insecurity adversely affected her relationship with B, and consequently M also. Although A had parental responsibility for his son, he too was worried because he felt unable to exercise it in the way that he wanted. He wanted M to stay with him on a regular basis so that he could build a real relationship with him.

In 2010, soon after M's first birthday, A applied for a defined contact order for himself. B and C applied for a joint residence order and for an order to limit A's exercise of his parental responsibility for M.

(ii) The decision in the High Court

After two interlocutory hearings, A was given 5 hours of contact with M, once a fortnight, in B and C's home. This was far less than he had wanted. At a final hearing before HHJ Jenkins J, A argued that his position was analogous to that of a divorced father who would normally be allowed staying contact with his children, which would increase in frequency and duration as the children grew older.

Although HHJ Jenkins J stressed the importance of the paramountcy of the child's welfare, and the importance of the checklist in s 1(3) of the Children Act 1989 in determining M's future, he appeared to show more concern about the needs of the two mothers. He acknowledged their stress and their relationship difficulties, which he accepted had been brought about, at least partly, by A's desire to play a greater role in M's life. The women maintained that their dream of an autonomous nuclear family in which M would be securely and lovingly nurtured was under threat. They wanted to have more children, and by an anonymous sperm donor. If A were allowed to play a bigger role in M's life, it would complicate the family dynamics.

HHJ Jenkins J regarded the nature of the discussions between all three friends prior to M's conception as important factors in determining M's future and concluded that:[48]

---

[48] Ibid, para 36.

> 'By agreement with the father, a child was conceived and born and on the basis of a relationship already created where the two mothers were to be the primary carers. The evidence is that they had prepared over a long period for parenthood on that basis, and the evidence is that they have established a regime of security and stability. It is plain that all three parties failed to get to grips with the nature of the relationship. The father never managed to establish an agreement to his satisfaction and he failed in the end to appreciate the way in which the mothers had thought through the stability of the relationship in the way that I have described.'

To accede to A's wishes and increase his contact with M significantly would, in effect, give M three parents and two homes. This, HHJ Jenkins J declined to do; it would be inappropriate because it had never been contemplated by B and C and any benefit which M might gain from such an order would be outweighed by:[49]

> 'confusion and disruption and the potential disruption of the relationship between the mothers and the child, and it is that relationship which provides the nurture, stability and security for M. That position is made more obvious by the particular anxieties which I have highlighted in this case, in particular the background of B and her family.'

HHJ Jenkins J granted B and C's request for a joint residence order and limited A's contact to a 5, or 6-hour visit once a fortnight in B and C's home but did not restrict A's parental responsibility as requested by the women. In reality, however, the court's orders did precisely that. According to the judge, M had a right to know that A was his father and should be allowed to develop a limited relationship with him. Whilst the judge did not specifically prohibit A from making a future application to vary the contact arrangements, he stated clearly that he did not see any likely basis for any variation in the near future. This led A to appeal on the grounds that the judgment was both unfounded and unprincipled.

(iii) The decision in the Court of Appeal

In the Court of Appeal, the women maintained that the judge's order did not exclude the possibility of a future variation of the contact arrangements. They also argued that the principles relating to contact with children after a heterosexual divorce or separation should not be applied to lesbian families where the biological father had never shared a family life with his child. To do so would risk the viability of the women's relationship and adversely affect the child. If agreements between lesbian couples and biological fathers, who were known to them, were ignored by the courts, the women would be forced to abandon using such men as a means of safe procreation. These agreements should be respected and rank alongside a child's welfare in the determination of parental contact disputes.

---

49 Ibid, para 37.

Thorpe LJ gave the main judgment and accepted that HHJ Jenkins J's final comments did impose, in effect, a bar on any application by A for variation of the contact order without the court's permission for some 3 to 4 years. His Lordship held that the judge had made a fundamental error in relying on Dr Sturge's paper on lesbian relationships, published in 2008.[50] Dr Sturge had described the stress and insecurity experienced by lesbians, particularly, non-birth mothers, vis-à-vis biological fathers. Such stress had a damaging effect on the women's relationship with each other and their children. Thorpe LJ maintained that a report specifically commissioned to consider the situation of A, B, C and M would have been more appropriate. The only principle relevant in the determination of contact between a child and a parent was that of the paramountcy of the child's welfare. HHJ Jenkins J had not followed this approach.

Thorpe LJ, highlighted A's involvement in the whole process of M's gestation and his commitment to him from birth. He suggested that A:[51]

> 'may be seeking to offer a relationship of considerable value. It is generally accepted that a child gains by having two parents. It does not follow from that that the addition of a third is necessarily disadvantageous.'

Thorpe LJ also thought that M should have been joined as a party to the proceedings. An experienced team could then have properly evaluated his welfare and ensured that the concerns of all three parents did not assume a greater importance. More particularly, Thorpe LJ was concerned about pre-conception or pre-birth agreements. He stressed the fact that:[52]

> 'Human emotions are powerful and inconstant. What the adults look forward to before undertaking the hazards of conception, birth and the first experience of parenting may prove to be illusion or fantasy. B and C may have had the desire to create a two-parent lesbian nuclear family completely intact and free from fracture resulting from contact with the third parent. But such desires may be essentially selfish and may later insufficiently weigh the welfare and developing rights of the child that they have created. No doubt they saw the advantages of A as first an ideal known father and later as a husband to ease problems in the maternal extended family. It would have been naïve not to foresee that the long-term consequences held disadvantages that had to be balanced against the immediate advantages.'

Thorpe LJ rejected Hedley J's views, in *ML and AR v RW and SW*,[53] on the importance of both the role of agreements and the use of the concept of principal and secondary parenting. He thought that to refer to a biological father, who was known to a lesbian mother, as a secondary parent might

---

50 C Sturge 'Current Issues in Relation to Gay and Non-Biological Parenting', a paper presented at the 2007 Dartington Conferences and published in *Integrating Diversity* (Jordan Publishing Ltd, 2008).

51 *A v B and C* [2012] EWCA Civ 285, para 24.

52 Ibid, para 27.

53 [2011] EWHC 2455.

demean his position and reduce him to the role of a mere sperm donor who left the stage once he had made his contribution. In some situations the biological father might have an important role to play in his child's life. It would be most unfair to A to categorise him as a mere secondary parent to M; he was not. Thorpe LJ preferred to employ the concept of primary and secondary carers and proceeded to rank the three parents in accordance with that concept. He accepted that the two mothers, B and C, were at present the primary carers whilst A was waiting in the wings and dependent on the court to determine whether he could actually care for M.

Thorpe LJ concluded that the High Court should have considered whether the relationship between M and A was one which should be encouraged to flourish and develop and leave open the issue of future contact to be decided on the basis of the available evidence at that time There were too many unforeseeable factors to have ruled out M having staying contact with A at some future date. A's appeal was allowed and the case was remitted to a Family Division judge to consider all the factors relevant to M's welfare. This would not take place for another year and would allow any future decision about contact to be made in the light of the success or failure of the current contact arrangements.

In spite of his emphasis on M's welfare, Thorpe LJ ended his judgment by implying that A's future contact with M might depend on whether the current stress experienced by the two mothers had lessened as a consequence of C having joint parental responsibility with B.

Black LJ added a short concurring judgment to that of Thorpe LJ. In her view, the intentions of A, B and C prior to M's conception were relevant but not determinative of A's parenting role once M was born. She acknowledged the tendency of individuals to change their plans over time when faced with the reality of the situation. Her ladyship accepted that it was right for those who contemplated entering into complex procreative arrangements:[54]

> 'to spell out in as much detail as they can what they contemplate will be the arrangements for the care and upbringing of their child. But no matter how detailed their agreement, no matter what formalities they adopt, this is not a dry legal contract. Biology, human nature and the hand of fate are liable to undermine it and to confound their expectations. Circumstances change and adjustments must be made. And above all, what must dictate is the welfare of the child and not the interests of the adults.'

Black LJ shared the implied view of Thorpe LJ that the emotional state of all the adults involved, or wishing to be involved, in the parenting of the child should be taken into account because of the potential, if indirect, effect to disrupt his or her security and stability. Black LJ thought that C might become less anxious and more secure, which could lead to the two mothers agreeing to more generous contact arrangements for A with M.

---

[54] *A v B and C* [2012] EWCA Civ 285, para 44.

(iv) Comment

Although HHJ Jenkins J stressed the importance of the paramountcy of the child's welfare, and the importance of the checklist in s 1(3) of the Children Act 1989 in determining M's future, he showed more concern for the needs of the two mothers. He also regarded pre-conception agreements as important factors in determining a child's future.

By contrast, in the Court of Appeal, Thorpe LJ took a firm stance and stated that the welfare of the child was more important than any other factors including agreements. He viewed A's commitment to M throughout B's pregnancy as important evidence of his ability to offer a relationship to his child which could be of considerable value. His Lordship saw the potential advantage of a child having three parents – a very realistic approach in circumstances where multiple parents are a reality.

It remains to be seen whether Thorpe LJ's attempt to use the concepts of parenting and caring to describe the role of fathers and mothers in their children's lives is so very different from Hedley J's terminology of primary and secondary parents.

Black LJ differed from Thorpe LJ in suggesting that agreements might be of relevance, albeit not determinative, in deciding a child's future relationship with his father. One must question the point of making detailed arrangements when Black LJ, herself, accepted that the views and emotions of the participants in procreation of a child may change once the child becomes a reality.

Black LJ, and Thorpe LJ (implicitly), thought that the effect of the father's involvement in his child's life on the mothers' relationship with each other should be taken into account because of the potential damage to the child. There is a danger that such an approach may lead to emotional blackmail by the mothers. To a certain extent, any involvement of a biological father will frustrate the desire of those lesbian mothers who wish to have a male-free family and lead to stress in their relationship. It is not the fault of the father or of the child; the sacrifice of their relationship with each other should not be the price they pay to ameliorate the mothers' stress.

(f) *Re G (a child) (sperm donor: contact order); Re Z (a child) (sperm donor: contact order)* (2013)

(i) The Human Fertilisation and Embryology Act 2008

In the two linked cases of *Re G and Re Z*,[55] the court had to consider, for the first time, the effects of the Human Fertilisation and Embryology Act 2008 (HFEA 2008) on biological fathers. The Act, which came into force on 6 April 2009, provides that, if certain conditions are met, the same-sex partner of a child's birth mother is entitled to become the child's legal parent. The new law

[55] [2013] EWHC 134 (Fam).

does not apply retrospectively. If a same-sex partner has become the legal parent of the birth mother's child and has acquired parental responsibility, no man may be treated as father of that child and apply for parental responsibility.[56]

(ii) The facts in Re G

D and E were lesbian civil partners who were friendly with S and T, also civil partners. They asked S to father children with E because they wanted their children to know their origins. However, they did not want S or T to have any serious involvement in the children's lives; they wished to be the children's sole parents and live as a nuclear family. They claimed that they had made it very clear to S before conception that there were conditions attached to his sperm donation. These were that:

- he would not have a parental title;
- he would have no parental responsibility;
- he would have no financial obligation towards any biological child;
- he would not be able to play a part in the upbringing of any child but that the two couples would continue to socialise together.

By contrast S thought that, although D and E would be the primary parents, he and T would be involved in the children's upbringing. He trusted the women and did not feel it necessary to record what he believed to be the arrangement in writing.

Two children were born, F, a girl, in 2008 and G, a boy, in 2010. The couples continued to socialise with each other and S saw F and G regularly in D and E's home. In 2011, D and E claimed that they noticed a change in the pattern of the visits which had become more regular. They thought, in retrospect, that this was because S had taken legal advice. S maintained that the visits were because

---

[56] The conditions are: if the couple are registered civil partners at the time of conception, which must be by artificial means and not by sexual intercourse and regardless of where that conception takes place, both the birth mother and her partner will be treated as the child's legal parents. The partner must have consented to the conception and will be presumed to have done so unless it can be shown that she did not. The partner has a right to be named on the birth certificate as a legal parent, and will acquire parental responsibility for the child together with the birth mother. If that happens, the biological father will acquire no parental status but may apply for a residence or contact order for his child with leave of the court. If the couple are not civil partners, the artificial conception must take place in a UK licensed clinic. Before conception, both partners must have signed forms electing to be the legal parents of the child. If the birth parent agrees, and is present at the registration of the birth, her partner may be named on the birth certificate as a legal parent and will acquire parental responsibility for the child together with the birth mother. If the non-birth mother becomes a legal parent, the biological father will acquire no parental status but may apply for a residence or contact order for his child with leave of the court. If she is not named on the birth certificate, she may only acquire parental responsibility by way of a court order. Unless she acquires parental responsibility, the biological father may apply for parental responsibility himself (see HFEA 2008, ss 42–55).

he had established a bond with G. The women maintained that these visits had been stressful. At one point, S's partner, T, had referred to the women as cheating lesbians who steal sperm. E accepted that, in response, she had described T as 'a manipulative little shit'.

The provisions of the HFEA 2008 prevented S from applying for parental responsibility for G because D had already obtained it. He, therefore, decided to apply for leave of the court to make an application for residence and contact orders.[57] His application was delayed because he was diagnosed with a brain tumour and admitted to hospital where D, E and the children visited him. After brain surgery and radiotherapy, there was no further contact between S and his children and he decided to pursue his application for leave to apply for residence and contact orders for G (separate proceedings were already in place with respect to F). He maintained that:[58]

> 'T and I are effectively being lost to the children, which will seriously weaken their lives and damage their well-being. I believe that a rich and rewarding relationship with their father and his partner, their extended families and their friends, will add to their security and their life experience. It will also be perfectly compatible with their family home life with D and E. That was the original arrangement we had and was what we provided until July 2011.'

He added:

> 'I will accept that the reality of becoming a parent to two new human beings was more wonderful than I had expected, and that I felt a stronger tie to both F and G than perhaps I imagined I would. I do not accept, however, that my expectations of the contact I would have with the children have changed ... I do not dispute that D and E are perfectly adequate parents; they are much more than that. However, I believe strongly that the children would benefit from the presence in their lives of me as a father, and would be deprived if they were not allowed it.'

S could not understand why if D and E:[59]

> 'had wanted a mere sperm donor who would have no involvement with the children ... why they would choose a close friend who was already living around the corner from them whom they saw on a very frequent basis.'

E responded that she believed that:[60]

> 'a donation [of sperm] is a gift freely given with no expectation of a return. Having a donor does not obligate a relationship between the donor and the resulting child. It does, however, allow the possibility of one if the child so desires. We will promise to facilitate contact with our children and S. This contact, however, will be when the children wish it and will be child led. That is what we always

---

57 Children Act 1989, ss 8 and 10.
58 [2013] EWHC 134 (Fam), para 22.
59 Ibid.
60 Ibid, para 23.

> promised ... We would propose that there is no contact until such time as G and F seek knowledge of their genetic background.'

She also denied that S had had a relationship with the children but had only seen them when socialising with her and D and had never wanted to engage with the children. She was prepared for a relationship to develop if it were to be led by the children and not the adults.

(iii) The facts in Re Z

In *Re Z* (2013), T and S were civil partners (the fathers of G above) who were introduced to X and Y, who were also civil partners, by D and E (the mothers of G above). According to T, it was agreed that his sperm would be used to impregnate X and that she and Y would be the parents of any child conceived but that he would play a fatherly role in his child's life. He maintained that he was unaware that he would not be the legal parent of the child because of the effect of the 2008 Act. X and Y insisted that they had made clear to T that he would have no parental or financial involvement with the child and that T had shown no interest in playing a future paternal role.

Z, a boy, was born in 2010 and T had regular contact with him, always in the presence of X or Y. These visits, according to X, were far in excess of what she and Y wanted but they felt that they had to show gratitude to T for giving them a child and that they wanted to keep the relationship positive for Z's sake. The women also agreed to T's proposal to set up a bank account for Z. One year after Z's birth, T's relationship with X and Y deteriorated and the two women attempted to reduce his contact with Z. At this point, T made an application for leave to apply for a contact order but withdrew it when S became ill. Six months later, T resumed his application and argued that:[61]

> 'I am Z's birth father. I donated sperm to X to enable her to conceive ... Z is a mixed race child and has a strong physical resemblance to me. I regard it as fundamentally important that Z grows up with a knowledge of his Sri Lankan heritage. This is something that I am best placed to help him with. I believe it is in Z's best interests to know me and have regular contact with a caring father, and to have me as a successful role model in his life. My child deserves to be given every opportunity in life and that includes having his father in his life ... I have no wish nor is it my intention to interrupt or disturb the family life enjoyed by Z with X and Y ... However, I do want to prevent my role in Z's life being relegated to that of an occasional visitor ...'

X maintained that she and Y had made clear to T what their expectations and boundaries were. She regretted not signing an agreement with him and claimed that he had refused to do so. She added that the stress was ruining her relationship with Y and that:[62]

---

[61] Ibid, para 35.
[62] Ibid, para 38.

> 'The brutal reality is that we have only enjoyed a few weeks of settled family life together in total since Z was born. I have lived in fear of Z suffering emotional manipulation, growing up in conflict, being confused about the differing roles of adults in his life and his happy life being disrupted.'

X and Y argued that the change in the law recognised them as Z's sole legal parents and specifically excluded T from being treated as Z's father for any purpose.

(iv) The conjoined decision

Baker J, in an extensive judgment, considered the meaning of family life under Art 8 ECHR and maintained that:[63]

> 'the relationship between a same-sex couple constitutes "family life" for the purposes of Art 8: see *Schalk and Kopf v Austria* [2010] ECHR 995. Thus, D, E, F and G have a family life together, as do X, Y and Z, that is entitled to respect under article 8. Thousands of children in this country are being brought up happily and successfully by same-sex couples.'

He cited the words of Lord Mansfield in *Barwell v Brooks* (1784): 'As the usages of society alter, the law must adapt itself to the various situations of mankind.'[64] Baker J held that, following the decision in *Anayo v Germany*,[65] although a biological kinship between a natural parent and child alone will not in itself be sufficient to attract the protection of Art 8 ECHR, it was arguable that the relationships which D and E allowed S to establish with G, and which X and Y allowed T to establish with Z, did amount to 'family life', or fall within the scope of 'private life'. A refusal to allow S and T, at least, permission to apply for residence and contact orders would amount to a breach of their rights under Art 8 ECHR.

Baker J considered whether, following the 2008 legislation, he could grant S and T leave to apply for residence and/or contact orders with G and Z respectively.[66] He explained that the policy underpinning the HFEA 2008 'is an acknowledgement that alternative family forms without fathers are sufficient to meet a child's need'.[67] However, he accepted that, in spite of this policy, it remained open to the court to grant leave to persons like S and T to apply for orders for contact and residence.[68] Although S and T were legal strangers to G and Z as a consequence of the Act, they were not strangers in any other sense of the word. D and E had chosen S, an old friend who lived very close by, to provide sperm to enable them to conceive G and his older sister, F. They had involved him throughout the pregnancy. They had invited him to see the baby

---

63 Ibid, para 113.
64 (1784) 3 Doug. 371.
65 *Anayo v Germany* [2010] ECHR 20578/07, [2011] 1 FLR 1883.
66 Applications for leave to apply for s 8 orders are governed by s 10 of the Children Act 1989.
67 *Re G and Re Z* [2013] EWHC 134 (Fam), para 113.
68 See the case comment, L Yeatman 'Lesbian Co-parents: Still Not Real Mothers' [2013] Fam Law 1581.

both immediately after the birth and thereafter on a regular basis. It was arguable that the relationship which D and E allowed S to develop was linked in some way to the children's biological relationship with him.

In the case of T, X and Y were well aware of S and T's involvement in the lives of D and E's children. Having been introduced to T by D and E, they went ahead with their plans for X to conceive a child with T. After Z's birth, X and Y allowed T frequent and regular contact with him for 18 months. It was an acknowledgement, in some sense, of T's biological relationship with Z. He could not be seen as a stranger to Z. Furthermore, X and Y had admitted that they wanted T to be a role model for Z.

Baker J interpreted the provisions of the HFEA 2008 in an interesting and creative way. He held that the Act permitted the exercise of parental responsibility, acquired by the same-sex partner of a birth mother, to facilitate a parental relationship between their children and a biological father (and his partner). If the latter were granted leave to apply for contact and residence orders for his children, it would not frustrate the legislative intention behind the Act's reforms. Had Parliament intended that a biological father should have no right to make such an application, it would have done so explicitly.

Baker J declined S's application for leave to apply for a residence order on the basis that it would be disproportionate and might undermine the autonomy of D and E's family. However, he did agree to grant him leave to apply for a contact order even though he acknowledged that this might cause stress and anxiety to D and E. There was a further compelling argument in favour of granting S leave; there were proceedings ongoing in respect of S and E's first child, F. Both children would be brought up knowing that S was their biological father. It would be somewhat unreal, and not in their interests, if G, but not F, were to be excluded from any consideration by the court of contact with his father.

Baker J also granted T's application for leave to apply for a contact order. In addition to T having established a relationship with Z, and X and Y's intentions that he should be a role model for Z, there was also his Sri Lankan racial and cultural heritage to consider.

(v) Comment

Baker J's decision draws attention to the absolutist provisions of the HFEA 2008. The Act has upgraded the role of a same-sex partner of a birth mother who obtains parental responsibility at the expense of downgrading that of a biological father who will be denied that right. It is questionable why the policy-makers felt that it was necessary to do so.

The decision is to be welcomed, however, for Baker J's attempts to ameliorate the statutory marginalisation of biological fathers. He limited, albeit minimally, the effects of the Act by giving fathers leave to apply for contact with their children. He also left open the possibility of granting leave to apply for residence orders.

Baker J's recognition of the right to family life for biological fathers under Art 8 ECHR could even lead to claims that the provisions of the HFEA 2008 are a breach of Art 8 ECHR.

III CONCLUSION

Family life and parenting in the twenty-first century have changed.[69] Many families today do not conform to the idealised model of the nuclear family of a happily married husband and wife, and two children, one male and one female (or so the media would have one believe), which may have existed for a comparatively brief period in the twentieth century.

One particular type of new family – the lesbian family – has been singled out by the judiciary as complex foreign territory which requires a search for special rules. The courts' approach to determining what those rules should be has proven to be muddled and uncertain. Mothers' demands for an autonomous family have tended to be treated sympathetically, sometimes at the expense of allowing a significant relationship between children and their biological fathers.

The courts have questioned the role of agreements made prior to the children's birth and, for the most part, have acknowledged that they are an important, albeit not the only, factor in determining future parental relationships. They have searched for a new vocabulary to describe these new forms of familial relationships. They have attempted to clarify the vague concept of parental responsibility and, throughout the decisions, they have insisted that the paramountcy of the welfare of the child must be the guiding light. Scant attention has been paid to the right to family life under Art 8 ECHR. They have sought to make sense of the HFEA 2008, which clearly negates the role of fathers in the lives of their biological children.

What possible solutions are there to the conflict between lesbian mothers and biological fathers who are known to them? Agreements made prior to conception or birth, no matter how well thought out, can never be the major factor in determining whether to exclude a father from a relationship with a child. The courts, whilst paying attention to agreements, have acknowledged that attitudes of both fathers and mothers have a tendency to change once a baby, anonymous in utero, emerges as a real person. This is well recognised in the law relating to surrogacy and adoption where the birth parent and any other person with parental responsibility has a 6-week period of grace after the baby's birth before they decide to relinquish it to a new family. If a biological

---

69 See Lady Hale 'New Families and the Welfare of Children', a paper presented at the Morgan Centre Conference, at the LSE 20 June 2013.

father genuinely prefers to be treated in the same way as an anonymous sperm donor and not play a part in his child's life, he could be permitted to make a legally binding statement to that effect once the child is 6 weeks old.

The constant search for a new vocabulary to describe familial relationships in the lesbian context appears to be more concerned with the needs of the women rather than the recognition of the right of a child to a paternal relationship. Why is a new familial language deemed to be necessary? Biological fathers who wish to have a relationship with their children are fathers. How different are they, in reality, from divorced or separated heterosexual non-resident fathers? The latter are rarely excluded from having a meaningful relationship with their children, regardless of the length of time spent with them prior to divorce or separation, or whether their children have a new parental relationship when their mother has acquired a new partner.

The emphasis on the elusive principle of the paramountcy of the best interests of the child has led lesbian parents to indulge in a form of emotional blackmail and maintain that the involvement of biological fathers in the lives of their children is stressful and threatens the stability of their relationship and hence their children's welfare. It appears that the courts are prepared to accept the claim of stress without any evidence that the biological father has set out deliberately to cause that stress. Children's welfare also demands a recognition of their right to know, and enjoy a relationship with, their parents of both genders; they need male role models in their lives. Children should not be denied this right because of the insecurity or frustration of their mothers, which may stem from a recognition that their dreams of a paternal-free family may be unrealistic.

The relationship between the parenting orders, under the Children Act 1989, which remain available to biological fathers, and the provisions of the HFEA 2008, which has the potential to deny these same fathers parental responsibility, is confusing. It is arguable that this statutory denial of paternal parental responsibility is a breach of Art 8 ECHR. There is no reason why fathers should not be allowed to have parental responsibility alongside lesbian mothers.

Biological fathers, who have made it possible for lesbians to become mothers, must not be ignored as important parental figures in their children's lives. Rather, they should be regarded as co-parents unless, of course, there are very serious reasons to exclude them or they choose to exclude themselves. Lesbians who wish to have children have a choice: they can use anonymous sperm and create nuclear families safe from the demands of biological fathers. If they choose to use men known to them because they regard them as a safer, and better, option for themselves and for their children, they may not have their cake and eat it too. They should not be allowed to demand that the relationship between a biological father and his children be downgraded, against his wishes, to that of a vaguely related, and infrequent, visitor in their lives.

FRANCE

A CHRONICLE OF FRENCH FAMILY LAW

*Centre for Family Law, University Jean Moulin, Lyon**

Résumé

Le droit français de la famille n'avait pas connu de période aussiagitée depuis bien longtemps. Certaines problématiques déjà anciennes continuent de faire parler d'elles sur des aspects particuliers, tellel'égalité des modes de conjugalité dans le droit au séjour des « compagnons » de Français (2), mais sur tout projet de réformes et réformes se multiplient, bienque le plus attendu de tous, la grande loi sur la famille n'ait cessé d'être différé, reporté, suspendu ... (1). En revanche, une modification de la loi sur l'interruption volontaire de grossesse est actuellement en discussion (3), une réforme des procédures judiciaires familiales est envisagée (4) et de nouvelles dispositions fiscales relatives au système du quotient familial sont déjà entrées en vigueur (5). Du côté de l'Union européenne, une prise de conscience de la nécessité d'un texte européen visant à simplifier la circulation des actes de l'état civil a donné lieu à une proposition de règlement (6). Quant aux difficultés liées à l'ouverture du mariage aux couples de même sexe par la loi du 17 mai 2013, elles ne cessent de surgir. En droit interne d'abord, le Conseil d'état a refusé aux officiers de l'état civil le droit d'invoquer une clause de conscience pour refuser de célébrer ces mariages (7). En droit international privé ensuite, les magistratsont été confrontés à la question de savoir si un mariage entre un Français et un Marocain de même sexe pouvait être célébré a lorsque les deux États sont liés par une convention bilatérale prévoyant l'application de la loi nationale au statut personnel et donc aux conditions de fond du mariage (8). Ces problèmes étaient inévitables et ils avaient été pointés du doigt avant même la promulgation de la loi. Tout aussi prévisibles étaient les difficultés liées à la situation des enfants nés à l'étranger avec l'assistance d'une mère porteuse. En revanche, la position adoptée par la Cour de cassation est des plus sur prenantetantelle est radicale (9). Elle contrasted'ailleurs très fortement de cellequ'elle a prise dans une toute autre affaire en refusant d'annuler, malgrél'empêchement existant en droit français, le mariage célébré entre une femme et son ex-beau-père au motif que celui-ci avait duré plus de vingt ans (10).

---

* A chronicle collectively written by the academic staff, PhD holders and PhD candidate at the Centre for Family Law at University Jean Moulin Lyon 3 (research team on private law – EA3707) aimed at presenting recent developments in family law in France. This collective chronicle was written under the leadership of Hughes Fulchiron and Christine Bidaud-Garon by Marine Bathias, Younès Bernand, François Chénedé, Jezabel Jannot, Aurélien Molière, Amélie Panet, Colin Reydellet (CREDIP), Stessy Tetard.

I MISADVENTURES OF THE 'GREAT FAMILY LAW': A FRENCH COMEDY (HUGUES FULCHIRON)

After the 2012 elections, the left-wing majority supported a major reform of family law among its societal projects. Beyond the symbolic aspect of same-sex marriage, the intent was to align French law with the realities and aspirations of society.

This vast project was launched in fall 2012 with a bill on 'marriage for all'. The text did not just open marriage to same-sex couples: marriage carried adoption along by arguing that, under French law, adoption by couples produced a marriage 'effect' (France allows adoption by a single person but rejects the adoption by or within a couple if unmarried). This admittedly clever approach to enact the 'homosexual family' through marriage, while avoiding the highly sensitive issues of PMAs (procréation médicalement assistée or assisted reproduction) in same-sex couples or GPA (gestation pour autrui or surrogacy), turned in fact against the government and its majority. To everyone's surprise, hundreds of thousands of people took to the streets to assert their commitment to 'traditional' marriage and, especially, to express their hostility towards homosexual families, on behalf of the interests of the child: the child is entitled to his father and mother; 'one child = one dad + one mom' was the demonstrators' motto.

It was to no avail that the President of the Republic and the Prime Minister declared that allowing PMA to single women, let alone lesbian couples, was far from their intent, and that they were radically hostile towards the GPA. Likewise, discordant voices in the majority and within government revived suspicions. The government, given the scale of a dispute going far beyond political divisions and religious beliefs, reconsidered its initial position: the law on marriage and adoption would be passed, but there would be no mention of PMAs or GPA, and the government would oppose any parliamentary initiative on the matter.

For the rest, it was necessary to allow some time for reflection; a 'great family law', assuming all consequences stemming from the recognition of marriage for all, while meeting the changing needs of families, would be built as part of a broad consultation; it would be presented in 2 months ... 6 months ... 9 months. Demonstrators did not stand down and the government delayed, consulted, reported and convened several expert groups (on parentage and parenthood, protection and child rights, early childhood, mediation etc), only to finally surrender in early 2014: it will not propose a 'great family law'. To appease critics in its majority, however, the Prime Minister hinted that he would not oppose a parliamentary initiative, since PMA or GPA would be out of the question anyhow.

Once experts appraised and commissions met (sternly instructed to keep absolute secrecy on their recommendations for fear of triggering new controversies – see the first report released in early April: Parentage, origin, parenthood, The Law before the new values of generational responsibility, Report of the Working Group on Parentage, origins, parenting, Irène Théry (Chair), Anne-Marie Leroyer (Rapp)), the only thing left was adding certain proposals – if possible of a consensual nature – to their conclusions.

A (first?) bill presented by Socialist deputies was made public at the beginning of April, a few days after the municipal elections. Up to that point, there was no question of reopening the debate. The bill, focused on 'parental authority and interest of the child', sought to strengthen the joint exercise of parental authority in the event of parent separation, providing in particular that, except in exceptional circumstances, the residence of the child was now set at the home of both parents; the parents' focus should therefore be on the practical arrangement of the time spent with the child, avoiding thus any conflicts around residence as such, whether exclusive, usual or shared. It was also envisaged to recognise the role of step-parents with the creation of a daily education mandate, allowing step-parents to perform the usual routines with the child, or redesigning rules on delegation and sharing of parental authority. Along the lines of previous proposals, family mediation was to be developed too. In particular, the judge should be entitled to order parents to participate in mediation sessions. Finally, the text seeks to ensure better consideration for the views of the child, specifying, if necessary, that: 'The minor is of course considered according to his/her maturity.'

These are indeed useful and for some (eg step-parenting issues) necessary measures, although the desire to avoid controversy led deputies to remove the most daring proposals. It is not unlikely, however, that the government had a say in it. Still, the matter of step-parents may stir certain controversy, in particular, as some find it hard to reconcile the principle of co-parenting with the recognition of the place of others. More importantly, really sensitive issues were largely ignored, including the alignment of parentage law with the recognition via adoption of same-sex families, opening of PMAs to singles and/or female couples, recognition of an ethical GPA or, at least, a status for children born abroad with the assistance of a surrogate mother, etc. In the near future, perhaps, they might inspire new parliamentary initiatives.

Towards a great, albeit piecemeal, family law?

II CONFORMITY WITH THE CONSTITUTION OF THE MONOPOLY OF MARRIAGE IN THE GRANTING OF A RESIDENCE PERMIT TO THE FOREIGN SPOUSE OF A FRENCH NATIONAL[1] (AURÉLIEN MOLIÈRE)

Presented with a priority issue of constitutionality referred by the State Council, the Constitutional Council ruled on the conformity of Art L 313-11, 4 with

1 Concerning ruling No 2013-312 QPC of 22 May 2013, *Mr Jory Orlando T* and No 2013-358 QPC of 29 November 2013, *Mr Azdine A*.

the rights and freedoms guaranteed by the Constitution. This provision of the code on entry and residence of foreign persons and asylum right (CESEDA) lays down the conditions for granting a residence permit. In particular, it is provided that a foreign person must be married to a French national to be eligible for such a permit. This condition was contested by the applicant, which considered that, by reserving the issue of residence permits to married foreigners and, therefore, denying the same to foreign persons bound through PACS (pacte civil de solidarité, which is the name of French registered partnership) to a French national, the text proved detrimental to the right to lead a normal family life, as well as to the principle of equality.

Such a question, though seemingly relevant, was doomed to failure. Article L 313-11, 4 of CESEDA concerns exclusively the conditions for obtaining a residence permit by foreigners married to French nationals. Therefore, it does not refer to obtaining of a residence permit by foreigners bound through a PACS to a French national. This situation is regulated by another text: Art 12 of the Law of 15 November 1999, codified in Art L 313-11, 7 of CESEDA. Consequently, all claims brought up on this matter were clearly ineffective, as they concerned the wrong text. The applicant, because he was engaged in a civil partnership, could not rely on the provisions of Item 4 of Art L 313-11, which is reserved for marriage. However, his conjugal mode allows him to apply for a residence permit –albeit under different conditions – on the basis of Art L 313-11, 7 from the Law of 15 November 1999. Moreover, it is precisely this law that allowed the review of the provision at issue here, since it had already been the subject of constitutional review a priori upon its establishment by the Law of 24 April 1997 (Dec No 98-389 DC, 22 April 1997). Only a 'change in circumstances' (Ord 58-107 of 7 November 1958 on the organic law on the Constitutional Council, Art 23-2, al 1st, 2) upon a text reform could justify one further review. The applicant sought undoubtedly to challenge this discrepancy in the conditions provided by the Items 4 and 7 of the Article in question, which vary depending on whether the foreigner applying for a residence permit is married or in a partnership. The Constitutional Council was nonetheless unable to comment, as the priority issue of constitutionality transmitted by the State Council did not concern this point.

However, the Constitutional Council took this opportunity to recall that 'the legislature could, without prejudice to the freedom to marry or disproportionately impairing the right to lead a normal family life, put forward the issuing by effect of law of a temporary residence permit to the foreign spouse of a French national' (Dec No 2013-312 QPC of 22 May 2013 *Mr Jory Orlando T*, Cons 6). This reminder is operated by the literal repetition of the motivation contained in a previous decision (Dec No 97-389 DC, 22 April 1997). Thus, it confirmed that conditions laid down in Art L 313-11, 4, organising a special regime for married couples, are justified by public interest objectives and undermine no right or freedom guaranteed by the Constitution.

Six months later, a new priority issue of constitutionality on the residence permit was presented to the Constitutional Council. This was no longer connected to the verification of issuing conditions but to the compliance assessment of renewal conditions with the Constitution. Once again, no verification was undertaken. The applicant considered that Art L 313-12, para 2, of CESEDA gave rise to certain discrimination as it reserves the benefit of such renewal for spouses. Even if the observation was indisputable, the grievance brought up proved again ineffective, as it was directed against the wrong text: the renewal of the residence permit is provided for by Art L 313-11, 7, for partners and cohabitants. The Constitutional Council was unable to comment on the text, as the question submitted by the State Council did not concern the former. By contrast, this decision has enabled the same to assert that the provisions of Art L 313-12, para 2, of CESEDA comply with the rights and freedoms guaranteed by the Constitution (Dec No 2013-358 QPC of 29 November 2013 *Mr Azdine A*).

III ABORTION – ON THE PROPOSAL TO ELIMINATE THE 'WOMAN IN DISTRESS' CIRCUMSTANCE (JEZABEL JANNOT)

'Equality remains unconquered territory':[2] the Bill for real equality between women and men, based on the observation of a 'gender equality, provided for by law albeit not translated into reality',[3] has the ambitious goal of fighting inequalities suffered by women through an 'integrated approach'. With a transversal logic,[4] the proposal intends to focus specifically on a third generation of women's rights, after the civil rights attained upon Liberation, and the economic and social rights of the 1970s and 1980s 'Now is the time to define the conditions of effective and clearly defined equality'.[5] The explanatory memorandum states 'this law is thus entirely geared towards the effectiveness of rights, experimentation and social innovation. Indeed, it will be the first to address equality from all angles'.[6]

Among the measures outlined in the Bill, the 1st Title groups 'provisions on equality between women and men in working life'(!) and, in particular, several provisions on voluntary interruption of pregnancy (VIP), with a view to strengthening the protection of women wishing to avail themselves of such a right. The Senate,[7] during its first reading of the Bill, has introduced an

---

2 Explanatory memorandum of the Bill for equality between women and men, text No 717 (2012-2013) of Ms NajatVallaud-Belkacem, Minister of Women's Rights, the government spokesman at the time, which was tabled in the Senate on 3 July 2013.

3 Bill, Impact Assessment, 1.

4 The method used is that of 'framework law'. The text deals with numerous issues including equality in working life, fight against precariousness, protection of women against violence and outrages against personal dignity, or the implementation of the constitutional parity goal.

5 Explanatory memorandum to the Bill, text No 717, above n 2.

6 Bill, Text No 717, above n 2.

7 Text No 214 (2012-2013) adopted by the Senate on 17 September 2013.

additional article, Art 5, which extends the definition of 'obstruction to voluntary interruption of pregnancy'[8] to acts intended to prevent access to information about VIP or its preliminaries. The National Assembly, also in its first reading of the Bill,[9] complemented this Article with two amendments adopted at the initiative of the socialist majority: Art 5 *d* B, which renames the title of the second part of the public health code, today entitled 'Health of the family, mother and child' to 'Reproductive health, women's rights and protection of child health'. As explained by the Law Commission in its report: 'The consecration of the concept of women's rights, beyond those of the *mother*, allows the full recognition of women's rights concerning their sexuality.'[10]

In line with this recognition, Art 5 *d* C of the text proposes amending Art L 2212-1 of the Code of Public Health, so that pregnant women can voluntarily request the interruption of their pregnancy, not only under a state of 'distress', as provided by positive law, but whenever they 'deem appropriate'. This amendment would aim, according to its promoters, to remove a useless and seldom demanded condition, while turning abortion into a real right for women. As already stated in 1980 by the State Council in its *Lahache* ruling,[11] women shall be entitled to independently assess whether the situation warrants the interruption of pregnancy, whereas abortion is permitted until the end of the 12th week of pregnancy. At this point, we note that abortion was legalised in France in 1975, initially on an interim basis by the famous Veil Law of 17 January 1975 (the so-called 'experimental' law), and finally by the Law of 30 December 1979. However, it was not until the reform of the penal code in 1992 that abortion was no longer regarded as an exception to an offence, a justification of sorts that allowed escaping prosecution. Later on, the law of 4 July 2001 removed, amongst other things,[12] the need to conduct a systematic preliminary interview with the woman. Today, even if abortion affects more than one in three women during their life (36%),[13] it is still regarded as an exceptional situation in current legislation. Moreover, it is interesting to note that, during the review of the constitutionality of the law of 2001 above, the Constitutional Council ruled that 'by reserving the right to resort to abortion' to 'pregnant women in distress', the legislature sought to exclude any evasion of the law and, more generally, any distortion of the principles posed by the same,

8 In the state of positive law (Art L 2223-2 Code of Public Health), it is punishable by 2 years' imprisonment and a €30,000 fine to prevent or attempt to prevent an abortion or its preliminaries: either by interfering in any way whatsoever with access to health facilities, free movement of people within those facilities, or working conditions of medical and non-medical personnel, or by exercising moral and psychological pressures, threats or intimidation on medical and non-medical personnel working in these facilities, and/or on women intending to undergo an abortion, or their entourage.

9 Text No 282 adopted by the National Assembly on 28 January 2014.

10 Report No 1663 for first reading.

11 EC, 31 October 1980, No 13028, *M Lahache Vincent*.

12 Law No 2001-588 of 4 July 2001 relating to abortion and contraception, which has also extended the statutory period of 10 to 12 weeks of pregnancy, removed the requirement of parental consent for minors, and put an end to discrimination against foreign women in an irregular situation.

13 Ibid.

among which we find, in Art L 2211-1 of the Code of Public Health, 'respect for the human being from the beginning of his life'.[14]

From a purely practical point of view, the removal of the 'distress' condition is essentially symbolic. Some consider it useless while others see it as the source of abortion trivialisation. It should be explained nonetheless that access to abortion encounters real obstacles in practice. Amongst others,[15] we note the reduction of human and material resources during the past decade, chiefly arising from the closure of many health facilities performing abortions. In this regard, the government has recently taken several measures to reduce these financial and territorial hindrances and guarantee the right of access to abortion including, inter alia, 100% reimbursement of the intervention for all women,[16] as well as increased rates. As a serious obstacle, however, we should mention the 'questioning of the legitimacy of abortion, in a context of widespread use of contraception, perceived thus as women's failure to control it and a source of guilt'.[17] Proof thereof can be found beyond French borders too: in late 2013, for example, the Spanish conservative government drafted a Bill to ban abortion except in cases of rape or danger to the health of the mother, albeit not that of the foetus, whereas the current Spanish legislation is one of the most permissive in Europe (abortion allowed until 14 weeks of pregnancy).

Back in France, and at the time of writing, the Bill for real equality between women and men is still being debated: it passed through the Senate for a second time on 17 April 2014. It has been decided to maintain Art 5 *d* C proposed by the House of Representatives that eliminates the condition of 'situation of emergency' for women in an abortion process. Indeed the Senate rejected an amendment proposed by various senators. The latter requested basically to suppress this new article, considering it went against the philosophy of the 1975 IVG Act (*Veil* Law for abortion) which lays out a balance between the principle of respect for the human being as at the beginning of life and the recognition that harm can be done only in case of necessity. The content of the Bill must be returned to the House of Representatives for a second reading before a possible mixed equal commission (CMP in France) in charge of looking for a common version to the two Houses in case of persistent disagreement.

---

14 Cons const, Decision No 2001-446 DC of 27 June 2001, Official Journal No 156 of 7 July 2001, 10828.

15 See in Report no 1663 of the National Assembly, prev, observations made in this respect by the High Council for Equality between Women and Men (HCEFH).

16 Law of Social Security funding of 2013.

17 Report no 1663, above n 15.

IV PREMISES FOR A REFORM OF FAMILY COURT PROCEEDINGS? ABOUT THE REPORT ON 'THE 21ST CENTURY JUDGE'[18] (MARINE BATHIAS)

The economic crisis, a pervasive reality in our society, demands an ambitious re-thinking of the legal practice as a whole. The Delmas-Goyon report, submitted to our Minister of Justice in December 2013, bears witness to this need by adopting a managerial vision of tomorrow's 'Justice'.

Simplification, clarification and expeditious procedures seem to inspire upcoming developments. Streamlining the practice of the judge tends to become the rule, to the point that the judge's intervention is now called into question in many areas of family law. A case in point can be found in the letter of proposal No 49 of the Delmas-Goyon report, envisaging the transfer of divorces by mutual consent to judicial clerks. Once again, they will become court officers with their own court responsibilities, which partly resemble those customarily lying with the judge.

Similarly, procedural simplifications initiated by the Guinchard commission are reflected in proposals found in the '21st century Justice' report. The total diversion of records and dissolution of PACS bear witness to this intent to reduce the burden on courts.

(a) Divorce by mutual consent: redefining the office of judge

In its proposal No 49, the Delmas-Goyon commission plans to redefine the office of the Family Court Judge by transferring divorces by mutual consent to judicial clerks. Although some regard this transfer as a diversion of the divorce process, this does not seem to be entirely the case. Literally speaking, 'diversion' involves removing from the scope of justice an activity hitherto entrusted to the judge. However, that is not the purpose of the proposal put forward in this report concerning divorce, inasmuch as the judicial clerk, an actor of the judiciary per se, would be assigned a fundamental competence in matters of divorce by mutual consent. Thus, it seems more appropriate to consider this development as a 'de-jurisdictionalisation', insofar as divorce will be pronounced by a judicial actor other than the judge, to be invested with real *jurisdictio* right. Specifically, the responsibilities of judicial clerks, a newly created body, would be akin to those of the Family Court Judge concerning divorce by mutual consent. They should verify the consent to divorce by spouses and approve the agreement regulating its consequences.

According to this report, the proposed de-jurisdictionalisation is justified by the need to rationalise justice. Indeed, the effectiveness and cost reduction in the

---

[18] Report under the direction of Pierre Delmas-Goyon, Counsel to the Court of Cassation, submitted to the Ministry of Justice on 9 December 2013. The report is available at www.justice.gouv.fr/la-garde-des-sceaux-10016/edification-de-la-justice-du-21eme-siecle-26387.html.

judiciary underlies the various initiatives. Regardless, the appropriateness of the solutions proposed may be open to further discussion. Some grey areas remain regarding the actual recruitment and remit of judicial clerks.

Other solutions relying on proven tools could also be considered. Likewise, it would be conceivable to introduce a simplified approval procedure by the judge of a lawyer's act in response to collaborative law requirements. In other words, even solutions intended to simplify judicial procedures can be reviewed and perfected in several areas.

(b) PACS: transfer of powers to registrars

Procedural simplifications proposed by the Delmas-Goyon report find a perfect example in the sensitive issue of transfer to registrars of PACS records and dissolutions. While the Guinchard report was totally opposed thereto because of the confusion that such a transfer could generate between PACS and marriage, the problem has been largely addressed by the law of 17 May 2013 opening marriage to same-sex couples.

Adoption of this reform necessarily entails a reduction in the symbolic significance of PACS. However, its categories and rupture procedures must necessarily change with its status. That is why this report seeks the right for partners to conclude and break their PACS before a single and same actor: the registrar.

V REFORM OF FAMILY POLICY: THE REDUCTION OF THE FAMILY QUOTIENT CAP (YOUNÈS BERNAND)

In early 2013, the French Government decided in the context of public spending cuts to initiate the reform of social and tax benefits, implemented under family policy. Several measures were proposed including the reform of family allowances. Without questioning the principle of universality of such allowances, the Fragonard report, submitted to the Prime Minister on 9 April 2013, proposed reducing the amount beyond a certain ceiling depending on the number of children. In the 2013 *International Survey*,[19] we noted that making such allowances conditional upon resources represented a shift from a system of horizontal redistribution (transfer from childless households to households with children), to one of vertical solidarity (from wealthiest to poorest households). Ultimately, this allowance 'verticalisation' may justify and inspire the reform in other sectors, eg health, with the ensuing risks of state disengagement and privatisation. The hypothesis of a family allowance reform was finally rejected during government negotiations in favour of a family taxation adjustment, the symbolic significance of which is certainly lower.

---

[19] Centre de la droit de la famille 'A Chronicle of French Family Law' in B Atkin (ed) *The International Survey of Family Law 2013 Edition* (Jordan Publishing Ltd, Bristol, 2013) 130.

Let us recall that, after the war, the legislature placed the tax as the cornerstone of family policy. As a way to increase the birth rate, the Finance Law of 31 December 1945 established the family quotient. This mechanism is based on a simple premise: the consumption budget per family depends on the number of dependants per household. 'Identical tax rate for identical living standards' stated its promoter, Adolphe Landry. It is thus a question of modulating income tax based on the number of household members: one share per adult, half-share for the first and second children, and one share for each additional child (Art 194 Tax Code – CGI). Therefore, a household with a married couple or in a civil partnership with two children has three shares, whereas the same couple with four children will have five of them.

Soon enough, however, the family quotient was criticised as the origin of a two-tier taxation, setting rich and poor families apart.[20] Furthermore, to avoid favouring affluent households, the effects of this 'tax shelter' were capped (art 197 Code Général des Impôts). It follows that the tax reduction resulting from the application of the family quotient cannot exceed a certain amount per half-share in addition to the share of a single person, or both shares of a married couple or in civil partnership.

The legislature has modelled the Finance Law 2014 along those lines – ie by lowering from €2,000 to €1,500 each half-share granted for dependency allowance. Similarly, the maximum tax benefit provided by the family quotient attached to the first dependent child, and granted to single or divorced taxpayers living alone with dependent children, is lowered by the same amount, ie from €4,040 to €3,540. In contrast, the overall cap of the family quotient effects for each half-share granted under specific provisions related to the taxpayer's situation (war veterans, invalids, maintaining of marital quotient of widowers with dependent children) remains unchanged, as the tax benefit provided by each additional half-share is held by the increase in additional tax cuts provided to offset the effects of the cap. These new provisions shall apply from fiscal year 2013.

From the family quotient example, we can make two concluding remarks. First, in economic terms, we measure how family policy can serve as a financial adjustment variable during periods of crisis and budgetary constraints. The budget is expected to increase by €1.03 billion. From an ideological standpoint, further to these savings, the draft Finance Law 2014 emphasises the need to reinforce vertical redistribution in family policy, reflecting the shift described above in *commutative justice* (horizontal logic) and the leaning towards an idea of *distributive justice* (vertical logic). The movement certainly has a life of its own.

---

[20] D Grillet-Ponton *On Family and Taxes* (puf, Paris, 1998) 57.

VI ISSUES REGARDING THE MOVEMENT OF FAMILY STATUS DOCUMENTS AND THE PROPOSED EU REGULATION ON CIVIL STATUS RECORDS (AMÉLIE PANET)

Administrative procedures to authenticate public documents, even if residual today given the large number of international conventions and internal practices, are not aligned with relations among member states. Furthermore, the legalisation of foreign public documents constitutes a source of indirect discrimination, given that it is precisely non-nationals who most often require the assertion of foreign documents. This measure, therefore, affects them more than nationals; in other words, it produces discriminatory effects.[21] In addition, the legalisation practice hinders freedom of movement, particularly because of costs and delays attached thereto.[22] Ultimately, it is not consistent with the law of the European Union, and incompatible with the principle of mutual trust. This is why the European Commission has proposed a regulation simplifying the acceptance of certain public documents in the European Union,[23] as a way to promote the free movement of citizens and businesses. Regulations would solely apply to the movement of public documents between member states. It would be implemented inasmuch as it will deal with the movement within 28 member states of a document covered by its material scope. At the end of section 3, a public document is a 'document issued by the authorities of a Member State and which has formal probative value regarding a) birth; b) death; c) name; d) marriage or registered partnership; e) parentage; f) adoption; g) residence; h) citizenship or nationality [...]'.

The great innovation of the proposed regulation lies in the exemption, for documents falling within its scope, from any form of legalisation or similar formality, including certification. The proposal also provides for the simplification of other formalities. Member states should no longer require the simultaneous presentation of the original of a public document issued by another member state authority and a certified copy thereof, but only a certified copy or uncertified copy accompanied by the original. Regarding translation, the proposed regulation provides for authorities to accept uncertified translations, except upon reasonable doubt, in which case the authorities may require a certified translation, and must accept those established in other member states. The proposal also establishes a residual control. If the authorities of a member state before which a foreign public document is produced hold doubts about its authenticity, they may submit a justified information request to the competent authorities of the member state where the document was issued. The overall verification system is directly inspired by

---

21 See the study 'The use of public documents in the EU' Study JLS/C4/2005/04, report presented in July 2007 by J Van de Velden at http://ec.europa.eu/civiljustice/news/docs/study_public_docs_synthesis_report.pdf, spec, 382 and following.

22 'The use of public documents in the EU', ibid, 395 and following.

23 Proposal for a Regulation of the European Parliament and the Council to promote the free movement of citizens and businesses by simplifying the acceptance of certain public documents in the European Union, and amending Regulation (EU) No 1024/2012, COM(2013) 228 final.

existing systems in international conventions or jurisprudence. Here, we adopt the principle of gratuitous verification and speed, with the introduction of a maximum period of one month to answer any request.[24] The verification process can be done either by communication between the central authorities of the states concerned, or via consultation of the Internal Market Information System (IMI) by the authority of the state in which the document was produced. The proposal also provides for the establishment of multilingual form[25] of the European Union, inspired by existing forms within the ICCS (International Commission on Civil Status)[26] concerning birth, death, marriage and registered partnership. These multilingual forms can be used in place of the existing equivalent national public documents, and provide the same probative force. They are exempt from legalisation or similar formalities.

While the proposed regulation helps optimise existing instruments such as IMI and the European Judicial Network, it also establishes a unitary whole, and provides greater legal certainty as to the question of the authenticity of foreign documents. Between member states, it replaces all international conventions which relate to areas covered by the proposed regulation, but does not affect the application of the same texts in relations with third states. Regarding multilingual forms, it is surprising that the proposed regulation does not rely on a slightly more developed information-coding approach, given the limited number of particulars it offers. This may be regrettable considering the recognition issues around registered partnerships between member states, due to the wide variety thereof. The name issue is addressed by the proposed form, but the effects on civil status are ignored: the form does not contain any indication of the impediments to marriage or partnership with a third party. The form regarding birth also presents a major flaw: it provides for 'father' and 'mother' checkboxes alone, whereas several states have already opened adoption to same-sex couples. For example, a couple of women in France can marry and adopt a child in plenary form. In this case, the new 'national' birth record of the child will not include a 'father' checkbox, and the multilingual form contained in the proposed regulation would be useless.

The abolition of legalisation and certification and even the creation of a European civil status certificate do not solve all problems, since the actual content and recognition of public documents still remain an obstacle.[27] Article 2.2 of the proposed regulation states clearly that it 'shall not apply to the recognition of the content of public documents issued by the authorities of other Member States'. Thus, the proposed regulation applies only to the recognition of the *instrumentum*, ie of the authenticity of the document. Therefore, the foreign authentic instrument is recognised solely as an instrument, attributing thereto the same probative value as a document that

---

24 Article 7.4 of the proposed Regulation.

25 Articles 11 to 15 of the proposed Regulation.

26 Convention No 16 on the issue of multilingual extracts from civil-status records signed at Vienna on 8 September 1976, http://ciec1.org.

27 In this sense, see the response of the ICCS to the Green Paper of 2010, on the website of the ICCS, at 2.

was established by this country. However, recognition of the *instrumentum* is not unrelated to the recognition of the *negotium*. Perhaps, it might have been necessary to attempt to go beyond the mere recognition of the document itself, and enact a recognition of the situation thereby represented, as well as of some of its effects.

VII REQUIREMENT FOR REGISTRARS TO CELEBRATE MARRIAGE BETWEEN SAME-SEX COUPLES (STESSY TETARD)

On 18 October 2013, the Constitutional Council made its decision about the absence, in the Law of 17 May 2013 opening marriage to same-sex couples, of a provision allowing for the conscientious objection of registrars. Presented with a priority issue of constitutionality by the State Council, its members refused to declare unconstitutional the impossibility for registrars and their deputies to evade their responsibilities regarding the celebration of marriage for same-sex couples. It all started with the circular of 13 June 2013 on the consequences of refusing to celebrate a marriage by a registrar. The law provides that the unjustified refusal to celebrate a marriage (no properly formulated objection, impediments to marriage or lack of compliance with the necessary formalism) constitutes an assault, allowing the judge to order the persons concerned to fulfil their mission under penalty. This order may be accompanied by compensation for the damage caused by the refusal. These civil penalties accompany criminal (Articles 432-1 and following of the Penal Code) and disciplinary sanctions (Article L. 2122-16 of the General Local Authorities Code).

In support of their request for recognising the unconstitutionality of several texts (arts 34-1, 74 and 165 of the Civil Code and Art 2122-18 of CGCT (Code Général des Collectivités Territoriales)), mayors argued that opening marriage to same-sex couples went against their personal beliefs, which they should be able to express via a 'conscience clause'.

The Constitutional Council has refused, in two stages, to recognise any upset to freedom of conscience, free administration of local communities and pluralism of ideas and opinions (cons 10). On the one hand, it recalled that the legislature is required to ensure proper operation and neutrality of the public service of civil status. In other words, it must ensure the uniform application of the law by state services. On the other hand, it claimed that the reason alleging infringement of freedom of conscience is inoperative regarding the registrar's functions. The judges of the Constitutional Council intend to recall here that the act at issue is a legal act, which does not involve the conscience of its author. The conditions under which marriage is celebrated are defined by law and do not entail any personal appreciation by the celebrating party. In comparison, the Constitutional Council has admitted a 'conscience clause' for physicians regarding abortion, which is justified by the refusal of the legislature to impose on professionals the performance of an action, as part of their profession, which directly clashes with their personal beliefs.[28] However, in this decision, it considers that mayors do not engage their consciousness in celebrating a union under conditions 'hardly comparable to those of medical diagnosis or treatment. There are peculiarities in the performance of medical procedures that are not found in the registrar's remit'.[29]

The experts have thus made a balanced decision that ensures the smooth and effective implementation of the law of 17 May 2013. It does not violate the freedom of conscience of registrars who, as agents of the state, should enforce the law without personal involvement.

This decision lies also in the wake of that rendered on 15 January 2013 by the European Court of Human Rights.[30] Acting on the case of a British registrar dismissed for refusing to perform civil unions between same-sex couples, the Court refused to admit a contradiction with Arts 9 and 14 of the Convention. The Court believed that the dismissal was justified by the desire of the employer to ensure a service provision policy without discrimination. Therefore, the appreciation leeway left to the British Government to find the right balance between the religious beliefs of the employee and the safeguard of rights of others by the employer was not overridden.[31]

VIII SAME-SEX MARRIAGE BETWEEN A FRENCH AND A MOROCCAN: CAN IT BE CELEBRATED WITH RESPECT TO THE FRANCO-MOROCCAN AGREEMENT? (COLIN REYDELLET)

With the entry into force of the law of 17 May 2013 opening marriage up to couples of the same sex,[32] French family law, including its private international law aspects, has been turned on its head. It is thus perhaps not surprising that the courts make, on the basis of this reform, decisions that arouse interest. Such is the case of the judgment commented on and publicised (it is useful to note this, since it is not a decision of the French Supreme Court, which usually attracts these honours) of 22 October 2013 of the Chambéry Court of Appeal.

The facts are not of great complexity: two men, one French and one Moroccan, wanted to get married in France. Not disputed by the registrar, the marriage was objected to by the public prosecutor. This opposition, however, was not upheld by the court of the first instance and the Court of Appeal, whose decision is the subject of comments. To understand the latter's motivation, we need to return to French positive law on international marriage.

---

28 Constitutional Council, DC No 2001-446, 27 June 2001.

29 Review available on the website of the Constitutional Council, www.conseil-constitutionnel.fr.

30 Eweida et al UK Req our 48420/10, 59842/10, 51671/10 and 36516/10.

31 Ibid at §107 et seq.

32 Law no 2013-404 of 17 May 2013: JO, no 0114, 18 May 2013, 8253.

Typically, the conditions for marriage are subject to the personal law of each spouse, while the formal requirements must respect the law in the place of celebration. The law of 2013 did not change this rule, but changed the foundation (the rule was previously deduced from arts 3 and 171-1 of the Civil Code: it is now clearly set out in arts 202-1 and 202-2 of the same Code). However, for the substantive requirements, art 202-1 introduced an exception to the conflicts rule governing substantive conditions: even when the personal law of one spouse or both prohibits marriage between persons of the same sex, marriage is possible provided that, for at least one of them, the law of nationality, domicile or residence permits it. The advantage for same-sex marriage is such that there is hesitation in the application of this rule: is it a contentious rule coloured by its alternative annexations, or an internationally valid substantive rule for same-sex marriage?[33] Still, it has been found to conform to the French Constitution, particularly as it does not create a breach of equality between heterosexual couples and homosexual couples in favour of the latter.[34]

The scope of this reform, however, is assessed in light of France's international commitments. Indeed, a circular dated 29 May 2013[35] was a reminder that there was a number of bilateral agreements on the issue, including the Rabat Convention of 10 August 1981 between the French Republic and the Kingdom of Morocco concerning the status of persons and family and judicial cooperation.[36] This reaffirms art 5 of the traditional rule regarding the conditions for marriage, without exception, while art 4 reserves recourse to public order if any of the applicable laws are 'obviously' contrary to international public order.

It is against this background that the ruling of the Chambéry Court of Appeal is assessed. The question seems to be that of which rule should apply: that of art 202-1 of the Civil Code or of art 5 of the Franco-Moroccan agreement. This was in any case, among others, based on the public prosecutor's argument. The question is similar to a school hypothesis, since art 55 of the French Constitution provides for the primacy of international treaties on the law. It should be noted that the National Assembly's Commission on Laws was well aware of this hierarchy, and that, as such, it has not considered it appropriate to include a specific provision in the text of the reform.[37]

The Court of Appeal adopted an original solution. After noting art 4 of the Franco-Moroccan agreement (the subject of public order) and the spirit in favour of gay marriage resulting from the reform of 2013, it held that French international public order was altered. The first notable feature is that the judges seem to base the development of this public policy on validation of the

33 Raising the same question: B Audit and L d'Avout *Private International Law* (7th edn, Economica, Paris, 2013), no 721.

34 Constitutional Council, 17 May 2013 no 2013-669 DC.

35 Circular dated 29 May 2013: BOMJ, no 2013-05, 31 May 2013.

36 Decree no 83-435 of 27 May 1983: JO, 1 June 1983, 1643.

37 Report no 628 of 17 January 2013.

law of 2013 made by the Constitutional Council.[38] Thus, acknowledging the new content of the public order, the Court of Appeal stated, by an ambiguous if not objectionable formulation, that:[39]

> 'it is best, for these reasons, to avoid the application of the Franco-Moroccan agreement in favour of the higher principles of the new international order, established by the law of 17th May 2013, and therefore does not recognise in this case the superiority of the treaty on the law according to the usual principle of hierarchy of norms.'

This sentence calls for several comments. First, there is no doubt that the conclusion thus made is dictated by considerations of legislative policy that the judge concedes to the legislators. In fact, there is no disputing the fact that the trend for marriage between persons of the same sex internationally breathed life into the law of 2013. However, as has been pointed out, it appears no more questionable that the legislative intent was to limit the previous set of bilateral agreements, which is also consistent with positive law (in this case, art 55 of the Constitution). In other words, the judgment sought to circumvent the obstacle of the hierarchy of norms emphasising the legislature's intention as to the influence of the reform, even though the same was intended to meet this challenge. The ruling is therefore open to criticism on this count. It is also liable to criticism in terms of the operation of private international law, including its clumsy wording on the implementation of the public order mechanism (you can read that the French international public order precludes the rule of conflict of laws contained in the Franco-Moroccan agreement from replacing it which, on the one hand, contrasts with its traditional role as a mechanism for avoidance of foreign law otherwise applicable and, on the other hand, leaves doubts about the shelving of the agreement by the public order mechanism based on art 4 of that agreement). But the solution remains worthy of approval and the ruling highlights this, since bilateral agreements such as the Franco-Moroccan agreement discriminate between couples of the same sex according to their nationality, between those who can access marriage and those who cannot. Some then risk, in case of the inverse solution, condemnation by the European Court of Human Rights.[40]

IX THE SITUATION OF CHILDREN BORN ABROAD WITH THE ASSISTANCE OF A SURROGATE MOTHER (CHRISTINE BIDAUD-GARON)

French law prohibits surrogacy on the basis of the principles of unavailability of the status of persons, respect for human dignity, especially that of women, and refusal of the commodification of the human body. The end of art 16-7 of the Civil Code states: 'Any agreement concerning procreation or gestation on

---

38 The formulation of the eleventh paragraph of the grounds of the judgment seems debatable.

39 Twelfth paragraph of the grounds.

40 H Fulchiron *'Marriage For All' is International Public Order* (Dalloz, Paris, 2013) 2576.

behalf of others shall be void.' While these principles seem admittedly solid and fully justify the ban, they fail to prevent the French from going abroad to seek a surrogate mother. Once the child is born, however, the question arises: how to reconcile the prohibition of surrogacy and the legal recognition of the child?

Now, as the legislator neither considered this international situation nor intends to do so in the upcoming bill of family law, the issue must be dealt with by the Court of Cassation. In the first cases ruled in 2011,[41] the Court refused the transcription on French civil status registers of foreign birth documents of these children on the basis of public order. No distinction is made according to the situation. The refusal is one of a general nature, disregarding the fact that some intended parents (father or mother) were also biological parents of the child. However, the Court was careful to note that these children were not deprived of parentage as they had one abroad. While the formula was certainly ambiguous and the situation of these children highly complex in France, one would think the Court could at least assert their parentage through their foreign civil status records, and thus enable the children to be legally attached to those raising them.

Presented again with these questions, the Court of Cassation adopted a more radical position in two rulings issued on 13 September 2013.[42] Acting on appeals against two rulings of the Court of Appeal of Rennes about children born in India through a surrogate mother, the court stated that 'when birth results from an overall process comprising an agreement for gestation on behalf of others, this agreement, deemed fraudulent in France albeit lawful abroad, is void on public order grounds pursuant to sections 16-7 and 16-9 of the Civil Code', parentage established abroad cannot be entered into the French civil status register. Taking a further step in its effort not to allow any effect to a GPA (gestation pour autrui or surrogacy) agreement concluded abroad, the Court confirmed the annulment for fraud under the Law of the recognition carried out in France by the biological father. The Court even stated that:

> 'in the presence of fraud, neither the interest of the child, as guaranteed by Article 3 §1 of the Convention on the Rights of the Child, nor respect for private and family life pursuant to Article 8 of the Convention for the Protection of Human Rights and fundamental freedoms, can be validly relied upon.'

By changing the basis and relying upon fraud, the Court placed children in a situation of lawlessness. The adage *fraus omnia corrumpit* has devastating

---

41 Cass Civ 1e, 6 April 2011, 3 orders: Appeal No 10-19053, 09-66486, 09-17130. Dalloz 2011, 1522 note D Berthiau and L Brunet; Dalloz 2011, 1585 obs F Granet-Lambrechts; JCP G 2011, No 441, obs F Vialla and M Reynier; RJPF-2011-6/12, obs M-C Le Boursicot; RTD civ 2011, 340, obs J Hauser, Rev crit DIP 2011, 722, note P Hammje.

42 Civ 1st, 13 September 2013, no 12-18.315 and no 12-30.138, Dalloz 2013, 2377, concl C Petit, Dalloz, 2013, 2384, notes M Fabre-Magnan, JCP, 2013, 985; plus H Fulchiron and C Bidaud-Garon, *In Legal Limbo: On the Situation of Children Born Abroad With the Assistance of a Surrogate Mother* (Dalloz, 2013) 2349 JCP, 2013, ed G 985 note A Mirkovic, AJ Fam, 579, obs F Chénedé, Family law 2013, comm no 151, note C Neirinck, A Gouttenoire, JCP 2014, ed G, Review of Family Law, doctr No 43, JDI 2014, pers No 1, note J Guillaumé.

effects, since it rends completely ineffective an act deemed fraudulent. Admittedly, the birth certificate cannot be entered in the civil status register; however, qualifying the birth itself as being the 'result of a fraudulent process' prevents establishing parentage in France. In addition, the Court failed to refer to its motivation of 2011, where it reported the parentage that the child had 'abroad'. Despite all the criticisms that can be made against this formula, it had at least the merit of suggesting that parentage established abroad could be considered in France. How could this still be the case after these 2013 rulings? Today, it is hard to imagine that such 'foreign parentage' can be enforced on French territory as the result of a fraudulent process reported by the Court of Cassation. Therefore, we deem the situation of these children as utterly unacceptable: French consulates have an obligation of issuing temporary travel documents to the 'parents' of these children and this allows them to enter on French territory; once in France, however, their foreign birth certificate cannot be entered in the civil status register, their parentage established abroad is unenforceable, and they cannot avail of any parentage determination mechanisms under French law.

What is more, as parentage underlies everything, no parental authority, no French nationality, no heir capacity, etc can ensue. With a decision of 19 March 2014,[43] the Court of Cassation confirmed its position, again on grounds of fraud, to deny the transcription of foreign birth certificates to French civil status records. However, it has not revisited its very questionable formula that the fundamental rights of the child 'cannot be properly relied upon'. While the abstention of the court is fortunate, as the statement itself is questionable, it fails to address any of the issues. As long as fraud serves as the basis for denial of the transcript of birth certificates and birth is deemed the result of a fraudulent process, affiliations established abroad shall remain unenforceable in France. The salvation of these children may come from the European Court of Human Rights, the court which must rule on one of the 2011 cases; in the meantime, however, they remain in 'legal limbo'.

X VALIDITY OF THE MARRIAGE BETWEEN A FORMER STEPBROTHER AND FORMER STEPSISTER (CASS CIV 1E, 4 DECEMBER 2013, APPEAL NO 12-26066) (FRANÇOIS CHÉNEDÉ)

In a landmark decision, the First Civil Chamber admitted, relying upon the right to respect for private and family life, the validity of a marriage celebrated between an ex-stepfather and an ex-stepdaughter, whereas this union between affines is expressly prohibited by art 161 of the Civil Code.[44]

---

[43] Cass Civ 1e, 19 March 2014, No 13-50.005: H Fulchiron and C Bidaud-Garon *The Child of Fraud: Reflections on the Status of Children Born With the Assistance of a Surrogate Mother* (Dalloz, 2014) 905.

[44] Cass civ 1, 4 December 2013, appeal No 12-26066 ; D 2013. 153, view of H Fulchiron; ibid

In this case, both parties to the dispute had been married from 1969 to 1980, during which period a girl was born (1973). Three years after their divorce, the ex-wife married the father of her ex-husband. Twenty years later, as the patriarch passed away, his son sought the annulment of the marriage, thus respecting the period of 30 years provided for in arts 184 and 187 of the Civil Code. Unsurprisingly, the court of appeal granted his request, noting also that the marriage had caused in the mind of the child from the first marriage 'a regrettable confusion between his father and grandfather'.

In support of the appeal, the wife relied on the ruling *B and L v United Kingdom*,[45] where the ECtHR ruled that English law, which holds a comparable solution to French law, infringes the very essence of the right to marriage guaranteed by Art 12 of the European Convention on Human Rights. This argument failed to convince the Court of Cassation, which based the appeal decision, on its own motion, not upon approval of Art 12 but that of Art 8 of the Convention, considering that the nullity of marriage was 'an unjustified interference with the right to respect for his private and family life, since this union, celebrated without opposition, lasted over twenty years'.

The choice of Art 8 to the detriment of Art 12 is by no means anecdotal. Indeed, it allows senior judges generally not to call into question art 161 of the Civil Code on behalf of the right to marry but to avoid instead its application in particular cases, because of its effects on the wife's private and family life lasting over 20 years. This is the message of the official statement issued by the Court of Cassation: 'Because of its foundation, the significance of this decision is limited to the particular case at issue. The principle of the prohibition of marriage between affines is not called into question.'

This decision is crucial because the Court of Cassation shifts, for the first time, from a conventionality verification in *abstracto* and *erga omnes* of the content of the law, to a verification *in concreto* and *relative* to its application to the present case: It does not rule out French law as a whole but disregards the same for particular cases.

In our view, such an approach appears highly questionable.

First, the Court of Cassation refused to apply a perfectly clear law (marriage between affines is void and can be attacked for 30 years), even though this rule, both in principle and in regard to the period, was solemnly reaffirmed by the legislature in 2013 (reform of marriage) and 2008 (reform of the regulation).

Secondly, the ad hoc non-application of the law, far from tempering the Court's boldness, adds legal uncertainty to usurpation of power. In apparent contradiction with its overarching purpose, ie to ensure compliance and unity

---

179; note F Chénedé; Family Law 2014. Comm 1, obs J-R Binet; JCP 2014 93, notes Mr Lamarche; Gaz Pal 21 January 2014, 30, obs J Casey; RLDC February 2014. 45, obs F Dekeuwer-Défossez.

[45] 13 September 2005 (req No 36536/02).

of law enforcement in the country, the Court of Cassation trampled the equality of citizens before the law by allowing the judge to ignore it in particular cases.

Finally, relying upon human rights cannot justify such an attitude. Indeed, even if we can understand the somewhat childish behaviour in regretting the limits imposed by law and society, it suffices to remind ourselves that such constraints to our goodwill and rights are nothing more than the expression of the rights of others and/or the public interest. Our case serves as a good example. While it is certain that the nullity of a marriage ordered by law violated the wife's individual rights, both on a personal (right to marry, right to respect for family life) and economic level (right to peaceful enjoyment of possessions), it is no less obvious that the Praetorian confirmation of its validity would be detrimental to those of the son (ex-husband), even those of the grandson, and after them, to whatever the legislature deemed to be the common interest.

By giving precedence, in a particular case, to its personal assessment over the arbitration made by the elected representatives of the people in 2008 and 2013, the First Civil Chamber of the Court of Cassation has certainly crossed a line.

GERMANY

REFORMING THE LAW ON PARENTAL RESPONSIBILITY

*Luise Hauschild**

Résumé

En 2012, en Allemagne, un enfant sur trois est né hors mariage, ce qui témoigne des changements importants dans une société moderne et nécessite que la loi soit adaptée. Ce chapitre présente une vue d'ensemble des modifications récentes mises en place par la loi allemande en matière d'autorité parentale. En 2010, la Cour constitutionnelle fédérale allemande a jugé les anciennes dispositions légales inconstitutionnelles car elles étaient contraires aux droits fondamentaux des pères célibataires. Suite à cette décision, les tribunaux ont écarté ces dispositions et le législateur allemand a été contraint de modifier la loi. Ce chapitre présente les principaux objectifs et principes de la nouvelle loi et examine les critiques de la doctrine et de la pratique.

I INTRODUCTION

One out of three children in Germany was born out of wedlock in 2012,[1] marking significant changes in modern society that the law has to be adapted to. The following chapter will present an overview of the recently implemented changes in German law on parental responsibility. As broached briefly in the 2013 *International Survey*,[2] the German Federal Constitutional Court found the former statutory regulation unconstitutional in 2010 due to basic rights violations to the detriment of unmarried fathers. Following the ruling, courts were prohibited from applying the provision and German legislators became obligated to change the written law accordingly. This chapter will outline the main goals and principles of the new provisions as well as examine the criticism that is voiced by scholars and practitioners alike.

---

* PhD-candidate and research assistant at the Institute of German, European and International Family Law, University of Bonn.

1 *Statistisches Bundesamt* 'Geburten in Deutschland' (2012), 18.

2 See Hauschild 'Abolition of Legal Discrimination and Implications of Highest-Court Case-law' in Bill Atkin (ed) *International Survey of Family Law 2013 Edition* (Jordan Publishing Limited, 2013) 133 at 134 et seq.

II THE NEW LAW

As of 19 May 2013, the reformed law[3] entered into force, amending in particular ss 1626a and 1672 of the German Civil Code.[4] Moreover, s 155a has been added to the Family Procedural Act,[5] introducing a simplified procedure in disputes on parental responsibility under s 1626a.

(a) Sole parental responsibility of the mother as a general rule

When a child is born out of wedlock, German law assigns sole parental responsibility to the mother.[6] This basic rule as such was not challenged by the Federal Constitutional Court which recognised that children can be born into a multitude of circumstances, some of which do not allow for joint parental responsibility. Furthermore, the court took as a basis the assumption that the mother is the only certain attachment figure the child is provided with upon the child's birth. Therefore, assigning sole parental responsibility to her was deemed constitutional.[7] However, by law at the time of the ruling, the child's father was only able to gain joint parental responsibility along with the mother if both parents issued joint declarations of responsibility or married each other.[8] Moreover, sole custody could be awarded to the father only if the mother gave her consent and the child's welfare was best served by this arrangement.[9] As a consequence, in the case of refusal on the mother's part, the father had no means to challenge her sole parental responsibility. In particular, there were no legal grounds on which judicial review could have been applied for. This was deemed unconstitutional by the Federal Constitutional Court, which found this situation to be in violation of the father's rights.

The German Constitutional Court's decision sprouted a lively debate during which the very foundations of the law on parental responsibility were challenged. Many favoured the basic concept of assigning joint parental responsibility to both parents upon the birth of the child, no matter whether the parents were married at the time or not. Adopted by several European countries, this solution was deemed to best take into account the fact that parental responsibility is not only a right, but also a duty assigned to the parent.[10] However, this road was not taken as the legislators believed that assigning joint parental responsibility to both parents by law would not be appropriate due to the fact that it would be forced upon them even if they were

---

3 *Gesetz zur Reform der elterlichen Sorge nicht miteinander verheirateter Eltern* of 16 April 2013, BGBl (*Bundesgesetzblatt*) I 2013, 795.

4 *Bürgerliches Gesetzbuch* (BGB).

5 *Familienverfahrensgesetz* (FamFG).

6 German Civil Code, s 1626a(3).

7 German Federal Constitutional Court (*Bundesverfassungsgericht – BVerfG*) NJW (*Neue Juristische Wochenschrift*) 2010, 3008 et seq.

8 German Civil Code, s 1626a (1) no 1 and 2.

9 German Civil Code, s 1672 (now abolished).

10 Dethloff 'Familienrecht' (CH Beck, 2012) § 13 at 32.

completely unable to come to a mutual understanding.[11] As a consequence, the legislators' first prerogative was to incorporate the possibility of judicial review into the written law.

(b) Possibility of judicial review

Besides issuing joint declarations of parental responsibility and getting married, the law now recognises a third option, allowing the family court to award joint parental responsibility to both unmarried parents fully or in part.[12] The necessary court proceedings are set in motion if one parent submits an application for joint parental responsibility.[13] This may also be the mother if she wishes to actively involve the father in the child's upbringing. However, this does not enable her to actually force parental responsibility upon the father if he is unwilling to take it. The court may award joint parental responsibility to both parents only if the transfer is not inconsistent with the child's best interests. Consequently, it is sufficient if the court cannot see any reasons why awarding joint parental responsibility would prove detrimental to the child in the particular case at hand (so-called 'negative evaluation'). This means that the court does not have to find that shared parental responsibility will actually benefit the child more than sole parental responsibility of the mother (so-called 'positive evaluation'). In this context, it should be noted that German law differentiates between several ways in which the child's best interests have to be considered. Other provisions require that changes made to the child's legal arrangements be most conducive to its best interests.[14] This lower threshold within the scope of s 1626a is based on the notion that, as a general rule, joint parental responsibility corresponds to the child's need to develop relationships with both parents.[15]

According to s 1671 of the German Civil Code, the father may now gain sole parental responsibility against the mother's wishes if the court finds that this is most conducive to the child's best interests. While the cases regulated by s 1626a only gain an additional holder of parental responsibility, the holder of parental responsibility changes in cases governed by s 1671; the court is therefore required to find that this change serves the best interests of the child.[16] Consequently, the threshold set by law is much higher within the scope of s 1671.

---

11 Federal Ministry of Justice, Draft Bill (*Referentenentwurf*), 15; earlier: German Federal Constitutional Court (*Bundesverfassungsgericht – BVerfG*) *Familie Partnerschaft Recht* (FPR) 2003, 205 et seq.

12 German Civil Code, s 1626a (1) no 3.

13 German Civil Code, s 1626a (2) sentence 1.

14 Eg German Civil Code, s 1671 (1) no 2.

15 *Entwurf eines Gesetzes zur Reform der elterlichen Sorge nicht miteinander verheirateter Eltern* of 17 October 2012, BT-Drs 17/11048, 12.

16 Heilmann 'Die Reform des Sorgerechts nicht miteinander verheirateter Eltern – Das Ende eines Irrwegs?' *Neue Juristische Wochenschrift* (NJW) 2013, 1473 at 1478.

(c) Simplified procedure according to s 155a of the Family Procedural Act

The procedural requirements corresponding to s 1626(2) – but not s 1671 – of the German Civil Code are governed by the newly inserted s 155a of the Family Procedural Act. According to this provision, the court serves the respondent and sets a period of time during which the application for joint parental responsibility has to be objected to. If the mother is the respondent, this period of time may not end sooner than 6 weeks after the child's birth. During this time the respondent may state facts indicating that parental responsibility would, in fact, contradict the child's best interests. If no such reasons are given, a legal presumption is created that joint parental responsibility is not inconsistent with the child's best interests.[17] In this case, the family court shall apply a simplified procedure that is conducted exclusively in writing.[18] As a consequence, neither the parents nor representatives of the youth welfare department (Jugendamt) have to be heard in person.

This is deemed highly problematic for two principal reasons: first, the simplified procedure shall be applied whenever the declaration of parental responsibility is not disputed, but in order for an objection to be effective, the reasons given must be specified. It does not suffice, for example, if the mother states that the relationship with the father had been brief or she did not wish to engage in further contact with him.[19] It is doubtful whether all parents are able to eloquently state those facts.[20] In any case, something as important as a decision considering parental responsibility for a child should not solely depend on a parent's written account of facts.[21] Section 1626a also states that, in addition to the reasons given by the opposing parent, no such reasons may be otherwise manifest. However, the only way the court is able to determine whether this is the case is relying on the parents' statements. This holds especially true since the youth welfare department is not involved either.[22] Secondly, the period of 6 weeks that has to elapse as the deadline before a possible objection is considered too short. Given the psychological and other difficulties that can arise when a child is born, it is feared that the necessity to deal with legal matters of this importance could overwhelm the mother.[23]

---

17 German Civil Code, s 1626a (2) sentence 2.

18 Family Procedural Act, s 155a (3) sentence 1.

19 Lambrecht and Bosse 'Plädoyer für eine gemeinsame elterliche Sorge' *Zeitschrift für Rechtspolitik* (ZRP) 2013, 9 at 10.

20 Lambrecht and Bosse 'Plädoyer für eine gemeinsame elterliche Sorge' *Zeitschrift für Rechtspolitik* (ZRP) 2013, 9 at 10.

21 Huber and Antomo 'Zum Inkrafttreten der Neuregelung der elterlichen Sorge nicht miteinander verheirateter Eltern' *Familienrechtszeitung* (FamRZ) 2013, 665 at 669.

22 Lambrecht and Bosse 'Plädoyer für eine gemeinsame elterliche Sorge' *Zeitschrift für Rechtspolitik* (ZPR) 2013, 9 at 10.

23 Huber and Antomo 'Zum Inkrafttreten der Neuregelung der elterlichen Sorge nicht miteinander verheirateter Eltern' *Familienrechtszeitung* (FamRZ) 2013, 665 at 669.

However, if reasons are given after the deadline's expiration but before the court's decision becomes effective, they will still have to be considered by the court.[24]

Once the application remains undisputed, the simplified procedure shall be applied. This means that a decision can be reached without an actual court hearing. Therefore, rightful criticism arose, stating that a decision considering the most important part of the child's legal situation should not be based solely on the records available to the court. Hearing the parents personally on this matter is deemed far too important to be abdicatable.[25] Because of these defects, it is very possible that the child's best interests are not being considered closely enough[26] for simple lack of information. In order to conduct a comprehensive evaluation of the child's best interests, the court needs to assess whether the parents' personal relationship allows for mutual decisions concerning the child's upbringing. The judges' personal impression of the parents is very important in this context.

The wording of s 155a allows for some discretion by the courts when considering whether the simplified procedure is applied. Originally, the wording stated that the courts were obligated to proceed accordingly, which was changed shortly before the provisions entered into force. As a consequence, even under the new law, it is possible for the court to apply the usual procedure if, for example, there are indications that the respondent is unable to properly voice his or her concerns.[27] Therefore there is hope that this problematic procedural provision will be applied with consideration by the courts on a case-by-case basis.[28]

III PROSPECTS

The new provisions show that – despite the fact that the changes have become necessary due to basic rights' violations to the detriment of the father – the child's best interests need to remain the primary focus of the law. They cannot be ignored whenever a decision concerning parental responsibility is to be made. It is doubtful whether the new provisions will serve to ensure this. The specific amendments are perceived to be stemming from political compromise rather than careful conception. The law on parental responsibility has been amended often in the past and due to this, some call it a 'patchwork of legal

---

24 Heilmann 'Die Reform des Sorgerechts nicht miteinander verheirateter Eltern – Das Ende eines Irrwegs?' *Neue Juristische Wochenschrift* (NJW) 2013, 1473 at 1476.

25 Salgo 'Ein Zwischenruf zum Regierungsentwurf eines Gesetzes zur Reform der elterlichen Sorge nicht miteinander verheirateter Eltern' *Familie Partnerschaft Recht* (FPR) 2012, 409 at 410.

26 Similar: Fahl '§ 1626a BGB und das Kindeswohl' *Neue Zeitschrift für Familienrecht* (NZFam) 2014, 155 at 156.

27 *Beschlussempfehlung und Bericht des Rechtsausschusses* of 30 January 2013, BT-Drs 17/12198, 4.

28 Huber and Antomo 'Zum Inkrafttreten der Neuregelung der elterlichen Sorge nicht miteinander verheirateter Eltern' *Familienrechtszeitung* (FamRZ) 2013, 665 at 670.

approaches'[29] that requires a comprehensive reform. The new provisions will be subject to review 5 years after entering into force. Then the Department of Justice will have to assess court decisions based on the new regulations and submit their report to the German Parliament. In light of the overwhelming criticism and subsequent lack of enthusiasm the new law was greeted with, its practical implications will certainly be of great interest.

29 Heilmann 'Die Reform des Sorgerechts nicht miteinander verheirateter Eltern – Das Ende eines Irrwegs?' *Neue Juristische Wochenschrift* (NJW) 2013, 1473 at 1478.

HONG KONG

REFORMING HONG KONG FAMILY LAW: STILL MORE TO DO?

*Anne Scully-Hill**

Résumé

Au cours de l'année 2013, l'évolution des mœurs et de la jurisprudence en matière familiale ont permis l'appréhension de nouvelles situations par le droit de la famille Hongkongais.

Plusieurs problématiques ont été abordées en matière familiale. Il a été question du mariage des personnes transsexuelles ayant acquis un nouveau genre, de la notion de « propriété matrimoniale » telle qu'envisagée par les auxiliaires de justice dans les dossiers dont ils acceptent la charge, et de l'audition des enfants mineurs dès lors qu'il doit être statué sur le droit de garde.

Globalement, ces changements ont promu l'égalité et le respect des personnes vulnérables, tout comme le droit des minorités.

Néanmoins, l'institution judiciaire peut constituer un frein à la mise en œuvre de ces changements. En effet, les évolutions du droit de la famille Hongkongais ne peuvent être initiées que par l'administration du Pays. Tel est le cas pour la création d'une Commission des enfants ou l'introduction d'une réforme d'ampleur en droit de la famille.

L'engagement du pouvoir exécutif s'avère être nécessaire afin de réformer en profondeur le droit de la famille Hongkongais.

I INTRODUCTION

Key areas of family law in which there has been significant development over the past year are the eligibility of post-operative transsexuals to marry in their acquired gender, the meaning of 'matrimonial property' in ancillary relief cases, and changes to the way in which the courts hear child custody cases. Each of these changes might be said to represent considerable positive reform of Hong Kong's family law. However, a closer look suggests that despite recent legal innovations, the need for further change may remain.

---

* Associate Professor, The Chinese University of Hong Kong.

II MARRIAGE: THE MEANING OF 'MAN' AND 'WOMAN': *W V REGISTRAR OF MARRIAGES*[1]

Section 40 of the Marriage Ordinance (MO)[2] incorporates the English case of *Hyde v Hyde*[3] into Hong Kong law so that a valid marriage is 'the voluntary union for life of one man and one woman to the exclusion of all others'. This is reiterated by s 20(1)(d) of the Matrimonial Causes Ordinance (MCO)[4] which states that a marriage will be void if the parties are not respectively male and female. This latter section is materially identical to the English legislative provision in s 1(c) of the Nullity of Marriage Act 1971. That statutory provision was introduced into English law following the decision in *Corbett v Corbett (otherwise Ashley)*[5] which held that parties to a lawful marriage be respectively male and female as designated at birth, based upon their biological characteristics.

At the handover of sovereignty of Hong Kong to China in 1997, Hong Kong's 'mini-constitution', the Basic Law, negotiated by the United Kingdom and China, came into force. This document not only sets up the constitutional arrangements for Hong Kong for the 50 years following the handover but also protects Hong Kong residents' fundamental rights, including the right to marry.[6] All legislation must now comply with the terms of the Basic Law or will be declared invalid. Within this constitutional framework, s 40 of the MO was the subject of an application for judicial review by a Hong Kong permanent resident who was registered at birth as male, was diagnosed with gender identity disorder, had undergone psychiatric assessment and hormonal treatment, lived for a period of 'real life experience' as a woman and was subsequently given sex reassignment surgery in Hong Kong.[7] The Hospital Authority then certified that the applicant's gender should now be recognised as female. The applicant's educational records, identity card and passport were amended to show her new name and acquired gender. However, when the applicant, W, sought confirmation from the Registrar of Marriages that she could marry her boyfriend in her acquired female gender, the Registrar stated that s 40 of the MO contemplated heterosexual marriage, for which purpose gender was determined by biological sex at birth.

The applicant challenged the lawfulness of the Registrar's decision, making two alternative submissions:

(i) the Registrar had misconstrued the meaning of 'male' and 'female' under the MO, specifically in s 40 and also in s 21 which repeats the *Hyde v Hyde* formula as part of the necessary words of the marriage ceremony;

---

1 [2013] 3 HKLRD 90.
2 Cap 181.
3 (1866) LR 1 P&D 130.
4 Cap 179.
5 [1971] P 83.
6 Basic Law Article 37. See also the Bill of Rights Ordinance Article 19.
7 *W v Registrar of Marriages* [2013] 3 HKLRD 90.

(ii) and if not, the provisions were unconstitutional in that they infringed her right to marry under art 37 of the Basic Law and/or art 19(2) of the Hong Kong Bill of Rights.[8]

The applicant lost at first instance and in the Court of Appeal before finally winning in the Court of Final Appeal.

On the first ground, the Court of Final Appeal found that the Registrar had not misconstrued the terms 'male' and 'female'. The court held the legislative intent in enacting s 20(1)(d) of the MCO to reflect the judgment in *Corbett* was sufficiently clear and so 'female' as used in the legislation was to be defined by biological sex fixed at birth. As s 40 of the MO covered in essence the same meaning as s 20(1)(d) of the MCO, the Registrar had not been mistaken in his interpretation.[9]

On the second ground of appeal however, the appellant was successful: the *Corbett* meaning of 'female' was based on biological aspects only of gender identity. This may have been acceptable at the time of that decision but with developments in medical knowledge it was now generally accepted that psychological aspects of gender identity were equally significant. The *Corbett* criteria were therefore an incomplete means of determining gender and as such represented an unlawful restriction on the right to marry and thus unconstitutional.[10] In so finding, the Court looked at the line of English cases following *Corbett,* via the European Court of Human Rights decision in *Goodwin v UK*[11] and culminating in the *Bellinger* decision in which the House of Lords, noting *Goodwin*, declared the relevant English legislation incompatible with the plaintiff's rights.[12] *Goodwin* stated that, whilst the member states were entitled to a margin of appreciation in how they defined access to marriage, this margin was to be understood within the context of medical and social developments over the intervening years from *Corbett* to the present.[13] In particular the European Court of Human Rights questioned the continued 'adequacy of purely biological criteria for determining sexual identity'[14] and found it lacking. The Court of Final Appeal agreed with *Goodwin*, declaring that the *Corbett* perspective had been driven by a view of marriage based on procreation but '[i]n present day multi-cultural Hong Kong ... procreation is no longer (if it ever was) regarded as essential to marriage. There is certainly no justification for regarding the ability to engage in procreative sexual intercourse as a sine qua non for marriage and thus as the premise for deducing purely biological criteria for ascertaining a person's sex for marriage purposes'.[15] Thus, '[t]o apply statutory criteria which are

---

8 Ibid at para 3.
9 Ibid at Section E of the judgment.
10 Ibid at paras 103–106.
11 (2002) 35 EHRR 18.
12 *Bellinger v Bellinger* [2003] 2 AC 467.
13 Cited in *Bellinger* at paras 20–24.
14 Cited in *W v Registrar for Marriages* [2013] 3 HKLRD 90 at para 77.
15 *W v Registrar for Marriages* [2013] 3 HKLRD 90 at para 89.

incomplete and which do not permit a full assessment of the sexual identity of an individual for the purposes of determining whether such person has the right to marry is inconsistent with, and constitutes a failure to give proper effect to the constitutional right guaranteed by art. 37 and art. 19(2)'.[16]

The court further found that the challenged statutory sections were unlawful because their meaning infringed the 'very essence of the right to marry'.[17] That is, because of the restrictive statutory meaning of 'man' and 'woman' the applicant, designated male at birth, was precluded from marrying a man, but in her acquired, and irreversible, female gender, and feeling herself in that gender to have a heterosexual sexuality, she wanted only to marry a man.

The Court of Final Appeal's decision further differed from the decisions of the courts below in that it did not find societal consensus on a changed meaning of 'male' and 'female' necessary. That societal consensus was necessary to establish change in legal meaning was an argument transplanted from the United Kingdom and European case-law. However, the Court of Final Appeal rejected this argument. It distinguished Hong Kong from Europe, suggesting that consensus may be of greater relevance in the regional setting of the European Court, where judges adjudicate on margin of appreciation within member states, than in Hong Kong where the judges interpret Hong Kong's own, singular constitution. Furthermore it held that, while consensus may be justification for extending the scope of a right, 'reliance on the absence of a majority consensus as a reason for rejecting a minority's claim is inimical in principle to fundamental rights'.[18]

What does this decision mean for the future of Hong Kong's law on marriage? The Court of Final Appeal made declarations of legislative invalidity in the applicant's favour but suspended the operation of the declaration for 12 months[19] to allow the Hong Kong Administration to introduce Basic Law-compliant legislation. The Court of Final Appeal indicated that the English Gender Recognition Act 2004 might serve as a possible template. In December 2013 a briefing document outlining draft proposals was submitted to the Legislative Council Panel on Security.[20] Those proposals now form the Marriage (Amendment) Bill 2014 and are limited to amending the meaning of 'male' and 'female' under s 20(1)(d) of the MCO, s 40 and s 21 of the MO to include Hospital Authority-certified post-operative transsexuals whose gender has been amended on their HK Identity Cards. The proposals have been criticised by the Equal Opportunities Commission, amongst others, for being 'inhumane' by requiring transsexuals to undergo reassignment surgery in order to fall within the proposed statutory amendment.[21]

---

16 Ibid at para 106.
17 Ibid at paras 108–112.
18 Ibid at para 116.
19 Ibid at para 150.
20 LC Paper No CB(2)588/13-14(08).
21 See www.chinadailyasia.com/hknews/2014-04/03/content_15128628.html.

However, the proposals are potentially an interim step only, designed to address the problem of legislative invalidity within the 12-month suspension period. The Administration has stated that 'it attaches great importance to the Court of Final Appeal's comments and problems facing transsexuals'[22] and has set up a working group to consider what further action should be taken. Whilst the group's terms of reference have not yet been set, it seems unlikely it will address reform beyond that relevant to transsexualism. Despite media coverage during the case which questioned whether a finding in W's favour would extend the way in which society conceives of marriage sufficiently to open the door to the possibility of same-sex marriage in Hong Kong,[23] briefing documents on the current legislative proposals expressly curtail discussion of same-sex marriage: indeed, the Court of Final Appeal's own statement that the facts of the case did not give rise to considerations of same-sex marriage is relied upon in support of the limited legislative reform proposal and it is noted further in the briefing document that nothing in the legislative proposals will change the heterosexual nature of marriage in Hong Kong.[24] This prompts one to ask whether, in the absence of an open debate about equality, gender and sexual identity, and the concept of 'family', the legislative amendment prompted by *W* is really about respect for minority rights and equality or simply the minimum measure necessary for the Executive to comply with a judicial order?

III ANCILLARY RELIEF: EQUAL DIVISION AND MATRIMONIAL PROPERTY

In late 2010 the Court of Final Appeal in *LKW v DD*[25] adopted the English *White v White*[26] 'yardstick of equality' in relation to determining what constitutes a fair ancillary relief award in cases where there is wealth surplus to meeting the couple's needs. The judgment set out the four steps to be taken by the court within the parameters of the guiding statutory framework: s 7(1) of the Matrimonial Proceedings and Property Ordinance (MPPO).[27] First, the

---

22 LC Paper No CB(2)588/13-14(08) at para 12.
23 *South China Morning Post*, 8 August 2010.
24 LC Paper No CB(2)588/13-14(08) at para 10.
25 [2010] HKEC 1727.
26 [2001] 1 AC 596.
27 Cap 192, s 7(1): 'It shall be the duty of the court in deciding whether to exercise its powers under section 4, 6 or 6A in relation to a party to the marriage and, if so, in what manner, to have regard to the conduct of the parties and all the circumstances of the case including the following matters, that is to say–
(a) the income, earning capacity, property and other financial resources which each of the parties to the marriage has or is likely to have in the foreseeable future;
(b) the financial needs, obligations and responsibilities which each of the parties to the marriage has or is likely to have in the foreseeable future;
(c) the standard of living enjoyed by the family before the breakdown of the marriage;
(d) the age of each party to the marriage and the duration of the marriage;
(e) any physical or mental disability of either of the parties to the marriage;
(f) the contributions made by each of the parties to the welfare of the family, including any contribution made by looking after the home or caring for the family;
(g) in the case of proceedings for divorce or nullity of marriage, the value to either of the parties

identification of the available assets: under s 7(1)(a), the court must have regard to 'the income, earning capacity, property and other financial resources' which each of the parties 'has or is likely to have in the foreseeable future'. Secondly, to assess the parties' financial needs, those needs being 'generously interpreted'. Thirdly, where there are assets surplus to the parties' needs the court will apply the 'sharing principle' so that the assets are divided equally between the parties unless there is a good reason to depart from equal division. Lastly, the court will identify good reasons, if any, for departure such as the various factors given under s 7(1) or the source of an asset: for example, an asset acquired during the life of the marriage by one party as a gift or an inheritance. The weight given to the source of the asset is within the discretion of the judge and considerations such as the duration of the marriage and any intermingling of property between the spouses will be relevant.[28]

While *LKW v DD* gives judicial recognition to the equal contributions of homemakers and breadwinners, parties themselves have sought to avoid the resulting equal division, either by claiming exceptional contribution or by trying to ring-fence assets as being unavailable for inclusion in the 'matrimonial pot'. In *KEWS v NCHC*[29] the Court of Final Appeal was asked to identify 'available assets' in circumstances where the husband had very little in the way of his own assets and the wife, suffering from considerable health issues, also had little or no assets of her own. However, both parties came from families that had previously supported them financially; the husband's family in particular was presented to the court as having consistently given considerable financial support to the couple during their marriage and as being able to do so with relative ease. The court was asked by the wife to make an award which would go beyond the husband's own assets and would 'judiciously encourage' his parents to continue to support him so that he could comply with the court order. The court determined that it was within its powers to shape such an award so long as it merely encouraged rather than put pressure[30] on the third party:[31]

> '... the court must look at the reality of the situation and have regard to matters of substance and not just form. In looking at reality, the court can take into account not only what a party actually has, but also what might reasonably be made available to him or her if a request for assistance were to be made ... in looking at what may occur in the foreseeable future, past conduct is often a useful guide ... Having ascertained the extent of the financial assistance provided by the third party and then finding on the evidence on a balance of probabilities that there is a likelihood of the continuation of such financial assistance in the foreseeable future, the court is then in a position in law first to take this into account in the identification of the financial resources of the parties and secondly, in determining

---

to the marriage of any benefit (for example, a pension) which, by reason of the dissolution or annulment of the marriage, that party will lose the chance of acquiring.'

28 [2010] HKEC 1727 at paras 89–94.

29 [2013] HKEC 226.

30 Ibid at para 50.

31 Ibid at para 12.

the appropriate ancillary relief to be granted. This is an approach that is entirely consistent with the court's duty under s 7(1) of the MPPO.'

Taking third party assets into account is not novel. Previously in English cases where beneficial ownership of assets by one spouse, either of company shares or property held under a discretionary trust, could be proven, or a bad faith attempt to dispose of assets by transferring legal ownership could be shown, then the relevant assets could be taken into account.[32] Indeed the court cited the English case, *TL v ML,* as authority that:[33]

> 'If the court is satisfied on the balance of probabilities that an outsider will provide money to meet an award that a party cannot meet from his absolute property then the court can, if it is fair to do so, make an award on that footing. But if it is clear that the outsider, being a person who has only historically supplied bounty, will not, reasonably or unreasonably, come to the aid of the payer then there is precious little the court can do about it.'

However, the judgment in *TL* went on to distinguish between a third party who is a member of the party's family and who has historically been supportive in an ad hoc manner and a third party who is in a fiduciary relationship with the party. In the former there is only a hope of assistance; in the latter the reason for the existence of the relationship is, at least in some way, to provide benefit for the party. The English court did 'not believe that it would be proper or principled ... to make an award that ranges outside the assets or income that are H's as of right'.[34] In *KEWS* the Hong Kong court did just that and thus, arguably, has gone beyond the factual matrices of the English decisions on which it relied, establishing a broad test which focuses on past provision of support and relies on what can, at best, be speculation as to whether those assets will continue to be provided. *KEWS* then is perhaps the high water mark of 'available assets'.

The question of 'available assets' arose again in the District Court in *LML v LSC.*[35] The wife applied for litigation funding from the husband. The husband's father, having previously supported the parties, expressly refused to continue to support either party. Given the father's unambiguous position, the judge made an award to the wife but only in the form, and on the basis that, the husband personally had the means to meet the order. Clarity of intent on the part of the third party donor was significant in this case and, it may be presumed, will be equally significant going forward for those third parties wishing to put themselves outside of the court's consideration of available assets under the *KEWS* test. Furthermore, in *CWYW v CPLA*[36] the court suggested that there should be not only clarity of intent but, to ensure third parties are not brought within the court's purview, ideally there should also be clear communication of

32 For example see *Prest v Petrodel Resources Ltd* [2013] 3 WLR 1, *Browne v Browne* [1989] 1 FLR 291; *Thomas v Thomas* [1996] 2 FCR 544.

33 [2006] 1 FLR 1263 at para 101.

34 Ibid at para 109.

35 [2013] HKEC 1235.

36 [2013] HKEC 1648.

that intent. In this case the court had to determine whether a sum given by the husband's parents to enable the couple to purchase a matrimonial home, had been a gift, and therefore an 'available asset', or a loan. The judge found, on the basis of the evidence from the husband, his mother and even on the wife's evidence as to her mother-in-law's considerable input as to which property to buy, that this was a loan. The judge however noted the lack of clear communication to the wife about the nature of the financial help and that subsequent confusion 'might have been avoided had the parties simply been more straightforward about it in the first place'.

That clarity of intent and communication thereof will become increasingly important in the aftermath of the *KEWS* judgment was confirmed in *TCWF v LKKS No 1*[37] in which the Court of Appeal handed down its judgment in the early days of January 2014. This case concerned a husband from an exceptionally wealthy family and seemed to fall squarely within the *LKW v DD* 'equal division' method. The case was complicated by the wife's allegations against the husband and his father of forgery of documents with the intent of disposing of assets previously held by the husband and by the father's counter-allegations of fraud on the part of the wife in cancelling, along with the husband, a marital property agreement (MPA) that the father had asked for and believed still to be in place.[38] Nonetheless, the key question remained: what assets were available to be included in the 'matrimonial pot'?

The main portion of the husband's assets was referred to as the 'Japanese business': real estate holdings in Japan developed by the husband with seed money and further financial support from his tycoon businessman father.[39] The trial judge, applying the *LKW v DD* framework, had found that the 'Japanese business' was an available asset, that therefore there were assets surplus to the needs of the parties, applied the sharing principle and made an order that the wife be paid a lump sum of approximately HK$1.4 billion. This represented around 20% of the assets identified by the judge as being available to the parties and the departure from equal sharing was due to the father's very significant support for the development of the business.[40]

The Court of Appeal disagreed, finding that the 'Japanese business' was not an available asset for two reasons. First, the father held a considerable degree of control over the business. The father had initially made a gift to the son of several billion Japanese Yen to start the business. This was recorded under a 'Framework Agreement' which entitled the father to a call option on shares subscribed to by the son in the Japanese companies which comprised the 'Japanese business'. If the father chose to exercise the right to the call option, the option would be executed on payment by the father of one US dollar to the son. Further, Special Articles were appended to the articles of incorporation of the companies requiring the father's consent for an extensive range of actions.

---

37 [2014] HKEC 47.
38 Ibid at para 19–22.
39 Ibid at paras 129–137.
40 Ibid at para 231.

In sum, the viability of the son's business was subject to the overarching control of the father. Secondly, the trial judge had been wrong not to consider the father's likely action on the breakdown of the marriage. In various ways the father had clearly communicated his intent that he would exercise his right to the call option in the event of a divorce between the parties and that in general he wished to protect the 'dynastic wealth' from claims by 'another man's daughter'.[41] The Court of Appeal concluded that these factors meant the 'Japanese business' was a 'non-asset' and therefore not available for distribution by the court. This is in contrast to a 'non-matrimonial asset' which is an asset owned by husband or wife and so may be considered but which, by virtue of its source, may ultimately be excluded from sharing.[42] As a consequence, the Court of Appeal found that the husband's remaining resources were insufficient to meet the needs of both spouses 'generously interpreted' and that therefore this was not a *LKW v DD* 'sharing' case but a 'needs' case. The wife's needs were calculated at HK$524.5 million and the husband was ordered to pay this sum less the wife's assets and some costs.

The Court of Final Appeal's landmark decision in *LKW v DD* introduced equality of spousal contribution into the language of Hong Kong law, and thus confirms marriage as a partnership of equals. However, the subsequent judicial decisions as to what exactly is 'in the matrimonial pot' to be shared equally could well mean that the ideal of equality is soon to be supplanted by the pragmatism of certainty, in the form of calls, as in England, for enforceable MPAs. Moreover, in the Hong Kong context, given the implications of the *KEWS* judgment, extended families may seek to ensure that any financial dealings amongst family members and their spouses are included in the MPA in order to protect dynastic interests.

IV CHANGING CHILD LAW? THE CHILDREN'S DISPUTE RESOLUTION PILOT SCHEME, THE UNCRC AND THE LAW REFORM COMMISSION

In late 2012 the Judiciary introduced Practice Direction 15.13: The Children's Dispute Resolution Pilot Scheme (CDR). This mirrors, and is to be read in conjunction with, the existing Practice Direction 15.11: The Financial Dispute Resolution Pilot Scheme (FDR).[43] The stated aim of CDR is:[44]

> 'to support mothers and fathers, so that they are able to effectively parent their children post separation or divorce. The intention is to ensure that whilst the best interests of children remains the court's paramount concern, that lasting

---

41 Ibid at para 206.

42 Ibid at paras 167–168.

43 Despite having first been introduced in 2003, revised in 2007 and again in 2012, the Financial Dispute Resolution Practice Direction is still titled a Pilot Scheme; the reasons for this are not entirely clear. The Children's Dispute Resolution Practice Direction is currently in its first incarnation.

44 Practice Direction 15.13 at para 3.

> agreements concerning children are obtained quickly and in a less adversarial atmosphere. The focus is therefore on the children's best interests together with the duties and responsibilities of their parents.'

CDR applies from October 2012 onwards to new disputes arising about children except those pertaining to adoption. The CDR process comprises a 'Children's Appointment' which serves to facilitate case management and promote a settlement ethos. This is followed by the CDR hearing at which the aim is to reach agreement on disputed issues. Parties' attendance at all hearings is mandatory. The process is not 'without prejudice', unlike the FDR, and so in the event of failure to reach agreement the judge running the CDR may also preside at the subsequent trial.

There are three particular points of interest in the CDR. First, parties must complete a 'Form J': the Children's Form.[45] The form is akin to a Parenting Plan and is designed to focus parents' minds on relevant issues, possible outcomes and the child's best interests. Secondly, the judge may direct that the parties attend counselling, a parenting education programme or stipulate third party involvement to help the parties.[46] This, like the Children's Form, is innovative and aims to diminish hostility and give parties the skills they need to co-parent effectively after separation. Lastly, where a child has requested to see the judge, the judge may speak directly to the child, if she deems it appropriate.[47]

The Judiciary have put in place a procedure which does much to implement Hong Kong's obligations as a signatory to the United Nations Convention on the Rights of the Child, particularly in terms of hearing the child's voice and focusing on the best interests of the child. In contrast, the Hong Kong Administration has this year been the subject of less than positive comment from the UN Committee on the Rights of the Child for, inter alia, its failure to provide children with an independent channel through which to voice their views. In its 'Concluding observations on the combined third and fourth periodic reports of China'[48] the UNCRC made the following observations with regard to Hong Kong's failure to act on past recommendations, and specifically on the need for an independent Children's Commission:

> '19. ... The Committee is further concerned that, contrary to its previous recommendations and despite the motion by the Legislative Council in June 2007 to establish an independent children's commission, Hong Kong, China has not taken any steps to set up such a commission.
>
> 20. The Committee draws attention to its general comment No. 2 (2002) and reiterates its recommendation that the State party promptly establish independent national human rights institutions on the mainland and in Hong Kong, China and Macao, China in accordance with the Paris Principles in order to systematically

---

45 Ibid at para 7.
46 Ibid at para 10.
47 Ibid.
48 16 September–4 October 2013: CRC/C/CHN/CO/3-4.

> and independently monitor and evaluate progress in the implementation of the Convention at the national and local levels and to deal with complaints from children in a child-sensitive and expeditious manner. The Committee, furthermore, recommends that a children's commission or another independent human rights institution with a clear mandate to monitor children's rights be established in Hong Kong, China and provided with adequate financial, human and technical resources.'

The Administration has consistently refused to establish a Children's Commission, despite creating Commissions for Women, Youth and the Elderly. Indeed it responded in October 2013 to this most recent round of Concluding Observations by saying that in 2007 it had established the Family Council which is tasked 'to examine, from the family perspective, the Government's policies and programmes designed for different age and gender sectors (including children)'.[49] This however is not the same as the child-centric model provided by a Children's Commission, as might be demonstrated by the fact that even the Bureau placed 'including children' in brackets when describing the role of the Family Council in its own press release.

Again in contrast to the Judiciary's innovative CDR, the Administration has also yet to implement proposals for the reform of the law on child custody. The Law Reform Commission published a report in 2005 recommending the abolition of the current regime of custody orders and the introduction of a system of parental responsibility based on that introduced by the English Children Act 1989.[50] The aim is to encourage both parents to maintain their relationships with their children after separation, whether they live with the child or not, and to diminish hostility in custody cases by removing the sense that the custodial parent is the 'winner' and the non-custodial parent the 'loser'. To date there have been two rounds of consultation, most recently in April 2012.[51] Nonetheless, despite general support for the reform proposals,[52] there is as yet no draft legislation.

V CONCLUSION

Over the course of 2013 formerly inviolable aspects of Hong Kong's family law, including the definition of marriage, have successfully been challenged or reformed to promote equality: equality between the sexes, for minority groups

---

49 www.info.gov.hk/gia/general/201310/09/P201310090635.htm: Press Release from Constitutional & Mainland Affairs Bureau.

50 www.hkreform.gov.hk/en/publications/raccess.htm.

51 www.lwb.gov.hk/eng/public_consultation/Custody_Consultation.htm.

52 The support for the reform has included overt judicial support: see *SMM v TWM* [2010] HKEC 895, where Cheung JA said at para 29: 'It should be noted that the Hong Kong Law Reform Commission Report on Child Custody and Access (7th March 2005) has recommended changes to the GMO, by, among other things, replacing custody orders with residence and contact orders. There has been no implementation of the recommendation yet. In my view the Administration should make a serious effort in implementing the recommendations by legislation soon.'

and for the previously disempowered, including children. Much of the change has come by virtue of steps taken and decisions made by the judiciary. Mostly this has been positive but the ongoing evolution of case-law has meant that landmark equality-based decisions such as *LKW v DD* have been applied in circumstances that may well result in greater change in future; change that will replace the 'yardstick of equality' with the certainty of MPAs. Time will tell.

Nonetheless, given Hong Kong's common law tradition, there is a limit to the change that can be effected by the judiciary alone, particularly because the courts are limited by the facts of the cases that come before them and must act within the bounds of existing legislation, unless that legislation is shown to be in contradiction of the Basic Law. Furthermore, some aspects of family law can only be delivered by the Administration: for example, the establishment of a Children's Commission or the introduction of far-reaching, and necessary, reforms to legislation across the spectrum of family law. It is therefore in the area of the Executive's engagement with family law that real change is needed in order to give Hong Kong a family law fit for families living in the 21st century.

INDIA

SURROGACY FOR SINGLE AND UNMARRIED FOREIGN PERSONS: A CHALLENGE UNDER INDIAN LAW

*Anil Malhotra and Ranjit Malhotra**

Résumé

La procréation assistée, incluant la gestation pour autrui, est en vogue en Inde depuis 1978, alors qu'on estime a 200 000 le nombre de cliniques qui, à travers le pays, offrent actuellement des services d'insémination artificielle, de fertilisation in vitro et de gestation pour autrui. Dans la foulée de leur contribution à l'édition 2013 du International Survey, les auteurs discutent de quelques récentes décisions en matière de gestation pour autrui, notamment dans des cas qui impliquent des étrangers, et ils analysent les réponses juridiques dominantes en la matière. Des directives administratives émises le 9 juillet 2012 par le ministère de l'Intérieur, stipulent que seuls les hommes et le femmes mariés depuis au moins deux ans peuvent soumettre une demande de visa médical en vue d'une gestation pour autrui projetée en Inde. Cette exigence affecte directement les célibataires et les couples non mariés qui voudraient obtenir de tels visas. Les auteurs sont d'avis que ces directives sont illégales et qu'elles sortent du champ de compétence du ministère.

I INTRODUCTION

At a time when the world's first test-tube baby (Louise Brown, born in 1978 in the United Kingdom), has now herself become a mother and high profile international adoptions by celebrities like Madonna and Angelina Jolie are glorifying international adoption, India does not lag behind. Noted Indian film actress Sushmita Sen inspires single women both in India and abroad to adopt children breaking conventional taboos and age-old practices. As a result, orphan girls are finding mothers in India and abroad. However, genuine adoptive foreign and non-resident would-be parents too are pitted against an insurmountable wall. Child adoption in India is a complicated issue. It is over-burdened with knotty legal processes and complicated lengthy procedures for those who want to give a new home and a new life to the reported 12 million Indian orphans. Even though the Indian Constitution ordains it to be a sovereign, socialist, secular, democratic republic, 65 years of independence have

---

* Malhotra & Malhotra Associates, India (Email: anilmalhotra1960@gmail.com).

not given a comprehensive adoption law applicable to all its citizens, irrespective of the religion they profess or the country they live in as non-resident Indians (NRIs), persons of Indian origin (PIOs) or overseas citizens of India (OCIs). Thus, those who cannot by law adopt and can be appointed only as guardians under personal Indian laws turn to options of IVF clinics or rent surrogate wombs. It is from this perspective that India now needs to adopt another law to turn to actual reality the dreams of those who live abroad rather than turning to unhappy and sometimes unethical practices.

A silent revolutionary change is fast heralding a new dawn in the matter of inter-country adoptions. However, the plethora of Indian laws does not improve the plight of 12 million orphaned children in India who need adoptive parents. The Guardian and Wards Act (GWA), 1890 permits guardianship and not adoption. The Hindu Adoption and Maintenance Act (HAMA), 1956 does not permit non-Hindus to adopt a Hindu child. Requirements of immigration create further hurdles even after adoption. May be the urge to be a parent has now taken over in the form of 'embryo adoption' whereby fertilized sperms and eggs developed into an embryo are successfully implanted in Indian clinics and nurtured by foreign mothers in their homeland ensuring hassle-free adoption of Indian embryos without complicated procedures. Technology has overtaken law.

As a background to the practice of surrogacy today, mythological surrogate mothers in the past are well known in India. Yashoda played mother to Krishna though Devki and Vasudeva were the biological parents. Likewise, in Indian mythology Gandhari made Dhritarashtra the proud father of 100 children though he had no biological relation with them. The primordial urge to have a biological child of one's own flesh, blood and DNA aided with technology and the purchasing power of money coupled with the Indian entrepreneurial spirit has generated the 'reproductive tourism industry'. This comes as a boon to childless couples all round the world. Clinically called 'assisted reproductive technology' (ART), it has been in vogue in India since 1978 and today an estimated 200,000 clinics across the country offer artificial insemination, in vitro fertilization (IVF) and surrogacy.

II RECENT CASES

In the decision of the Supreme Court on 29 September 2008 in *Baby Manji Yamada v Union of India & Anr*,[1] a Japanese baby Manji, born on 25 July 2008 to an Indian surrogate mother with IVF technology upon fertilization of her Japanese parents' eggs and sperm in Tokyo and the embryo being implanted in Ahmedabad, triggered off complex, knotty issues. The Japanese biological parents got divorced and the mother disowned the infant upon her birth in India. The grandmother of the infant petitioned the Supreme Court challenging the directions given by the Rajasthan High Court relating to the reproduction

1 *Baby Manji Yamada v Union of India & Anr* AIR 2009 SC 84.

and custody of baby Manji Yamada. The grandmother's request to the Apex Court for permission for the infant to travel with her and for issuance of a passport under consideration with the central government was directed to be disposed of expeditiously. Following the directions of the Supreme Court, the Regional Passport Office in Jaipur issued an 'Identity Certificate' to the baby. Hence, there was an implied recognition of the status of single parent since the divorced father as a single parent got custody of the child after which he flew to Japan.

In another case, Israeli gay couple, Yonatan and Omer Gher, became parents in India on 12 October 2008, when their child was conceived with the help of a Mumbai based surrogate mother in a fertility clinic in Bandra. It is reported that a 3.8 kilo baby boy was born to them at Hiranandani Hospital in Powai (Mumbai). Reportedly, Yonatan and Omer had been together for the past seven years and had decided to start a family. But since Israel reportedly does not allow same-sex couples to adopt or have a surrogate child, India became their choice to find a surrogate mother. Yonatan and Omer reportedly first came to Mumbai in January 2008 for an IVF cycle when Yonatan is stated to have donated his sperm. Thereafter, they selected an anonymous 'mother'. Accordingly, the child was conceived with the help of a Mumbai based surrogate mother in a fertility clinic in Bandra. After the child was born, the gay couple left for Israel with the child. In this case, a same-sex couple was able to achieve surrogacy arrangements in India without any objections.

Subsequently, in the year 2010, another gay couple, Dan Goldberg and Arnon Angel from Israel to whom twin baby boys were born in Mumbai from an Indian surrogate mother, were stranded in India after the refusal of the Jerusalem Family Court to allow a paternity test to initiate the process for Israeli citizenship for the twins. The issue was debated in The Knesset (Israeli Parliament) where Prime Minister Benjamin Netanyahu had to intervene so that the infants could be brought to Israel following legal procedures. Ultimately, on appeal, the Jerusalem District Court accepted the claim that it was in the best interest to hold a DNA paternity test to establish that Dan Goldberg was the father of the twin baby boys, Itai and Liron. The DNA samples of Goldberg and the twins were brought to the Sheeba Medical Centre in Israel which established Goldberg as the father of the infants. After being stranded in Mumbai for over 3 months, Goldberg and his twin baby boys returned to Israel in May 2010 after being granted Israeli passports.

After a frustrating two year legal battle in India on behalf of their surrogate sons – Nikolas and Leonard – German couple, Jan Balaz and Susan Anna Lohald, got to go to Germany after the Supreme Court of India intervened and in a Court hearing on 26 May 2010, the Indian Government agreed to provide them exit permits. The twin babies were born in the State of Gujarat in January 2008 and registered as children born of a foreign couple through an Indian surrogate mother. Upon being declined birth certificates, Jan Balaz moved the Gujarat High Court which ruled that since the surrogate mother is an Indian national, therefore, the children would also be treated as Indian nationals and would be entitled to Indian passports. However, the Government of India challenged this decision stating that the toddlers, being surrogate children, could not be granted Indian citizenship, which rendered the twins stateless as they got neither German nor Indian citizenship. The German authorities had also refused visas to the twins on the ground that German law did not recognize surrogacy as a means to parenthood. Ultimately, Jan Balaz and Susan Lohald went through an inter-country adoption process in India, upon which the Indian Government granted exit permits to the German surrogate twins to enable their journey back home to Germany.

III PREVAILING LEGAL POSITION

In the absence of any law to govern surrogacy the Indian Council of Medical Research (ICMR) issued *National Guidelines for Accreditation, Supervision and Regulation of ART Clinics in India, 2005* [Guidelines], to check the malpractices of ART. The preface of these guidelines clearly states that in the Indian context, where barrenness is looked down upon, infertile parents look up to ART as the last resort for parenthood. These Guidelines are said to be widely publicized, discussed and debated by experts and practitioners of ART involving over 4000 participants. Para 3.5.2 of these Guidelines, setting out 'Desirable Practices/Prohibited Scenarios', states that there would be no bar to use of ART by single women and the child thus born will have all the legal rights in relation to the woman or the man, as follows:

> '3.5.2 There would be no bar to the use of ART by a single woman who wishes to have a child, and no ART clinic may refuse to offer its services to the above, provided other criteria mentioned in this document are satisfied. The child thus born will have all the legal rights on the woman or the man.'

A reading of the above indicates that these Guidelines clearly permit single parents to commission surrogacy and prescribe that no ART clinic may refuse to offer it services to single women/men. These Guidelines are still prevalent to date.

In a phenomenal exercise to legalise commercial surrogacy, the Assisted Reproductive Technology (Regulation) Bill and Rules, 2010 (ART Bill), a draft bill prepared by a 12-member committee including experts from ICMR, medical specialists and other experts from the Ministry of Health and Family Welfare, Government of India, has been posted online for feedback. Also earlier floated in 2008 for comment, the ART Bill is stated to be an Act to provide for a national framework for the regulation and supervision of assisted reproductive echnology and matters connected therewith or incidental thereto as a unique proposed law to be put before the Indian Parliament. Abetting surrogacy, it legalizes commercial surrogacy stating that the surrogate mother may receive monetary compensation and will relinquish all parental rights. Single parents can also have children using a surrogate mother. Foreigners, upon registration with their embassy, can seek surrogate arrangements. It also legalizes commercial surrogacy for single persons and married or unmarried couples, stating that the surrogate mother shall enter into a legally enforceable surrogacy agreement. The 2010 draft bill states that foreigners or NRIs coming to India to rent a womb shall have to submit documentation confirming that their country of residence recognizes surrogacy as legal and that it will give citizenship to the child born through the surrogacy agreement from an Indian mother.

The proposed bill which is called an Act 'to provide for a national framework for the regulation and supervision of assisted reproductive technology and matters connected therewith or incidental thereto' provides the constitution of a National Advisory Board for Assisted Reproductive Technology, comprising of members not exceeding 21, whose functions are confined to promoting the cause of reproductive technology. The salient details are:

- The new Assisted Reproductive Technology (Regulation) Bill and Rules, 2010, legalises commercial surrogacy, stating that the surrogate mother may receive monetary compensation for carrying the child in addition to health-care and treatment expenses during pregnancy.
- Both the couple or individual seeking surrogacy through the use of ART, and the surrogate mother shall enter into a surrogacy agreement which shall be legally enforceable.
- The surrogate mother will relinquish all parental rights over the child once the amount is transferred and birth certificates will be in the name of commissioning parent/s.
- The prescribed age-limit for a surrogate mother is between 21–35 years. The proposed bill also states that no women shall act as a surrogate mother for more than five children including her own.
- Single persons, men or women or single parents, and unmarried couples can also have children using a surrogate mother. In the case of a single man or a woman, the baby will be his or her legitimate child. A child born to an unmarried couple using a surrogate mother and with the consent of both the parties shall be their legitimate child.
- All foreigners seeking infertility treatment in India will first have to register with their embassy. Their notarised statement will then have to be handed over to the treating doctor. The foreign couple will also state whom the child should be entrusted to in case of an eventuality such as a genetic parent's death.
- A foreigner or foreign couple not resident in India or an NRI individual or couple seeking surrogacy in India shall appoint the local guardian legally responsible for taking care of the surrogate child during and after pregnancy.
- The party seeking surrogacy must ensure and establish to the ART clinic that the party would be able to take the child born through surrogacy outside India to the country of the party's origin or residence as the case may be.

- A child born out of surrogacy shall be the legitimate child of both the parties or of the single man or woman as the case may be. The birth certificate will contain the name or names of the genetic parent or parents (as the case may be) who sought such use. If parties get divorced or separated, the child shall be the legitimate child of the couple. The birth certificate of a child born through the use of ART shall contain the name or names of the parent or parents, as the case may be, who sought such use.
- If a foreigner or a foreign couple seeks sperm or egg donation, or surrogacy, in India, and a child is born as a consequence, the child, even though born in India, shall not be an Indian citizen.
- Foreigners or NRIs coming to India seeking surrogacy in India shall appoint a local guardian who will be legally responsible for taking care of the surrogate during and after pregnancy until the child is delivered to the foreigner or foreign couple or the local guardian. Further, the party seeking surrogacy must ensure and establish through proper documentation that the country of their origin permits surrogacy and that the child born through surrogacy in India will be permitted entry in the country of their origin as a biological child of the commissioning couple/individual. If the foreign party seeking surrogacy fails to take delivery of the child born to the surrogate mother, the local guardian will be legally obliged to take the child and be free to hand over the child to an adoption agency. In the case of adoption or the legal guardian having to bring up the child in India, the child will be given Indian citizenship.
- Surrogacy may be recommended for patients for whom it is medically impossible/undesirable to carry a baby to term.
- ART clinics must not advertise surrogacy arrangements. The responsibility should rest with the couple or a semen bank.
- ART clinic must ensure that the surrogate woman satisfies all the testable criteria (no sexually transmitted or communicable disease that may endanger the pregnancy).
- A prospective surrogate mother must be tested for HIV and shown to be seronegative for this virus just before embryo transfer.

A reading of the above bill, which recognises the rights of individuals as well as couples to commission surrogacy by approaching ART clinics, identifies even unmarried couples and individuals besides married couples as prospective parents. The ART Bill in Chapter IV dealing with duties of an ART clinic clearly stipulates that individuals or couples will be provided with professional counselling, knowledge about choices of treatment and other information to create awareness about ART. Likewise, Chapter VII dealing with Rights and Duties of Patients, Donors, Surrogates and Children in Section 32 states as follows:

'32.Rights and duties of patients –

> (1)Subject to the provisions of this Act and the rules and regulations made thereunder, assisted reproductive technology shall be available to all persons including single persons, married couples and unmarried couples.'

It is abundantly clear that the competent authority in the matter has spelt out the legislative intent of making ART available to all persons including single persons, married couples and unmarried couples. This policy decision is already clearly in vogue today in the shape of the ICMR Guidelines. Hence, surrogacy and ART, which is a subject-matter to be dealt with as a portfolio, have been appropriately dealt with by the Ministry of Health and Family Welfare, which is competent to take decisions with respect to issues pertaining to them.

It is also pertinent to point out that the Law Commission of India in Report No 228 of August 2009 entitled '*Need for legislation to regulate assisted reproductive technology clinics as well as rights and obligations of parties to a surrogacy*'[2] has given its views on surrogacy achieved through ART. After examining all the issues and various viewpoints besides discussing actual cases of foreign nationals who have utilised ART for commissioning surrogacy in India, various recommendations have been made by the Law Commission of India in its said Report and in Chapter IV of the Report dealing with conclusions and recommendations, para 4.2 reads in the following terms:

> '4.2 The draft Bill prepared by the ICMR is full of lacunae, nay, it is incomplete. However, it is a beacon to move forward in the direction of preparing legislation to regulate not only ART clinics but rights and obligations of all the parties to a surrogacy including rights of the surrogate child. Most important points in regard to the rights and obligations of the parties to a surrogacy and rights of the surrogate child the proposed legislation should include may be stated as under:
>
> [1] to [3] xxxxxx
>
> [4] One of the intended parents should be a donor as well, because the bond of love and affection with a child primarily emanates from biological relationship. Also, the chances of various children of child-abuse, which have been noticed in case of adoption, will be reduced. In case the intended parent is single, he or she should be a donor to be able to have a surrogacy child. Otherwise, adoption is the way to have a child which is resorted to if biological (natural) parents and adoptive parents are different.'

Clearly, the Law Commission of India which recommends that a pragmatic approach should be adopted by legalising altruistic surrogacy arrangements recommends and approves of surrogacy arrangements for single parents as well. Hence, there is no move indicated by the Law Commission to propose that single parents should not be allowed use of ART for surrogacy and its position is to the contrary.

---

2 http://lawcommissionofindia.nic.in/reports/report228.pdf. Law Commission of India, New Delhi, 2009.

IV LAW FOR ENTRY OF FOREIGNERS INTO INDIA

The entry, stay and exit of foreigners into India is governed by the Passport (Entry into India) Act, 1920, the Passport (Entry into India) Rules, 1950, the Foreigners Act, 1946, and the Registration of Foreigners Rules, 1992. The Policies, Acts and Rules relating to entry of foreigners into India are framed by the Ministry of Home Affairs, Government of India. To facilitate an easy understanding of purposes of the above Acts, a tabulated account is as below:

1	The Passport (Entry in India) Act, 1920 and the Passport (Entry into India) Rules, 1950.	It prescribes specific authorization of foreign nationals on their valid travel documents/passports for allowing entry into the country. Under this Act and the Rules made thereunder, the foreigners coming to India are required to get visa from Indian Missions/Posts
2	The Foreigners Act, 1946 and the Foreigners Order, 1948.	It regulates the entry of foreigners into India, their presence therein and their departure therefrom.
3	The Registration of Foreigners Act, 1939 and the Registration of Foreigners Rules, 1992.	It mandates that certain categories of foreigners whose intended stay in India is for more than the specified period, or as provided in their visa authorization, are required to get themselves registered with the Registration Officer.

From a reading of the above, it is evident that under the provisions, the Ministry of Home Affairs can make provisions for prohibiting, regulating or restricting the entry, departure and presence of foreigners into India by enacting justifiable and legitimate Visa Rules and Regulations with a classification for different purposes. The basic principles of the visa policy is non-discrimination. Though the decision to grant a visa in a particular category may depend upon requisite conditions, it cannot create an unjust classification by debarring any category of persons from being ineligible to apply for a particular category of a specific visa in violation of Articles 14 & 21 of the Constitution of India which provides equality of laws besides protection of life and personal liberty to all persons including foreign nationals.

V BAR ON SINGLE AND UNMARRIED PERSONS

Even though the Ministry of Health and Family Welfare does not prohibit or debar single persons or unmarried couples from commissioning surrogacy through ART in India, the Ministry of Home Affairs by administrative guidelines dated 9 July 2012 has stipulated that only married foreign men and women whose marriage has sustained for at least two years would be eligible to apply for medical visas for the purposes of surrogacy in India. Consequently, all single persons and unmarried couples have been declared ineligible from even applying for a visa in any category whatsoever for coming to India for the purposes of surrogacy. This unreasonable classification, violative of Articles 14 and 21 of the Constitution, has no nexus with the object sought to be achieved and directly curtails/ interferes with 'the right of reproductive autonomy' which is a facet of the 'right of privacy' under Article 21 of the Constitution. No reasons, justification, logic or explanation is forthcoming as to why single persons or unmarried couples have been debarred and excluded from commissioning surrogacy in India. None of the grounds made out in the impugned Guidelines justify or validate this arbitrary exclusion and unfounded ineligibility of single persons/unmarried couples who have been debarred from even applying for visas to India even though the ICMR Guidelines, ART Bill, and Law Commission Report do not contemplate any such restrictions.

VI INDIAN LAW ON SURROGACY

(a) Surrogacy in India is legitimate for married couples/unmarried couples/single persons because no Indian law prohibits surrogacy. To determine the legality of surrogacy agreements, the Indian Contract Act would apply and thereafter the enforceability of any such agreement would be within the domain of Section 9 of The Indian Code of Civil Procedure (CPC). Alternatively, the biological parent/s can also move an application under the Guardian and Wards Act seeking an order of appointment to be declared the guardian of the surrogate children.

(b) In the absence of any law to govern surrogacy, the 2005 ICMR Guidelines apply to all couples/single persons. Under para 3.10.1 a child born through surrogacy must be adopted by the genetic (biological parents). However, this may not be possible in the case of non-Hindu foreign parents who cannot adopt in India but can be appointed as guardians under the Guardians and Wards Act. Under para 3.5.2 of the ICMR Guidelines, there would no bar to the use of ART by single women and a child born will have all the legal rights as against the woman or man as the case may be.

(c) Under Section 10 of the Indian Contract Act, 1872 all agreements are contracts, if they are made by free consent of parties competent to contract, are for a lawful consideration, are with a lawful object, and are not expressly declared to be void. Therefore, if any surrogacy agreement of a married/unmarried couple/single parent satisfies these conditions, it is an enforceable contract. Thereafter, under Section 9 of the Code of Civil Procedure, 1908 prescribing that the Courts may try all civil suits unless barred, it can be the subject of a civil suit before a civil Court to establish all/any issues relating to the surrogacy agreement and for a declaration/injunction for the relief prayed for.

(d) Other issues, which have now cropped up for opinion, are as to whether a single parent or unmarried couple can be considered to be the custodial parent of a surrogate child. As of today, it may be stated that a single parent or unmarried couple can be considered to be the custodial parent by virtue of being the genetic or biological father of the surrogate child born out of a surrogacy arrangement. Japanese baby Manji Yamada's case[3] and the Israel gay couple's case who fathered the child in India are clear examples to establish that this is possible. Under paras 3.16.1 and 3.5.2 of the 2005 ICMR Guidelines dealing with legitimacy of children born through ART (which were the basis of the claim in the Japanese baby's case in the Supreme Court), this claim can be made. However, only in a petition for guardianship under GWA and/or in a suit for declaration in a civil Court can the exclusive custodial rights be adjudicated by a court of competent jurisdiction upon appreciation of the evidence and considering all claims made in this regard.

(e) What would be the status of divorced biological parents in respect of the custody of a surrogate child? Essentially, this is a question which will require determination in accordance with the surrogacy agreement between the parties. There would be apparently no bar to either of the divorced parents claiming custody of a surrogate child if the other parent does not claim the same. However, if the custody is contested, it may require adjudication by a court of competent jurisdiction under the provisions of Civil Procedure Code.

(f) Would biological parent/s be considered the legal parent of the children? In answer to this question it can be stated that the biological parents would be considered to be the legal parents of the children by virtue of the surrogacy agreement executed between the parties and the surrogate mother. Under para 3.16.1 of the 2005 ICMR Guidelines dealing with legitimacy of the child born through ART, it is stated that 'a child born through ART shall be presumed to be the legitimate child of the couple, born within wedlock, with consent of both the spouses, and with all the attendant rights of parentage, support and inheritance'. Under para 3.5.2 of the ICMR Guidelines a single man/woman can have a child by ART through surrogacy. Even in the 2010 Draft Bill and Rules, a child born to a married couple, an unmarried couple, a single parent or a single man or woman shall be the legitimate child of the couple, man or woman as the case may be.

(g) The Law Commission of India Report, in its conclusions and recommendations in para 4.2 (4), stated that, where the intended parent is single, he or she should be a donor to be able to have a child through surrogacy. Clearly, in the views of the Law Commission, there is a clear recommendation to the Government of India to permit surrogacy for single parents.

(h) POSITION OF LAW UNDER THE 2010 BILL

Under the ART Regulation Bill 2010, 'assisted reproductive technology', 'surrogacy', 'gamete', and 'surrogacy agreement' have been defined as follows:

---

[3] JT 2008 (11) SC 150.

> 'assisted reproductive technology', with its grammatical variations and cognate expressions, means all techniques that attempt to obtain a pregnancy by handling or manipulating the sperm or the oocyte outside the human body, and transferring the gamete or the embryo into the reproductive tract;
>
> 'surrogacy', means an arrangement in which a woman agrees to a pregnancy, achieved through assisted reproductive technology, in which neither of the gametes belong to her or her husband, with the intention to carry it and hand over the child to the person or persons for whom she is acting as a surrogate;
>
> 'gamete', means sperm and oocyte (that is egg);
>
> 'surrogacy agreement', means a contract between the person(s) availing of assisted reproductive technology and the surrogate mother.

Chapter 2 of the Bill describes the constitution of authorities to regulate assisted reproductive technology. A 21-Member National Advisory Board comprising of various experts is sought to be created with functions to promote assisted reproductive technology related issues. State Boards are recommended in States and State Registration authorities are sought to be created for procedural purposes. Proceedings before the National and State Boards are deemed to be Civil Court Proceedings for limited purposes and are sought to be treated as Judicial Proceedings even though the constitution of the National or State Advisory Board have no Judicial Officers, Judges or Designated Courts as constituents.

Chapter 3 of the Bill sets out procedures for registration and complaints in respect of assisted reproductive technology clinics. Chapter 4 sets out the duties of such clinics. Chapter 5 talks of sourcing, storage, handling and record-keeping for gametes, embryos and surrogates. Chapter 6 relates to 'Regulation of Research on Embryos'.

Chapter 7 discusses 'Rights and Duties of Patients, Donors, Surrogates and Children' in extenso. The rights and duties are well defined and determination of the status of the child is laid out in detail irrespective of the status of parties as a couple, as an unmarried couple, as single parents, gay parents or otherwise. The duty to take children born through surrogacy from India to the country of origin or residence of the biological parents or residence is spelt out.

Chapter 8 is about 'Offences and Penalties' for contravening the provisions of the Act and Chapter 9 in the miscellaneous part covers maintenance of records, power to search and seize, power to make regulations and rules. The Bill is stated to be in addition to and not in derogation with any other law for the time being in force.

The National and State Advisory Boards are only authorities which will promote ART, surrogacy arrangements and related procedures. The proceedings of these Boards have been deemed to be 'Judicial Proceedings' before civil courts for limited purposes.

VII CHALLENGES TO RESTRICTIONS ON SURROGACY BY SINGLE AND UNMARRIED FOREIGN PERSONS

In the face of the above factual and legal position enunciated by the ICMR Guidelines, ART Bill, 2010 and the Law Commission Report, which reflect the policies, decisions and the mandate of the Ministry of Health and Family Welfare, who are competent and authorised to opine and decide such matters, there is no bar on surrogacy in India for foreign single persons or foreign unmarried couples. In fact, there is no statutory law made or policy decision taken by the Ministry of Health and Family Welfare, whereby surrogacy by single persons or unmarried couples of foreign nationality has been prohibited or banned. In the face of such a factual situation, the Ministry of Home Affairs has no authority under law to lay down the Guidelines restricting surrogacy only to married foreign couples with two years of marriage. Hence, the Guidelines to this extent are illegal, without any authority of law and are beyond the competence of the Ministry of Home Affairs. Therefore, para 2(i) restricting surrogacy only to married foreign men and women is illegal without sanction of law and it is beyond the competence to make such guidelines. The following points reinforce this position.

(a) Under the 1920 Act read with the 1950 Rules, the Foreigners Act, 1946, read with the Foreigners Order, 1948 and the provisions of the Registration of Foreigners Act, 1939 read with the Registration of Foreigners Rules, 1992, it is beyond the competence, authority and power of the Ministry of Home Affairs to debar, prohibit and exclude single persons and unmarried couples from commissioning surrogacy agreements through ART. Under the above provisions the entry of foreigners into India can be regulated and conditions can be prescribed for their stay in India on valid travel documents thereby restricting the entry, departure and presence of foreigners into India by making justifiable and legitimate visa regulations. This however cannot empower the Ministry of Home Affairs to restrict the entry of single persons or unmarried couples into India for surrogacy purposes. It is beyond the competence and authority of the Ministry of Home Affairs to lay down any guidelines to impose any such restriction debarring single persons or unmarried couples from coming to India for surrogacy. No such power or authority is vested in law under the enactments/rules whereby such a bar can be imposed by the Ministry of Home Affairs. Therefore, para 2(i) of the Guidelines is illegal and ultra vires the provisions of Articles 14 and 21 of the Constitution of India since they take away the protection of law and invade the right of privacy guaranteed to people and thus deserve to be struck down.

(b) The Ministry of Home Affairs cannot interfere with and abrogate to itself functions and powers which cannot be attributed to it. The Ministry of Health and Family Welfare is the competent authority which is duly empowered under the Rules of Business of the Government of India to enact laws and make policies which are within the domain of their appropriate functions dealing with subjects under the portfolio of Health and Family Welfare. The Ministry of Home Affairs cannot take over the functions of the Ministry of Health and Family Welfare nor the Indian Council of Medical Research. A team of dedicated experts has enacted the Guidelines and a similar team of experts has made the ART Bill. The Law Commission itself through its members appointed by the Government of India has given its recommendations to the Government in its Report. The Ministry of Home Affairs therefore cannot start taking decisions beyond its competence and start dictating policies which run contrary to the mandate of the Ministry of Health and Family Welfare. Therefore, para 2(i) of the Guidelines are illegal, beyond the authority of law and are ultra vires the provisions of the Constitution of India since the Ministry of Home Affairs cannot usurp powers and functions of the Ministry of Health and Family Welfare, to make policies in contravention of Articles 14 and 21 of the Constitution of India.

(c) Para 2(i) of the Guidelines infringe upon the right of privacy guaranteed to foreign nationals under Article 21 of the Constitution of India. The right of privacy is a facet of Article 21 of the Constitution. The Apex Court in *Govind v State of MP*[4] and *Kharak Singh v State of UP*[5] have identified the right of privacy as a constitutionally protected right as a facet of Article 21 of the Constitution. The personal decision of a single person about the birth of a baby through surrogacy called 'the right of reproductive autonomy' is a facet of the right of privacy guaranteed under Article 21 of the Constitution. Thus, the right of privacy of a single person to be free from unwarranted governmental intrusion into matters fundamentally affecting a single man and his decision to bear or beget a child through surrogacy cannot be taken away by the Ministry of Home Affairs, particularly when the Ministry of Health and Family Welfare does not bar or restrict any such right of single persons or unmarried couples. Therefore, this discriminatory policy advocated by the Ministry of Home Affairs infringes the right of privacy under Article 21 of the Constitution, has no nexus with the objects sought to be achieved and is invading the protection of Article 14 of the Constitution. Para 2(i) of the Guidelines directly curtails and interferes with the right to make a decision in the matter of procreation by banning a man's entry into India for the purposes of surrogacy as a single person. Such a restriction is constitutionally impermissible in the context of the rights guaranteed under Article 21 of the Constitution. Hence, para 2(i) of the Guidelines are ultra vires the provisions Article 21 of the Constitution and deserve to be struck down since they create an unreasonable restriction on the right of procreation by surrogacy of a single parent in India.

(d) Para 2(i) of the Guidelines create an unjust and arbitrary classification by meting out unequal treatment to equals. In effect, para 2(i) of the Guidelines discriminates between Indian nationals and foreign citizens by debarring only foreign single men/women and unmarried couples from commissioning surrogacy through ART in India. Single Indian men/women or unmarried Indian couples can commission surrogacy

---

4 *Govind v State of MP* AIR 1975 SC 1378.

5 *Kharak Singh v State of UP* AIR 1963 SC 1295.

arrangements in India through ART since the Ministry of Health and Family Welfare does not impose any bar or embargo on surrogacy for single Indian nationals or unmarried Indian couples. Hence, the ban by the Ministry of Home Affairs on foreign single persons or foreign unmarried couples from commissioning surrogacy in India through ART is wholly unjustified, illegal, arbitrary, discriminatory and is a wholly unjust classification, not authorised by any law. The Ministry of Home Affairs which has no competence to take a policy decision on the subject of surrogacy within the domain and portfolio of Health and Family Welfare has thus made a policy decision which beyond the law. This classification treats equals unequally thereby violating equality of law and equal protection of laws. Foreign nationals, overseas citizens of India, and person of Indian Origin cannot be discriminated in the matter of surrogacy upon comparision with Indian nationals. Therefore, imposing a ban on surrogacy by foreign single persons or foreign unmarried couples under para 2(i) of the Guidelines amounts to an unreasonable, unjust and arbitrary classification which has no nexus with the object sought to be achieved. The purpose, if any, of protection and other suggested beneficial factors are adequately taken care of by the other conditions contained in para 2 of the Guidelines. Therefore there is no justification for imposing restrictions on foreign single persons or unmarried couples in commissioning surrogacy in India.

(e) It is not within the authority of the Ministry of Home Affairs to enact rules, make policies or issue guidelines which impinge upon the functions, duties, portfolios and subjects of the Ministry of Health and Family Welfare. At the most, the Ministry of Home Affairs can issue Guidelines requiring all foreign applicants to apply for a medical visa if they want to visit India for purposes of surrogacy through ART. However, it is not within the domain or authority of the Ministry of Home Affairs to issue guidelines to state that single foreign persons or unmarried couples will not be granted medical visas for purposes of surrogacy in India. Such a guideline contained in para 2(i) of the Guidelines is unjustified, beyond the authority of law and violates Article 14 of the Constitution. This classification is wholly beyond the scope of power of the Ministry of Home Affairs. Therefore, the Guidelines are not authorised by virtue of the powers conferred upon the Ministry of Home Affairs under the Enactments, Orders and Rules.

(f) Para 2(i) of the Guidelines clearly militates against the position of law stated by the Apex Court in *Baby Manji Yamda*, the judgment in which a single divorced parent was allowed to take a surrogate baby to Japan.[6]

From a reading of the above, it is evident that under the above provisions, the Ministry of Home Affairs can make provisions for prohibiting, regulating or restricting the entry, departure and presence of foreigners into India by enacting justifiable and legitimate visa rules and regulations with a classification for different purposes. The basic principles of the visa policy is non-discrimination.

---

[6] See above n 1.

The decision to grant a visa in a particular category may depend upon requisite conditions, but it cannot create an unjust classification by debarring any category of persons from being ineligible to apply for a particular category of a specific visa in violation of Articles 14 and 21 of The Constitution of India which provides equality of laws besides protection of life and personal liberty to all persons including foreign nationals.

VIII CONCLUSION: AN UNJUSTIFIED BAR ON SINGLE AND UNMARRIED PERSONS

Even though the Ministry of Health and Family Welfare does not prohibit or debar single persons or unmarried couples from commissioning surrogacy through ART in India, the Ministry of Home Affairs by administrative guidelines dated 9 July 2012, has stipulated that only married foreign men and women whose marriage has sustained for at least two years are eligible to apply for medical visas for the purposes of surrogacy in India. Consequently, all single persons and unmarried couples have been declared ineligible from even applying for a visa in any category whatsoever for coming to India for the purposes of surrogacy. This unreasonable classification violative of Articles 14 and 21 of the Constitution has no nexus with the object sought to be achieved and directly interferes with 'the right of reproductive autonomy' which is a facet of the 'right of privacy' under Article 21 of the Constitution. No reasons, justification, logic or explanation are forthcoming as to why single persons or unmarried couples have been debarred and excluded from commissioning surrogacy in India. None of the grounds made out in the impugned Guidelines justifies or validates the arbitrary exclusion and unfounded ineglibility of single persons and unmarried couples who have been debarred from even applying for visas to India, and the ICMR Guidelines, the ART Bill, and the Law Commission Report do not contemplate any such restrictions.

IRAN AND ARMENIA

RIGHTS AND OBLIGATIONS OF SPOUSES IN IRAN'S LAW COMPARED WITH ARMENIA'S

Grigor Bekmezyan and Gholam Reza Shirazi[*]

Résumé

L'objet de cette étude est de faire état des droits et des obligations des époux dans le cadre du droit de la famille en Iran et en Arménie. Les deux systèmes prévoient que l'amour et le respect mutuels ainsi que l'obligation de secours et d'assistance constituent les fondements de l'institution de la famille et que toute ingérence intentionnelle dans les affaires familiales est prohibée. En droit arménien, les biens acquis pendant la vie commune sont la propriété commune des époux, sauf convention contraire, alors qu'en droit iranien ces biens appartiennent au mari, sauf stipulation contraire. En Iran, même si la responsabilité de l'entretien de la famille repose sur les épaules des maris, les femmes travaillent souvent à l'extérieur du foyer et contribuent ainsi aux dépenses.

I INTRODUCTION

According to the social history of mankind, humans have to adjust to the rules and regulations in order to coexist. Diversity of cultures, rituals and customs has resulted in a diversity of structures and frameworks into which conventions fall. The family is the smallest social unit with the minimum members being wife and husband. This institution is the oldest and most important social group, the notion of which has continued to change throughout the history of mankind and it has followed social transformations. It has a firm connection to culture. Ruth Benedict believes that most behavioural features of families are in harmony with the social culture and civilisation.[1]

Each regulation in legislation must meet a social necessity, paying due attention to the fact that the behaviour within a family is the most private aspect of life

* Professor Bekmezyan is Doctor of Law, Associate Professor in Yerevan State University, Guide Professor, and Gholam Reza Shirazi is Doctor of Law candidate in Yerevan State University, Correspondent Author (Shirazi.llb@gmail.com).

1 Saei Arsi, Iraj *An Introduction to Sociology and Pathology of Disordered Family* (Abhar Azad University Press, 2003) 22.

and to enter this basic social unit the law is faced with difficulties. This study attempts to analyse the enforceable rules and regulations stipulated for spouses in the current codes of Iran and Armenia. It is a study based on related Codes, books and other written materials. First, the related articles in Iran's Codes will be discussed and in second part the Codes of Armenia will be dealt with.

II A SPOUSE'S RIGHTS AND DUTIES UNDER IRAN'S LAW

A permanent marriage is a social contract and its consequences are not limited to the parties. Not only does the children's future depend on the stability and continuing of family, but also public order necessitates this institution be safe and stable. Because of the importance of this, legislators have taken the husband–wife relationship out of their scope of powers, upholding the duty of family order.[2]

This legal institution can only be dissolved if the law permits it to happen. Even in the case of mutual consent to dissolve it, the court should refer the case to a family consulting centre. Parties to the contract can start from consulting centres and if they still want to divorce, the centres should refer the case back to the court for a final verdict, and this is where the certificate of the impossibility of compromise is issued (arts 25 and 26 of the Family Support Act). Cancellation is invalid in relation to marriage and, because an illegal condition does not invalidate the contract, without a shadow of doubt, the contract is valid. This issue has been elucidated at the start of art 1069 of the Civil Code: 'A provision in the marriage contract reserving the right of cancellation of the contract, if made, will be null and void.'

Where a marriage was concluded in the correct manner, there are rights and duties for both husband and wife, which jurists call 'the consequences of marriage'. Article 1102 of the Iranian Civil Code states that: 'As soon as marriage takes place in due form, relations of matrimony will automatically exist between the marriage parties and rights and reciprocal duties of husband and wife will be established between them.'

The matrimonial relationship in its absolute sense has a very extensive meaning which comprises all personal non-financial and financial relations between the parties. Since marriage, first, is a non-financial contract, in other words, non-financial relations are more important, we will discuss non-financial relations first, then financial ones.

III NON-FINANCIAL RELATIONS BETWEEN SPOUSES

Family manners, social conventions and behaviours have ordained certain reciprocal duties for the husband and wife, which in turn classify their rights. In

2 Katuzian, Dr Naser *Civil Law, Family* (7th edn, Enteshar Co, 2006) vol 1, at 135.

couples' personal relations, some duties are common and some specified to one party being either the husband or the wife. First, we will study common duties and then those specified to one party.

(a) Communal duties of spouses

These duties are those that both parties are bound to meet and fulfil.

(i) Friendly association

Friendly association is one of the spouses' communal obligations. This has been emphasised in art 1103 of the Civil Code: 'The husband and wife are bound to treat each other as good companions.' The partnership of husband and wife means that their relations should be cordial, friendly and amicable. Spouses' friendly association or good behaviour is related to social conventions and customs and its requirements change in accordance with time and place. In short, we can say all the behaviour that is socially offensive, for example, swearing, assaulting, arguing and humiliating or actions that are in opposition to family affection and the requirements of love between spouses, eg family abandonment, ignoring one's partner or his or her wishes, developing bad habits, are instances of bad association in the family.[3]

Shared life is a requirement for good association, so a husband is bound to accept his wife into his home and a wife is bound to live in the man's house. Having sexual intercourse in due manner is conventionally another requirement for good association and whenever a husband or wife refrains from doing so he or she has gone against good association.

The legal department of the Judiciary in the announcement No 7977/7 dated 18 February 2007 declared that, under art 1103 of the Civil Code, the husband and wife are bound to have good association. Therefore maltreatment or mistreatment by a wife towards her husband can be considered as a breach of the aforementioned provision in the marriage contract. If a wife's mistreating of others is so acute that it disturbs the husband's life, a court can also consider that as being directed at her husband and it can be regarded as an instance of harsh treatment.

Although the duties relating to friendly association are ethical, they can also be established legally. A wife's bad association eliminates the right to receive alimony. As mentioned in art 1108 of the Civil Code 'if a wife refuses to fulfill her duties as a wife without legitimate reason, she will lose her entitlement to receive maintenance'.

When a husband's bad association is so acute that it makes life unbearable for the wife, with reference to para 4 of the note to art 1130, she can refer to the court and apply for divorce. The Code declares 'beating or any ongoing harsh

---

3 Ibid at 81–82.

treatment, which customarily considering the wife's situation is unbearable, is an instance of a difficult and undesirable condition'. In verdicts from the Supreme Court, argument and ill treatment, assaulting and beating have been considered as instances of bad association.[4]

(ii) Cooperation in family welfare and education of children

Article 1104 of the Iranian Civil Code requires the cooperation and collaboration of spouses in two cases: (i) family welfare; and (ii) education of children. The article stipulates that 'husband and wife must cooperate with each other for the welfare of their family and the education of their children'.

The husband and wife should cooperate with each other to run the family, and in illness and in distress help and sympathise with each other. What helps the welfare of a family is not confined to marriage but it is required that husband and wife do not refrain from any actions which strengthen the family. The important legal consequence from this fact that imposes a duty on the husband and wife is that neither of them has the right to ask for remuneration for the services provided for the family and help offered to the other spouse.[5]

The non-cooperation of the wife in this regard can be an instance of disobedience and can nullify the right to maintenance and husband's non-cooperation is an instance of a difficult and undesirable situation that can be a cause for a court to order a divorce. Another common and important duty is the education of the children who are the fruits of their life. The law has emphasised the couple's cooperation in relation to the children's education. If the husband or wife educates their children as they wish, it will cause discordance and duality. This in turn, in addition to causing numerous problems, disturbs the children's education and the children can abuse the situation. In such families children are the primary victims of this disharmony over education.

(iii) Loyalty

In Iranian law this matter has not been dealt with explicitly. Perhaps the lawmaker did not deal with this matter as it is very obvious. Faithfulness can be considered one of the instances of friendly association or fortifying family ties. The husband or wife's being unfaithful to each other is a betrayal and in addition to being disgraceful, it is criminal.

In Iranian law there is no difference between a man and a woman in this regard. In 'Islamic Criminal Law' the punishment for a married woman or married man who commits adultery may be as severe as capital punishment. A

---

4 Bazgir, Yadollah *Supreme Court Verdicts on Civil Law Affairs* (Ghoghnoos Publication, 1998) vol 3, at 81–82.

5 Katuzian, Dr Naser *Civil Law, Family* (7th edn, Enteshar Co, 2006) vol 1, at 220.

wife or husband's committing adultery is a public crime and the very same fact clearly demonstrates the significance of faithfulness and its relation with public order.

A husband's falling into the habit of adultery can be an instance of bad association and can be a ground for applying to the court for divorce. Marrying another woman according to the relevant rules is not in conflict with faithfulness as defined here.

(b) Allocated rights and obligations of spouses

As it was mentioned earlier, some rights and duties are specific to the husband or wife. We will discuss these under the husband's headship of the family and wife's obedience.

(i) Headship of the family

Establishing order in each community is conditional upon someone governing it. Family, which is the smallest social unit, is not an exception to this rule and its survival and stability is impossible except through choosing a leader. With regard to the wife's individual rights, equality of man and woman is reasonably justified. The majority of women and sometimes men claim that the family should be run jointly and its being governed should be based on mutual agreement. But, it goes without saying, that social obligation imposes restrictions on individual freedom. If a man and woman's authority over regulating family affairs is the same, how should differences be resolved? Maybe, in some families the woman is more competent than the man, but the law governs the majority.

A family, on its own, is not left without a manager, and the authority of the manager depends on various factors among which the law is the least influential. Whoever is the manager of the family cannot exceed the limits determined by conventions, customs and factors governing it although the law may have authorised the manager. Exceeding these limits is the beginning of disagreement, argument and instability in the family.[6]

Article 1105 of the Iranian Civil Code reads: 'In relations between husband and wife; the position of the head of the family is the exclusive right of husband.' From arts 1104 and 1105 collectively it can be concluded that in family welfare and children education the wife is her husband's helper and assistant.

The concept of husband's headship of the family

Maybe in the past it was believed that the man was the dictator in a family and supporter of incapacitated people called his wife and children. Nevertheless, nowadays, a man's leadership is a social obligation rather than exercising

---

[6] Ibid at 221–225.

individual rights. The lawmaker's goal was not to privilege the man compared to the woman or to gratify his desire. It was rather burdening him with responsibility. Leadership is a responsibility laid upon him, not a right that he exercises, and the wife is exempted from this responsibility compared with the husband.

By leadership we mean ultimate decision-making in family affairs and serving their interests, some of which have been specified by the lawmaker, eg allotting a dwelling, controlling the woman's choice of work etc are within the man's scope of powers. Other cases that are not specified by the lawmaker will be defined according to customs, conventions and common sense.[7]

The man's leadership of the family means sound and just management. Justice is a lofty, ethical concept. So, if leadership does not diverge from governing and reigning, it will go against justice and would be absolutely unethical and disgraceful. It is better for the family that this management is delegated to the man and it does not mean assertion, self-centredness, domination, and discrimination so that one can say the concept of equality of the parties in family associations is not observed. Actually it is serving and leading this small (at the same time basic) unit. In other words it is the same sound and democratic leadership.[8]

For instance, the husband cannot prevent his wife from fairly visiting her relatives and friends. It should be noted that the canonisation of the right to leadership is to achieve ultimate social rights, so that family, by regulating its inter-relationships, does not experience crisis. Thus, the right to head a family should serve the paramount and vital interest of the family and its members. Sharia (Islamic jurisprudence) supports this right as far as it is does not result in the harm of family members. If due to the family leader's incompetency or his imprudence or his intention to harm family members suffer damage, this is an instance of exercising the right beyond the scope of the powers because the leader has abused his power. Iran's Constitution in this regard in art 40 explicitly declares: 'No one may inflict loss on another or violate public interests by means of the exercise his rights.'

Since the position of the head of the family is given to the man to protect and safeguard family interests, he may not give his right to a woman according to a contract or his unilateral will, because male headship of a family in its present sense is related to public order.[9]

---

7 Mohaghegh Damad and Seyed Mostafa, *Religious Jurisprudential (Feghhi) Consideration of Family Law* (15th edn, Islamic Science Publication Center, 2008) at 287.

8 Zareei, Mohammad Mehdi 'An Introduction to the Position of Ethics in Marriage and Family' (2011) 34 Islamic Studies 87/1 at 85.

9 Gorgi, Abolghasem et al *A Comparative Study of Family Law* (University of Tehran Press, 2005) 184.

The consequence of the husband's headship of the family

The position of the head of the family is the exclusive right of the husband and it has consequences including:

- the wife can use the husband's family name with his consent;
- the wife must obey him;
- allotting a dwelling is basically the husband's right;
- the husband can prevent his wife from choosing a job that is against family interests or a job which is below her dignity;
- legal guardianship of children is the exclusive right of father;
- the alimony of the family is father's responsibility.

Compliance

Obedience, also like the position of heading the family, depends on customs, conventions, traditions and ethics in society. Obedience in Iranian law has two different meanings: general and specific. General obedience means accepting the man's position as the head of the family, respecting his management of the children's education, financial and ethical management within the scope of the law and custom with a view to safeguarding family interests. Specific obedience is fulfilling the man's legal sexual needs. In other words specific obedience means the woman's acceptance of sexual relations with the man and acceding to her husband's sexual requests customarily and in cases where there is no acceptable excuse.

The husband also is bound to have sexual relations with his wife to the customary extent. In all these cases final judgment is based on conventions and ethics. Therefore specific obedience does not mean ignoring the woman's emotions.

The criterion of obedience is the behaviour of a conventional person living in that special situation which in this case has two aspects: typical and personal. In obedience the woman's readiness is important. In relation to this specific duty of the woman, there is no effective legal guarantee, and its fulfilment depends on the partners' good-will and temperament. A wife who does not obey her husband is not entitled to maintenance and the man can divorce her with the permission of the court, but, even with a court decree and a police force, no one can oblige a woman to obey and to have a good temperament.

Obedience can be considered as an instance of friendly relations. Being good-tempered in the family is an ethical guideline and it helps to meet their needs in different aspects. In contrast, harsh treatment takes away peacefulness.

The emergence of ethics and its being blended with family law and regulations is actually a guarantee of its implementation and the family components with these ethical laws and duties can contribute to strengthening family bonds. To make this happen in the family, in comparison to other fortifying factors including beauty, health, social titles and education, ethics plays a pivotal role.[10]

Allotting the dwelling house

In this regard art 1114 of the Civil Code states: 'the wife must stay in the dwelling that the husband allots for her unless such a right is reserved to the wife.' This article providing the right of allotting dwelling places gives the exclusive right to the husband. This, in turn, can be one of the consequences of the husband's holding the position of heading the family and the wife will have the right to choose the dwelling house only if this right is explicitly reserved to her. This right may be in the marriage contract or in a different contract or in a separate contract granting the right to the woman. If this is an absolute right, in addition to choosing the city it is enforceable for choosing the house as well.

The Supreme Court in verdict No 776 on the issue states: 'if it is stipulated in the marriage certificate that the wife has an absolute right to allot the dwellinghouse for 30 years the condition includes specifying the house, and it is not possible to confine her right to choosing the city so that her staying in her paternal home and not going to her husband's does not result in disobedience'. Another verdict, No 176 Division 8, declares, if according to the marriage certificate the right to allot the dwelling place is granted to the wife, action taken by the husband forcing her to obey and return to the dwelling that she herself allotted is null and void. Of course, the wife must not abuse this right or intend to harm or bother her husband, or else in such a case by reference to 'abuse of rights' it can be followed through the court.

Since the right to allot dwellings is the exclusive right of husband, to prevent him from abusing this right, the law permits the wife to choose a separate dwelling. Article 1115 of the Civil Code provides: 'if the co-existence of the wife and husband in the same house involves the risk of physical injury, financial loss or injury to the wife's dignity, she may choose to live in a separate dwelling. If the alleged risk is proved, the court will not order her to return to the matrimonial house and, so long as she is authorized to remain in a separate home, her husband will be liable for her alimony.'

Verdict No 366 issued by Division 6 of the Supreme Court in this regard says that art 1115 of the Civil Code has granted the right to the woman that, in cases of physical injury, financial loss or injury to the dignity of the wife, she can choose another house different from that of her husband's. This is not a case of disobedience. Therefore, where the wife rightly fears injuries that are normally unbearable, she can leave the husband's house. Avoiding injuries is a

---

[10] Zareei, Mohammad Mehdi 'An Introduction to the Position of Ethics in Marriage and Family'(2011) 34 Islamic Studies 87/1 at 69–70.

general principle and it also governs family relations, and none of them, wife, husband, or children, is allowed to put others in difficult and undesirable conditions.

Opposing the wife's occupation

Woman's freedom is somehow limited after marriage. Fulfilling conjugal duties prevents the wife from freely choosing a legal occupation as a single woman can. Based on art 1117 of the Civil Code the husband can prevent his wife from undertaking an occupation or technical work which is incompatible with the family interests or the dignity of himself or his wife. The lawmaker's aim was to safeguard family interests and spouses' dignity. There are activities that go against the family interest and weaken the basis of the family or disturb the rearing and education of children or destroy spouses' social dignity or throw the family economic system into disarray. There are no strict guidelines to determine them, because family interests or spouses' social dignity depend on the specific conditions of each family. Maybe an occupation with the same characteristics does not jeopardise the family interests of a specific family but for another family it does so. Family interests depending on time, place and family conditions differ. All the occupations done out of house more or less prevent the woman from fulfilling some of her wifely or maternal duties.

The aim of providing art 1117 of the Civil Code was to ensure that the challenges of an occupation do not impede the wife from running the house and educating the children. The husband as the head of the family – the individual in charge of protecting this institution – can prevent her from choosing a job that threatens family interests. Therefore, the husband right – the subject of the article – is not exclusive and is conditioned by family interests and his wife's interests.

Prior to the enactment of the Family Support Bill, there was disagreement about the issue whether determining family interests is the man's right, as a result of which, he – as the head of the family – can prevent the wife from choosing any occupation that he considers against the spouses' interests or not. Should the wife be required to prove the abuse of this right or should the husband like other claimants refer the matter to the court and, after proving his claim, ask the court to give a verdict on it? From the wording of arts 1105 and 1117 it can be inferred that it is not required for the husband to provide evidence and, he, as head of the family can authoritatively determine family interests. So, it is the wife who should prove the opposite.

Article 15 of the Family Support Act 1967 has provided for this: the husband, with the approval of the court can prevent his wife from choosing an occupation which is against family interests or the wife's dignity. Then, under the current Iranian legal system, the husband should initiate an action as a claimant in the court, and, after proving the wife's occupation to be against family interests or his wife's dignity, ask the court to prevent her.

Guardianship of an incapable person is an exception to this general principle. In this case, the husband's consent is required and proving it to be against family interests is not required. As mentioned in art 1233: 'A woman cannot accept guardianship without the consent of her husband.' Theoretically we can say that accepting guardianship is not a job and the aforementioned article has not followed the requirement in art 18 of the Family Support Act on this matter about the necessity to obtain the court's approval. It goes without saying that accepting guardianship sometimes necessitates managing the incapable person's properties and doing business and handling affairs and that this is a full-time and lucrative job. Therefore the husband's consent actually in this case is an occupational limitation for the wife and it is a consequence of the husband's heading the family.

It should be added that the husband's right is not only enforceable for occupations that the wife has after marriage but it can be enforced for occupations prior to the marriage. Hence, if a man marries a woman who is a flight attendant and then realises that her continuing this job threatens the family interests, he has the right to ask the court to prevent her. The husband's consent does not deprive him of his right because preventing the woman is not his exclusive right: one cannot claim that, because he has given his consent, he has waived his right. The retention of this right is one in the public order domain and exercising it is the duty and responsibility of the husband in managing the family.[11]

Under the Family Support Act 1967, only men could appeal to the court to prevent women from choosing certain occupations while the chance that the man's job was a threat to family's interests and his wife's dignity was ignored. It was against the principle of men and women's equality of rights. Some Islamic scholars believe that men and women's equality of rights is the most important criterion, declaring that the exception is against the principle and it should be limited to specific or consensus cases.[12]

Under the Family Support Act 1974 the wife became entitled to the right, whenever she considered her husband's job to be against family interests and her or her husband's dignity, to apply to the court to prevent him. It has been added to the end of art 18 that 'if the family livelihood is jeopardized, the court will prevent the husband from having that specific occupation'.

Therefore, theoretically one cannot consider the husband's right to prevent his wife from choosing an occupation that is against family interests as a consequence of the husband's headship. The family's avoiding such occupations and respecting the partner's dignity are among mutual duties and violating them entitles either party to refer the case to the court to force the violator to observe the rule.

---

[11] Katuzian, Dr Naser *Civil Law, Family* (7th edn, Enteshar Co, 2006) vol 1, at 234–235.

[12] Ezat, Hebeh et al *The Other Half* (Trans Mehdi Sarhadi, Naghed Publication, 2003) at 187.

The culture in Iranian society still has not eliminated the conventional division of tasks. If lunch is not ready or the laundry is not done, the wife is the person at fault, as when the ends are not met this is the man's rather than the woman's fault. The necessity for friendly association makes women help more inside home and encourage the man to be active outside the home.

IV FINANCIAL RELATIONS BETWEEN SPOUSES

(a) Spouses financial independence principle

Prior to the 20th century under the European legal system, a wife was not financially independent from her husband and after marriage she was one of the 'incapacitated'. Since the late 19th century laws in countries were amended and in most countries wives became financially independent. Still, in the legal system of most of these countries husbands and wives according to law or mutual consent can decide to be financial partners, and that is why regulating their financial relations is not easy.[13]

Under Iranian law, the property of a husband and wife do not become 'common property', but the property of each party is separated from the other party's. The principle of husband and wife sharing their talents will entail free will, resulting in the enjoyment of freedom of thought and will, which is the same as having authority to act freely. Therefore, a wife can in all aspects of her personal and social life, with the exception of cases for which there are impediments, act independently.[14]

Article 1118 of the Civil Code on the issue declares 'the wife can independently do what she likes with her property'. This is an advanced right that in some civilised and developed countries women could achieve after years of resistance. The payments to a woman are also considered her property and she does not have to share them with her husband gratuitously, unless the job which according to conventions and customs and having regard to friendly relations or contributions is considered her duty. So she cannot demand remuneration for that. Iranian laws are not gender-based regarding ownership.[15] A wife can demand remuneration for what she does for her husband on his orders. Of course if the woman intends to do something gratuitously, she is not entitled to remuneration.

At the beginning of art 29 of the Family Support Bill it is stated that on divorce, in addition to the verdict and considering conditions stipulated in marriage contract, the court must decide about dowry, marriage portion, wife's alimony and pay parity for the marital period according to a note to art 336 of the Civil

---

13 Katuzian, Dr Naser *Civil Law, Family* (7th edn, Enteshar Co, 2006) vol 1, at 137.

14 Tabatabaei, Mohammad Hossein *Almizan fi Tafsir Alquran* (Trans Mosa Hamadani, Darolelme Tehran Publication, 2006) vol 7, at 274.

15 Kar, Mehrangiz *The Structure of the Family Legal System in Iran* (Roshangaran Publication,1999), at 47.

Code. A wife's pay parity is the sum for the work she did on her husband's order and cannot be confined to divorce. It is a general principle which can be applied to other situations as well. To confirm this idea, one can refer to art 336 of the Civil Code which declares: 'If a person carries out an act on the order of another and a wage is payable for such an act according to custom and usage, or if the person carrying out the act is accustomed and available to undertake such work, then he may claim payment for his work, unless it can be shown that he has acted gratis.' This principle is called 'Exploitation' which includes the wife working at her husband's home as well. The lawmaker also noted the point recently and added a note to art 336 on 13 January 2007 as follows: 'If the wife carries out acts which according to Sharia are not her duties and there is payment for them according to custom and usage, at the order of her husband and she intended to do them non-gratuitously and this is proved for the court, the court will calculate the pay for those acts and will order to be paid.'

As we have seen, in husband-wife financial relations, the issue of common property that in some countries is acceptable does not come up in Iran.[16] Nevertheless, husband-wife financial relations may be considered in two cases: the marriage portion, and alimony.

(b) Marriage portion

In the pre-Islam era financial relations governed the marriage contract, marriage portion being an example. Islam also has emphasised this fact and has made a firm recommendation on its not being excessive. However, specifying its amount was delegated to parties, based on considering facts such as the husband's ability, the wife's dignity, conventions and customs of different people. The marriage portion is the sum that the husband, according to the marriage contract, undertakes to pay to the wife.

The obligation imposed for the payment of the marriage portion is rooted in law and is not dependent on contract. Therefore, the silence of both parties while concluding the marriage contract or even agreeing on the wife not being entitled to receive a marriage portion does not breach the husband's duty in this regard. Article 1087 of the Civil Code states 'if a dowry is not mentioned in the marriage contract or if the non-payment of the marriage portion is stipulated as a condition for permanent marriage, that marriage will be valid and parties may subsequently agree a dowry by mutual consent. If intercourse between the married couple has already taken place before such a mutual agreement, the wife is then entitled to receive the amount of dowry normally due.'

As mentioned earlier, although the conditions in the marriage contract may be based on mutual consent, the occurrence of their consequences is out of the spouses' power. As husband and wife accept the marriage contract, they are in

---

[16] Kar, Mehrangiz *The Structure of the Family Legal System in Iran* (Roshangaran Publication, 1999) at 134.

a position under which they have to face its unavoidable consequences. Thus, a marriage portion is a legal obligation imposed on the man and the parties, while concluding the marriage contract or after it, specifying the marriage portion by mutual consent. Article 1080 of the Civil Code related to this issue states: 'fixing the amount of the marriage portion depends upon the mutual consent of the marrying parties'. The legal department of the Judiciary in an announcement No 7/414 dated 2 April 2008 declared that the increased marriage portion after concluding a marriage contract is not a dowry and it is not governed by the Civil Code. In practice it is debt undertaken by the husband.

Obliging the wife to obey her husband results directly from the law and it must not be attributed to the husband and wife's consent. Therefore the relationship between the marriage portion and obedience cannot be compared with compensatory financial relations. Human ethical character distinguishes humans from creatures and entities in the world. Humans are always entitled to a right or obliged to observe it but will never be the subject of a right.

The marriage portion is not the price paid for a wife. Rather, she concludes a contract with her husband, the inevitable consequence of which obliges the husband to pay the marriage portion and the wife to undertake the duty to obey him. That is why cancellation of the marriage portion does not nullify the marriage contract and does not exempt her from fulfilling her duties.[17] Article 1081 emphasises that 'If a condition is set in the marriage contract that the marriage portion must be paid within a fixed period of time or that marriage will be annulled, the marriage contract and the agreed dowry will remain valid but the condition will be null and void'.

(c) The wife's lien

It is mentioned that there is no causative relationship between the marriage portion and marriage and one may not compare a marriage contract with ordinary contracts for consideration. Nevertheless, art 1085 of the Civil Code in certain cases has extended laws on compensated contracts to the marriage contract. Under this article 'so long as the marriage portion is not delivered to her, the wife can refuse to fulfil the duties thereto she has undertaken toward her husband, if the marriage portion is payable at once. This refusal does not debar her from the right of maintenance'. This right is known as 'the wife's lien'. Although one of the wife's duties to her husband is living in his dwelling, she can refuse to go to her husband's dwelling. Notwithstanding the fact that the wife's duties towards her husband are not legally related to the husband's obligation to pay the marriage portion, by custom it governs the whole matrimonial life. Having said that, according to art 1086 it seems that the lawmaker aimed at specific obedience. The article reads: 'if the wife voluntarily proceeds to fulfil the duties that she undertakes toward her husband, she

---

[17] Katuzian, Dr Naser *Civil Law, Family* (7th edn, Enteshar Co, 2006) vol 1, at 139.

cannot subsequently avail herself of the provisions of foregoing article, but she will not in any case forfeit her right to demand payment of the dowry due to her'.

Even an instalment of dowry does not lead to the forfeiture of the right to the wife's lien. A precedent from a High Court jury No 708, dated 12 August 2009, giving approval to this, declares that additionally, on the establishment of the husband's hardship, he can pay by instalments. According to art 1085, which mentions the dowry as a whole sum being fixed by mutual consent, the issuing of an order to pay by instalment, which is only due to husband's being indigent and in constrained circumstances, does not nullify the right to the wife's lien. This is because, first, the wife's right of lien and the husband's poverty are two separate matters that do not affect each other. Secondly, the marriage portion in the foregoing article means that the reception of the whole and collection of one or some instalment(s) do not mean the reception of the marriage portion as intended by the wife when concluding the marriage contract. The right of lien is abolished under two circumstances under which the husband can demand that his wife fulfil her matrimonial duties prior to the payment of the marriage portion: first, although a definite time has been specified for the payment of the marriage portion, the wife agrees to collect the marriage portion later. Matrimonial relations start from the time of concluding the marriage contract and each party must fulfil his or her duties. This judgment is mentioned in the last part of art 1085. Secondly, if the wife obeys of her own free will, following that, she cannot exercise the right of lien.

(d) Provision of family expenses

According to art 1106 of the Civil Code the cost of maintenance of the wife in permanent marriages is the responsibility of the husband. Notwithstanding the fact that the lawmaker has bound the husband to provide alimony for the family because of being the head of the family, the spouses should cooperate in managing the family affairs. This duty arises from obligatory law, so conditions contrary to it do not breach the duty.

Article 1107 of the Civil Code provides that the wife's maintenance costs, including all her ordinary needs proportionate to a woman's circumstances, declaring that the cost of maintenance includes accommodation, clothing, food and furniture appropriate to the wife's situation on a reasonable basis and provision of a servant if the wife is accustomed to having servants or if she needs one owing to illness or disability, are the husband's responsibility.

In relation to the cost of maintenance as inferred from the aforementioned article, the wife's situation and needs according to her custom are the criterion in practice, not the husband's financial circumstances. Therefore, if the wife is from an opulent family, the husband is bound to provide the necessities for life in proportion to familial and social situations and status.

Considering the wife's or husband's situation as the criterion for specifying the quality and quantity of the cost of maintenance is contrary to justice and fairness. Because if a rich man married a woman from a poor family he must not humiliate her by paying the cost of maintenance parsimoniously or vice versa.[18]

The husband, due to the cost of maintenance and observing ethical principles, should meet all the ordinary needs of his wife. This exempts the wife from obligatory and boring tasks. She does not have to shoulder the financial responsibility of the family but only suffer the unbearable burden of pregnancy which is her inherent responsibility from God. It is her husband's ethical duty to support her financially and spiritually.[19]

The cost of maintenance in comparison with the wife's blood relatives has the peculiarities and advantages as follows:

- if there is a wife and one or more relatives who are to be supported, the claim to support of the wife precedes that of others (art 1203). The wife can always and in any case make a claim for her past expenses, and her right to these expenses is preferential, but relatives entitled to provision towards maintenance expenses can claim only their expenses for a future period (art 1206);
- the cost of the wife's maintenance is not conditioned by the man's poverty or opulence. Even a rich wife can demand the cost of maintenance from her husband. If the husband refuses to pay the cost of his wife's maintenance and if it is impossible to enforce the verdict of the court to induce him to pay the alimony, the wife can refer to the judge and apply for divorce and the judge will compel the husband to divorce her (art 1129). However, for the cost of the maintenance of relatives, the poverty of one party and the opulence of the other is the condition;
- the cost of the wife's maintenance is not a reciprocal duty – it is an individual duty. Under the Iranian legal system, the wife is never bound to pay the cost of maintenance to her husband while the relatives' cost of maintenance is a reciprocal duty (art 1201);
- the cost of the wife's maintenance is a preferential claim and, in the case of the husband's bankruptcy or death and inadequacy of properties to pay all the debts, it is preferred to other debts, while the cost of maintenance for other relatives, with the exception of that for children, is not of same nature.[20]

---

18 Ghazizadeh, Kazem et al 'The Legal-religious Jurisprudential Basis and Nature of a Wife's Alimony in Quran' (2009) 6 Scientific-Propagation Quarterly Journal of Shieit Women 20, at 127.

19 Zareei, Mohammad Mehdi 'An Introduction to the Position of Ethics in Marriage and Family' (2011) 34 Islamic Studies 87/1 at 71.

20 Safaei, SH Emami *A Concise Family Law* (12th edn, Mizan Publication, 2007) at 138.

(e) The wife's alimony guarantee

It was mentioned that the husband's obligation for payment of the maintenance costs is the result of an obligatory principle, not agreement. This duty on the husband has civil and criminal guarantees. Under art 1111 of the Civil Code, a wife may make a claim to the court if her husband refuses to provide maintenance costs. In such cases the court will set the amount of maintenance costs and induce the husband to pay it. Now, if the husband refuses to execute the court verdict or execution of such a verdict is impossible due to inaccessibility of the husband's property or his inability to do so, the wife is entitled to the right of divorce and the judge will compel the husband to divorce his wife (art 1129).

In making a claim to the court for the maintenance cost, just proving the marriage contract suffices on behalf of the wife for her to be entitled to the alimony. Therefore, if the husband claims the wife's disobedience which abolishes the right to maintenance costs, he must prove the issue. The Supreme Court also in verdict No 2612–1316 declared that the proof of a marital relationship is enough to claim for the maintenance costs. If a husband, contrary to his financial ability and wife's obedience, does not pay the maintenance costs to his wife and the wife sues for it, the husband will be punished with imprisonment for the term of 6 months to 2 years.

V A SPOUSE'S RIGHTS AND DUTIES IN THE REPUBLIC OF ARMENIA

According to art 1 of the Family Code in the Republic of Armenia's law, the institution of the family is under the protection of society and the state; and the family's rights are the result of the necessity of family solidarity. The foundation of family relationships is based on the mutual love and respect, cooperation and mutual responsibility of all family members, and any self-willed interference is inadmissible. Its regulations are based on the realisation of family members' rights and the necessity of juridical protection of these rights. The third Provision of art 1 claims that man and woman should enjoy equal rights at the moment of the marriage conclusion, during the marital life, and in the case of marriage cancellation. Provision 4 of the same article has emphasised that legal regulation of family relations is realised in accordance with the principles of free will of a man and woman's marital union, the equality of spouses' rights in the family, the solution of family issues by mutual consent, taking care of mutual well-being, the primary provision of the rights and best interests of minor and incapable family members. This article conforms to art 16 of the Convention on Eradicating any Inequality Against Women that was passed by the United Nations in 1979.

If the relations between family members are not regulated by family legislation or the parties' consent, and there are no norms directly regulating them, the norms of family and/or civic law regulating such relations (if they do not contradict their essence) are applicable with regard to them (law analogy). In cases of impossibility of a law analogy, family members' rights and duties are established proceeding from family principles or civic rights (rights analogy) (art 5).

According to the first paragraph of art 25, spouses are free to choose an occupation, job, profession and residence. The second clause of the same article stipulates that the spouses deal with the issues of maternity, paternity, rearing and education of a child, as well as other issues of family life proceeding from the principle of equality of spouses' rights.

In the third clause of the above-mentioned article couples have been obliged to build their relations on the basis of mutual cooperation and respect, contribute to the stability of the family, and take care of the well-being and bringing up of their children. This article conforms to art 1104 of the Civil Code in Iran.

Issues related to the common shared property of spouses are regulated by the Civil Code as well as the marriage contract concluded between them (art 26). Spouses' rights and obligations during the marital life and at the time of dissolution are specified by the marriage contract that is based on the spouses' agreement or consent (art 27). According to art 29, by concluding a marriage contract spouses can change the scope of common property in order to establish common, shared, or private property in relation to all the property of the spouses. A marriage contract may be concluded in relation to present assets and what will be obtained in the future. Through the marriage contract they may establish mutual rights and obligations of meeting each other's living expenses, ways of participation in each other's income, and how each is to provide for family expenditure. Meanwhile, they can specify any mutual obligation at the time of divorce and also specify in this contract any possible criterion for financial relations. Rights and obligations stipulated by a marriage contract can be restricted for a certain period or depend on the emergence of certain circumstances or vice versa.

Property acquired by spouses during the marital life is in their joint ownership unless a contract between them establishes otherwise. Property that belonged to each of the spouses before entry into marriage, as well as property acquired by one of the spouses during marriage by gift or by way of inheritance, is in this spouse's ownership. Property for individual use (clothing, etc) with the exception of jewellery and other luxury items, although acquired during the marital life at the expense of the general assets of the spouses, shall be recognised as owned by the spouse that uses them. The property of each of the spouses may be recognised as in their joint ownership if it is established that during marriage, at the expense of common property of them or personal property of the other spouse, investments were made that significantly increased the value of this property. This rule shall not be applied if a contract between them provides otherwise. For obligations of one of the spouses, execution may be levied on property that is in that spouse's ownership, as well as on his or her ownership share in the common property of the spouses (art 201 of the Civil Code).

According to third Provision of art 29 of the Family Code, there are occasions where spouses are not allowed to make an agreement on:

- depriving of the right of applying to the court by either one;
- non-financial relations between couples;
- couples' rights and duties in relation to children;
- limiting the rights of an incapable spouse about demanding the means of living;
- other regulations which create unfavourable conditions for either one of the spouses;
- any agreement that contradicts the major principles of family legislation.

Conditions that are in contrast to the conditions stated in Provision 3 of art 29 are invalid. Article 30 stipulates the revision in content or the revocation of the marriage contract as follows: with the spouses' consent the marriage contract can be altered or cancelled at any time. The marriage contract is altered and cancelled by the procedure established for the conclusion of it. Unilateral rescission of the marriage contract is forbidden. On the application of one of the spouses, the marriage contract may be altered or revoked by judicial procedure according to the basis and procedure established by the Civil Code for alteration and cancellation of treaties. The validity of terms specified in the marriage contract expires with the cancellation of the marriage, except for the obligations that are stipulated for the period after the revocation of the marriage.

Based on the regulations on invalidity of transactions in the Civil Code, the court can recognise a marriage contract as invalid partly or completely. Additionally, if the conditions stated in the marriage contract specify severely unfavourable conditions for either one of the couple, the court can revoke a part or the whole of the marriage contract if the objecting spouse makes a claim.

VI CONCLUSION

Under Iran's law, the family is an institution with a certain framework in which the rights and responsibilities of its members have been defined and determined. Agreement contrary to some of these conditions is null and void without having effect on the contract. Some conditions are so essential that a contrary agreement makes the marriage contract null and void. Under the law, the husband is the head of the family and the family is recognised in his name. Providing the means of living is the husband's duty, and maybe because of this responsibility, in consultation with the other family members, he makes the final decision about family affairs. Abuse of headship by the husband is prohibited. Nowadays despite the fact that wives generally work outside and help husbands provide the means of living for the family, legally they are never responsible for it, even when they are rich. This is a sign of mutual assistance that is customary rather than in accordance with the law. So, an amendment is necessary to recognise the property acquired during the marital life as being in common ownership. Under Iran's law independence of property ownership has been stipulated, each spouse's property obtained before marriage being in his or her ownership and that acquired after marriage as well, unless otherwise provided.

Under Armenia's law, the family is set up on the basis of mutual love, respect and assistance but habitually the provision of family income is the responsibility of the man. Spouses may agree on all their property regardless of whether it was acquired before or after marriage. There is no hindrance on this issue under Armenia's law. In the latter legal system it is the principle that property acquired by spouses during marriage is in their joint ownership unless a contract between them establishes otherwise. Property acquired by one of the spouses during the marital life by gift or by way of inheritance is in this spouse's ownership.

IRELAND

IRISH ABORTION LAW – LEGISLATING TO STAND STILL?

Maebh Harding[*]

Résumé

La légalité de l'avortement en Irlande fait l'objet d'un débat public divisant la population depuis plus de 30 ans. La Constitution irlandaise reconnaît autant le droit à la vie de l'enfant à naître que le droit à la vie de la mère. Le 1er Janvier 2014, la loi relative à la protection de la vie durant la grossesse de 2013 est entrée en vigueur. Cette loi est le premier texte réglementant la pratique de l'avortement sur le territoire irlandais. L'Irlande conserve l'un des droits les plus stricts du monde dans ce domaine. L'avortement n'est autorisé que si la pour suite de la grossesse comporte un risque direct pour la vie de la mère. L'accès à l'information sur les possibilités d'avortement legal dans d'autres pays demeure limité aux femmes enceintes. Cet article retrace l'évolution du droit irlandais, passé d'une interdiction constitutionnelle expresse de l'avortement à la création d'un droit constitutionnel limité à l'avortement. Il montreque de fréquents rappels de l'impact pratique de la loisur les individus sont essentiels.

I INTRODUCTION

The legality of abortion in Ireland has been the subject of hugely divisive public debate for over 30 years. Article 40.3.3 of the Irish Constitution acknowledges the right to life of the unborn as equal to the right to life of the mother and places a duty on the Irish state to respect and defend the right to life of the unborn.

On 1 January 2014, the Protection of Life During Pregnancy Act 2013 came into force. The Act is the first piece of legislation to regulate the provision of domestic abortion. Ireland retains one of the most restrictive abortion regimes in the world. Abortion is permitted only where continuation of the pregnancy is of direct risk to the life of the mother. Access to information about legal abortion services in other countries remains restricted to pregnant women.

This chapter maps the development of Irish law from an express constitutional ban on abortion to legislation for a limited constitutional right to abortion.

* Assistant Professor, University of Warwick.

Throughout the decades of debate, official focus on the abstract morality of abortion has distracted from the need to provide adequate care for pregnant women. It is argued that, for progress to be achieved on divisive moral issues such as abortion, frequent reminders of the practical impact of the law on individuals are essential.

II THE GENESIS OF ARTICLE 40.3.3

In 1987, Art 40.3.3 was inserted into the Irish Constitution following a national referendum:

> 'The State acknowledges the right to life of the unborn and, with due regard to the equal right to life of the mother, guarantees in its laws to respect, and, as far as practicable, by its laws to defend and vindicate that right.'

Article 40.3.3 acknowledges the right to life of the unborn as equal to that of the mother. The dependency of the unborn child on the continued life and health of the pregnant mother is not acknowledged. The amendment has been described as 'uniquely misogynistic' setting up a conflict between the rights of the mother and the unborn and anticipating that the time would come when someone would have to choose between them.[1]

The Irish Constitution as adopted made no express reference to the unborn child. Abortion was always illegal in the Irish state under the Offences Against the Person Act 1861 which rendered it a criminal offence to 'procure a miscarriage' or to assist a woman doing so.[2] The continued existence of the 1861 Act created a lingering uncertainty for medical professionals as to the circumstances in which deliberate abortions, carried out to in order to save a mother's life, would be immune from criminal prosecution.

From the 1970s onwards both the courts and the legislature began to adopt an express anti-abortion stance as sale of contraceptives was legalised in Ireland. In 1974, the Supreme Court held that the existing legislative ban on contraception was incompatible with the constitutional right to marital privacy.[3] Walsh J drew a clear line between contraception and abortion expressly recognising the right to life of the unborn child as an unenumerated right protected by the Irish Constitution.[4] The Health (Family Planning) Act 1979 which legislated for sale of contraception on prescription to married couples specifically prohibited the importation, sale and distribution of abortifacients.[5]

---

1 Ivana Bacik 'Legislating for Article 40.3.3' (2013) 3 IJLS 18–35, 18.

2 British statute law in force in Ireland before 1922 remains in force until repealed by Irish statute or found to be repugnant to the Irish Constitution.

3 *McGee v Attorney General* [1974]1 IR284.

4 Ibid 312. This position was reiterated by in *G v An Bord Úchtala* [1980]1 IR 32, 69 and *Norris v Ireland* [1984] 1 IR36, 103.

5 Section 10.

In spite of these legal safeguards, it was feared that the right to marital privacy, established in *McGee v Attorney General*, would be extended by the courts to encompass a constitutional right to abortion on demand, mirroring the approach of the US Supreme Court in *Roe v Wade*.[6] A Pro-Life constitutional amendment was seen by Catholic groups as a line in the sand in the defence of Irish morals.[7]

Opponents of the amendment argued the right to life of the unborn child was already protected in the Constitution.[8] Anti-amendment campaigners drew attention to the consequences for individual women, warning that the amendment would threaten the current medical practice of therapeutic abortion.[9] The Attorney General emphasised that the wording could put women's lives in danger as doctors would have to treat the two lives as equal and could not prefer the life of the mother.[10]

The campaign surrounding the amendment was unprecedentedly bitter and divisive.[11] The amendment was passed by 841,233 votes in favour and 416,136 against.[12]

III THE EXTENT OF THE DUTY IMPOSED BY ARTICLE 40.3.3

From 1983 until 1992,the Irish courts interpreted Article 40.3.3 as imposing a very heavy duty and prioritised the right to life of the unborn over other competing constitutional rights such as the right to travel and the right to disseminate information. A series of cases action was taken by the Society for the Protection of Unborn Children (SPUC) against individuals who provided information about legal abortion services in other countries. The actions, taken on behalf of the unborn, were abstract and the court did not have to consider the reality of its ruling on any particular woman.

---

6 410 US 113 (1973). See for example, William Binchy 'Privacy and Family Law: A reply to Mr O'Reilly' (1977) 66 Studies: An Irish Quarterly Review 330–335.

7 Sandra Mc Avoy 'From Anti-Amendment Campaigns to Demanding Reproductive Rights' in Jennifer Schweppe (ed) *The Unborn Child, Article 40.3.3. and Abortion in Ireland* (The Liffey Press, Dublin, 2008) 17–24.

8 *Finn v The Attorney General* [1983] 1 IR 15.

9 Sandra Mc Avoy 'From Anti-Amendment Campaigns to Demanding Reproductive Rights' in Jennifer Schweppe (ed) *The Unborn Child, Article 40.3.3. and Abortion in Ireland* (The Liffey Press, Dublin, 2008) 24–29.

10 'Attorney General rules out wording' *Irish Times* 16 February 1983.

11 See further Brian Girvin 'Social Change and Moral Politics: The Irish Constitutional Referendum 1983' (1986) 24 Political Studies 61–81; Tom Hesketh *The Second Partitioning of Ireland: The Abortion Referendum of 1983* (Bransma Books, 1990).

12 Department of the Environment, Community and Local Government, 'Referendum Results 1937-2013' available at www.environ.ie/en/LocalGovernment/Voting/Referenda/PublicationsDocuments/FileDownLoad,1894,en.pdf (accessed 30 March 2014).

In 1992, the right to life of the mother and the right to life of the unborn child came into direct conflict in the *X* case.[13] The courts ruled that an abortion was lawful under Irish Law where there was a real and substantial risk to the life of the mother. Following X, the scope of the duty to protect the life of the unborn child was reconsidered. Women who sought a lawful abortion had a right to travel and to information.

IV BLANKET RESTRICTIONS ON OTHER CONSTITUTIONAL RIGHTS

In *AG (SPUC) v Open Door Counselling Ltd,*[14] SPUC took legal action against counselling services provided by Open Door Counselling Ltd and Dublin Well Woman Centre Ltd. Both organisations provided non-directive counselling to pregnant women, which included the discussion of abortion as an option. If the pregnant woman wished to explore the option of abortion she was referred to clinics in the UK, which had been inspected by the organisations. Post-abortion counselling was provided on the woman's return to Ireland.

The High Court held that Art 40.3.3 imposed a heavy burden on the courts to protect the life of the unborn against threats from whatever source.[15] The constitutional rights of freedom of expression and the right to disseminate information simply could not interfere with the right to life of the unborn.[16] The decision was upheld by the Supreme Court. The organisations were restrained, in perpetuity, from assisting pregnant women to travel by referral to clinics, making travel arrangements or informing them of the location and contact details of abortion clinics.[17]

SPUC next sought injunctions against the student unions who disseminated information about abortion and the contact details for abortion clinics in an annual welfare guide. In *SPUC v Coogan,*[18] the Supreme Court held that SPUC had *locus standi* to seek such an injunction without the imperator of the Attorney General. Walsh J emphasised the vulnerability of the unborn child and the urgency of these kinds of cases.[19] McCarthy J dissented, holding that the implications to a free society of such power to prevent a group of citizens from engaging in future conduct was alarming.[20]

In *SPUC v Grogan (No 1)*[21] the students claimed their right to publish and distribute information under EU law. Pregnant women had a right to travel to

---

13 *Attorney General v X* [1992] 1 IR 1.
14 [1988] IR 593.
15 Ibid 599.
16 Ibid 617.
17 Ibid 627.
18 [1989] IR 734.
19 Ibid 744.
20 Ibid 751.
21 [1989] IR 753.

avail of legal abortion services in other EU member states and a corollary of that right was the right to obtain and distribute information about such services. In the High Court, Carroll J refused to grant the sought injunctions distinguishing the case from *Open Door* and referred the issue of the right to distribute information to the ECJ.

On appeal to the Supreme Court, Finlay CJ held that the distribution of such information was unlawful and could not be distinguished from *Open Door*. It was the fact that information was conveyed to pregnant women that created the constitutional illegality.[22] Walsh J emphasised that all procedural questions must be subordinated to the defence of right to life.[23] All those who assisted a pregnant woman in obtaining an abortion were acting in violation of the constitution.[24]

Both *Open Door* and *SPUC v Grogan* were based on the assumption that restricting information about abortion would reduce the numbers of women who went abroad for foreign abortions.[25] Neither case involved the provision of information to a particular woman. The court did not consider the real effects of Irish women seeking information. Only McCarthy J considered the practical consequences of the injunctions, stating in *Open Door* that they were unlikely to save the life of a single unborn child as women would obtain the information they needed from other sources.[26]

The cases had a dramatic effect on the availability of information in the late 1980s and early 1990s as counselling services closed down and English newspapers containing advertisements for abortion clinics were seized.[27] Underground groups providing information were set up such as the Women's Information Network (WIN) and the London-based Irish Women's Abortions Support Group (IWASG).[28]

The rulings also affected the attitudes of medical practitioners. The 1981 and 1984 Ethical guidelines of the Irish Medical Council had advised doctors to adopt a sympathetic and supportive role in caring for women who travelled abroad for abortions to deal with unwanted pregnancies. The codes also emphasised the duty of doctors to make every effort to save life, both born and

---

22 Ibid 764.

23 Ibid 766.

24 Ibid 767.

25 Ivana Bacik 'Legislating for Article 40.3.3' (2013) 3 IJLS 18–35, 22.

26 [1989] IR 771.

27 Caroline McCamley 'Censoring newspapers will not prevent women having abortions' *Irish Times* 22 May 1992.

28 Sandra Mc Avoy 'From Anti-Amendment Campaigns to Demanding Reproductive Rights' in Jennifer Schweppe (ed) *The Unborn Child, Article 40.3.3. and Abortion in Ireland* (The Liffey Press, Dublin, 2008) 29.

unborn.[29] By 1989 the express duty to both lives was removed and the code drew doctors' attention to the changing legal position.[30]

In 1991, the ECJ ruled on the preliminary reference[31] holding that medical termination of pregnancy performed in accordance with the law of the state in which it is carried out is a service within the meaning of the Treaty.[32] However, the court held that the link between the students and the clinics was too tenuous for the prohibition on distribution of information to constitute a restriction on the freedom to supply services. The students were not working in cooperation with the clinics but merely exercising a freedom of expression which was independent of economic activity carried on by the clinics.[33]

In 1992,*Open Door and Well Woman Ireland* brought their case to the European Court of Human Rights.[34] The ECtHR found that there had been an interference with the rights of counsellors to impart information and the rights of women to receive it.[35] The restriction pursued a legitimate aim; abortion was morally wrong in the view of the majority of Irish people as expressed in the 1983 referendum.[36] Although the ECtHR acknowledged the wide margin of appreciation given to states in the matter of morality, the restriction was found to be overbroad and disproportionate.[37] The injunction had created a risk to the health of women who were now seeking abortion at a later stage due to lack of proper counselling and was a violation of Art 10 of the European Convention of Human Rights.[38]

The ruling by the ECtHR was not binding on Ireland but the ruling by the ECJ meant that EU law had the potential to conflict with the Irish Constitution.[39] This threat to Ireland's identity as a 'pro-life' nation complicated national debates about European integration.[40] As a result of the ruling in *Grogan*, Ireland negotiated a protocol to the Maastricht Treaty to prevent abortion

---

29 The Medical Council, *A Guide to Ethical Conduct and Behaviour and to fitness to Practise* (Dublin, 1981) 14–15; The Medical Council, *A Guide to Ethical Conduct and Behaviour and to fitness to Practise* (2nd edn, Dublin, 1984) 21–22.

30 The Medical Council, *A Guide to Ethical Conduct and Behaviour and to fitness to Practise* (3rd edn, Dublin, 1989) 32.

31 *Society for the Protection of Unborn Children Ireland Ltd v Grogan*, Case C-159/90, [1991] ECR 468.

32 Ibid [16].

33 Ibid [26].

34 *Open Door and Dublin Well Woman v Ireland* (App No 14234/88; 14235/88) [1992] ECHR 68.

35 Ibid [60].

36 Ibid [63].

37 Ibid [74].

38 Ibid [77].

39 Diarmuid Rossa Phelan 'Right to Life of the Unborn v Promotion of Trade in Services: the European court of Justice and the Normative Shaping of the European Union' (1992) 55 MLR 670–689; Gráinne de Búrca 'Fundamental Human Rights and the Reach of EC Law' (1992) 13 OJLS 283–319.

40 Siobhán Mullally 'Abortion Law: Rights Discourse, Dissent and Reproductive Autonomy' in Jennifer Schweppe (ed) *The Unborn Child, Article 40.3.3. and Abortion in Ireland* (The Liffey Press, Dublin, 2008) 215–226.

being introduced surreptitiously by EU law.[41] This fear was still relevant in 2008 and was identified as one of the reasons for the rejection of the Lisbon Treaty by the Irish People.[42] In 2009, the Irish Government obtained a legally binding decision of the heads of state of the 17 member states, which included an assurance that nothing in the Treaty of Lisbon would affect the protection of the unborn under the Irish Constitution.[43]

V THE LAWFUL ABORTION

In *X v Attorney General*[44] the Supreme Court considered a case which raised national awareness about the real life impact of protecting the life of the unborn from all possible threats. X, a 14-year-old girl was pregnant as the result of an alleged rape following a sustained period of sexual abuse. X was deeply traumatised and had expressed wishes to commit suicide to her parents, the Gardaí and to a consultant clinical psychologist. Her parents brought her to England to obtain an abortion but enquired whether DNA evidence obtained during the abortion would be admissible in criminal proceedings against the alleged rapist.

When made aware of the case, the Attorney General obtained an interim injunction from the High Court to prevent X from travelling for 9 months or from obtaining an abortion within Ireland.

The High Court held that the Attorney General had a constitutional duty to apply for the injunction.[45] Activities assisting pregnant women to travel for abortion were a direct threat to the life of the unborn. Costello J distinguished the cases from situations in which the pregnancy itself posed a physical risk to the life of the mother where abortion was permissible.[46] The proposed abortion posed 'a real and imminent danger' to the life of the unborn.[47] The risk to the life of the mother was by contrast 'much less and [is] of a different order of magnitude than the certainty that the life of the unborn will be terminated if the order is not made'.[48]

---

41 'Nothing in the Treaty on European Union, or in the Treaties establishing the European Communities, or in the Treaties or Acts modifying or supplementing those Treaties, shall affect the application in Ireland of Article 40.3.3 of the Constitution of Ireland.'

42 Richard Sinnott et al 'Attitudes and Behaviour in the Second Referendum on the Treaty of Lisbon' (July 2010) available at http://gnothai-eactracha.net/uploads/documents/ucd%20geary%20institute%20report.pdf (accessed 30 March 2014).

43 Presidency Conclusions – Brussels, 18/19 June 2009 (11225/2/09 REV 2) available at www.consilium.europa.eu/uedocs/cms_data/docs/pressdata/en/ec/108622.pdf (accessed 30 March 2014).

44 *Attorney General v X* [1992] 1 IR 1.

45 Ibid 9.

46 Ibid 11.

47 Ibid.

48 Ibid.

Costello J failed to acknowledge the dependency of the foetal life on the mother and regarded both lives as separate and equal. This was not a simple choice between a mother and a child; both mother and foetus would die if suicide was successful.

On appeal, the Supreme Court held that the abortion sought was permissible under Irish law and so the injunction should be lifted. Abortion was legal in Ireland if it was established, as a matter of probability, that there was a real and substantial risk to the life of the mother, which could only be avoided by termination of the pregnancy.

Most judges carried out a simple balancing act between the two lives and focused on the evidence of the level of risk to the life of the mother. The psychologist concluded in his expert report that X was capable of suicide and that carrying the pregnancy to term would cause damage to her mental health that would be 'devastating'.[49] Finlay CJ held that the level of evidence of risk of suicide in this case was enough to satisfy the test.[50]

McCarthy J expressly considered the contingent nature of the life of the unborn child:[51]

> 'The right of the girl here is a right to a life in being; the right of the unborn is to a life contingent; contingent on survival in the womb until successful delivery.'

The judges did not expressly consider whether there was sufficient evidence that the risk of suicide could only be avoided by termination. The evidence of the psychologist was that 'minimising the episode' would be best for the child.[52]

The *X* case was criticised by anti-abortionists as attaching too much weight to the risk of suicide[53] and failing to recognise the equal worth and dignity of the mother and child;[54] creating a superior right to life for pregnant women in certain circumstances.[55]

VI LIMITED RIGHTS TO TRAVEL AND INFORMATION

In *X*, Costello J had ruled that restricting on X's right to travel under EU law was a proportionate derogation based on Irish public policy to prevent illegal

---

49 Ibid 9.
50 Ibid 55.
51 Ibid 80.
52 Ibid 68.
53 Theresa Iglesias 'The X Case: A Lego-moral Consideration' (1996) 18 DULJ 187-197.
54 William Binchy 'Article 40.3.3 of the Constitution: Respecting Dignity and Equal Worth of Human Beings' in Jennifer Schweppe (ed) *The Unborn Child, Article 40.3.3. and Abortion in Ireland* (The Liffey Press, Dublin, 2008) 198–213.
55 Alibhe Smyth 'The 'X' Case: Women and Abortion in the Republic of Ireland, 1992' (1993) 1 Feminist Legal Studies 167.

abortions. He noted that in the absence of such a power to restrict the movement of women, the protection provided to the unborn would be useless in many cases.[56]

The Supreme Court, finding X to be entitled to travel abroad for a lawful abortion, did not rule on the legitimacy of restricting travel for an unlawful abortion. However, two of the majority judges made obiter statements that a mother's right to travel under the Irish Constitution could be limited by injunction to protect the life of unborn child.[57] Finlay CJ stated that such injunctions would do little to effectively defend the right to life of the unborn child but would have deterrent effect.[58]

McCarthy J, concerned by the implication of the idea that the Attorney General could prevent an individual from leaving the country for the purposes of abortion,[59] reasoned simply that X had the right to travel and her purpose for doing so was irrelevant.[60]

Following the ruling in *X*, the government admitted that persons entitled to travel abroad for a lawful abortion must be entitled to have appropriate access to information in relation to facilities for such operations either in Ireland or abroad.[61] This was confirmed by the Supreme Court in *Information (Termination of Pregnancies) Bill 1995*.[62]

In *SPUC v Grogan (No 5)*,[63] members of the Supreme Court questioned the validity of *Open Door* following the *X* case. Denham J held Open Door to be erroneous following the ruling in *X* that Irish law permitted abortion in limited circumstances. A blanket ban on information to a class of people that might include those who had a right to information was in error.[64] Keane J held that *Open Door* was only compatible with an absolute right to life of the unborn child and was impossible to reconcile with X.[65]

VII THE 1992 AMENDMENTS TO THE CONSTITUTION

The *X* case provoked outrage in Ireland and received wide coverage in the international media. The ruling introduced lawful abortion to Ireland,

56 Above n 44, 16.
57 Ibid 59 per Finlay J and 92 per Egan J.
58 Ibid 59.
59 Ibid 84.
60 *Attorney General v X* [1992] 1 IR 1, [1992] ILRM 410, [1992] 2 CMLR 277, McCarthy J at 153.
61 *Open Door and Dublin Well Woman v Ireland* (App No 14234/88; 14235/88) [1992] ECHR 68, [25].
62 [1995] 1 IR 1, 33.
63 [1998] 4 IR 343.
64 Ibid 375.
65 Ibid 391.

undermining the campaign of the anti-abortion movement who demanded a new referendum to reinforce the ban on abortion in Article 40.3.3.[66]

The ruling also had the potential to permit future injunctions to prevent women travelling abroad for abortion undermining the efforts of pro-choice groups. Such groups opposed the protocol to the Maastricht Treaty which ensured EU travel rights could be restricted to protect the unborn child and campaigned against the ratification of the Treaty.[67] In an effort to ensure that Maastricht was ratified at a referendum the government obtained a 'Solemn Declaration' that the protocol would not limit travel between member states or the dissemination of information relating to services lawfully available in other member states.[68] It was also agreed that the right to information and the right to travel would be protected by constitutional referendum.

Three separate amendments to Article 40.3.3 were considered by the Irish people in a referendum in December 1992.

The Thirteenth Amendment of the Constitution Bill 1992 amended Art 40 to safeguard the right to travel.[69] This was adopted by a margin of 1,035,308 to 624,059.

The Fourteenth Amendment of the Constitution Bill, 1992 amended Art 40 to allow information to be disseminated about abortion services in other countries subject to legislative safeguards.[70] This was adopted by a smaller margin of 992,833 to 665,106.

The Twelfth Amendment of the Constitution Bill, 1992 proposed limiting life-saving abortions to cases where the risk to the mother's life was due to physical illness rather than risk of suicide.[71] The wording was designed to prevent a development of the *X* case jurisprudence to provide for a right to abortion where there was a risk to the mother's health.[72] The amendment was opposed by pro-choice groups who wanted to maintain the right to abortion

---

[66] Brian Girvin 'Moral Politics and the Irish Abortion Referendums, 1992' (1994) 47 Parliamentary Affairs 206.

[67] Sandra Mc Avoy 'From Anti-Amendment Campaigns to Demanding Reproductive Rights' in Jennifer Schweppe (ed) *The Unborn Child, Article 40.3.3. and Abortion in Ireland* (The Liffey Press, Dublin, 2008) 32–34.

[68] Declaration adopted at Guimaraes, Portugal, by the High Contracting Parties to the Treaty on European Union, 1 May 1992, P 26. See Brian Girvin 'Moral Politics and the Irish Abortion Referendums, 1992' (1994) 47 Parliamentary Affairs 207–210.

[69] 'This subsection shall not limit freedom to travel between the State and another state.'

[70] 'This subsection shall not limit freedom to obtain or make available, in the State, subject to such conditions as may be laid down by law, information relating to services lawfully available in another state.'

[71] 'It shall be unlawful to terminate the life of an unborn unless such termination is necessary to save the life, as distinct from the health, of the mother where there is an illness or disorder of the mother giving rise to a real and substantial risk to her life, not being a risk of self-destruction.'

[72] Brian Girvin 'Moral Politics and the Irish Abortion Referendums, 1992' (1994) 47 Parliamentary Affairs 211–219.

established in *X* and anti-abortion groups who advocated a complete constitutional ban on abortion. The amendment was rejected by a margin of 1,079,297 to 572,177.

As a result of the referendum, the right of women to travel abroad could no longer be restricted to protect the life of the unborn and legislation was enacted to regulate the dissemination of information about foreign abortion. The rejection of the twelfth amendment meant that abortion in accordance with the *X* case principles remained lawful in Ireland. Attempts to legislate to implement *X* resulted in a protracted consultation process and yet another referendum in 2002.

VIII A CONSTITUTIONAL FREEDOM TO TRAVEL

In the 'C' case[73] the High Court considered whether the thirteenth amendment had created a positive right to travel abroad for an abortion. C was a 13-year-old member of the traveller community who was pregnant as the result of rape. She wanted to have an abortion. She had been placed in state care with foster parents who intended to bring her to England for an abortion with the consent of C's parents. When the parents changed their minds, the Eastern Health Board applied to the District Court for an interim care order with directions for the termination of the pregnancy as a 'medical treatment'. The court made the direction after hearing evidence from two psychiatrists that C was suicidal. The parents sought judicial review.

In the High Court, Geoghegan J held that the facts satisfied the test laid down in *X*; a real and substantial risk to the life of the mother established on the balance of probabilities.[74] The lawfulness of the abortion sought was crucial. The amendment merely prevented the courts from granting an injunction to prevent travel but did not create a positive right to travel to obtain an abortion.[75] When considering the welfare of an Irish child in Ireland the court could not make a positive direction for travel to another jurisdiction for the purposes of obtaining an unlawful abortion.

Pro-choice campaigners argued that the case demonstrated the necessity of legislating to implement the *X* case test.[76] Pro-life campaigners felt that the facts in *C* had been manipulated to satisfy the *X* case criteria and lamented the characterisation of a deliberate abortion as medical treatment, arguing that abortions were not necessary to deliver care to pregnant women.[77]

---

73 *A and B v Eastern Health Board* [1998] 1 IR 464.

74 Ibid 480.

75 Ibid 482.

76 Ivana Bacik 'Editorial: C, Re (Unreported – Ireland) (HC)' (1997) MLJI 83, 84.

77 William Binchy 'Editorial: C, Re (Unreported – Ireland) (HC)' (1997) MLJI 85.

In *D (A Minor) v District Judge Brennan*,[78] the nature of the right to travel as a freedom rather than an entitlement was again emphasised. D was a minor in the care of the local authority. Her foetus was given little or no chance of surviving outside the womb. A social worker had notified the Gardai that D was not permitted to leave the state. The High Court gave an ex tempore oral judgment that D could not be prevented from travelling to the UK for an abortion as this right was protected by the thirteenth amendment.

IX LEGISLATIVE RESTRICTIONS ON INFORMATION

The Information (Termination of Pregnancies) Bill was drafted in 1995 and referred to the Supreme Court for an a priori ruling on its compatibility with the Irish Constitution.[79] The Supreme Court upheld the Bill as compatible with the Constitution as amended.[80] The Act makes a distinction between information relating to abortion services disseminated to the general public[81] and information given directly to pregnant women.[82]

The Supreme Court ruled that it was not unlawful to publish information about abortion directed at the general public, as long as the conditions of the Act were complied with. The information must not advocate or promote the termination of pregnancy and must be truthful and objective.[83] Specific information about providers of abortion services is permitted if services are lawful in the place they are provided and the publication of such information is lawful within the law of that other country. Section 4 of the Act specifically outlaws distributing published information about abortion without solicitation or publishing information by notice in a public place.

Sections 5–7 of the Act place additional restrictions where information is given directly to pregnant women. Individuals who provide counselling or advice to pregnant women may not obtain any financial or other benefit from abortion providers. When a pregnant woman requests information about abortion, it is not lawful for a counsellor or medical practitioner to advocate or promote abortion. The woman must be advised in a truthful and objective manner of *all* courses of action open to her. This means that doctors may not advise a woman to have an abortion under any circumstances but they are permitted to inform the patient of the consequences of the pregnancy on her health and life, leaving the decision up to the mother.[84]

---

78 Unreported judgment of the HC, 9 May 2007. See further Jennifer Schweppe, '"A Constitutionally Permissible Abortion?" The Right to Travel, the Role of the Medical Profession and the Duty of the HSE' in Jennifer Schweppe (ed) *The Unborn Child, Article 40.3.3. and Abortion in Ireland* (The Liffey Press, Dublin, 2008) 349–371.

79 A Bill can be referred by the President to the Supreme Court for an a priori ruling on its constitutionality under Art 26 of the Irish Constitution.

80 *Information (Termination of Pregnancies) Bill 1995* [1995] 1 IR 1.

81 Sections 3 and 4.

82 Section 5.

83 Section 3.

84 *Information (Termination of Pregnancies) Bill 1995* [1995] 1 IR 1, 50.

Where a woman decides to take the option of abortion she must book the appointment at a foreign clinic herself, no one can make the appointments on behalf of the woman seeking the termination.[85] Upon booking her doctor can liaise with the doctor at the abortion clinic but direct referrals are prohibited.[86]

The ruling of the Supreme Court did not dispel criticism; anti-abortionists argued that the Act diluted the protection of the unborn[87] bringing Ireland closer to legalising abortion on demand.[88] Despite the intense criticism, the Irish Government advocated that the Act did remove legal uncertainty.[89] Following the Supreme Court ruling, the 1995 Act is immune from future constitutional challenges.[90] The Supreme Court will never consider the constitutionality of the Act as implemented.

Despite the legalisation of non-directive counselling services the government noted the inadequacy of available counselling services in 1999.[91] The Irish college of general practitioners had produced an information leaflet in 1995, but doctors were not obliged to provide women with information about how to obtain an abortion and some did not.[92] The availability of post-abortion counselling and post-abortion medical check-up remained an issue of concern.[93] The 1999 report linked the issues of counselling women and provision of information about foreign abortion to a policy goal of reducing the numbers of women who travelled abroad for abortion. The government was concerned that the significant numbers of women travelling to England and Wales[94] must be offered practical options to deal with their crisis pregnancies to feel that they had real alternatives to abortion.[95]

In 2000, the Constitutional Review Committee stressed the urgent need to deal with crisis pregnancy in Ireland, including preventative measures, options in crisis pregnancies and post-abortion counselling.[96] The Committee considered the experience of women in travelling abroad for abortion but noted that no

---

85 Regulation of Information (Services Outside the State for Termination of Pregnancies) Act 1995, s 8(1).

86 *Information (Termination of Pregnancies) Bill 1995* [1995] 1 IR 1, 49.

87 'Knights strongly criticise abortion Bill' *Irish Times* 28 February 1995; Andy Pollak 'Hierarchy criticises Supreme Court' *Irish Times* 1 July 1995.

88 Micheal O'Regan 'Leading Judge Condemns Abortion Information Act' *Irish Times* 10 July 1995.

89 Trish Hegarty 'Court decision removes doubt, says Noonan' *Irish Times* 13 May 1995.

90 Article 34.3.3 of the Irish Constitution.

91 Department of the Taoiseach, *Green Paper on Abortion* (Dublin 1999) [5.64].

92 Ibid [6.24].

93 Ibid [6.35] and [6.36].

94 Ibid [6.01]. The only official data on abortion trends of Irish women is published by the Department of Health in London and covers abortions carried out in England and Wales only; Steve Clements and Roger Ingham *Improving Knowledge regarding abortions performed on Irish women in the UK* (CPA report 19, 2007).

95 The 1999 report noted that almost 6,000 women had abortions in England and Wales in 1998, most for social/economic reasons [7.97].

96 The All Party Oireachtas Committee on the Constitution *5th Progress Report: Abortion* (Stationery Office, Dublin, 2000).

person had requested to see the Committee about the actual experience of abortion.[97] The Committee noted that the ready availability of abortion facilities abroad reduced the pressure in Ireland to provide abortion facilities and the secrecy available in Britain would always be more attractive to Irish women than facilities provided in Ireland.[98]

The Crisis Pregnancy Agency was established in 2001.The agency refers women to approved counselling services, identifying agencies who will discuss the issue of abortion and provide contact details for abortion services if appropriate.

In 2005, CPA[99] interviews with women experiencing crisis pregnancy revealed widespread lack of knowledge of the availability of counselling, particularly in rural areas. Women who were contemplating abortion were unclear as to whether counsellors could or would provide information about abortion or contact details of abortion providers.

In 2010, Human Rights Watch reported that media coverage of cases such as *C* and *D* coupled with the lack of clear information about abortion in the public sphere left women in genuine doubt about their right to travel abroad for abortion.[100] Many of the women who had travelled abroad did not have access to adequate information and counselling in Ireland. In order to comply with the 1995 Act many counsellors read from a script rather than actively discussing the option of abortion.[101]

Human Rights Watch criticised the actions of the CPA in dealing with rogue agencies who gave women false information about the medical and psychological consequences of abortion as well as using inappropriate imagery and delaying tactics to prevent women from travelling abroad for abortion.[102] In 2009 after 67 complaints and newspaper coverage the CPA finally announced that it would clamp down on rogue agencies.[103] The CPA website now carries a warning that other agencies may have a hidden agenda, can seek to delay the counselling process and in certain cases show inappropriate images or use other tactics to influence a decision.

---

97 Ibid 85. The Committee relied on a study published in 1998, Evelyn Mahon et al *Women and Crisis Pregnancy* (Stationery Office, Dublin, 1998).

98 The All Party Oireachtas Committee on the Constitution *5th Progress Report: Abortion* (Stationery Office, Dublin, 2000) 35.

99 Catherine Conlon *Mixed Methods Research of Crisis Pregnancy Counselling and Support Services* (CPA report 12, 2005).

100 Human Rights Watch *A State of Isolation: The State of Abortion for Women in Ireland* (2010) 13. This problem had been identified by the CPA in 2004 where it was noted that flexibility of interpretation of the law was required for a truly client-centred experience. *A Summary of Research conducted by Drs S Nic Gabhain and V. Batt on crisis pregnancy counselling, to inform the development of The Strategy to Address the Issue of Crisis Pregnancy* (CPA report 4, 2004) 17.

101 Human Rights Watch *A State of Isolation: The State of Abortion for Women in Ireland* (2010) 23.

102 Ibid 24–26.

103 Ibid 40 and see Kitty Holland 'Warning on biased crisis pregnancy "counselling": campaign to highlight secret anti-abortion agenda' *Irish Times* 21 July 2009.

X LEGISLATING FOR *X*

Although the *X* case established that a right to abortion in Ireland existed where there was a real and substantive risk to the mother's life, no legislation was drafted to allow such abortions to take place in Ireland. A 10-year process of consultation was followed by a second referendum on the *X* case criteria in 2002. Much of the stalemate related to the question of establishing the risk of suicide. Although the rulings in *X* and *C* had established that risk of suicide was a real issue in difficult cases, anti-abortion campaigners failed to accept the decision as correct. Allowing a woman to request an abortion where she was at risk of taking her own life was an acceptance of the principle of abortion by demand.

The 1996 Constitutional Review Group advocated legislation to provide for abortion services in Ireland where there was a real and substantial risk to the life of the mother.[104] Following a broad consultation the 1999 Green Paper on Abortion by the Department of An Taoiseach outlined seven options ranging from an absolute constitutional ban on abortion, to amending the Constitution to allow abortion in a broader range of circumstances. It was hoped that the report would lead to a constructive discussion of the options rather than a polarised debate about the morality of abortion.[105]

The 1999 Group noted that although many submissions had been received favouring a complete ban on abortion in Ireland in all circumstances this was not feasible as in very rare cases termination was needed to save a woman's life.[106] For some anti-abortion campaigners there was a distinction between direct and indirect abortion to save the life of the mother.[107] Indirect abortion where termination of the pregnancy was an inevitable result of another medical treatment was morally acceptable and not considered to constitute abortion. Direct abortion was never acceptable. Anti-abortion campaigners simply insisted that there was no medical condition which would require a direct abortion in order to save the mother's life. The 1994 Medical Ethics code noted that the necessity for abortion to preserve the life or health of the sick mother remained to be proved.[108] The 1998 Medical Ethics code stated expressly that deliberate destruction of the unborn child was professional misconduct although cases where the child in utero lost its life as a side-effect of standard medical treatment were not unethical.[109]

---

104 *Report of the Constitutional Review Group* (Stationery Office, Dublin, 1996).

105 Department of the Taoiseach, *Green Paper on Abortion* (Dublin, 1999).

106 Ibid [7.96].

107 Ibid [5.07].

108 The Medical Council, *A Guide to Ethical Conduct and Behaviour and to fitness to Practise* (4th edn, Dublin, 1994) [39.03]-[39.05].

109 The Medical Council, *A Guide to Ethical Conduct and Behaviour* (5th edn, Dublin, 1998) [26.5].

In 2000,the Constitutional Review Group[110] considered the case for constitutional change, examining the evidence of the medical necessity of abortion to save a mother's life.

The vast majority of submissions to the consultation favoured a referendum for an absolute constitutional ban on abortion. Anti-abortion campaigns advocated the ban as a 'principled moral position',[111] the only option compatible with the equal and inherent value of each life. Anti-abortion campaigners did not accept that a direct abortion was ever necessary to save the life of the mother.[112] Statistics were produced to show that there was a very low rate of maternal death in Ireland and a very low rate of suicide amongst pregnant women in general.[113] It was not accepted that the level of risk in any one case might be much higher. The *X* and *C* cases were criticised for their failure to properly examine the medical evidence of the risk of suicide; the experiences of *X* and *C* were rendered irrelevant to the debate.[114] The key concern of anti-abortion campaigners was that any provision for abortion to deal with exceptional cases would inevitably lead to abortion on demand.[115]

The Group endeavoured to examine current medical practice. No official statistics on the numbers of terminations carried out in the state existed. Instead the Committee relied on evidence given by leading obstetricians about their own practice. Medical intervention to save the life of the mother, which resulted in the unavoidable death of the unborn, was routinely carried out and not regarded as abortion by obstetricians.[116] Pregnancies were sometimes ended for therapeutic reasons by inducing very early birth but the babies delivered were not expected to survive.[117] The three masters of the Dublin hospitals, which dealt with 40% of all births in the country, warned that a total constitutional ban on abortion would end in the deaths of women.[118] They stated that direct abortions to save the life of the mother were being carried out in Ireland in cases of cancer, ectopic pregnancies, pre-eclampsia and heart conditions. They warned that emergency situations were encountered at least once a year and in such cases the mother would be far too ill to be moved abroad for abortion. Evidence from psychiatrists noted that it was often difficult to predict suicide[119] but emphasised that this was not the same as saying that no pregnant woman would commit suicide.

As a result of the medical evidence, the Committee was united in the recommendation that an absolute ban on abortion could not be recommended

[110] The All Party Oireachtas Committee on the Constitution, *5th Progress Report: Abortion* (Stationery Office, Dublin, 2000).
[111] Ibid 35.
[112] Ibid 44.
[113] Ibid 28–30.
[114] Ibid 119.
[115] Ibid 33–34.
[116] Ibid 45.
[117] Ibid 46.
[118] Ibid 47–51.
[119] Ibid 57–59.

because it would put the lives of considerable numbers of pregnant women at risk.[120] The Committee disagreed about the medical case for abortion where there was a risk of suicide and put forward three options for consideration by the Legislature: leaving abortion to be regulated by the principles laid down in the *X* case, legislation to regulate medical intervention to safeguard the life of the mother or a referendum to remove the right to a lawful abortion where the risk posed to the life of the mother was one of suicide.[121]

The Fianna Fáil Government committed to a constitutional referendum on abortion. The wording of the new amendment was published in October 2001. The Twenty-fifth Amendment of the Constitution (Protection of Human Life in Pregnancy) Bill, 2001 was the most complex amendment, designed to regulate abortion in Ireland through the Protection of Human Life in Pregnancy Act 2002. This associated Act was given constitutional protection so that it could not be amended except by referendum.[122]

The proposed Protection of Human Life in Pregnancy Act defined abortion as excluding any procedure which was, in the reasonable opinion of a medical practitioner, necessary to prevent a real and substantial risk of loss of the woman's life other than by self-destruction.[123] All other abortions were criminalised and those who carried them out or procured them would face a maximum prison term of 12 years. The right to travel for an abortion was expressly preserved.[124]

Advocates of a no vote included pro-choice campaigners who hoped that rejection of the amendment would maintain the ruling in *X*, and anti-abortion campaigners who felt the amendment did not go far enough to protect unborn life.[125] The campaign also split the medical profession into Doctors for Choice who claimed that the Bill devalued women's mental health by excluding suicide as a grounds for abortion and Doctors for Life who pointed out that where abortion was available, suicide rates did not improve.[126]

In March 2002, the amendment was rejected by 629,041 votes to 618,485. Following the defeat, the Taoiseach delegated the task of abortion legislation to the next government.[127] Although the government was re-elected, no further action was taken to legislate for abortion. The availability of lawful abortion in

---

120 Ibid 115.

121 Ibid 120.

122 This unusual format was challenged in *Morris v Minister for Environment* [2002] 2 JIC 0105 but upheld.

123 Section 1(2).

124 Section 4.

125 Eamon O'Dwyer '"No" campaigners hope rejection will open door to abortion' *Irish Times* 27 February 2002.

126 Muiris Houston 'Doctors take up opposing sides on abortion debate' *Irish Times* 2 March 2002.

127 Mark Hennessy 'Referendum result is for next Government to act on – Ahern' *Irish Times* 9 March 2002.

Ireland remained unregulated, although the 2004 Code of Medical Ethics[128] provided for direct abortion where the unavoidable death of the baby was necessary to protect the life of the mother.

XI INTERNATIONAL PRESSURE FOR CHANGE

From 2000 onwards, international human rights bodies reiterated concerns about the very restrictive grounds under which abortion was available to women in Ireland.[129] Domestic focus remained on the less controversial solution of providing services in Ireland to prevent and manage crisis pregnancies while providing information about safe legal abortion services in the UK.[130]

In 2007, the Council of Europe Commissioner for Human Rights showed concern about the unavailability of abortion services even in circumstances where it was theoretically permitted by Irish law. He noted that the absence of legislation gave no legal certainty to doctors asked to perform life-saving operations which jeopardised women's health. The availability of lawful abortions to save the lives of women remained sporadic and uncertain. Yet at that stage, the Irish Government had no plans to implement legislation to ensure abortions permitted by the *X* case were happening in practice.[131] The Commissioner reiterated his concerns on a return visit in 2011.[132]

In 2010 Human Rights Watch[133] was unable to find any evidence that a single legal abortion had been carried out in Ireland since the *X* case. It criticised the response of the Irish Government to the issues of abortion as erratic and divisive[134] and condemned the Irish public debate about abortion as creating a climate of shame and fear in which the voices of women were entirely absent.

It would take a ruling of the European Court of Human Rights, enhanced scrutiny by the Council of Europe and a high profile maternal death, before legislation implementing the *X* case was finally put forward.

---

128 Medical Council *A Guide to Ethical Conduct and Behaviour* (6th edn, Dublin, 2004) 44.

129 Eg *Concluding Observations of the Human Rights Committee: Ireland* (24 July 2000) A/55/40,paras 422–451,[24]; Convention for the Elimination of Discrimination Against Women 33rd Session July 2005 (CEDAW/C/IRL/4-5) [38]–[39]. 3rd Report of Ireland on observance of the UN Covenant on Civil and Political Rights (CCPR/C/IRL/CO/3 dated 30 July 2008) [13]CCPR/C/IRL/CO/3 [13].

130 See for example 3rd Report of Ireland on observance of the UN Covenant on Civil and Political Rights (2007) CCPR/C/IRL/3 [139]–[144].

131 Report of the Commissioner for Human Rights, Mr Thomas Hammarberg on his visit to Ireland, 26–30 November 2007, adopted on 30 April 2008, CommDH(2008)9 [78]–[80].

132 Report by Thomas Hammarberg, Commissioner for Human Rights of the Council of Europe, following his visit to Ireland from 1 to 2 June 2011 adopted Strasbourg, 15 September 2011 CommDH(2011)27 [15].

133 Human Rights Watch 'A State of Isolation: The State of Abortion for Women in Ireland' (2010) 2–3.

134 Ibid 1.

XII EUROPEAN COURT OF HUMAN RIGHTS' SCRUTINY OF IRISH ABORTION LAW

The European Court of Human Rights reviewed the availability of abortion in Ireland on two occasions. In neither case did the court directly consider the legal grounds for abortion but rather the practical reality facing women who sought an abortion.

In *D v Ireland*[135] the Court considered the provision of services for pregnant women whose foetus had a fatal abnormality. The applicant D was pregnant with twins when, at 14 weeks, she discovered that one foetus had stopped developing and the other had severe chromosomal abnormalities and was unlikely to live longer than 6 days after birth. D travelled to the UK for an abortion in 2002. D complained that the need to travel abroad for abortions and the restrictions imposed by the 1995 Act on information about foreign abortion violated her rights under the ECHR.[136]

The government maintained that D should have initiated an action in the High Court to obtain a declaration that Art 40.3.3 allowed abortion in the case of a fatal foetal abnormality and had not exhausted domestic remedies.[137]

The ECHR held that there was a feasible argument that the balance between the right to life of the mother and of the foetus could have shifted in favour of the mother where the unborn suffered from an abnormality incompatible with life.[138] The availability of D's abortion was uncertain under Irish law and she had not exhausted domestic remedies.[139] By a majority the court held the application to be inadmissible.

In *ABC v Ireland*[140] the Court considered the question of the availability of abortion where there was a real and substantial risk to the mother's life. There were three applicants in the case; A and B had travelled to the UK for abortions and challenged the prohibition on abortion in Ireland for reasons relating to health and well-being. C complained that the failure to implement the constitutional right to abortion in Ireland where there was a risk to the life of the woman violated her Art 8 rights.

The Court held that the availability of abortion fell with the Art 8 right to respect for private life.[141] In relation to the first two applicants, the prohibition on abortions for reasons of health or well-being of the mother did interfere with

---

135 (2006) Application no 26499/02.

136 Lisa Smyth 'From Rights to Compassion: the D case and Contemporary Abortion Politics' in J Schweppe (ed) *The Unborn Child, Article 40.3.3 and Abortion in Ireland: Twenty-Five Years of Protection?* (Liffey Press, Dublin, 2008) 47—65.

137 (2006) Application no 26499/02 [64].

138 Ibid [90].

139 Ibid [102].

140 (2010) Application No 25579/05.

141 Ibid [214].

their right to a private life.[142] However, the prohibition pursued the legitimate aim of the protection of morals of which protection of the right to life of the unborn was part.[143] The prohibition was considered proportionate given the broad margin of appreciation accorded to the Irish state.[144] The court had regard to the fact that Irish law permitted the first two applicants to travel abroad for an abortion with access to appropriate information and medical care in Ireland.[145]

The situation of C was quite different. C had been undergoing chemotherapy for a rare form of cancer. She became pregnant unintentionally when the cancer was in remission. Given the uncertainty of the risks involved in taking the pregnancy to term she travelled to England for an abortion. C complained that there was no regulatory framework in Ireland by which a risk to her life could be assessed and her entitlement to a lawful abortion in Ireland could be established.[146]

The Court accepted that C had travelled for abortion because of a fear that her pregnancy would cause her cancer to return and that she would be unable to get treatment for the cancer in Ireland due to the pregnancy.[147]

The Court held that ordinary medical consultation could not be considered effective in determining whether an abortion could be lawfully performed on the ground of risk to life.[148] There were no obstetric guidelines on determining whether or not an abortion should be carried out and a doctor ran a risk of criminal conviction under the Offences Against the Person Act 1861 if he carried out an abortion that was later found to be unlawful.[149] It was also inappropriate to resort to legal proceedings where a constitutional right to an abortion in the case of a qualifying risk to life was undisputed.[150]

The Court noted that there was now a striking discordance between the theoretical right to a lawful abortion in Ireland and the reality of its practical implementation.[151] No convincing reason for the failure to legislate could be ascertained.[152] The Court held that the absence of a procedure by which C could have established whether or not she qualified for a lawful abortion in Ireland in accordance with Article 40.3.3 constituted a violation of Art 8.

---

[142] Ibid [216].
[143] Ibid [227].
[144] Ibid [232].
[145] Ibid [241].
[146] Ibid [130].
[147] Ibid [125].
[148] Ibid [255].
[149] Ibid [254].
[150] Ibid [258]–[259]
[151] Ibid [264].
[152] Ibid [265].

ABC has been criticised for its focus on European consensus about the availability of abortion[153] where determining whether highly restrictive abortion laws violate women's rights. However, the ruling that, when a right to abortion exists under national law, it must be accessible to individual women was to change the availability of abortion in Ireland.[154]

XIII THE RESPONSE TO *ABC*

The response to the *ABC* judgment was limited, focused and pragmatic. The case was placed under enhanced supervision by the Council of Europe. This required the government to keep to a timetable and allowed NGOs to feed concerns about implementation of the judgment directly to the Committee of Ministers. This international scrutiny meant that the experience of C could not be ignored, unlike the experiences of the women in the *X* case and the *C* case.

By June 2011 the Irish Government had submitted an action plan to the Committee of Ministers that an expert group would examine the judgment and make recommendations to the government about how to implement the judgment.[155] The committee underlined the importance of putting substantive measures in place and keeping to an express timeline.[156]

By September 2012 the Irish Council for Civil Liberties expressed concerns that religious and political opposition to reform had been mounting. Anti-abortion groups had called for yet another referendum and a vocal minority of politicians had signalled opposition to any proposal put forward by the government to provide for abortion.[157]

On 28 October 2012 Savita Halappanaver died in University Hospital Galway. The death sparked an international debate about Irish abortion law.[158] Savita, who was 17 weeks' pregnant, had been diagnosed with inevitable miscarriage. She was kept in hospital and given antibiotics to combat the risk of infection. The consultant stated that he could not induce a miscarriage under Irish law while there was a foetal heartbeat unless the risk to the mother increased. At the time that the abortion was requested there was only a theoretical risk of death by infection. Savita's condition rapidly deteriorated and she died 7 days' later from septic shock.

153 Fiona de Londras and Kanstantsin Dzehtsiarou 'Case Comment Grand Chamber of the European Court of Human Rights, A, B and C v Ireland, decision of 17 December 2010' (2013) 62 ICLQ 250–262; Sheelagh McGuinness 'A, B and C Leads to D (For Delegation!)' (2011) Medical Law Review 476.

154 See also *Tysiac v Poland* (2007) (Application no 5410/03) and *P v Poland* (2013) Application no 57375/08.

155 DH–DD(2011)480E available at https://wcd.coe.int/ViewDoc.jsp?id=1802037&Site=CM.

156 11120th meeting 14 September 2011 available at https://wcd.coe.int/ViewDoc.jsp?id=1829853.

157 DH-DD(2012)882 available at https://wcd.coe.int/com.instranet.InstraServlet?command=com.instranet.CmdBlobGet&InstranetImage=2154679&SecMode=1&DocId=1931236&Usage=2.

158 Una Mulally 'Savita story resonates around the world' *Irish Times* 17 November 2012.

Anti-abortion campaigners tried to marginalise the event as a failure in medical care with nothing to do with the law on abortion.[159] A number of medical professionals argued that the case highlighted the greyness of the law in establishing risk to life that put women's lives in serious danger.[160] The final report by the Health Service Executive (HSE) concluded that the medical team had failed to recognise the gravity of the increasing risk to the mother, inadequately monitored the patient and failed to offer her all management options for her condition.[161]

The Expert Group's report following *ABC* was published in November 2012. The government's report to the Council of Europe in December 2012 put forward an interim procedure making it the responsibility of an individual doctor to determine when a real and substantial risk existed to the life of the mother.[162] The Committee of Ministers noted the view of the Expert Group that only a legislative solution was the preferred method of implementation and urged Irish authorities to expedite implementation.[163]

The Expert Group[164] noted that a deep-seated division still existed in Irish society between groups who felt that risk of suicide should not be a basis for abortion and those who wished to extend the right to abortion in Ireland to situations beyond a direct risk to the life of the mother.[165] Following the ruling in *ABC* it was accepted that a right to abortion in certain circumstances had existed in Ireland since the enactment of the eighth amendment.[166]

The report conceptualised lawful abortion as a medical treatment.[167] A framework was required to ensure that the treatment was clinically appropriate before a decision to proceed could be made by the patient.[168] Doctors were considered to be the most appropriate decision-makers in determining whether a real and substantial risk to the mother existed. The agreement of two doctors was recommended except in situations where risk to life was imminent and

---

159 David Quinn 'Even without legislation, we're going to have more abortions in Irish hospitals' *Irish Independent* 26 April 2013; Breda O'Brien 'Latest report provides more evidence that change in law not needed to save Savita' *Irish Times* 12 October 2013.

160 Paul Gartland 'Medical Council ready to reconsider guidance if law changed: Savita Halappanavar case Reaction' *Irish Times* 17 November 2012.

161 HSE *Investigation of Incident 50278 from time of patient's self referral to hospital on the 21st of October 2012 to the patient's death on the 28th of October, 2012* (June 2013).

162 DH-DD(2012) 1124. Available at https://wcd.coe.int/com.instranet.InstraServlet?command=com.instranet.CmdBlobGet&InstranetImage=2203972&SecMode=1&DocId=1958946&Usage=2.

163 1157th meeting 6 December 2012. Available at https://wcd.coe.int/ViewDoc.jsp?id=2010979&Site=CM&BackColorInternet=C3C3C3&BackColorIntranet=EDB021&BackColorLogged=F5D383.

164 Sean Ryan, *Report of the Expert Group on the Judgment in A,B and C v Ireland* (November 2012).

165 Ibid 3.

166 Ibid 7.

167 Ibid 28.

168 Ibid 29.

inevitable, where the opinion of one medical practitioner should suffice.[169] The group considered that a right to conscientious objection should be provided for but this would be limited by a right to inform the patient of her right to ascertain whether abortion was lawful and a duty to refer to another doctor as well as an overriding duty to treat where risk of death was inevitable and imminent.[170]

The HSE investigation into the death of Savita had recommended the prompt introduction of a Maternity Early Warning Scoring System and a review of national guidelines on infection and pregnancy.[171] A second report[172] into the standards of services provided by the HSE noted wide variation in local clinical and corporate governance arrangements across the 19 maternity units in Ireland and inconsistency in the provision of maternity services.[173] A review of national standards and the implementation of consistent models for the delivery of maternity services was recommended as a matter of priority.[174] The report noted inconsistencies in reporting data about maternal deaths and noted that 8/19 maternity units produced no annual clinical report.[175] In February 2013, the HSE announced the launch of a national maternity early warning system for the early detection of life-threatening illness in pregnant women.

XIV THE PROTECTION OF LIFE ACT 2013

The Protection of Life During Pregnancy Act 2013 is an Act to protect human life during pregnancy rather than an Act to legislate for abortion. It repeals ss 58 and 59 of the Offences against the Person Act 1861 and provides for a new criminal offence of intentional destruction of unborn human life carrying a sentence of a 14-year imprisonment.[176]

An abortion is lawful where two medical practitioners have jointly certified in good faith that there is a real and substantial risk of loss to the woman's life from physical illness and if the risk can only be averted by carrying out the procedure. The procedure must also be carried out by an obstetrician at an appropriate institution.[177]

---

169 Ibid 36.
170 Ibid 43.
171 HSE *Investigation of Incident 50278 from time of patient's self referral to hospital on the 21st of October 2012 to the patient's death on the 28th of October, 2012* June 2013 (HSE incident investigation)
172 Health Information and Quality Authority, *Investigation into the safety, quality and standards of services provided by the HSE to patients including pregnant women, at risk of clinical deterioration, including those provided in University Hospital Galway and as reflected in the care and treatment provided to Savita Halappanaver* (7 October 2013).
173 Ibid 16–17 /[3.6].
174 Ibid [3.7].
175 Ibid [3.8].
176 Section 14.
177 Section 7.

In emergency situations it is lawful to carry out such a procedure where a medical practitioner believes in good faith that there is an immediate risk of loss of the woman's life from physical illness and the medical procedure is immediately necessary.[178]

The Act provides for a special procedure where the pregnant woman poses a suicide risk. In this scenario three medical practitioners[179] must jointly certify in good faith that there is a real and substantial risk of loss of life by way of suicide and the risk can only be averted by carrying out the medical procedure.[180]

Women may seek a review of any decision not to allow an abortion.[181]

The Act has been criticised as a failure to address the needs of women who have received a diagnosis that their foetus will not survive outside the womb.[182] This basis for abortion had been presented as tenable by the state in *D v Ireland.* The Irish Minister for Justice argued that Art 40.3.3 prevented the government from providing for abortion in such circumstances and anticipated another referendum in years to come.[183] A case on the issue is pending before the United Nations Human Rights Committee.[184] Pro-choice campaigners have already launched petitions for the repeal of Art 40.3.3.

Anti-abortion campaigners have condemned the Act as introducing an abortion regime into Ireland.[185]

The first legal abortion was carried out in Ireland in August 2013[186] and the Act came into force in January 2014. The College of Psychiatrists continues to express concern about the lack of clinical guidelines to assess the risk of suicide during pregnancy which are still being drafted by the HSE.[187]

---

178 Section 8.

179 Two of whom must by psychiatrists.

180 Section 9.

181 Sections 10–12.

182 S Donoghue and S Claire Michelle 'Abortion for Foetal Abnormalities; the Limited Scope of the Irish Government's Response to the A, B and C Judgment' (2013) 20 European Journal of Health Law 117–145; Ivana Bacik 'Legislating for Article 40.3.3' (2013) 3 IJLS 18–35.

183 Ruadhn Mac Cormaic 'Abortion law should go further – Shatter: Lack of option here in cases of rape and fatal foetal abnormality "a great cruelty"' *Irish Times* 25 July 2013.

184 Pamela Duncan 'Woman forced to travel to UK for Abortion takes case to UN' *Irish Times* 14 March 2014.

185 'Pro Life Campaign says "flaws" showing in Law' *Irish Times* 4 January 2014.

186 Henry McDonald 'Ireland's first legal abortion carried out in Dublin' *The Guardian* 23 August 2013.

187 Kitty Holland 'College tells psychiatrists not to do abortion assessments: Psychiatrists say implementation of new abortion Act "completely unsatisfactory"' *Irish Times* 3 January 2014.

XV CONCLUSION

Ireland retains one of the most conservative abortion regimes in the world. The Protection of Life During Pregnancy Act 2013 does nothing to liberalise the basis on which abortion is available in Ireland. It merely provides for abortions to be carried out in accordance with the principles laid down in the *X* case in 1992.

Since 1983 the principle of an abortion to save the life of the mother has been generally accepted by all sides except those who believe that such a necessity could never arise. Why did legislation to provide for this life-saving treatment take so long? Pragmatic attempts to legislate for *X* were turned into polemics about the moral-legal aspects of abortion rather than focusing on health care issues or women's rights.[188] The tendency of the Irish public has been to polarise the issue of life-saving abortion, viewing it as either an unacceptable step towards a regime that would eventually lead to abortion on demand or as inferior commitment that does not go far enough. The women whose lives were put at risk by the continuation of their pregnancies were lost in the middle ground.

The polarisation of the debate can be understood by the invisibility of the reality of abortion in Ireland. Accurate empirical evidence of the numbers of women seeking abortion has never been available. Although women's experiences of abortion are now given great prominence in the media,[189] the significance of individual experiences of Ireland's restrictive abortion policies was never properly addressed in the official consultations leading up to domestic reforms. Cases such as *X*, *C* and *D* were dismissed as rare, incorrectly decided and not reflective of the majority of Irish women who did not need or want abortion.

The adoption of the Protection of Life During Pregnancy Act represents a shift in the national debate. For even minor progress to be achieved on divisive moral issues where ideological positions have become entrenched, frequent reminders of the practical impact of law on individuals are essential. Enhanced scrutiny of the ECtHR ruling in *ABC v Ireland* meant that the reality of C's experience could not be swept aside. The death of Savita Halappanaver reinforced the necessity of urgent change. The new Act places an obligation on the state to monitor the numbers of abortions carried out in Ireland and there has been a widespread review of maternity services. It is hoped that this more pragmatic approach to facing the reality of abortion as an Irish problem may lead to substantive legal reform with a proper consideration of women's reproductive rights.

---

188 Ivana Bacik 'Legislating for Article 40.3.3' (2013) 3 IJLS 18–35, 18.

189 For example, the *Irish Times* ran a series of stories on abortion published on 25 February 2012 and 24 March 2012.

ITALY

JOINT CUSTODY OF CHILDREN ON SEPARATION AND DIVORCE: THE CURRENT LAW IN ITALY: AN OVERVIEW OF THE LAW AND HOW IT IS APPLIED

*Federica Giardini**

Résumé

Le présent texte analyse la législation qui, depuis 2006, régit la garde partagée. Un des principes fondamentaux en la matière est que les enfants, tant légitimes que naturels, doivent pouvoir entretenir des relations continues avec chacun de leurs parents, même après la séparation de ceux-ci. C'est la raison pour laquelle les tribunaux doivent donner priorité à la garde partagée et n'accorder de garde exclusive que lorsqu'il est démontré que la garde partagée n'est pas dans l'intérêt de l'enfant. La loi de 2006 prévoit également que l'autorité parentale est exercée conjointement, en matière d'éducation ou de santé par exemple. À l'occasion d'une réforme législative en 2012, l'expression 'autorité parentale' a été remplacée par celle de 'responsabilité parentale'.

I INTRODUCTION

The way the custody of children is organised when a situation of crisis arises in the relationship between the parents, or on any occasion where a court decision on custody becomes necessary, is a part of the broad subject that makes up family law. It is a salient area in the relationship between law and society itself and confirms family law as a legal field that is very much 'law in action'.

In this context, developments in Western law have seen a steady and continuous evolution from the granting of custody to one parent only, often the mother, to forms where the relationship with both parents, and hence also the father, are viewed as being essential to the minor, as well also as the right of the child to maintain a relationship with both of the parental figures as well as the grandparents and relatives on both sides.

* Professor, Dipartimento di Diritto Privato e Critica del Diritto, Scuola di Giurisprudenza, Università degli Studi di Padova.

II THE TRADITIONAL CUSTODY MODEL IN ITALIAN LAW UP TO 2006

The Italian civil code of 1942 recognised civil marriage as indissoluble and did not therefore expressly deal with the question of custody in the event of its breakdown. The decisions of the court tended to fill in the lacunae in the law by recourse to the criteria set forth in art 147 of the civil code (cc), which attributed particular importance to the principles of morality for the education and upbringing of the children. The family in the legal sense consisted only of the lawful family, that is to say the family based on matrimony. Law number 898 of 1 December 1970 introduced divorce into Italian law and posed the question of the problem of custody in this situation.

Looking at the question from a historical perspective, it should be noted that before the reform of 1975 the custody of children of unmarried parents came under the provisions of art 333 cc, which limited parental authority as a kind of sanction against the unfit parent (even though before that time the interpretation of art 333 cc saw a broader view being taken through the consideration of objectively prejudicial situations, irrespective of any parental blame). As regards the financial aspect, reference was to the duty to make maintenance payments and the corresponding procedures (art 433 cc et seq) involved a distribution of competence between the juvenile court and the ordinary court that remained in operation until very recent times.

The family law reform approved small changes with law 151 of 1975, introducing a new perspective into the Italian system. From a hierarchical view of the traditional family, in which the husband was at its head, there was a move or a trend, towards a more egalitarian view, with both spouses having the same rights and duties. Changes were also made to art 155 of the civil code and provision was made, in the case of separation, for the children to be put in the custody of the parent deemed most fit by the court on the basis of the moral and material interests of the offspring.

The family law reform of 1975 also introduced changes in the area of custody where the parents were not married. Article 317 bis cc, which was a departure from all previous law, governed inter alia the custody of unmarried parents following the breakdown of their own cohabitation and with the children, as well as when no such cohabitation had ever been established. This law gave notably discretionary powers to the court (the juvenile court), which could in the interests of the minor exclude the parental authority of both parents and appoint a guardian. In this field the provisions in law diverge greatly from art 155 cc which deals with the question of custody of children of parents who are married and separated. There is no doubt that the introduction of art 317 bis cc led to the independence of the proceedings in question with respect to the limitations of and loss of parental authority. Nevertheless the reference to the exercise of parental authority in the provisions, the wide discretionary powers afforded to the judge, the jurisdiction being given to the juvenile court and consequently the proceedings in camera of the counsel, as in arts 737 et seq cpc, contributed to keeping it within in context of proceedings under arts 330, 333 and 336 cc. On the contrary, however, the proceedings before the ordinary courts achieved some autonomy as regards maintenance payments. For its part the reform of 1975 clearly specified in the new art 261 cc that the parent who recognises paternity of the child is attributed all the rights and duties in regard to the child that the married parent has. It is therefore a matter of maintenance rather than alimony, and the action brought in the ordinary courts for recognition of the child, brought with a writ, meant the procedure was closer to that for separation and for divorce as regards the provisions relating to the children.

With law number 74 of 1987, which reformed the law on divorce (no 898/1970), the Italian legislation considered for the first time the concepts of joint custody and of alternate custody. This latter envisages the parents working in shifts as regards to where the child stays, as well as in regards to the exercise of parental authority at the time the child is living with the parent. Despite its shortcomings the reform of 1987 did introduce for the first time the notion of dual parenthood.

III THE REFORM BROUGHT IN WITH LAW 54 OF 8 FEBRUARY 2006: ITS GUIDING PRINCIPLES AND CONTENT

(a) The guiding principles of the reform

According to the traditional conception of matrimonial breakdown, the crisis of the couple leads to the end of the family. This idea was finally superseded with the reform of 2006, which is based on the principle according to which with the crisis of the family the relationship of parent survives (forever) and more generally the relationship between parents and children continues. The question of joint custody needs to be seen according to this precise logic.[1]

Among the fundamental principles driving the reform of 2006 is that all minors (legitimate and 'natural'[2]) should have the right to a continuing and stable relationship with both parents even in the event of the breakup of the family unit. Joint custody amounts to a restatement and broadening of the principle of dual parenthood in the sense of the right of the child to a full and stable relationship with both parents, even where the family is going through the pains of the separation or the divorce of the spouses. Joint custody seeks to divide in a balanced way the specific responsibilities of and the time spent with each of the parents while maintaining unchanged the status of the parenthood

---

1 On the subject see: De Sisto, On the feasibility of joint custody even where the parents live far apart or even in different countries in *Giurisprudenza di merito*, 2007, no 12, Giuffrè, 3110; and Spalazzi Caproni, Affido condiviso e interesse del minore, in *Vita notarile*, 2006, no 3, Edizioni Giuridiche Buttitta, 1625.

2 The distinction between 'legitimate children' and 'natural children' was abolished in Italian law with law 219 of 2012: see below, section IX.

of each and hence protecting the relationship between the children and the parents. With this process the Italian legal system has since 2006 appeared to be in line not only with the principles enshrined within its own constitution (arts 2, 3, 29, 31), but also with international conventions (the European Convention on Human Rights signed in Rome on 4 November 1950, the United Nations Convention on the Rights of the Child signed in New York on 20 November 1989, and the European Convention on the Exercise of Children's Rights adopted by the Council of Europe in Strasbourg on 25 January 1996).

The Italian civil code, by virtue of law 54 of 2006, establishes that the court, as regards the custody of minors, must decide as a matter of priority in favour of joint custody even though the legislators kept as a 'system safety valve' the possibility of sole custody where it deems that otherwise joint custody would go against the interests of the minor. In making its appraisal the court must take account of the emotional and psychological aspects and not only material aspects of the situation.

Joint or sole custody may not be awarded according to blame for the separation: if one of the spouses is deemed to be 'responsible' for the breach of matrimonial obligations it does not follow that for that reason custody of the children may not be awarded to that parent. What counts is that the children are assured an environment capable of affording them the best development of their personality. In the end the court must give preference to joint custody and if it decides to opt for sole custody it must give reasons for this solution (in the interest of the minor), stating why custody to the other parent would be against the interests of the minor. As regards the choice of the parent who has custody of the offspring, the court must apply the fundamental criterion provided for in art 155, para 1 cc, which is solely the interest of the offspring. The judge must therefore prefer that parent who seems most suited to reduce the damage from the breakup of the family and able to ensure the best possible development of the minor in the environment most suited to the satisfaction of the material, emotional and psychological needs of that child, taking account of the specific situations that exist in that environment in which the minors will be living in after the separation.

Article 155 cc, as altered by the law of 2006, also gives some indications on the suppositions for and characteristics of the child maintenance payments that the parents must pay for the children. The law expressly introduces in this area the general principle already established by the Court of Appeal, by which each parent should provide for the maintenance of the children in proportion to their income, with the further provision that the court may order, where necessary, the payment of a period payment to realise this 'proportionality' principle.

(b) The content of the reform

The institution of joint custody of children in the event of the separation or the divorce of the parents was introduced as the general rule in Italian law in 2006.

Law number 54 of 8 February 2006 was published in the Official Journal of Italy (no 50 of 1 March 2006) and came into force on 16 March 2006.

The provision changes both substantive law and procedural law on family matters, amending the Italian civil code and also the code of civil procedure (cpc). In detail, as regards substance, art 155 cc is replaced so that the 'Provisions regarding the children' explicitly state that even if the parents personally separate the minor child has the right to maintain a balanced and continuous relationship with each of them, to receive care, to be brought up properly and to have an education from both and to also maintain important relationships with the grandparents and relatives on each side. To achieve this aim prescribed by the law a court that decrees that the spouses are separated shall adopt measures in relation to the children with sole reference to the moral and material interest of such children. Having made an appraisal as a priority of the possibility of custody being awarded to both of the parents, it determines the times and manner of their presence with each parent, establishing also the extent to which each must contribute to the maintenance, care, education and upbringing of the children. It takes into account any agreements made between the parents themselves, provided these do not run counter to the interest of the children. It then makes any orders required in relation to the children.

The law further provides that parental authority be exercised by both parents and the decisions most relevant to the interest of the children with regard to their upbringing, education and health are taken jointly by common agreement, taking account of the ability, natural inclination and the aspirations of the children. If the parents are not in agreement the decision is remitted to the court. As regards decisions simply of ordinary administration, the court may establish that the parents exercise their parental authority separately. On the question of the maintenance to which the child is entitled, the law intervenes to provide that, unless otherwise agreed in writing by the parties, each of the parents shall provide for the maintenance of the children in proportion to that person's own income. Finally the court orders, where necessary, the payment of a periodic maintenance payment to realise the principle of proportionality, to be calculated according to a series of factors that are expressly listed in the legislation, such as the current needs of the child, the standard of living enjoyed by the child when living with both parents, the amount of time spent with each parent, the financial resources of each of the parents and the economic value of domestic chores and care undertaken by each parent. The maintenance payment is automatically indexed to the ISTAT indices where no other variable is indicated by the parties or by the court. If the information of an economic character provided by the parents is not sufficiently well documented, the court orders an assessment by the inland revenue police on contested assets even if held in the name of different persons. After art 155 cc, the new arts 155 *bis* to 155 *sexies* cc are introduced. They deal respectively with custody to a sole parent and opposition to joint custody, a review of the orders concerning the custody of the children, the assigning of the family home and orders on the subject of residence, provisions in favour of children that are of age and the powers of the court to listen to the views of the minor.

As regards custody awards to a sole parent and opposition to joint custody, the law says that the court can provide for custody of the children by just one of the parents where it seems to the court, and the court must give reasons, that the custody to the other would be against the interests of the minor.

Each of the parents may moreover at any time request sole custody of the child where the circumstances here apply, ie where joint custody is against the interests of the child. If the court accepts the application, it orders custody solely to the applicant partner save however as far as possible with respect to the child's right under art 155 to maintain a balanced and continuous relationship with each of its parents, and to receive care, upbringing and education from both and to maintain important relations with the grandparents and relatives on both sides of the family.

If the application for sole custody made by one of the parents is manifestly unfounded, the court may consider the conduct of the applicant parent for the purposes of determining the orders to make in the interest of the children, without prejudice to art 96 cpc, which permits the court to penalise the applicant parent by ordering him or her to pay compensation to the other parent for the mischievous application brought before the court. On the question of the review of provisions concerning the custody of children, the general principle is that expressly established by the law in art 155 *ter* cc, that is to say that the parent has the right at any time to request a review of the orders concerning the custody of the children, the attribution of the exercise of parental authority over them and any provisions made regarding the extent and the manner of the contribution for maintenance of the children themselves. On the matter of the assignment of the family home and the subject of residence, the law of 2006 provides that the enjoyment of the family home is, by priority, to be assigned having regard to the interest of the children. With the assignment the court shall take account of the regulation of the financial relations between the parents, also taking account of the ownership of the property as the case may be. The right to enjoyment of the family home ceases where the person to whom the home is assigned does not live there or stops generally living there or lives with a partner *more uxorio* or marries another person. Finally the order for the assigning and that of its revocation are registerable and opposable against third parties under the terms of art 2643 cc. Where one or other of the spouses changes residence or domicile, the other spouse may request, if the change interferes with the manner of exercising custody, the determination of the agreements or provisions adopted, including those of a financial nature.

Specific provisions are also set forth in the law of 2006 with regard to children of age. In this area the court, having duly assessed the circumstances, may make an order in favour of child of age who is not yet economically independent for a periodic maintenance payment. Such payments, unless determined otherwise by the court, are to be paid directly to the interested person. Grown up children who suffer from serious disabilities in the terms provided for in art 3, para 3 of law 104 of 5 February 1992 are protected fully by the laws in place for minors. With regard to the powers of the court and that of listening to the views of the minor, *before* the issuing, even on an interim basis, of the orders under art 155, the court may take evidence on the application of either of the parties or ex officio. The court may further be disposed to hear the minor who has reached the age of 12 years or even if the child is younger where the child is capable of making discerning judgments. If, finally, the court deems it advisable, after hearing the parties and after obtaining their consent, it may adjourn the adoption of the orders under the terms of art 155 to permit the spouses, with the assistance of experts, to seek mediation to find an agreement, with particular regard to the safeguarding of the moral and material interests of the children.

The law of 2006 also has a significant effect on the legal process. It provides in the first place that, when temporary and urgent orders are made by the court on the first appearance of the spouses in the process for their separation, an appeal may be brought to the Court of Appeals, which will make its decision in counsel chambers. The complaint must be brought within the mandatory term of 10 days from notification of the order. The new art 709 *ter* cpc on the subject of the settlement of disputes and provisions in the case of breach or infringement, provides specifically that, for the settlement of disputes arising between parents in relation to the exercise of parental authority or the matter of custody, the court of competence is that of the pending proceedings. For those proceedings to change the provisions relating to the separation of the spouses, as in art 710 cpc, the competent court is that of the place of residence of the minor. Following the appeal, the court calls the parties and takes the appropriate measures. In the event of serious breaches or actions that bring prejudice to the minor or obstruct the proper process of the awarding of custody, it may change the order currently in force and by express provision in law may also warn the parent in breach and order the payment of damages by one of the parties to the minor; order the payment of compensation for damages by one of the parents to the other or, finally, order the parent in breach to pay a monetary fine of from a minimum of €75 to a maximum of €5,000 to the Fines Fund. The orders taken by the court can be challenged in the ordinary ways. From the point of view of the criminal law, it should be emphasised that the breach of financial obligations gives rise to the offence of failure to meet family financial assistance duties under art 570 of the criminal code.[3]

---

[3] The law in art 570 of the Italian criminal code, 'The breach of the duty of family assistance', provides that:
'Anyone, abandoning the domestic domicile, or in any way conducting him or herself in a way that is contrary to the order and morality of the family, fails to fulfill the obligations of assistance that are the duty for the person with parental authority or as spouse, shall be punished with prison for up to one year and a fine of from two hundred thousand to two million lire [€103 and €1,032].
The aforesaid punishments also apply to any person who: 1) misappropriates or dissipates the assets of the minor child or ward or spouse; 2) removes the means of sustenance of minor offspring, or offspring who are unable to work, parents or a spouse, who is not legally separated because of his or her own fault. The offence is punishable on a complaint from the victim save in those cases provided for in number 1 and when the offence is committed in

The range of innovations introduced by the reform of 2006 is at least potentially extended also to those situations already decided in the past, that is before the new law came into effect. In this case, when the decree of approval of the consensual separation agreement, the judicial separation order, the dissolution, the annulment or the cessation of the civil effects of the marriage were already issued as of the date of the coming into force of the law of 2006, each of the parents may request, in the manner provided for in art 710 cpc or art 9 of law 898 of 1 December 1970, as subsequently amended, the application of the provisions of the new law.

Finally, with the last important innovation, the law expressly provides that all the provisions contained within it apply also in the case of the dissolution, cessation of the civil effects or the nullity of the marriage as well as to proceedings relating to children of parents who are not married to each other.

IV CRITICAL POINTS EMERGING AFTER THE APPROVAL OF THE LAW

The provisions brought in with the so-called joint custody law did not fail to arouse notable critical commentary, including from those working in this field. Certain critical points were evident from the outset.

From the substantive standpoint and in terms of definitions of terms, the Italian legislature could have grasped the opportunity in 2006 to go beyond the concept of parental authority over children and custody and put the law in line with the EEC law whose regulations on the recognition and the execution of decisions on family matters uses the notion of 'parental responsibility',[4] in the place of the traditional Roman law idea of parental authority. The change would not have just been terminological but would also have been substantial. The traditional notion of 'potestà' (parental authority) has inherent in it the idea of 'power over the minor', while the notion of parental responsibility, as well as having the advantage of placing the parents at a level of equality with their children, would also have had the advantage of expressly affirming, through a precise stance on the part of the legislature, the centrality of the recognition of the actual rights of the minor, even within the family unit itself.[5]

It would moreover have been able to expressly provide for the need to appoint a guardian in those cases where there was seen to be conflict of interest with the parent.

---

relation to minors, from number 2 of the previous paragraph.
The provisions of this article do not apply if the facts come into a category of more serious crimes in other provision in law.'

4 As in EEC Regulation no 1347 of 2000, later replaced by EEC Regulation no 2201/03 which came into force on 1 March 2005.

5 The sensitivity towards such changes was in any case already in progress since the Italian legislature returned to radically modify these concepts with the more recent reform in the area of filiation, introduced with law 219 of 2012 and its subsequent implementation.

It was commented, once again,[6] that the text of the law as presented after its approval imposes in reality on all separations a single custody model, neglecting to consider some situations where the cases put before the court may have fundamental importance for the safeguarding of the interests of the minor. Such a risk is that the law aggravates rather than solves a series of practical problems that could have negative consequences for the balanced growth of the minor.

The absence, in terms of the legislation, of the need to specify which should be the usual place of residence of the minor is considered an omission capable of giving rise to numerous disputes between parents, for example in relation to the choice of school that the minor will have to attend: given the parity of the parents, if the two parents for example live in different school catchment areas.

The same can be said for the necessarily joint exercise of parental authority, for example in the case of disagreement between the parents on the most important decisions for the children, such as the choice of school and medical care choices. The need for recourse to the court, which is a consequence of the legislative system adopted in Italy, inevitably leads to increased costs and a potential increase in conflict between parents, to the detriment of the interests of the child.

The provisions on the subject of the revocation of the assignment of the family home in the case of a new cohabitation by the parent to whom the home was assigned gives rises to a certain perplexity since such an automatic result fails to consider what might in the actual case be the real interests of the minors involved.

No less confusion reigns with regard to the provision for direct payments, unless otherwise ordered by the court, to the child of age who is not yet financially independent. It may be in fact that in those cases where a child who has just turned 18 years of age that child will become the only person with the locus standi to bring a legal action against his or her own parent who fails in the duty to provide maintenance.

The law of 2006 also makes it mandatory, and this too has given rise to perplexity, to hear the views of the child who has reached the age of 12 years. It seemed to have been unnecessary to make this mandatory. Situations may arise in reality where the dispute is in areas to which the minor is an outsider (eg the case in which the proceedings concern maintenance of one parent payable to the other). The question for example of appointing a special guardian in these circumstances was also overlooked.

Another opportunity missed by the legislation of 2006 was that of establishing a special 'Court for the person and the family', with sole competence for family law matters and organisational autonomy. Today in the Italian legal system

---

6 As in the Juvenile Chamber of Milan, a non-profit lawyers association that with its articles of association has the aim of promoting the centrality of rights of minors. Cf www.cameraminorilemilano.it.

family matters are largely left to the ordinary courts and to the judges themselves, who always pass work of the same kind, eg family law matters, to the same divisions of an ordinary court, with a de facto functional sharing out between the judges.

From the perspective of competence by subject, between the juvenile court and the ordinary court, the imperfect legislative technicalities have required the intervention of the Sezioni Unite della Suprema Corte di Cassazione Italiana. Its now established position on the question regarding the shared jurisdiction of the juvenile court and the ordinary court in cases, regarding children born outside of marriage, specifies that custody cases for parents who are not married to each other are a matter completely for the juvenile court. This moves on from the previously contradictory precedents whereby the juvenile court decided on custody but the ordinary court intervened, insofar as competent, on the maintenance of these and the assigning of the family home.[7]

(a) The effects of the reform of 2006

(i) The effects of the reform of 2006 on filiation outside wedlock (formerly called 'natural filiation'): the application of law no 54/2006 on 'proceedings regarding parents who are not married'

Law no 54 of 2006 made an evident choice to harmonise the legal situation for children of unmarried parents and those who are the issue of matrimony, as regards custody decisions, saying that 'the provisions in this law also apply (. . .) to proceedings relating to children whose parents are not joined in marriage'.

The rules introduced by the aforesaid law on separation and divorce also apply, therefore, in this sector too. That is to say with regard to the exercise of the *potestà* or parental authority by both parents, the decisions of principal interest are by common agreement (with the intervention of the court in the case of disagreement): that minor decisions may be taken separately; the preference for joint custody rather than to one or the other of the parents, though sole custody may in any case be ordered where the former solution seems to be contrary to the interests of the minor; maintenance payments for the child only as a subordinate matter since the prevailing principle is that of direct maintenance of the child on the part of each parent; the mandatory hearing of the views of the child who has reached the age of 12 years; the possibility of a review of the custody terms, and more besides. In addition to the above changes in substantive law introduced by law no 54 there also followed a number of problems with regard to legal procedure insofar as the changes gave rise to the final independence of proceedings under art 317 *bis* cc, taking the procedures under arts 330, 333 and 336 cc and in some ways assimilating the procedures relating to minors with those operating in the area of separation and divorce.

---

7 Cass SU no 8362 of 2007.

With the coming into force of law no 54/2006 it nevertheless seemed that conflict was at the same time generated with some of the law contained in the civil code, and it was only with the intervention of legal writers and court judgments, both on the merits and on the law, that the lacunae have to some extent been filled.

With law no 54/2006, the problem was posed as to how to reconcile the new institution of 'joint custody' (which according to art 4, para 2 of the previously cited law applies also to 'proceedings relating to the children of parents who are not married to each other'), and the principle expressly sanctioned therein, that of dual parenthood, with the law enshrined in the civil code.

While the new art 155, para 3 cc – as replaced by art 1, para 1 of law no 54 of 8 February 2006 – said 'the potestà genitoriale, [parental authority] is exercised by both parents', art 317 of the Italian civil code said that the parental authority in the case of the natural child (outside wedlock) was exercised by the parent with whom the child lived. There was a need on this point for legal academics and the courts to intervene to find a consistent manner of interpreting the law.

On this question two court decisions on the merits[8] – among many the Supreme Corte di Cassazione[9] (court of appeals) – concluded by recognising the tacit repeal of art 317 *bis* cc by the law of 2006 according to the rules that govern the superseding of a law by another law passed later in time where the two laws were incompatible with each other on the points in question.

V SOME SIGNIFICANT LEGAL PERSPECTIVES RESULTING FROM THE APPLICATION OF THE REFORM OF 2006

(a) Quarrelling between parents and its influence on joint custody

Joint custody embraced by the law of 2006 as a general rule presupposes agreement on educational objectives, a good association between the parents and profound respect for the respective roles of each parent, requisites which in fact may well not present themselves to the court due to the quarrelsome nature of the relationship between the parents.

If on the one hand it may be regarded as normal that within the family unit there are frequent episodes of conflict between the parents (especially when the stage of breakdown in their personal relationship is reached), on the other hand

---

8 Cf among others: Giudice tutelare di Palestrina, 18 September 2006, in Riv notar, 2007, 517, and Trib Roma, 3 May 2010, no 9656, in Guida al dir, 30, 2010, 83.

9 Cf among others, eg Cass Civ, 30.10.2009, no 23032; Cass Civ, sez I, sentenza 04.11.2009 no 23411; Cass, no 10265/2011.

the responsibility of the individual spouse in the breakup of the family unit and the difficulties between spouses should not be considered as directly affecting the parent-child relationship, though the specific repercussions on the child are recognised. Parental suitability has to be ascertained by the court through an overall appraisal that takes account not only of the moral aptitude, the totality of the personality of the parent, the emotional support the person can bring, the parent's willingness to provide assiduously, and the environment in which the person lives but also the material, moral and psychological needs of the child, that have to be considered together as the priority factors in the whole situation.

The non-legal sciences such as psychology, the science of education and pedagogics that the jurists draw on every day in this field have recognised for some time that where there is a situation of keen antagonism between the parents this in most cases is not only perceived by the child but may also have a salient and negative impact on the child's peace of mind. The traumas deriving from the child's inability to metabolise the manifestations of conflict in the family and contextualise them, processing them properly and seeing them as relative to a larger picture, may give rise in the child to fears, anxiety, difficulties with relationships and social difficulties in general and even to problems in the maintenance of an emotional relationship and bond of trust with the individual parent. It may be that the arguments between the parents even lead to the loss of the assurance of protection and safety that the child should naturally perceive.[10]

Repeated and heated quarrelling and access may even in the most serious cases lead to negative, real and immediate effects for the daily management and care of the offspring. The two parents assailed by their reciprocal conflict may no longer even be able to identify and deal with the most elementary needs of their offspring.[11] Practical experience shows that high conflict levels between parents may cause them to oppose any form of interaction with the professional persons whose job it is to help find solutions to such conflict (eg social workers).

Given all of the foregoing, the law of 2006 does not specify what the consequence of this conflict between parents may be and specifically fails to take account of the possibility that the very conflict may feed on the circumstance of the parental authority itself and the decisions of major importance that the parents have to take together. On the subject of separation, the conflict between the spouses, which often runs parallel to the breakup of the family unit, does not preclude recourse to the preference given to joint custody if the level of conflict is kept within tolerable limits as regards the distress caused to the child. It becomes positively obstructive to the application of the

---

10 R Luberti and MT Pedrocco Biancardi *La violenza assistita intrafamiliare* (Franco Angeli edizioni, Milano, 2005).

11 V Santarsiere *Paralisi educativa del figlio minorenne per conflitto senza soluzione dei genitori, decadenza della potestà*, in *Giur merito*, 2011.

rule where it takes forms likely to jeopardise and seriously endanger the equilibrium and psychological and physical development of the children, and hence prejudice their interests.[12]

Where therefore the children find themselves in a situation of very serious psychological distress caused by the bitter arguments between the spouses, the court may even order custody to be given to the social services in order to ensure that the minor has living conditions suitable to his or her age and psychological resources. The question of the awarding of custody of the offspring is remitted to an assessment and discretion of the judge on the merits and the rule in favour of joint custody provided for in art 155 cc may be departed from when its application would be prejudicial to the interests of the minor.

The awarding of custody to one parent may be made only when the court believes, giving its reasons, that custody also to the other parent would be contrary to the interests of the minor, where the excluded parent has manifest failings or is clearly unfit for the upbringing of the child to the extent that such custody would be in fact prejudicial for the minor. It must therefore amount to a specific and negative condition of the parent who is excluded: conflict between the parents, a situation that concerns both of them, may not it should be stressed translate into a judgement of unsuitability of one of the two and certainly may not provide of itself any indication as to which of the parents should be chosen. This is all the more so where practically the same opinions have been expressed on the suitability of each of the parents at the time of the judicial appraisal. Where the quarrelsome nature of the relationship between the parents is found to stem from just one of the parents the court decisions have suggested that custody may be denied to this parent.[13] This may for example happen where at the time of the judicial appraisal there are serious and repeated displays of contempt for the ex-spouse; displays that are the result of the prolonged and steady deterioration in the relationship, possibly and as the case may be, favoured by 'forced' continued cohabitation of the parties. These factors, assessed together and as a whole, may justify the denial of joint custody if it is deemed prejudicial to the psychological development of the minor.

There thus emerges from the court judgments in Italy a recognition of the potential irrelevance of conflict between the parents when deciding on the question of joint custody. Indeed, in some cases where there is such a conflictual situation the application of the general rule for joint custody may contribute to the confrontational attitudes being overcome and the recovery of a more peaceful atmosphere from which the minor is the first person to benefit. It has however to be said that the courts have made decisions which can also be regarded at times as themselves conflicting with each other.

---

12 Cass Civ, sez I, 19 giugno 2008, no 16593, Cass Civ, sez I, 17 dicembre 2009, no 26587 e Cass Civ, sez IV, ord 2 dicembre 2010, no 24526.

13 Such as for example in Cass no 16593/2008; no 1202/2006,Cass Civ, sez I, 11.08.2011, no 17191.

There are cases where the very decision on the awarding of custody to one parent alone has been justified as a way of developing a sense of responsibility in both parents where their attitudes have been equally reprehensible.[14]

A study of the cases also reveals the criteria that may be relevant to ascertaining whether there would be prejudice to the minor where there is a situation of conflict between the parents. The maltreatment of one parent by another may also be seen as violence meted upon the minor where this latter has been a witness to it.[15]

Another factor that may be the subject of judicial assessment is where the children are used as pawns by the parents in the attempt to gain advantages in proceedings one from the other.[16]

(b) Denial of joint custody where the children refuse to entertain a relationship with the parent

Joint custody may also not be awarded by the court where there is a categorical refusal on the part of the minor to entertain a relationship with the parent. This has been the view of the Corte di Cassazione,[17] rejecting an appeal brought by one of the parents against the judgment of the Court of Appeal that had confirmed the award of custody solely to the other parent. The court found that the firm refusal on the part of the child to have any kind of relationship with the parent, as well as the ability of the parents to avoid arguments between them, prevented, according to paramount interest of the child, the making of any other decision. Following the same logic the appeal decision seems to comply with the requirement of the law in arts 155, 155 *bis* and 155 *sexies* cc on recognising sole custody of one parent.

In cases such as these, joint custody may be seen as conflicting with the greater and prevailing interest of the children, on the basis also of what emerges from the meeting for the hearing of the views of the children in the case.

(c) Joint custody even where one of the parents is living abroad

The physical distance between the two dwellings of the parents also does not amount to good reason to depart from the principle of joint custody of the minor.[18]

The general rule now in favour of joint custody means that it can be departed from only in the presence of serious and ascertained reasons. Sole custody, considered as a merely residual option, applies only where there are

14 As for example in Cass 29.3.2012 no 5108.
15 As for example in Trib Min L' Aquila, 15 giugno 2007, in *Giur merito*, 2008, 134.
16 As for example in 28.6.2013, no 28292.
17 As for example in Cass, 15.9.2011, no 18867.
18 Cass Civ, sez VI, ord 2.12.2010 no 24526.

circumstances such that joint custody will run counter to the interest of the minor, for example in the case of manifest failings or unfitness for the upbringing of the child on the part of one of the parents. According to this, therefore:

> 'the objective distance between the places of residence of the parents does not preclude the possibility of the joint custody of the minor by both parents since the distance will only affect the governing of the times and manner of presence of the minor with each parent (art 155, para 2, and 155 *quater*, para 2, cc).'

Account in fact has to be taken of the circumstance that the choice of residence of a parent to whom custody or placement is awarded amounts to the exercise of an inviolable freedom guaranteed by art 16 of the Italian Constitution. The other parent may complain about this only by using arguments directly connected to the interest of the offspring, as in the case where there is an evident obstacle to the exercise of the right to visit the child, with the consequent possibility under the provisions of art 155 *quater* cc, of restructuring the custody conditions.

(d) Joint custody and provisions regarding the assigning of the matrimonial home

According to the provisions of the civil code, as a result of the amendments made to it by the law of 2006 (art 155 *quater*), the enjoyment of the family home is determined by giving priority to the interests of the children. On assigning the home the court takes account of how the financial relations between the parents are regulated, considering as the case may be the ownership of the property. The right of enjoyment of the family home ceases if the person to whom it is assigned does not live there or ceases to normally live in the family home, or lives with a partner *more uxorio* or marries again. The order assigning the family home, as well as that revoking it, is registerable and opposable against third parties under the provisions of art 2643 cc. Where one of the spouses changes residence or domicile, the other spouse may request, if the change interferes with the workings of the custody order, the redrawing of the agreements and the orders made, including the financial orders.

The right to live in the conjugal home of the parent who lives there with the children is aimed at safeguarding the interests of the offspring, to ensure they are not subject to changes in their lifestyle. The right to live in the conjugal home remains with the spouse and the children until the children come of age, or else achieve financial independence. Following the logic of this, proof that the children have gained financial autonomy, having found work suited to their expectations having regard to their social status and the educational qualifications that they have, has to be furnished by the spouse who wishes to have the home back. For the ex-spouse to have the right to live in the house it is therefore not enough that the child who has reached the age of majority has for example found a temporary job outside of the city, when it is shown in proceedings that this offspring returns to the conjugal home when compatible with his or her work commitments. The order can then be changed only when the permanent link between child and dwelling that is assigned to the parent in the assigning order has been broken.[19]

VI HEARING THE VIEWS OF CHILDREN

The provisions on custody of children cannot consist of forced experimentation, during the course of which the real and actual needs of the offspring are sacrificed in the attempt to have the conduct of parents conform to generally more mature and responsible models, which may be contradicted by actual situations already encountered. With this in mind the hearing of the views of the minor by the court not only makes it possible to have the child present at the proceedings but also certainly ensures that the court takes due account of such a hearing, save for any different evaluations the court may come to, while giving its reasons, in relation to the level of discernment attributed to the minor.[20]

VII JOINT CUSTODY AND FAMILY MEDIATION

Family mediation may be a tool that can be effectively used in the joint custody process.[21] The aims of family mediation include offering support for the couple to confront the breakdown in family relations, fostering cooperation in the reorganisation of the new relationship that will come out of this. The old concept of family mediation is prescribed only where the couple intending to separate is not able unaided to reach an agreement. It may also be offered on consensual separation where an agreement has already been achieved. The mediation may be seen as an alternative means of reaching an understanding that seeks to govern the new family situation such as to assure the minor's right to maintain a balanced and continuous relationship with each of the parents, to receive care, an upbringing and education from both of the parents and maintain significant relationships with the grandparents and relatives on both sides. In such a context, therefore, sending the couple to family mediation can be seen as the opportunity to face up to the needs to build an atmosphere of trust and a collaborative environment in which it is possible to reach an agreement that is in the primary interest of the minor children.

---

19 Cass Civ, sez I, sentenza 22.03.2010 no 6861.

20 Così Cass, sez I civ, 17.5.2012, no 7773, in www.affidamentocondiviso.it.

21 Cf Tribunale Lamezia Terme, sez civile, ord 11.03.2010.

VIII THE RELATIONSHIP BETWEEN JOINT CUSTODY AND CONTRIBUTIONS TO THE MAINTENANCE OF THE CHILD

Events relating to the contribution to the maintenance of the child, by the parent, are reflected in joint custody. It may in fact happen that one parent (the father for example) fails to make the monthly maintenance payment and that this behaviour is viewed by the court as part of a more general situation regarding the relationship between the parent and the child. A potential consequence of the failure to make the payment may lead to the application of a general rule under the law on the matter of joint custody. If the parent regularly fails to make the monthly payment, the order for joint custody may be revoked insofar as the omissions may be shown in court as indicative of the lack of fitness of the parent to look after the offspring, inferred moreover by the lack of interest displayed in relation to the children.[22] Also in cases such as this one, therefore, the fundamental ratio decidendi of the court is that such joint custody runs counter to the interests of the minor.

As with any possible application in which the court may decide to depart from the norm and use the sole parent custody model, the judge must give reasons for the order made. Such reasons must explain what impediment there was to the general legal rule, with particular reference not only to the fitness of the parent to whom sole custody is awarded to bring up the children but also and above all to the unfitness of the other parent which leads the court to exclude him or her from the exercise of parental authority.

IX JOINT CUSTODY AFTER THE FILIATION REFORM (LAW NO 219 OF 10 DECEMBER 2012 'PROVISIONS ON THE ACKNOWLEDGMENT OF "NATURAL" CHILDREN')

At the end of 2012 the Italian legal system approved a new and profound legislative reform in the field of family law. Its importance can perhaps be compared with the great family law reform Act of 1975. The law of 2012, which came into force in 2013, provides for legal equality as between all categories of children. The law abolishes the distinction between legitimate children and natural children and expressly affirms that all children have the same legal status. The changes introduced with the new legislation are many and wide-ranging, as was said at the time, for the whole field of Italian family law.

From the perspective of what is particularly of most interest for this chapter, the law replaces the definition adopted since 2012, of '*potestà genitoriale*', or parental authority, with that of parental responsibility. The joint custody rule for the children is confirmed as the general rule in Italian law, drawing also on

---

[22] Cass Civ, sez I, sentenza 17.12.2009 no 26587.

the notion of parental responsibility, which is that of both parents even in the event of the breakup of the family unit.

TWO LANDMARK DECISIONS OF THE SUPREME COURT: ONE TOO LATE; THE OTHER STILL EARLY

Yangwhan Kim[*]

Résumé

En 2013, la Cour suprême du Japon a rendu deux décisions qui feront date. Dans la première, la Cour a jugé que la disposition du Code civil qui prévoit que la part *ab intestat* d'un enfant naturel doit être la moitié de celle qui échet à un enfant légitime était inconstitutionnelle. Dans la seconde affaire, un enfant était né par insémination artificielle avec un tiers donneur, au profit de la mère et de son mari. Le mari ayant auparavant souffert de désordre de l'identité, il avait subi une chirurgie de changement de sexe de femme à homme. Bien que les rapports sexuels aient été physiquement impossibles, la Cour a décidé que l'enfant était l'enfant légitime du père. La première décision était attendue depuis longtemps. La seconde est prématurée parce que, d'une part, le Japon n'a pas encore de législation sur les techniques de procréation médicalement assistée, et, d'autre part, car la présomption de paternité semblait en l'espèce réfutée par les faits.

I INTRODUCTION

In 2013, the Supreme Court of Japan handed down the two landmark decisions: in September, the Court held that the Civil Code, Article 900, Section 4, providing that the intestate share of an illegitimate child should be one-half of the intestate share of a legitimate child violated the Constitution, Article 14, Section 1, securing the equal protection under the law (hereinafter referred to as 'the illegitimate child case');[1] in December, the Court found that a child born by artificial insemination by donor to a mother, and a father who had suffered from gender identity disorder and underwent sex reassignment surgery from female to male was the legitimate child of the father (hereinafter referred to as 'the AID case').[2]

---

* Associate Professor of Law, Law School of Yamanashi Gakuin University.

1 The decision of the Supreme Court's grand bench on 4 September 2013 reported at vol 67 no 6 *Minshu* 1320.

2 The decision of the Supreme Court's 3rd petty bench on 10 December 2013 reported at 1593 *Saibansho Jiho* 4.

Concerning the illegitimate child case, it is certain that the decision puts an end to a long struggle to get rid of discrimination against an illegitimate child in Japan, but it cannot be denied that the Court's decision is too late, considering the trend to grant equal rights to an illegitimate child. On the other hand, in relation to the AID case it could be said the Court recognised a diversity in family units. However, considering current circumstances, that there is no regulation for assisted reproductive technologies such as artificial insemination by donor (hereinafter referred to 'AID') nor legislation for parenthood of a child who is born as the result of such technologies, it might be said that the Court's decision was too early.

In this chapter, the illegitimate child case and the AID case will be introduced and some consideration will be given to the Court's opinions delivered in both cases.

II THE ILLEGITIMATE CHILD CASE

(a) Facts

The heirs of the decedent, who died in July 2013, are four legitimate children (two of them are per stripes; hereinafter referred to 'Xs') and two illegitimate children (referred to 'Ys'). The Xs and Ys had not reached an agreement concerning a division of the estate, and the Xs filed a motion for the court's adjudication[3] with the Tokyo Family Court. In the proceeding, the Ys claimed that the Civil Code, Article 900, Section 4, was unconstitutional as it violated the equal protection under the law secured by the Constitution, Article 14, Section 1, which prohibits discrimination in political, economic or social relations by reason of race, creed, sex, social status or family origin, so the Ys had an equal share to the Xs. The court, however, rejected the Ys' claims citing the precedent of the Supreme Court's grand bench on 5 July 1995, which held that the disputed Civil Code provision was not unconstitutional. The Tokyo High Court also rejected the Xs' appeal for the same reason. The Ys filed a special appeal[4] with the Supreme Court.

(b) Court's opinion

Note: the translation below is made up of excerpts from the original, and paragraph numbers and titles are placed by the author as a matter of convenience.

---

3 It is referred to as '*Shimpan*' in the Japanese legal system.

4 It is referred to as '*Tokubetu Kokoku*' in the Japanese legal system. Tokubetu kokoku is allowed only if the high court's decision is unconstitutional.

(i) Standard of judicial review

'We repeatedly confirmed that the Constitution Article 14 Section 1 did not prohibit all kinds of discriminatory provisions. If we assume that the provision is based on reasonable reasons, it would not be unconstitutional.'

'In establishing an inheritance system in a certain country, the factors such as domestic tradition, social backgrounds, feeling of a people, etc should be taken into consideration. Moreover, the current inheritance system is closely involved with the notion of what the family is in that country, so it could not be established without consideration for the control over marriage, parenthood and for the opinion of the people. Therefore, it is left to the legislature's broad discretion to establish the inheritance system from all those considerations.'

'What is raised in front of us is whether or not discrimination in the intestate share of an illegitimate child compared to a legitimate child by the disputed Civil Code provision is based on reasonable reasons, and, if not, it would be unconstitutional even though the legislature has the broad discretion.'

(ii) Constitutionality of the provision

'The Constitution Article 24 provides that "Marriage shall be based only on the mutual consent of both sexes and it shall be maintained through mutual cooperation on the basis of the equal rights of husband and wife" in Section 1 and "with regard to choice of spouse, property rights, inheritance, choice of domicile, divorce and other matters concerning marriage and family, the law shall be enacted based on the dignity of an individual and the essential equality of the sexes" in Section 2. And under these provisions, the Civil Code Article 739 provides that "Marriage shall take effect on registration pursuant to Family Register Act (No. 224 of 1947)." It means the Civil Code has adopted civil registration marriage, not *de facto* marriage. On the other hand, with regard to our inheritance law, the amendments in 1947 had established the system that basically the spouse and child should be heirs, but the provision on the intestate share, the Civil Code Article 900 Section 4, had not been amended.'

'In 1995, the Supreme Court held that the disputed provision had not been unconstitutional on grounds as follows: as the result of civil registration marriage which the Civil Code had adopted, it is sure that the disputed provision had put the legal spouse and legitimate child at an advantage. The provision, however, had also granted certain protection to an illegitimate child, and this would not be beyond the legislature's broad discretion.

'However, even under civil registration marriage, the intestate share of a legitimate child and an illegitimate should be decided after considering all the factors mentioned in (1), and those factors would change with time, so we should keep the constitutionality of the disputed provision under review in the light of the dignity of an individual and the equal protection under the law secured by the Constitution.'

'From this point of view, we could take what has occurred since amendments to the Civil Code in 1947 into consideration: there have been the transition in social mobility and in the form of the family unit accompanied with the people's notion of what a family is like; the trends of foreign countries' legislation to abolish discrimination against an illegitimate child; ratification of the "International Covenant on Civil and Political Rights" in 1979, the "Convention on the Rights of the Child" in 1994 and the CCPR Human Rights Committee's recommendation[5] requiring the improvement of an illegitimate child's rights in 1998; the Court's holding that the Nationality Act Article 3 Section 1 which had discriminated in naturalization between an illegitimate child and a legitimate was unconstitutional in 2008; the development of "Tentative Proposal for the Amendment of the Civil Code" which suggested that the intestate share be equal by the Legislative Council in 1996; delivery of the dissenting opinions so far against the majority opinions which hold the disputed provision is not unconstitutional in the same cases repeatedly.'

'Considering all these together, we assume it to be apparent that respect for an individual in the family unit has become even more definitely appreciated. Even though the Civil Code has adopted civil registration marriage, it is not acceptable that the law disadvantages illegitimate children on the basis of the marital status of their parents, which children cannot help themselves, and today it can be said the notion that children should be esteemed as individuals and their rights be secured has been established.'

'Therefore, we assume that the reasonable reasons for discrimination in the intestate share between an illegitimate child and a legitimate had vanished in July 2001, when the inheritance in this case commenced, at the latest. The disputed Civil Code provision in this case has been unconstitutional since that time.'

(iii) On the binding nature of the decision in this case

'The decision in this case does not affect other inheritance cases which were settled pursuant to the disputed Civil Code provision from July 2001 through the day of the decision.'

(c) Comment

As cited in this decision, it was in 1995 that the constitutionality of the Civil Code, Article 900, Section 4, was disputed in the Supreme Court (hereinafter referred to as 'the 1995 decision'). The 1995 decision held that the provision was not unconstitutional from the viewpoint of the protection of civil registration marriage. After the 1995 decision, seven cases[6] had been brought before the Supreme Court's petty bench and in six of them it had been

---

5 CCPR Human Rights Committee, Concluding observations of the Human Rights Committee: Japan (1998/11/19, CCPR/C/79/Add.102) Section 12 says: 'The Committee continues to be concerned about discrimination against children born out of wedlock, particularly with regard to the issues of nationality, family registers and inheritance rights. It reaffirms its position that pursuant to article 26 of the Covenant, all children are entitled to equal protection, and recommends that the State party take the necessary measures to amend its legislation, including article 900, paragraph 4, of the Civil Code.'

6 Two cases in 2000, two cases in 2003, one case in 2004, one case in 2009 and one case in 2011.

concluded that it was constitutional; one[7] had come to an end by settlement by the parties. Finally, this eighth decision brought about great change 18 years after the 1995 decision.

The Court found that the disputed Civil Code provision had become unconstitutional in July 2001 at the latest. However, from the viewpoint of legal stability, already settled cases pursuant to that provision from July 2001 through to this decision were not affected by this decision. In other words, the unsettled cases where the inheritance had commenced after July 2001 are within the reach of this decision, while the unsettled cases before July 2001would be out of reach.

The decision is broadly welcomed,[8] but some question it from the viewpoint of the protection of the legal spouse,[9] especially the wife, as this kind of case often involves the husband's infidelity and the Civil Code does not give sufficient protection for a married couple and their child. Also, it has been pointed out that the decision exerts influence on other related fields such as inheritance tax, finance, life insurance and so forth. Moreover, the standard adopted by this decision would generate another dispute whether or not a case had been 'settled'.[10]

After the decision, the amendment to the Civil Code, Article 900, Section 4, was promulgated on 11 December 2013 and took effect on the same day. However, the amendment is only on the intestate share. The Civil Code still has other provisions regarding illegitimate child's status such as establishment of parentage (Article 779 provides it shall be established by acknowledgment), family name (Article 790, Section 2 provides it shall be mother's), parental authority (Article 819, Section 4 provides the mother has it in principle) and so forth, and it is time to examine the rationality of those provisions.[11]

III AID CASE

(a) Facts

A was born female but had suffered from gender identity disorder (hereinafter referred to as 'GID'). A underwent sex reassignment surgery female to male in 2004 and A was given permission to change sex from female to male pursuant

---

7 The case in 2011.

8 Shuhei Ninomiya 'What We Learn from the Supreme Court's Decision on Intestate Share of Illegitimate Child Unconstitutional' (2013) 703 *Koseki Jihou* 2; Masayuki Tanamura, 'The Supreme Court's Decision on Intestate Share of Illegitimate Child Unconstitutional' (2014) vol 65 no 1 *Jiyuu To Seigi* 97.

9 Noriko Mizuno 'The Supreme Court's Decision on Intestate Share of Illegitimate Child' (2013) 1066 *Houritu Jihou* 1.

10 Noriko Mizuno 'The Unconstitutionality of Intestate Share of Illegitimate Child and its Influence on Other Cases' (2014) 401 *Hougaku Kyoushitu* 25.

11 Atsushi Motoyama 'The Supreme Court's Decision on Intestate Share of Illegitimate Child Unconstitutional' (2014) 1436 *Kinyu Shoji Hanrei* 32.

to an 'Act on Dealing with the Sex of an Individual with Gender Identity Disorder' (hereinafter referred to as 'the GID Act'), Article 3, Section 1, which provides that the Family Court can give permission to change by statute the sex of an individual with GID[12] on the individual's application, only if the applicant meets all of the following conditions: the applicant is 20 years and over; is not married at present; has no minor child; has no gonads, or persistently lacks the function of gonad; and has genitalia which have a similar appearance to the opposite sex. A got married to B in 2008 and B gave birth to C by AID under A's consent in 2009 as A had lost the capacity for reproduction.

In 2012, A and B attempted to register the birth of C as their legitimate child in the city office, but the office did not enter the name of C's father in the family register ('*koseki*') on the ground that the Civil Code, Article 772, should not be applied to C, which provided that 'A child born after 200 days from the formation of valid marriage or within 300 days of the day of the dissolution or rescission of marriage shall be presumed to have been conceived during marriage' in Section 2 and the 'child conceived by a wife during marriage shall be presumed to be a child of her husband' in Section 1, because it was impossible for B to conceive A's child and A had no blood ties to C.

A and B filed a motion for correction of their family register pursuant to the Family Register Act, Article 113, with the Tokyo Family Court. The court, however rejected the motion. On appeal, the high court also rejected on the ground that judging by entry on family register, if it is apparent that husband is an individual who had changed the sex under the GID Act and has no blood ties with his alleged legitimate child, then the child is not covered by the Civil Code, Article 772. A and B appealed to the Supreme Court.

(b) Court's opinion

Note: translation below is made up of excerpts from the original.

> 'As an individual who had been permitted to change sex from female to male under the GID Act Article 3 Section 1 he is hereafter regarded as male by application of the Civil Code or other laws except as otherwise provided in relevant laws. Therefore, he can get married under the Civil Code and if his spouse conceived a child in wedlock, the child was presumed his child pursuant to the Civil Code Article 772.'

> 'It is well established in our case law that if it is apparently impossible for a marriage couple to have sexual intercourse such as when they are in a *de facto* divorce and lack substance as a married couple when the wife conceived a child, the Civil Code Article 772 should not be applied to the child as a matter of

12 GID Act, Article 2 defines an individual with GID as an individual who psychologically identifies persistently with the opposite sex from the biological one, although it is apparent which sex the individual biologically belongs to, and he or she has the intention to adapt himself or herself to the opposite sex with which the individual psychologically identifies and has been diagnosed by at least two professions.

substance. Surely it cannot be assumed that an individual who had been permitted to change sex pursuant to GID Act could make a child by sexual intercourse, but it would not be acceptable that, while he was permitted to get married on one hand, he was not permitted to have applied the provision on the presumption of paternity, which is one of the important effects of marriage, on the other hand. So the Civil Code Article 772 should be applied to an individual who had been permitted to change sex from female to male pursuant to GID Act.'

'In this case, we cannot find that A and B lack substance as a married couple. Therefore, the Civil Code Article 772 should be applied to A, so C is the legitimate child of A under the provision.'

Reversed and affirmed

Justice Kiyoko Okabe and Justice Takehiko Ohtani delivered the dissenting opinion.

Justice Okabe stated that:

> 'the establishment of legal parentage should be determined whether or not the parties meet the requirements for it, and the GID Act has no provision on the establishment of legal parentage. Therefore, the establishment of legal parentage should be determined on the relating law. The presumption of the Civil Code Article 772 is based on the fact that there is an opportunity to have sexual intercourse between a married couple. So if it is biologically apparent that a married couple is incapable of having the opportunity, and the fact is shown on *Koseki* under the relevant law, there is no basis for the presumption. Surely our case law has allowed the presumption in some cases even though a father has no blood ties with a child whom his wife has given birth to, but it could be said that the parties may have an opportunity to have a sexual intercourse in those cases, in other words, those cases have the basis for the presumption. On the other hand, this case has no such basis.'

Justice Ohtani stated that:

> 'the GID Act does not assume that an individual who is permitted to change sex from female to male under the GID Act has a biological child, and this is apparent by the entry on *Koseki*. Therefore, this case is not covered by the presumption of the Civil Code Article 772.'

(c) Comment

It could be said that this decision raises questions from two directions.

One direction is on regulation for assisted reproductive technologies and the parentage of a child as the result of them. In Japan, while there has been related medical societies' self-regulation over assisted reproductive technologies without legally binding effect, it has not been regulated by law.

In 2003, the Ministry of Health, Labour and Welfare released 'Report on the Regulation over Sperm, Egg and Embryo Donated Assisted Reproductive Technologies' and the Ministry of Justice did the 'Intermediate Report on the Parenthood of Children Born by Sperm, Egg and Embryo Donated Assisted Reproductive Technologies'. According to these reports, AID should be allowed in cases where there is proper indication for it, and the legal father of a child born by it should be the husband who gave consent and the sperm donor should not claim the child born by his donated sperm. In fact these reports are thought to aim at legislation on assisted reproductive technologies. However, it has not been realised so far.

Meanwhile a posthumously conceived child case in 2006[13] and a surrogate mother case in 2007[14] have been brought before the Supreme Court. The former was a mother who gave birth to a child by AID using the deceased husband's cryopreserved sperm and who claimed that the child was the deceased father's legitimate child. The Court rejected the mother's claim on the ground that the current provisions on legitimacy of children in the Civil Code enacted in the end of the nineteenth century had assumed natural reproduction, and the problem should be resolved by proper legislation after due consideration of the people's views, ethical problems, etc. The latter was a Japanese married couple who claimed they were legal parents of a child whom an American woman in Nevada had conceived by transplantation of the couple's embryo under a surrogacy agreement. The Court had also rejected the couple's claim on the ground that this problem should be resolved by proper legislation. In short, under the current circumstance that lacks proper legislation dealing with the problems regarding assisted reproductive technologies, the Court cannot help deciding the cases pursuant to legislative intent and established principle of the current law. The concurring opinions delivered in both of them urged the legislature to enact rapidly.

In spite of those careful decisions so far, this latest case made a decision on parentage of a child conceived and born by AID on the premise that the performance of AID was permitted. It could be said the decision was legislation by justices.

The presumption of parentage points in the other direction. Basically the Civil Code, Article 772, providing for the presumption of parentage is based on marriage and blood ties, but the provision also makes an exception. That is to say, if a father did not exercise the right to rebut the presumption of parentage by bringing an action within one year of becoming aware of the birth of a child, the father shall lose the right (see the Civil Code, Articles 774, 775 and 777), ie parentage without blood ties shall be established. The purpose of the presumption of parentage system in Japan is respect for a child's interests, and the father's intent.

---

13 The Supreme Court's decision on 4 September 2006 reported at vol 60 no 7 *Minshu* 2563.

14 The Supreme Court's decision on 23 March 2007 reported at vol 61 no 2 *Minshu* 619.

However, the Supreme Court has established by case-law that, even though a child was born during the period provided in the Civil Code, Article 772, if it was apparently impossible for a married couple to have sexual intercourse such as where they are in a de facto divorce, or the husband is in prison, so they lack substance as a married couple when the wife conceived the child, the Civil Code, Article 772 should not be applied to the child as a matter of substance.[15]

Literally construing the provision, the same conclusion as in majority opinion could be possible in this case. However, as the dissenting opinions pointed, the provision assumed that it was possible to have sexual intercourse between husband and wife, so this case had no basis to apply the provision. Moreover, comparing the purpose of the GID Act with that of the presumption of parentage in the Civil Code, it could be said that the former is one thing and the latter is another.

As mentioned, it could be said in the AID case that the Court recognised a diversity in family units. However, considering current circumstances that there is no regulation for assisted reproductive technologies nor legislation for parenthood of a child who was born by one of those technologies, it could be said that the Court's decision was still early.

IV CONCLUSION

This chapter has been aimed at the introduction of two landmark decisions of the Supreme Court in 2013: the illegitimate child case and the AID case. The former could be said to be too late, but indicates a new step in Japanese family law. The latter could be said to be still too early and it might be said the drastic decision confused the essence of our family law: 'What is the presumption of parentage?'

Regarding the AID Case, it might be justified on the ground that the Court could fill any lacuna in the family law as the amendment of the family law is too late to catch up with the rapid transition of family and society. When we fill a lacuna, however, it could be said that we should pay due attention to the balance with the existing system and its construction. If not, instead of filling one lacuna, another lacuna could be made.

---

[15] The Supreme Court's decision on 29 May 1969 reported at vol 23 no 6 *Minshu* 1064; on 14 March 2000 reported at 189 *Saibanshu Minji* 497.

KENYA

CHANGING THE CONSTITUTION AND CHANGING ATTITUDES: RECENT DEVELOPMENTS IN KENYAN FAMILY LAW

*F Banda**

Résumé

Ce chapitre donne un aperçu de quelques récents développements en droit familial au Kenya, en commençant par la Constitution de 2010 qui a provoqué des changements radicaux en droit de la famille, dont l'adoption de la loi sur la propriété matrimoniale. Celle-ci reconnaît pour la première fois la notion d'apport non monétaire, c'est-à-dire les services domestiques, qui sont surtout le fait des femmes. Un projet de loi sur le mariage tente de rationnaliser les différents systèmes de mariage au Kenya, mais ce texte datant de 2007 fait l'objet de critiques car maintient la polygynie. Le travail des tribunaux dans une distribution plus juste des biens en cas de décès mérite également d'être souligné. Par contre, il existe un regrettable vide juridique en ce qui concerne les personnes transgenres à qui l'on nie encore et toujours la possibilité d'obtenir des documents d'identité sans les obliger à indiquer s'ils sont de sexe masculin ou féminin. Ce problème est exacerbé par le fait que les tribunaux supérieurs refusent de protéger cette catégorie de personnes sans droits.

I INTRODUCTION

Kenya has experienced a tumultuous decade. Violence following a disputed election result in 2008 led to charges being brought against leading politicians by the International Criminal Court in The Hague. Two of the accused went on to win the next election in 2013, and to assume the positions of President and Prime Minister. The indictments still stand and the trial of one, the Prime Minister, has begun. As all who have lived in politically turbulent times will attest, family life continues. This chapter considers recent developments, starting with the adoption of a new constitution which came into effect on 27 August 2010.[1] The chapter also considers the provisions of the Matrimonial Property Act 2013[2] as well, as case-law brought challenging gender

* Professor of Law, School of Oriental and African Studies, University of London.

1 Constitution of Kenya 2010.

2 Matrimonial Property Act, Kenya Gazette Supplement No183 (Acts No 49), commenced on 16 January 2014.

discrimination in the distribution of property on death. It will also consider the difficulties that arise when the law does not recognise intersex people.

II CONSTITUTION

The 2010 Constitution has been hailed as an exercise in democracy having been drafted by a Committee of Experts on Constitutional Review who, via a process of national consultations and meetings, heard from a broad range of Kenyans. Following the finalising of the draft Constitution, a referendum was held to seek the approval of the population. Reflecting the rise of the human rights discourse globally, and in keeping with the trends in constitution-making on the African continent, the Kenyan constitution attempts to be human rights compliant and removes many of the discriminatory provisions within family law. It does this by specifying that all the treaties and conventions ratified by Kenya will form part of the law of Kenya.[3] Furthermore, it is made clear that inconsistency of any law, including customary law, with the provisions of the Constitution are invalid.[4] It is further noted that 'every person is equal before the law and has the right to equal protection and equal benefit of the law'.[5] This provision is reinforced by s 27(3) which guarantees 'Women and men the right to equal treatment' and s 27(4) and (5) which enumerate the grounds on which the state and private actors cannot discriminate. These include 'race, sex, pregnancy, marital status, health status, ethnic or social origin, colour, age, disability, religion, conscience, belief, culture, dress, language or birth'.[6] In contrast to previous constitutions, there is no attempt to ring-fence customary family law from the non-discrimination or equality provisions.

While the Constitution continues to recognise the existence of plural family law forms this is made subject to the injunction that, in enacting legislation recognising marriages conducted in line with customary, religious or traditional tenets, the state should ensure that the laws are consistent with the Constitution.[7] In keeping with Kenya's commitment under art 16(1) of CEDAW, the Constitution also guarantees equality between the spouses from the outset of marriage to its dissolution.[8] However, it is worth noting that there is provision made for Kadhi courts for which jurisdiction is limited to 'the determination of questions of Muslim law relating to personal status, marriage, divorce or inheritance in proceedings in which all the parties profess the Muslim religion and submit to the jurisdiction of the Kadhi courts'.[9] The

3 Constitution 2010, s 3(6). In its concluding observations to the seventh report of Kenya, the Committee on the Elimination of all Forms of Discrimination (CEDAW) commended Kenya on the progressive provisions in its new Constitution. CEDAW/C/KEN/CO/7, 5 April 2011, paras 4, 5, 6 and 8.

4 Constitution 2010, s 3(5).

5 Constitution 2010, s 27(1).

6 Constitution 2010, s 27(3).

7 Constitution 2010, s 45(4).

8 Constitution 2010, s 45(3). Convention on the Elimination of all Forms of Discrimination against Women, 1979 (CEDAW) 1249 UNTS 13.

9 Constitution 2010, s 170(5).

provision and its antecedents generated criticism not least from Christian leaders who queried what they saw as the privileging of Islam and Kadhi courts in a supposedly secular state.[10] An additional issue continues to be whether the retention of jurisdiction in family matters by Kadhi courts will lead to, or entrench, discrimination against women. If the Constitution is the supreme law of the country and it guarantees equal protection before the law for all, and prohibits discrimination, including on grounds of sex, does this mean that Kadhi courts have to ensure their decisions are discrimination free, or, is the provision for their continued jurisdiction in personal status matters, an indication that they are exempt from the equality provisions of the Constitution? The Committee on the Elimination of all Forms of Discrimination against Women favours the former interpretation, noting that the alternative would constitute a breach of arts 2 and 16, on state obligations and family responsibilities, of the Convention which Kenya has ratified without entering any reservations.[11] The Committee enjoined the state to: 'Harmonize religious and customary law with article 16 of the Convention and consider bringing Kadhi courts under the specific equality provision enshrined in the new Constitution.'[12]

Controversial from an international human rights perspective, but in keeping with regional trends on the issue of sexual orientation, the Constitution defines marriage in narrow heteronormative terms: 'Every adult has the right to marry a person of the opposite sex, based on the free consent of the parties.'[13] Despite this provision, case-law seems to leave open the possibility of the continued recognition of woman to woman marriages practised by some groups.[14] The *Katam* case is on point.[15] This case involved a dispute over who should be given letters of administration over the property of an elderly Nandi woman who had died. The petitioner, a woman of 35 with two children, claimed that she was the legitimate heir, while the other petitioners claimed to be relatives. The petitioner said that the deceased, who had not had children of her own, had approached her father and asked if she (the deceased) could enter into a woman to woman marriage with her (the petitioner). Her father agreed and an engagement ceremony which was followed by the exchange of bridewealth. Thereafter the petitioner said she went to live with the deceased whom she looked after. The respondents contested the existence of the woman to woman marriage and argued that the first petitioner had merely acted as the deceased's servant. Part of the dispute involved whether the deceased had left a will (two were produced) and which one of these was valid. After evidence was led on whether either of the wills should be taken into account, the court decided that neither

---

10 Ndzovu, Hassan J 'Is the Inclusion of the Kadhi Courts in the Kenyan Constitution Against the Principle of a Secular State?' (18 September 2013). Available at SSRN: http://papers.ssrn.com/sol3/papers.cfm?abstract_id=2327775.

11 CEDAW CO Kenya, CEDAW/C/KEN/CO/7 (2011) para 11.

12 Ibid para 12(d).

13 Constitution 2010, s 45(2).

14 Woman to woman marriages are different from same-sex marriages because they are not regarded as including sexual intimacy.

15 *Monica Jesang Katam v Jackson Chepkwony & another*, Succession Cause 212 of 2010, [2011] eKLR (HC).

was valid, thus making it an intestate case. The court further considered whether a woman to woman marriage had taken place. Again the court considered evidence of witnesses who had been present at both the engagement and bridewealth ceremonies and academic opinion, and concluded that, while Kenyan society was evolving, there were certain groups, including the Nandi, to whom the deceased belonged, which did recognise that a woman who had not had children (sons) of her own could give bridewealth for a younger woman who would bear children with the older woman's male kin. The older woman would be regarded as the 'father' of those children as she was the 'husband' of their mother. This practice, the court noted, could be considered to fall within the protections envisaged by art 11, the culture provision of the 2010 Constitution. The court was persuaded that a woman to woman marriage had indeed taken place in accordance with Nandi customary law and therefore granted letters of administration to the young widow.[16]

Under the Constitution, children are guaranteed the right to a name and nationality from birth, health, education and the right to be protected from abuse, neglect and harmful cultural practices.[17] It is not made clear in this section when childhood ends and adulthood begins. However, the Children Act 2001 (CRC) defines a child as being under the age of 18, again in keeping with the United Nations Children's Rights Convention 1989 and the African Charter on the Rights and Welfare of the Child 1990 (ACRWC).[18]

The granting of nationality to all children is important in light of a case brought on behalf of Nubian children to the African Committee of Experts on the Rights and Welfare of the Child (ACERWC).[19] It was filed before the Constitution was finalised, but long after the same guarantees to nationality had been given in the Children Act 2001. Bringing a complaint to the ACERWC, Nubian children in Kenya alleged that, by failing to provide them with identity documents, the state had violated their right to a nationality at birth guaranteed in art 6(3) of the ACRWC. Additionally they averred that, in so denying them, the state was also in breach of its obligation to prevent statelessness. Finally, the children's representatives argued that the systematic denial of Kenyan nationality constituted discrimination because the Nubian children were not able to enjoy rights including to health and education which were provided for other Kenyan children. This unjustifiable distinction in treatment breached art 3 of the African Children's Charter. In the absence of a submission from the state, the Committee found for the authors. It noted that the longstanding historic disenfranchisement of the Nubian people had resulted

---

16 Ibid 22–23.

17 Constitution 2010, s 53(1)(a)–(d). See also s 12(1) on the entitlements of citizenship which include a passport and identification documents.

18 Children Act 2001 [CAP 141], s 2. Convention on the Rights of the Child, 1989, 1577 UNTS 3; African Charter on the Rights and Welfare of the Child, 1990, OAU Doc CAB/LEG/24.49.

19 African Committee on the Rights and Welfare of the Child, Communication No 002/2009 *Institute for Human Rights and Development in Africa (IHRDA) and Open Society Justice Initiative on Behalf of Children of Nubian Descent in Kenya v The Government of Kenya*, Decision No 002/Com/002/2009, 22 March 2011 (hereafter 'the Nubian children case').

in the multiple disadvantages complained of.[20] Specifically the Committee linked the state's failure to provide birth certificates to Nubian children, amongst other groups, with a denial of their nationality rights.[21] Furthermore, the Committee found that there was unfair discrimination against the Nubian children which resulted in consequential violations, including of their rights to health and education.[22] Without making a finding on the issue, the Committee also highlighted that the discrimination faced by the Nubian children impacted on their ability to fulfil their obligations to the community under art 31 of the Charter. It was up to the state to remedy the discrimination against the children.[23] As the decision was handed down after the adoption of the 2010 Constitution, the Committee was able to acknowledge the improvements that it had made.[24] However, it noted continued concern about the provision guaranteeing children under the age of 8 citizenship.

Also remedied by the 2010 Constitution is longstanding discrimination against women with respect to their ability to pass on citizenship to children born in marriage or to an alien spouse. The provision on citizenship in the new Constitution gives many avenues to citizenship. Crucially, it provides: 'Citizenship is not lost through marriage or the dissolution of marriage.'[25] Previously married women were to take on the nationality of their husbands. This created difficulties for women married to alien men, whose right to live in Kenya was not guaranteed. The new Constitution permits anyone who was born in Kenya and has renounced their citizenship to apply to regain their Kenyan citizenship.[26] Moreover, the Constitution permits the spouse of a Kenyan citizen to apply for citizenship provided they have been lawfully resident in the country for the preceding 7 years.[27] All of these provisions augur well for the enjoyment of all to the right to family life.

Crucially, married women are now also allowed to pass on nationality to their children because of the neutral drafting of the Constitution allowing citizenship to pass to a child born within, or outside of Kenya, to a mother or father who is a citizen.[28] Similarly a citizen may adopt a child who is not a citizen and pass to that child their citizenship.[29] Generously, the Constitution also gives citizenship to any child 'who is, or appears to be, less than eight years of age, and whose nationality and parents are not known, is presumed to be a citizen by birth'.[30] This provision is particularly important in light of the number of children who are orphaned early and who do not have identification documents, or the many who find themselves stateless because their parents

---

20 *IHRDA and OSJI (for Nubian Children) v Kenya*, Com 002/2009, para 69.
21 Ibid paras 54–57.
22 Ibid paras 58, 59, 63 and 65.
23 Ibid para 66.
24 *IHRDA and OSJI (for Nubian Children) v Kenya*, Com 002/2009, para 53.
25 Constitution 2010, s 13(3).
26 Constitution 2010, s 14(5).
27 Constitution 2010, s 15(1).
28 Constitution 2010, s 14(1) and (2).
29 Constitution 2010, s 15(3).
30 Constitution 2010, s 14(4).

who may be dead or with whom they have lost contact, were displaced from neighbouring states following wars and unrest.[31]

Under the 2010 Constitution, children are also entitled to 'parental care and protection, which includes equal responsibility of the mother and father to provide for the child, whether they are married to each other or not'.[32] A constitutional challenge has already been brought alleging that parts of the Children Act on parental responsibility breach art 53(1)(e) of the Constitution on parental duties of support.

In *ZAK and Another v MA and Another*[33] a man challenged the constitutionality of provisions of the Children Act which gave precedence to the mother of children born out of wedlock in the acquisition of parental responsibility, while also providing that a stepfather could be asked to pay maintenance for his stepchildren if he had treated them as children of the family.[34] There was provision made for subsequent acquisition of parental responsibility for the father, or a person who took on the role of parent. The petitioner had met a woman who had two children from a previous relationship. They cohabited (with her children) for 2 years, during which time the two went on to have twins. The man ran off with the maid. He provided maintenance in the form of a deposit for food with a local shop for his own twin children, but only for 2 months. Faced with the possibility of having to provide for all four children, the man brought a petition to the Supreme Court alleging a breach of his right to equal protection of the law and also alleging that s 53(2)(e) of the Constitution, which required parents to provide for their children, was a duty targeted specifically and solely at biological parents, not those who had acted as social parents. While the court did strike down the provision of the Children Act on parental responsibility as being unconstitutional as it constituted discrimination against children born out of wedlock who were treated differently to those born to married people, it dismissed the petition noting that the determination of liability for the payment of child support, including by step-parents, was to be done by a court following the criteria set out in the Children Act. The court ruled that s 53(2)(e) was about maintenance of a child by a responsible adult. A person who had acted as a parent and treated a child as a member of the family could not, on the ending of the relationship with the child's biological parent, walk away from their responsibilities to the child.

Echoing art 4 of the ACRWC, which is replicated in the Kenyan Children Act, is art 53(2) of the Constitution which provides that a child's best interests are of paramount importance in every matter concerning the child.[35]

---

31 The ACERCW thinks that this provision does not go far enough. See *IHRDA and OSJI (for Nubian Children) v Kenya,* Com 002/2009, para 53.

32 Constitution 2010, s 53(2).

33 *ZAK and Another v MA and Another*, Petition 193 of 2011, reported in 2013 eKLR. Available at: www.kenyalaw.org/CaseSearch/view_preview1.php?link=51993230494601146271507.

34 Children Act 2001, ss 23, 25 and 94 respectively.

35 Children Act 2001, s 4(2). See also CEDAW, art 16(1)(d) and (f).

A key problem facing women in family law has been inequitable access to, and distribution of property, including land, during marriage, and, at the point of death or divorce.[36] It is important therefore that, as noted, the Constitution guarantees equality from the beginning of marriage to its dissolution.[37] Elaboration of this provision with respect to land and marital property can be found in the principles of land policy which require 'the elimination of gender discrimination in law, customs and practices related to land and property in land'.[38] To ensure that equality is guaranteed, the Constitution requires Parliament to enact laws which protect both dependants and wives of deceased landholders who are in occupation of the land.[39] Given the dependence of many women on land for subsistence and livelihood, this recognition of their legal entitlements to land is particularly important. Moreover, Parliament is required to enact legislation which regulates the recognition and protection of the family home during and on the ending of the marriage.[40] It has most recently tried to fulfil this obligation by enacting the Land Registration Act 2012 and the Matrimonial Property Act 2013.

III MATRIMONIAL PROPERTY ACT 2013

The promulgation of the Matrimonial Property Act on 16 January 2014 brought Kenya into line with many other Commonwealth countries in respect to the division of marital property on divorce. Hitherto, Kenya had relied on the English Married Women's Property Act 1888 whose provisions had long been abandoned in the originating jurisdiction.[41] Section 17 of the Married Women's Property Act permitted either spouse to apply to court for a determination of entitlement to title or possession of property. In interpreting the Married Women's Property Act judges usually worked on the principle of 'he', and it was usually a he, 'who pays for the property, owns the property'. This worked against women whose inferior earning capacity, due to structural discrimination, often meant that they were not in a position to purchase or to contribute cash to pay for assets. Furthermore, the pay-ownership nexus ignored the huge contributions made by wives by way of their unpaid labour within the home.[42] This discrimination was best exemplified by a case discussed by Nyamu-Musembi in an earlier volume of the ISFL where a wife who was

---

36 Federation of Women Lawyers (FIDA) in Kenya and United States' Georgetown University Law Centre 'Empowering Women with Rights to Inheritance – A Report on Amendments to The Law of Succession Act Necessary to Ensure Women's Human Rights' (2009) 40 Georgetown Journal of International Law 127.

37 Constitution 2010, s 45(3).

38 Constitution 2010, s 60(1)(f).

39 Constitution 2010, s 68(c)(vi). See also Matrimonial Property Act 2013, s 11 and 11(c).

40 Constitution 2010, s 68(c)(iii).

41 Married Women's Property Act 1882, Statutes of General Application applied in Kenya by virtue of Section 3(1)(c) of the Judicature Act (Cap 8). A Commins 'Dividing Matrimonial Property on Divorce: Colonialism, Chauvinism and Modernism in Kenya' June [2010] IFL 167.

42 Action Aid *Making Care Visible – Women's Unpaid Care Work in Nepal, Nigeria, Uganda and Kenya* (Action Aid, 2013).

claiming a share of the matrimonial assets was told dismissively by the judge that she wanted to 'sit on her husband's back with her hands in his pockets'.[43]

Due to lobbying by women's rights activists within Kenya and criticism from human rights bodies, this position has been slowly changing with judges prepared to take on board indirect contributions made by women to the acquisition or improvement of family assets and by extension dividing marital property more equitably.[44]

However, the pendulum swung back with the Court of Appeal's much criticised decision in *Echaria v Echaria*.[45] By the time of the divorce the couple had been married for 23 years, during which time the wife had supported the husband in his various diplomatic postings. She had taken care of their four children and looked after their home. On their return to Kenya she took up a teaching post. From her salary, she contributed to the payment of loans taken out by the couple. They had substantial land holding and other assets. She asked for a 50% share of the property but was only awarded a 25% share. The Court of Appeal stated that where property was registered in the name of one spouse, then the other spouse did not acquire a beneficial interest unless she could point to direct financial contribution. The Court stated that domestic contribution would not suffice. It went on to say that the presumption of equality in properties registered in joint names was rebuttable and that equal division was not a rule. The proportionate contribution of each spouse had to be taken into account. The Court then passed the baton to the Legislature and noted that, if reform of the law was needed, then Parliament should lead the way.[46] Although the Court made reference to Kenya's ratification of international and regional human rights instruments including the Covenant on Economic, Social and Cultural Rights,[47] the African Charter and CEDAW, as providing a source of

---

[43] C Nyamu-Musembi '"Sitting on her husband's back with her hands in his pockets": Commentary on Judicial Decision Making in Marital Property Cases in Kenya' in A Bainham (ed) *International Survey of Family Law 2002 Edition* (Bristol, Jordan Publishing Ltd, 2002) 229.

[44] See for example cases discussed at Kenya Law Resource Centre 'Courts response to matrimonial property rights' at: http://kenyalawresourcecenter.blogspot.co.uk/2011/07/courts-response-to-matrimonial-property.html -accessed 28 March 2014.

[45] *Echaria v Echaria* Civil Appeal No 75 of 2001, [2007] eKLR. This case was singled out for criticism by Federation of Women Lawyers – Kenya (FIDA-Kenya) and the International Women's Human Rights Clinic, Georgetown University Law Center, Washington DC, USA *Kenyan Laws and Harmful Customs Curtail Women's Equal Enjoyment of ICESCR Rights* A Supplementary Submission to the Kenyan Government's Initial Report under the ICESCR, scheduled for review by the Committee on Economic, Social, and Cultural Rights during its 41st session (Nov 3–21, 2008), October 3, 2008, para 6. See also CEDAW –CEDAW CO Kenya, CEDAW/C/KEN/CO/7 paras 45 and 46(b). A Commins, n 41 (2010) 169; M Hallward-Driemeir and T Hasan *Empowering Women: Legal Rights and Economic Opportunities in Africa* (World Bank, 2013) 103.

[46] *Echaria v Echaria* [2007] eKLR 26 et seq.

[47] International Covenant on Economic, Social and Cultural Rights, 1966, 993 UNTS 3; African Charter on Human and Peoples' Rights, 1981, 21 ILM 58, 1520 UNTS 217.

law 'which, in appropriate cases, the courts in this country may tap from' it did not itself utilise said instruments, thus reinforcing gender inequality.[48]

Fortunately, human rights norms have begun to be embedded within the judiciary yielding more positive outcomes. In *CMN v AWM*[49] the husband sought a declaration that he was the sole owner of the matrimonial home because he had paid for it and all the related outgoings. The wife, with whom he had four children, who was registered as a joint owner, counter-sued for half. Citing s 2(5) of the 2010 Constitution enshrining international law, and s 45(2) on equality between spouses from entry to dissolution of marriage, the judge proceeded to list provisions from a raft of international instruments including the Universal Declaration of Rights,[50] the African Protocol on the Rights of Women and CEDAW to hold that the property should be shared equally.

The Matrimonial Property Act made two key changes: first, it sought to mitigate the shortcomings of the Married Women's Property Act by recognising marriage as a partnership, including in terms of property ownership, and secondly, it introduced prenuptial contracts into Kenyan law. In addition to providing that husbands and wives have equal rights to enter into contracts and to acquire, own or dispose of property,[51] a major development has been the recognition that 'contribution' to the acquisition of property counts in the determination of the shares that each party should receive. Contribution is defined as including 'monetary and non-monetary contribution including– domestic work and management of the matrimonial home; child care, companionship, management of family business or property, farm work'.[52] Marital property includes the family home, goods therein and any other moveable or immoveable property that the parties have acquired during the course of the marriage.[53] The CEDAW Committee criticised the draft bill to the Act for its narrow construction of matrimonial property, which the Committee said included: 'tangible property alone, so that such assets as pension rights, life insurances etc., although accumulated during the marriage, may be left out of the property distributed upon dissolution'.[54] The Committee's recommendation that matrimonial property should include tangible and non-tangible assets does not appear to have been taken up.[55]

Section 7 of the Matrimonial Property Act gives ownership of the marital property to both spouses, but according to their respective contributions to its acquisition. While the property is to be divided between the spouses, there is no requirement that this division be equal. The division very much rests on how

48 Ibid 27.

49 *CMN v AWM* Environmental & Land Case 208 of 2012, [2013] Eklr.

50 Universal Declaration on Human Rights, 1948 UN GA Res.217 A (III) art 16(1); Protocol to the African Charter on Human and Peoples' Rights on the Rights of Women in Africa, OAU/AHG/Res.240, art 7(d); CEDAW art 16(1)(h).

51 MPA 2013, s 4.

52 MPA 2013, s 2.

53 MPA 2013, s 6.

54 CEDAW CO Kenya, CEDAW/C/KEN/CO/7 para 45.

55 Ibid para 46(c).

judges choose to weigh non-monetary contribution. Again, in its consideration of Kenya's last report, the CEDAW Committee advised that the Matrimonial Property Bill, as it then was, should ensure: 'that non-monetary contribution to matrimonial property is accorded equal value and women are awarded equal share in matrimonial property regardless of the nature of their contribution'.[56]

With regard to property that does not become part of the joint marital estate either because it is acquired before, or during the marriage, in a personal capacity, s 9 of the Act provides that, where the other party makes a contribution towards the improvement of that property, then the contributing party 'acquires a beneficial interest in the property equal to the contribution made'.[57] Again, it will be left to a judge to decide how much of the property should be acquired by the holder of the beneficial interest which is dependent on the weighting given to contribution. This has proved controversial and subject to criticism by the UN Working Group on Laws that Discriminate against Women and some UN Special Rapporteurs who have argued:[58]

> 'Women will effectively have no security of tenure, or place to live with their children if their husband leaves them or dies, which will also increase their risk of experiencing violence ... The passage of the Act will have a detrimental impact on the right to food, the right to adequate housing and the right to an adequate standard of living for Kenyan women, children and communities.'

It may well be that the experts have prejudged the way in which contribution will be interpreted. It is significant that the definition of contribution takes on the caring roles traditionally taken on by women as well as their contribution to family farms by way of unpaid labour. A different consideration is whether the statute should simply have put the matter beyond doubt by providing for a presumption of equal sharing of all matrimonial property in monogamous marriages.

In recognition of the plural marriage forms in existence, the MPA makes provision for polygynous unions in s 8. Where property was acquired by the man and his first wife before he took on other wives, then the property is held equally by the husband and first wife.[59] If there are multiple wives when the property is acquired, then the property is to be: 'regarded as owned by the man and the wives taking into account any contributions made by the man and each of the wives'.[60] The statute has a proviso to the joint ownership presumption providing, 'where it is clear by agreement of the parties that a wife shall have her matrimonial property with the husband separate from that of the other wives, then any such wife shall own that matrimonial property equally with the

---

56 Ibid para 46(b)

57 MPA 2013, s 9.

58 UN Working Group and the Special Rapporteurs on extreme poverty, food, housing and violence against women, 'UN Human Rights Experts Urge Kenya to Repeal Discriminatory Sections in Matrimonial Property Act' 17 February 2014 at: www.ohchr.org/EN/NewsEvents/Pages/DisplayNews.aspx?NewsID=14254&, accessed on 28 March 2014.

59 MPA 2013, s 8(1)(a).

60 MPA 2013, s 8(1)(b).

husband without the participation of the other wife or wives'.[61] The question is how clear such agreements are and when this separate property holding is to be determined? One can envisage a situation where the remaining wife or wives 'agree' to the husband's suggestion that they say disputed property in fact belongs to them and the husband to the exclusion of the claimant wife. Again, here the non-financial contribution likely to be made by wives can be easily discounted: how much can she have contributed by way of labour if there are two or three other wives claiming to have worked harder and longer? Given the fluidity of entry into marriage, especially in customary law, is it really that easy to ascertain when a formal marriage comes into being and by definition when property rights start to accrue? Finally, the Act presumes gender equality in decision-making between husband and wives which is belied by the evidence.

The Matrimonial Property Act exempts Islamic law and provides that adherents '*may* [my emphasis] be governed by Islamic law in all matters relating to matrimonial property'.[62] Does the use of 'may' instead of the peremptory 'shall', suggest an opt-out for those who would prefer to be governed by the MPA rather than Islamic law? The question whether a person born a Muslim can opt out in this way has occupied legal and religious jurists and commentators for centuries. The explicit recognition given to Kadhi courts to determine personal status law issues in the 2010 Constitution also suggest that the ring-fencing of Islamic law is deliberate.[63] It is noteworthy that the Constitution provides that those professing the Islamic faith can have their property determined by Islamic law.[64]

Trust property, including property held in trust under customary law, is excluded from the definition of marital property in s 6. Does this exclusion raise problems of gender-based discrimination as women are often excluded from accessing land in this way? Arguably, the application of the constitutional principles of gender equality encapsulated in the land principles will protect women from suffering disadvantage. Similarly, s 11 provides for consideration to be given to the customary law(s) of the parties in property distribution on divorce or dissolution, but notes that this is subject to the Constitution. The court is required to consider constitutional principles including rights to access and use ancestral land and the cultural home by a wife or wives or former wife or wives.[65]

The Act operates on the basis of a series of presumptions which include that where property is acquired during the marriage by one spouse, it is presumed to

61 MPA 2013, s 8(2).
62 MPA 2013, s 3.
63 The case of Fatia Essa v Mohamed Alibhai (no citation given) is said to be one where the courts used the now repealed Married Women's Property Act 1888, to give a Muslim woman an equal share of marital property in recognition of her financial contribution on divorce. See Kenya Law Resource Centre 'Courts Response to Matrimonial Property Rights' at: http://kenyalawresourcecenter.blogspot.co.uk/2011/07/courts-response-to-matrimonial-property.html (accessed 28 March 2014).
64 MPA 2013, s 3.
65 MPA 2013, s 11.

be held in trust for the other. Where the property is acquired jointly, the presumption is that the parties own the property in equal shares.[66] If either party gives the other a gift during the marriage, the gift is held by the recipient personally.[67] Debts which were incurred before the marriage remain the personal responsibility of the person who entered into the original agreement. Marriage does not automatically lead to the creation of joint and several liability.[68] However, if the property has become marital property or was acquired during the marriage and the parties have agreed, then liability is shared.[69] Do these provisions only apply to marriages which remain monogamous? How is liability to be determined in polygynous relationships? Important to note is s 12 which protects against what Fehlberg has called 'sexually transmitted debt', that is the loss by one spouse, usually the wife, of property rights arising from the re-mortgaging or use of the house or other common property as security on a loan which the borrower spouse then cannot repay.[70] The Act is clear that a spouse cannot be evicted nor can the home be mortgaged or sold without the explicit consent of both parties to the marriage.[71] Are all the 'houses' in a polygynous set up protected, or only the one(s) under direct threat?

Perhaps one of the most significant changes made in the Matrimonial Property Act is the introduction of prenuptials in s 6(3).This allows parties to decide how they wish to arrange their property affairs before they marry. The statute allows a spouse to challenge the prenuptial on three grounds: fraud, coercion or by alleging that the settlement is manifestly unjust. While prenuptials are often praised for giving parties autonomy and respecting their right to make decisions that suit them, it is as well to remember the dissenting judgment of the only female Supreme Court justice in England and Wales, Lady Hale in *Radmacher v Granantino*.[72] Lady Hale pointed out that the case, which involved the husband of a rich heiress challenging their prenuptial contract, was unusual because it was more often than not, the man who had the money. She also identified the inequality of bargaining power between men and women in the drawing up of the contracts and in post-marital work and contribution, including within the home. She noted that these inequalities may be difficult to factor into an agreement reached before the marriage begins to the detriment of the weaker party, usually the woman. The discrimination became even worse the longer the marriage subsisted. The difficulty of foreseeing changing circumstances was an issue that needed attention. It was therefore important for courts to take into consideration fairness in the ascertainment of interests at the point of divorce, remembering that marriage is built on a fundamental principle of reciprocal duties of support between the parties, and towards any children they may have. Without proper scrutiny and each party receiving independent and impartial

---

66 MPA 2013, s 14.
67 MPA 2013, s 15.
68 MPA 2013, s 16.
69 MPA 2013, s 10.
70 B Fehlberg *Sexually Transmitted Debt* (Clarendon, 1997). MPA 2013, s 12(1) and (2).
71 MPA 2013, s 12(4) and (5).
72 *Radmacher v Granantino* [2010] UKSC 42.

legal advice, prenuptial contracts may return Kenya to the bad old days of the Married Women's Property Act, and its money-property ownership nexus, to the exclusion of domestic and other non-monetary contribution.

IV INHERITANCE

It is in the determination of entitlement to intestate property that Kenyan courts have been the most gender aware. They have been guided in their decision-making by Kenya's ratification of human rights instruments which guarantee equality and freedom from discrimination. In *Rono v Rono*[73] a polygynous man died intestate leaving two wives and nine children. He had three sons and two daughters with the first wife and four daughters with the second wife. All the children were adults. Initially letters of administration were, by family agreement, given to the two wives and eldest son. However, there followed a protracted dispute about the distribution of the property which included land and moveables. The deceased had also left debts. It was argued for the first family that sons should get more than daughters because the daughters would marry and should therefore not benefit twice. The first family also noted that many of the assets had been acquired before the second marriage and so they were entitled to a bigger share. They were more generous in their proposals for sharing the deceased's liabilities. The first judge seemed to have been won over by the argument that the daughters would marry, and gave them each 5 hectares, compared to the 30 hectares each given to the sons. To 'compensate' for the second wife's failure to produce sons, she was given 50 hectares while the first wife got 20. The liabilities were divided 60/40 between first and second houses respectively.[74] Section 40 of the Law of Succession Act provides that where a deceased is married polygynously, then the children and wife of each house are to be given a child's portion after all liabilities have been met.[75]

On appeal, the court reversed the division giving each child of the deceased an equal share of 14.44 hectares. The Court of Appeal also equalised the distribution of the land between the wives giving each 30 hectares. Two hectares were kept as joint family property. As they were not in contention, the liabilities were left untouched. The Court noted that the Law of Succession Act provided that dependants of the deceased included the wife and children of the deceased.[76] It did not say anything about the marital status of the children, thus daughters could not be excluded because they were married, or might marry in the future. Rather ungallantly perhaps, the lead judge noted that the daughters were past their first bloom and were therefore unlikely to get married. In reaching its decision to share the property equally, the Court cited the Commonwealth Bangalore principles to the effect that courts should have

---

73 *Rono v Rono and Another* (2008) 1 KLR (G&F) 803.

74 Ibid 808–809.

75 The concept of house (a wife and her children in a polygynous marriage) is defined in s 3 of the Law of Succession Act (cap 160).

76 Law of Succession Act, s 29.

regard to international commitments undertaken by a country whether or not that country has incorporated the conventions into national law.[77] The Court then cited art 1 of CEDAW which explains discrimination and also art 18(3) of the African Charter on Human and Peoples' Rights which enjoins states parties to 'ensure the elimination of every discrimination against women and also ensure the protection of rights of the woman and the child as stipulated in international declarations and conventions'.[78] Furthermore, the Court also cited the repugnancy clause which allows a court to disregard customary law if it is 'repugnant to justice and morality or inconsistent with any written law'.[79] The Court did this in part to get round the provision in the previous constitution which had included, by way of amendment in 1997, sex as a prohibited ground for discrimination, but then clawed back that gain, by exempting customary law from its reach in family matters including 'devolution of property on death'.[80]

Building on the *Rono* case was *Ntutu*.[81] Mr Ntutu, a Masai, had died leaving several wives and children. The deceased's daughters who were described by the court as educated and who 'are exposed to the modern trends of Kenya', challenged their stepbrothers who wanted to exclude them from sharing in the inheritance.[82] The brothers argued that Masai customary law did not recognise the right of women to inherit.[83] They also argued that the Constitution ring-fenced customary law from the prohibited grounds which included sex. Excluding daughters from inheritance was therefore legal.

While acknowledging that it had been the case that many customary laws did not recognise married women as entitled to inherit from their deceased fathers' estates, the court noted that this had been overridden by the Law of Succession Act which made provision for *all* the dependants of the deceased, including wives and children, to inherit. The judge noted that the statute did not say anything about distinctions on grounds of sex or marital status, so all daughters, whether married or unmarried, were to be counted as children, and therefore entitled to an equal share.[84] The court disagreed with the brothers' interpretation of the Constitution, noting that the 1997 constitutional amendment which had introduced sex into the non-discrimination provision (discussed in *Rono*) had been as a direct result of Kenya's exposure to

---

77 Commonwealth Secretariat, Report of Judicial Colloquium on the Domestic Application of International Human Rights Norms, Bangalore, India, 1988, reprinted 'The Bangalore Principles on the Domestic Application of International Human Rights Norms'(1988) Commonwealth Law Bulletin 14, 1196.

78 *Rono v Rono* (2008) 1 KLR (G&F) 803, 813.

79 Section 3 of the Judicature Act, Cap 8, Laws of Kenya in *Rono* at 811.

80 Constitutional Amendment Act 9 of 1997, ss 82(3) including sex, and 83(4) excluding customary law from the non-discrimination provision. *Rono v Rono* (2008) 1 KLR (G& F) 803, 812.

81 *In Re the Estate of Lerionka Ole Ntutu (Deceased)* Succesion [sic] Cause No 1263 of 2000, [2008] eKLR.

82 Ibid 1.

83 Ibid 1.

84 Ibid 2. The court cited s 29 of the Law of Succession Act (cap 160).

international laws and its acknowledgement thereafter that it was no longer tenable to continue discriminatory treatment of women.[85] Finally, the court noted that any attempt to exclude the daughters was repugnant, and therefore the brothers' interpretation of customary law, which was grounded in an unjustified distinction on grounds of sex, fell within the scope of exclusion anticipated by s 3(2) of the Judicature Act.[86]

Marking a break from the past and showing how the 2010 Constitution works in practice is *Rukunga v Rukunga*.[87] The deceased who had been a polygynist in life left 12 children; six daughters and six sons. All the daughters are listed as being married. Interestingly, the sons' marital status is not recorded. The dispute arose when one of the sisters challenged an attempt to evict her from a plot of land which had belonged to her mother, the deceased's second wife who had died after him. The first wife predeceased him. Also in dispute was the ownership of a stone house which one of the sons of the first wife had built and given to his stepmother. The son said that his sister, being married, was not entitled to inherit. He also said that the stone house belonged to his brother who was living in the United States. The objecting sister said that she was no longer married. She had returned to her father's home when her own marriage ended and had continued to live on the family homestead farming her late mother's allocated fields and living in the house which had been given to her mother by her stepbrother. Both the house and fields should therefore pass to her. The Court cited the land and equality provisions of the new 2010 Constitution to find for the daughter. Specifically the judge noted that art 60(1)(f) called for the 'elimination of gender discrimination in law, customs and practices related to land and property in land'. He also cited s 27 on equality before the law. He highlighted provisions which reinforced women's right to equal treatment and access to opportunities, and noted that discrimination was prohibited, including on grounds of status. He concluded by noting that the Constitution prohibited all direct and indirect discrimination on any of the prohibited grounds which included sex.[88] These combined meant that a daughter could not be excluded simply because she was married as this would constitute discrimination on grounds of status. The court gave her all her mother's land, plus the buildings thereon including the stone house which had become her mother's property by virtue of gift.[89]

Clearly Kenya has, in the cases discussed above, adhered to its international obligations. However, there are still areas where pockets of resistance remain. The final section looks at the challenges faced by intersex people.

---

85 Ibid 7-8. *Ntutu* 5–6.

86 Ibid 9.

87 *In the Matter of the Estate of Rukunga Kaimathiri (Deceased). Rukunga v Rukunga* Succession Cause 308 of 1994, [2011] eKLR.

88 Constitution 2010, s 27(3), (4) and (5) respectively.

89 *Rukunga v Rukunga* [2011] eKLR 5.

V INTERSEXUALITY

In *RM v Attorney General and 4 Others*[90] the courts were confronted with a claim for sex discrimination and degrading and inhuman treatment brought by an intersex person. RM was born intersex, that is, 'having reproductive organs or sex chromosomes that are not exclusively male or female'.[91] His parents had not felt able to register the birth of RM but had decided to bring RM up as a boy, giving him the name Richard.[92] RM led a troubled life which resulted in him committing a violent robbery which led to imprisonment in a male prison. There RM experienced taunting and assaults from both prison warders and fellow inmates. RM brought a claim for multiple violations of his rights. The ones that concern us are the claim for discrimination on grounds of sex and status and the claim that intersexuals were not free to marry or to adopt.[93]

The petitioner contended that, while the Births and Deaths Registration Act required every birth to be registered, the list of prescribed particulars, which included sex, did not allow for intersex people to be registered because the statute only recognised two categories under sex: male or female. Failure to tick one of these boxes would result in a birth certificate being denied. Without a birth certificate, the intersex person could not access a number of other services or enjoy the related rights including education and health care. Additionally, without a form of identity, the petitioner could not apply for a passport. The inability to get a birth certificate constituted discrimination against RM solely because of intersexual status. Furthermore, the male-female only recognition in the Births Act denied intersexual people the right to marry because marriage in Kenya was defined as being between a man and a woman.[94] This last claim is now even more pertinent since, as earlier discussed, the 2010 Constitution reinforced this definition of marriage. The petitioner claimed that the Births and Deaths Registration Act was inconsistent with constitutional principles and should be struck down to the extent of its inconsistency.

The court was presented with a wealth of medical and comparative jurisprudence on intersexuality, from a range of Commonwealth countries and other jurisdictions including the United States and Colombia. All the evidence showed a move from denial to recognition of intersex identity and the granting of equal rights to people belonging to this group.[95] However, the Court decided to ignore all the evidence and to find against the petitioner and the interested parties who had joined the petition in support on the key issues that concern us. The Court acknowledged that the term sex in the Births and Deaths Registration Act comprised two categories: male and female. It further noted that the sex of a child was formed within the womb and fixed. All that had to

---

90 *RM v Attorney-General* Petition 705 of 2007, [2010] eKLR.

91 Ibid at para 15 citing the Australian Legislation Act 2001.

92 While conscious of the importance of respecting intersex identity, I will use the pronoun 'he'. This is for clarity and not a deliberate slight or attempt to render invisible RM's plural identity.

93 *RM v Attorney General* [2010] eKLR, para 3(h).

94 *RM v Attorney General* [2010] eKLR, paras17–23.

95 Ibid. See for example, paras 37–44, 106–111,125–126, 138–139 and 146–147.

be determined in the case at hand was on 'which side of the divide the petitioner fell particularly for purposes of registration of the birth'.[96] The answer is clearly 'neither', but this was not the view of the Court. Taking a discredited view, the Court said that it was possible to take a view on sex by picking the dominant characteristics and assigning the child a sex in that way. That is what the petitioner's mother had done.[97] This being the case, the petitioner had not been denied a birth certificate, but had simply not been registered.[98]

The petitioner also claimed that the term 'sex' in the Constitution, listed as a prohibited ground of discrimination, should be read as including intersex people.[99] However, the Court rejected the contention that intersex constituted a 'form of gender identity to which discrimination on the grounds of sex relates'.[100] Instead the Court noted that it interpreted sex as denoting male or female only because that was the 'ordinary meaning' of the word 'which is inclusive of all persons including intersex persons within the broad categories of male and female'. Apparently this was in conformity with international instruments such as the UDHR which guaranteed equality before the law for all.[101] Confused? It got worse; on status discrimination the Court went on to note that the recognition of 'intersex in the category of "other status" ... would result in the recognition of a third category of gender which our society may not be ready for at this point in time'.[102] The Court decided that the petitioner was indeed covered by the law and had not suffered any disadvantage. The examination of social stigma by the Court revealed its real fear. It was afraid of being seen to expand sexual identity as this might be seen as condoning other practices such as homosexuality: 'Few seem to appreciate the fact that the issue of gender definition for an intersex person unlike a transsexual or a homosexual, is a matter of necessity and not choice.'[103] In short societal, or more accurately judicial, prejudice and lack of preparedness had to trump the rights of a minority. However, the Court did say that this was an issue that the Legislature should address.[104]

On the claim about the violation of the right to marry, the court again reiterated the male to female requirement for marriage. Although a doctor had given evidence after examining RM, the Court said that it did not have sufficient medical evidence about the petitioner's condition to say where on the male to female spectrum RM sat. It also noted that RM's mother (who had assigned him the status of a man) and his grandmother had attested to his small penis. As he was incapable of consummating a marriage, the court decided, he

96 Ibid para 128.
97 J Greenberg *Intersexuality and the Law: Why Sex Matters* (NYU Press, 2012).
98 *RM v Attorney General* [2010] eKLR, para 129.
99 Ibid paras 22 and 23 respectively.
100 *RM v Attorney General* [2010] eKLR – this argument was made by the second interested party, the Kenya Gay and Lesbian Trust, at para 46.
101 Ibid para 132.
102 Ibid para 133. See also para 130.
103 Ibid para 145.
104 Ibid para 148.

could not marry. While noting that same-sex marriages were not permitted in Kenya,[105] the Court still ruled: 'His handicap is biological rather than legal.'[106] On adoption, the court was short; as the petitioner had neither adopted, nor indicated an intention to adopt, there was no need to address the issue.[107]

The lack of imagination, compassion and legal nous of the Court in the *RM* case is disheartening. Interesting is the reference to the lack of judicial purposiveness in *RM* articulated by another judge in *Ntutu* which was about the wholly unrelated matter of inheritance property. There it was noted of *RM*:

> '[The] Constitution of any country of the world should not represent a mere body or skeleton without a soul or spirit of its own. I would not like to discard as the Court of Appeal did in *RM and Another* ... even after taking a strict interpretation, the possibility of the court adopting a broader view or using the living tree principle of the interpretation of the Constitution where there are "**amongst others, ambiguity, unreasonableness, obvious imbalance or lack of proportionality or absurd situation.**"[emphasis in the original].'[108]

VI CONCLUSION

The chapter has given an overview of some of the recent legal developments in Kenya, starting with the 2010 Constitution which has led to radical change of the legal landscape with respect to family law. The constitutional injunction that the state amend and repeal legislation that contravenes constitutional provisions has already resulted in the passing of the Matrimonial Property Act which gives recognition, for the first time, to non-monetary contributions made, often by women, in looking after the home and family. Pending is legislation on marriage. There is a Marriage Bill which tries to rationalise the plural marriage system in existence in Kenya. However, the 2007 draft has been criticised by the CEDAW Committee for retaining polygyny.[109] Also worthy of note is the work of the judiciary not least in determining fairer distribution of property on death. Problematic is the legislative vacuum with respect to intersex people and the failure to provide them with the means to acquire identity documents without having to declare themselves as either male or female, the only two options available. The problem has been exacerbated by the reluctance of the upper judiciary to intervene to provide protection for this disenfranchised group. It is hoped that the new constitutional dispensation, with its focus on human rights and equality, will permeate the consciousness and practice of all Kenyans, citizens and those tasked with interpreting and applying the law alike. Passing the law is one thing, ensuring that those who

---

[105] Ibid para 139.
[106] Ibid para 141.
[107] Ibid.
[108] *In Re Estate of Lerionka Ole Ntutu (Deceased)* [2008] eKLR 8.
[109] CEDAW CO Kenya, CEDAW/C/KEN/CO/7, paras 45 and 46.

need to seek its protection are able to do so without difficulty is another. It is important that access to justice and legal literacy about peoples' rights and entitlements be prioritised.

KOREA

WHEN A REVEALED AFFAIR IS A CRIME, BUT A HIDDEN ONE IS A ROMANCE: AN OVERVIEW OF ADULTERY LAW IN THE REPUBLIC OF KOREA

Ann Black and Kwang-Soo Jung[*]

Résumé

La République de Corée est considérée comme une des puissances économiques mondiales. Sa récente industrialisation et son développement, connus sous l'expression «le miracle du fleuve Han», ont eu pour résultat que ses 50 millions d'habitants sont bien éduqués, riches, urbanisés et doués en technologie. De plus, ils sont les héritiers d'une riche histoire ainsi que de traditions juridiques qui s'étendent sur quatre millénaires. La modernité n'a pas complètement jeté cet héritage par-dessus bord. En particulier, le néo-confusianisme propre à la Corée continue d'influencer les fondements de la vie des Coréens, surtout en ce qui a trait aux relations familiales et aux concepts de moralité, de convenance et d'éthique. Les règles en matière d'adultère se situent dans cette lignée et elles sont à la jonction de la tradition et de la modernité. L'esprit communautaire coréen et la priorité des valeurs familialesoccupent la même place que les valeurs modernes individualistes tels que le droit au respect de la vie privée, à la liberté sexuelle et au bonheur qui sont désormais inscrits dans la Constitution. Une des missions de la Cour constitutionnelle de Corée est de pondérer ces intérêts divergents et, depuis son adoption en 1988, le crime d'adultère figure parmi les dispositions légales dont la constitutionnalité est régulièrement contestée devant cette instance. En plus d'analyser le raisonnement de la Cour dans les quatre arrêts qui jusqu'à ce jour se sont penchés sur la constitutionnalité des dispositions légales relatives à l'adultère, le présent texte situe ces dispositions dans leur contexte historique et il analyse les différentes dimensions juridiques de l'adultère, c'est-à-dire en tant qu'infraction pénale, motif de divorce et source de responsabilité civile. Chacun de ces volets est analysé à la lumière de la jurisprudence, particulièrement celle de la Cour suprême,

[*] Ann Black is an Associate Professor of Law at the TC Beirne School of Law and Deputy Director of the Centre for Public, International and Comparative Law. Kwang-Soo Jung is a Prosecutor, Seoul Central District, South Korea and a research scholar at the Centre for Public, International and Comparative Law, Korean Law Program. Special thanks and appreciation goes to Jung Wook-Lee, legal research assistant and assistant translator for this chapter. The Republic of Korea is internationally referred to as South Korea. For the purposes of this chapter the more colloquial 'Korea' will be used instead of the Republic of Korea or South Korea. For background on the law of Korea, see Korean Legislation Research Institute *Introduction to Korean Law* (Springer, Verlag Berlin Heidelberg, 2013).

ainsi que de la législation civile et pénale. Ce texte fait également état des débats sur ces questions, tant dans les milieux judiciaires qu'académiques ainsi qu'au sein des médias et il constate que si la dimension pénale de l'adultère pourrait bientôt changer, le volet civil semble bien destiné à demeurer inchangé.

I INTRODUCTION

It was a scandal that riveted South Koreans. In 2007, popular actor Park Chul accused his equally high-profile actress wife, Ok So-ri of adultery, that is, of having an extra-marital sexual affair, with two other men. The story played out in the Korean media just as stories of celebrity adultery are relished by the media around the world. Whether it is a member of the British royal family, a professional sportsperson, a President or politician, a film or television star engaging in an extra-marital affair that becomes public, the moral transgression will fuel drama, outrage, and intrigue in most communities. Social consequences inevitably flow from violating the trust that lies in marriage and the promise of marital fidelity. Arnold Schwarzenegger gave an emotional public apology, General Petraeus resigned as head of the CIA, Tiger Woods lost lucrative sponsorship deals, the marriage of the Prince and Princess Wales came to an end, and President Clinton's denials led to impeachment charges. Shame abounds. At a private level, emotional pain, betrayal, embarrassment, and sometimes an urge for revenge are felt by the individuals, their families, friends, colleagues and supporters. In the West, that is generally where it ends. For Park Chul and Ok So-ri, and for other Koreans whose secret romance is publicly revealed there are significant legal consequences. These can include a criminal conviction for a married adulterer and his or her illicit partner, with up to 2 years' imprisonment as punishment;[1] the adulterer can be required under civil law to pay damages to his or her (victim) spouse;[2] adultery is a valid ground for divorce[3] as well as a factor to be considered in custody,[4] visitation rights,[5] and property distribution[6] after divorce. In addition, there can be consequences for one's employment notably the public service, where acts of adultery can be seen as breaching the 'dignity' of an institution.[7]

The gamut of these consequences played out for Park and Ok in the following ways. First, Park filed for divorce based on the ground of Ok's adultery. She admitted to an extra-marital relationship with Park's opera-singer friend, Jung, but did deny the other alleged affair. Secondly, Ok So-ri was indicted in the Uijeongbu District Court for the criminal offence of adultery, pursuant to art 241 of Korea's Criminal Act, where she faced the possibility of up to 2 years' imprisonment. Ok So-ri challenged the constitutionality of this law in the

---

1 Criminal Act, art 241 (Adultery) and Criminal Procedure Act, art 229 (Accusation by Spouse)
2 Civil Act, arts 843 and 806.
3 Civil Act, art 840.
4 Civil Act, art 909.
5 Civil Act, art 837.
6 Civil Act, art 839.
7 National Public Service Law, art 63.

Constitutional Court, but its validity was upheld. Ok and Jung were ultimately convicted but they received suspended sentences of 8 and 6 months respectively. Thirdly, Park brought a civil claim against Ok and her lover for damages.[8] The personal lives of these individuals were open to public commentary not only because of the legal proceedings but because the media was invited to report on it. Ok called a news conference in which she confirmed the affair and revealed, in considerable personal detail, the reasons why she had resorted to having one.[9] Park responded with a media conference disputing Ok's version of events. Whether there are merits or not in the public laundering of their story, it did not only draw attention to the efficacy of adultery laws of Korea, but opened a wider debate on the place for morality, gendered roles and tradition in modern Korean society vis-à-vis rights of individuals to privacy and to happiness now guaranteed in the Constitution of the Republic of Korea ('the Constitution').[10] Although the revealed affair of Ok and Jung became a prominent case, convictions for adultery are not unusual. In 2008 it was estimated that each year over 1,200 people are indicted under this criminal law, with around half convicted and sentenced for the offence of adultery.[11] Five years later it is felt the numbers actually receiving a prison term have decreased as suspended sentences have become more prevalent, but it is not a moribund provision. At the time of writing, several more cases challenging the constitutionality of the criminalising adultery have been lodged with the Constitutional Court. The division in public opinion on this issue has meant reluctance from both the Constitutional Court and the Legislative Assembly to implement adultery law reform. In the meantime the debate goes on.

The romance between Ok and Jung may have had the trappings of an old-fashioned love affair, just like the ones portrayed in novels and films, but it is also an important one in highlighting the different legal consequences that a revealed affair can bring and the culture that it supports. This chapter examines the laws, both criminal and civil, which govern adultery in today's Korea and place them in their historical and also contemporary socio-legal context. The aim is to use these laws as a vehicle to gain insight into the complexity of factors that impact upon the role of law, and of law reform in a society that has a legal tradition and culture stretching back to 2333BC,[12] in which philosophical and religious forces, Confucianism, Neo-Confucianism and Buddhism have informed notions of morality and family. In addition, the colonisation by Japan has left a legacy for the legal system including for the adultery laws, but the Korean assertion of distinction from that colonial era and also from contemporary Western values of individualism and modernity is

---

8 Anthony Bessette 'Regulating and Punishing Adultery in Korea and East Asia' (July 27, 2009). Available at SSRN: http://papers.ssrn.com/sol3/papers.cfm?abstract_id=1439830.

9 Choe Sang-hun, 'Court challenge on adultery rocks South Koreans', *Taipei Times*, 21 May 2008.

10 The Constitution of the Republic of Korea. Available in English at:www.ccourt.go.kr/home/att_file/download/Constitution_of_the_Republic_of_Korea.pdf.

11 Choe Sang-hun 'Court challenge on adultery rocks South Koreans' *Taipei Times*, 21 May 2008.

12 *Paljobubgum of Gojosun* (The Eight Legally Prohibited Acts of Gojosun, BC 2333~108) is considered to be the first legal document in Korea.

equally significant. Korea is a modern, innovative and affluent nation but its cultural identity lies in thousands of years of tradition which reinforce long held values of ethics and morality.

Korea is just one example of how Asian traditions and notions of gender and family inform contemporary practice. The dimensions of adultery are also relevant to understanding law and morality in Asia. Many nations in the Asia-Pacific region have criminal sanctions for adultery, including the Republic of China (Taiwan)[13] with almost identical legislation to Korea's; the Philippines,[14] Cambodia,[15] Burma,[16] Laos,[17] Papua New Guinea,[18] as well as the Syariah informed laws against *zina* (adultery) and *khalwat* (inappropriate conduct) for Muslims in Indonesia, Malaysia and Brunei Darussalam. In all these Asian nations adultery is lauded as an important vehicle for preserving the integrity of marriage, ensuring the family unit is the foundation of society, and guaranteeing the moral integrity of its people. Religion, whether it is Buddhism, Christianity or Islam, or Confucian philosophy and other moral traditions, continues to inform the efficacy of laws against adultery.

The chapter is divided into six sections. Following this introductory section, section II reflects on adultery in an historical context where the criminal and civil consequences of marital infidelity on the Korean peninsula have ebbed and flowed for several millennia. Section III looks at the crime of adultery including the current legislative provisions and how they are applied and interpreted in the District and Supreme Courts and the vexed issues of proof that can arise. This includes how such prosecutions proceed, how the evidentiary requirements needed to prove adultery are met, and the consequences when such evidence is obtained illegally, for example by trespass. It will highlight the interplay between criminal complaints and divorce proceedings which is a distinctive feature of the Korean system. Section IV will review and assess the constitutionality of adultery as a crime though analysis of the reasoning of the Constitutional Court of Korea, which has retained the validity of the offence on four separate occasions. Section V will focus on the civil consequences of adultery, both in terms of divorce outcomes and compensation claims. Section VI will assess the viability of adultery laws in light of changes within Korean society and discuss tensions between traditionalism and individualism, and some of the unusual alliances that have arisen, for example, Confucianists aligning with feminists to support the retention stance. The chapter concludes that, whilst there are divergent views on adultery remaining a crime, there is still an acceptance that it has a role to play in the civil law realm. The Constitutional Court may be leaning towards reform but some obstacles still

13 Criminal Code (Republic of China), art 239. See: Lisa Tran 'Sex and Equality in Republican China' (2009) 35 Modern China 191–223.

14 Revised Penal Code (The Philippines), arts 333 and 334.

15 Law on Monogamy 2006 (Cambodia). For background see: Hugi Hotte and Geneveive King Ruel 'A Comparative and Legal Analysis of the Cambodian Law on Monogamy', at: www.ieim.uqam.ca/IMG/pdf/etude-de-cas-hotte-king.pdf.

16 Penal Code (Burma), s 498.

17 Criminal Code (Laos), art 117.

18 Adultery and Enticement Act (Papua New Guinea) 1998, art 2.

remain. Whilst the detail and discussion of these laws will be distinctively Korean, the core of the debate will resonate with tensions in family and moral issues prevalent across Asia.

II HISTORICAL PERSPECTIVES ON ADULTERY

(a) From ancient kingdoms

The general view is that adultery was criminalised under *Paljobubgum of Gojosun* (The Eight Legally Prohibited Acts of Gojosun) BC 2333–108, which is the oldest written legal code of Korea. From that time penalties for adultery have been in place.[19] In the time of the ancient northern kingdom of *Buyeo* (BC 200–494) and the *Baekjae* kingdom located in the southwest of the peninsula (BC 18–660) records show that adultery was prosecuted as a criminal offence.[20] Both men and women could be prosecuted with proven adultery resulting in capital punishment. A right to compensation also existed.[21] In the time of the Three Kingdoms there may have been a lull, but during the *Koryo* Dynasty (918–1392), from which the nation of Korea takes its name, a new ideology based on the doctrines of Chu-tzu found its way into the dynasty through King Chungryul. The focus of Chu-tzu doctrine was practical ethics with emphasis on social ethics through loyalty, honour and morality. Towards the end of the *Koryo* Dynasty scholars were critical of sexual promiscuity within their society and began to again officially regulate adultery through the application of Confucian ethics. Adulterers could be punished by lashings, with the husbands and children of adulterous wives held unable to serve as public officials or live as nobles.[22] Collective responsibility flowed from a culture where the family, not the individual, was the recognised legal entity. This was also the time when the restrictions on marriage between relatives were introduced,[23] and when married women were forbidden from entering Buddhist temples.

(b) During the *Chosun* Dynasty

The *yangban* (nobles of the scholarly class) who rose to power during the *Chosun* Dynasty (1392–1910) also emphasised ethical morality. Neo-Confucianism was at its zenith and its teachings on honour and loyalty instilled

---

19 Constitutional Court Decision 2007 Hun-Ka17.21, 2008 Hun-Ka7.26.

20 Hoon-Dong Lee 'Hankook Sung Munha wa HyungsaBup' ['The Sexual Culture and Criminal Law of Korea'] (2007) 2 Korea University of Foreign Studies Law Research Institute Journal 49 [Kwang-Soo Jung trans].

21 Gung-Sik Jung 'Hankuk eui Kantongchoe eui byeopjesajeol kochal' ['Historical Review of the Crime of Adultery in Korea'] (1991) 10 Korea Institute of Criminology 211 [Kwang-Soo Jung trans].

22 Choi Yoon-Jung 'Choisum Choi Gi Gangtong Gwanhan Younggu' ['The Study of Adultery during the Chosun Dynasty'] (1996) Catholic University of Daegu 4–8 [Kwang-Soo Jung trans].

23 Inter-marriage between Koreans of the same family name from the same region continued to be illegal until 1997. The Constitutional Court held the relevant provision (art 809 of the Civil Code) to be unconstitutional. Constitutional Court Decision, 95Hun-Ka 6–13, 16 July 1997.

a psyche of absolute obedience to the king and restored fastidious order to the Korean hierarchy of class and rank which had fallen into disarray during the later days of the *Koryo* Dynasty. In seeking to establish its moral ethics, the *yangban* at the apex of the *Chosun* social hierarchy[24] emphasised education for men and chastity for women.[25] Laxity in women's morals was identified as one of the main causes of the demise of the *Koryo* Dynasty.[26] Unlike today, chastity then was mandated for unmarried as well as married women, so that any sexual relationship between an unmarried woman and man was also categorised as adultery and subject to punishment.[27] Teachings of chastity and fidelity for women are found in the principle of *Bubuyubyul* (the principle of differentiation of husbands and wives), which was one of five core principles of Confucianism. *Bubuyubyul* taught separation of roles between husbands and wives and responsibilities and duties to each other.[28] In the *yeojayusamjongjido* (the Three Teachings for a Woman) a woman must follow three principles. First is *jaegajongbu* (following the father), where you must follow the wishes of your father; the second is *jukinjongbu* (following the husband), where you must follow the wishes of your husband once you get married; the last is *busajongja* (following the son) where you must follow the wishes of your son once your husband dies. It established a strong patriarchal society in which women were subservient to men and where their fidelity within marriage was prescribed to ensure the purity of the paternal lineage and to enable ancestral rites to be performed.[29] At first, a wife's refusal to remarry after the death of her husband was seen as virtuous, but by 1477 it become a prohibition, with offspring prevented from undertaking the examinations needed to succeed in government ranks.[30] By contrast, a husband could remarry, and could take a second wife or adopt a son if his wife had not produced a male heir. A husband was allowed concubines[31] in addition to his legally recognised first wife. A husband could

---

24 Four classes: royalty, *Yangban* (nobles), commoners (which included agricultural workers and professionals such as physicians and entertainers) and slaves. See Han Hee-sook 'Women's Life during the *Choson* Period' (2004) 6 International Journal of Korean History 113, 129.

25 Byungin Jang *Josun Jongi Honinje Sungchabyul* [*The Marriage Laws of Sexual Discrimination During the Early Chosun*] (Il Ji Sa, South Korea, 1997) 307 [Kwang-Soo Jung trans].

26 Han Hee-sook 'Women's Life during the *Choson* Period' (2004) 6 International Journal of Korean History 113, 117.

27 Pae-yong Yi *Women in Korean History* (Ewha Woman's University Press, Seoul, 2008) 44.

28 Seung Hae Kim, in her article 'Bubuyubyul Haesuk Hak Chuk Yoksawa Hyun dai Chonmang' ['The Historical Analysis and the Outlook of Bubuyubyul'] (1998) The Korean Society of Confucian Studies 58,71, wrote that 'the original teachings of Mencius on *Bubuyubyul* centred around the respect for deity, manners and mutual responsibility for each other between married couples. Some scholars, including the author, believe that there was no differentiation between genders when it came to the practice of moral ethics [Kwang-Soo Jung trans].

29 Han Hee-sook, 'Women's Life during the *Choson* Period' (2004) 6 International Journal of Korean History 113, 135.

30 Han Hee-sook 'Women's Life during the *Choson* Period' (2004) 6 International Journal of Korean History 113, 121–122.

31 A concubine is a recognised stable sexual partner for a married man, akin to a de facto wife, who frequently will have entered a contract with the man in which she is guaranteed financial protection in exchange for her sexual fidelity. Her status is different to that of the lawful wife, and the arrangement is not regarded as polygamy. 'Concubine' was a recognised category in the

also divorce his wife[32] if her conduct came under one of the 'seven sins' of which adultery was one, as was failure to produce a male heir.[33]

In keeping with the Neo-Confucianism, the *Daemyungryul* (Commentary of the Great Ming Dynasty Code) was enacted as the general criminal code. Article 390 of this Code stated that 'a person will receive 80 lashes if they commit adultery while single, 90 lashes if married, 100 lashes if they were deceptive in their adultery ... if the adultery was through deception and/or the adultery was with a married person, then the punishment shall be the same for both man and woman'.[34] The *Daejunhusokrok*, a code of the *Chosun* Dynasty during its middle years, read in part 'where a woman married to a scholar [*yangban*] acts on her carnal desires and corrupts, disturbs and disgraces teachings on good public morals, the woman, together with the adulterous man, shall be sentenced to death'. This allowed an adulterous wife and her lover to be killed. Where a woman was not married to a *yangban*, *Daemyungryul* with its lashings would have applied to adultery.[35] Some scholars, such as Choi Yoon-jung, suggest that in reality it was unlikely that the authorities would have always acted in cases of adultery[36] because, despite the teachings and the punishments, romances involving extra-marital sexual encounters, as in other eras, were still prevalent during the *Chosun* Dynasty. However, the tone was set. Adultery by a married woman was a sin that could end her marriage and ruin her children's future, and it was a crime with severe consequences.

(c) Era of modernisation

Following Japanese success in the Sino-Japanese War, Korea established a council to consider how best to implement modernising reforms along Japanese lines. These Japanese inspired reforms of the Kabo movement led to the *Hyeongbeop Daecheon* (The Great Penal Code) of 1905,which continued the criminalisation of adultery. After the Meiji Restoration in Japan adultery had been made a criminal offence for married women and their lovers.[37] This was incorporated into the *Hyeongbeop Daecheon* and when Korea was colonised

---

legal system and was socially acceptable. On the principle, see: Kuk Cho 'The Crime of Adultery in Korea: Inadequate Means for Maintaining Morality and Protecting Women' (2002) 2 91 Journal of Korean Law 81, 85.

32 Han Hee-sook 'Women's Life during the *Choson* Period' (2004) 6 International Journal of Korean History 113, 122.

33 Han Hee-sook 'Women's Life during the *Choson* Period' (2004) 6 International Journal of Korean History 113, 124.

34 Even in the early days of the *Chosun* Dynasty, there was some evidence to suggest that *Daemyungyul* was not followed completely, but in some circumstances, more severe punishments were handed out (eg The Annals of the Chosun Dynasty 5th year of Sejong).

35 Cho ji Man *Chosunsidae hyungsabup: Daemyungryu, Gookchun* [*The Criminal Law of the Chosun: the Daemyungryu and National Code*] (2nd edn, Kyeongin Munhwasa, Seoul, 2007) 202–206 [Kwang-Soo Jung trans].

36 See Byungin Jang *The Marriage Laws and Sexual Discrimination During the Early Chosun* (Il Ji Sa, South Korea, 1997) 296–297 [Kwang-Soo Jung trans].

37 Imperial Penal Code of Japan, 1880 and 1907, s 183.

by Japan (1910–1945) the Japanese Penal Code took effect in Korea, as it had done in Taiwan. It meant that only married female adulterers and their 'fornicating' partners could be imprisoned for up to 2 years based on the husband's accusations.[38]

After Korea was liberated from Japan, further reforms occurred. Unlike Japan, which abolished the offence of adultery during the time of American Occupation, the Korean Criminal Act of 1953 retained the offence but made both male and female married adulterers equally punishable upon the accusations of their spouses. It was a contentious issue at the time. The National Assembly's Committee for Legal Institution and Administration submitted a draft for de-criminalising adultery. However they lacked the number of votes required, and a subsequent proposal criminalising adultery was submitted and passed in 1953 by one vote.[39]

During the 1980s' era of Korean democratisation, law reform was back on the national agenda. The Constitutional Court was established in 1988[40] and it would play an important role in maintaining the status quo on adultery.[41] In 1985, the Ministry of Justice set up a Special Review Committee to develop guidelines for revising the entire Korean criminal legal system.[42] The Petit Committee under the Special Review Committee, by a vote of 8 to 2, decided in January 1989 to abolish the offence of adultery. Initially the Justice Ministry accepted that opinion as seen in the official summary of Criminal Act Revision. However after the 1990 Constitutional Court's decision upholding the constitutionality of Korea's adultery law (89 Hun-Ma 82, 10 September 1990), the Ministry returned to its former position and retained the offence.

Again in April 1992, it seemed adultery as a crime could be removed. The Ministry of Justice cited six reasons for its abolition:[43]

---

38 See Jung Gung-Sik 'Hankuk eui Kantongchoe eui byeopjesajeol kochal' ['Historical Review of the Crime of Adultery in Korea'] (1991) 10 Korea Institute of Criminology 211, 233–237 [Kwang-Soo Jung trans]. Also comments in Constitutional Court Decision 2007 Hun-Ka 17.21, 2008 Hun-Ka 7.26.

39 See Dong-Woon Shin 'Hyung Bup Gaijong Gwalyunhayo Bun Gangtongjai Yongu' ['A Study on Adultery and the Abortion from the Viewpoint of Criminal Law Reform in Korea'] (1991) 6 Korean Institute of Criminology 151 [Kwang-Soo Jung trans].

40 Constitutional Court Act and the Ninth Amendment to the Constitution. For an overview see Tom Ginsberg 'The Constitutional Court and the judicialization of Korean Politics' in Andrew Harding and Penelope Nicholson (eds) *New Courts in Asia* (Routledge Law, Abingdon, 2010) 145–157; and for a summary see Youngjoon Kwon 'Korea: Bridging the gap between Korean substance and Western form' in E Ann Black and Gary F Bell *Law and Legal Institutions of Asia; traditions, adaptations and innovations* (Cambridge University Press, Cambridge, 2011) 166–167.

41 This is discussed in section IV.

42 Presidential Order, No 11601.

43 These are cited in the dissenting opinions of Justices Kim Jong-dae, Lee Dong-heub, Mok Young-joon in Constitutional Court Decision, 2007 Hun-Ka 17·21, 2008 Hun-Ka 7·26, 2008 Hun-Ba 21·47 (consolidated), 30 October 2008 (at 298–299). Constitutional Court Decisions are translated into English by the Court and are available at: http://english.ccourt.go.kr.

> '... first, adultery crimes are ones that involve ethical issues between individuals and are being abolished worldwide; second, it is inappropriate for the State to intervene in an individual sexual life, which should remain private; third, it is often taken advantage of as a threat or means to receive compensation; fourth, the significance of incrimination has weakened as a means of State punishment as accusations are mostly withdrawn in the trial procedures; fifth, there is little deterrence or re-socialization effect as intended for criminal policy purposes; sixth, the effectiveness of protecting families and women is also in doubt.'

One month later in May 1992, the Ministry of Justice finalised the draft for the Criminal Act Revision composed of 405 articles. Despite the arguments of the Ministry, the offence of adultery was retained but the statutory punishment of 2 years' or less imprisonment was lowered to a year or less, with an option for fines up to five million Won. However this revision was not enacted. The Criminal Act, revised by Act No 5057 on 29 December 1995, retained both the prohibition and the maximum of 2 years' imprisonment.[44] The reason why the criminalisation of adultery and the 2-year imprisonment period were retained was discussed by the members of the Constitutional Court in 2008. They believed that, whilst there was an attempt to find a compromise for retentionist and abolitionist views, community consensus supported retention. Legislators accordingly accepted that abolition was premature.[45] As well, the Constitutional Court of Korea had just upheld the constitutionality of the existing law.[46]

III OVERVIEW OF THE CURRENT CRIMINAL LAW ON ADULTERY

(a) Elements of the crime of adultery

The offence of adultery is set out in art 241 of the Criminal Act, namely:

> '(1) A married person who commits adultery shall be punished by imprisonment for not more than two years. The same shall apply to the other participant.'

Adultery is not defined in the Criminal Act. However, the meaning is taken from the words 'married persons' which are gender neutral, and from cases[47] which have established that adultery is a voluntary consensual act of extra-marital sexual intercourse between a man and woman, one of whom is

---

44 Criminal Act (enacted on 18 September 1953 by Act No 293, and revised on 29 December 1995 by Act No 5057). The Criminal Act is translated into English on the Ministry of Government Legislation website as an unofficial translation. It can be accessed at: www.moleg.go.kr/english/aboutMgl.

45 Constitutional Court Decision, 2007 Hun-Ka 17·21, 2008 Hun-Ka 7·26, 2008 Hun-Ba 21·47 (consolidated), 30 October 2008.

46 Constitutional Court Decision, 89 Hun-Ma 82, 10 September 1990.

47 Supreme Court Decision of 20 August 1985 85 Do 1171. Selected Supreme Court decisions are translated into English at: http://eng.scourt.go.kr/eng/decisions/guide.jsp. However, the majority of cases in this section have been translated in English by Kwang-Soo Jung.

lawfully married to another person. A married person engaging in this act is an adulterer, and, if the sexual partner is unmarried but aware the person he or she is with is married, the label 'fornicator' is applied. Adultery does not extend to sexual intercourse between an unmarried man and woman, nor to same-sex relationships. The essential ingredient of the offence is a violation of the marital relationship. This is confirmed by s 2 of art 241 where the crime of adultery can only be prosecuted where there is an accusation by the victimised spouse. Unlike other jurisdictions, such as Malaysia, where there are religious police who can bring a prosecution, in Korea the prosecution can only be initiated by an aggrieved spouse.

The meaning of 'spouse' is found in the Civil Act, art 812, where de jure marriage applies to include only one's lawfully married spouse, even where they do not live together. Questions have arisen regarding marriages contracted outside Korea. The Supreme Court[48] looked at an adultery complaint made in a case involving two South Korean citizens both of whom immigrated to the State of Maryland in the United States and married in accordance with that state's laws. They did not register their marriage in Korea but lived as a lawfully married couple in America. They subsequently obtained their American citizenship and relinquished their South Korean citizenship. When one returned to Korea and married a Korean citizen, an adultery complaint was filed against two defendants. The question arose as to whether a marriage between a non-citizen of South Korea, whose marriage was not registered in South Korea, is capable of committing and/or making complaint for adultery under art 241 of the Criminal Act. In the original judgment, the Court found that because the complainant and the second defendant's marriage was not recognised or registered in accordance with the South Korean marriage laws the complainant was not a 'spouse' who had the right to make a complaint of adultery under art 241 of the Criminal Act. The case was dismissed. However, on appeal the Supreme Court held that the meaning of a 'spouse' used in art 241 was not limited to couples who wed within the borders of South Korea. The Court looked to s 1 of art 15 of the Private International Law Act, to hold that a marriage validly conducted in accordance with the applicable laws of the state where the marriage took place, which is legally recognised by that state, must be recognised as valid in Korea (even if it was not formally registered in South Korea). These are 'spouses' for the purposes of art 241 of the Criminal Act. The Court overturned the original decision. So a broader definition of spouse applies which extends to all lawful marriages whether conducted within, or outside, Korea.

The courts have also held that the act of sexual intercourse outside the marital relationship constitutes a single act of adultery (or fornication). The Supreme Court (Decision of 20 August 1985 85 Do 1171) held that the unique nature of the adultery offence is that each act of sexual intercourse constitutes a separate

---

[48] Supreme Court Decision of 13 December 1983, 83 Do 41.

offence and, in order to prosecute for all instances of sexual intercourse, each must be specifically complained of, and a complaint of one act of adultery cannot be extended to another.

(b) Nature of the prosecution

Section 2 of art 241, states:

> 'The crime in the preceding section shall be prosecuted only upon the accusation of the victimized spouse. If the victimized spouse condones or pardons the adultery, accusation can no longer be made.'

This section establishes that the only legal trigger for a prosecution is an accusation from the victimised spouse. This section is to be read with art 229 of the Criminal Procedure Act, which states that 'the accusation in Article 241 of the Criminal Act shall not be made unless the marriage is void or divorce action is instituted'.[49] Hence there is a nexus between the end of a marriage, usually by divorce proceedings, and a complaint made about spousal adultery. If couples remarry, or withdraw their divorce action, then any accusation of adultery is automatically considered to be withdrawn.[50] Also an accusation can be withdrawn prior to the judgment at first instance[51] and a prosecution terminated.[52] The period in which an accusation should be made is 6 months after learning the identity of his or her spouse's lover.[53] There is, in addition, the 3-year statute of limitations.

As noted earlier, for an offence to be prosecuted a complaint must be initiated by the wronged spouse. An exception is made in circumstances where the victimised spouse is legally incapable of making the complaint. This arose in a case where the wife was in a vegetative state.[54] Although her husband (the adulterer) was her legal guardian, the court allowed her mother, as the nearest blood relative, to make the adultery complaint against the husband. The court relied on art 226 of the Criminal Procedure Code to hold that where a victim is declared incompetent and the accused is the guardian of the victim, other blood relatives of the victim may bring proceedings against the guardian including for adultery.[55]

(c) Condoning adultery

If it can be established that the victimised spouse condoned adulterous acts, the prosecution will not proceed. Cases have established that 'condoning' can be either express or implied. The Supreme Court held there is an implied

[49] Revised by Act No 8496, 1 June 2007.
[50] Criminal Procedure Act, art 229(2).
[51] Criminal Procedure Act, art 232(1).
[52] Criminal Procedure Act, art 327(1).
[53] Criminal Procedure Act, art 230(1).
[54] Supreme Court Decision of 29 April 2010, 2009 Do 12446.
[55] Supreme Court Decision of 29 April 2010, 2009 Do 12446.

condoning of adultery when both husband and wife were in agreement that the marriage should not continue.[56] Such agreement should be viewed as a form of a prior consent or an inducement for extra-marital relationships. In the Decision of 10 July 2008, the Supreme Court, 2008 Do 3599 stated that, in examining whether or not there was an agreement to divorce, the intention to do so need not be in writing, but can be derived from the consistency in the couple's actions and words. In this case the couple had agreed to divorce and moved out of their marital home. This was seen as evidence of an intention to divorce and as a consequence could be construed as implied consent to adultery. Similarly, where a separate or a joint divorce application is made, but there are differences on the property settlement, the fact of their agreement to divorce is sufficient. However, even when there have been divorce applications filed, the conduct of the parties is relevant on the issue of implied consent for adultery. The Supreme Court found that the fact that a couple had returned to their marital home, although not engaging in sexual intercourse, was significant to the issue of whether or not she condoned adultery.[57] In this case the wife had pleaded that they continue to live together as husband and wife and as such could not be seen as giving consent for her husband to have sexual relations with another.[58]

(d) Pardoning adultery

There are quite a few cases which set out what amounts to pardoning adultery. A leading case is Decision of 26 November 1991, the Supreme Court, 91 Do 2049. In this case, a wife suspected infidelity by her husband and reported him to the police. The police then arrested the husband with another woman. At the time of the arrest, they were both present in a same room but both were dressed and strenuously denied adultery. The wife said she would 'forgive everything if you simply made a statement confessing that you had an affair'. He provided a statement confessing adultery which his wife promptly provided to the police in support of her complaint. The question arose as to whether her initial promise to forgive was in fact a pardon. In the first judgment it was found that, even though she had no real intention of pardoning her husband and the women he was with, she had made a statement to that effect and her husband had believed the assurance to be genuine. As such based on s 2 of art 241 of the Criminal Act, the court found the pardon to be genuine and dismissed the case against the two defendants. However, on appeal, the Supreme Court stated that the pardon allowed under s 2 of art 241 of the Criminal Act was a form of forgiveness after the fact and was designed to facilitate situations where a spouse may wish to work at retaining the marriage even after there was awareness of a spouse's infidelity. The motivation behind the law was to respect the desire of the victimised spouse's 'honourable intentions' and to give it legal effect in order to prevent dissolution of marriages where possible. A genuine pardon must first be made with the prior knowledge of the adultery by the

[56] Supreme Court Decision of 22 March 1991, 90 Do 1188.
[57] Supreme Court Decision of 11 December 2008, 2008 Do 3656.
[58] Supreme Court Decision of 11 December 2008, 2008 Do 3656.

victimised spouse and secondly there must be a clear believable declaration of a desire to maintain the marriage. The Court found that a simple promise of forgiveness did not constitute a full pardon and overturned the original verdict.

This can be contrasted with a case[59] where the adulterous wife sought to sever all contact with her lover, once her husband became aware of the affair. Her lover sought the return of all gifts previously given, and advised the husband 'after this memorandum of understanding has been made, I will not meet your wife any more and if this memorandum is breached, then this memorandum is void and I will accept any punishment'. The husband replied in writing: 'if you agree not to see my wife any more, I will end it all here and pretend it never happened.' The question arose as to whether this was a valid pardon or not. The Supreme Court held that, because the husband was aware of the affair at the time he issued a pardon to the defendants and because the husband and wife were still living together, it should be construed a true pardon.[60]

(e) Proof of adultery: direct versus circumstantial evidence

After a complaint of adultery is made by a spouse, the prosecution needs evidence to prove whether or not sexual intercourse with another person has, in fact, occurred. Given the private and often secretive nature of these affairs, the courts will allow circumstantial evidence provided there is more than one incriminating piece of evidence. A collective case can satisfy the court beyond reasonable doubt. While medical evidence of live semen in vaginal discharge may be direct proof, the absence of semen is not conclusive that intercourse did not occur because contraceptive devices may have been used.[61] A case in 2008 shows how collective evidence can be used.[62] The complainant followed her spouse and the second defendant to a motel. About an hour and twenty minutes after the defendants had entered the room, the police requested the motel manager to knock on their door. When there was no response the police used a master key to enter the room. When they entered, the defendants were naked lying on the bed together. The question was whether this was sufficient evidence for adultery. At first the couple denied any adultery. Later they wrote a statement confessing adultery, but subsequently recanted saying the statement was false and was in response to a police officer's advice that they could be released earlier if they confessed. The Court at first instance found that there was insufficient evidence for adultery and declared them not guilty. On appeal, the Supreme Court took a more comprehensive view to find that the defendants had engaged in sexual intercourse and overturned the original decision. Some of the factors examined by the Court included the relationship of the defendants; their age and health; the time they spent in the motel; their mannerisms towards

---

59 Supreme Court Decision of 24 August 1999, 99 Do 2149.
60 Supreme Court Decision of 24 August 1999, 99 Do 2149.
61 Supreme Court Decision of 25 July 1997, 97 Do 974.
62 Supreme Court Decision of 27 November 2008, 2007 Do 4977.

the complainant and others at the time of their arrest; their mannerisms at the motel and the police station after arrest; and the fact that the defendants had visited the same motel 4 days prior.[63]

The Supreme Court outlined that in criminal cases the evidence must prove an offence beyond reasonable doubt.[64] Where there is insufficient evidence to convince a judge beyond reasonable doubt that sexual intercourse has occurred, the judge must rule in favour of the defendants, even if the evidence gives rise to suspicion. However, the evidence need not be only direct evidence. A conviction can be derived from circumstantial evidence based on good logic and experience. Where collective evidence conclusively proves adulterous criminal activity, the crime can be established. Because adultery by its very nature is a discreet and secretive crime, it is difficult to expect conclusive evidence or eye witness testimony. The Court concluded that in this case there was sufficient circumstantial evidence to prove beyond reasonable doubt an adulterous affair had occurred.[65]

(f) Evidence of adultery gathered through trespass

The Supreme Court has allowed evidence obtained by trespass, an illegal act, to be used in determining whether sexual intercourse has occurred. A case which went to the Supreme Court in 2010 involved evidence obtained by a wife who illegally entered the residence of her husband (the defendant) to obtain bloodstained tissues and bed sheets in order to prove sexual intercourse between him and the second defendant had taken place. The question arose as to whether such evidence was admissible. The Court found that there is a duty on the state to ensure the personal dignity and privacy of individual citizens and this duty does also extend to criminal proceedings. However, this did not mean that any and all evidence collected from the private lives of citizens was inadmissible because the courts also have a duty to balance a citizen's privacy with the public interest in having a fair and effective criminal justice system which can get at the truth. In this particular case the primary evidence submitted by the complainant was crucial to the prosecution's case and therefore was in the interest of the public at large. The Court ruled it must be admissible even if it was obtained by trespassing and was to the detriment of the defendants' privacy. The public interest in finding the truth with the consequence of a rightful criminal prosecution (regardless of the illegal trespass to obtain the evidence) outweighed the private interests of the defendants. They were found guilty of adultery.[66]

However, trespass is an illegal act. What happens to the suspicious spouse who illegally trespasses in order to obtain evidence to establish the other spouse's infidelity? The answer will turn on a construction and application of art 20 of

---

63 Supreme Court Decision of 27 November 2008, 2007 Do 4977.
64 Supreme Court Decision of 27 November 2008, 2007 Do 4977.
65 Supreme Court Decision of 27 November 2008, 2007 Do 4977.
66 Supreme Court Decision of 9 September 2010, 2008 Do 3990.

the Criminal Act,[67] which can excuse a 'righteous act' such as trespass provided it 'does not violate the social rules'. This played out in Decision of 26 September 2003, the Supreme Court, 2003 Do 3000. The wife who suspected that her husband was having an affair, followed him and saw him enter the residence of the woman she suspected was his lover. The wife then unlawfully entered the residence to collect evidence of adultery. The question arose as to whether the defendant had committed a trespass. In the original decision, the court cited the following reasons to find that she was not guilty of trespass as it was a righteous act according to art 20 of the Criminal Act. First, she had a lawful motivation for entering the residence, namely to collect evidence of her husband's adultery; secondly, she did not use violence or force but demanded they open the door which was lawful; thirdly, there was urgency as she had to catch the adulterous couple red-handed; and fourthly, she had sought help from the police but the police refused to cooperate in this instance.[68]

However, the Supreme Court focused on the requirement in art 20 that for a criminal act to be excused[69] it must be one 'that does not violate the social rules'. The Court took the view that the provision was designed to excuse behaviours that are acceptable by the social ethics and norms of the day and so when applying the provision the Court must take into consideration the surrounding circumstances of the illegal act in its entirety including the act itself, the circumstances of the act, motivation, reasons behind the act and its social implications. The Court went on to state that it must satisfy the following five elements for an illegal act to be excused under the aforementioned provision: first, the motivation, purpose and object of the act must be just; secondly, the means of the act must be fair and considerate; thirdly, it must strike a good balance between the need to preserve and the need to encroach; fourthly, the urgency of the situation; and fifthly, that there must be no other real alternate means of achieving the same goal. In applying these requirements to the facts of the case, the court found that the means used were not fair and considerate, nor was there a genuine urgency to collect photographic evidence of the adultery which overrode the right of the victim to peace and her privacy.[70] The court overturned the original non-guilty verdict for trespass.

(g) Other criminal sanctions

The suggested 1992 revision in the Ministry of Justice's draft for the Criminal Act Revision would have allowed monetary fines in addition to imprisonment for adultery. Although this was not introduced, Professor Cho makes the interesting observation that monetary sanctions can be granted for other

---

67 Article 20 (Justifiable Act): An act which is conducted in accordance with Acts and subordinate statutes, or in pursuance of accepted business practices, or other action which does not violate the social rules shall not be punishable.

68 Supreme Court Decision of 26 September 2003, 2003 Do 3000.

69 Article 20 (Justifiable Act) see n 67.

70 Supreme Court Decision of 26 September 2003, 2003 Do 3000.

offences in violation of sexual morality, namely, brokering obscene conduct, distributing obscene materials and public indecency.[71]

IV INSIGHTS FROM THE CONSTITUTIONAL COURT ON THE CRIMINALISATION OF ADULTERY

Since its inception in 1988, the Constitutional Court[72] has been the final adjudicator of constitutional issues. One of its important features is to allow for 'constitutional petitions'[73] or complaints to be filed by a party at trial who believes a fundamental right guaranteed under the Constitution has been infringed.[74]

On four occasions, the Constitutional Court has adjudicated a constitutional complaint about art 241 on the ground it impinges on rights guaranteed under either art 10[75] which provides for dignity and the right to pursue happiness, or art 17 which guarantees the privacy of citizens.[76] However, rights are not unlimitedly guaranteed, and can be restricted by law under art 37[77] when this is necessary to ensure national safety and public order and welfare. Any restriction however cannot violate an essential right. This requires the court to balance the rights of citizens with the duties of the state. In adultery cases the duty comes from art 36 of the Constitution, which charges the state with a duty to maintain social order and ensure sustainable marriage and family life.[78] This balancing, known as the 'proportionality test', is frequently cited in the Court's reasoning in constitutional cases and is referred to by constitutional lawyers and scholars as the 'rule against excessive restriction'.[79] This means that, if the public interest can be achieved only by infringing individual rights, it will be

---

71 Criminal Act, arts 242–245.

72 For background on the Constitutional Court, see: Jonghyun Park 'The Judicialization of Politics in Korea' (2008) 10 Asian-Pacific Law & Policy Journal 63–113; Constitutional Court of Korea *Twenty Years of the Constitutional Court of Korea*, at: www.ccourt.go.kr/home/att_file/library/20year.pdf.

73 Constitutional Court Act, art 68.

74 See generally Youngjoon Kwon 'Korea: Bridging the gap between Korean substance and Western form' in E Ann Black and Gary F Bell *Law and Legal Institutions of Asia; traditions, adaptations and innovations* (Cambridge University Press, Cambridge, 2011) 166.

75 Article 10: All citizens are assured of human worth and dignity and have the right to pursue happiness. It is the duty of the State to confirm and guarantee the fundamental and inviolable human rights of individuals.

76 Article 17: The privacy of no citizen may be infringed.

77 Article 37: (1) Freedoms and rights of citizens may not be neglected on the grounds that they are not enumerated in the Constitution. (2) The freedoms and rights of citizens may be restricted by law only when necessary for national security, the maintenance of law and order, or for public welfare. Even when such restriction is imposed, no essential aspect of the freedom or right shall be violated.

78 Article 36: (1) Marriage and family life are entered into and sustained on the basis of individual dignity and equality of the sexes, and the State must do everything in its power to achieve that goal. (2) The State endeavours to protect mothers. (3) The health of all citizens is protected by the State.

79 Jonghyun Park 'The Judicialization of Politics in Korea' (2008) 10 Asian-Pacific Law & Policy Journal 63, 95.

constitutional only when the public interests outweigh the individual rights. This balancing standard is regarded by scholars such as Park as providing the judges of the Constitutional Court with a wide range of discretion.[80] Thus far, public interest has prevailed although in the most recent case brought by Ok in 2008 the opinions were more sharply divided. The reasoning of the justices of the court gives insight into the rationale for the law but also highlights shifting views amongst the judiciary, which reflect broader changes in the mores of Koreans.

The first case to determine the constitutionality of adultery was in 1990 – Case 89 Hun-Ma 82, 10 September 1990. Its importance lies not only in its reaffirmation and elucidation of the law and its societal rationale, but also in the impact it may have had on the Ministry of Justice rescinding a revision to the law designed to repeal the criminalisation of adultery. In the 1990 case the issue was whether the right to 'human worth and dignity and the pursuit of happiness' guaranteed by art 10 of the Constitution was violated by art 241. The majority, 6 to 3, accepted that the law did impinge on that right by restricting 'sexual autonomy' which it determined was part of the right to self-autonomy which is essential for human worth and the pursuit of happiness. That said, restricting sexual autonomy was justified on the grounds that it ensured: 'continued good sexual morality and monogamy, guarantees of family life, protection of marital obligation for faithful sexual relationship and prevention of social harms caused by adultery'.[81] The majority found that sentencing adultery offenders for up to 2 years was a minimal restriction on a person's sexual autonomy and did not amount to an infringement of the essence of art 10's guarantee of freedoms and rights. The majority also ruled that art 241 conformed to the principle of 'equality before the law' as it is gender neutral, either spouse can make a complaint and either can be the recipient of punishment. Two of the dissenting judges agreed that, whilst any abolition of the offence of adultery should be left to legislature, the fact that imprisonment was the only punishment provided for in the legislation was incompatible with the Constitution. Three years later there was another constitutional challenge – Decision of Case 90 Hun-Ka 70, 11 March 1993 in which constitutionality of the law was upheld with similar reasoning.

A decade later in the Decision of Case 2000 Hun-Ba 60, 25 October 2001 the constitutionality and reasoning of the earlier cases were maintained, 8 to 1, in favour of constitutionality, but the majority noted the legal consciousness of the public regarding sex had changed and that the laws could be abused to obtain consolation awards. They called for the legislators (in the National Assembly) to take a serious approach to determining whether to retain or abolish the crime of adultery.[82] Interestingly, one judgment expressed the view that

---

80 Jonghyun Park 'The Judicialization of Politics in Korea' (2008) 10 Asian-Pacific Law & Policy Journal 63, 95. See also the 'balancing role' undertaken by the Court: Ann Black and Jeong-Seop Yoon 'The Blind Masseurs' Case' (2006) LAWASIA Journal 249–254.

81 Constitutional Court Decision 89 Hun-Ma 82, 10 September 1990.

82 Discussed in Kuk Cho '*Nullum Crimen, Nulla Poena Sine Lege* in Korean Criminal Law' (2006–2007) 6 Journal of Korean Law 147, 160.

committing adultery is a breach of contract that violates the duty for faithful sexual relationship which is part of the marriage contract. Therefore adultery should be punished in accordance with general principles of the contract law, rather than be a matter of criminal punishment.

The most recent case was the one brought by Ok and two others in 2007 with the decision delivered in 2008.[83] The Constitutional Court, in an opinion 4 to 5, which fell short of the quorum of six votes required for a decision of unconstitutionality, ruled that the anti-adultery provision does not violate the Constitution. This case is most significant in setting out the constitutional arguments for and against retaining adultery as a criminal offence.

(a) The reasoning of the Justices *for* the constitutionality of art 241[84]

> 'Marital relationships are the cornerstone of family life that serve as the foundation for the state and society ... [they] function as a valuable social system based on tradition and culture.'

Three Justices[85] gave the essential rationale for art 241 as protecting marital relationships which in turn preserve Korea's social order. Adultery and fornication, they argued, cause marriages to break down causing social problems and family disintegration. In light of the duty imposed under art 36 of the Constitution, adultery goes beyond a personal matter of ethics and morality, and means that the criminalisation of adultery is adhering to a legitimate legislative purpose.[86] They recognised that the global legislative trend is to not punish adultery but that there were traditional Koran ethics and moral standards supporting sexual fidelity within marriage. Accordingly, they saw a strong societal demand for preventing adultery. Given the proposition that Korean legal awareness sees adultery as harming the social order and demands its pre-emptive prevention, the legislature's role in criminally punishing adultery is not arbitrary. Also, whilst privacy[87] interests of individuals including to sexual autonomy will be infringed by art 241, such individualistic interests are insignificant when compared to the public interest. In this way, it achieves the right balance of interests pursuant to art 37(2) of the Constitution.[88]

On the issue of proportionality, these Justices reasoned that the scope of the punishment should be left to the legislators, who should take into account

---

83 Constitutional Court Decision 2007 Hun-Ka 17·21, 2008 Hun-Ka 7·26, 2008 Hun-Ba 21·47 (consolidated), 30 October 2008.

84 Constitutional Court Decision, 2007 Hun-Ka 17·21, 2008 Hun-Ka 7·26, 2008 Hun-Ba 21·47 (consolidated), 30 October 2008 at D (2).

85 Justice Lee Kang-kook, Justice Lee Kong-hyun, Justice Cho Dae-hyen.

86 Constitutional Court Decision, 2007 Hun-Ka 17·21, 2008 Hun-Ka 7·26, 2008 Hun-Ba 21·47 (consolidated), 30 October 2008 at D (2).

87 Article 17 of the Constitution: The right to privacy of all citizens shall not be infringed.

88 Constitutional Court Decision, 2007 Hun-Ka 17·21, 2008 Hun-Ka 7·26, 2008 Hun-Ba 21·47 (consolidated), 30 October 2008 at D (1).

factors such as 'Korean history and culture', the 'values or legal awareness of the general public' and 'crime prevention'.[89] However, they rejected the argument that the penal provision is excessive and did not allow for proportional punishment by noting that 2 years is the maximum sentence and for a 'low degree of adultery' it can be a fully suspended sentence. A 'light fine' they argued would not have the required deterrent effect. Therefore, it does not violate the rule against excessive restriction.

Justice Min, Hyeong-ki, concurred that punishing adultery through the Criminal Act is not in itself unconstitutional, but recommended that the National Assembly revisit the penalty to determine whether imprisonment is appropriate or excessive. It is in the national interest, he opined, for the legislature to do this rather than for the 'judicial body to actively intervene'.[90]

(b) The reasoning of the dissenting Justices *against* art 241's constitutionality[91]

> 'In recent years the growing awareness of the Korean society, along with rapid spread of individualism and liberal views on sexual life, is that sexual life and love is a private matter not subjected to legal control.'

Three of the justices who wrote the joint dissenting opinion[92] looked at changes within Korean society believing that there has been a shift away from the 'social interest of sexual morality and families' to the more liberal 'private interest of sexual autonomy'.[93] This shift they argue had shaken the foundation for adultery law 'to its roots, making it no longer sustainable'.[94] In addition to changing public attitudes, they found criminal punishment for adultery was no longer appropriate. The first reason was that some aspects of life should be regulated by moral law whilst others should by directly regulated by law. They reasoned by analogy that there were many anti-social acts which were morally reprehensible like 'unfilial piety, malignant default, begging, suicide, and squandering'[95] which were not punished as crimes, whilst adultery was, concluding that it is inappropriate for the state to remedy social immorality though criminal punishment. The second reason was that sexual acts and expressions of love between consenting adults are a matter of personal freedom and where there is no harm, there should not be restrictions. They noted that

---

89 Constitutional Court Decision, 2007 Hun-Ka 17·21, 2008 Hun-Ka 7·26, 2008 Hun-Ba 21·47 (consolidated), 30 October 2008 at D (4).

90 Constitutional Court Decision, 2007 Hun-Ka 17·21, 2008 Hun-Ka 7·26, 2008 Hun-Ba 21·47 (consolidated), 30 October 2008 at E.

91 Constitutional Court Decision, 2007 Hun-Ka 17·21, 2008 Hun-Ka 7·26, 2008 Hun-Ba 21·47 (consolidated), 30 October 2008 at F (C) (1).

92 Justice Kim Jong-dae, Justice Lee Dong-heub, Justice Mok Young-joon.

93 Constitutional Court Decision, 2007 Hun-Ka 17·21, 2008 Hun-Ka 7·26, 2008 Hun-Ba 21·47 (consolidated), 30 October 2008 at F (C) (1).

94 Constitutional Court Decision, 2007 Hun-Ka 17·21, 2008 Hun-Ka 7·26, 2008 Hun-Ba 21·47 (consolidated), 30 October 2008 at F (C) (1).

95 Constitutional Court Decision, 2007 Hun-Ka 17·21, 2008 Hun-Ka 7·26, 2008 Hun-Ba 21·47 (consolidated), 30 October 2008 at G (C) (2) (A).

there were other reprehensible and immoral acts including 'incest, bestiality and group sex' that do not attract punitive regulations. The third reason cited was the worldwide trend in modern criminal law to abolish adultery crimes. They also drew on public opinion in Korea, but differed from the majority, arguing that the public view about sexual conduct is evolving. They noted that in Korea one can see an increase in suspended sentences as an indication of the change in judicial and societal attitudes.

The effectiveness of criminalisation was also called into question. Because an adultery complaint can only be made if there is a divorce action instituted[96] it is apparent that the crime of adultery does not protect marriage or the family. However a criminal record can lead to 'social ruin' making it unlikely that a person punished for adultery would remarry the spouse who made the accusation. The family breakdown would be complete and the process of collecting evidence against a suspected spouse could serve to intensify mistrust, which of itself can negatively impact on a marriage. The court debunked the deterrence argument on the basis they doubted whether fear of punishment would be effective, and that preserving families should be left to mutual affection rather than coercion by fear of criminal punishment. In addition, there are the civil law consequences for adultery (discussed later) which result in significant disadvantage to the adulterer and a corresponding advantage to his or her injured spouse. These consequences may be sufficient to outweigh the need for criminal punishment.

A further reason provided was that no longer could it be said that criminalisation of adultery protected women. They questioned the traditional rationale that it was mostly husbands who committed adultery, making wives the economic beneficiaries of adultery law. Doubts were raised as to whether the adultery provisions did in fact protect women in this way.

Central to their determination that art 241 was unconstitutional was that it contradicts the principle which prohibits excessive restriction. This it does through excessive restrictions on an individual's right to sexual autonomy and privacy. Given this and their conclusion that on balance the law is ineffective in protecting monogamy and keeping families intact, art 241 did not, in their view, meet the requirement for the appropriateness of means and the least restrictive means.

Justice Song Doo-hwan also found art 241 to be unconstitutional. His reasoning was that a criminal penalty was an excessive restriction in line with art 37(2) on the right to pursue happiness which includes sexual autonomy to decide 'whether to or with whom to have sexual acts'.[97] However, whilst he opined that self-autonomy including sexual autonomy does not mean infinite liberty, there does need to be proportionality between the 'gravity of the crime and the responsibility of the offender'. He found it difficult to say that acts of

[96] Criminal Procedure Law, art 229, see overview earlier at section III(b).

[97] Constitutional Court Decision, 2007Hun-Ka17·21, 2008Hun-Ka7·26, 2008Hun-Ba21·47 (consolidated), October 30, 2008 at H (1)(B)

adultery and fornication imply major illegality warranting prevention which is so desperate that all acts must be punished without exception. Article 241 imposes imprisonment as a statutory sentence without taking into account that the gravity of the crime can vary according to the modes of acts. Accordingly as art 241 does not take into account the 'specificities of the specific case it violates the principle of proportionality'.[98] Banning adultery and imposing criminal penalties does not violate the Constitution, but contradicts the principle of proportionality and in this regard does violate the Constitution.

(c) Reasoning of the dissenting Justice that art 241 was incompatible with the Constitution

Justice Kim Hee-ok followed a similar line of reasoning to Justice Song Doo-hwan but did not find art 241 to be unconstitutional. He did however find it to be incompatible with the Constitution.[99] This was because criminal punishment could be imposed on acts which are merely morally reprehensible and are not 'extremely harmful' to society. The state should not provide criminal punishment where civil, administrative and socio-legal sanctions could be more appropriate. He reasoned that there are different 'modes of adultery and fornication' which vary greatly in intention, family life, frequency, and method and also in the extent to which an act is 'anti-social and morally reprehensible'. For this reason there should be a range of sanctions. Some acts of adultery may warrant criminal sanctions, whilst civil consequences would be more appropriate for others. Because art 241 provides that all modes of adultery are subject to criminal sanctions, including ones that are not, or are barely subject to reprehension, it is non-conforming with the Constitution. Until the legislators revise the Article, Justice Kim Hee-ok, held it should continue, albeit temporarily, to apply.

(d) Conclusion: Article 241 is constitutional

Four justices found Article 241 constitutional, four found it unconstitutional, and one found it incompatible with the Constitution. Although five justices found violations, the decision fell short of the six persons required for a determination of unconstitutionality. The criminalisation of adultery was upheld. The reasoning of the Justices provides another example of what Chaihark Hahm has described as the 'clash or two opposing narratives' on the definition of family and marriage, and Confucian tradition in contemporary

98 Constitutional Court Decision, 2007Hun-Ka17·21, 2008Hun-Ka7·26, 2008Hun-Ba21·47 (consolidated), October 30, 2008 at F.

99 Justice Kim Hee-ok, Constitutional Court Decision, 2007Hun-Ka17·21, 2008Hun-Ka7·26, 2008Hun-Ba21·47 (consolidated), October 30, 2008 at F.

Korean society.[100] It gives weight to Cho's thesis that the Constitutional Court is reluctant to 'strike down provisions which are moralistic in nature'.[101]

V IMPLICATIONS OF ADULTERY IN CIVIL LAW

(a) Overview

The adultery provisions in the Criminal Act are not the only legal consequences that can flow from extra-marital affairs. It means that even if art 241 was repealed a number of civil law ramifications would remain to regulate and, in theory, deter adultery.

The civil law does not specifically set out an obligation of chastity between husband and wife, but chastity has long been considered the norm in spousal relationships. Article 826, s 1 of the Civil Act states in part that 'spouses should live together, supporting each other and being cooperative'. Spousal duties are implied from the monogamous nature of marriage reflected in the anti-polygamy provision in art 810 of the Civil Act.[102] Although in earlier times concubinage[103] was widespread amongst the upper classes in Korea, today 'contracts for concubines',[104] regardless of the consent of the first spouse, are illegal and the contract deemed void. The Supreme Court found that because these contracts are used to disrupt the public order and good morals both the man who enters into a second sexual relationship by contract and the person who facilitates such activity are acting illegally in breaching the rights of the legally married first wife.[105]

Korea has two avenues for divorce. One is consensual by mutual spousal agreement[106] and the other is 'fault-based' divorce. Adultery is one of the legally recognised grounds of fault that can be used by a victimised spouse (art 840, s 1 and art 841 of the Civil Act)[107] seeking to end a marriage. The

---

100 Chaihark Hahm 'Law, Culture, and the Politics of Confucianism' (2003) 16 (2) Columbia Journal of Asian Law 253, 289.

101 Kuk Cho '*Nullum Crimen, Nulla Poena Sine Lege* in Korean Criminal Law' (2006–2007) 6 Journal of Korean Law 147, 159.

102 Article 810 (Prohibition of Bigamy): No one who has a spouse shall enter into another marriage.

103 See above n 31.

104 Supreme Court Decision of 29 September 1960, 4293 Minsang 302.

105 Supreme Court Decision of 29 September 1960, 4293 Minsang 302.

106 Re consensual divorce see: Jinsu Yune 'Reform of the Consensual Divorce Process and Child Support Enforcement System in Korea' (2012) 2 Journal of Korean Law 247.

107 Article 840 (Causes for Judicial Divorce): Either husband or wife may apply to the Family Court for a divorce in each case of the following subparagraphs: [Amended by Act No 4199, 13 January 1990] 1. If the other spouse has committed an act of unchastity.
Article 841 (Extinguishment of Right to Apply for Divorce due to Unchastity): With respect to the cause mentioned in subparagraph 1 of Article 840, if the spouse has given a previous consent or an ex post facto tolerance to the other party, or if six months have passed since the spouse was aware of such act of unchastity of the other, or if two years have passed since the happening of such event, the spouse may not apply to the court for a divorce.

rationale is that a guiltless spouse should not be forced into an unwanted divorce.[108] Unofficial figures suggest that in 2006, 11,244 couples used adultery as the basis for their divorce application in Korean courts.[109] Adultery is also taken into consideration when a court rules on custody and visitation rights. In both matters, the courts are required to take into consideration the welfare of a child. In examining the welfare of a child, the courts have demonstrated that they are willing to consider the misconduct of a spouse including adultery to the detriment of the offending spouse.[110] The impact on property entitlements has lessened since the significant 1993 case in which the Supreme Court held that spouses who had committed adultery still retained their right to claim half of the marital property.[111]

In addition, an offending spouse can be required to pay damages to the victim of his or her adultery (arts 843 and 806 of the Civil Act).[112] This covers both property and psychological damages from the offending spouse. It was in 1959 that the Supreme Court[113] first ordered an adulterous wife and her lover to pay damages to the victimised husband. The Court stated:[114]

> 'it is clear that the plaintiff had suffered psychological damage as a result of the offending spouse and the adulterous partner's adultery. As such, it is only just that the victimised spouse is appropriately compensated for the damage suffered.'

However, damages do not extend to psychological harm suffered by children of a marriage. The Supreme Court held[115] that a woman who chooses to have a de facto relationship with a married man that causes damage to his lawful wife incurs the legal responsibility to pay her appropriate damages. However, the issue for the Court was whether she could also be responsible to pay damages to his children. The Court found that, unless it can be established that the woman intentionally and proactively prohibited the man from providing such

---

108 Jeremy Morley 'Korean Law of Divorce' International Family Law, at: www.international-divorce.com/d-korea.htm.

109 Jeremy Morley 'Korean Law of Divorce' International Family Law, at www.international-divorce.com/d-korea.htm.

110 Family Court of Seoul, Decision of 29 March 1996, 95De58781 demonstrates that the Family Court takes seriously the question as to which partner caused the breakdown of the marriage. However, it is just one factor as Supreme Court Decision of 4 March 1993, 93se3 showed that even if one parent has committed the 'misdeed such as adultery' the parent who will provide better welfare to the child must be established.

111 Supreme Court Decision of 11 May 1993, 93Seu 6.

112 Article 843 (Provisions to be Applied Mutatis Mutandis): The provisions of Articles 806, 837, 837–2 and 839–2 shall apply *mutatis mutandis* to the case of judicial divorce. [Amended by Act No 4199, 13 January 1990] Article 806 (Dissolution of Matrimonial Engagement and Claims for Damages): (1) When a matrimonial engagement has been dissolved between parties, one party may claim against the other party in negligence the damages therefrom. (2) In paragraph (1), the negligent party shall be liable for damages from mental anguish in addition to property damages.

113 Supreme Court Decision of 5 November 1959, 4219 Minsang 77; see also Chungyee Hong 'Adultery & Damages' (1994) 8 Family Law Examiner 249–256.

114 Supreme Court Decision of 5 November 1959, 4219 Minsang 77.

115 Supreme Court Decision of 13 May 2005, 2004 Da 1899, Decision of 28 July 1981, the Supreme Court, 80 Da 1295.

paternal love, care and emotional support to his children, she should not be found liable to the children for any damages.[116] This was due to insufficient proximity.

An interesting case in 1987 considered whether or not a person could be found liable for adulterous conduct through negligence arising from not properly checking whether the person with whom they were having a sexual relationship was, or was not, married.[117] The Supreme Court upheld the original judgment which ruled that '[t]raditionally, when a man and a woman have a sexual relationship, it cannot be said that they each have an obligation to check the marital status of each other. The defendant, at the time of the sexual activity, thought that the man she was with was unmarried, and, even though she did not make any attempts to discern his marital status, one cannot find her liable in tort for her negligence. Nor can that person be liable for damages to the victimised spouse through the adulterous partner's negligence.[118]

(b) Connection between criminal and civil proceedings

The connection between criminal and civil proceedings can be seen in the case of Decision of 12 April 1994, the Family Court of Seoul, 93 De 22429. In this case, the wife was the applicant in the divorce proceedings. She had married her husband (respondent) in March 1987. After registering their marriage, the couple lived with the husband's parents. The relationship between the wife and her in-laws deteriorated, and to save the marriage she demanded that the couple move and live away from his parents. The husband refused. So in January 1991, the wife left her in-laws' home with her children and started working in a coffee shop. While working there, she met a new man and a romance commenced. She committed adultery with him on several occasions. When her husband found out about the affair, he made an application for divorce while making a criminal complaint at the same time. The wife was convicted of adultery and given a sentence of 10 months' imprisonment. Upon the sentence being imposed the husband discontinued his divorce application.[119]

Once the wife had served her sentence, she made a divorce application of her own. Even though the husband (respondent) seemed uncooperative, he conceded that there was no real prospect of reconciliation. In the mediation process he demanded damages of W10,000,000 (AUD $10,000.00). Even though the decision of the mediated agreement was that a sum of W10,000,000 would be paid to him, he then objected to the mediated agreement claiming that he would only cooperate in the divorce proceedings if the money was paid first. The Court ruled that the marriage had broken down irrevocably and the

---

116 Supreme Court Decision of 13 May 2005, 2004 Da 1899.
117 Supreme Court Decision of 18 August 1987, 87 Me 19.
118 Supreme Court Decision of 18 August 1987, 87 Me 19.
119 Because adultery is an accepted ground for divorce, he would have succeeded in being granted a divorce from his adulterous wife.

perpetrator who caused the breakdown of the marriage was the wife (applicant). Where the applicant is the offending spouse, normally the divorce should not be granted. However, the court made an exception in this case. Because the husband had conducted himself in a manner that was contrary to any reconciliation and to the continuation of the marriage, it could be gleaned that he too wanted the divorce but was only refusing to cooperate out of 'spitefulness and resentment'. The Court ruled that in such circumstances, despite the fact that the wife as applicant was the offending spouse, the divorce should be granted. However, the instances where a divorce is granted when the divorce application is filed by an offending spouse have been rare.

VI CHOICES FOR KOREA: THE FUTURE FOR ITS ADULTERY LAWS

This chapter started with the prominent case of Ok So-ri. However the media spotlight on adultery in Korea is seldom lifted. Reports of infamous cases of adultery have continued, including that of a Christian pastor who had an affair with a woman at whose marriage he had officiated 10 years earlier,[120] and of two well-known Korean corporate chief executive officers.[121] However, in late 2013 reports of an extra-marital affair in one of the most respected institutions in the Korean legal system, the national Judicial Research and Training Institute (JRTI),[122] dismayed many Koreans. For two JRTI students, their romance has had disastrous consequences. The female student commenced her affair with the married male student in August 2011. She did not learn of his marital status until 2013 when he confessed all, and indicated he planned to leave his wife to be with her. He had not informed his wife of any of this. Shortly after this revelation, he ended the affair, but the female student felt betrayed and made the decision to reveal his infidelity to his wife. There were calls and a series of text messages. The couple separated. Shortly afterwards his wife committed suicide. The wife's mother held a protest outside the gates of JRTI to shame her son-in-law and his former lover, with a sign outlining their adulterous conduct and its tragic consequences. It is reported that JRTI expelled the male student and suspended the female student for 3 months for 'inappropriate behaviour that harmed the dignity of the institution'[123] in violation of the National Public Service Law, art 63. The difference in the outcome was because she was unaware he was married when their romance started, making her less culpable.

---

[120] 'South Korean Pastor jailed for adultery', Inquirer net, 26 November 2011, at: http://newsinfo.inquirer.net/100875/south-korean-pastor-jailed-for-adultery.

[121] Park Han-na 'Korean CEO arrested for adultery', *The Korean Herald*, 5 October 2012, at:http://news.asiaone.com/News/AsiaOne+News/Asia/Story/A1Story20121005-375691.html.

[122] All judges, lawyers and prosecutors must pass the difficult entrance exam and study at the JRTI for 2 years. On the affair, see: Nam Hyun-woo 'Adulterous Legal Trainees Punished', *The Korean Times*, 3 October 2013, at: www.koreatimes.co.kr/www/news/nation/2013/10/116_143694.html.

[123] Harold Olsen 'Adultery at Korea's Elite Law School ends in Suicide', *Donga Newspaper*, 7 October 2013, at: www.koreabang.com/2013/stories/adultery-scandal-at-koreas-elite-law-school-ends-in-suicide.html. The discussion thread show some strong comments in support of the current law.

Given that in recent years there have been several additional constitutional complaints brought by aggrieved citizens against art 241 lodged with the Constitutional Court and together with a constitutional review request from the Uijeongbu District Court[124] in 2011 there would seem to be increasing pressure placed on the Court to find the law unconstitutional. Such a finding would result in its repeal. For the Constitutional Court to declare a law unconstitutional there must be a minimum of six concurring votes from a bench constituted by seven to nine Justices. However, in addition to a determination of constitutional or unconstitutional, there are gradations between the binary choices, including a ruling of non-conforming, which sends an instruction to the National Assembly to amend the legislation. The range of possibilities open to the Court, Ginsberg reasons, places the 'Court in dialogue with the legislative and executive agencies and gives it some flexibility',[125] especially when handling politically sensitive issues, such as reform of adultery laws.

The way forward appears to be in the direction of abolishing the crime of adultery whilst retaining its civil law dimensions. The Ministry of Justice has recommended this on several occasions.[126] There are several forces that are propelling Korea towards abolition, including the current composition of the Constitutional Court, the political parties and advocacy groups which align in support of abolition, and shifts in public sentiment which acknowledge the primacy of individual rights over collective interests of Korean society. It would appear that economic and social changes are having an impact on long held social mores and values. These factors will be briefly considered as 'the tug of war' on retaining or abolishing the law continues to be debated.

(a) The evolving Constitutional Court

Whilst the judicial reasons for retaining, or for abolishing, the offence of adultery have already been canvassed in some detail in section IV, this was based on a decision from 2008. Five years later, the composition of the Constitutional Court has changed. Three of the justices (Lee Kong-hyun, Kim Hee-ok and Cho Dae-hyun) who held that art 241 was constitutional are no longer on the Court. Based on decisions given in other recent cases, there are predictions that the quorum of six needed for unconstitutionality would be reached by the current members of the Court. Korea's *Joongang Daily* predicts that seven of the nine judges 'are leaning towards abolition of the adultery law' as a criminal offence.[127]

---

124 An ordinary court can request a constitutional review under art 41 of the Constitutional Court Act and art 111(1) (1) of the Constitution. Bae Ji-sook 'Adultery law faces constitutional review', *The Korea Herald,* 10 August 2011.

125 Tom Ginsberg 'The Constitutional Court and the Judicialisation of Korean Politics' in Andrew Harding and Penelope Nicholson (eds) *New Courts in Asia* (Routledge, Abingdon, 2012) 146.

126 James M West and Dae-kyu Yoon 'The Constitutional Court of the Republic of Korea: Transforming the Jurisprudence of the Vortex?' (1992) 40 American Journal of Comparative Law 73, 112.

127 Ser Myo-ja 'Court mulls redefining adultery constitutionality', *Korea Joongang Daily*, at: http://koreajoongangdaily.joins.com/news/article/Article.aspx?aid=2972624.

A shift in the thinking of the Court away from criminalisation of any extra-marital relations was seen in the 2009 case[128] which reviewed the constitutionality of the crime in art 34 of the Criminal Act – 'Sexual Intercourse under Pretence of Marriage'. Like adultery, this article also provided for up to 2 years' imprisonment, but with an alternative of W5,000,000 (AUD $4,300) in fines for anyone engaging in illicit intercourse with a woman under the pretence of marrying her.[129] A majority of six[130] Justices held that a man's fundamental rights to sexual self-determination and to privacy meant he should be able to have a sexual relationship without state interference, provided no violence was involved. More importantly, they reasoned that, because the law is to protect women, it 'runs afoul of the state's constitutional duty to create and maintain a gender equal society'[131] and 'den[y] women's right to self-determination regarding sexual activity under the guise of protecting women, by treating them as not being mature enough to have the capacity to voluntarily make such a decision'.[132] The court held the law was unconstitutional because it violated the rule against excessive restriction in art 37(2) of the Constitution. Tellingly, they went on to explain changes in Korean society regarding sex and marriage, opining that it is 'at the heart of people's privacy to have any kind of sexual or romantic relationships *whatsoever*' (emphasis added). It can be read expansively to extend to adultery and fornication.

This 2009 case is also significant for another reason. Some men who had been convicted of the art 34 crime prior to the declaration of unconstitutionality filed suits for compensation against the state and were awarded it.[133] This is because art 47(2) of the Constitutional Court Act which deals with the effect of a decision of unconstitutionality states: 'Any statute or provision thereof decided as unconstitutional shall lose its effect from the day on which the decision is made: Provided, that the statutes or provisions thereof relating to criminal penalties shall lose their effect retroactively.' Similar retroactive consequences could flow were the Constitutional Court to similarly rule that art 241 was unconstitutional. The concern that retrospectivity could go back to the 1953 date of enactment gives rise to the possibility that an extremely large amount of state compensation could be demanded by former convictees. The media has estimated 100,000 people convicted under the Article could seek

---

128 Constitutional Court Decision 200 8Hun-Ba 58, 2009 Hun-Ba 191 (consolidated).

129 Criminal Act, art 304: 'A person who induces a female who is not prone to an obscene act into sexual intercourse under pretence of marriage or through other fraudulent means, shall be punished by imprisonment for not more than two years or by a fine not exceeding five million won'.

130 Three Justices found the Article constitutional on the basis that 'a man's conduct of lying to a woman about marriage without intention to do so, does not fall into the category of privacy to be protected by Article 17 of the Constitution. It is wrongful and disturbs the social order. The need to maintain social order is far more important than the need to protect private life of the parties to the case.'

131 Constitution, art 36(1).

132 Constitutional Court Decision 2008 Hun-Ba 58, 2009 Hun-Ba 191 (consolidated).

133 Newspaper reports a 58-year-old man, who had served 8 months' imprisonment in 1998, received W12,000,000 (AUD $11,000) from the government as compensation. See Ser Myo-ja, 'Court mulls redefining adultery constitutionality', *Korea Joongang Daily*, at http://koreajoongangdaily.joins.com/news/article/Article.aspx?aid=2972624.

compensation.[134] Responses to this possibility have included the need for the National Assembly to revise the Criminal Act to restrict the retroactive consequences in some way. One suggestion discussed in the National Assembly was to limit any retroactive operation to the date of the last Constitutional Court decision.[135] For adultery this would be 2008.[136]

(b) Social mores

Scholars and legal sociologists have long held the view that the criminal law is designed to reflect and prioritise the underlying mores of a society. As the guardian of what is acceptable and what is a transgression, the state entrusts punitive sanctions to the criminal law alone. Throughout the decisions of the Constitutional Court and the Supreme Court two lines of reasoning were employed to justify the continued operation of art 241. The first is what Ginsberg refers to as 'Confucian constitutionalism'.[137] Confucian teachings are not referred to. However notions of Confucian values and traditionalism are evident in the phrases setting out the need to preserve 'marriage as the cornerstone of family life' because it is the 'foundation for the state and society';[138] is part of 'Korean tradition';[139] goes against the sound 'morality called for in our society';[140] and obtaining evidence of a spouse's infidelity can be excused as a 'righteous act'.[141] By design, criminalising adultery is seen to preserve traditional Korean values which correspond with the Confucian perspectives on family[142] and social order. It is paternalistic in that it seeks to protect Koreans from harm and temptation, and to guide them in a righteous and moral path. Chaihark Hahm sees many instances of law reinforcing a norm derived from a cultural tradition when its relevance is being questioned.[143] Yet, Confucian dominance is waning as seen in the National Assembly's 2005

---

134 Ser Myo-ja 'Court mulls redefining adultery constitutionality', *Korea Joongang Daily*, at: http://koreajoongangdaily.joins.com/news/article/Article.aspx?aid=2972624.

135 Discussion of the National Assembly debate can be accessed (in Korean) at: http://likms.assembly.go.kr/bill/jsp/BillDetail.jsp?bill_id=PRC_Y1J3E0T4J1T0S1T4F5Y8K0Z6X0U5H3. Also, reported by Ser Myo-ja 'Court mulls redefining adultery constitutionality', *Korea Joongang Daily*, at: http://koreajoongangdaily.joins.com/news/article/Article.aspx?aid=2972624.

136 Ser Myo-ja 'Court mulls redefining adultery constitutionality', *Korea Joongang Daily*, at: http://koreajoongangdaily.joins.com/news/article/Article.aspx?aid=2972624.

137 Tom Ginsberg 'The Constitutional Court and the judicialization of Korean Politics' in Andrew Harding and Penelope Nicholson (eds) *New Courts in Asia* (Routledge, Abingdon, 2012) 151.

138 Constitutional Court Decision, 2007 Hun-Ka 17·21, 2008 Hun-Ka 7·26, 2008 Hun-Ba 21·47 (consolidated), 30 October 2008 at D (2).

139 Constitutional Court Decision, 2007 Hun-Ka 17·21, 2008 Hun-Ka 7·26, 2008 Hun-Ba 21·47 (consolidated), 30 October 2008 at D (3)

140 Constitutional Court Decision, 2007 Hun-Ka 17·21, 2008 Hun-Ka 7·26, 2008 Hun-Ba 21·47 (consolidated), 30 October 2008 at B (1).

141 Supreme Court Decision of 9 September 2010, 2008 Do 3990.

142 Youngjoon Kwon 'Korea; Bridging the gap between Korean substance and Western form' in E Ann Black and Gary F Bell *Law and Legal Institutions of Asia: traditions, adaptations and innovations* (Cambridge University Press, Cambridge, 2011) 176.

143 Chaihark Hahm 'Law, Culture, and the Politics of Confucianism' (2003) 16(2) Columbia Journal of Asian Law 253, 279.

abolition of the bedrock institution of the *hoju* system,[144] and the Constitutional Court's declaration in 1997 that the statute which prohibited marriage between those with the same surname and family origin was unconstitutional.[145]

The second dimension to the reasoning is that retaining the crime of adultery reflects the public will. This is set out in the Constitutional Court's decision of 2008:[146]

> 'Given the Korean legal awareness that adultery harms social order and violates others' rights in *addition to the strong demand for preemptive prevention of adultery*, the legislature's judgment to criminally punish adultery is not arbitrary.' (emphasis added)

There is some anecdotal support for the view that the majority of Koreans do support the current law. It is reported that a survey in 2008 found 70% of Koreans supported retaining the law[147] with a 2010 survey by the Korea Research Centre concluding that 7 out of 10 married women favoured its retention on the basis that any repeal would serve to encourage marital infidelity.[148] These findings accord with comprehensive research taken some 15 years earlier in 1991 by Professor Shim Young-Hee.[149] She found that 73.2% of those surveyed supported the criminalisation of adultery (mainly for the reason that it goes to preventing broken families) with 74.3% of respondents indicating that the criminalisation of adultery acted as a deterrent and believed the incidence of adultery would increase if it were decriminalised. She did detect double standards as respondents were more tolerant of males engaging in adulterous behaviour as opposed to females, with 77.8% of respondents indicating they would never accept a female engaging in adulterous behaviour, while only 53.4% of respondents said the same for a male counterpart engaging in the same.[150]

---

144 *Hoju* was an inherited but permanent position for a male family member. Women were prohibited from being appointed *hoju*.

145 Constitutional Court Decision, 95 Hun-Ka 6–13, 16 July 1997. See generally the analysis of Chaihark Hahm 'Law, Culture, and the Politics of Confucianism' (2003) 16(2) Columbia Journal of Asian Law,253, 287. Note also a contrary outcome in Supreme Court Decision, 1998, 96Da52670, moral principles of implicit filial piety were used to modify the application of a legal right.

146 Constitutional Court Decision, 2007 Hun-Ka 17·21, 2008 Hun-Ka 7·26, 2008 Hun-Ba 21·47 (consolidated), 30 October 2008 at 1 (A).

147 Survey by RealMeter, reported by Brian Lee 'Is hanky-panky a crime?' *Joongang Daily*, 12 March 2008. And www.hancinema.net/is-hanky-panky-a-crime–12966.html.

148 John Power 'Should Adultery be a crime?' *The Korea Herald*, 13 May 2013, at: www.koreaherald.com/view.php?ud=20130513000676.

149 Kantong eui Siltae mit Euisik e Kwanhan Yeonku 1991 [An Empirical Study of Adultery in Korea: Focusing on the Extent and Attitude] [Shim Young-Hee trans] which is cited by Kuk Cho 'The Crime of Adultery in Korea: Inadequate means for Maintaining Morality and Protecting Women' (2002) 2(1) Journal of Korean Law 81, 87.

150 Kuk Cho 'The Crime of Adultery in Korea: Inadequate means for Maintaining Morality and Protecting Women' (2002) 2(1) Journal of Korean Law 81, 86–87.

Surveys are not always reliable indicators. The Justices who found the law unconstitutional argued the public view was changing.[151] The data from the Constitutional Court in 2008 shows that the number of criminal cases on adultery is between 3,000 and 4,000 a year, which means most acts of adultery either were not discovered, or were not brought to the court by the victimised spouse.[152] Less than 10% filed proceed to prosecution and accusations of adultery are often cancelled, which shows that it is 'losing its function as a regulative norm'.[153] Advocates for abolition point out that actual social practice shows that the criminal adultery laws do not act as deterrents and do the opposite to preserving and protecting families. This is because a marriage must be dissolved or divorce suit filed along with the criminal complaint of adultery. As the complaint takes place alongside the breakdown of a marriage, the law is not designed to promote marriage, but rather is a recourse action after the fact. Some, like Ok, would suggest it is purely a revenge action.[154] In addition, a criminal complaint is unlikely to assist with reconciliation between the two parties, increasing its counter-productivity. Even if the law can act as a deterrent, the question becomes what is it really preserving? Justice Kim Yang-Kyoon, in his dissenting opinion in the 1990 Constitutional Court decision, reasoned that 'fidelity through criminal punishment is not genuine fidelity'.[155]

(c) Political parties and advocacy organisations

Ginsburg notes the Constitutional Court is routinely called on to resolve issues of social policy, as well as significant political conflicts,[156] which he describes as a gradual 'judicialisation of Korean politics in which major social and political questions' are determined in a court room rather than in a conventional political institutions.[157] It seems on this issue the National Assembly done just that. It has avoided tackling the question in favour of a judicial resolution. There have been legislative motions to repeal the law, but each time it has been unsuccessful.[158] In 1953, 1985 and 1992[159] repeal of the Article has been on

---

151 See earlier section IV(b).

152 Constitutional Court Decision, 2007 Hun-Ka 17·21, 2008 Hun-Ka 7·26, 2008 Hun-Ba 21·47 (consolidated), 30 October 2008, D 4.

153 Constitutional Court Decision, 2007 Hun-Ka 17·21, 2008 Hun-Ka 7·26, 2008 Hun-Ba 21·47 (consolidated), 30 October 2008, D 4.

154 In Ok's petition to the Constitutional Court, she claimed the adultery law has degenerated into a means of revenge by the spurned spouse, rather than a means of saving a marriage. This was cited in Anthony Bessette 'Regulating and Punishing Adultery in Korea and East Asia' (27 July 2009), at SSRN: http://papers.ssrn.com/sol3/papers.cfm?abstract_id=1439830.

155 Constitutional Court Decision of 10 September 1990, 89 Heon Ma 81.

156 Tom Ginsberg 'The Constitutional Court and judicialization of Korean Politics' in Andrew Harding and Penelope Nicholson (eds) *New Courts in Asia* (Routledge Law, Abingdon, 2010) 145.

157 Tom Ginsberg 'The Constitutional Court and judicialization of Korean Politics' in Andrew Harding and Penelope Nicholson (eds) *New Courts in Asia* (Routledge Law, Abingdon, 2010) 145.

158 Anthony Bessette 'Regulating and Punishing Adultery in Korea and East Asia' (27 July 2009). Available at SSRN: http://papers.ssrn.com/sol3/papers.cfm?abstract_id=1439830.

159 See earlier discussion in section I.

the reform agenda and the Constitutional Court in 2001[160] called on the legislators to seriously consider reform of the law. In 2005, a member of the National Assembly[161] introduced a revision to the National Assembly's Legislation and Judiciary Committee. His aide told the media that the 'lawmakers sitting on the committee are conservative and for them the issue is not pressing'.[162] In 2010, it was reported that a special committee of 24 legal experts was tasked with revising the Criminal Act, including the adultery law.[163]

The law has had some strong political support over many decades. One such advocate was former Prime Minister and law Professor Lee Soo-Sung. He argues that a criminal law should not simply be 'dead law', which merely establishes standards and the limits of criminal sanctions; it should go further to become a 'living law', which enhances the order of values and the moral standards of a community.[164] It also becomes a counterpoint to Western values and individualistic notions. Professor Lee expressed concern that Korean culture's adoption of Western ideas and ethics, with the subsequent deviation from oriental ideas and ethics, had led to the decay of morals within Korean society. This argument resonates in many Asian cultures where laws like this are seen as a bulwark against corrupting Western values and practices, popularly referred to as the 'free-sex culture' of the West.[165]

Over the decades this law brought strange bedfellows as Confucianists, women's rights groups, and the bar association[166] aligned in support of preserving the criminalisation of adultery. Women's advocacy groups were staunch proponents of retaining the crime of adultery. They focused on the point borne out in Professor Shim Young-Hee's study that there exists a double standard in Korea that makes it acceptable for men to engage in adulterous behaviour, but not for women. However, the criminal law of adultery in Korea is gender neutral and this equality sends an important message to society at large. Kwak Bae-Hee, a leading women's rights activist, says the laws of adultery protect women's rights in Korea.[167] There are economic benefits as

---

160 Constitutional Court Decision 2000 Hun-Ba 60, 25 October 2001.

161 Yeom Dong-yong of the United New Democrat Party. This is based on the newspaper report in Brian Lee 'Is hanky-panky a crime?' *Joongang Daily,* 12 March 2008, at: www.hancinema.net/is-hanky-panky-a-crime–12966.html.

162 Yeom Dong-yong of the United New Democrat Party. This is based on the newspaper report in Brian Lee 'Is hanky-panky a crime?' *Joongang Daily*, 12 March 2008, at: www.hancinema.net/is-hanky-panky-a-crime–12966.html.

163 'Korea considers ending law criminalising adultery law' in *dalje.com*, 18 March, 2010.

164 Hankuk eui Munhwa Cheontong Kwa Hyeongbeop 1994 [Cultural Tradition of Korea and Criminal Law] [Professor Lee Soo-Sung trans], writings are cited by Kuk Cho 'The Crime of Adultery in Korea: Inadequate means for Maintaining Morality and Protecting Women' (2002) 2(1) Journal of Korean Law 88.

165 Choe Sang-Hun 'Koreans Agog as Off-Screen Soap Becomes Courtroom Drama', 19 May 2008, *New York Times,* at: www.nytimes.com/2008/05/19/world/asia/19adultery.html?pagewanted=print&_r=0.

166 Tom Ginsberg 'Confucian Constitutionalism' (2002) 27 Law and Social Inquiry 763, 787.

167 Discussed in Kuk Cho 'The Crime of Adultery in Korea: Inadequate means for Maintaining Morality and Protecting Women' (2002) 2(1) Journal of Korean Law 81, 89.

well. Dr Yang Jung-Ja hones in on the role that the enforcement of criminal adultery plays in protecting women's economic interests in divorce suits instituted as a result of their husbands' committing adultery. Dr Yang explains that women are often hard done-by in divorce proceedings being denied their rights to marital property or consolation awards due to their husbands' hiding or moving assets, or changing ownership of assets in the interim to avoid paying their ex-wives. Therefore, the criminal adultery provision, which allows a woman to immediately accuse her husband of engaging in adultery, provides an effective and necessary means for women to protect their economic rights.[168] Adultery charges are a lever to secure child custody and a better financial settlement post-divorce.

However, increasingly there are signs that some women's groups[169] are shifting their views. Ju Jin-woo, an official at the Ministry of Gender Equality, stated in 2008 that the existing adultery law can in reality put women at a disadvantage, because 'if a man gets caught, women tend to drop the charges or get a divorce. But if a woman gets caught, she is charged just about every time'.[170] In another line of reasoning, Kwak Bae-hee, director of the Korean Legal and Aid Centre for Family Relations, once a staunch supporter, is now reported as saying that the government has no right to meddle with the intimate affairs of married couples, and that establishing 'other protective schemes for the victims of spouses' adultery would be more effective'.[171] In addition, she argues that gender roles are changing. The economic disparity between the genders is decreasing and, whereas adultery was once seen as something only husbands would do, today wives are more likely also to engage in extra-marital relationships than in the past. As in Ok's case, it means there is an increasing number of men who can use this law against their wives.[172]

There is significantly more questioning of whether criminal law should protect social morals, and whether intrusion in the private lives of individuals can be justified. In addition to Justices on the Constitutional Court applying the principle of proportionality and its prohibition on excessive restriction in line with art 37(2) of the Constitution[173] to find the law unconstitutional, scholars such as Kuk Cho have advocated a minimalist approach in respect of moral issues. Criminal law should serve its role as *ultima ratio* as opposed to *prima*

168 Discussed in Kuk Cho 'The Crime of Adultery in Korea: Inadequate means for Maintaining Morality and Protecting Women' (2002) 2(1) Journal of Korean Law 81, 90.

169 Lee Hye-kyung of Minwoo Women's Right's Group rejects the 'law's intrusion into private parts of adult sexual life' cited by Anthony Bessette 'Regulating and Punishing Adultery in Korea and East Asia' (27 July 2009), at: SSRN: http://papers.ssrn.com/sol3/papers.cfm?abstract_id=1439830.

170 Brian Lee 'Is hanky-panky a crime?' *Joongang Daily*, 12 March 2008, www.hancinema.net/is-hanky-panky-a-crime–12966.html.

171 Bae Ji-sook 'Adultery law faces constitutional review' *The Korea Herald*, 10 August 2011.

172 Choe Sang-Hun 'Koreans Agog as Off-Screen Soap Becomes Courtroom Drama' May 19, 2008 *New York Times*, at: www.nytimes.com/2008/05/19/world/asia/19adultery.html?pagewanted=print&_r=0.

173 See earlier discussion in section IV.

ratio,[174] which means that restricting individual freedoms on the ground of preserving social morality may be disproportionate. He follows the reasoning of the dissenting Justice Kwon Sung's in the 2008 Constitutional Court decision. If incest, bestiality, masochism, and group sex are not criminalised in Korea, how can it be argued these 'immoral' behaviours are any less in comparison to adultery? Justice Kwon Sung wrote:[175]

> 'Adultery is an object of ethical reprehension and moral remorse, not criminal sanctions ... Sexual relationships essentially belong in the realm of the most private and secret spheres of an individual's life, and thus fidelity should never be forced upon and should not be the object of state supervision and conditioning through criminal punishment.'

VII CONCLUSION

For many thousands of years, through the Gojoson era and the kingdoms and dynasties which followed,[176] acts of adultery have had serious social, legal and economic ramifications for any Koreans who find that their private romance has become public. This was true too in many other societies, including most Western nations, but in the last few decades the numbers of nations which criminalise adultery has markedly decreased and no-fault divorce regimes are more common. The result is that acts of adultery are legally inconsequential. When adultery is relegated to this private sphere, social reprobation is the one and only consequence. In many ways, Asia goes against this trend with fault divorce still prevalent and criminalisation of adultery not only retained but in some states re-introduced.[177]

Modern Korea has struggled to find the ideal way to deal with marital infidelity. Any change must resonate with its citizens whilst recognising Western liberal and individualistic notions of rights to privacy, to happiness, to dignity, to autonomy, but not jettisoning traditional values of family, morality and Confucian societal norms. The tensions between these two dimensions have been evident right from 1953. Despite the National Assembly's Committee recommendations of that year to de-criminalise adultery, it failed by one vote. Throughout the decades that followed, including the era of democratisation, there has been a 'buck-passing' between the legislature and the judiciary

---

174 Kuk Cho '*Nullum Crimen, Nulla Poena Sine Lege* in Korean Criminal Law' (2006–2007) 6 Journal of Korean Law 147, 159; also Kuk Cho *Aggravated Punishment on the Homicide of Lineal Ascendants in the Korean Penal Code: Maintain Filial Piety by Criminal Law?* International Conference on Criminal Law: Protection of Life in Criminal Law (Seoul, 2001); Kuk Cho 'The Crime of Adultery in Korea: Inadequate Means for Maintaining Morality and Protecting Women' (2002) 2(1) Journal of Korean Law 81, 92.

175 Decision of 25 October 2001, the Korean Constitutional Court, 2001 Heon Ba 60 (Justice Kwon Sung, dissenting opinion).

176 See discussion in section II.

177 Cambodia, the Philippines, and Papua New Guinea, with Aceh (now an autonomous province in Indonesia) and Brunei Darussalam strengthening their Syariah criminal law to provided a greater penalty for adultery.

including the Constitutional Court on whether or not to reform, or to abolish, art 241. The balance between retentionists and abolitionists has been a fine one. Despite the six reasons given by the Ministry of Justice in 1992 for abolition, the National Assembly decided that, as there was a preponderance of community support for the law, to do so would be premature. Similarly, the Justices of the Constitutional Court have on regular occasions[178] called for the legislature to seriously address the issue, whilst the Court itself has retained the status quo. Perhaps this is about to change, as once again the Constitutional Court ponders the constitutionality of art 241. Signs are that a majority of the current bench could endorse reform, and that women's advocacy groups, which once opposed change to art 241, now see it 'as a fetter and not a shield for women's rights, especially given the rapid growth in Korean women's consciousness of their fundamental rights to privacy and freedom over sexual decisions'.[179]

Regardless of the fate of art 241 itself, adultery will, for now, remain of significance in the lives of Koreans, as divorce and custody outcomes, and the requirement to pay damages by way of compensation for psychological harm and financial loss, will continue. The descriptors 'draconian',[180] 'anachronistic',[181] 'outdated'[182] and 'ineffective'[183] are used for art 241, but not for the other aspects of adultery with many scholars,[184] judges[185] and commentators advocating that the civil law,[186] not the criminal law, is the more appropriate vehicle by which marital infidelity can be addressed. Perhaps that is a compromise that both sides could accept.

---

178 1990, 1993, 2001, and 2008, for example, the judgments of Justices Cho Kyu-Kwang, and Kim Moon-Hwe, Constitutional Court Decision, 1990, 89 Hun-Ma 82; Justices Hyeong-ki Min, Lee Kang-kook, Justice Lee Kong-hyun, Justice Cho Dae-hyen, Constitutional Court Decision, 2007 Hun-Ka 17·21, 2008 Hun-Ka 7·26, 2008 Hun-Ba 21·47 (consolidated) 30 October 2008.

179 Kuk Cho 'The Crime of Adultery in Korea: Inadequate means for Maintaining Morality and Protecting Women' (2002) 2(1) Journal of Korean Law 81, 81.

180 Kim Junghyun 'South Korean Actress Avoids Jail for Adultery', 17 December 2008, *Il San South Korea*, at: http://uk.reuters.com/article/2008/12/17/uk-korea-adultery-idUKTRE4BG0KH20081217.

181 John Power 'Should Adultery be a crime?' *The Korea Herald*, 13 May 2013, at: www.koreaherald.com/view.php?ud=20130513000676.

182 'Korea considers ending law criminalising adultery law' in *dalje.com*, 18 March 2010.

183 Kim-Shin Myung Sook cited in Kim Myun Joong 'Should Adultery be a Crime?', at: www.international-divorce.com/Korea:SHOULD-ADULTERY-BE-A-CRIME.htm.

184 For example, Kuk Cho 'The Crime of Adultery in Korea: Inadequate means for Maintaining Morality and Protecting Women' (2002) 2(1) Journal of Korean Law 81.

185 For example, Justice Kim Hee-ok, Constitutional Court of Korea, 2007 Hun-Ka 17·21, 2008 Hun-Ka 7·26, 2008 Hun-Ba 21·47 (consolidated), 30 October 2008 at F.

186 John Power 'Should Adultery be a crime?' *The Korea Herald*, 13 May 2013, at: www.koreaherald.com/view.php?ud=20130513000676.

LESOTHO

PROTECTING ORPHANS AND VULNERABLE CHILDREN IN LESOTHO: AN ASSESSMENT OF THE CHILDREN'S PROTECTION AND WELFARE ACT 2011

*Julia Sloth-Nielsen**

Résumé

La loi du Lesotho de 2011, relative à la protection et au bien-être des enfants, a été inspirée par la nécessité de mettre en place des mécanismes légaux efficaces de protection des enfants vulnérables, dont la situation est particulièrement critique. L'adoption de cette loi résulte de la constatation de l'avancée significative du virus du SIDA et de son impact sur les enfants. Néanmoins, la loi présente des insuffisances relativement à la prise en charge des enfants vulnérables. Deux remarques peuvent être formulées. Tout d'abord, les dispositions légales n'instaurent aucun cadre juridique solide pour l'adoption entre Etats et le placement en famille d'accueil. Ensuite, la loi ne prévoit pas de protection particulière quant à la santé sexuelle des adolescents confrontés au SIDA, et plus spécifiquement pour l'accès à la contraception et aux préservatifs. Cela démontre bien que la loi a été adoptée dans un contexte social conservateur, aujourd'hui totalement dépassé.

I INTRODUCTION

This chapter reviews specific aspects of the Children's Protection and Welfare Act 2011 of Lesotho, insofar as they pertain to the situation of orphans and vulnerable children. The chapter commences with a brief outline of the context in which the legislation was adopted, including a brief overview of relevant country data. The substantive aspects of the Act pertaining to orphans and vulnerable children are thereafter discussed. Notably provisions relating to non-discrimination, to health, to registration of orphans and vulnerable children, to protection of surviving children's property and provisions concerning fostering and adoption are featured. Finally an overall assessment of the scheme of the Act in addressing the plight of orphans and vulnerable children is given.

* Professor of Law, University of the Western Cape and Professor of Children's Rights in the Developing World, Leiden.

II THE CONTEXT

Lesotho is a small mountainous country surrounded on all sides by the Republic of South Africa. Then called Basotholand, it was annexed by the British after approaches from the then king (Moshoeshoe) in the 1860s for assistance against the Boers, who went to war against the Basotho in search of land. National elections were held in 1960, and full independence was achieved in 1966; however, the elected head of state, Chief Leabua Jonathan was not popular and when defeated at the polls subsequently, he deposed the king (Moshoeshoe II), and suspended the constitution. Chief Jonathan was deposed in a military coup in 1986 and the king restored to the throne. But ongoing power disputes between the king and the coup leader raged until the king was deposed in favour of his son, King Letsie III. From time to time, political discord has continued to reign, such as in 1998 when the Southern Africa Development Community (SADC) was called in to help restore order in the country. Democracy remains fragile.

Lesotho, however, remains a kingdom, with King Letsie III still at the helm, although he does not exercise executive power. Real power lies with the cabinet, headed by a prime minister and a bi-cameral Parliament (a national assembly and a non-elected senate, comprising 22 chiefs and 11 nominated members).

Lesotho ranks among the poorest countries in the world.[1] It has little in the way of natural resources (the exception being water, which led to the building of the Lesotho Highlands Water Project[2] some years ago for the purposes of exporting water and hydroelectric power to neighbouring South Africa), and the 2 million inhabitants of the country are largely pastoral people. Significant numbers of Basotho work as migrant labourers on the mines of South Africa; remittances are key to the national economy, and labour remains Lesotho's major export, with at its peak, 60% of males working in South Africa, primarily in the mining sector.

With high levels of migration for economic reasons, it is no surprise that Lesotho is regarded as having the third highest per capita incidence of HIV/Aids in the world, with obvious impact on the numbers of children who are left orphaned or vulnerable due to the impact of the scourge. Poverty and worsening economic outcomes further impact on food security which is tenuous: nearly 60% of the population lives below the poverty line. A combination of ongoing migration (especially of adult males) and the devastating impact of HIV have shattered the traditional social safety nets

---

1 56.6% of Lesotho population (1,876,633 million people) live below the national poverty datum line, while 43.3% live on one dollar a day.

2 See www.lhda.org.ls/portal/home (accessed 19 February 2014).

which had characterised this largely rural society.[3] It must be pointed out that gender inequality is pervasive and culturally sustained.[4]

Having been colonised by the British, previous legislation dealing with aspects of child law bore some of the hallmarks of a previous colonial dispensation. For instance, under the 1952 Adoption of Children Proclamation, a Mosotho child could be adopted only by a non-national, Basotho were legally prohibited from adopting their own clanspeople (although it appears that in recent times Basotho people did participate in adoption).[5]

Recognising the need for modernisation of the law, the Lesotho Law Reform Commission was tasked shortly after the turn of the Millennium with investigating proposals for a children's law that would comply with international treaties such as the Convention on the Rights of the Child and the African Charter on the Rights and Welfare of the Child. The first Bill was available in 2004, and an updated version is dated 2009. The legislation was finally signed into law in 2011.[6] The new law of 2011 replaced the outdated Children's Act of 1980, which was silent on social needs and challenges of the children, rather focusing on children in trouble with the law. Launching the Act in January 2012, the Queen of Lesotho depicted the new Act as a 'special law that greatly differs with any previous law ever enacted', saying that 'it combines numerous laws from the country, regional and international levels while maintaining Basotho cultural values which put children's interest at the forefront'.[7]

The new Children's Protection and Welfare Act 2011 purports to be a comprehensive enactment to domesticate international children's rights. It covers both child protection and juvenile justice, as well as parentage, custody and guardianship, maintenance of children, employment of children, and protective measures related to child health. It drew inspiration from amongst

---

3 The average life expectancy is currently 48 years, which is indicative of the impact of HIV/Aids (www.dataworldbank.org/country/Lesotho (accessed 22 March 2014)).

4 Concluding observations of CEDAW to Lesotho's initial and combined 1st, 2nd, 3rd, and 4th country report, para 34: 'While noting the various initiatives taken by the State party to prevent and combat HIV/AIDS, including the adoption in 2011 of the National HIV/AIDS Strategic Plan and the National Action Plan on Women, Girls and HIV/AIDS 2011-2016, the CEDAW Committee notes with deep concern that the State party faces a serious epidemic and that women and girls are disproportionately affected by HIV. In this respect, the CEDAW Committee is concerned that women and girls may be particularly susceptible to infection owing to gender-specific norms, and that the persistence of unequal power relations between women and men and the inferior status of women and girls may hamper their ability to negotiate safe sexual practices and increase their vulnerability to infection.' (CEDAW/C/LSO/CO/1-4 of 8 November 2011).

5 Dr I Kimane presentation on adoption and foster care at the UWC/Miller D Toit Cloete conference on child and family law (2009).

6 The lengthy period between the finalisation of the Lesotho Law Reform Commission's work, and the conclusion of the legislative process, explains why there is now a measure of disconnect between the law and the policy objectives contained in the National Strategic Plan for Vulnerable Children, 2012–2017, to which this chapter pays some attention.

7 Lesotho has a plural legal culture similar to those of other British colonies in the SADC region; i e a mix of Roman Dutch law, civil law and customary law.

others the South African Children's Act 38 of 2005 as well as that of Botswana (2009).[8] Nevertheless, it contains some unique features not as prominent in the laws of South Africa or Botswana, such as some of those highlighted further in this chapter. As indicated in the chapter title, the focus is on provisions of the children's statute impacting upon children orphaned or made vulnerable, largely due to HIV/Aids.

III THE HIV/AIDS CONTEXT IN LESOTHO

The Lesotho National Strategic Plan on Vulnerable Children April 2012 to March 2017, replaced the outgoing National OVC Strategic Plan (2006–2010) that came to an end in December 2010. The key achievements of the 2006 OVC plan included the development of the National OVC Policy (2006), the establishment of the National OVC Coordinating Committee (NOCC) at national level, as well as structures at the district level respectively. A Child Help Line was established in 2008. Through the 2006 OVC plan, the Department of Social Welfare defined the essential services package for OVC that included education, health, food security and nutrition, and protection, care and support. Attempts were made to develop a national OVC database over the lifespan of this initial plan. However, despite efforts to improve strategic information management, the 2012 Plan records that reporting on progress on OVC service provision has been poor. It identified the greatest challenges with the implementation of the 2006 OVC response as a weak policy and legal framework, and inadequate human and financial resources both in government and among civil society organisations.

The 2012 Plan records that, while the directed focus on orphanhood status in the 2006–2010 Plan has had some benefits, it had not been sufficient to provide meaningful support to vulnerable children, and that it is now felt to be stigmatising by selecting only orphans.

In the latest Plan 2012–2017, it is said that the response will shift from focusing on orphanhood status to a child's vulnerability, with orphanhood being one of the many possible causes of vulnerability. Also, the Plan notes that a family setup provides the most important social safety net for vulnerable children. In most cases vulnerable children live in vulnerable households, and hence it is important to address the needs of individual vulnerable children in the context of the needs of their families.

A situation analysis of orphans and other vulnerable children conducted in Lesotho in 2011 estimated that vulnerable children in Lesotho are between 10% and 13% (125,000) of all children (1,072,974) between the ages 0–17

---

[8] Members of the Lesotho Law Reform Commission task teams visited South Africa, and information on legislative developments were also shared by South Africans who provided some technical assistance to Lesotho during the course of the work of the Law Commission.

years.[9] The situation analysis found that there are 363,526 orphans.[10] The analysis indicates that of the total number of orphans, 58.7% (213,248) were paternal orphans, and 17.8% (64,647) were maternal orphans.[11] The total number of double orphans (who have lost both parents) is estimated as 23.6% (85,631). It is this latter group who are now regarded as being targeted by the National Strategic Plan. The increase in the number of orphans and vulnerable children has in particular been fuelled by HIV and AIDS. In 2009, the National HIV and AIDS estimates noted that there were 180,000 orphans in Lesotho of whom 122,000 were as a result of AIDS. The high adult HIV prevalence rate of HIV/AIDS amongst the general population (estimated at 23%) has caused increased mortality among parents, which has in turn resulted in rapidly increasing numbers of orphans and other vulnerable children in the country.[12]

The Plan clearly identifies the 2011 Child Welfare and Protection Act as a major milestone and complementary tool in the protection of children made vulnerable by HIV/AIDS. Amongst the priorities the Plan identifies are strengthening social, legal and judicial protection of vulnerable children and their families, inter alia via implementation of the Act.[13] Hence the Plan and the Act are, to this extent, inextricably linked.

---

9 The 2012–2017 Plan (at 11) discussed the meaning of vulnerability as follows: 'The [previous] National Policy on Orphans and Vulnerable Children (OVC) has defined an orphan as a "person who is below the age of 18, who has (sic) lost one or both parents due to death". The Children's Protection and Welfare Act (CPWA, 2011) has defined a vulnerable child as "a person who is below the age of 18, who has one or both parents who have deserted or neglected him (her), to the extent that he has no means of survival and as such is exposed to dangers of abuse, exploitation or criminality and is therefore in need of care and protection". The Situation Analysis of OVC in Lesotho (2011) redefined a vulnerable child as "a child whose rights to survival, development, protection and participation are not met" because of certain conditions or circumstances. This means that children become vulnerable when their rights to survival, development, protection and participation in social and economic issues affecting them are not fulfilled. All three definitions above are broad, and inclusive of most children.' It seems that the quantification of 'vulnerability' links to the Situational Analysis which counted orphans but discounted those being adequately cared for by kin, and added other children whose socio-economic circumstances meant that there was no or inadequate means of survival in the family setting.

10 The National Policy on Orphans and Vulnerable Children (OVC) 2006–2010 defined an orphan as a 'person who is below the age of 18, who has lost one or both parents due to death'. The Children's Protection and Welfare Act, 2011, has defined a vulnerable child as 'a person who is below the age of 18, who has one or both parents who have deserted or neglected him (her), to the extent that he has no means of survival and as such is exposed to dangers of abuse, exploitation or criminality and is therefore in need of care and protection'. Analysis of this definition shows that it is limited to vulnerable children being deserted or neglected and hence does not cover all issues that make children vulnerable or put them in harm's way, according to the 2012 OVC policy. The new Plan clearly seeks to broaden the concept of vulnerability encompassed in the Act.

11 The number of maternal orphans is significant as mothers are traditionally the primary care-takers of children, and this is exacerbated in the context of male migration in Lesotho.

12 The Lesotho Child Poverty Study (2011) noted that the major underlying drivers of social change in Lesotho are unemployment and HIV and AIDS. The Government of Lesotho has put in place some social protection strategies and programmes that include the Old Age Pension Scheme, the Child Grants Programme, the Public Assistance Scheme, bursaries for secondary schools, free primary education and a school feeding programme.

13 There are five priorities established in the Plan (the one cited in the text is priority 3). The

IV THE PROVISIONS OF THE ACT

(a) Guardianship and child rights

The Children's Protection and Welfare Act defines a guardian as 'any person who, in the opinion of the Children's Court having cognisance of any case in relation to the child or in which the child is involved, is for a time being in charge of and/or has control over the child'. This is a far cry from the traditional Roman-Dutch legal definition of a guardian based on biological ties, and is indicative of the uncertain parental status of many children who may come to the attention of the Children's Court. The definition accords primacy to the role played by the person factually caring for the child, the traditional response to the death of a parent usually being that another member of the extended family steps in. There is also a definition of a 'member of the family' which accords with African custom, insofar as it refers to 'parent or guardian or member of an extended family who is a household member'.

The short chapter on the 'Principles'[14] at the outset of the Act already contains provisions pertinent to children affected by HIV/AIDS. Thus the non-discrimination provision forbids discrimination on a whole list of grounds, which include the child's health status.[15] This is important given the stigmatisation that frequently occurs in respect of children who themselves are HIV positive. In the following chapter, titled 'Rights of a child and responsibilities of parents and the State', a unique provision concerns the right of orphaned and vulnerable children to registration.[16] Section 9(1) provides for this, and it is explained in more detail in s 9(2):[17]

> 'The Department responsible for registration of births and deaths shall maintain and administer a systematic and comprehensive data in relation to all groups of orphaned and vulnerable children.'

It could be suggested that maintaining a separate registry of orphaned children sets them up for potential discriminatory practices, and downplays the extent to which their life can be 'normalised' through absorption into family and kinship structures, through informal fostering and even through formal adoption. On the other hand, knowledge of their consequent vulnerability could equally assist various organs of state and community structures to ensure that these children

---

others are: raising awareness and commitment to vulnerable children's rights and needs through advocacy and social mobilisation; strengthening the capacity of families and communities to protect, care for, and support vulnerable children; scaling up availability and access to services by vulnerable children and their families; and systems strengthening.

14 Containing only three overarching principles, namely the best interests of the child, recognition of children's evolving capacity and non-discrimination.

15 Article 6.

16 Although, as noted above, the Plan 2012–2017 describes this registration endeavour as having been less effective than desired. The provision in the Act is indicative of the fact that the Act was developed largely in a previous era when registration was thought to be an appropriate response to identifying vulnerable children.

17 Section 9(3) continues that the Bureau of Statistics shall have access to this data.

do not fall through the cracks (as it were), and contribute to ensuring that appropriate alternative care is in fact provided to all children left without families. Such is indeed a state duty under s 22(i) of the Act (s 22 listing a range of state responsibilities in relation to children with disabilities, the provision of primary education, the protection of children from all forms of maltreatment, etc): s 22(i) requires that the state provide 'special protection for a child deprived of a family environment' and that the state must 'ensure appropriate alternative family care or institutional placement' for such children.

(b) Protection of property rights

The Children's Protection and Welfare Act is unusual (amongst comparable legislation in the region) insofar as it singles out for dedicated treatment the protection of children's property. Property grabbing by relatives and others upon the AIDS-related death of a parent or care-giver is a well-known phenomenon, and deprives affected children further of available safety nets, including housing, livestock and land for grazing or crop cultivation. One of the listed children's rights – in s 19 – is the right of the child to the property of his parents, save where the child is born out of wedlock in which case the child has the right to inherit the property of his biological mother (irrespective of the mother's marital status).[18]

Part 5 of the Act deals with the administration of the property of children by the Master of the High Court. The Master of the High Court, the statutory body protecting children's rights to inherit, has been decentralised to all districts to protect orphans' and widows' inheritance rights.[19] The Act provides for a system of community reporting of the death of a parent of minor children to the Master within 2 months of the death of the parent.[20] Alienation, disposal or sale of the child's (inherited) property is forbidden without the permission of the Master, and contravention of this provision (s 39(1)) is a criminal offence with a tariff of a fine or imprisonment not exceeding 5 months.

---

18 This is a statutory assimilation of the customary law rule that children born of unmarried mothers do not share in the inheritance of the estate of their fathers. The 2012–2017 National Strategic Plan records that Lesotho has initiated a process where inheritance laws will be reviewed and harmonised. This is because 'the majority of families in Lesotho depend on the Laws of Lerotholi (customary law) in determining inheritance. The cornerstone of the laws of inheritance in Lesotho is Section 11 of the Laws of Lerotholi. The direct effect of this law on vulnerable children is that younger siblings cannot inherit family property, as this is a preserve of the eldest boy child. However, among the elite Basotho an increasing number of families prepare wills to determine how their property should be inherited upon their death. Until recently women had no decision-making role in inheritance issues. However, the Legal Capacity of Married Persons Act 2006 has established a legal framework for equality among men and women and has empowered women to make family decisions, including preparing a family will. A key aspect is articulating the management (handover) of important documents such as birth certificates and title deeds of movable and immovable property' (National Strategic Plan on Vulnerable Children 2012–2017, 14).

19 National Strategic Plan on Vulnerable Children 2012–2017, 20.

20 The obligation is placed first on any surviving parent, the child's guardian or closest relative: s 38.

The Master has specific duties in relation to safeguarding children's property. Alienation or disposal of property – with permission – may not result in a child being left destitute or homeless; negligent use of property by heirs can result in the concerned person being required (upon application to court) to pay for such negligence. The Master is empowered to pursue a surviving spouse for maintenance towards the upkeep of the children. Employers of deceased persons are required to remit any monies due (pension payouts, for instance) to the Master for him to administer in favour of surviving children and s 43 of the Act provides that no financial institution shall open or operate any account in respect of an orphaned child without the prior consent of the Master of the High Court. Both employers and financial institutions' misconduct in this regard is subject to criminal sanction.

Section 205 of the Act deals with testamentary guardianship, a useful corollary to the provisions on the administration of the inherited property of orphans discussed above. It enables a parent of a child to appoint by will any person to be guardian of a child after the parent's death.[21] The guardian of a child (including one appointed by will him or herself)[22] may in turn appoint by will or deed another individual to take his place as the guardian of the child in the event of his death. A child, member of the family or appointed guardian may approach a children's court for various orders, including appointing a relative to act jointly with the guardian, or refusing to make any order confirming guardianship.[23] The children's court is enjoined not to appoint the guardian, if the guardian is not a relative of the child unless the circumstances are such that it is 'prudent to do so'. This indicates a clear preference that children are placed with relatives. Various further provisions relating to the duties and roles of guardians spell out, inter alia, their duty to protect and safeguard any assets forming part of the child's estate.[24]

These provisions seek to mitigate the most detrimental consequences of becoming an orphan, by ensuring as far as possible the preservation of assets of the deceased parent in favour of the child; given the high levels of poverty and food insecurity that prevail generally in Lesotho, this seems to have been a wise step.[25]

---

21 The National Strategic Plan on Vulnerable Children 2012–2017 foresees succession planning becoming an important tool in the fight against vulnerability: 'Succession planning is an important component of mitigating children's and widow's vulnerability. It can alleviate emotional distress and anxiety, fear of death and loss of inheritance, of being abandoned, abused or separated from other siblings. Succession planning helps parents plan for their children's future, and the children's preparedness of a future without their biological parents. Despite its importance, succession planning is still not a routine or common practice' (13).

22 See s 203 which includes under the definition of guardian (for the purposes of this section) a person appointed by a parent in a will.

23 Section 205(5).

24 See ss 210 and 211 for instance.

25 Training of officials attached to the Master's Office on their fiduciary duties under the Act took place in December 2013. Orphan's estates that require administration by the Office of the Master of the High Court increased from 161 in 2011 to 200 in 2014/15, and are estimated to comprise 250 by March 2017 (National Strategic Plan for Vulnerable Children 2012–2017, 21).

(c) Health-related provisions

In Lesotho, as a result of food insecurity and poor nutrition children's stunting has become a common occurrence with 39% of children under 5 years being stunted, of whom 15% were severely stunted.[26] A survey of 2009 quoted in the National Strategic Plan for Vulnerable Children 2012–2017 further reports 4% of wasting among children of whom 1% are severely wasted. Children who are underweight constitute 13% of children under 5 years, and 4% are severely underweight. Commencing with s 11, health-related provisions of the Act include that a child has a right to access (inter alia) medical attention or any other service required for the child's development. Amongst the listed state duties and responsibilities in s 22 (dealing with the responsibilities of the state) are that the state has a duty to formulate policies that will ensure a child's survival and development (s 22(c)) and that there must be special emphasis on the provision of primary and preventive health care, public health education, reduction of infant mortality and measures to ensure that no child is deprived of access to effective health services (s 22(j)).

It is further provided that a child has a right to sexual and reproductive health information and education appropriate to his age.[27] This right is elaborated in a dedicated chapter of the Act entitled 'Protective measures relating to the health of children'.[28] Some of these are clearly inspired by the impact of HIV upon the fulfilment of children's rights in Lesotho.

First, the section which details that children's consent to surgical operations must be effected with the assistance of a parent, guardian or care-giver of the child is an implicit acknowledgement of the difficulties that arise when children require invasive medical treatment and no living parent is available to provide such consent. Hence broadening the list of persons potentially able to provide such consent is a rights-enhancing step.[29]

Consent to HIV testing is separately provided for, and children of 12 or older are empowered to provide independent consent to the performance of an HIV test. A parent, guardian or care-giver may furnish consent for younger children below that age, or for children above that age who lack the maturity or mental

26 National Strategic Plan for Vulnerable Children, 30.

27 Section 11(6), falling under the chapter headed 'Rights of a child and responsibilities of parents and the state'.

28 Part XXV of the Act.

29 The problem of care-giver consent has arisen in other neighbouring countries such as South Africa where the HIV/AIDS pandemic has led to many children being cared for in the extended family. However, in South Africa's Children's Act, the capacity of care-givers to furnish consent is confined to medical treatment and is not extended to (the more invasive) surgical operations. Section 232(4) of the Lesotho Act empowers parents, guardians or caregivers to consent to medical treatment *or surgical operations* of a child under the age of 12 year, or a child above that age who is of insufficient maturity or does not have the mental capacity to understand the benefits, risks and social implications of the treatment or operation. A child of 12 is able to furnish independent consent to medical treatment, provided he or she has sufficient understanding, but needs adult assistance for consent to surgical operations.

capacity to understand the benefits, risks and implications of an HIV test. If a child has no parent or guardian and there is no child protection organisation arranging the placement of a child, the consent may be given by the person who is in charge of the hospital where the test is to be performed. This provision equates substantially to the provision of s 130 of the South African Children's Act 38 of 2005, with the subtle distinction that the South African equivalent permits independent consent by a child who is younger than 12, where the child is able to comprehend the consequences of undergoing an HIV test.[30]

This right is complemented – to an extent – by the provision contained in s 234: this section requires that a child who is a survivor of sexual abuse and exploitation be provided with emergency legal, medical or health assistance. Although the section does not say this in so many words, it seems that the health assistance may include post exposure prophylaxis (PEPs) (to combat the possibility of HIV/AIDS having been transmitted). This is suggested by the wording of the ensuing subsection (2) which provides that no person may refuse to provide reproductive health information to a child who has been a subject of any form of abuse.

That the section is inspired by s 134 of the South African Children's Act 38 of 2005 seems evident: the drafters of the Lesotho Act were fully aware of the South African section which also falls within the short (four section) Part dealing with the protection of children's health rights in the South African version.[31] However, the Lesotho formulation differs markedly insofar as it is limited to children who are victims of sexual abuse, and insofar as it does not mention access to contraception eo nomine at all, referring rather to remedial interventions. This would have been occasioned by the strong traditional and customary attitudes to adolescent sexuality which prevail under Basotho culture.[32] The provisions as currently formulated, though not unwelcome, do

---

30 See J Sloth-Nielsen 'Chapter 7: Protection of Children' in CJ Davel and A Skelton *Compendium on the Children's Act* (2nd rev ed, Juta and Co, Cape Town, 2013).

31 Section 134 of the South Africa law reads as follows:
'(1) No person may refuse –
to sell condoms to a child over the age of 12 years; or
to provide a child over the age of 12 year with condoms on request where such condoms are provided or distributed free of charge.
(2) Contraceptives other than condoms maybe provided to a child on request by the child and without the consent of the parent or care-giver of the child if –
(a) the child is at least 12 years of age;
(b) proper medical advice is given to the child; and
(c) a medical examination is carried out on the child to determine whether there are any medical reasons why a specific contraceptive should not be provided to the child.
(3) A child who obtains condoms, contraceptives or contraceptive advice in terms of this Act is entitled to confidentiality in this respect, subject to section 105.'

32 Earlier draft provisions relating to children's access to reproductive health information and provision of reproductive health devices and technologies 'on request by the child and without the consent of the parent or guardian of the child provided that the child is at least twelve years of age, proper medical advice to be given to the child, and a medical examination is carried out on the child to determine whether there are any medical reasons why a specific contraceptive should not be provided to the child' did feature in the Bill (clause 245). The Bill was clearly altered in the Cabinet and Parliamentary process in favour of the much more restrictive version

not comply with the requirements of the Committee on the Right of the Child as spelt out in General Comment no 3 (HIV AIDS and the Rights of the Child) and General Comment no 4 (Adolescent Sexual Health and the Rights of the Child). Both require confidential access to reproductive health promoting services to be freely available to sexually active adolescents.

(d) Fostering and adoption

In the words of the National Strategic Plan on Vulnerable Children 2012–2017:[33]

> 'in the Basotho culture, legal adoption of children is not a common practice, as children who are vulnerable would normally be placed under the care of a relative in the family. This system has however broken down as more families are unable to provide care and support let alone meet their basic needs due to the socioeconomic impacts of HIV and AIDS, and poverty. A review of the MOHSW Annual Joint Review Report for 2010/2011 fiscal year confirmed the low local adoption rates compared to adoptions outside the country facilitated by international adoption agencies.'

However, the National Strategic Plan for Vulnerable Children 2012–2017 identifies alternative care to be an important component of the national response to child vulnerability, including as a response to orphanhood as a result of HIV/AIDS. Alternative care methods identified in the strategic plan include foster care, adoption, and institutional care. The Plan envisages that communities will be encouraged to foster or adopt vulnerable children as the first choice. Institutional care will be considered as the last option. All of these – foster care, adoption and institutional care – relate to provisions in the 2011 Act, as discussed below.

Lesotho ratified the Hague Intercountry Adoption Convention of 1993 on 24 August 2012, and the Convention entered into force on 1 December of that year.[34] This follows the recommendations of a judicial commission of inquiry into adoption appointed in 2004, which was occasioned (inter alia) by reports of two Basotho boys found in Thailand, one of whom who had died in prison, without any indication as to how they had come to be there. There were fears

that was eventually passed into law (see African Child Policy Forum 'Harmonisation of law in Eastern and Southern Africa: Lesotho' (2013 update) 94 (available at www.africanchildforum.org (accessed 26 February 2014)).

33 By 2011 approximately 1,980 OVC were placed in 34 institutions that were registered with the Department of Social Welfare (as it then was), and in 2010/11, the Department facilitated 50 international and seven local adoptions (National Strategic Plan for Vulnerable Children 2012–2017, 32).

34 Lesotho also ratified the Hague Abduction Convention of 1980 on that date, and the 1996 Hague Convention on Applicable Law, Recognition, Enforcement and Co-operation in respect of parental responsibilities and measures for the protection of children of 10 October 1996, which entered into force on 1 June 2013. These ratifications, coupled with the finalisation of the 2011 Children's Protection and Welfare Act, constitute the principal reason why the African Child Policy Forum accorded Lesotho a position of fourth on the child friendly states index as regards legal measures to protect children (2013 African Child Wellbeing Report, 31).

that they had been trafficked, and absent a proper system of adoption and adequate record-keeping, such suspicions could not be ruled out. The inquiry, which was headed by Lady Justice Majara, completed its report in 2008.[35] The Commission expanded its work to include foster care, as well as adoption, and produced a detailed report spanning three volumes. It was discovered that there was no way of determining how many children were in fact being adopted in Lesotho due to a lack of standardised record keeping at both the Department and the Courts. The Commission did find clear indications that intercountry adoption was being practised, but details of the adoptive parents and circumstances of the children placed for adoption were seldom clear from the perused records.[36]

With ratification of the Hague Convention, the Ministry of Social Welfare, which has been quite newly established as an independent ministry, is the designated Central Authority. The suspension on adoption was lifted by 2009, and since then, working agreements with four agencies for the purposes of intercountry adoption have been concluded.[37]

The Act provides for fosterage and adoption in Part VII. This Part provides a framework for adoption and fosterage, whilst leaving it clear that the detail will be spelt out in standards and guidelines to be developed by the Ministry of Social Welfare (as it now is an independent Ministry).[38] Eligibility to apply to be an adoptive parent and to serve as a foster parent is, however, legislatively defined.[39] The role of the Ministry in assessing suitability of prospective adoptive and foster parents is spelt out, as is the role of the High Court, the body which must authorise any adoption. The requirement of parental (and, where a child is over the age of 10 years, the child's) consent is detailed as is also the effect of an adoption order on parental rights, which severs these and ensures that the adoptive child is for all purposes 'a member of the clan, lineage or other group, and as such will be entitled to all rights to the family rituals in accordance with customary law'.[40]

As far as intercountry adoption is concerned, an adoption order involving transborder placement of a child is made for an interim period of no less than 2

---

35 Due to suspicions of untoward practice in adoption, especially intercountry adoption, all adoptions were suspended in 2007. They have now been resumed.

36 There was also evidence of adoption according to customary or traditional practice (ie without the formal involvement of the courts), but this always occurred between members of the extended family. For a South African case confirming the practice of customary adoption see *M v M* 2010 ZAGPJHC 74.

37 See in general for a discussion of the commission on adoption, Dr I Kimane 'Presentation on adoption and foster care' at the UWC/Miller Du Toit Cloete Conference on Child and Family Law, 2009 (available at www.millerdutoitcloeteinc.co.za/Paper%20-%20Dr%20Itumeleng%20Kimane.ppt).

38 See s 52 of the Act.

39 Sections 51, 54 and (for intercountry adoption) 61.

40 Obviously this formulation is aimed more at in-country than intercountry adoption.

years, subject to supervision of the child by social workers in the country where the adoptive parents reside.[41] It can only then be made final, according to the Act.

The Act requires that a child be informed, under the guidance of a social worker, of the fact that he or she is adopted (unless it is not in the best interests of the child to have that fact disclosed to him or her).[42] No person other than an adoptive parent may make this disclosure.[43] If the child who is to be adopted has siblings, the child is to be informed of any siblings and helped to maintain a link with them, through visits, letters or other forms of communication.[44] The importance of a child knowing his or her roots is also evident from art 60(3), which requires, where possible, an adopted child to have access 'to photos, letters or any form of artifacts that might help him to understand his roots better'.

Foster care – by relatives or by persons not related to the child – is rather less well defined in the Act as a whole.[45] Although the children's court is empowered to place a child in foster care,[46] and the eligibility criteria for foster parents are set out in the same vein as those of adoptive parents, as well as the Act including a provision requiring assessment for suitability by the Ministry,[47] there is no scheme for the development of a more elaborate foster care system set up by the Act: there are far fewer provisions on foster care than on adoption, for instance, and far fewer than in the foster care chapter of the South African Children's Act 38 of 2005 (seen together with the package of regulations to the South African Act on this topic). This may well militate against the enhancement of foster care as an alternative care option for children orphaned or made vulnerable by HIV/AIDS, and tends to indicate a preference for adoption over foster care as a placement option insofar as adoption receives more elaborate treatment in the law. However, in recent times (2012), the

---

41 In this way the Act gives effect to Art 24(f) of the African Charter on the Rights and Welfare of the Child (1990) which requires signatory states to establish machinery to monitor the well-being of children who have been adopted internationally.

42 Section 60(1). He or she must also be 'of an understanding age'. It is not clear whether the provisions of this section apply also to intercountry adoption but there is nothing to indicate that they do not. See the text at n 41 above.

43 Section 60(2).

44 Section 60(4).

45 The definitions clause defines 'family foster care' as placement of a child by the Department of Social Welfare with family members who are not the child's biological parents. 'Foster parent', in turn, is defined as a person not being a parent of a child, who undertakes the responsibility of providing for the care, accommodation and upbringing of the child, with or without financial reward. This latter definition clearly contemplates persons unrelated to the child as well as relatives. The separate definitions of family foster care and foster parent do not appear to play any material role in the provisions of the Act.

46 Section 37(1)(e).

47 Section 54(1): 'section 53 provides that the foster parent in whose care a child is placed shall have the same rights in respect of the child's care and guardianship as the parent of the child while the child remains in his care.' It is possibly unusual for foster parents to have legal powers in all respects equitable to those of parents or guardians, but maybe this is a practical solution in a country not well served by social work authorities who can step in to fulfil parental and guardianship roles when required (eg for medical reasons).

Ministry has developed policy and guidelines on adoption and foster care, which can assist to develop these forms of alternative care further.

Institutional care is also somewhat neglected in the Act. Whilst there are provisions empowering the designation of establishment of places of safety for the care and protection of children, the detail of the conditions, and requirements, not to mention management and functioning of these are left for Ministerial determination, presumably in guidelines and policy.[48] There is no general chapter or Part dealing with residential care establishments outside of this limited provision. Far more attention is accorded, however, to places of detention or custody for children in conflict with the law, which occupy a further 16 substantive sections in this Part (the sections on places of safety are only three in number).

V CONCLUSIONS

The Lesotho Children's Protection and Welfare Act of 2011 was self-evidently inspired by the need to put in place effective legal mechanisms for the identification and provision of services to alleviate the plight of orphans and vulnerable children in the country. Several concrete provisions highlighted in this chapter bear testimony to the social phenomenon of HIV/Aids and its impact upon children as a motivating factor for the Act as a whole, and for the inclusion of certain specific provisions.

However, two main concerns are that the Act is light on detail on the specifics of alternative care, including a sound framework for intercountry adoption and its processes, as well as foster care and the regulation of a comprehensive alternative care framework to include private facilities (which may or may not seek designation as a place of safety). The linkages between private child care institutions and intercountry adoption have emerged as a source of concern in African countries in recent times, especially where they become 'feeders' for agencies abroad at the expense of potential domestic placements. Concern about the rights and protection of children in alternative care is underscored by the 2009 UN Guidelines for Children in Alternative Care (the adoption of which post-dates the drafting (but not the finalisation) of the Lesotho Act).

Secondly, the Act shies away from comprehensively addressing adolescent sexual health in the HIV context, notably as far as access to contraception and condoms is concerned. This is no fault of the original drafters, it would appear, but provides some evidence of the rather conservative social environment within which the Act was eventually passed into legislation.

However, the fact that the Lesotho National Strategic Plan for Vulnerable Children 2012–2017 affirms the centrality of the Act's judicial measures for

---

48 Section 175(1) and (2) of the Act. Compare Chapter 15 of the South African Act (Child and Youth Care Centres) and the detail contained in the accompanying regulations.

combating vulnerability attests to the enduring value that the provisions have, and the important complementary role that the Act can play in the years to come.

MACEDONIA

FAMILY LAW IN THE NEW CIVIL CODE OF THE REPUBLIC OF MACEDONIA: KEY ISSUES AND NECESSARY REFORMS

*Dejan Mickovik and Angel Ristov**

Résumé

La République de Macédoinerédige actuellement son Code civiletle droit de la familleen sera partieintégrante. Les auteursprésentent une analysedela place du droitde la familledanscette codification. Ils suggèrentqu'il devrait y avoirune réforme dudroit de la famille. Ils formulentdes propositionsd'amendements à lalégislation macédoniennerelative à la réglementationde la cohabitation. Ils préconisent une réglementationdu contrat demariage. Les auteurs proposentl'adoption de laresponsabilité parentaleconjointe après le divorce etinsistent surla nécessité de créer un système d'audition de l'enfant pour recueillir son avis lorsque les parents et les institutions prennent des décisionsrelatives à ses droits et ses intérêts.Ils recommandent une réglementation du statutjuridique et de la protection du logement familial.

I INTRODUCTION

The most significant reform of family law in Macedonia was made in 1992, when the Family Law Act was enacted,[1] which was a 'mini codification' in this area, because the parts of family law – marital law, parental rights, adoption and guardianship – which hitherto had been regulated in separate laws, were united in one legal text. Since then, despite the rapid and dynamic changes in the field of family and family relationships,[2] family law experienced a few

---

* * Dejan Mickovik PhD, Professor at the Faculty of Law 'Iustinianus Primus', University 'Saints Cyril and Methodius', Skopje, Republic of Macedonia. Angel Ristov PhD, Assistant Professor at the Faculty of Law 'Iustinianus Primus', University 'Saints Cyril and Methodius', Skopje, Republic of Macedonia.

1 *Official Gazette of Republic of Macedonia*, n 80/92, 9/96, 38/2004, 33/06, 84/08, 157/08, 67/10, 39/12, 44/12.

2 In the last several decades in all European countries dramatic changes in marital and family relations are happening: the number of divorces is increasing, as well as the number of non-marital couples, children born out of wedlock and single parent families, the number of marriages is decreasing and there is a dramatic fall in the birth rates in European countries. For more on the changes in modern family, see Martine Segalen *Sociologie de la famille*(Armand Colin, Paris, 2004); Mary Daly Changing family life in Europe: significance for state and

changes, regarding the procedure of adoption, regulation of domestic violence and deprivation of parental rights. Significant reform of family law is expected to be completed during the development of the Civil Code of the Republic of Macedonia that will include regulation of family relations as well. The Government of Macedonia in 2010 decided to form a Commission for drafting the Civil Code of the Republic of Macedonia[3] and this Commission to date has prepared the draft versions of Obligations (Book II of the Civil Code)[4] and Succession[5] (Book IV of the Civil Code). The Commission is working on the preparation of Book V of the Civil Code, which will regulate family relations.

This chapter will assess the place of family law in the Civil Code of the Republic of Macedonia, and the authors will propose amendments to family law in the sphere of regulation of cohabitation, divorce, exercise of parental rights, protection of the rights and interests of children and regulation of the status of family home. We believe that these changes in regulation of family relations in Macedonia will be aligned with changes in the family, the most important international documents, and the basic tendencies of regulation of family law in European countries.

II PLACE OF FAMILY LAW IN THE CIVIL CODE OF THE REPUBLIC OF MACEDONIA

During the preparation of the Civil Code of the Republic of Macedonia, there were certain opinions according to which family law should not be an integral part of the civil codification, but that family relations should be regulated by a special law. The idea that family law should not be included in the civil codification is based on the division of civil relations on personal relationships (which should be regulated in a separate family code) and proprietary relationships (which should be regulated in the Civil Code). However, it is not easy to separate personal and proprietary relationships, because they are closely intertwined. In addition, there are other, more important reasons why family law should be an integral part of civil codification. The main aim of codification is to cover a wide field of law and to be the most important source of law in a particular area. Codification must not have gaps and its introduction should reduce the number of sources of law. Moreover, codification should be simple and understandable for every citizen.[6] Thus, the main reason for the inclusion of family law in the Civil Code is to provide

society (2005) 7(3) *European Societies*; Graham Allan, Sheila Hawker and Graham Crow, 'Family Diversity and Change in Britain and Europe' (2001)22(7) *Journal of Family Issues*.

3 *Official Gazete of Republic of Macedonia*, n 4/2011.

4 See the Civil Code of the Republic of Macedonia, Book II, Obligations, Draft version prepared by the Commission for drafting the Civil Code of the Republic of Macedonia, Skopje, July 2013.

5 See the Civil Code of the Republic of Macedonia, Book IV, Succession, Draft version prepared by the Commission for drafting the Civil Code of the Republic of Macedonia, Skopje, July 2013.

6 See more Gunther A Weiss 'The Enchantment of Codification in the Common-Law World' (2000)25 *Yale Journal of International Law* 435.

regulation of all issues important to the citizens, from birth to death, in one legal text, in a comprehensive and systematic way.[7] Furthermore, family law is an integral part of the most significant civil codes in Europe, such as the French and German Civil Codes,[8] and this is the situation in all countries of Western Europe that have civil codifications.[9]

Only in the former socialist countries that were influenced by the legislation of the Soviet Union was family law not an integral part of civil codifications. After the October Revolution of 1917, the reform of family law was a top priority, and it had already started in the same year, even though the country fought a civil war.[10] The main objective of the Soviet authorities was to change the old family model and build a new one, in accordance with the basic principles of Marxism-Leninism, which is why the Soviet Union has built a family law system radically different from systems in Western Europe.[11] One of the main features of Soviet law was the separation of family law from civil law. The main reason for this deviation from the European civil law tradition had an ideological character: Soviet Bolsheviks believed that the family should be distinguished from bourgeois families in Western countries, and that family relations should be based on love, respect and support, not a property interest.[12] Under the influence of Soviet law, this concept of separation of family law from civil codifications was accepted in all other countries of the socialist bloc. In this sense Zbigniew Radvanjski pointed out that Communist doctrine determined that family law should be separated from civil law, and consequently, in the USSR, as in other 'popular democracies', family law was regulated in a special Family Code.[13]

After the dissolution of the Soviet Union, and after the democratic changes in the former socialist countries, significant reforms were made in the sphere of civil law. All former socialist countries that have adopted or are in the process of adopting civil codifications have abandoned the communist ideological

---

7 L Chanturia *Introduction to the Civil Code of Georgia* (Tbilisi, 2001) 2.

8 According to James D Apple and Robert P Deyling, formal and comprehensive codification of civil law norms in the modern period started in France and Germany. In the French Civil Code Family Law was included in Book I and in the German Civil Code Family Law was regulated in Book IV. For more on the history of the process of the codification of civil law in the countries of continental Europe, see J D Apple and Robert P Deyling, *An example of the Civil-Law System* (Federal Judicial Center, Washington DC, 1995).

9 Family Law was an integral part of the Italian Civil Code from 1865, Portuguese Civil Code from 1867, Spanish Civil Code from 1889, Dutch Civil Code from 1838, Austrian Civil Code from 1811, Swiss Civil Code from 1907, Turkish Civil Code from 1926. Family Law was an integral part of the Serbian Civil Code from 1844 (brought under the influence of the Austrian Civil Code), that has for a long time been applied in Macedonia as well.

10 For more on the development and characteristics of the Soviet Family law, see M V Antokolskaia 'Development of Family Law in Western and Eastern Europe: Common Origins, Common Driving Forces, Common Tendencies' (2003) *Journal of Family History*.

11 See at O A Khazova, 'Family Law on Post-Soviet European Territory: A Comparative Overview of Some Recent Trends' (2010) 14(1) *Electronic Journal of Comparative Law* 5.

12 Ibid.

13 Z Radwański *GREEN PAPER, An Optimal Vision of the Civil Code of the Republic of Poland* (Ministry of Justice, Warsaw, 2006) 21.

matrix, returned to the original European legal tradition and all have included family law in their civil codes. For example, the former Soviet republics of Estonia, Lithuania and Latvia have included family law in their civil codes, which were brought about upon their separation from the Soviet Union,[14] and family law was included in the Civil Code of Georgia, passed in 2001.[15] Similarly, Slovakia has abandoned the influence of Soviet law, and the Government of the Slovak Republic in 2009 decided to start a process of drafting of a new Civil Code under which family law will be regulated in Book II of the Civil Code.[16] Hungary follows the example of other former socialist countries, so family law will be included in Hungarian Civil Code.[17] In Poland the Civil Code contains five parts, which are expected to be adopted soon,[18] and that is so in the newest version of the Civil Code of the Czech Republic, and family law is regulated in Book II, as an integral part of civil codification.[19] Due to the fact that family law is an integral part of civil codifications of nearly all European countries, as well as the need to regulate all relations in the sphere of civil law in one legislative text, in a coherent and comprehensive way, the Commission for the preparation of the Civil Code of Macedonia has decided that family law should be included in Book V of the Civil Code.

III CHANGES IN THE REGULATION OF COHABITATION

Cohabitation in Macedonia has been regulated by the Family Law Act since 1992,[20] and this provision, without any changes, is in force today. In many European countries there are provisions that no marital impediments should exist for nonmarital partners, but according to art 13 of Family Law Act, no marital impediments are envisaged for nonmarital partners in Macedonia. As a

---

14 For more on the process of bringing Civil Codes into the countries of Central and Southeast Europe, see P Cserne *Drafting civil codes in Central and Eastern Europe, A case study on the role of legal scholarship in law-making* (Pro Publico Bono Online, *Támop Speciál*, 2011). Also see O A Khazova, above n 11, 1–2.

15 In the Civil Code of Georgia, Family law is regulated in Book IV. See more in L Chanturia, above n 7, 2.

16 See more in M Jurčova, *Re-codification of Slovak Civil Law,* Paper presented at the international conference: Perspectives on European Private Law, 7–8 May 2009 at the Faculty of Law, University of Santiago de Compostela.

17 For more on the Procedure for bringing the Hungarian Civil Code, see P Cserne, above n 14, 12–23.

18 For the arguments in favour of including family law in the Civil Code of Poland, see Z Radwański, above n 13, 21–25.

19 P Cserne, above n 14, 8. For the arguments in favour of including family law in the Civil Code of the Czech Republic see D Elischer, 'The new Czech Civil Code. Principles, perspectives and objectives of actual Czech civil law recodification: On the way to monistic conception of obligation law' (2010) 19(2) *Dereito*. See also Z Kralickova, 'Czech Family Law: The right time for re-codification' in B Atkin (ed) *The International Survey of Family Law 2009 Edition* (Jordan Publishing Limited, 2009) 157.

20 In art 13 of the Family Law Act, cohabitation is defined as: 'The living community of a man and woman, which has not been established according to the provisions of this law (non-marital cohabitation) and has endured at least one year, is equal to the marriage in the right of mutual maintenance and the property acquired during the time of endurance of that cohabitation.'

result of this provision in the Family Law Act, in reality there are cases where a man or a woman can have simultaneously marital and nonmarital partners. Also, there is no prescribed form for proof of the existence and duration of cohabitation, because Macedonian Family Law Act has accepted the concept of unregistered nonmarital cohabitation. The exact moment of the establishment of nonmarital cohabitation is known only to nonmarital partners, which creates problems of proving the existence and the duration of the common life after the dissolution of the nonmarital community. For these reasons, and the fact that the existing legal framework for cohabitation creates numerous problems in practice,[21] certain changes are necessary in the regulation of cohabitation. We have already pointed out the need for changes in the regulation of cohabitation.[22] We believe that the reform of the civil law in Macedonia that began with the drafting of the Civil Code is a good opportunity to amend the current inadequate regulation of cohabitation in the Macedonian legal system. The Macedonian legislature should envisage in the new Civil Code that there should be no marriage impediments between the individual nonmarital cohabitation partners in order for their nonmarital cohabitation to produce legal effects. Moreover, to make it easier to prove its existence, nonmarital partners should be able to register their community with a two-sided statement which could be certified and deposited with a notary. Nonmarital partners who do not want to register their union will be exposed to greater risk and problems of proving the existence and duration of their nonmarital union in the case of termination of the common life. Moreover, bearing in mind that the number of nonmarital unions is constantly increasing, we believe that nonmarital partners who live together for more than 5 years, or more than 3 years if they have common children, should have the right to lawful inheritance, according to the rules applicable to spouses.

IV INTRODUCTION AND REGULATION OF MARITAL AGREEMENTS

The marital contract is one of the most controversial contracts in family law and the law generally. It has many opponents who believe that this agreement does not correspond with the nature of marriage in contemporary societies, which is based on love that is diametrically opposed to any property calculations. On the other side, the marital contract has many supporters, who

---

21 Failure of the Macedonian legislature to envisage the marital impediments for non-marital couples creates serious problems, because it opens the possibility of non-marital union producing legal effects despite the fact that one or both of the nonmarital partners are married or are relatives.

22 See more Dejan Mickovik and Angel Ristov 'The Legal Regulation of the Nonmarital Cohabitation in the Macedonian Family Law' in B Atkin (ed) *International Survey of Family Law 2012 Edition* (Jordan Publishing Ltd, 2012); Dejan Mickovik and Lidija Stojkova, 'Non-marital Cohabitation in Contemporary Societies' *Eurodialogue* No 15, Student's Word, Skopje 1999. Dejan Mickovik 'Legal Regulation of Non-marital Cohabitation' *Lawyer*, Lawyers Association of the Republic of Macedonia, Skopje, 2008. Angel Ristov 'Non-marital Cohabitation and the Status of Non-marital Partners in the Law of Inheritance', *Association Iuridica*, Strumica, 2010.

think that it allows for the realisation of the spouses' free will, which can change the rigid legal framework regulating property relations in marriage. Proponents of the marital contracts believe that this agreement lessens the problems during the divorce, because the spouses do not have to stretch out a long, difficult and uncertain 'war' on the division of the property in the case of a divorce.

Overall, the basic problem of the marital contract, according to its opponents, is that it introduces the principle of interest and desire for profit in the marriage, which is characteristic of market relations, and promotes egoism and selfishness in a relationship which should be based on love, respect, support, and readiness for sacrifice for the partner. In this sense, a prominent New York lawyer who specialised in divorces said: 'You cannot regulate the human heart with contract. You should have confidence in the person you marry, not in the legal document'.[23] Other authors suggest that the basic problem with marital agreements is that, with their conclusion, distrust is expressed towards the marital partner.[24] In addition, a major objection regarding marital agreements is that they 'destroyed' romance in marriage.[25] Some authors believe that the acceptance of the marital contract in the legal system means that much more attention is paid to the interests and welfare of the individual, rather than the welfare of the couple, which ultimately negatively affects the stability and success of the marriage and often leads to divorce.[26] The marriage contract is often an indicator that there is no trust between spouses and that they try to protect their property and financial interests by concluding a marital agreement. According to Servidea the conclusion of a marital agreement is a strong indicator that the spouses are preparing for divorce as early as the time of the celebration of the marriage.[27]

Despite these criticisms of the marital agreement, there are many arguments that it should be accepted and regulated in the legal system and that it has positive effects on spouses and their children. With the ability to conclude a marital agreement spouses can exercise their free will in regulating their relationships during the marriage and in the event of divorce. This contract

---

23 Citation by Allison A Marston 'Planning for Love: The Politics of Prenuptial Agreements' (1997) 49(4) *Stanford Law Review* 889.

24 According to Ralph Underwager and Holida Wakefield, marital contracts disrupt the confidence between spouses, see Ralph Underwager and Holida Wakefield 'Psychological Considerations in Negotiating Premarital Contracts' in *Introduction to Premarital and Marital Contracts: A Lawyer's Guide to Drafting and Negotiating Enforceable Marital and Cohabitation Agreements* (Edward L Winner & Lewis Becker (eds), 1993).

25 According to Mary Rowland, the biggest challenge in creating financial arrangements during the celebration of the marriage is not whether it will be accepted by the courts, but whether money interfering with love does not destroy the romantic relationship: 'Linking Love and Money' *New York Times*, 25 February 1990.

26 In this sense Underwager and Wakefield pointed out that the marital contract glorifies the independence and individual interest. According to them, this disrupts the feeling of partnership and equality which are necessary for successful marriage. See more Ralph Underwager and Holida Wakefield, above n 24, 280.

27 For the arguments in favour of marital contracts, see K Servidea 'Premarital Agreements and Gender Justice'(1994) 6 *Yale Journal of Law & Feminism* 279.

allows them to regulate their property relations differently from the provisions provided by the law. Supporters believe that the marital contract is not an expression of a lack of confidence between the spouses, but that it is an expression of genuine sincerity, which is the basis for a successful marriage, as well as confirmation that the spouses have no hidden intentions in marriage. According to some authors the fact that spouses discuss the signing of a marital contract is 'a reflection of the stability of the relationship and the maturity of the spouses'.[28] One of the strongest arguments in favour of the marital agreement is that it protects spouses in divorce, because it deals with all property issues and prevents lengthy, expensive and traumatic procedures for settlement of property relations after divorce.

The marital contract is not regulated in the Family Law Act of the Republic of Macedonia, unlike many European countries, such as France, Germany, Switzerland, and several former socialist countries (Croatia,[29] Serbia,[30] Russia,[31] Bulgaria,[32] Montenegro, Republic of Srpska, and Hungary)[33] where the spouses are allowed to choose or create a regime of marital property. There are authors who think that any marital property regime is not always suitable and adequate to meet the needs of each couple. Different couples have not only different needs and desires, but their requirements in terms of property relationships may change during marriage. It is very important to allow the spouses, according to their specific needs and interests, to regulate their property relations themselves.[34] We believe that the marital agreement should be introduced in the Civil Code of the Republic of Macedonia.[35] This will allow the spouses to be able in front of a notary to regulate their mutual rights and

---

28 See Irena Majstorovic *Marital agreement – Novelty in Croatian family law* (Zagreb, 2005) 225.

29 For the Croatian law, see M Alinčić, D Hrabar, D Jakovac-Lozić and A Korać-Graovac, *Family Law (*Narodne Novine, Zagreb, 2007) 514–518.

30 For marital contracts in Serbian law, see Slobodan Panov, *Family Law* (Faculty of Law, University of Belgrade, Belgrade, 2010) 356–368; Gordana Kovacek-Stanic, *Family Law* (Faculty of Law Novi Sad, Novi Sad, 2007) 125–129; Marija Draškić *Family Law and Child's Law* (JP Službeni glasnik, Belgrade, 2009) 408–412; Milan Počuča *Family Law* (Univerzitet Privredna Akademija, Novi Sad, 2010) 324–326.

31 For the changes in Russian law, see A M Нечаева, Семейное право (Юрайт, Москва, 2011) 77–78.

32 According to E Матеева: 'Introduction of the marital agreement may be defined as the heart of the legislative reform in the field of matrimonial property relations in the new Family Law Act'. E Матеева, Семейно право на Република България (ВСУ „Черноризец Храбър', София, 2010) 164. See more on the marital contract: Ц Цанкова, М Марков, А Станева, В. Тодорова, Коментар на новия Семеен Кодекс (ИК „Труд и право', София, 2009) 105–133; М Марков, Семейно и наследствено право (Сиби, София, 2009) 58–63.

33 For marital contracts in comparative law, see Gordana Kovacek-Stanic, *Uporedno porodično pravo* (University of Novi Sad, Novi Sad, 2002) 62–72.

34 See Mary Ann Glendon *The Transformation of Family Law* (University of Chicago Press, Chicago and London, 1999) 135–136.

35 For the arguments in favour of introducing the marital contract in Republic of Macedonia, see Dejan Micković and Angel Ristov, 'Marital Contracts in Macedonian and Comparative Law', *Legal Life* (Association of Lawyers of Serbia, Belgrade, 2012), Angel Ristov 'Do We Need the Marital Contract in Macedonia's Family Legislation', *Notarius*, Notary Chamber of the Republic of Macedonia, Skopje 31–45.

obligations in relation to title to property, with which the partners independently will regulate property relations for the duration of their union and in the case of its termination.

V REPLACEMENT OF THE TERM 'PARENTAL RIGHTS' WITH 'PARENTAL RESPONSIBILITIES'

In the last few decades in all European countries significant changes have occurred in the content of parental rights, changes that have put in the foreground the obligations and responsibilities of parents, as well as the need for greater respect for the interests and autonomy of the will of the child. These changes are closely associated with the adoption of the UN Convention on the Rights of the Child in 1989. This is the most important international document for children's rights that has been adopted and ratified by the vast majority of member states of the United Nations. This Convention uses the concept of parental responsibility, and the children in the Convention are treated as subjects of rights, rather than as objects whose protection is guaranteed by the parents and the state. The new concept of the rights and responsibilities of parents, based on their obligations to the child, and which provides rights to the parents only if they are aimed at caring for the upbringing, education and protection of the child, led to changing the term used for labelling of parental rights and responsibilities. In many international documents, as well as in several European countries, instead of 'parental rights', a term used in the Family Law Act of the Republic of Macedonia,[36] the term 'parental responsibility' is used more often.[37] The term 'parental responsibility' better signifies the essence of the relationship between parents and children. In contemporary societies parents have primarily obligations and responsibilities towards their children, and the rights that are prescribed by law for the parents are envisaged only to allow them to fulfil their obligations towards their children. Several of the most important international documents concerning the rights of children in recent decades have used the term 'parental responsibility'.[38] This term is gradually accepted in many European jurisdictions, suggesting a substantial change in the conception of the rights and

---

36 Parental rights in the Family Law Act of the Republic of Macedonia are regulated in Part 3, art 44-95.

37 The term 'parental responsibility' is used in the revised Brussels II Regulation, in the Council's of Europe Recommendation No R (84) 4 on 'Parental Responsibilities' and in the White Paper on Principles Concerning the Establishment and Legal Consequences of Parentage (2002) CJ-FA(2001) 16 Rev.

38 In art 18, para 1 of the UN Convention on child's rights it is determined that the countries will make every effort to accept the principle that both parents have mutual responsibility for the child's development. The term 'parental responsibility' is used in the Hague Convention for the protection of children and cooperation in the field of international adoption from 1993, and in the European Convention on the exercise of the rights of the child from 1996. This concept is accepted in Recommendation 1121 of the Parliamentary Assembly of the Council of Europe. For more on the acceptance of the term 'parental responsibility' see S Gratalou *L'enfant et sa famille dans les norms européenes* (LGDJ, Paris, 1998) 315.

obligations of parents towards their children.[39] We believe that the Civil Code of the Republic of Macedonia, in Book 5, which will regulate family relationships, should abandon the term 'parental rights' which is used in the current Family Law Act and accept the term 'parental responsibilities'. By accepting the term 'parental responsibilities' Macedonian legislation will be conformed to the most important international documents and the general trend in European legislation. This change has not only terminological meaning, but it expresses more appropriately the new ideas and ideology in the exercise of parental responsibilities, which are primarily based on the obligations of parents towards their children.

VI PREDICTING THE POSSIBILITY FOR CHILDREN TO EXPRESS THEIR OPINION IN ALL PROCEEDINGS CONCERNING THEIR RIGHTS AND INTERESTS

In the context of the exercise of parental responsibilities, it is important to take account of the child's autonomy and the influence of the child's will and wishes, especially if, given the age and maturity, the child is capable of forming an opinion on relevant issues concerning rights and interests. Connected with this, of great importance is the question of the possibility for the child to be heard in procedures before the state authorities who decide on specified issues relating to the rights and interests of the child. These are essential questions, because only if parents and state agencies really take account of the views, opinions and wishes of the child, can we speak of a real application of the UN Convention on the Rights of the Child, which considers the child as a subject of rights, rather than as a passive object of care.[40] This concept is accepted in the most important European convention in this area, the European Convention on the exercise of rights of the child.[41]

---

39 In France the term 'parental power' was used until 1970 because of the dominant role of the father in caring for the child. In 1970, this term was replaced by 'parental authority'. After the adoption of the UN Convention on the rights of the child, France adopted the term 'parental responsibility' in 1993. The State Council of France stated that the replacement of the term 'parental authority' with 'parental responsibility' is justified by the need to take into account the evolution of the parental role in French society. See more in Huet–Weiller, Ganghofer, R (ed) *Le droit de la famille en Europe, Son évolution de l'antiquité à nos jours* (Presses Universitaires de Strasbourg, Strasbourg, 1992). In England, the term 'parental responsibility' is used in Children Act 1989. According to Cretney, words like 'rights' and 'authority' have unpleasant connotations and therefore he considers that the responsibilities of parents should be described as 'responsibility' and 'commitment'. See SM Cretney, *Family Law* (Sweet & Maxwell, London, 1997) 168. The term 'parental responsibility' is used in Belgium (see H. De Page, *Traité élémentaire de droit civil belge, T. II (Les Personnes)*, Vol. 2 (by J.-P. Masson) (Brussels: Bruylant, 1990) 947. The term 'parental responsibility' is used in the Norwegian Children Act 1981, and in Portugal, in Law 61/2008. See more in Nigel Lowe *A Report for the attention of the Committee of Experts on Family Law*, CJ-FA (2008) 5, 13.

40 In art 12, para 1 of the UN Convention on the Rights of the Child it is determined that states parties shall assure to the children a right to their own opinion, right of free expression of opinions in all matters affecting the child, giving due weight to the opinion of the child in accordance with the age and maturity of the child.

41 In Art 3 of the European Convention on the exercise of the rights of the child from 1996 it is

Much European legislation explicitly stipulates the obligation of parents, in the exercise of parental responsibilities, to take into account the opinions and views of the child. The Italian Civil Code provides that parents have the right and obligation to support, educate and raise their children, taking into account their abilities, natural inclinations and aspirations.[42] Courts in Italy take account of the wishes and autonomy of minors. The court in Bologna in 1973 ruled that the minor may leave the parental home in order to maintain the relationship that the parents tried to forbid.[43] The child's right to autonomy is provided in case-law in other European countries, and the child's right to make decisions for themselves and their rights and interests are accepted in the particularly important and influential case *Gillick v West Norfolk and Wisbech Area Health Authority* in the UK.[44] Based on the decision in this case, in the English case-law a new concept appeared: the mature minor under 16, which opens numerous dilemmas. Namely, it is unclear how it will be determined whether the minor has sufficient understanding and intelligence to be able to make decisions for themselves and their rights and interests, and whether this could lead to possible danger to the rights of children. According to Cretney, it is a factual issue that should be resolved in each case, depending on the complexity of the issues in question, and the emotional and intellectual maturity of the juvenile.[45]

The child's right to express an opinion that should be taken into account is provided in other European jurisdictions. The Swiss Civil Code stipulates the obligation on the parents, when they make important decisions for the child, to take account of the child's opinion.[46] Moreover, the children in Switzerland, who have reached a certain level of maturity, have the right to independently organise their lives.[47] In the Czech Republic, the legislature has also taken into

---

determined that: 'A child considered by internal law as having sufficient understanding, in the case of proceedings before a judicial authority affecting him or her, shall be granted, and shall be entitled to request, the following rights: a. to receive all relevant information; b. to be consulted and express his or her views; c. to be informed of the possible consequences of compliance with these views and the possible consequences of any decision.'

42 See more in L Lenti *Droit de la famille: Italie, Juris-Classeur de Droit Comparé* (Michèle Klein (ed), Paris, 1997).

43 See more in F Boulanger *Droit civil de la famille, Aspects comparatives et internationaux* (Economica, Paris, 1994) 238.

44 [1986] AC 112 (HL). In this case, the mother of four girls under 16 years disputed the decision of the Department of Health and Social Security, according to which doctors, in exceptional cases, can give advice and prescribe treatment in the field of contraception for girls under 16 years of age, without the consent of parents. Ms Gillick asked the court to revoke this decision, because it violated her rights as a parent. The House of Lords rejected the appeal. In explanation of the judgment, the House of Lords stated: 'The right of parents comes behind children's rights to make their own decisions when they reach the age and intelligence sufficient to form an opinion and decide on areas and issues that require a decision.' See more in MT Meldeurs-Klein *La personne, la famille et le droit, Trois décennies de mutations en occident* (Bruylant, Brussels, LGDJ Paris, 1999) 359.

45 Cretney, above n 39, p 170.

46 See art 144, para 2 of the Swiss Civil Code.

47 See more G Guillod *Droit de la famille: Suisse, Juris – Classeur de Droit Comparé* (Michèle Klein (ed), Paris, 1999).

account the views of the child.[48] The Family Law stipulates that, when a child is capable of forming opinions and of understanding the measures that relate to the child, the child has the right to obtain all necessary information and to speak freely about all decisions of the parents in essential matters affecting the child.[49] In France, the child's right to express their opinion is based on the amendments to the Civil Code of 1993,[50] and the children's right to express their opinion in some countries, such as Poland, is provided in the Constitution.[51]

Macedonia does not provide consistent application of Art 12 of the UN Convention on the Rights of the Child, although the Act on protection of children provides that the opinion of the child should be taken into account when deciding for the child and in relation to the child's rights and interests.[52] However, the Family Law Act, which regulates the most important issues relating to the rights and interests of children, does not contain any general provision that parents and state institutions should take into account the opinion and the wishes of the child when deciding about the child's rights and interests. Certain articles of the Family Law Act, pertaining to the maintenance of personal contact of the child with the parent, when parents do not live together,[53] or adoption,[54] or designation of a guardian,[55] provide for an obligation to take into consideration the wishes of the child. However, for some extremely important situations, such as, for example, the question whether the child should live with the father or the mother after divorce, the Family Law Act does not provide an obligation for the Court and Centre for Social Work to hear the child and to take into consideration the child's wishes and opinions. Because of this, we believe that the Civil Code of the Republic of Macedonia should provide a general obligation for the parents, as well as for all public

---

48 Generally, the child has a right to be heard in any proceedings in which essential matters relating to the child are decided (s 31, para 3 of the Czech Family Code).

49 M Zuklinova, *Droit de la famille: République Tchèque, Juris-Classeur de Droit Comparé* (Michèle Klein (ed), Paris, 1999) 11.

50 According to art 388–1 of the French Civil Code (since the Act of No 93–22 of 8 January 1993) the minor child can be heard before the court or before the person appointed by the court, in any proceedings related to the child.

51 Article 72, s 3 of the Polish Constitution provides a rule, according to which, when assessing a child's rights, the public authorities and persons responsible for the child should hear the child and, to the extent possible, take the child's opinion into consideration.

52 In art 3 b from the Act on the Protection of Children it is determined that the state has a duty to ensure the right of the child to express their views on all matters that concern them and that the views of children should be given due weight in accordance with their age and maturity.

53 In art 79, para 2 of the Family Law Act it is prescribed that the Centre for Social Work will inform the child and take into account the child's views and opinions depending on the age and level of development of the child, when it is deciding about maintaining personal relations of the child with the parent.

54 Article 103, para 1 of the Family Law Act prescribes that the adoptee who is older than 12 years should give consent to the adoption.

55 In art 135, para 4 of the Family Law Act it is determined that, in deciding about the guardian, the Centre for Social Work should take into account the wishes of the person under guardianship.

authorities, when making decisions for the child, to have an obligation to hear the child, and to take child's views into consideration, according to the age and the maturity of the child.[56]

VII PREDICTING SPECIFIC LEGAL PROTECTION OF THE FAMILY HOME

Under the family law of the Republic of Macedonia there are no provisions for separate legal status and protection of the family home. At the same time, it is undisputed that the family home is a necessity without which we cannot imagine the existence of the family and the exercise of its main functions. It is a central hub that connects spouses, parents and children in the exercise of family rights and duties.[57] Despite these features, the family home, for a long period of time, has not enjoyed special legal protection in family law in European countries.[58] It became the object of interest of legal theory and modern reform legislation in the last several decades, and has acquired special legal protection. In modern legislation the family home is regulated by special legal rules in a way that limits ownership rights in order to protect the interests of the children. The question of the specific status of the family home is becoming important in situations where a spouse to whom the children are entrusted after divorce has not been provided with a house or an apartment. Therefore, selling the family home after divorce and moving the children into new environment is very common, which has a negative influence on the children's development.[59] Given this, legislators are faced with the dilemma of how to establish a balance between the interests of spouses and children and the interests of creditors in respect of the family home.[60]

The most important argument in favour of predicting specific legal protection for the family home is the interests of the children to have a stable environment.[61] In most cases of divorce, children who are entrusted to the

---

[56] For the opportunity to take into account the position of the child in determining questions relating to the child, see Bo Borce Davitkovski, Gordana Buzarovska, Gordan Kalajdziev and Dejan Mickovik *Comparative Review of the Legislation in the Republic of Macedonia and the Convention on the Rights of the Child* (UNICEF, Ministry of Justice, Skopje, 2010) 104–112.

[57] See more in Angel Ristov 'The Legal Status of the Marital Home in the Macedonian and Comparative Law' (2012) *Iustinianus Primus Law Review*, Skopje.

[58] See P Petot, *Histoire du Droit Privé Français, La Famille* (Editions Loysel, Paris, 1992); J Bart, *Histoire du droit privé* (Montchrestien, Paris, 1998).

[59] In theory there are more reasons and arguments for predicting specific legal protection of the family home. See more in T Altobelli 'The Family Home in Australian Law', *Australian Institute of Family Studies Conference*, University of Wollongong; Kovaks 'Matrimonial Property Law Reform in Australia: The "Home and Chattels" Expedient. Studies in the Art of Compromise' (1978–1980) *University of Tasmania Law Review* p 227; P Wessner, 'Le divorce des époux et l'attribution judiciare à l'un d'eux de droits et obligationas résultant du bail portant sur le logement de la famille', 11 e Séminaire sur le droit du bail (Neuchâtel, 2000) 3; Withnall, 'Negligence and the House that Jack Built' (1990) 7(2) *Otago Law Review* 189.

[60] T Altobelli, above n 59, 12.

[61] See more on the measures for protecting the child: S Bubić and N Traljić, *Parental and Guardianship Rights* (Faculty of Law in Saraevo, Saraevo 2007) 193–218.

custody and education of one spouse, and it is usually the mother, are forced to move out of the family home. Changing the home and the environment in which the children lived is a very emotional experience that negatively affects their development.[62] Because of this, the treatment of the family home is increasingly becoming a concern for the courts and the legislators, who must take account of the principle of the best interests of the child after divorce. These interests in practice are accomplished by the child's remaining living in the family home, close to their friends and their school.[63] An argument for predicting the special protection of the family home is a common trend of non-payment of alimony by the spouse, which is present in almost all societies, including the Macedonian,[64] and the fact that the special regime of the family home allows greater flexibility for judges, when deciding the child's fate. This confirms the rich case-law in states where it is left to the discretion of the courts.

Because of all this we believe that there is a need to provide specific legal protection for the family home in the Civil Code of the Republic of Macedonia. This protection would have effect during the marriage, as well as in the event of divorce. During the marriage, it is necessary to provide a solution under which the disposition of the family home is limited, and subject to the approval of the other spouse, even though the family home is the exclusive property of one of the spouses. In the event of divorce, the legislature could envisage provisions in the Civil Code whereby the court can make a decision regarding the family home, based on the interests of the children, the legal regime of the family home, as well as the income and the needs of the spouses. These solutions would significantly improve the situation of the children, taking into account the principles contained in the UN Convention on the Rights of the Child that decisions should be made in the best interest of children.[65]

In addition to these changes in the family law in Macedonia, we propose that the Civil Code should accept the concept of joint execution of parental responsibilities after divorce,[66] and to introduce the possibility for a notary public, not the court, to dissolve the marriage by mutual consent, when partners have no children. Also, we propose that in the case of a divorce by mutual consent, there should be an obligatory requirement for the partners, other than agreement about the guardianship of the children, to agree on

---

62 According to statistics from 1996 in Australia almost 19% of families (467,200) consisted of one parent and child. The family home was sold in 40% of the cases.

63 See more in M F Davis 'The marital home: equal or equitable distribution?' (1983) 50(3) *University of Chicago Law Review* 1089–1090.

64 M F Davis, above n 63, 1089–1090.

65 In art 3, para 1 of the UN Convention on the rights of the Child it is provided that 'In all actions concerning children, whether undertaken by public or private social welfare institutions, courts of law, administrative authorities or legislative bodies, the best interest of the child should be a primary consideration.'

66 In the Republic of Macedonia there are no precise legal provisions that parents continue to conduct joint parental rights after divorce. See more Dejan Mickovik and Angel Ristov 'The Exercise of Parental Rights After Divorce in Macedonian Family Law' in B Atkin (ed) *International Survey of Family Law 2013 Edition* (Jordan Publishing Limited, 2013) 251–265.

alimony and division of joint property. Moreover, it is necessary to simplify the procedure for adoption, which is now very complicated and lengthy, and to provide for payment to a guardian, making the guardian more efficient and more accountable in performing custody functions. We propose creation of a special law on domestic violence, and to allocate all the provisions for domestic violence, which are now included in Family Law and Criminal Law, to this separate law on domestic violence. We believe that these changes to family law in Macedonia, which would be included as part of the Civil Code, would be in accordance with international standards and with the general trends in the legal regulation of family relations in European countries, and that these changes will provide greater protection of the rights and interests of all family members, especially children.

MOZAMBIQUE

THE RIGHT TO ALTERNATIVE CARE FOR CHILDREN DEPRIVED OF A FAMILY ENVIRONMENT: OVERVIEW OF INTERNATIONAL NORMS AND THE LEGISLATIVE FRAMEWORK OF MOZAMBIQUE

Usang Maria Assim and Aquinaldo Mandlate[*]

Résumé

Ce texte fait état des obligations internationales bien établies en ce qui a trait au placement des enfants en dehors de leur famille lorsque celle-ci fait défaut. Au Mozambique, la Loi sur les enfants et le Code de la famille font partie des initiatives prises par le pays en vue d'intégrer les normes internationales en droit interne. Cette intégration est une bonne chose mais il reste des défis à relever. Ainsi, on attend toujours la réglementation qui doit faciliter la mise en œuvre de ces législations. Il est également nécessaire d'encadrer l'adoption internationale et d'énoncer clairement que la prise en charge d'enfants au sein de la famille élargie fait partie des solutions possibles, tout en continuant à accepter que des enfants soient placés de manière informelle dans la parenté.

I INTRODUCTION

Mozambique is a relatively small country in Southern Africa. According to a World Bank report (2012), it has a population of around 25 million people. Children make up more than half of the population.[1] Many socio-economic and political challenges affect the lives of children.[2] For instance, the HIV and AIDS pandemic affecting many Southern African countries continue to claim

* Usang Maria Assim is a post-doctoral research fellow at the Children's Rights Project, Community Law Centre, University of the Western Cape (UWC), LLD (UWC), LLM (Pretoria), email at usassim@gmail.com and Aquinaldo Mandlate is at the Children's Rights Project, Community Law Centre, University of the Western Cape (UWC), LLD (UWC), LLM (Pretoria), *Licenciatura em Direito* (Mozambique), email at aquinaldo101@gmail.com.

1 See Report of the Special Rapporteur on extreme poverty and human rights – Mission to Mozambique (A/HRC/26/28/Add.1), 3 June 2014, para 31, available at www.ohchr.org/EN/Countries/AfricaRegion/Pages/MZIndex.aspx (accessed 16 June 2014).

2 See generally Aquinaldo Mandlate (2012) 'Assessing the Implementation of the Convention on

the lives of many people in the region. Mozambique is no exception as the country has high numbers of people perishing due to deaths caused by HIV and AIDS. In situations like this, many children are orphaned and sometimes forced into child labour to obtain basic needs for their survival.[3] There are many other factors impacting negatively on the lives of children in Mozambique.[4] A collection of these factors exacerbate their poor living conditions by depriving them of basic needs such as educational rights and the essentials of living within the confines of a family environment (which are essential for their survival and development).[5]

This chapter looks at the protection of the right to alternative care for children deprived of their family environment. Mainly, the chapter discusses the Mozambican normative framework, but also takes into account the country's commitments under international human rights norms relevant to the subject. The international norms concerned are mainly the United Nations Convention on the Rights of the Child (CRC) and the African Charter on the Rights and Welfare of the Child (ACRWC), which Mozambique has ratified. These instruments place stringent obligations on state parties to adopt additional measures of protection and assistance for children deprived of their original family environment.[6] Reference is also made to the United Nations Guidelines on Alternative Care for Children (UN Guidelines, 2009), which expand on the provisions of the CRC and the ACRWC.

First, the chapter provides an overview of the standards contained in the international law instruments mentioned above, insofar as they speak to the right to alternative care for children deprived of their family environment. Thereafter, it assesses the legislative measures taken by Mozambique to give effect to the provisions of these instruments on the right to alternative care for children deprived of a family environment in the country's own jurisdiction. The conclusion sums up the paper and provides some recommendations on how to improve the situation of these children in Mozambique.

II INTERNATIONAL AND REGIONAL FRAMEWORK GOVERNING THE RIGHT TO ALTERNATIVE CARE

There are many international (global and regional) law instruments speaking to the importance of a family environment, and the need for alternative care when that environment is absent or at risk. Examples of these include the Hague Convention on Protection of Children and Cooperation in Respect of Intercountry Adoption (Hague Adoption Convention, 1993) the CRC, the

---

the Rights of the Child in Lusophone Africa (Angola and Mozambique)', unpublished LLD thesis submitted to the Law Faculty of the University of the Western Cape, 17–44.

3 Ibid 39–41.

4 See Mandlate (2012) above n 2, for more details on the factors impacting negatively on the lives of Mozambican children, at 17–44.

5 See para 4 of the UN Guidelines for the Alternative Care of Children, 2009.

6 See generally, Art 20 of the CRC and Art 25 of the ACRWC.

ACRWC, and the UN Guidelines for the Alternative Care of Children (UN Guidelines). However, the CRC and the ACRWC are key to the discussions in this chapter as they have both been ratified by Mozambique. The UN Guidelines, which are non-binding, will also be discussed. This is because they serve as a reference text for the governments of states parties, policy makers and all other stakeholders involved in realising alternative care for children, by providing detailed information for the practical implementation of the right to alternative care.[7] Their importance lies in the fact that they build on the provisions of the CRC and ACRWC, and provide more detailed standards and principles for filling the implementation gaps in the CRC and the ACRWC (see further discussions in Section II(b) below).

The above instruments attach significant value to the importance of children growing up within the confines of a family environment, which is generally considered to be crucial for the full and harmonious development of a child until adulthood.[8] Thus, the drafters conceived standards that place significant weight on the need for additional measures of protection and assistance for children deprived of their original family.[9] The rationale behind this is the fact that children deprived of a family environment are at greater risk of having all their other rights (such as education and health) violated.[10] Put in simple terms, this means that the family is potentially capable of protecting children from facing various abuses which amount to violations of their rights. Consequently, to understand fully the notion of alternative care for children deprived of a family environment, first of all, it is imperative to understand the notion of family environment and what it means to be deprived of such environment. To this end, the next section unpacks the concept of 'family environment' and 'what deprivation of a family environment' entails. This will be followed by an analysis of the legal framework on the right to alternative care, and examination of the forms of alternative care provided in the relevant international and regional instruments.

(a) The family environment in international law and deprivation of a family environment

International law does not provide any specific definition for the concept of 'family environment', and the same applies to 'family' and 'family life', generally. This is as a result of the variations in the understanding and practice of 'family', as well as its implications for child upbringing around the world.[11] In the same vein, international law does not accord to anyone the 'right to a family'. The term 'family environment' is however a new concept introduced by

---

7 See para 1 of the UN Guidelines.

8 See para 4 of the Preamble to the ACRWC; para 6 of the Preamble to the CRC; para 1 of the Preamble to the Hague Adoption Convention, and para 3 of the UN Guidelines.

9 See generally, Art 20 of the CRC and Art 25 of the ACRWC.

10 See para 4 of the UN Guidelines.

11 CRC Committee General Comment No 7, 'Implementing child rights in early childhood' 2005, para 19.

the CRC and adopted by the ACRWC; it has been suggested that all three terms (family, family life, family environment) are overlapping concepts that are generally used interchangeably.[12]

The word 'family' is derived from the Latin word '*familia*' which simply means household.[13] The family environment is distinguished from other social groups by the underlying assumption of it being 'a close physical, economic and emotional unit within which children are planned, born and reared'.[14] It is a non-institutional living arrangement to the extent that it is not established on the basis of any state initiative and is ordinarily not subject to state supervision or intervention.[15] Thus, the importance of a family environment is not premised on the mere existence of a physical structure but on the psychological elements it ideally represents and provides.[16]

While there is no 'right to a family' under international law,[17] the near complete dependence of children on adult care, particularly in their early years, necessitates 'social (and legal) patterns that protect, nurture and teach children'.[18] Customarily, the family is regarded as the basic unit of society.[19] It is uniquely a place of intimate relations as well as a social institution upon which society rests.[20] This implies that the family plays a fundamental role in shaping the society as a whole.[21] In effect, the absence of a family environment not only destroys childhood but also has damaging impacts on both the future of the child and, ultimately, the society at large.[22] As the building block of society, the importance of the family is premised on its stability or continuity in a 'non-exploitative caring' relationship among family members.[23]

---

12 G Van Bueren *The International Law on the Rights of the Child* (Kluwer, Amsterdam, 1998) 68–69.

13 D Hodgson 'The International Legal Recognition and Protection of the Family' (1994) 8 Australian Journal of Family Law 219.

14 A Adepoju (ed) *Family, Population and Development in Africa* (Zed Books, London and New Jersey, 1997) 28; E Terpstra 'Children on the Move: A Perspective from the Netherlands' in J Doek et al *Children on the Move: How to Implement their Right to Family Life* (Martinus Nijhoff, The Hague, 1996) 22.

15 CMI Moolhuysen-Fase 'Opening Speech' in J Doek et al (1996), above n 14, 3.

16 E Bartholet *Nobody's Children: Abuse, Neglect, Foster Drift, and the Adoption Alternative* (Beacon Press, Boston, 1999) 60.

17 See J Sloth-Nielsen, BD Mezmur and B van Heerden 'Inter-country Adoption from a Southern and Eastern African Perspective' (2010) International Family Law 86–96.

18 J Garbarino et al *Children and Families in the Social Environment* (Aldine, New York, 1992) 74.

19 See among others, Arts 12 and 16(1) UDHR; Preamble and Art 23 ICCPR; Art 10 ICESCR; Art 18 ACHPR; Art 16 of the European Social Charter and Art vi of the American Declaration of the Rights and Duties of Man, 1948.

20 Garbarino *et al*, above n 18, 71.

21 Cicero Offices, *Essays and Letters,* translated by T Cockman (1690), London (1909) I, xvii cited in D Hodgson *Individual Duty Within a Human Rights Discourse* (Ashgate, Aldershot, 2003) 147.

22 Bartholet (1999), above n 16, 60.

23 S Goonesekere 'Human Rights as a Foundation for Family Law Reform' (2000) 8 The International Journal of Children's Rights 84.

International law therefore guarantees additional levels of protection and assistance to children deprived of their family environment due to their increased vulnerability caused by the loss of a family environment.[24] The family environment plays a vital role in the realisation of a child's right to life, survival and development.[25] The significance of this right goes beyond the inherent right to life to an all-embracing approach determined by the quality of life available to the child, physically, psychologically, socially and otherwise.[26] By making room for emotional and other forms of contact (tangible and intangible), the family environment enables children to acquire the stability and security they need for proper development.[27]

From the foregoing, it is quite clear that children deprived of their family environment indeed require special assistance and protection. The concept of 'deprivation' within the framework of the right to alternative care is contextual in that the focus is on the loss of the intimate attachments or relationships, as well as the psychological and emotional elements, and not just the physical loss of parents or caregivers.[28] The term 'deprived' therefore draws attention to a child's loss of the general or ideal components of a family environment such as a warm relationship based on acceptance, the formation of strong bonds over time, and stimulation from infancy to enhance the developmental traits of language and intelligence, among other pertinent aspects.[29] The absence of these crucial elements from or during childhood may result in irreversible consequences in the individual's future as an adult.[30]

In specialised studies, the concept of 'deprivation' is also used to describe the consequences of living in state-run institutions resulting in the absence of affection, personal care and deep emotional relationships, presumably present in a family environment.[31] Thus, deprivation in the context of the right to alternative care does not necessarily indicate 'a deliberate act by a third party', it rather denotes any reason why and situation (justified and lawful or not) where a child is lacking in parental and family care.[32]

---

24 See generally Art 20 of the CRC and Art 25 of the ACRWC, both of which will be analysed subsequently.

25 See Art 6 of the CRC.

26 D Fottrell (ed) *Revisiting Children's Rights: 10 Years of the UN Convention on the Rights of the Child* (Kluwer, The Hague, 2000) 5.

27 See para 5 of the CRC preamble; Art 18(1) of the ACRWC.

28 D Tolfree *Roofs and roots: The Care of Separated Children in the Developing World* (Arena, Aldershot, 1995) 24.

29 Tolfree (1995), above n 28, 19.

30 P Parkinson 'Child Protection, Permanency Planning and Children's Right to Family Life' (2003) 17 International Journal of Law, Policy and the Family 154.

31 SOS Kinderdorf International 'A Child's "Right to a Family": Family-Based Child Care, the Vision and Experience of SOS Children's Villages, Position Paper' 2008 edn, 18.

32 N Cantwell and A Holzscheiter 'Article 20: Children Deprived of their Family Environment' in A Alen et al *Commentary on the United Nations Convention on the Rights of the Child* (Brill, Leiden, 2008) 38; CRC Committee, General Comment No 3, 'HIV/AIDS and the Rights of the Child' (2003).

(b) Analysis of the legal framework: the CRC, the ACRWC and the UN Guidelines

Article 20 of the CRC is the main provision on the right to alternative care for children deprived of their family environment while Art 25 of the ACRWC is the regional equivalent of the same provision. Article 20(1) of the CRC provides that:

> 'A child temporarily or permanently deprived of his or her family environment, or in whose best interests cannot be allowed to remain in that environment, shall be entitled to special protection and assistance provided by the state.'

Similarly, Art 25(1) of the ACRWC provides that:

> 'Any child who is permanently or temporarily deprived of his family environment for any reason shall be entitled to special protection and assistance.'

The scope of the provisions above covers both situations of temporary or permanent deprivation, and refers to categories of children who have either 'lost' or become 'separated' from their families for various reasons.[33] Causes of loss or separation include the death of parents, abandonment or relinquishment by parents, armed conflict, internal displacement, temporary or permanent incapacity of parents (due to imprisonment, illness or disability) and children removed from parental care, in their best interests, by an administrative or judicial decision.[34] 'Children deprived of their family environment' is thus a generic term covering a wide range of children including orphans due to HIV/AIDS and other causes of death or destitution.[35]

Further, in recognition of the different forms of family environments in existence, the CRC and the ACRWC refer to a child deprived of 'his or her' family environment and not of 'a' or 'the' family environment.[36] In addition to this, Art 20 of the CRC makes reference to 'family' and not merely 'parents'. This distinction is in recognition of a broad understanding of the concept of 'family' (or 'family environment') as going beyond the mere existence of parents.[37] This is especially important within the African context and other non-Western cultures where attachments are formed with a wide variety of

---

33 An obvious example of 'loss' would be orphanhood, while there are situations where children may be separated from their existing family environment as a result of factors such as abuse or neglect of the child by the parents . See for instance, Art 9(1) of the CRC and Art 19(1) of the ACRWC.

34 CRC Committee, Day of General Discussion, 'Children without Parental Care', 2005, para 8.

35 UNICEF (Child protection from violence, exploitation, and abuse) 'Children without parental care', available at www.unicef.org/protection/57929_58004.html; CRC Committee General Comment No 6 'Treatment of unaccompanied and separated children outside their country of origin' (2005) paras 7, 8 and 39; Tolfree (1995), above n 28, 38.

36 Cantwell and Holzscheiter (2008), above n 32, 32; Art 20 CRC and Art 25 ACRWC. Note that the ACRWC refers to 'his' in a generic sense as evidenced by the reliance on that pronoun in several of the provisions contained therein.

37 See Art 20(1) of the CRC; R Hodgkin and P Newell *Implementation Handbook for the Convention on the Rights of the Child* (UNICEF, Geneva, 2007) 278.

people who play distinct but active and complementary roles in the upbringing of children.[38] Thus, while 'family' and 'family environment' may be used interchangeably as earlier indicated, the latter expression is significant as it keeps the emphasis on the nature rather than the structure of a family, and on the function rather than the form.

While neither the CRC nor the ACRWC defines 'alternative care', reference to 'family environment' implies that the child's right to alternative care comes into effect upon the loss of or deprivation of not just parental care but more broadly, a family environment (which, in the African context, would include care of the child by members of the extended family).[39] Indeed, the UN Committee on the Rights of the Child (CRC Committee), which is the body that monitors the implementation of the CRC, noted as follows:[40]

> 'The basic institution in society for the survival, protection and development of the child is the family. When considering the family environment the Convention reflects different family structures arising from the various cultural patterns and emerging familial relationships. In this regard the Convention refers to the extended family and the community and applies to situations of nuclear families, separated parents, single parent family, common law family and adoptive family.'

It must however be noted that the more recent UN Guidelines[41] departs from the approach of the CRC and ACRWC in terms of when or how the right to alternative care is activated. The UN Guidelines define the child's family as primarily comprising the child's parent(s), thereby implying that 'a child's right to alternative care springs into effect when he or she is deprived of "parental care"'.[42] Thus, while the phrase 'children deprived of their family environment' can be inferred from the CRC and the ACRWC, the phrase, 'children deprived of parental care' is that which runs through the UN Guidelines.[43] Consequently, the Guidelines define 'children without parental care' as 'all children not in the overnight care of at least one of their parents, for whatever reason and under

---

38 Tolfree (1995), above n 28, 24.

39 Hodgkin and Newell (2007), above n 37, 278.

40 CRC Committee, Day of General Discussion, 'Role of the Family in the Promotion of the Rights of the Child', 1994, para 2.1.

41 The UN Guidelines were approved and welcomed by the UN General Assembly on 20 November 2009, on the occasion of the 20th anniversary of the CRC. The guidelines were developed by a consortium of international non-governmental organisations, 15 states parties, young persons with care experience and the CRC Committee.

42 See para 3 of the UN Guidelines: 'The family being the fundamental group of society and the natural environment for the growth, well-being and protection of children, efforts should primarily be directed to enabling the child to remain in or return to the care of his/her parents, or when appropriate, other close family members.' See also para 4 which provides that children with 'inadequate or no parental care' are at the risk of being denied 'a supportive, protective and caring environment that promotes [their] full potential'.

43 See among others, paras 1, 4, 7, 14, 15, 18, 53, 69 and 70 of the UN Guidelines; para 1 of the UN Guidelines sets out the purpose of the guidelines as follows: 'The present Guidelines are intended to enhance the implementation of the Convention on the Rights of the Child and of relevant provisions of other international instruments regarding the protection and well-being of children who are deprived of parental care or who are at risk of being so.'

whatever circumstances'.[44] This shift is due in part to the structural and socio-economic factors that have impacted on the demography of the traditional family in many parts of the world, particularly in Africa in recent years.[45] The effect of this is that the UN Guidelines expressly locate care by extended family members within the framework of alternative care as further discussions in the next part of this chapter will show.

From the above therefore, the scope of Art 20 of the CRC (and Art 25 ACRWC) covers children who for whatever reason have become deprived of parental (and family) care whether due to the non-availability or inadequacy of such parents, or having been separated from them, and who are not being informally cared for by members of their extended family.[46]

In providing for alternative care, both the CRC and the ACRWC oblige state parties to give 'due regard' to ensuring continuity in the child's upbringing, with reference 'to the child's ethnic, religious, cultural and linguistic background'.[47] 'Continuity in upbringing' does not however mean that alternative care provided should be as exact as the child's original family environment. It rather refers to the importance of continuity in 'childhood care' with due consideration to the elements present in the child's previous background, for example language and religion.[48] The focus is on providing a stable environment to ensure that the child continues to grow and develop harmoniously, and not merely continuity in a particular socio-cultural setting.[49] A rigid interpretation of continuity in upbringing would be incompatible with the flexible nature of the principle in accordance with the best interests of the child.[50] It is submitted, however, that where it is deemed possible and necessary, improvements must be made to improve the living conditions of children.

The ACRWC goes further by obliging states parties to take necessary measures to re-unite children with their parents or original family environment, in cases where their 'deprivation' was as a result of factors such as armed conflicts and natural or man-made disasters.[51] Such phenomena have become quite frequent occurrences on the African continent for a number of years.

While both the CRC and the ACRWC provide the international and regional legal framework for the care and protection of children deprived of a family

---

44 See para 29(a) of the UN Guidelines. This includes children without parental care who are outside their country of habitual residence or who are victims of emergency situations.

45 See UM Assim 'Understanding Kinship Care of Children in Africa: A Family Environment or an Alternative Care Option?' unpublished LLD thesis, University of the Western Cape (2013) 44. See also J Backhouse 'Grandparents Raising Their Grandchildren: Impact of the Transition From a Traditional Grandparent Role to a Grandparent-as-Parent Role', unpublished PhD thesis, Southern Cross University (2009) 1–2.

46 Cantwell and Holzscheiter (2008), above n 32, at 9, 32 and 63.

47 Aee Art 20(3) of the CRC and Art 25(3) of the ACRWC.

48 Cantwell and Holzscheiter (2008), above n 32, at 60.

49 Cantwell and Holzscheiter (2008), above n 32, at 62.

50 Cantwell and Holzscheiter (2008), above n 32, at 61.

51 See Art 25(1)(b) of the ACRWC.

environment, they do not provide detailed guidelines as to the practical application of their provisions on alternative care. In other words, Art 20 of the CRC (and Art 25 of the ACRWC) provides a broad framework for the protection of children deprived of a family environment, but establishes no rules for the implementation of the provisions contained therein. This was the case until 2009 when the UN Guidelines were 'adopted'.[52]

As previously indicated, the purpose of the 2009 UN Guidelines is to enhance the implementation of the CRC and other relevant international instruments by filling implementation gaps with regard to state obligation towards children without parental care and, more broadly, family care.[53] The guidelines are comprehensive in terms of providing a broad range of alternative care measures that can be provided for children who cannot be kept in or returned to care of their family.[54] Thus, a combination of the CRC, the ACRWC and the UN Guidelines provides a comprehensive package of law, policy, and practice standards for the proper implementation of the right to alternative care for affected children.

There are two main principles (or 'pillars') underlying the UN Guidelines regarding alternative care for children. These are namely, the 'necessity principle' and the 'suitability principle'. These principles translate the idea that realising the right to alternative care requires making sure 'that such care is genuinely needed (the "necessity principle"), and that, when alternative care is deemed necessary, the most appropriate alternative for the child concerned be made available (the "suitability principle")'.[55] Through these principles, the UN Guidelines place great emphasis on the need to exhaust all measures to keep children in their original family environment (where there is ordinarily no need for alternative care) without compromising the need to safeguard their best interests while living within that environment.[56] Such measures include the need to prevent family disintegration through state support, measures to ensure that siblings are kept together, and to ensure that children in alternative care are well prepared for adult life.[57] The next section provides an overview of the alternative care options, which can be made available for children deprived of

---

52 The development of the UN Guidelines was a culmination of a process which began in 2005 during the CRC Committee's Day of General Discussion on the theme: 'Children without Parental Care'.

53 See para 1 of the UN Guidelines.

54 See para 2 of the UN Guidelines.

55 See generally, paras 3–7 and 9–10 of the UN Guidelines. See also N Cantwell, J Davidson, S Elsley, N Quinn and I Milligan Moving Forward: Implementing the 'Guidelines for the Alternative Care of Children' (Centre for Excellence for Looked After Children in Scotland, Glasgow, 2012) 22–23. The suitability principle is also described as the 'appropriateness' principle. See Save the Children, 'Guidelines for the Alternative Care of Children: Policy Brief', November 2012, at http://resourcecentre.savethechildren.se/library/guidelines-alternative-care-children-save-children-policy-brief (accessed 28 August 2013).

56 See para 2(a) of the UN Guidelines.

57 See paras 1–2 of the UN Guidelines. See also SOS Children's Villages, 'International Guidelines for the Alternative Care of Children: A United Nations Framework' at www.coe.int/t/dg3/children/childrenincare/SOS-ISS%20Guidelines%20Publication.pdf (accessed 7 August 2013).

their family environment. The discussions are intended to inform the section dealing with the domestic implementation of alternative care measures in the Mozambican normative framework.

(c) Forms of alternative care

It was noted above that states have an obligation to provide alternative care for children deprived of their family environment.[58] While there are no limitations to other suitable solutions, the alternative care options contained in the CRC, the ACRWC and the UN Guidelines that states can provide for these children include adoption, foster care, institutional placement, Islamic kafalah, and kinship care.[59]

The UN Guidelines categorise alternative care measures into two forms, these being formal and informal, depending on whether a specific form of alternative care concerned is privately arranged or arranged at the initiative and by the power of a competent authority of the state.[60] Importantly, where there is proven need for alternative care, the UN Guidelines, like the CRC and the ACRWC, give 'priority to family-like and community-based solutions' including care by extended family members (kinship care).[61] The inclusion of kinship care in the Guidelines as one of the forms of alternative care is compatible with the non-exhaustive nature of the list of alternative care options provided by the CRC and the ACRWC as follows:[62]

> 'Such care shall include, inter alia, foster placement, *kafalah* of Islamic law, adoption or, if necessary, placement in suitable institutions for the care of children.'

And:[63]

> '... shall be provided with alternative family care, which could include, among others, foster placement, or placement in suitable institutions for the care of children.'

In providing for alternative care options,[64] Art 20 of the CRC and Art 25 of the ACRWC give priority to family-based options such as foster care, kafalah and adoption while making institutional care a subsidiary option where necessary, thereby making placements in institutional care facilities a secondary form of

---

58 See Art 20(2) of the CRC and Art 25(2)(a) of the ACRWC, and para 5 of the UN Guidelines.

59 See Art 20(3) of the CRC and Art 25(2)(a) of the ACRWC.

60 See para 29(b)(i)(ii) of the UN Guidelines.

61 See Art 20(3) of the CRC and Art 25(2) of the ACRWC; para 53 of the UN Guidelines; Cantwell et al (2012), above n 55, 22 and 79.

62 See Art 20(3) of the CRC.

63 See Art 25(2)(a) of the ACRWC.

64 The use of 'inter alia' in Art 20(3) of the CRC (and 'among others' in Art 25 of the ACRWC) indicates the non-exhaustive nature of the alternative care options listed in the article(s), leaving states the discretion of making available other options 'in accordance with their national laws [and circumstances]'.See Art 20(2) of the CRC.

alternative care in the hierarchy of care options.[65] Although the idea of ranking or hierarchy is contested in international law (and it is not expressly stated that there is a hierarchy to be followed in deciding on a placement option), the apparent priority given to family-based options serves to underscore the importance of a family environment to the proper development of the child.[66] Arguably, this reaffirms the 'superiority of the family environment, be it the "natural" family environment or an alternative family placement (foster care, adoption), over other types of alternative care'.[67] The implication of this is that between the time when a child 'loses' his or her original family environment and the time of placement in institutional care, other suitable alternatives should be explored, unless it is necessary to place the child in such care in the first place, especially if for a temporary period of time. In other words, institutional placement options should be avoided at all times, unless family-like settings or community-based alternative care solutions for children deprived of a family environment are unavailable or inadequate. The principle of the best interests of the child however remains the primary focus in any circumstance, when deciding on an alternative care placement option for a particular child.[68] The forms of alternative care provided in the CRC, the ACRWC, and the UN Guidelines namely, foster care, kinship care, kafalah, adoption, and institutional placement are discussed below.

Traditionally, *foster care* is defined as the legal placement of children in the care of individuals to whom they are unrelated, biologically.[69] According to the UN Guidelines, this form of alternative care entails the placement of a child in a family environment other than his or her original family environment, subject to the approval and supervision of the state.[70] Historically, foster placement was temporary, pending reunification with the family.[71] However, over time, it evolved into a child care option, which could be employed permanently until the child became an adult or when the placement itself was transformed into an adoption or quasi-adoption.[72] The unique characteristic of foster care in the classic sense is that parental responsibilities for the child are shared between the

---

65 See Art 20(3) of the CRC and Art 25(2)(a) of the ACRWC; Cantwell and Holzscheiter (2008), above n 32, 16. The use of the phrase 'if necessary' before listing or permitting institutional placement is indicative of this.

66 Cantwell and Holzscheiter (2008), above n 32, 19.

67 Cantwell and Holzscheiter (2008), above n 32, 19. The options listed (prior to institutional placement) appear to be ranked in order of permanence, that is, from the least permanent form of alternative care to the most permanent. The order provided in Art 20(3) of the CRC reads as follows: 'foster care', 'kafalah' and 'adoption'; Art 25(2)(a) of the ACRWC reads: 'among others, foster placement, or placement in suitable institutions for the care of children'. In effect, options that are 'family-based' should be considered before considering institutional care.

68 See Art 3(1) of the CRC and Art 4(1) of the ACRWC.

69 J Williamson *A Family is for a Lifetime* (The Synergy Project, Washington, 2004) 12.

70 See para 29(c)(ii) of the UN Guidelines.

71 N Cantwell 'Improving Protection for Children without Parental Care: Developing Internationally-accepted Standards' Paper presented at the European Congress in Gmunden, June 2005, at www.crin.org/bcn/details.asp?id=11692&themeID=1001&topicID=1007 (accessed 28 August 2013) 8.

72 SL Waysdorf 'Families in the AIDS Crisis: Access, Equality, Empowerment and the Role of Kinship Caregivers' (1994) 3 Texas Journal of Women and Law 145.

state and the foster parents, making it a form of social parenting that is subject to some measure of state control and financial support.[73] Although foster care in this formal sense is not commonly practised across many African states, there is a wide variety of forms and models of foster care all over the world.[74] One of the outcomes of the ongoing child law reform process across the African continent is the introduction of foster care as an alternative care option for children deprived of their family environment. To this end, the place of foster care, among other alternative care options in Mozambican law will be discussed later in this chapter.

Unlike foster care *kinship care* is not explicitly listed in the CRC and the ACRWC. However, pursuant to the interpretation of these instruments in the UN Guidelines, and the background earlier provided, it is recognised as an alternative care option in terms of both the CRC and the ACRWC.[75] Kinship care is premised on a broad interpretation of family to include all the people involved in caring for a child through a wide range of social relationships.[76] It is an age-old form of child care built on the extended family network.[77] Unlike foster care, kinship care is a common child care practice in Africa, and is usually practised informally, either spontaneously or at the request of parents, and generally places no legal responsibilities on the caregivers.[78] The UN Guidelines define kinship care as 'family-based care within the child's extended family or with close friends of the family known to the child, whether formal or informal in nature'.[79] The rationale for the express inclusion of kinship care in the UN Guidelines is, among others, the need to respect and promote traditional coping mechanisms for children in need of parental care, particularly in developing countries where the economic, social and cultural dimensions or issues are different.[80] Under the UN Guidelines, kinship care is broadly categorised into two types: formal and informal. Kinship care is formal if the placement was ordered by a competent administrative body or judicial authority, and informal if the placement is based on a private arrangement initiated by the child, his parents (or relatives) or other person without the involvement of any administrative body or judicial authority.[81]

---

73 A Bainham *Children: The Modern Law* (Family Law, Bristol, 1998) 191.

74 See generally V Nott and C Brisbane *Alternatives to Institutional Care for Orphaned and Vulnerable Children: A Model for Transitional Care* (Pietermaritzburg, Built Environment Support Group & Child Advocacy Project, 2008) 1; D Tolfree Facing the Crisis: Supporting Children Through Positive Care Options (Save the Children Fund, London, 2005) iv; L Lee-Jones 'Foster Care and Social Work From the Perspective of the Foster Child' unpublished master's thesis, University of Cape Town (2003) 1.

75 UNICEF and International Social Service 'Improving Protection for Children Without Parental Care, Kinship Care: An Issue for International Standards' (UNICEF and ISS, New York and Geneva, 2004) 2.

76 M Mutua 'The Banjul Charter and the African Cultural Fingerprint: An Evaluation of the Language of Duties' (1995) 35 Virginia Journal of International Law 339.

77 C R O'Donnell, 'The Right to a Family Environment in Pacific Island Cultures' (1995) 3 The International Journal of Children's Rights 90.

78 Cantwell and Holzscheiter (2008), above n 32, 19.

79 See para 29(c)(i) of the UN Guidelines.

80 Cantwell et al (2012), above n 55, 82.

81 See generally paras 29(b)(i)(ii), 56, 7—79 of the UN Guidelines.

Kafalah is an Islamic practice developed under Islamic (Shariah) law. It is predominantly practised in countries where the Islamic Shariah law constitutes a part of or serves wholly as state law.[82] Kafalah refers to 'the commitment to voluntarily take care of the maintenance, of the education and of the protection of a minor, in the same way as a father would do it for his son'.[83] However, this form of alternative care does not permit the altering of the child's original kinship status (in the way an adoption would do).[84] Thus, in kafalah placement, the child is not entitled to take up the family name (as his or her surname) and is not entitled to an automatic right of inheritance from the new family.[85] Usually, a child is placed in a family that is closely related to his or her natural family (as much as possible) without the new parents totally displacing the original parents.[86] The UN Guidelines recognise the need for kafalah to be considered as an alternative care option in appropriate circumstances.[87]

Adoption is yet another alternative placement option, which is listed in the instruments under analysis. This form of placement option entails the creation of a legal and permanent parent-child relationship through a child's acquisition of new family ties which are equivalent to biological ties and extinguish (completely or partially) a pre-existing (biological) parent-child relationship.[88] Broadly speaking, adoptions may be 'full' or 'simple' on the one hand or, 'open' or 'closed' on the other hand.[89] An adoption is full where the pre-existing parent-child relationship is terminated and the child is fully integrated as part of the new family, including the extended family.[90] On the other hand an adoption is simple where the pre-existing parent-child relationship is not

---

82 Examples of these countries include jurisdictions like Bangladesh, Lebanon, Iran, Pakistan and Syria. Kafalah is also practised in the majority of states that make up the Northern part of the African continent, such as Egypt and Libya, and on a more limited basis in other countries in the sub-Saharan Africa region with large Muslim populations (including, for example countries like Mali, Nigeria and Sudan). See generally K Hashemi 'Religious Legal Traditions, Muslim States and the Convention on the Rights of the Child: An Essay on the Relevant UN Documentation' (2007) 29 Human Rights Quarterly 220; AA Sonbol 'Adoption in Islamic Society: A Historical Survey' in EW Fernea *Childhood in the Muslim Middle East* (University of Texas Press, Austin, 1995); D Olowu 'Children's Rights, International Human Rights and the Promise of Islamic Legal Theory' (2008) 12 Law, Democracy and Development 73; R Hodgkin and P Newell *Implementation Handbook for the Convention on the Rights of the Child* (2007), above n 37, 294.

83 See Art 116 of the Family Code of Algeria, quoted in ISS/IRC 'Fact Sheet No 50: Specific case: KAFALAH' (2007) 1 available at www.iss-ssi.org/2009/assets/files/thematic-facts-sheets/eng/50.kafala (accessed 6 August 2013).

84 Hashemi, above n 82, 221.

85 Van Bueren (1995), above n 12, xxi.

86 Better Care Network 'Adoption' (undated) available at www.cin.org/bcn/topic.more.asp?topicID=1014&themeID=1002 (accessed 4 May 2014).

87 See paras 2(a), 123, 152 and 161 of the UN Guidelines.

88 S Vite and H Boechat 'Article 21: Adoption' in Alen et al *A Commentary on the United Nations Convention on the Rights of the Child* (2008), above n 32, 19.

89 Vite and Boechat (2008), above n 88, 16; W Duncan 'Children's Rights, Cultural Diversity and Private International Law' in G Douglas and L Sebba (eds) *Children's Rights and Traditional Values* (Ashgate, Abingdon, 1998) 17; W Duncan 'Intercountry Adoption: Some Issues in Implementing the 1993 Hague Convention on Protection of Children and Cooperation in Respect of Intercountry Adoption' in Doek et al (1996), above n 14, 84.

90 Vite and Boechat (2008), above n 88, 16.

terminated but a new parent-child relationship is established between the child and the adoptive parents, upon whom parental responsibilities for the child are conferred.[91]

Furthermore, adoption placements may be domestic or international/intercountry. While the former takes place in the same country as the one in which the child was born, the latter involves bringing children from one country to live in the country of their adopted parents.[92] In essence, domestic adoptions are governed by domestic law, but the rules governing intercountry adoptions extend to the 1993 Hague Adoption Convention. The Hague Adoption Convention is supplementary to the CRC and the ACRWC in that it brings into practical effect the general provisions on adoption contained in Art 21 of the CRC (and Art 24 of the ACRWC).[93] Broadly, adoption placements represent the most permanent form of alternative care for children without parental care (or a family environment as may be the case). This is due to the fact that once an adoption process is completed it is no longer alternative care strictly speaking because it confers full parental responsibilities on the adoptive parent(s) and is no longer subject to periodic reviews or state supervision.[94]

The last form of alternative placement option for children deprived of a family environment, which is regulated in the instruments under analysis is *institutional care*. This form of placement option refers to 'a group living arrangement for children in which care is provided by remunerated adults who would not be regarded as traditional caregivers within the wider society'.[95] Although the only form of non-family based alternative care option listed in the relevant instruments, there are different types of facilities which fall under the umbrella of institutional or residential care, and many of them are further classified based on specialisation or the categories of children that they cater for (for example, 'orphanages' for orphans). These include 'residential units' like 'group homes', 'family homes', 'family-type orphanages' and 'family-like boarding schools', 'community-based care' centres, 'temporary stay solutions' and, 'placement for day or night' among others.[96] A major goal of the UN Guidelines is ensuring that all such facilities are as family-based as possible in order to encourage intimate relationships and interactions, which are vital for

---

91 Permanent Bureau, Hague Conference on Private International Law *The Implementation and Operation of the 1993 Hague Intercountry Adoption Convention: Guide to Good Practice* (HCCH, The Hague, 2008) 121.

92 Van Bueren (1995), above n 12, 96.

93 Hague Conference on Private International Law *Hague Intercountry Adoption Convention – Outline* (2008); Vite and Boechat (2008), above n 88, 5; G Parra-Aranguren *Explanatory Report on the 1993 Hague Intercountry Adoption Convention* (HCCH, The Hague, 1994) 3.

94 Cantwell and Holzscheiter (2008), above n 32, 52; D Quinton et al *Joining New Families: A Study of Adoption and Fostering in Middle Childhood* (John Wiley, New York, 1998) 6.

95 M Peterson-Badali, M Ruck and J Bone 'Rights Conception of Maltreated Children Living in State Care' (2008) 16 The International Journal of Children's Rights 6.

96 C Phillips *Child-headed Households: A Feasible Way Forward, or an Infringement of Children's Right to Alternative Care?* (Dissertation, Amsterdam, 2011) 134.

child development.[97] Having stated the above, the next section looks at how Mozambique is faring in terms of ensuring domestic protection of children deprived of a family environment in its jurisdiction.

III THE MOZAMBICAN LEGAL FRAMEWORK: AN ANALYSIS

By ratifying the CRC and the ACRWC, Mozambique created opportunities to further children's rights at domestic level. It was stated in the introduction of the chapter that these instruments place obligations upon states parties to take measures to protect children. Relevant to the subject under discussion, states parties are required to take additional measure to protect and assist children, especially when they are deprived of a family environment. It was also stated earlier that this is due to the significance of the family in ensuring full development of the child until adulthood.

In the Mozambican context, the passing of a Family Law Code[98] in 2004 and the enactment of a comprehensive statute (Act No 7/2008 of 9 July 2008)[99] governing children's rights represent significant milestones to domesticate the standards contained in the international and regional norms discussed. The chapter now turns to evaluate the extent to which these domestic laws of Mozambique give effect to the country's obligations under international law norms on the right to alternative care for children. The Family Code and the Children's Act contain the principal standards applicable to children, including the right to alternative care. The following sections provide an overview of the domestic norms contained in these laws highlighting the progress achieved thus far and the gaps that need to be addressed.

(a) The right to alternative care as protected under the Children's Act

The Children's Act of Mozambique was enacted in 2008. It is the principal instrument regulating children's rights in Mozambique. The statute sets out clear rules binding the government, parents and the society at large, to promote the implementation of children's rights.[100] It also sets out basic rules of family law on subject matters that interact with children's rights. Article 1 of the Children's Act states the aim of the law as being to protect the child and to strengthen, promote and protect children's rights as entrenched in the CRC, the ACRWC, and other child-rights instruments. As part of the Mozambican child

---

[97] See para 29(c)(i)–(v) of the UN Guidelines. See also LG Baladon 'A Child's Journey Across International Frontiers: The Asian Experience' in Doek et al (1996), above n 14, 124; Council of Europe 'Children in Institutions: Prevention and Alternative Care' (2005) presentation at the CRC Committee Day of General Discussion (2005).

[98] The Family Law Code was enacted in 2004 (Family Code).

[99] Mozambican Children's Act or Act No 7/2008 of 9 July 2008 ('the Children's Act').

[100] See generally A Mandlate (2012), above n 2.

law reform process therefore, the Children's Act seeks to harmonise all laws concerning children with the standards contained in the CRC and the ACRWC.[101]

To this end, the Act contains key provisions of the CRC and ACRWC that are considered to be the core principles of children's rights,[102] namely, non-discrimination,[103] the best interests of the child,[104] the right to life, survival and development,[105] and child participation.[106] The interpretation and implementation of all children's rights, including the right to alternative care, are said to be hinged on these four interrelated principles.[107] With reference to the best interests of the child principle, for example, it is important to note that the principle does not mean the same thing for every child. This is because the determination of the best form of alternative care for a particular child will depend on the child's particular circumstances. To this end, the principle is re-stated in both Art 20 of the CRC and Art 25 of the ACRWC on alternative care, emphasising the importance of the principle to the situation of children deprived of a family environment.[108] Other basic rights including the right to education, the right to health and the right to a name and nationality are also protected by the Act.[109] All of these rights are important for ensuring the survival and development of the child, and providing life opportunities for children, and more so for children requiring alternative care.

In line with the international standards expressed in the CRC and ACRWC, together with the UN Guidelines, the Children's Act promotes the importance of a family environment in ensuring the proper upbringing of the child. To this end, Art 5 of the Act, which deals with the child's living environment, is termed 'special rights'. Its subsection (1) states that every child has the right to grow surrounded with love, care and understanding. This provision also states that the child shall be brought up in an environment where there is happiness, security and peace. Article 5(2) adds flavour to the discussions as a whole by stating that every child has the right to live in a family where the Mozambican identity, tradition and socio-cultural values are strengthened. This provision highlights the element of continuity in upbringing within the Mozambican socio-cultural context, as earlier discussed.[110] It arguably points to a preference for domestic rather than international forms of alternative care in cases where

---

[101] See Art 1 of Mozambique Children's Act.

[102] J Sloth-Nielsen 'Of Newborns and Nubiles: Some Critical Challenges to Children's Rights in Africa in the Era of HIV/Aids' (2005) 13 The International Journal of Children's Rights 73; Hodgkin and Newell (2002), above n 37, 42.

[103] See Art 2 of the CRC, Art 3 of the ACRWC and Art 6 of the Children's Act.

[104] See Art 3 of the CRC, Art 4 of the ACRWC and Art 9 of the Children's Act.

[105] See Art 6 of the CRC, Art 5 of the ACRWC and Art 11 of the Children's Act.

[106] See Art 12 of the CRC, Art 7 of the ACRWC and Art 5 of the Children's Act.

[107] CRC Committee, General Comment No 1 'The Aims of Education' (2001) paras 6 and 7.

[108] CRC Committee, General Comment No 14 (2013) 'The right of the child to have his or her best interests taken as a primary consideration', para 3.

[109] See Arts 28 (right to education), 12–13 (right to health), and 26(2)(4) (right to a name and nationality) of the Children's Act.

[110] See Section II(b) above.

Mozambican children become deprived of parental care or a family environment. This will be discussed in greater detail later.

Articles 27, 28, 36 and 37 of the Children's Act are the main provisions on alternative care for children deprived of a family environment. The provisions of Art 27 are similar to those in Art 20 of the CRC and Art 25 of the ACRWC. It provides as follows:

> '... a child temporarily or permanently deprived of his or her family environment, or in whose best interests cannot remain integrated in his or her natural family, has the right to alternative protection and special assistance provided by the State within the terms prescribed by law.'

Article 28 of the Act provides further that:[111]

> '[e]very child has a right to be brought up and educated within his or her family and exceptionally, within a foster or adoptive family and he or she has a right to relate with his or her family and community.'

From a reading of the two provisions above, and with particular reference to the word 'exceptionally' in Art 28, it is clear that the aim is to ensure that the provision of alternative care is an absolute necessity after it is certain that the child can no longer be cared for within his or her original family environment. This speaks to the 'necessity principle' of the UN Guidelines as discussed earlier in Section II(b) above.

In reading Art 28 it is clear that there is no mention of kinship care as an alternative solution for children lacking parental care or a family environment. However, it is submitted that, although Art 28 makes no explicit reference to that form of care (or care by extended family members), 'family', as expressed in the provision, encompasses members of the extended family and does not necessarily refer only to biological parents. This explains why even when the child is exceptionally placed in foster care and adoptive families he or she maintains the 'right to relate with his or her *family and community*'.[112]

In addition, farther in the Act, Art 36(1) provides more clearly that 'children lacking parental care must be placed either under a tutor, or an adoptive family, or in foster family defined in the terms of the law'. In this case, the Act expressly refers to a lack of 'parental care', as is the case in the UN Guidelines, before providing for possible alternative care options while including 'tutorship' in the list. Each of these alternative care options will be discussed later in this chapter as they are defined in the Family Code (the next law to be examined in this discussion).

In addition to tutorship, foster care and adoption, Art 37 of the Act provides for institutional care as follows:

---

111 See Art 28(1) of the Children's Act.

112 Emphasis added.

> '[w]hen it is not possible to attend the child in his or her natural family or when no alternative measure has been adopted, provisionally the child shall be attended to at vocational institutions, where the fulfillment of his or her basic needs must be secured.'

From this provision it is quite clear that institutional care was conceived as a secondary measure to be applied strictly temporarily in the event that other primary alternative care options for the affected children as set out in Art 36 are unavailable. This is in accord with the standards of international law as discussed in terms of the CRC and the ACRWC, and as expanded by the UN Guidelines requiring temporary institutional placements when family-like options are unavailable for the children concerned.

Despite the progressive nature of the Children's Act, its implementation is challenged by a lack of regulations.[113] To this date,[114] regulations have not been drawn to provide guidance on how to implement the law. This is in breach of Mozambique's obligation to undertake additional measures for the implementation of all children's rights as regulation would add clarity to the interpretation of the Act.[115] However, some guidance may be found in the Family Code which contains provisions speaking to family matters and includes provisions on alternative care options for children deprived of a family environment. The law can be used to address some of the limitations of the Children's Act. Thus, the next section discusses at the Family Code, generally, and the provisions of the law that are relevant to the subject, specifically.

(b) The right to alternative care in the Mozambican Family Code of 2004

Under the Family Code, family ties are determined mainly by factors such as marriage and lineage. Family ties are also enhanced by factors such as procreation and adoption.[116] The Code defines lineage as the link between two people as a result of one of them descending from the other or the link between two people descending from a common ancestor.[117] This supports the understanding of family to include members of the extended family, which presupposes recognition of kinship care as subsequent discussion will show.

With specific reference to alternative care, the Family Code, like the Children's Act, also provides for tutor placements, adoptions and foster family care as possible alternative care options for children deprived of their family environment. There are different legal implications for children and caregivers in each of the alternative care options provided for in the Code. The differences

---

[113] This view was expressed earlier by Mandlate. His study assesses the implementation of the CRC in Portuguese-speaking countries in Africa. See generally Mandlate (2012), above n 2, 108–176.

[114] The date of writing is reported as end May 2014.

[115] See Art 4 of the CRC and Art 1(1) of the ACRWC.

[116] See Art 6 of the Family Code .

[117] See Art 8 of the Family Code.

derive from the objectives sought to be achieved through each option in providing care for affected children. These are discussed below to highlight their specificities and provide further guidance for the implementation of the provisions of the Children's Act on alternative care.

Under the Family Code, a tutor is a person designated by the parents of a child or someone indicated by the court to provide care for children lacking parental care.[118] Tutorship is a placement option which involves putting the child in the care of persons who are directly related to the child or to any person linked to the child's biological family as determined by the court.[119] In terms of this law, tutorship therefore translates into what the UN Guidelines refer to as kinship care which also speaks to the understanding of the family under the Mozambican Children's Act discussed previously. A tutor is responsible for ensuring the education and well-being of the child.[120] Furthermore, the tutor is tasked with administering the property of the child and with exercising those rights that the child cannot exercise alone.[121] The appointment of tutors depends largely on a judicial order following an application by the (competent) authority while the child remains naturally and legally connected to his or her biological family.[122] The tutor thus exercises measure of parental responsibility over the child, on behalf of the parents or the state, where the appointment is initiated by the court or other competent authority.

However, since the appointment of a tutor is subject to a judicial order, the Family Code falls short of the standards of the UN Guidelines in that it provides no room for kinship care (tutorship) that results from informal arrangements within families. This is problematic given the fact that in the Mozambican context kinship care is a common practice occurring informally. As a result, primary caregivers of children in kinship care are unable to lay claim to measures of assistance from the government in fulfilling their role as caregivers. This challenge needs to be addressed to improve the situation of children in Mozambique.

Furthermore, foster care is provided for as yet another form of alternative care particularly for orphaned and abandoned children (including children of unknown parents).[123] According to the law, foster family care consists of care given to a child by a family that receives and integrates the child into the family and takes responsibility for his or her daily care and well-being. As is the case with tutorship, an order granting foster placement must be obtained from the court before the child is put into a foster family setting. In terms of the law, a child cannot be placed in a foster family unless it is proven that he or she could not be adopted or placed under a tutor.[124] In effect, the preferred option for

---

118 See Art 338 of the Family Code.
119 See Art 338 of the Family Code.
120 See Art 337(2) of the Family Code.
121 See Art 337(2) of the Family Code.
122 See Art 335(1) of the Family Code.
123 See Art 381(1) of the Family Code.
124 See Art 381(2) of the Family Code.

orphaned children, and those who have no one to serve as tutors, is adoption ahead of foster care placement. This approach is derived from the permanent and stable nature of an adoption which eliminates the need for regular renewals of the placement or moving the child from one family to another at regular intervals.[125] Otherwise, such constant movements would not be in the best interests of the child given the need for stability and continuity in upbringing during childhood as already discussed. Under the Family Code therefore, foster care is envisaged to serve as a temporary placement option until a more permanent solution is secured, as is traditionally understood. However, where an adoption or tutorship cannot be secured for the affected children, foster care will be considered even if such a placement will be maintained until the child becomes an adult. The above suggests that in the Mozambican context, the hierarchy of alternative care options shows a preference first for tutorship (akin to kinship care which may offer the closest alternative to the child's original family environment), followed by adoption, and lastly foster placement.

With reference to adoption as an alternative care option, the Family Code provides for it as a placement solution that is expected to bring concrete advantages to the lives of the adopted children.[126] As previously discussed, an adoption is distinguished from other forms of alternative care by the fact of its finality. Essentially, it leads to a complete rupture of the child's previous biological ties and fully integrates the child into a new family.[127] Adoption placements therefore require a judicial decision to that effect before the placement itself is made.[128] While the importance of adoption for children deprived of parental care and the seriousness with which it should be regulated cannot be overstated, many of its peculiar aspects remain unregulated. For instance, the Mozambican laws have no provisions speaking to intercountry adoption, which entails the placement of children with parents from another country different from their own country of origin. It is submitted that the lack of standards dealing with intercountry adoption is a violation of children's rights principles contained in the relevant instruments under discussion. This is because both the CRC and the ACRWC call state parties that recognise the system of adoption (including intercountry adoption) in their countries to ensure that the child concerned enjoys safeguards such as the placement of laws and procedures to protect them.[129] Intercountry adoption is common in Mozambique. Yet there are no laws and procedures regulating the practice and the state is not party to the 1993 Hague Intercountry Adoption Convention.[130] Nowadays, intercountry adoption is a subject of great international concern because of the risks that it presents to many innocent children who may fall victim to trafficking, prostitution, and pornography, among others.

---

[125] This is described as the 'foster care drift' and has been condemned as being detrimental to the proper growth and development of children.

[126] See Art 391(1) of the Family Code.

[127] See Art 400(1) of the Family Code.

[128] See Art 389 of the Family Code.

[129] See Art 21 of the CRC and Art 24 of the ACRWC.

[130] See Mandlate (2012), above n 2, 144 and 155.

Consequently, there is a need to enact laws to regulate intercountry adoptions while protecting children from such abuses and incidents that are increasing annually.[131]

IV CONCLUDING REMARKS

The chapter showed that there are clear international obligations for the realisation of the right to alternative care for children deprived of a family environment. Every state party is required to meet the obligations of the relevant instruments. In the Mozambican context, the Children's Act and the Family Code are part of the country's efforts to domesticate international law standards on alternative care. The fact that these laws incorporate a multiplicity of standards captured in international norms discussed is positive, but still there are challenges needing to be addressed. These include lack of regulations to guide the implementation of the laws, provision for inter-country adoption, and the need to clearly designate kinship care as part of the solutions for children deprived of a family environment (or parental care) while making room for informal kinship placements. Indeed, the fact that the affected children need additional protection and assistance in practical and tangible ways cannot be over emphasised.

[131] See Mandlate (2012), above n 2, 144 and 155.

THE NETHERLANDS

DUTCH CO-MOTHERHOOD IN 2014

*Ian Curry-Sumner and Machteld Vonk**

Résumé

Depuis le 1er avril 2014, il est possible pour les couples de lesbiennes de devenir des parents sans passer par la procédure usuelle de l'adoption. Le certificat de naissance fera alors état d'une mère ainsi que d'une mère qui a donné naissance à l'enfant. Deux nouvelles lois ont été adoptées à ce sujet. Ce chapitre explique les conséquences de ces législations pour les co-mères et pour les enfants et, le cas échéant, pour d'autres groupes de parents. La première partie du texte examine la situation lorsque les deux femmes sont néerlandaises et que l'enfant est né au pays. La deuxième partie aborde les situations qui ont un élément d'extranéité, par exemple lorsque l'enfant est né aux Pays-Bas alors que les deux femmes sont des citoyennes américaines vivant aux Pays-Bas.

I INTRODUCTION

As of 1 April 2014 it is possible for Dutch lesbian couples to become legal parents without the previously required adoption procedure. The birth certificate will show a *mother* and a *mother who has given birth to the child.* How the woman who has *not* given birth to the child will become a legal mother will depend on two questions: (1) is she married to or in a registered partnership with the birth mother, and (2) have the couple made use of artificial insemination in a clinic or hospital with sperm from a donor unknown to them? Two recent new Acts are of importance for answering the above questions: a new Act that regulates the legal parenthood of the birth mother's female partner[1] and a new Act that aims to abolish a number of differences between the legal consequences of marriage and registered partnership.[2] This chapter

---

* Dr Ian Curry-Sumner is a private legal consultant for Voorts Legal Services. In this capacity he provides legal teaching and legal advice to attorneys-at-law, civil-law notaries, judges, legal officiers, civil registrars. See for more information www.voorts.com.

1 Act on Lesbian Parentage (Wet van 25 november 2013 tot wijziging van Boek 1 van het Burgerlijk Wetboek in verband met het juridisch ouderschap van de vrouwelijke partner van de moeder anders dan door adoptie, *Stb.* 2013/480).

2 Act Removing a Number of Differences between Registered Partnership and Marriage (Wet van 27 november 2013 tot wijziging van het Burgerlijk Wetboek en het Wetboek van Burgerlijke Rechtsvordering in verband met de evaluatie van de Wet openstelling huwelijk en de Wet geregistreerd partnerschap, *Stb.* 2013/486).

will explain what the consequences of these two Acts are for co-mothers and their children in the Netherlands and, where relevant, the consequences for other groups of parents. The first part of this contribution will focus on the Dutch substantive law and the situation where the women concerned are Dutch and the child is born in the Netherlands. The second part of this contribution will focus on those cases that have an international element, for instance where the child is born in the Netherlands but both women are American nationals living in the Netherlands.

PART I: SUBSTANTIVE LAW

II LEGAL MOTHERHOOD FOR THE BIRTH MOTHER'S SPOUSE/REGISTERED PARTNER BY OPERATION OF LAW

The combination of the two new Acts mentioned earlier provides for motherhood by operation of law for a specific group of married or registered female couples with regard to a child born during their marriage/registered partnership. The birth mother's female spouse or registered partner will automatically become the child's legal parent if the couple can submit a declaration from the Donor Data Foundation on the registration of the child's birth.[3] This declaration needs to state that the birth mother has made use of artificial insemination in a clinical setting in line with the Donor Data Act[4] *and* that the identity of the sperm donor is not known to her. This declaration can be obtained from the Donor Data Foundation before the child's birth.[5] The fact that the donor needs to be unknown to the birth mother does not mean that the identity of the donor will remain unknown to the child. The professional who performs the artificial insemination with donor sperm has an obligation to submit specific information about the donor to the Donor Data Foundation. This includes relevant medical information, some specific information about the donor's appearance and education, and information about his identity. The Donor Data Foundation will keep this information and supply it to the child upon his or her request. Once the child reaches the age of 12, the child has access to information about the donor's physical and social characteristics. Once the child reaches the age of 16, the child may request information about the donor's identity. This personal identification information will be provided to the child, unless the donor can prove that he has very strong personal arguments against his identity being revealed.

---

3 Birth registration needs to take place within 3 days of the child's birth in the Netherlands (Art 19e(6) Dutch Civil Code).

4 For more information on this Act see: Janssens et al 'A New Dutch Law Regulating Provisions of Identifying Information of Donors to Offspring: Background, Content and Impact' (2006) *Human Reproduction,* vol 21, no 4, 852–856.

5 www.donorgegevens.nl/wetswijziging.asp.

If the spouses or registered partners submit this declaration upon the registration of the child's birth, both women will be regarded as legal parents from the moment of birth. In case the spouse/registered partner passed away before the child's birth, she will nevertheless become the child's legal mother, provided that the birth mother submits the declaration on the registration of the child's birth.[6] Female spouses or registered partners who have made use of a known sperm donor, will not be able to obtain such a declaration and will therefore not both become legal mothers by operation of law. The same applies to couples who travelled abroad for medical treatment with (anonymous) donor sperm or bought sperm via the internet. In these cases the birth mother's spouse/registered partner will *not* become a legal parent by operation of law.

III LEGAL MOTHERHOOD FOR THE BIRTH MOTHER'S PARTNER OR THE KNOWN SPERM DONOR THROUGH RECOGNITION

A co-mother who does not become a legal mother by operation of law has been given the chance to 'recognise' the birth mother's child, which will give her the same legal relation to the child as legal parenthood by operation of law. For recognition, the female partner will need the birth mother's consent if the child is younger than 16, and if the child is between 12 and 16 years of age, she will need both the mother's and the child's consent.[7] The possibility of recognising a child is not at all new, but was reserved for men until 1 April 2014. As of that same date some progress has also been made in the recognition of male same-sex parents. If a child has only a father as a legal parent, this father may give his male or female partner consent to recognise the child. Since a child always has a mother, the woman who gives birth, and anonymous delivery of a child is not allowed in the Netherlands, use of this possibility will not be widespread. Should the birth mother pass away, this would not terminate her legal motherhood; legal motherhood can only be terminated through adoption. Thus, the only circumstance in which a child will have only a father as a legal parent is after a one-parent adoption by this father. Adoptions like these are most common among male same-sex couples, who may encounter difficulties in adopting jointly outside the Netherlands. This new option makes it far easier for the adoptive father's male partner to become the child's second legal parent.

If the birth mother refuses to consent to the recognition of her child by the co-mother, she can file an application with the court for substitution of the birth mother's consent. She has this right on the basis of the fact that she is or was the birth mother's partner (whether married, registered partners, co-habiting, or living together) at the moment that she consented to the act that led to the conception of the child by her partner. This act may be the artificial insemination with donor sperm in a clinic, the self-insemination with the sperm

6 Article 1:198(1)(b) Dutch Civil Code.
7 Article 1:204(1)(c) and (d) Dutch Civil Code.

from a known donor at home, or actual intercourse with a 'donor'.[8] She is, however, not the only person who can apply to the court for substitution of the birth mother's consent; this also applies for the man who had sexual intercourse with the birth mother or the known sperm donor with 'family life'. This means that there are three categories of persons who may apply to the court for substitution of consent to recognition:

(a) the begetter of the child (the man who had intercourse with the mother) (Art 1:204(3)(a) Dutch Civil Code);
(b) the biological father who did not have intercourse with the mother but has 'family life' with the child (usually a sperm donor) (Article 1:204(3)(b) Dutch Civil Code); and
(c) the birth mother's female or male partner who consented to an act that may have resulted in the conception of a child by the birth mother (Article 1:204(4) Dutch Civil Code).

There are two different criteria that the court needs to apply to such requests: one for biological fathers (covering both begetters and sperm donors with family life), and one for consenting partners. In case the application stems from a biological father the court will substitute the birth mother's consent to recognition *unless this would infringe on the mother's interests in an undisturbed relationship with her child or would endanger the balanced emotional and social-psychological development of the child.*[9] This criterion is very similar to the criterion that was to be applied before 1 April 2014, with the exception that the definition that the Dutch Supreme Court gave of the concept *damage to the child's interests* is now included in the criterion.[10] This very same Supreme Court decision provided another important guideline with regard to the balance of interests that the court needs to apply in such cases, namely that the child and the begetter in principle have a right to have their biological relationship recognised as a legal parent-child relationship.

The criterion that the court must apply when a non-biological parent applies for the substitution of the birth mother's consent reads as follows: the court may substitute the birth mother's consent *if this is in the child's best interests.*[11] The possibility for a consenting partner to apply for substitution of consent was introduced into this new Act by an amendment in Parliament, which means that the Explanatory Memorandum does not contain any guidance on the application of this criterion. It may be of importance that the criterion for biological fathers states that consent may be substituted by the court *unless* this infringes on the mother's interests or endangers the child's development, whereas the criterion for consenting partners reads that consent may be

---

8 This also applies in case a child of 12 years and older does not consent to the recognition, but in this discussion is limited to the case where the birth mother refuses her consent.
9 Article 1:204(3) Dutch Civil Code.
10 Dutch Supreme Court 31 May 2002, *NJ* 2002/407.
11 Article 1:204(3) Dutch Civil Code.

substituted *if* this is in the best interests of the child. Time will tell as to how these criteria will be applied in practice, and with what result.

(a) What happens if the birth mother gives a third party consent to recognise her child?

(i) The birth mother gives her consent to her female partner while the known sperm donor with 'family life' meant to recognise the child

The birth mother first chooses to whom she will give consent to recognise her child, as is the intention of the legislature.[12] However, if she decides to give her consent to her female partner while the known sperm donor with *family life* meant to recognise the child (for instance because he had been promised by the birth mother that she would give him her consent), he has access to a very limited remedy to invalidate the recognition by the female partner. This remedy cannot be found in the Dutch Civil Code itself. Article 1:205 of the Dutch Civil Code, which concerns the invalidation of recognition by a non-biological parent, does not provide for such a request by a person other than the child's legal mother, the person who recognised the child, or the child. However, the Dutch Supreme Court decided that under very specific circumstances the begetter of a child may apply for the invalidation of recognition by a third person if it is clear that the mother misused her right to give or withhold consent to recognition.[13] If the begetter has simply waited too long to seek consent to recognise the child, the court may only invalidate the recognition by a third party if the mother gave her consent to this third party for no other reason than to infringe on the rights of the begetter. If the begetter has not had time to seek consent before he is faced with recognition by a third party, the court may invalidate the recognition by this third party if it finds that the mother could not reasonably have come to the decision to give consent to this third party, taking into account the interests of the other parties involved all in relation to the best interests of the child.

If the known donor with *family life* has been told that he will be given consent to recognise the child but finds that the birth mother has given her consent to her female partner instead, he may apply to the court to have the recognition invalidated and apply for a substitution of the birth mother's consent. The court will base its decision on a balance of the interests of the parties involved, all in relation to the best interests of the child. This will also be the case where no clear agreement was made between the birth mother, the known sperm donor with *family life* and the co-mother about the recognition of the child, and the known donor is faced with recognition by the co-mother shortly after the birth. However, we do think that the fact that there is agreement or not on who may recognise the child will have to play a role in the subsequent court proceedings. The idea behind the earlier mentioned decision by the Dutch Supreme Court

12 *Parliamentary Proceedings II* 2011-2012, 33032, No 3, 8.
13 Dutch Supreme Court 12 November 2004, *NJ* 2005, 248.

and subsequent case-law is that the begetter and the child in principle have a right to establish a legal parent-child relationship and the birth mother may not infringe on this right without good reason. However, the begetter's possibilities are limited because the legislature aimed at a regulation that would protect the status of legal parenthood based on recognition with the mother's consent, and thus the interest of the child, from arbitrary invalidation by a biological parent.[14] The child as such has the right to invalidate recognition by a non-biological parent, but the begetter has only been given a very limited right to do so.

(ii) The birth mother gives her consent to the known sperm donor but the co-mother meant to recognise the child

The second question that needs to be addressed is what happens when a co-mother is faced with recognition of the child by the known donor with the birth mother's consent? Can she also apply to the court for an invalidation of the recognition by the sperm donor and subsequently for a substitution of the birth mother's consent? Does it make a difference that the recognising person in this case is a biological parent? The basis for invalidation of recognition is the fact that the recognising person is not a biological parent, whereas in this case he is. In 1998 Dutch parentage law was revised and the procedure that allows for the application to a court to substitute the birth mother's consent to recognition was introduced to forge a closer link between biological reality and parentage law.[15] This is of course also the idea that underpins the above-mentioned case-law. However, the recent changes in the law that allow for the legal motherhood of co-mothers either automatically or through recognition has introduced social parenthood as a basis for legal parenthood in Dutch parentage law. Whether biological parenthood and social parenthood have equal status as a basis for legal parenthood remains to be seen. Article 1:205 of the Dutch Civil Code, as it reads today, does not allow for the invalidation of recognition by a biological father. However, it may still be argued that in cases where the birth mother has promised to give her consent to the co-mother to recognise the child and she subsequently gives her consent to the known donor, the birth mother has misused her right to give or withhold consent. A court would subsequently have to judge such a request on the balance of interests of the parties involved. What the outcome of such procedures will be remains to be seen. Invalidating the sperm donor's recognition in favour of the co-mother would mean a fundamental shift in Dutch parentage law.

Things become even more complicated if the birth mother refuses consent to recognise the child to both the known sperm donor with *family life* and the co-mother, and both parties file an application to substitute the birth mother's consent. The legislature has provided no guidance as to a preference for the

---

14 Dutch Supreme Court 12 November 2004, *NJ* 2005, 248 §3.5.4.

15 Dutch Supreme Court 12 November 2004, *NJ* 2005, Conclusion AG De Vries Lentsch-Kostense §9.

biological father or the co-mother in such cases. The court will have to apply different criteria to these two applications and again the circumstances of the case will probably play a crucial role in the court's decision.

IV LEGAL PARENTHOOD FOR THE CO-MOTHER THROUGH JUDICIAL ESTABLISHMENT

As of 1 April 2014 it is possible to judicially establish the legal parenthood of a co-mother who consented to the conception of a child by her female life partner on the basis of Article 1:207 of the Dutch Civil Code. The birth mother and the child can request the judicial establishment of the co-mother's legal parenthood. The parenthood of a known sperm donor with *family life* cannot be judicially established. Judicial establishment will usually occur when the parent concerned is unwilling to become the child's legal parent through recognition or has passed away before recognition could take place.

V REBUTTING THE CO-MOTHER'S LEGAL PARENTHOOD

Just as legal fatherhood established by marriage or recognition can be rebutted if it turns out the legal father is not the child's biological father, the legal motherhood of a co-mother can be rebutted if she is not the biological mother of the child. If her legal parenthood came about automatically on the basis of Article 1:198(1)(b) (in the case of marriage or registered partnership as discussed earlier) her legal parenthood can be denied on the basis of Article1:202a of the Dutch Civil Code. However, this is only possible if she is not the child's biological parent. In the Explanatory Memorandum the concept 'biological parent' in this context has been further explained. Normally the biological mother would be the woman who gave birth to the child, but in this context the biological mother includes the woman who supplied the egg (normally referred to as the genetic mother).[16] This means that if woman A supplies her egg to woman B and the fertilised egg is placed in woman B, who carries the child to term, and both women subsequently become the child's legal parents, the legal motherhood of neither of the women can be rebutted. This form of egg donation between partners without medical necessity is not available in the Netherlands. It is, however, available in neighbouring countries. As was discussed earlier, if women travel abroad for fertility treatment they will not be able to obtain the required declaration from the Donor Data Foundation which would bestow legal parenthood automatically on both spouses or registered partners. In such cases the possibility for the co-mother to recognise her partner's child will of course be available.[17]

---

16 *Parliamentary Proceedings II*, 2011-2012, 33032, No 3, 16.

17 This also leads to interesting questions in the context of consent to recognition. If the birth mother fails to give her consent, would the co-mother have a stronger case if she supplied the egg? We would think so.

The mothers cannot rebut the legal motherhood of the co-mother if the co-mother consented to an act that may have led to the conception of the child by her partner, or if the co-mother was aware of the fact that the birth mother was pregnant at the time the marriage or registered partnership was concluded.[18] It is difficult to think of a situation in which either the birth mother or the co-mother can rebut the legal motherhood of the co-mother. Given the fact that her legal motherhood only comes about if the earlier mentioned declaration is submitted upon the registration of the child's birth, it seems unlikely that the women will be able to prove that the co-mother did not consent to the conception of the child. All this has no relevance to the possibilities for the child to rebut the legal motherhood of the co-mother. The child can file such an application with the court up until 3 years after reaching the age of majority.

Legal parenthood established by a non-biological parent through recognition with the mother's or the court's consent can also be terminated through the invalidation of the recognition by the co-mother.[19] For the mothers, this option is only open if they can prove that the consent or the act of recognition was not given or undertaken freely, but under duress or fraud.[20] For the child, such requirements do not exist. The child can request the invalidation of recognition by a non-biological parent up until 3 years after reaching the age of majority. Again the concept of 'biological parent' includes the woman who is the supplier of the egg, which means that her recognition cannot be invalidated.

The possibility for female partners to adopt each other's children will continue to exist.[21] This option may, in particular, be relevant for female couples that plan to spend part of their life abroad and want to be certain that the legal motherhood of both mothers is recognised abroad. Some say that legal motherhood for the co-mother is more likely to be recognised if it was established though a legal adoption procedure which involves an inquiry into the child's best interest, whereas automatic legal motherhood or legal motherhood through recognition does not involve such an inquiry. I think the fact that the Dutch legislature introduced these possibilities in Dutch parentage law without having to adopt, indicates that it considers legal motherhood for both mothers automatically or through recognition to be in the child's best interest.

---

18 Article 1:202a Dutch Civil Code.

19 Article 1:205a Dutch Civil Code.

20 Article 1:205a Dutch Civil Code.

21 See an earlier chapter by these authors on this topic: 'Something Old, Something New, Something International and Something Askew' in B Atkin (ed) *The International Survey of Family Law 2012 Edition* (Jordan Publishing Ltd, Bristol, 2012).

PART II: PRIVATE INTERNATIONAL LAW CONSEQUENCES

VI INTRODUCTION

The entry into force of the Act on Lesbian Parentage, as well as the Act Removing a Number of Differences between Registered Partnership and Marriage have substantially changed the applicable private international law in this field. Although the concept of private international law refers to the three separate issues of jurisdiction, applicable law, and recognition and enforcement of foreign decisions and facts,[22] this contribution will focus on the changes that have been made to the applicable law rules in this field. The rules on international jurisdiction have remained completely unchanged, and therefore the vast majority of parentage issues that will reach the courts will do so on the basis of Article 3 of the Dutch Code of Civil Procedure. This article ensures that the Dutch courts have international jurisdiction if the petitioner has his or her residence or habitual residence in the Netherlands at the time the petition is filed. If this is not the case, then the Dutch courts also retain jurisdiction if the Dutch courts are sufficiently connected with the case.

VII APPLICABLE LAW RULES

(a) Introduction

In a similar fashion to the domestic parentage rules, Dutch private international law draws a distinction between various methods that can be used to establish parentage. The applicable law rules in this field are contained in Title 5, Book 10 of the Dutch Civil Code. Book 10 of the Dutch Civil Code was enacted on 1 January 2012 and was the result of many years of piecemeal codification.[23] The final text is a consolidation text drawing together all the piecemeal legislation in the field of private international law in the Netherlands. The provisions in the field of parentage are largely transposed from the previously applicable Private International Law (Parentage) Act (*Wet conflictenrecht afstamming*).[24] Title 5 comprises six different sections: birth during marriage or registered partnership (Articles 10:92–10:94, Section 1, Title 5), recognition and judicial determination of parentage (Article 10:95–10:97, Section 2, Title 5), legitimisation (Article 10:98, Section 3, Title 5), the content of legal familial ties (Article 10:99, Section 4, Title 5), the recognition of judicial decisions and legal

---

22 L Strikwerda *Inleidjng tot het Nederlands Internationaal Privaatrecht* (Kluwer, Deventer, 2012) 3.

23 P Vlas *Weekblad voor Privaatrecht Notariaat en Registratie* (Hcch, The Hague, 2011) 6892.

24 See in general L Strikwerda in T De Boer and F Ibili (eds) *Nederlands internationaal personen- en familierecht* (Kluwer, Deventer, 2012) 74 *et seq.*

acts and facts from abroad (Articles 10:100–10:101, Section 5, Title 5), and transitional provisions (Article 10:102, Section 6, Title 5). This division will also be followed in this chapter.

(b) Children born during marriage or registered partnership

(i) Determination of parentage

According to Article 10:92 of the Dutch Civil Code a choice of law cascade applies to children born in the Netherlands in order to determine which law applies to parentage that arises by operation of law. The first connecting factor is that of the joint nationality of the parties at the time of the birth of the child. In the event that the parties do not possess a common nationality, then reference is made to the common habitual residence of the parties. In the absence of this connecting factor, then reference is made to the habitual residence of the child.[25] The same rule applies regardless of whether the child is born to a different-sex married couples or a female same-sex married couple. Furthermore, since 1 April 2014 this rule also applies to different-sex and female same-sex registered partners.

With respect to the connecting factor of nationality, Book 10 did introduce a particular rule to avoid the need to resort to an effectiveness or reality test. Nominal possession of the nationality is sufficient in this context.[26] Therefore, if the mother of the child possesses Dutch nationality, for example, whereas the father possesses both Belgian and Dutch nationality, according to Article 10:92(1) and (2) of the Dutch Civil Code, the couple will be regarded as having a common nationality, namely the Dutch nationality. As a result, this law will apply to determine the question whether both mother and father have legal familial ties with respect to the child. If the mother and father, on the other hand, both possess a double nationality, as long as they possess only one common nationality, this nationality will prevail.[27] If, however, they both possess the same double nationality, then according to Article 10:92(2) of the Dutch Civil Code, it will be assumed that the parties do not possess a common nationality, and instead reference will be made to the next rung on the choice of law cascade, namely the common habitual residence of the parties. For example, if the father and the mother both possess Dutch and Belgian nationality, reference instead will be made to the law of common habitual residence.

In the context of different-sex married couples, this rule rarely caused substantial problems. However, in simply applying this rule analogously to

---

25 See further, K Saarloos *European Private International Law on Legal Parentage?* (Océ, Maastricht, 2010).

26 APMJ Vonken *Internationaal privaatrecht. Internationaal personen-, familie en erfrecht* (Kluwer, Deventer, 2012) 216, No 241.

27 For example, imagine that the mother possesses Dutch and Belgian nationality, whereas the father has Belgian and German nationality, then both parties possess Belgian nationality, and thus this law will apply.

female same-sex couples, the legislature has failed to provide for the somewhat perverse results that this may have in practice.

> *Example 1*
>
> Anna and Barbara, both German citizens living in the Netherlands wish to have a child utilising the newly enacted Act on Lesbian Parentage. The couple have lived in the Netherlands all of their lives and have no bond with Germany whatsoever. According to Article 10:92(1) of the Dutch Civil Code, as this couple possesses a common nationality, namely the German nationality, German law will apply to the question of which parties automatically acquire parentage rights over this child. As a result, this couple may well have satisfied all the necessary requirements of Dutch law to enable their parentage to be determined automatically and by operation of law. However, due to the choice of law rule applicable in this case, the non-birth mother would instead need to either recognise the child, or her parentage would have to be judicially determined.

According to the general rules on private international law contained in the First Title to Book 10 of the Dutch Civil Code, a number of general correction mechanisms could be used in this case.[28] For example, reference can be made to Article 10:8 of the Dutch Civil Code, which allows for a reference to be made to a different law from the law applicable on the basis that the different law is more closely connected. Although all the requirements of Article 10:8 of the Dutch Civil Code would be satisfied in this case, it is questionable whether the Dutch civil registrar would be willing to apply this correction mechanism *ex officio*. Instead, it is the authors' opinion that the civil registrar would be more likely to apply foreign law, and inform the parties that if they wish for an exception ground to be applied they should go to court. As a result, one of the main reasons for introducing this legislation (avoidance of unnecessary court procedures) would therefore not be achieved in this case. This problem could easily be rectified by ensuring that Article 10:92 of the Dutch Civil Code provided for an exception on the basis that the law applicable does not allow for parentage to be determined automatically in same-sex relationships. A similar result was also introduced in Dutch legislation when registered partnership was introduced to ensure that account was taken of the fact that the institution was not widely accepted across the globe.[29]

(ii) Denial of parentage

According to Article 10:93 of the Dutch Civil Code, the same law will apply to the denial of parentage as applied to the establishment of parentage according to Article 10:92 of the Dutch Civil Code.[30] The aim of this provision is to ensure symmetry between the law applicable to the creation of the legal familial

---

28 Reference could also possibly be made to the Dutch public policy exception (Article 10:6 Dutch Civil Code) or obviously a more general reference to human rights provisions that are directly applicable in Dutch law (Article 8 ECHR).

29 See, further, I Curry-Sumner *All's Well That Ends Registered?* (Intersentia, Antwerp, 2005).

30 If the establishment of the parentage occurred abroad, then, following the reasoning of the Dutch Supreme Court of 1 October 2004 (*NJ* 2004/622, ECLI:NL:HR:2004:AP2680), it would be correct to presume that the law applicable to establish the legal familial ties abroad

ties and the possible annulment thereof.[31] In practice, this will rarely cause specific issues with respect to the denial of parentage established in lesbian relationships. The reason for this is that the denial of parentage regulated in Dutch law, according to which the non-birth mother may attempt to deny her parentage, would be applicable in practice only if the parentage had already been established. As the number of jurisdictions in which this is possible is relatively limited, the chances are currently relatively high that Dutch law will be the governing applicable law to the establishment of the parentage rights, and thus Dutch law will also govern the denial of those rights. As the number of states around the world allowing for this kind of parentage by operation of law continues to increase, the more issues may arise in this context.[32]

(iii) Birth outside of marriage

If the parentage of the legal father has not or cannot be established, then Article 10:94 of the Dutch Civil Code will apply. This provision ensures that the law of the nationality of the birth mother applies with respect to the question whether legal familial ties are created by virtue of the birth. Nevertheless, if the woman has her habitual residence in the Netherlands, legal familial ties will always be deemed to have been created in accordance with the third sentence of Article 10:94 of the Dutch Civil Code.

> *Example 2*
>
> Carla, a French citizen, living in the Netherlands gives birth to baby boy in Amsterdam. Her spouse, Davina (also a French citizen) also lives in the Netherlands. Despite the fact that the couple satisfy the conditions in Dutch domestic law to have their parentage automatically registered (Article 10:92 Dutch Civil Code), Article 10:94 applies to determine whether legal familial ties are created between Carla and the child. Primarily reference would be made to French law, that being the law of the nationality of the birth mother. However, French law requires the birth mother to formally recognise the child. This would in principle prevent the automatic creation of legal familial ties between Carla and the child. Nevertheless, according to the final sentence of Article 10:94 of the Dutch Civil Code, as Carla has her habitual residence in the Netherlands, legal familial ties will be created regardless of the applicable law.

(c) Recognition of the child by non-birth mother

(i) Establishment of parentage

According to Article 10:95 of the Dutch Civil Code a distinction must be drawn between:

---

will also be applicable to the annulment of those ties in the Netherlands, instead of reference being made to the choice of law rule laid down in Article 10:92 Dutch Civil Code.

31 *Parliamentary proceedings II*, 1998-1999, 26 675, No 3, p 10.

32 In the Netherlands, problems have arisen when the law applicable does not allow for the denial of parentage. See, for example District Court Breda 24 May 2005, *NIPR* 2005/317, District Court Haarlem, 12 July 2005, *NIPR* 2005/231, District Court The Hague, 4 July 2011, *NIPR* 2011/430.

(i) the law applicable to the capacity of the person intending the recognise the child (Article 10:95(1) Dutch Civil Code); and
(ii) the law applicable to the consent of the legal mother of the child (Article 10:95(3) Dutch Civil Code).

With respect to the first category, namely the capacity of the recogniser, it is important to note that this rule is based on the principle of favouring a particular outcome.[33] In this case, an outcome is favoured in which the person wishing to recognise the child is actually permitted to recognise the child; this principle is regarded to be in the best interests of the child. Ultimately, this will mean that with respect to female recognisers, as long as one of the connecting factors points to Dutch law, the recognition will in principle be possible. The choice of law cascade involves the application of the law of the following legal systems in the following order:

(a) the nationality of the recogniser;[34]
(b) the habitual residence of the child;
(c) the nationality of the child;
(d) the habitual residence of the recogniser.

Although the connecting factors must be applied in this order, as soon as a legal system is identified that would permit the recognition, this law must be applied. One cannot compare the various solutions in order to identify the 'best solution' for the recogniser.[35] As soon as an applicable law has been identified the civil registrar must note this in the deed of recognition (Article 10:95(2) Dutch Civil Code).

With respect to the second category, namely the consent of the birth mother, this question is subject to a different cascade of applicable law rules. Article 10:95(3) of the Dutch Civil Code refers primarily to the law of the nationality of the birth mother to determine whether she must provide her consent for the recognition. The problem arises when this law does not allow for women to recognise the children (as is the case with the vast majority of countries around the world at this moment in time). Article 10:95(3) of the Dutch Civil Code states that reference may only be made to the next rung in the

---

[33] *Parliamentary proceedings II*, 1998-1999, 26 675, No 3, p 13.

[34] As a result of the principle of favouring a desired outcome, no effectiveness of reality test is applied in the context of the nationality test. Nominal possession of a nationality is thus sufficient for satisfaction of this connecting factor.

[35] See in general L Strikwerda in T De Boer and F Ibili (eds) *Nederlands internationaal personen- en familierecht* (Kluwer, Deventer, 2012) 80. Criticism of this rule in the context of male recognisers has been levied by Saarloos, see K. Saarloos *European Private International Law on Legal Parentage?* (Océ, Maastricht, 2010) 140. Saarloos has criticised this article as it forces the civil registrar to analyse as many as four legal systems with respect to the legal conditions for recognition prior to being able to confirm the applicable law. In the authors' opinion the same criticism could be levied at this article with respect to female recognition, albeit that the task is somewhat simpler due to the limited number of systems that currently allow for female recognition.

cascade (ie the law of the habitual residence of the birth mother) if the law of the nationality of the birth mother does not **know** of the institution of recognition. The question arises whether a country that permits recognition but does not permit female same-sex couples to recognise is sufficient to allow for a different law to be applied. This is a question that will be the subject of debate in the case-law and academic literature on this topic. At this moment, the gates are wide open for debate!

(ii) Annulment of recognition

According to Article 10:96 of the Dutch Civil Code, the law that will apply to a petition to annul a recognition will be the same law as is applicable to the recognition in accordance with Article 10:95 of the Dutch Civil Code. In a similar fashion to Article 10:93 of the Dutch Civil Code, the problem arises if the recognition took place abroad. The Attorney General has suggested that the aim of Article 10:96 is to ensure concurrence between the law applied to the recognition and the law applied to the petition for annulment thereof. Accordingly, it would tend to suggest that the law that *had been applied* abroad will also be applicable to the annulment, rather than the law that *would have applied* in accordance with Article 10:95 of the Dutch Civil Code. Once again, in the context of lesbian parentage, this issue will more-than-likely not be a pressing one, as there will be relatively few jurisdictions that even permit female recognition, thus narrowing down the choice of jurisdictions that could be applicable to the recognition in the first place.

(d) Judicial determination of parentage

As mentioned in the substantive law section of this contribution, Dutch law also permits the judicial determination of the parentage of the non birth-mother who had consented to the conception of a child by her female life partner. In international cases, the question is when reference to this provision may be made. According to Article 10:97 of the Dutch Civil Code, the law applicable to a petition for judicial determination of parentage is subject to an applicable law cascade. Reference will first be made to the common nationality of the birth mother and the person whose parentage is being judicially determined. Where there is no common nationality, reference will be made to the law of the state in which the parties have their common habitual residence. In absence thereof, then reference will be made to the law of the state in which the child has his or her habitual residence.

This applicable law cascade is based on the principle of closest connection, and not on the principle of favouring one of the parties, nor the best interests of the child. Accordingly, it can occur that the parties possess a common nationality that does not permit for the parentage of the non-birth mother to be judicially determined. The question then is whether any exceptions to this rule can be made. The same problem has also arisen in the context of judicial determination of paternity in different-sex couples. In a number of cases Dutch courts have deemed Article 10:97 of the Dutch Civil Code (as well as its predecessor, Article 6 Private International Law (Parentage) Act, *Wet conflictenrecht afstamming*) to be in contravention of Article 8 ECHR. In the case-law this has happened with respect to a number of jurisdictions that do not permit a form of judicial determination of paternity including the Netherlands Antilles,[36] Morocco,[37] Nigeria,[38] Egypt,[39] and Suriname.[40] Whether this approach is permissible with respect to petitions involving the judicial determination of the parentage of a female partner is debatable. In our opinion serious doubts could be raised as to whether such a petition falls within the realm of Article 8 ECHR. Reference to Article 10:6 of the Dutch Civil Code (Dutch public policy exception) would also be difficult, as the legislature has made an explicit decision to ensure that the applicable law cascade is not based on the principle of favouring one of the parties, but instead on the closest connection. As a result, in the Dutch Government's opinion, if the applicable law does not permit the judicial determination of paternity, then no reference should be made to other possible applicable laws.

(e) Recognition of foreign judicial decisions and foreign legal acts and facts

Article 10:00-101 of the Dutch Civil Code applies to the recognition of foreign birth certificates, foreign judicial determinations of parentage etc. These rules have been left virtually untouched by the recent statutory amendments. In practice these rules will only be referred to in a limited number of cases of lesbian parentage, as there are relatively few jurisdictions outside the Netherlands that currently permit lesbian parentage outside of adoption to be formally registered.

The only real change is that, as the prohibition on a married man from recognising the child born to a woman other than his wife has been repealed from Dutch domestic substantive legislation, this too has been removed from the private international law rules. Nonetheless, the authors note particular concerns with respect to the possible consequences of this repeal for illegal adoption. If a married man recognises the child of another woman abroad, the resulting instrument of recognition will be able to be recognised in the Netherlands. In order to deny recognition to this deed one will need to refer to the general public policy exception. This will, therefore, allow married men to travel abroad and perform a civil act of recognition and have this recognition recognised in the Netherlands as long as this recognition creates legal familial ties according to the law of the state in which the recognition was conducted,

---

36 District Court Rotterdam 21 December 2006, ECLI:NL:RBROT:2006:AZ6489; Court of Appeal The Hague 20 February 2008, ECLI:NL:GHSGR:2008:BC6649.

37 District Court The Hague 3 November 2008, ECLI:NL:RBSGR:2008:BG8815, *JPF* 2010/63; Court of Appeal 's-Hertogenbosch 27 November 2008, ECLI:NL:GHSHE:2008:BG6114, *JPF* 2010/62; Court of Appeal Amsterdam 23 February 2006, ECLI:NL:GHAMS:2006:AV2119.

38 District Court Haarlem 11 December 2012, ECLI:NL:RBHAA:2012:BY6564, *JPF* 2013/131.

39 District Court Den Haag 14 May 2013, ECLI:NL:RBDHA:2013:CA2355.

40 Court of Appeal The Hague 3 October 2007, ECLI:NLGHSGR:2007:BB8333, *JPF* 2008/32; Dutch Supreme Court 12 December 2008, ECLI:NL:HR:2008:BG1113.

and that this was performed by a competent authority in that state in accordance with the law applicable in that state.[41] Accordingly, the Netherlands does not apply a so-called 'choice of law' test and thus ensure that the birth certificate also be drawn up in accordance with the law that would have been applicable had the birth certificate been drafted in the Netherlands. Accordingly, the possibility of having such legal acts conducted abroad recognised in the Netherlands has dramatically increased as of 1 April 2014.

VIII CONCLUSION

The new Acts discussed bring substantial changes for the legal position of lesbian couples and their children in the Netherlands and for Dutch parentage law in general. It is not yet clear to what extent sociological and biological parenthood will be regarded as equally important for the attribution of legal parenthood. This is one of the questions Committee of State *Recalibrating Parenthood* will need to look into the next 2 years.[42] This committee will be installed to look into questions relating to multi-parent families and surrogacy and is expected to present its final report in March 2016. Despite the progress these Acts signify in the equal treatment of same-sex and different-sex families, enough challenges remain for families, lawyers, and judges in applying the law when conflicts arise or when an international element is involved. It remains to be seen how these issues will be dealt with in practice.

---

41 For an extensive discussion of these conditions, see I Curry-Sumner and M Vonk 'The Netherlands' in K Trimmings and P Beaumont *International Surrogacy Arrangements* (Hart, 2013) 273–293.

42 http://leidenlawblog.nl/articles/dutch-committee-of-state-to-recalibrate-parenthood-a-broad-and-challenging.

CHILD POVERTY IN NEW ZEALAND – DEFINITIONS, CONSEQUENCES, AND POSSIBLE LEGISLATIVE RESPONSES

*Mark Henaghan and Ruth Ballantyne**

Résumé

La pauvreté infantile est actuellement endémique en Nouvelle-Zélande où un quart des enfants (approximativement 270 000) vivent dans des conditions de précarité. Le présent texte s'intéresse à ce problème qui est en croissance, à la difficulté de définir avec précision le concept de pauvreté infantile, aux conséquences immédiates et futures de celle-ci, ainsi qu'aux raisons qui devraient pousser la Nouvelle-Zélande à prendre des mesures législatives pour contrer ce phénomène. Dans la dernière partie, le texte analyse quatre projets de loi (le Projet de loi sur la réduction et l'élimination de la pauvreté infantile, deux projets de loi portant sur l'alimentation à l'école et le Projet de loi sur les enfants vulnérables) qui devraient être adoptés afin de réduire le niveau de pauvreté des enfants.

I INTRODUCTION

New Zealand is currently experiencing a child poverty epidemic with as many as 25 per cent of New Zealand children (approximately 270,000 children) presently living in impoverished conditions.[1] Child poverty incorporates a significant amount of deprivation and prevents children from accessing basic social and educational life prerequisites. According to the Expert Advisory Group on Solutions to Child Poverty ('the Expert Advisory Group'):[2]

> 'Child poverty involves material deprivation and hardship. It means, for instance, a much higher chance of having insufficient nutritious food, going to school hungry, wearing worn-out shoes or going barefoot, having inadequate clothing, living in a cold, damp house and sleeping in a shared bed. It often means missing out on

* Mark Henaghan is Professor and Dean of Law, Faculty of Law, University of Otago, Dunedin, New Zealand and Ruth Ballantyne is professional Practice Fellow, Faculty of Law, University of Otago, Dunedin, New Zealand.

1 Expert Advisory Group on Solutions to Child Poverty *Solutions to Child Poverty in New Zealand: Evidence for Action* (Children's Commissioner, Wellington, 2012) at 1.

2 Expert Advisory Group on Solutions to Child Poverty *Solutions to Child Poverty in New Zealand: Evidence for Action* (Children's Commissioner, Wellington, 2012) at 1.

> activities that most New Zealanders take for granted, like playing sport and having a birthday party. It can also mean much narrower horizons – such as rarely travelling far from home […] This is not the kind of country most New Zealanders experience or know much about. But it is the harsh reality for many of our children.'

Such poverty has immediate and long-term negative consequences, not just for the children affected, but New Zealand society as a whole. Worst of all, child poverty is not a new problem in New Zealand. As Jonathan Boston states:[3]

> 'New Zealand has tolerated significant levels of relative child poverty for more than two decades. For a country which once prided itself on being comparatively egalitarian and, more particularly, on being a great place to bring up children, this is surprising. It is also concerning.'

This chapter considers the growing child poverty problem in New Zealand and the difficulty of defining exactly what counts as child poverty. This is followed by a general analysis of the immediate and long-term consequences of child poverty, which leads to an examination of the reasons why New Zealand needs to implement child poverty legislation. This involves a discussion of the child poverty legislation enacted in the United Kingdom and Wales in 2010. The chapter concludes with an exploration of four proposed pieces of legislation (the Child Poverty Reduction and Eradication Bill, the Education (Breakfast and Lunch Programmes in Schools) Amendment Bill, the Education (Food in Schools) Amendment Bill, and the Vulnerable Children Bill), which should be enacted to help reduce the high level of child poverty in New Zealand.

II WHAT IS CHILD POVERTY?

Child poverty is notoriously difficult to define. Consequently, New Zealand has no agreed definition of precisely what constitutes living in poverty. This is problematic, in that it is hard to reduce child poverty, when no one can agree exactly what child poverty is. This also makes it difficult for statistics on child poverty to be gathered accurately and consistently across different organisations. The Expert Advisory Group, who were tasked with investigating possible solutions to child poverty in New Zealand, believes that the first step in reducing child poverty is to create a clear definition of child poverty. As the Expert Advisory Group said:[4]

> 'New Zealand has no agreed definition of poverty or official poverty measures. Without an authoritative definition and widely accepted measures we will lack a common purpose or agreed goals. Likewise, we will be less able to develop focused

---

3 Jonathan Boston 'The Challenge of Securing Durable Reductions in Child Poverty in New Zealand' (2013) 9 Policy Quarterly 3 at 3.

4 Expert Advisory Group on Solutions to Child Poverty *Solutions to Child Poverty in New Zealand: Evidence for Action* (Children's Commissioner, Wellington, 2012) at 2.

> solutions to child poverty or evaluate their success in achieving specified poverty-reduction targets. Accordingly, we need a clear definition and agreed measures.'

The group proposes the following definition of child poverty:[5]

> 'Children living in poverty are those who experience deprivation of the material resources and income that is required for them to develop and thrive, leaving such children unable to enjoy their rights, achieve their full potential and participate as equal members of New Zealand society.'

This definition incorporates 'the socioeconomic rights of children as citizens' and 'affirms that children should be given the opportunity to achieve their full potential – both for their own future well-being and for the economic and social well-being of society'.[6] The Expert Advisory Group are not the only individuals who believe in the importance of children being given their best chance. As Robert Stephens said:[7]

> '[C]hildren should be given the opportunity to achieve their full potential, both as children, receiving full educational and social opportunities, and as adults so that they can achieve their own economic and social well-being.'

The proposed definition is also consistent with international concepts of child poverty and integrates the rights guaranteed by the United Nations Convention on the Rights of the Child to which New Zealand is a signatory. The Convention ensures (among other things) that children have a universal right to education,[8] 'the enjoyment of the highest attainable standard of health',[9] and 'a standard of living adequate for the child's physical, mental, spiritual, moral and social development'.[10]

Regardless of whether the above definition is adopted, New Zealand needs an approved and consistent definition of child poverty before any real progress can be made in reducing child poverty. The definition (however formulated) will

---

5 Expert Advisory Group on Solutions to Child Poverty *Solutions to Child Poverty in New Zealand: Evidence for Action* (Children's Commissioner, Wellington, 2012) at 2.

6 Expert Advisory Group on Solutions to Child Poverty *Solutions to Child Poverty in New Zealand: Evidence for Action* (Children's Commissioner, Wellington, 2012) at 2.

7 Robert Stephens 'Dimensions of Poverty Measurement' (2013) 9 Policy Quarterly 18 at 19.

8 United Nations Convention on the Rights of the Child 1990, Art 28. Further, Art 29 declares that education shall be geared towards the 'development of the child's personality, talents and mental and physical abilities to their fullest potential.'

9 United Nations Convention on the Rights of the Child 1990, Art 24.

10 United Nations Convention on the Rights of the Child 1990, Art 27. Article 27 further states: 'States Parties, in accordance with national conditions and within their means, shall take appropriate measures to assist parents and others responsible for the child to implement this right and shall in case of need provide material assistance and support programmes, particularly with regard to nutrition, clothing and housing.'
This article clearly imposes an international obligation on signatories to assist children and their families who are suffering from the effects of poverty. However, the provision is qualified by the proviso 'in accordance with national conditions and within their means'.

need to be consistently used by all relevant government organisations and agencies to better allow for the collection of accurate, comparable and useful statistics.

III THE COSTS AND CONSEQUENCES OF CHILD POVERTY

The negative consequences of child poverty are far easier to agree upon. There is little room for debate that living in poverty detrimentally affects children in a myriad of ways. As John Hancock states:[11]

> 'High levels of child poverty have stark social implications. It is now well documented that children who grow up in poor households are also more likely to experience adverse outcomes in other facets of their life. This includes low educational attainment, poor physical and mental health, and exposure or susceptibility to harmful phenomena such as substance abuse and crime.'

Likewise as the White Paper for Vulnerable Children declares:[12]

> 'Material hardship or poverty has significant adverse effects on children's development and wellbeing, including on brain development, physical health, learning, psychological wellbeing and behaviour.'

What is less known is that a child's age may have a significant impact on the ultimate consequences caused by their impoverished living conditions. There is recent evidence that suggests the causal link between child poverty and child-focused health, social and education disadvantages has a temporal dimension, in that children who are exposed to poverty in their early years may be more affected by their living conditions than those children who experience poverty later in their childhood. As Greg Duncan and Katherine Magnuson explain:[13]

> 'It is not solely poverty that matters for children's outcomes, but also the timing of child poverty. For some outcomes later in life, particularly those related to achievement skills and cognitive development, poverty early in a child's life may be especially harmful.'

This is clearly illustrated in an educational context where children living in poverty find it much harder to succeed academically and generally do worse at school than their more prosperous classmates. This is particularly concerning

---

11 John Hancock *Legislating to Reduce Child Poverty: Considering the UK Child Poverty Act 2010 and Its Application to New Zealand* (Report for Winston Churchill Memorial Trust Board, Auckland, 2014) at 5.

12 New Zealand Government *The White Paper for Vulnerable Children: Volume II* (Ministry of Social Development, Wellington, 2012) at 19–20.

13 Greg Duncan and Katherine Magnuson 'The Importance of Poverty Early in Childhood' (2013) 9 Policy Quarterly 12 at 14.

when one considers that these educational differences can be seen before such children even start school. As Duncan and Magnuson elucidate:[14]

> 'Poor children begin school well behind their more affluent age mates, and, if anything, lose ground during the school years. On average, poor kindergarten children have lower levels of reading and maths skills and are rated by their teachers as less well behaved than their more affluent peers. Children from poor families also go on to complete less schooling, work less and earn less than others.'

However, it is not just individual children and families that are negatively affected by child poverty. There is also an immense societal cost brought to bear by child poverty. From a purely economic point of view, the current estimated costs of child poverty in New Zealand are in the range of NZ$6–8 billion per year. This extraordinary cost cannot help but affect New Zealand's long-term financial security. As Boston states 'the empirical evidence suggests that substantial rates of child poverty reduce a nation's prosperity. Hence, on economic grounds alone there is a case for seeking lower child poverty rates'.[15]

The impact of the economic costs of child poverty is much wider than the direct monetary costs alone. A recent UNICEF report describes the significant costs of childhood poverty thus:[16]

> 'Failure to provide this protection brings heavy costs. The biggest price is paid by individual children whose susceptible years of mental and physical growth are placed at risk. But societies also pay a heavy price – in lower returns on educational investments, in reduced skills and productivity, in the increased likelihood of unemployment and welfare dependence, in the higher costs of social protection and judicial systems, and in the loss of social cohesion ... the economic argument, in anything but the shortest term, is therefore heavily on the side of preventing children from falling into poverty in the first place.'

IV WHY NEW ZEALAND NEEDS CHILD POVERTY LEGISLATION

The extremely serious societal and economic costs produced by child poverty are experienced not just by the individual children and families affected, but also by society as a whole. Consequently, child poverty cannot be considered as a solely individualistic problem. A degree of collective responsibility is required to avoid subjugating children to unacceptable levels of deprivation, especially

---

14 Greg Duncan and Katherine Magnuson 'The Importance of Poverty Early in Childhood' (2013) 9 Policy Quarterly 12 at 13.

15 Jonathan Boston 'The Challenge of Securing Durable Reductions in Child Poverty in New Zealand' (2013) 9 Policy Quarterly 3 at 3.

16 UNICEF Innocenti Research Centre *Measuring Child Poverty: New League Tables of Child Poverty in the World's Rich Countries – Innocenti Report Card 10* (Innocenti Research Centre, Florence, Italy, 2012) at 27.

because impoverished children have no real voice of their own and have very limited choices (if any) about their own living conditions. As the Expert Advisory Group points out:[17]

> 'Children do not choose to be poor. They do not select their parents. Even though they are citizens, they lack a democratic voice and the choices available to adults. Society has a responsibility to protect the powerless and vulnerable. Children, above all, deserve our collective protection and best endeavours.'

It has long been recognised that children are inherently vulnerable and need to be protected. Indeed, current New Zealand family law legislation, such as the Care of Children Act 2004 (which primarily concerns whom children should live with), is child-focused to the degree that in proceedings under that Act the 'welfare and best interests of a child in his or her particular circumstances *must* be the first and paramount consideration'.[18] This 'first and paramount' principle could also be applied (within reason) to considerations of child poverty. As UNICEF states:[19]

> 'Childhood by its nature, and by its very vulnerability, demands of a civilized society that children should be the first to be protected rather than the last to be considered. This principle of "first call" for children holds good for governments and nations as well as for the families who bear the primary responsibility for protection. And because children have only one opportunity to grow and to develop normally, the commitment to protection must be upheld in good times and in bad. It must be absolute, not contingent.'

The only real way to begin to eradicate child poverty is to introduce a 'systematic policy approach aimed at measuring, targeting and reducing child poverty'.[20] According to Hancock this needs to involve the 'implementation of a suite of poverty measures, both income and non-income based, and a comprehensive monitoring, reporting and accountability framework'.[21] As if this was not a difficult enough exercise already, political realities also need to be acknowledged. As Boston states:[22]

> 'It is one thing to identify possible strategies, and related policy frameworks, for minimising child poverty; it is quite another to implement them and sustain the required political support over long periods of time.'

---

17 Expert Advisory Group on Solutions to Child Poverty *Solutions to Child Poverty in New Zealand: Evidence for Action* (Children's Commissioner, Wellington, 2012) at 68.

18 Care of Children Act 2004, s 4.

19 UNICEF Innocenti Research Centre *Measuring Child Poverty: New League Tables of Child Poverty in the World's Rich Countries – Innocenti Report Card 10* (Innocenti Research Centre, Florence, Italy, 2012) at 27.

20 John Hancock *Legislating to Reduce Child Poverty: Considering the UK Child Poverty Act 2010 and Its Application to New Zealand* (Report for Winston Churchill Memorial Trust Board, Auckland, 2014) at 5.

21 John Hancock *Legislating to Reduce Child Poverty: Considering the UK Child Poverty Act 2010 and Its Application to New Zealand* (Report for Winston Churchill Memorial Trust Board, Auckland, 2014) at 5.

22 Jonathan Boston 'The Challenge of Securing Durable Reductions in Child Poverty in New Zealand' (2013) 9 Policy Quarterly 3 at 7.

The only viable way of introducing such wide-ranging changes is via legislation specifically targeted at reducing child poverty. The Expert Advisory Group suggests that the purpose of such child poverty prevention legislation should be to '[a]chieve a sustainable reduction' in both the 'number and proportion' of child poverty and to '[a]lleviate the socio-economic disadvantage experienced by children living in poverty in New Zealand'.[23] The legislation would also need to set out clear measures for poverty. This is a complex task, which will require significant economic and statistical expertise. Rather than merely focusing on income poverty, measures should also be implemented in other areas such as housing, education and health and support services. A significant aspect of the legislation would be to place a duty on the Minister responsible to gather relevant consistent data each year and to show Parliament where progress has or has not been made. This way child poverty becomes a matter of public debate and pressure can be brought to bear to ensure that progress is made. Such over-arching legislative intervention may not please everyone. However, at the very least, we should be able to agree as a society to be accountable for providing the best possible environment for children to thrive, even if we disagree on the specific means of getting there.

V INTERNATIONAL CHILD POVERTY LEGISLATION

Both the United Kingdom and Wales provide legislative models that define child poverty, set out targets and strategies for eliminating child poverty, and place duties on government ministers and local authorities to act in ways designed to reduce child poverty. This ensures that child poverty is considered when policy decisions are made. Each country's legislative approach is examined in turn below.

(a) United Kingdom

The Child Poverty Act 2010 came into force in March 2010 in the United Kingdom with the primary purpose of eradicating child poverty.[24] The legislation provides targets relating to the reduction of child poverty and introduces a variety of accountability mechanisms. The machinery of the Act does not actually correspond to an abolition of all child poverty across the United Kingdom, but rather aims to achieve 'certain baseline levels (which are deemed to be low rates)'.[25] The Act provides four targets ranging from the 'relative low income target' to the 'persistent poverty target'.[26] The Child Poverty Act 2010 also ensures the government develops child poverty reduction strategies and the government must report back to Parliament on the progress

---

[23] Expert Advisory Group on Solutions to Child Poverty *Working Paper No 6 – Legislative Mechanisms to Reduce Child Poverty* (Children's Commissioner, Wellington, 2012) at 15.

[24] Child Poverty Act 2010 (UK), Introductory text.

[25] Expert Advisory Group on Solutions to Child Poverty *Working Paper No 6 – Legislative Mechanisms to Reduce Child Poverty* (Children's Commissioner, Wellington, 2012) at 10.

[26] Child Poverty Act 2010 (UK), ss 3–6.

of these strategies each year.[27] Section 14 of the Child Poverty Act 2010 requires the Secretary of State to 'lay an annual report in Parliament on progress in meeting the statutory targets and in implementing the national child poverty strategy'.[28] The Act also established the Child Poverty Commission to provide advice on the construction of national strategies.[29] The Act also imposes duties on local authorities and bodies to work with the government to mitigate the effects of child poverty in their local area.[30]

At this stage it is too early to know how successful the Act has been. However, as the Expert Advisory Group states:[31]

> 'The most recent set of Households Below Average Income (HBIA) statistics released by the Department for Work and Pensions in June 2012, indicates that over the last year there has been a small drop in the levels of child poverty from 20 percent to 18 percent (approximately 2.3 million children), a reduction of around 300,000. However, this figure rises to 3.6 million, or 27 percent, when housing costs are included in the income measurement. Nevertheless, this figure is still 200,000 less than the after-housing cost measurement for the previous year.'

While this downward trend is encouraging it is too soon to draw any firm conclusions as to the Act's long-term effectiveness in meeting its targets, especially because some of the numbers involved have actually increased since the implementation of the Act. For example, in the 2011/2012 financial year the number of children experiencing 'severe levels of income poverty has become significantly worse'.[32] Even more concerning is the prognosis that children poverty rates in the United Kingdom 'are projected to rise steadily through to the end of the decade'.[33]

(b) Wales

The Welsh Assembly also passed legislation in 2010 that specifically tackles child poverty, among other issues. The Children and Families (Wales) Measure 2010 ('the Measure') aims to:[34]

> '[M]ake provision about contributing to the eradication of child poverty; to provide a duty for local authorities to secure sufficient play opportunities for

---

[27] Child Poverty Act 2010 (UK), ss 9–13.

[28] Expert Advisory Group on Solutions to Child Poverty *Working Paper No 6 – Legislative Mechanisms to Reduce Child Poverty* (Children's Commissioner, Wellington, 2012) at 11.

[29] Child Poverty Act 2010 (UK), s 8.

[30] Child Poverty Act 2010 (UK), ss 19–25.

[31] Expert Advisory Group on Solutions to Child Poverty *Working Paper No 6 – Legislative Mechanisms to Reduce Child Poverty* (Children's Commissioner, Wellington, 2012) at 12.

[32] John Hancock *Legislating to Reduce Child Poverty: Considering the UK Child Poverty Act 2010 and Its Application to New Zealand* (Report for Winston Churchill Memorial Trust Board, Auckland, 2014) at 13.

[33] John Hancock *Legislating to Reduce Child Poverty: Considering the UK Child Poverty Act 2010 and Its Application to New Zealand* (Report for Winston Churchill Memorial Trust Board, Auckland, 2014) at 13.

[34] Children and Families (Wales) Measure 2010, introductory text.

> children; to make provision about arrangements for participation of children in local authority decisions that might affect them; to make provision about child minding and day care for children; to make provision establishing integrated family support teams and boards; to make provision about improving standards in social work for children and persons who care for them; to make provision about assessing the needs of children where their parents need community care services or have health conditions that affect the needs of the children; and for connected purposes.'

The Measure provides a number of 'broad aims' which include increasing income for households with one or more children, ensuring that, so far as reasonably practicable, children living in households in the relevant income group are not materially deprived, to reduce inequalities in educational attainment between children, to ensure that all children grow up in decent housing, to help young persons participate effectively in education and training and to help young persons participate effectively and responsibly in the life of their communities.[35] The measure places a duty on Welsh Ministers and local authorities to prepare and publish child poverty strategies, which must be then enacted into regulations.[36] Local authorities must also provide free childcare services and implement free heath and parental support services.[37] The legislation requires Welsh Ministers to have due regard to the rights of children and the United Nations Convention on the Rights of the Child 1990.

VI PROPOSED NEW ZEALAND LEGISLATION

The biggest challenge does not lie in deciding that New Zealand needs to take action against child poverty, but rather in determining the best action to take. Arguably (as discussed above), the most effective way to take collective action against child poverty is to pass legislation specifically designed to reduce child poverty. Such legislation would make the government directly accountable for reducing child poverty and ensure that decreasing the number of children living in poverty became a fundamental priority. However, as yet, no such over-arching legislation has been passed in New Zealand. However, four Bills have been proposed which address child poverty to differing degrees. The Child Poverty Reduction and Eradication Bill, the Education (Breakfast and Lunch Programmes in Schools) Amendment Bill, the Education (Food in Schools) Amendment Bill, and the Vulnerable Children Bill are discussed below in turn.

(a) Child Poverty Reduction and Eradication Bill

Labour Party Member of Parliament (MP) Jacinda Ardern has proposed new legislation entitled the Child Poverty Reduction and Eradication Bill. The Bill is currently in the Parliamentary Members' Bills Ballot and will not be addressed by the government unless and until it has been pulled from the ballot. As its

35 Children and Families (Wales) Measure 2010, s 1.
36 Children and Families (Wales) Measure 2010, ss 3–6.
37 Children and Families (Wales) Measure 2010, ss 7–10.

name would suggest, this Bill is directly concerned with reducing the amount of children living in impoverished conditions in New Zealand. As the explanatory note to the Bill states:[38]

> 'The purpose of this Bill is to achieve a sustainable reduction in the numbers and proportion of children living in poverty in New Zealand, and to alleviate the socio-economic disadvantage these children experience. It does so by putting child poverty at the heart of government policy development and decision making, and establishing targets to reduce and eradicate the impact of child poverty.'

To this end, the Bill would start by defining and measuring child poverty.[39] As the explanatory note to the Bill explains, measuring child poverty 'is an important starting point',[40] because '[s]imply put, you cannot manage what you have not measured, nor can the Government be held to account on an issue without agreed measurements'. The Bill would then require 'the Government to set targets to reduce the number of children living in poverty'.[41] Measures of child poverty are not to be solely income-focused as the Bill seeks 'child poverty reduction indicators under the headings of education, health, socio-economic, and child quality of life'.[42] The Bill also focuses on a need for transparency and accountability, alongside cross-agency commitment. As the explanatory note elucidates:[43]

> 'In order to deliver genuine change for children it is necessary to establish a transparent mechanism to hold the Government to account on poverty reduction. This Bill provides that mechanism by requiring the Minister for Social Development to establish long-term and short-term targets, and to report against them to the House of Representatives. The Minister of Finance must also include a child poverty reduction statement in the annual Budget Policy Statement.
>
> To ensure true cross-departmental collaboration on child poverty, the Bill also establishes a Child Poverty Reduction Board, which brings together the heads of all the relevant government departments to deliver a reduction in child poverty and associated indicators.'

The Bill itself is relatively brief, consisting of only 15 clauses, but what it may lack in size, it makes up for by the far-reaching impact of the possible changes. The Bill aims to 'achieve a sustainable reduction' in both 'the numbers and proportion' of New Zealand children living in poverty by alleviating 'the socio-economic disadvantage they experience'.[44] At first glance, these aims seem disingenuously simple, but they are underpinned by the Bill's more practical and reality-focused objectives, which aim to achieve the Bill's purpose by:[45]

---

38 Child Poverty Reduction and Eradication Bill, explanatory note.
39 Child Poverty Reduction and Eradication Bill, explanatory note.
40 Child Poverty Reduction and Eradication Bill, explanatory note.
41 Child Poverty Reduction and Eradication Bill, explanatory note.
42 Child Poverty Reduction and Eradication Bill, explanatory note.
43 Child Poverty Reduction and Eradication Bill, explanatory note.
44 Child Poverty Reduction and Eradication Bill, cl 3.
45 Child Poverty Reduction and Eradication Bill, cl 4.

'(a) providing a statutory definition of children living in poverty;
(b) setting objectives towards meeting the purpose of the Act;
(c) establishing criteria for the measurement of the numbers and proportion of children living in poverty;
(d) requiring the establishment of periodic targets for reducing the numbers and proportion of children living in poverty;
(e) requiring the issuing of periodic child poverty reduction strategies and reports of progress made towards meeting those targets;
(f) establishing indicators for the purpose of alleviating the socio-economic disadvantage of children living in poverty;
(g) establishing mechanisms for monitoring progress, implementing policies, and co-ordinating services.'

These objectives provide a blueprint for the rest of the Bill. First and foremost, they establish the need for child poverty to be properly defined. The definition of child poverty proposed in the Bill provides as follows:[46]

> '**children living in poverty** means all persons under the age of 18 years who experience deprivation of income and the material resources required for them to develop and thrive, enjoy their rights, achieve their full potential, and participate as full and equal members of New Zealand society, and **child poverty** has a corresponding meaning.'

This definition is clearly based upon the one provided by the Expert Advisory Group (as set out above) in that both definitions refer to limited material resources and income that impact upon children's rights to 'develop and thrive', 'achieve their full potential' and participate as 'equal members of New Zealand society'.[47] Such definitions as those proposed are not without their difficulties, in that it is extremely problematic to legally quantify or define what it means for a child to 'thrive', to reach their 'full potential', or to participate as 'equal members' of society.[48]

The majority of the remaining objectives are concerned with establishing consistent measures of child poverty and establishing 'periodic targets' and 'indicators' for reducing the number of children experiencing impoverished living conditions due to socio-economic disadvantages.[49] To this end, the Bill provides an extensive list of possible steps 'aimed at reducing the proportion of children living in poverty and alleviating the socio-economic disadvantage they experience'.[50] The proposed steps include:[51]

---

[46] Child Poverty Reduction and Eradication Bill, cl 6.
[47] See Expert Advisory Group on Solutions to Child Poverty *Solutions to Child Poverty in New Zealand: Evidence for Action* (Children's Commissioner, Wellington, 2012) at 2 and cl 6 of the Child Poverty Reduction and Eradication Bill.
[48] See Expert Advisory Group on Solutions to Child Poverty *Solutions to Child Poverty in New Zealand: Evidence for Action* (Children's Commissioner, Wellington, 2012) at 2 and cl 6 of the Child Poverty Reduction and Eradication Bill.
[49] Child Poverty Reduction and Eradication Bill, cl 4.
[50] Child Poverty Reduction and Eradication Bill, cl 7(2).
[51] Child Poverty Reduction and Eradication Bill, cl 7(2).

'(a) increasing the income of households with 1 or more children with a view to reducing the proportion of children living in poverty;
(b) reducing the material deprivation of children living in poverty;
(c) improving educational outcomes for children living in poverty;
(d) improving health outcomes for children living in poverty;
(e) enhancing social inclusion for children and their families living in poverty;
(f) ensuring that all children grow up in adequate and decent housing;
(g) ensuring that all children grow up in safe and cohesive communities;
(h) enabling more cost-effective, co-ordinated service support;
(i) enabling effective community responsiveness;
(j) identifying any legislative measures necessary for promoting policy measures to reduce and mitigate child poverty by having due regard to the requirements of the United Nations Convention on the Rights of the Child;
(k) identifying any legislative measures necessary for promoting policy measures to reduce and mitigate child poverty by having due regard to the principles of the Treaty of Waitangi.'

Some of these steps will be easier to achieve than others. For example, enhancing the health of children living in poverty could be realised by specifically targeted New Zealand healthcare system spending, media campaigns and increased funding for social support organisations in low decile areas. However, 'enhancing social inclusion' for poor families and children and ensuring all children 'grow up in safe and cohesive communities' will be much more difficult to achieve and will require significant time, funding and creativity.[52]

The Bill also calls for the establishment of robust accountability and reporting measures to ensure that forward progress is maintained. The Bill seeks to achieve this objective in two main ways: through the creation of a Child Poverty Reduction Board and imposing strict obligations on the Ministry of Social Development (and inter alia the Minister for Social Development). The Child Poverty Reduction Board is to be made up of the following members: the Director-General of Health, the Secretary for Education, the Secretary to the Treasury, the chief executive of the Department of Prime Minister and Cabinet, the chief executive of Te Puni Kōkiri, the chief executive of the Ministry of Pacific Island Affairs, the Government Statistician, the Secretary of Justice, the Police Commissioner and the Children's Commissioner.[53] The Board will be responsible for developing 'annual poverty measurements' and 'child poverty reduction indicators' relating to a child's education, health, socio-economic position and quality of life.[54] In recognition of the fact that child poverty will not be a quick fix, the Board will be obliged to develop a '10-year child poverty reduction strategy'.[55] This strategy is to be published publicly and its results

---

52 Child Poverty Reduction and Eradication Bill, cl 7(2).
53 Child Poverty Reduction and Eradication Bill, cl 15.
54 Child Poverty Reduction and Eradication Bill, cl 8.
55 Child Poverty Reduction and Eradication Bill, cl 14(a).

closely monitored.[56] All progress made pursuant to the strategy will need to be reviewed and reported upon annually to the Minister of Social Development.[57]

The Minister of Social Development will be obliged to 'set periodic child poverty reduction targets' every 3 years for short-term poverty reduction targets, and every 10 years for more long-term reduction targets, as well as provide progress reports (obtained annually from the Chief Executive of the Ministry of Social Development) to the House each year.[58] The Minister must also 'support locally-initiated child poverty reduction strategies by local authorities, community organisations, iwi, and social services providers'.[59]

It remains to be seen if/when the Child Poverty Reduction and Eradication Bill will be drawn from the Parliamentary Members' Bills Ballot and, following that, if it will receive the required political support to become enacted law. However, regardless of its eventual status, the Bill provides an important starting point for talking about child poverty and provides a practical model of the kind of legislation that is required to properly address this vast problem on the premise that children 'are the most vulnerable members of our community and the Government has a responsibility to act [to] improve the conditions in which 1 in 4 of our children are growing up'.[60]

(b) Education (Breakfast and Lunch Programmes in Schools) Amendment Bill and Education (Food in Schools) Amendment Bill

These two private Members' Bills (the Education (Breakfast and Lunch Programmes in Schools) Amendment Bill and the Education (Food in Schools) Amendment Bill) essentially aim to achieve the same thing – to ensure children that attend low decile schools are adequately fed to enable them to reach their full academic potential. The New Zealand Ministry of Health estimates 'that as many as 80,000 children turn up to school each week without having had breakfast'.[61] This is problematic due to the wealth of evidence suggesting 'that hunger has a significant impact on children's cognitive development, learning, and classroom behaviour'.[62] This is a substantial number of children whose learning is disadvantaged on a regular basis. Poverty is one of the primary causes of this problem. As the explanatory note to the Education (Breakfast and Lunch Programmes in Schools) Amendment Bill explains:[63]

---

56 Child Poverty Reduction and Eradication Bill, cl 14.
57 Child Poverty Reduction and Eradication Bill, cl 14.
58 Child Poverty Reduction and Eradication Bill, cl 10.
59 Child Poverty Reduction and Eradication Bill, cl 11.
60 Child Poverty Reduction and Eradication Bill, explanatory note.
61 Education (Food in Schools) Amendment Bill (154-1), explanatory note.
62 Education (Food in Schools) Amendment Bill (154-1), explanatory note.
63 Education (Breakfast and Lunch Programmes in Schools) Amendment Bill (85-1), explanatory note.

> 'Growing levels of poverty in New Zealand have resulted in too many parents being unable to afford to provide their children with breakfast before school and/or lunch at school, or being unable to afford to provide their children with sufficiently nutritious meals before and during school.'

The Education (Breakfast and Lunch Programmes in Schools) Amendment Bill is a private Members' Bill brought in the name of New Zealand Mana Party MP Hone Harawira. It was introduced to the House on 8 November 2012, but as of May 2014 has not progressed any further. It would provide free nutritious breakfasts and lunches to all children enrolled in decile one and two schools (in New Zealand's most socio-economically deprived areas).[64] Schools receiving the breakfast and lunch programmes would be monitored each year to 'ensure they are providing meals each day they are open for instruction and that the meals follow nutritional guidelines'.[65] The programmes would be evaluated after the first 3 years of their implementation to 'further develop and improve their effectiveness'.[66]

The Education (Food in Schools) Amendment Bill is a private Members' Bill brought in the name of New Zealand Labour Party MP David Shearer. It was introduced to the House on 26 September 2013, but also has subsequently failed to make any headway since. The explanatory note to the Bill proclaims that ensuring children are adequately fed before beginning school each day 'is one of the most important actions we can take to lift New Zealand's educational achievement'.[67] The Bill would ensure that the New Zealand Government was 'more hands-on, partnering with communities and voluntary organisations to put free food in all primary and intermediate schools that want and need it'.[68] The Bill is intended to be 'permissive rather than prescriptive' providing for all decile one, two and three schools to receive the required food, but also permitting other schools to be included 'as funding permits'.[69] The stated purpose of the Bill is to 'ensure that the Crown supports organisations to deliver food to students in schools where a need for food can be identified'.[70] This programme was also to be reviewed within 3 years of its implementation.

The implementation of one of these Bills would be a relatively inexpensive exercise compared to some of the other wider costs associated with the proposed Child Poverty Reduction and Eradication Bill, and could significantly assist children living in poverty by improving both their short and long-term educational and health outcomes. As the explanatory note to the Education (Food in Schools) Amendment Bill explains, '[i]f kids turn up to school not

---

64 Education (Breakfast and Lunch Programmes in Schools) Amendment Bill (85-1), explanatory note.

65 Education (Breakfast and Lunch Programmes in Schools) Amendment Bill (85-1), explanatory note.

66 Education (Breakfast and Lunch Programmes in Schools) Amendment Bill (85-1), explanatory note.

67 Education (Food in Schools) Amendment Bill (154-1), explanatory note.

68 Education (Food in Schools) Amendment Bill (154-1), explanatory note.

69 Education (Food in Schools) Amendment Bill (154-1), explanatory note.

70 Education (Food in Schools) Amendment Bill (154-1), cl 4.

having eaten breakfast, without shoes, or sick because their house is cold and damp, it is obvious they will not get the best start'.[71]

(c) Vulnerable Children Bill

The Vulnerable Children Bill seeks to 'protect and improve the well-being of vulnerable children'.[72] It is not directly concerned with child poverty per se, but it does contain provisions that could improve the plight of some New Zealand children currently living in poverty if they also qualify as vulnerable children. The Bill envisages improving the well-being of vulnerable children by promoting their best interests (focusing on both their current and future lives).[73] The Bill includes several aims relevant to vulnerable children that could also be applicable to children living in poverty including 'improving their physical and mental health',[74] 'improving their education',[75] 'increasing their participation in decision-making about them, and their contribution to society'[76] and, most importantly, 'improving their social and economic well-being'.[77]

The Bill does not specify exactly who is to be classified as a vulnerable child. Instead the Bill states that the phrase vulnerable children 'means children of the kind or kinds (that may be or, as the case requires, have been and are currently) identified as vulnerable in the setting of Government priorities'.[78] These government priorities have not yet been set. However, it seems likely that some children living in poverty will be caught by the priorities if the Bill is passed, despite the fact the legislation is not specifically geared towards children experiencing impoverished living conditions.

The Bill (if ultimately passed) would introduce financial provisions that may prevent some vulnerable children from having to live in poverty. It would place an obligation on the Chief Executive of the Ministry of Social Development to provide specific types of financial assistance to carers under s 388A of the Children, Young Persons, and Their Families Act 1989.[79] The Bill would also

---

[71] Education (Food in Schools) Amendment Bill (154-1), explanatory note.

[72] Vulnerable Children Bill 2013 (150-1), explanatory note. The Vulnerable Children Bill (150-1) was introduced to New Zealand's Parliament on 2 September 2013. The Social Services Committee reported their findings on the Vulnerable Children Bill (150-2) on 25 March 2014. The Committee recommended that the Bill be passed, but called for substantial amendments – especially the removal of the proposed child harm prevention orders.

[73] Vulnerable Children Bill 2013 (150-2), cl 6.

[74] Vulnerable Children Bill 2013 (150-2), cl 6(b).

[75] Vulnerable Children Bill 2013 (150-2), cl 6(c).

[76] Vulnerable Children Bill 2013 (150-2), cl 6(e).

[77] Vulnerable Children Bill 2013 (150-2), cl 6(f).

[78] Vulnerable Children Bill 2013 (150-2), cl 5(1).

[79] See cl 131A of the Vulnerable Children Bill 2013 (150-2), which would insert s 388A into the Children, Young Persons, and Their Families Act 1989. Under the original version of the Vulnerable Children Bill 2013 (150-1) a similar provision was to be inserted into s 389 of the Children, Young Persons, and Their Families Act 1989 by cl 132 of the Vulnerable Children Bill 2013 (150-1).

introduce a Family Court review or appeal process for permanent caregivers who considered that the Chief Executive had wrongfully or unreasonably declined their request for financial assistance.[80] These provisions may help a child living with carers that are unable to adequately financially support themselves and the child. Moreover, the Bill would increase the financial and non-financial support to be provided to 15–20 year olds leaving care to live independently.[81] This may help older children who wish to live independently from ending up in impoverished circumstances.

The Bill may also be helpful in the quest for the eradication of child poverty in that it provides an example of what government legislation imposing cross-agency measures (similar to those that may be required for possible child poverty prevention focused legislation) might look like. The Bill's current cross-agency measures would impose a great deal of responsibility and direct accountability on a variety of government agencies that administer particular legislation relevant to the protection of children.[82] If passed, the Bill would also send a clear message that the government is prepared to legislate to better protect vulnerable children in New Zealand. This could potentially smooth the way for broader legislative measures to work towards eradicating child poverty.

The Bill received unanimous support at its first reading, an indication of early cross-party support for the relatively bold proposed changes. Nevertheless, there have been criticisms of the philosophical ideas underpinning the Bill. For example, it has been submitted that the proposed regime was not the appropriate way to target child abuse, as it considered individuals in isolation, rather than in their wider social environment.[83] Evidence demonstrates that there is a strong correlation between child abuse, poverty and income inequalities.[84] The 2013 Child Poverty Monitor revealed that hospital admissions for conditions with a social gradient are much higher for children from more socio-economically deprived areas.[85] In particular, children living in poverty are 5.6 times more likely to be hospitalised for 'injuries from assault, neglect or maltreatment' than children who do not live in poverty.[86] This strong

---

80 See cl 133 of the Vulnerable Children Bill 2013 (150-2), which would insert ss 389A and 389B into the Children, Young Persons, and Their Families Act 1989.

81 See cl 131 of the Vulnerable Children Bill 2013 (150-2), which would insert s 386A into the Children, Young Persons, and Their Families Act 1989.

82 The relevant children's agencies are defined in cl 5(1) of the Vulnerable Children Bill 2013 (150-2) as the state departments or Crown instruments responsible for the administration of the Children, Young Persons, and Their Families Act 1989, the Education Act 1989, the New Zealand Public Health and Disability Act 2000, the Policing Act 2008, the Sentencing Act 2002 or any other Act subsequently prescribed.

83 (17 September 2013) 693 NZPD 13391.

84 (17 September 2013) 693 NZPD 13401.

85 Elizabeth Craig, Anne Reddington, Andrew Wicken, Glenda Oben and Jean Simpson *Child Poverty Monitor: 2013 Technical Report* (New Zealand Child and Youth Epidemiology Service, University of Otago, Dunedin 2013) at 62. Such conditions include a range of medical conditions and injuries, infant mortality and sudden unexpected death in infancy (SUDI), and hospital admissions for injuries arising from assault, neglect and maltreatment.

86 Elizabeth Craig *New Zealand Children's Social Monitor 2011 Update* (New Zealand Child and Youth Epidemiology Service, University of Otago, Dunedin, 2011) cited in Expert Advisory

connection between child poverty and the vulnerability of children is not explicitly reflected in the Bill. Consequently, Labour Party MP Jacinda Ardern suggested that poverty measures should be inserted into the Vulnerable Children Bill. Her Supplementary Order Paper to the Bill would have seen child poverty measures, targets and indicators inserted into the Vulnerable Children's Plan, alongside the current targets in terms of reducing child abuse and protecting vulnerable children.[87] The Supplementary Order Paper would have amended cl 9 of the Vulnerable Children's Plan so that it was additionally required to establish:[88]

> '(a) criteria for the measurement of the numbers and proportion of children living in poverty; and
> (b) periodic targets for reducing the numbers and proportion of children living in poverty; and
> (c) indicators for the purpose of alleviating the socio-economic disadvantage of children living in poverty; and
> (d) mechanisms for monitoring progress, implementing policies, and co-ordinating services.'

These changes would have widened the impact of the Vulnerable Children Bill and ensured more children would have been protected by the proposed legislation. However, this part of Ardern's Supplementary Order Paper was voted down (63 votes to 56 votes) on 13 May 2014.[89] This means that her proposed changes will not be added to the Vulnerable Children Bill, which is unfortunate, as the additions would have been a positive step forward, especially considering that all children living in poverty can properly be considered to be vulnerable.

The Bill illustrates a political interest in promoting and indeed prioritising the protection of children, and indicates that the government is prepared to provide funding, systematic improvements and practical tools to achieve this goal. It remains to be seen whether the Bill will continue to attract such widespread parliamentary support past the Select Committee stage, but any discourse raising awareness of vulnerable children issue is valuable in itself, even though the Bill is not specifically designed to reduce child poverty.

VII CONCLUSION

New Zealand can no longer afford to ignore the severe levels of child poverty currently experienced by too many New Zealand children. If left unchecked, the devastating short and long-term effects of child poverty will continue to deprive an inherently vulnerable sector of society of their opportunity to

---

Group on Solutions to Child Poverty *Solutions to Child Poverty in New Zealand: Evidence for Action* (Children's Commissioner, Wellington, 2012) at 15.

87 Supplementary Order Paper 2014 (436) Vulnerable Children Bill 2013 (150-2) (explanatory note) at 2.

88 Supplementary Order Paper 2014 (436) Vulnerable Children Bill 2013 (150-2) at 1.

89 (13 May 2014) 698 NZPD 17813.

'achieve their full potential and participate as equal members of New Zealand society'.[90] New Zealand's duty to deliver and uphold the rights of children under the United Nations Convention on the Rights of the Child can only be met if the government steps up and makes child poverty a legislative priority. As the Expert Advisory Group declares:[91]

> 'New Zealand can be a great place for children – where all children can enjoy their rights, achieve their full potential and participate as equal members of our society. But to achieve this goal we must address the problem of child poverty. Moreover, unless a concerted effort is made now to reduce child poverty, the costs that it imposes today, both social and economic, are likely to be magnified in generations to come.'

New Zealand has already made a move in the right direction via the aspirational *White Paper for Vulnerable Children* and the progress of the Vulnerable Children Bill. However, much more remains to be done to ensure that no more New Zealand children experience the debilitating effects of living in poverty. There is now, more than ever, a need for legislation specifically targeting child poverty to be enacted along the lines of the Child Poverty Reduction and Eradication Bill. The prompt implementation of either of the Education (Breakfast and Lunch Programmes in Schools) Amendment Bill, or the Education (Food in Schools) Amendment Bill would also suitably assist in the reduction of some of the unwanted consequences of child poverty, especially from an educational point of view.

The large number of children living in poverty in New Zealand shows no signs of abating of its own accord. Therefore, until the government and relevant agencies are prepared to step up and acknowledge the causes and consequences of child poverty, and take real (financially supported) steps to address the problem, nothing will change for the children detrimentally affected by poverty. As the explanatory note to the Child Poverty Reduction and Eradication Bill proclaims:[92]

> 'It is time that New Zealand became a champion on behalf of its own children, and put their needs at the heart of government decision making.'

---

90 Expert Advisory Group on Solutions to Child Poverty *Solutions to Child Poverty in New Zealand: Evidence for Action* (Children's Commissioner, Wellington, 2012) at 2.

91 Expert Advisory Group on Solutions to Child Poverty *Solutions to Child Poverty in New Zealand: Evidence for Action* (Children's Commissioner, Wellington, 2012) at 67.

92 Child Poverty Reduction and Eradication Bill, explanatory note.

PAPUA NEW GUINEA

CUSTOMARY POLYGAMY, HUMAN RIGHTS AND THE CONSTITUTION IN PAPUA NEW GUINEA

*John Y Luluaki**

Résumé

La polygamie, plus précisément la polygynie, c'est-à-dire lorsqu'un homme est marié avec deux femmes ou plus, est une forme traditionnelle de mariage qui a fait l'objet de beaucoup de discussion en Papouasie-Nouvelle-Guinée. Les principales raisons avancées par ceux qui sont hostiles à la polygamie sont qu'elle serait non chrétienne, inconstitutionnelle, discriminatoire à l'égard des femmes dont elle bafoue les droits, qu'elle serait une cause de séparation et de violence, qu'elle serait mauvaise sur le plan économique, néfaste pour les enfants, qu'elle contribuerait à la surpopulation et, finalement, qu'elle mènerait au VIH et au SIDA. Le présent article entend essentiellement critiquer la plupart de ces affirmations. Il entend démontrer que le point commun de ces arguments est une méconnaissance de l'essence même de la polygamie coutumière. En d'autres mots, l'idée n'est pas tant défendre ici la polygamie que d'expliquer que les critiques qui lui sont adressées en méconnaissent la réalité.

Cet article suggère également que la question devrait être analysée dans le cadre plus large des droits fondamentaux et des principes constitutionnels. La polygamie n'est pas nécessairement mauvaise en soi. Le vrai problème est celui de son organisation qui nuit à de nombreuses personnes. La polygamie n'est pas contraire non plus aux principes fondamentaux des droits de la personne. Elle est aussi une question de choix. Or la liberté de choix est un droit fondamental. Une discussion objective sur la polygamie dans le contexte des droits de la personne n'est possible que si l'on met de côté les préjugés, les expériences personnelles et les idées préconçues. La culture est un autre aspect important des droits de la personne. La culture n'empêche pas nécessairement le libre choix; le défi est de faciliter ce libre choix dans les paramètres du contexte culturel telles que dictées par la constitution. La polygamie permet également au pays de développer des normes locales d'un droit sous-jacent qui reflètent la diversité de culture, de coutumes et de traditions. Quoi qu'il en soit, le servile copier-coller des normes étrangères et internationales en droit interne a eu pour résultat de freiner le développement de thèmes locaux indépendants en matière des droits de la personne dans un pays pourtant aussi diversifié qu'est la Papouasie-Nouvelle-Guinée.

* School of Law, University of Papua New Guinea, PO Box 317, University PO, NCD, Papua New Guinea.

I INTRODUCTION

The practice of polygamy is known to exist in many countries including many societies in Africa and in Melanesia. In Papua New Guinea as elsewhere, this has been the subject of much comment generally as well as being the focus of academic inquiry by social and legal anthropologists and legal academics.

Schedule 2.1 of the Constitution provides the constitutional basis for the recognition of custom in the country. It provides that 'custom is adopted, and shall be applied and enforced, as part of the underlying law' unless, 'and to the extent that it is inconsistent with a Constitutional Law or a statute, or repugnant to the general principles of humanity'. Similar restrictions are imposed by s 3 of the Customs Recognition Act, Ch 19 and s 4(2) of the Underlying Law Act 2000.

In respect of customary marriage in particular, s 3 of the Marriage Act Ch 280 confers legal validity on customary marriages provided that they are entered into (a) between indigenous Papua New Guineans, neither of whom is a party to an existing (monogamous) statutory marriage with another person, and (b) in accordance with relevant customary marriage procedures. A customary marriage that satisfies these requirements is valid and effectual for all legal purposes. This means that, if one of the parties is already a party to a subsisting customary marriage, the second customary marriage is a valid polygamous marriage. However, if the first marriage is a monogamous statutory one, the second purported customary marriage would be bigamous. Section 3 is in the following terms:

> **'3. Customary marriages**
>
> (1) Notwithstanding the provisions of this Act or of any other law, a native, other than a native who is a party to a subsisting marriage under part V, may enter, and shall be deemed always to have been capable of entering, into a customary marriage in accordance with the custom prevailing in the tribe or group to which the parties to the marriage or either of them belong or belongs.
>
> (2) Subject to this Act, a customary marriage is valid and effectual for all purposes.'

In 2008, the Constitutional and Law Reform Commission of Papua New Guinea, by Supreme Court Reference No 03 of 2008, sought an advisory opinion from the Supreme Court on the constitutionality of polygamous marriages. At the time of writing, no determination had been made and the matter was still awaiting legal arguments to be presented to the Court.

(a) Purpose of discussion

This discussion has a number of purposes: first, to help clearly identify the subject (polygamy) so that there is unity in understanding of it. This is necessary to avoid confusing what it is that is the focus of the present discourse. The second and related purpose is to restate some of the more common reasons that have been put forward to either justify retaining this marriage practice or force its discontinuation and the likely response to each of these arguments. The third purpose is a general one. This is to use the discourse on polygamy to reveal an underlying contradiction or opposition between an aspiration to build this nation based on Papua New Guinea ways, on the one hand, and the almost religious adoption and domestication of international values and standards that, despite them having no parallels in our communities, challenge our right as a collective set of peoples to chart our own course, develop on our own terms, develop our own jurisprudence and, together, determine our collective *independent* destiny, on the other hand.

(b) What is polygamy?

Polygamy is a term used to refer to marriage situations in which a person has a plurality of spouses. Just as there can be a principal male or a principal female in a polygamous marriage, there are two types of polygamy: polygyny and polyandry. The former involves a plurality of wives while the latter a plurality of husbands. In other words, it is polygynous polygamy when a man is married to two or more wives at the same time and polyandrous polygamy when a woman is married to two or more husbands simultaneously. Polyandrous polygamy is the rarer form of polygamy. This has been reported to exist in societies as widely separated from one another as the eastern Inuit (Eskimos), Marquesan Islanders of Polynesia, and Tibetans.[1]

Polyandry can take a number of forms and may serve different purposes. The most common type is when a woman is married to two or more men who are not related to each other. However, if the husbands are related, they are usually brothers. Anthropologists call this 'adelphic' or 'fraternal' polyandry. This is the form of polygamy favoured by the patrilineal Tibetans and perpetuates principally for economic reasons. Because arable land is in such short supply, the marriage of brothers to one wife averted the danger of constantly subdividing farmlands among all the sons of any one landholder while ensuring, at the same time, a good life by having access to family resources including land and animals.[2]

Polyandrous marriages must however be distinguished from situations in which males in certain circumstances are tolerated to have sex with someone else's wife or wives (polygyny). The custom of allowing other males to have sexual access to the wife or wives of other males is known as polykoity in anthropology. A form of polykoity found in the Pacific including Papua New

---

1 W Haviland *Cultural Anthropology* (6th edn, Holt, Rinehart and Winston, Fort Worth, Chicago, San Francisco, 1990) 229.

2 W Haviland *Cultural Anthropology* (6th edn, Holt, Rinehart and Winston, Fort Worth, Chicago, San Francisco, 1990) 229 and M Goldstein 'When Brothers Share a Wife' in N Flowers *Cultural Anthropology* (3rd edn, McGraw Hill Inc, New York, St Louis, San Francisco, 1990) 274.

Guinea is associated with hospitality. It is also reported in the Old Testament. This involves offering to a visitor a sleeping companion who may be the host's wife or daughter. Literature on this in Papua New Guinea uses the term 'wife-lending' to refer to this form of expressing customary hospitality.

(c) Polygamy in Papua New Guinea

In Papua New Guinea, polygamous marriages are almost invariably polygynous, meaning that polygamous marriages involve co-wives, not co-husbands. Despite the dominance of polygyny in many of our communities, there is anecdotal evidence, as well as unverified reports of women having a plurality of 'husbands' or at least male partners who have been regarded as husbands.

Polygynous polygamy has been observed mainly in patrilineal societies even though the matrilineal Trobriand Islanders and the Siwai of North Bougainville also practise this as a form of marriage. Otherwise, the practice is found mainly in the Highlands, the Sepiks, and Papuan communities. However, while we know that polygynous marriage is the dominant if not the only form of polygamy in the country, what is not known is why men choose to marry polygynously whereas women generally do not readily consider polyandry as a serious marriage option.

A number of explanations may be considered, but sex is perhaps not one of them; first, compared to polyandry, polygynous polygamy performs certain important social and economic functions for society as a whole and serves a number of needs that cannot be met through polyandrous polygamy or monogamy. In this scenario, and in the absence of an effective alternative social security system to respond to crisis situations of widowhood in particular, polygyny was necessary and unavoidable. Secondly, polygyny operated as an effective method of increasing the labour force required to materialise ambitions motivated by selfish gain.

Thirdly, polygyny, but not polyandry, marks the difference in views regarding a man's as opposed to a woman's domain in a society's social and economic life. In this view, women are regarded as being primarily interested with private and particularistic concerns that benefit only themselves and their children without much or any direct regard for larger social interests. Women are regarded and women themselves regard themselves as being located in the 'domestic' domain with family concerns and welfare matters dominating their responsibilities. This can be contrasted with the position regarding men who are seen as having concerns that extend beyond the limited parochial domestic domain to include the welfare of the social whole. In other words, even though the man's primary concern lies in the public domain, his sphere of concern also includes aspects located within the wife's domestic domain. Polygyny then provided men the very tool required to be an effective manager of his public domain concerns by forging new alliances, networks and relationships. Both monogamy and polyandry fail to deliver in that regard.

Managing his universalistic concerns and assisting his wife to manage her domestic domain is an onerous task for the man but something he must do. He must be skilled enough to strike the right balance between these concerns or risk the stability in family relationships and social life. For this, he would have to rely on his wife's cooperation, and the situation becomes even more challenging if he has several wives. Among the Hageners for example, Professor Marilyn Strathern found that women in their everyday lives:[3]

> 'are very much concerned with focusing men's attention upon their wives, mothers, sisters, and so on. A polygynist's wives demand that he manage their separate relations with scrupulous fairness – men say ruefully that a polygynist never rests, for whichever house he sleeps in he always has to remember the others.'

In more ways than one, however, both/all parties know that the successful discharge of the wife's or wives' responsibilities in the domestic domain has a direct positive impact on his public domain concerns.

A fourth explanation is perhaps that men, more than women, are, by nature, plural. The presence of sexual or intimate temptation or desire for another woman in men including married men attests in some way to the plural nature of the man. As pluralists, men will always welcome at least a second alternative source of sexual or relationship intimacy. This is, without exception, universal. Polygyny avoids or limits infidelity among men. From a Papua New Guinea point of view, that men have monogamist relationships is by choice and therefore not natural. The point is true in both the mating (sex) and long-term relationship (marriage or de facto unions) senses. A final explanation is that unlike polyandry, polygyny makes paternity easier to establish for a whole host of reasons including inheritance.

II POLYGAMY, WOMEN'S RIGHTS AND THE INTERNATIONAL COMMUNITY

The issue of polygamy must also be considered in the context of three international instruments relating to human rights generally, marriage, family relationships and women's rights. They are the International Covenant on Civil and Political Rights, the UN Convention on the Elimination of Discrimination against Women (CEDAW) and the Universal Declaration of Human Rights 1948. It must be noted, however, that in none of these instruments is specific reference made to polygamy as a form of marriage even though some have attempted to interpret the provisions of the latter as proscribing its practice.

---

[3] M Strathern 'Self-interest and the social good: Some Implications of Hagen Gender Imagery' in SB Ortner and H Whitehead *Sexual Meanings. The Cultural Construction of Gender and Sexuality* (Cambridge University Press, Cambridge and New York, 1981) 166–191, at 186.

(a) Convention on the Elimination of Discrimination against Women (CEDAW)

The main purpose of the Convention on the Elimination of Discrimination against Women (CEDAW) is to address the issue of discrimination against women in all areas of human activity, cultural, economic, social, personal and family relations, employment and workplace. Papua New Guinea ratified the CEDAW on 12 January 1995. The CEDAW makes no specific reference to polygamous marriage. Nevertheless, it is the view of the CEDAW Committee on the Elimination of Discrimination against Women[4] that polygamy does in fact violate Art 5(a) and any constitutional provision that establishes equal rights between men and women.[5] Article 5(a) is in the following terms:

> '5. State Parties shall take all appropriate measures:
>
> (a) To modify the social and cultural patterns of conduct or men and women, with a view to achieving the elimination of prejudices and customary and all other practices which are based on the idea of the inferiority or superiority of either of the sexes or on stereotyped roles for men and women.'

It has not been possible to find any explanation as how polygamy is prejudicial to women generally, or that it is based on a position of inferiority of women compared to men, or discriminatory to women. There is clearly nothing inherently prejudicial or discriminatory to a woman who chooses to marry polygamously and becomes a man's additional wife if both parties give their full and free consents and she is of marriageable age. That an existing wife or wives will naturally object is distinctly a different matter altogether. Further, how is the conduct of the woman who chooses to marry polygamously discriminatory to the woman who is already married to him?

On the contrary, the right of a woman of marriageable age to choose when and with whom she marries and whether she wishes to marry monogamously or polygamously must be respected, protected and enforced by both domestic and international law. How is this to be regarded as indicating her inferior or her husband's superior position, and how can her decision to exercise her right of choice be discriminatory to her or to her competitor? That this may cause violence involving her, any existing wife and/or the husband is a criminal matter for which the relevant criminal process will be applied.

It is clear that until the cultural and economic reasons which make polygynous polygamy attractive to women disappear or are rejected, it must be continued despite opposition to it. The serious social and economic realities confronting scores of women today make polygynous polygamy a necessary evil. What is required therefore and urgently is to find ways to remove the social and economic vulnerabilities that make women feel they need polygamy. Abolishing

---

4 Recommendation No 21, para 14.

5 In Papua New Guinea for example, this would be s 55(1) of the Constitution.

polygamy and dissuading women from it without replacing it with a reliable or functional alternative is to punish these women further for being poor and vulnerable.

(b) International Covenant on Civil and Political Rights

This international agreement is important because Art 23 states in very clear terms that it is the right of every person, male and female, to marry and found a family. Article 23(1) recognises the family as the fundamental basis of human society and for it to be respected and protected. Article 23(2) and (3) declare that it is 'the right of men and women of marriageable age to marry and to found a family' provided that it is entered into with 'the free and full consent of the intending spouses'.

It will be noted that this Article does not discriminate forms of marriage, between monogamous and polygamous marriages or between polygynous and polyandrous polygamy. It also does not favour one form of marriage over another or others. But it can be assumed nevertheless that the reference to 'marriage' means heterosexual marriage. Thus, since the focus is on the rights of the intending spouses to the marriage, the interests of any other party or person are irrelevant.

Article 23(2), which provides for free and full consent, is not contingent upon whether the marriage is customary or not or whether it is potentially or actually polygamous. The law against bigamy is not a prohibition against customary polygamy. Bigamy is the outcome of marriage procedure rather than marriage itself. Both polygamy and monogamy are embraced by Article 23. In relation to a woman therefore, the requirement of free and full consent is satisfied by protecting, by law, their right to choose an equally eligible and consenting man to whom she can marry and found a family. This means that so long as the requirements of marriage age and consent are in order, the interests of relatives and other persons including first wives in polygamous marriages are essentially irrelevant.

(c) Universal Declaration of Human Rights 1948

The Universal Declaration of Human Rights ('the Declaration') is the forerunner of all international agreements including treaties and conventions on human rights matters generally. Even though it has no direct means of enforcement, its provisions are in general terms and apply to all people rather than to specific groups such as family and children or matters such as marriage, adoption, disability or poverty. As expected, however, the Declaration reveals a certain Western bias. It emphasises rights as opposed to duties on individuals rather than on group or collective rights.[6]

---

6 M Freeman *Human Rights. An interdisciplinary approach* (Polity Press, Cambridge (UK) and Malden (Massachusetts), 2002) 36.

Article 1 declares that all human beings are born free and equal in dignity and rights. This is followed by Art 2 which confers on every human being an equal right to enjoy the rights established by the Declaration regardless of any criterion such as 'race, colour, sex, language, religion, political or other opinion, national or social origin, property, birth or other status' that may distinguish them.

Article 16, upon which Art 23 of the International Covenant on Civil and Political Rights is based, is of particular relevance here. It states that men and women of full age have the right to marry and to found a family without any limitation due to race, nationality or religion and have the same rights as to marriage both during and at its dissolution. Importantly, marital status is not one of the criteria. If the man and woman to the proposed marriage meet these criteria, it seems clearly irrelevant that one of them is already married or that a first wife or spouse objects. In relation to societies that observe the custom of polygamy, it is the eligibility of the parties to the proposed polygynous marriage rather than the objections of existing wives, the married status of the husband, and the likely negative consequences that must ultimately determine the matter.

Compliance with these international prescriptions regarding marriage appears clearly to be met in the case of polygynous polygamy in Papua New Guinea.

III ARGUMENTS FOR AND AGAINST POLYGAMY

All comments regarding polygamy have seesawed between two arguments: one supporting the custom of polygamy and for it to continue and the other opposing its continuation with calls for direct action to be taken to forbid the practice.

The major arguments in support of polygamy (meaning polygyny) is that it is a distinguishing feature of customary marriage practices in traditional societies that should be preserved. It is also argued that polygamy served certain important functions that ensured the stability of families and society as a whole. On the other hand, opponents of polygamy have denounced it as being evil because it is unchristian, the cause of domestic violence, and unconstitutional because it devalues women and violates women's human rights and is in any case no longer appropriate to today's Papua New Guinea.

An underlying characteristic of arguments against polygyny is their portrayal of men as perpetrators of abuse against and exploiters of women because they stand directly to benefit by committing polygyny. While it is true that young females are more likely than their older counterparts to be forced into marrying a man who is already married, it is unjustified to think that polygyny is always forced upon women thereby amounting to a violation of their rights as humans. Secondary wives are known to have stood their grounds against first wives in defending *their decisions* to become secondary wives. That first wives will object is totally irrelevant because this is not the issue.

A further important point to note is that not all attempts to marry polygynously succeed, and there are many or a combination of reasons that might produce such an outcome. It may fail simply because of the different motives of the husband and his second wife in entering into the marriage. Thus, if the second wife entered into the marriage in the hope that this will cause or force the first wife to leave and this does not happen, she will simply give up and leave or even be driven out by the first wife. In many such situations, the use of magic and other spells as agents to cause a competitor to leave is not unusual or uncommon. Also, if the husband is unable to marshal enough support from his kinsmen in putting together the required wealth to make the required payments as bride price, the proposed second marriage will fail.

The present discussion identifies some of the major and other points that have been advanced regarding the subject and seeks to provide some parallel perspectives on each of the points that have been put forward.

(a) Arguments supporting polygamy

(i) A distinguishing feature of customary marriage practices

It is often said that polygamy is an aspect of traditional marriage that is unique and must therefore be preserved. Prohibiting it would be a great loss to our cultural heritage.

It is clear that polygamy is not a common cultural heritage in Papua New Guinea. The custom of polygamy is not universal in Papua New Guinea. However, even though the custom of polygamy is not practised in all societies, it is common among the Highlands societies, the Sepiks, some Papuan communities, as well as among the matrilineal Trobriands society which observes a hierarchical form of social organisation headed by a paramount chief. Its disappearance therefore will have only a limited application in that it will only be of concern to societies that practise polygamy.

(ii) Polygamy performs certain important functions

One of the major reasons put forward to justify the continuation of the polygynous polygamy custom is that it performs certain important functions in society and that its forced discontinuation will impact negatively on families and community as a whole. This is because polygyny acted as a remedy for barrenness and allowed young widowed or divorced mothers to continue life as normally as possible after the husband's death or divorce and ensured that existing family relationships continued.

In all societies, regardless of whether or not the custom of polygamy is practised, the state of being unmarried attracts social rejection and single people have never been known to become successful social beings in society. They are instead the subject of stigmatization, avoidance, targets for discrimination, outright rejection, and exclusion from important customary rituals, ceremonies and events. Many never make it to becoming 'adults'. Polygynous polygamy provided the facility for widows and divorcees to re-enter society and for life to continue as normal. It was a perfectly legitimate response to crisis situations such as those mentioned. By enabling widows, divorcees and single mothers to enter marriage, it enhanced their dignity more than would be the case if they remained unmarried.[7]

Polygamy is an obvious remedy for childlessness as has been reported among the Enga where a barren first wife would assist the husband secure a second wife on account of her own barrenness.[8] If the wife is barren, and because offspring is a universally accepted important criterion for marriage, polygamy offers the best alternative to divorce to correct what is really an incomplete marriage. Divorcees are not regarded as suitable marriage partners for men who have never married. While barrenness may precipitate polygamy or divorce, childlessness itself cannot always justify such outcomes. This is because barrenness is not always the cause of childlessness in a marriage because impotence and sterility in the man can also be the cause of childlessness. In this situation, neither polygamy nor divorce and remarriage will improve the situation. Both barrenness in women and sterility or impotence in men are permanent fatalities.

Polygamy also enabled husbands who had lost their wives to debilitating illness or medical conditions to continue life in the community. Also, what if she is involved in a car or other accident and is paralysed? What should a husband do if because of these conditions his wife is no longer able to be a wife to him? Should he divorce her and return her to her family of origin or keep and look after her with the assistance of a second wife? What option should he take; to send her away and invite the wrath both of his own and his wife's family or marry a second wife who will also act as a substitute mother to the first wife's children? It seems clear enough that justice would require that he chooses the latter, but if a law is made prohibiting polygamy he can neither divorce his wife nor marry a second wife polygamously to help him out. Generally, too, any ground justifying a man to divorce his wife is a reason for polygyny.

It has been argued that these justifications are no longer relevant, maintainable or appropriate to the present circumstances of the country. Is this truth or an assertion? There are still childless marriages, divorce and family disintegration in non-marriage families are on the rise, the number of wives surviving husbands is also increasing, the number of destitute children dependent on their unemployed mother is increasing, and a social protection mechanism is still not in sight. So what are the circumstances that render irrelevant the traditional social security function performed by polygyny?

---

7 F Banda *Women, Law and Human Rights: An African Perspective* (Hart Publishing, London, 2005) 116–119.

8 A Kyakas and P *From Inside The Women's House: Enga Women's Lives and Traditions* (Robert Brown & Associates (Qld) Pty Ltd, Buranda, 1992) 158.

(iii) It is a man's customary 'right' to marry polygamously

The concept of 'rights' clearly excludes the claim that a man has a right based on custom to marry polygamously. Custom itself recognises no such right. Despite claims to the contrary, a man does not have and has never had a 'right' to take on additional wives as and when he wished or at his volition. It is a privilege at best and optional at worst. There has not at any time been recognised such a right as confirmed by the absence of any procedure to enforce a right against an unwilling partner or family. If a man attempted to do so today, it would be both criminal and unconstitutional. The fact that forced marriages are acceptable under custom is not based on a right but on the wishes of those in charge of her such as parents to marry the woman off to the man.

(b) Arguments against polygamy

(i) Polygamy leads to HIV and AIDS

There is no empirical data to support this claim. HIV and AIDS are the result of unsafe sex, not polygamy. So, if a man remains faithful to his wives and wives to their husband, this claim falls flat on its face. HIV and AIDS are by-products of sex, not marriage let alone polygyny.

To the extent that AIDS and sex are related, it is erroneous to think that polygamy and therefore marriage is only about sex. Sex is important but not the defining element of marriage. Marriage is a package, which includes sex. If one marries for sex, the emphasis is unfortunate. Sex is more frequent than marriage and there is today more sex outside of marriage than within the bonds of marriage. A whole industry and profession thrive on it. They are social and moral issues of their own, issues which threaten marriage itself, including polygamous ones. In other words, why marry for sex when it can be obtained with relative ease and without the complications presented by marriage anyway?

(ii) Polygamy leads to population increase

Again, there is no data to support this assertion. Like HIV and AIDS, population increase is the result of sex, not marriage let alone polygamy. Population is also influenced by human appetites for sex. Compared to women, men generally have a greater appetite for sex than their women counterparts. And since sex is today more frequent both within and outside marriage, population will naturally increase. Moreover, if, as seems likely, the frequency of sex outside of marriage is higher than in marriage, it is predictable that the time when the nation's legitimate population will be overtaken by persons conceived outside of marriage cannot be far away.

Polygamy is also relevant in the context of sex ratios in relation to the availability of eligible marriage partners. According to the 2000 census figures, out of a total population of just over 5.1 million, 48% were females while 52% were males. Of these, 69% of all males and females over the age of 15 years had had a marriage experience. The figures also indicate that 75% of women eligible for marriage were already married meaning therefore that only 25% were available for a first-marriage experience. This can be compared to a large 37% of eligible men who had yet to have a first-marriage experience. The figures clearly indicate that there were fewer women than men and even fewer females available for marriage for an increasing population of unmarried men. In other words, there is no surplus of women to cater for polygamous marriages without also depriving more men of their right to marry and found a family. In this scenario, polygynous polygamy has an undesirable effect by further reducing the number of females eligible for marriage.

The converse argument is that polygyny is a remedy for situations in which the ratio of females to males favours females. Polygyny inhibits population growth by reducing the number of available child-bearing females.

(iii) Polygamy leads to a thinning of available resources

This is not unique to polygamous families. It applies to all large families whether based on marriage or not. Resources are determined predominantly by economic factors, not marital status or form of marriage. Polygamy has the advantage of 'pooling' resources if each spouse is gainfully employed. This is clearly absent in non-polygamous relationships. The experience of some polygamous families cannot be used to predict the outcome in all other cases let alone provide the justification for making unscientific and outrageous claims.

Polygamy is as much about marriage as it is about putting together a functionally effective economic team in society. It allows for putting together people with different skills and strengths to pursue life's goals as a single team composed of units headed by the number of wives. Only polygynous polygamy makes provision for this.

(iv) Polygamy causes domestic violence

Polygamy presents very real and serious problems regarding violence within marriage. Polygamy has been responsible for many instances of violence among co-wives leading, in many cases, to the death of one wife. Polygamy will continue to send women and mothers to prison but only convicted criminals are sent there. It is true that polygynous polygamy today poses a much greater risk to family stability than in the past in traditional communities because daily life between men and women today brings them into more conflicting situations than was the case in the past. However, despite its seriousness, it must be accepted that violence of this type is not unique to polygamous unions.

The removal of polygamy will not halt sexual jealousy related domestic violence. The competition and competitors will not go away. If polygamy is criminalised, polygynous marriage as we know it will come to an end. Or will it? How will the law respond if, in observing this legal prohibition, the man decides to 'marry' his lover outside the formal legal system by living in 'sin' with her in a de facto union? What will be the argument against polygamy then? Alternatively, and to avoid sexual jealousies and conflict, he may instead decide to divorce the first wife and marry her competitor. Is this desirable? Will those who are opposed to polygyny be there to look after her and her children? Putting together a dossier against polygamy composed of cases involving polygamy-related violence and killings is skirting the issues of legal and constitutional relevance which is the primary focus of the views presented here.

Prohibiting polygamy by legal fiat is too simplistic, irresponsible and may in fact be counterproductive. Criminalising or otherwise banning polygamy may have the undesired effect of bringing down more monogamous families than might be intended by such action. Unless we achieve the impossible by removing all situations in which women will compete for men's love, it will continue to be the bane of domestic violence in domestic and family relationships in the country. Scapegoating polygamy in this way is therefore clearly objectionable. It is worth noting that in a 2001 Institute of National Affairs study on family and sexual violence in the country led by an international feminist, sexual jealousy, not polygamy, was stated as one of the reasons for family violence.[9] This is not surprising because sexual jealousies arise in all situations of plural lovers including polygyny.

Criminalising polygamy, declaring it unconstitutional or otherwise outlawing it is counterproductive and destined to cause more harm than good to those whose interests its banning seeks to promote and ensure. If polygamy goes underground, it must be expected that it will be even more difficult to protect the interests of those who stand to suffer most because of their generally weaker and vulnerable positions.

(v) Polygamy is unconstitutional

A number of reasons have been put forward to support the claim that polygamy is unconstitutional.

(1) Customary law does not recognise women as having a corresponding 'right' or 'privilege' to marry polygamously

This argument is based on s 55 of the Constitution, which prohibits discrimination of any form including sex. It is however not known if there really does exist in polygamous societies rules forbidding women from being married simultaneously to more than one husband, the typical polyandrous marriage. That women choose not to enter into plural marriages does not of itself point to the presence of a rule prohibiting polyandrous marriage.

If there is no customary rule forbidding women from marrying polyandrously, why then do women choose not to enter into plural marriages? Is it because it is

---

9 'Family and Sexual Violence in PNG: An Integrated Long-Term Strategy', Report to the Family Violence Action Committee of the Consultative Implementation and Monitoring Council, 2001, Discussion Paper No 84, at 10.

not their nature? If women did choose to marry polyandrously, how then is one to view the increased yet legitimate demands her husbands would naturally place on her for her sexual services or even to give them offspring in equal numbers? Would this be unconstitutional or otherwise illegal? Whatever the case, if women choose not to marry more than one man at any one time, or choose not to marry monogamously and choose instead to become a man's second wife, what constitutional or other legal justification can there be to demonise them and propose to make them criminals because of their choice to become a man's second or third wife? The present situation is perfectly constitutional, nor has any violation of core human rights prescriptions occurred. On the contrary, to deny these women their right of choice may itself be unconstitutional. Moreover, if women choose not to marry polyandrously while men choose to marry polygynously with consenting women, why blame men for women not choosing polyandrous polygamy?

(2) It is illegal because it forces young women to marry older men

It is universal that women marry men older than themselves and up in social rank (hypergamy) and rarely down (hypogamy). It is illegal to force any woman to marry a man she does not want, but the problem is not polygamy. The problem of legal concern is the 'force' used to 'contract' the marriage rather than the polygamous nature of the union. The task here is to deal with the criminal nature of the forced marriage, not its polygamous form. There already exist provisions under the criminal laws to charge and prosecute alleged offenders.

There are men who promise polygamy to women but continue to live unmarried with them, causing so much misery for both his wife and children and his proposed new wife and yet taking no steps to comply with the required marriage procedures. They are interested only in the object, not the subject. This constitutes abuse and a violation of her rights as a person and woman. They are a shame to polygamy and polygamists. Many failed or incomplete polygynous marriages such as these are perhaps a reflection of the different expectations men and women have about relationships. While women are looking for romance in relationships, men want sex.

(3) Polygamy does not allow an existing wife to successfully object to her husband taking additional wives

This is wrong. Under customary law, women have always protested and are expected to 'protest'. The protest can take many forms including in particular violence. Sometimes, the most powerful weapon against her husband's plan to take an additional wife (or generally for having wandering eyes) is not her physical might but her 'tongue'. Nowadays, and depending on the situation, she can use her tongue to her great advantage (at her husband's great expense) in public places like busy streets, at shopping places, market places, church, school grounds, his office or workplace, or even at public gatherings where he is present.

The rights to marry or associate or enter into a relationship with any willing person are fundamental rights of all humans. The wife has the right to 'protest' her husband taking on additional wives, but she should not expect to succeed in any court action against the husband or his lover to prevent them seeing each other or to associate with any other woman who chooses to associate with him. The National Court has held that any such expectation by the wife is unconstitutional as it violates ss 47 and 52 (freedom of assembly and association, and right to freedom of movement) of the Constitution.[10]

Her competitor also has a right to choose a man to be her husband. If she chooses to marry polygamously, her right to make that decision should be respected, indeed protected, even by law. If she chooses to be a second wife, the important issue is the legal relationship that is created between her and the husband, and even though the interests of the existing wife or wives are important, the critical legal issue must ultimately revolve around the new relationship. The marriage contract is between the husband and his second wife. She is marrying the husband, not his first or any future wife. Each additional wife entails a separate contract and demands, at least in the legal sense, separate exclusive attention to determine its legality both in substance and form. The social ramifications of their contract are irrelevant when the issue for scrutiny is legal in essence such that any relationship between the second and first wife is social rather than legal.

(4) Polygyny is discriminatory to women

There is no social, economic or legal justification to support the argument that polygamy is discriminatory to women generally. Competition among women for a man's love in marriage is not discrimination. This is a situation of conflict among equals which requires separate attention. It does sometimes create social problems, but there is nothing inherently discriminatory of women generally or against the first wife if another woman, in exercising her constitutional right, decides to marry the same man as his second wife. One must accept that by doing so she has exercised her right to choose a husband. Of course, it is going to be very difficult for the first wife and will rightly feel injured by the husband's conduct, but it can hardly be discriminatory to the woman who is joining the family or to the first wife.

It is also argued that polygyny licenses a husband to use the services of his wives to further his own interests at the expense of his wives. Appearance can be deceptive. Women and men belong to separate domains as mentioned earlier. It is a difference based on a common relationship of interdependence. The difference is not one of opposition but that of complementarity and mutual dependence. People who lack the capacity or refuse to acknowledge the strength of this bond will continue to knock polygyny on this ground. Allied to this is the argument that men use polygyny to become wealthy and achieve the 'big man' status, which is therefore exploitative of women. However, this is

---

10 *Emmanuel v Norman* (2003) N2427.

neither the full nor only story because in many instances men take on additional wives not because they want to become big men but because they are big men.

A stronger case against polygynous polygamy is that it is discriminatory to women because, while the husband enjoys exclusive rights over his wives' sexual, social, and economic services, the most they can expect is to share his services in these departments with other wives. It would be too simplistic however to use this reality to denounce all polygynous polygamy. In responding to this argument, the focus must essentially be on the first wife because the secondary wives will have known the claims of the first wife before consenting to becoming his secondary wife. It must also be borne in mind that plural marriages are separate contracts and sharing is not the same as competing for services.

The concept of monogamy as commonly known in the Western sense is generally absent in our societies. Customary marriages have always been potentially polygamous in societies whose marriage practices include polygyny. Our marriage laws are designed to accommodate both monogamy and polygamy. Under s 3 of the Marriage Act, Ch 280, customary marriages including polygamous marriages are valid provided they comply with the relevant customary marriage procedure and neither party is already married to another person statutorily and hence monogamously under the Act. Under s 360(1) of the Criminal Code Act, a person commits bigamy if he, while already married to another person, marries someone else unless both marriages are customary as provided for by s 3 of the Marriage Act.

(iv) Polygamy is unchristian and immoral

Polygamy is not unchristian nor is it non-Biblical or immoral. A Christian view in Papua New Guinea is that polygamy is as Christian in the New Testament as it is biblical in both the Old and the New Testaments. God created three institutions for man's benefit: church, authority/government, and marriage. Marriage is God's command and sex outside marriage (polygamous or monogamous) is sin. God created every species of animals including humans, male and female respectively for a very important reason – to regenerate the species they represent. But he reserved marriage only for the human species. He did so to facilitate the orderly process of regeneration of the human race.

There is no provision in the Constitution stating that Papua New Guinea is a Christian country. The Preamble to the Constitution, which is the only source from which this erroneous view hinges, does not provide the constitutional or other legal basis to make this assertion. While the dominant religion is Christian, pledging to adopt Christian principles does not make Papua New Guinea a Christian country. Section 45 of the Constitution (freedom of conscience, thought, and religion) makes this claim non-constitutional, not unconstitutional.

Under the disguise of having adopted Christian principles, the lobby against polygamy argues that banning polygamy would be in accordance with Christian principles. Is this true? There is no Scripture condemning polygamy as sin. The Scripture which many use to justify their condemnation of polygamy is at best opinion or advisory and at worst wrong and a hypocritical misinterpretation of the relevant Scriptures. The Scriptures clearly support marriage. Marriage is for life. It is a contract between the marrying parties and a covenant between them and God. This is clear by its condemnation of divorce, except in certain circumstances.

The most commonly cited Scripture 'Christians' use to anchor their argument is the 'two shall become one flesh' consequence of marriage on the persons marrying. The principal text is Genesis 2:24, referenced in Matthew 19:5–6, Mark 10:8, 1 Corinthians 6:16 and Ephesians 5:31. When the Scriptures mention 'one flesh' they are referring to sex, the act of having sexual intercourse, and not marriage. Thus, a man is 'one flesh' with each woman with whom he copulates, whether in marriage or with an unmarried woman or a prostitute.

1 Corinthians 6.16 makes it clear that just as a married or unmarried man can be 'one flesh' with a prostitute, a married man can be 'one flesh' with more than one woman including his wife. This being the case, a man can be 'one flesh' with more than one wife. The texts in Matthew 19:5,6 and Mark 10:8 which refer to the original 'one flesh' verse of Genesis 2.24 were dealing with divorce, not polygamy.

In his book, *Sex in the Bible*,[11] Tom Horner makes the important point that some time prior to the time of the New Testament, Jews seemed to have come to accept that having one wife at a time was sufficient for their needs. Because of Christianity's close affinity with Jewish morality, the custom of monogamy increasingly became part of the Christian doctrine and eventually became law itself. It should be noted too that the time these changes were taking place, both Judaism and Christianity were living in the midst of a Greek and Roman world that was also monogamous.

IV POLYGAMY IN THE COURTS

Even though the issue of customary polygamy has come up in the National Court, this has been only indirectly because of its link to substantive questions requiring the court's determination. In other words, its constitutionality or otherwise has not been the subject of focused legal arguments or specific judicial inquiry. Almost all the instances in which the issue of polygamy has attracted judicial attention have been because of its connection with the substantive issues of bigamy and violence involving co-wives and the husband. In many such instances, this has resulted in the death of a co-wife.

---

[11] T Horner *Sex in the Bible* (2nd printing, Charles E Tuttle Company, Rutland, 1982) at 34.

It is widely accepted, and the courts acknowledge, that polygamy is a source of stress and anger for wives leading invariably to marriage instability, violence and in many cases fatalities. In *State v Peter*,[12] the husband was already married to two wives. He then added a third wife. The second wife became angry with him for taking on the third wife in an environment she considered was already overcrowded. His action angered her even more by comparing her unfavourably with the newcomer who was said to be more educated than her. She went on to kill her competitor with a kitchen knife by stabbing her twice as she lay asleep. She pleaded guilty to murder and was sentenced to 12 years' imprisonment in hard labour.

In handing down his decision, Kirriwom J acknowledged polygamy as the source of the provocation that led to the prisoner killing the victim. He also noted the seriousness of the social implications of the practice of polygamy and that it was a matter of general concern requiring appropriate legislative attention. His Honour called for laws to be made to 'outlaw' polygamy for good and for severe penalties to be prescribed for offenders.[13]

A similar view was taken by the court in *State v Sinowi*.[14] In that case, the first wife assaulted the second wife 'to teach her a lesson' for frequently neglecting her duties as a mother and leaving the first wife to also take care of her five children. Even though the court understood her reason for assaulting the second wife, it did not relieve her of criminal responsibility and proceeded to impose a suspended non-custodial sentence of 6 months with conditions. In relation to polygamy, it was in the presiding judge, Kandakasi J's view that it was men who created the problems characteristic in polygamous families. It was therefore their responsibility to minimise disputes between co-wives and ensure that there was peaceful coexistence between and among co-wives and their children. Unless a man is capable of ensuring this, he should not marry more than one wife. He went on to say that:[15]

> 'Presently, there are calls for an end to polygamy … Cases like this demonstrate the need to enact such laws … The duty is on Parliament to enact such laws quickly for the security, peace and harmony of our society. There should really be no difficulty in Parliament enacting such laws promptly … The call for such laws to be enacted has been around for a long time and is yet to be enacted … I believe the reluctance of Parliament enacting such a law is because Parliament is dominated by men who rather prefer to have more wives than just one. They appear not to care about the problems polygamy brings upon a family and society as a whole. If they still wish to allow polygamous relations, they could enact laws to punish those men who are not able to maintain peace and harmony between himself and his wives, between his wives and children of such marriages.'

It will be noted that, while the judge in the earlier case proposed to punish men who married polygamously, the judge in this case proposed instead that a man

[12] *State v Peter* [2000] PNGLR 307.
[13] At 310.
[14] *State v Sinowi* (N2175 (13 December 2001).
[15] At 4.

who failed to maintain peace among (or) between wives and their children should be punished. In Kandakasi J's view, any legislative action must also seek to punish husbands who are unable to maintain peace between or amongst co-wives and their children.

In the more recent case of *Kumbamong v State*,[16] the Supreme Court, while expressing similar sentiments regarding the family hardships caused by polygamy and the need for appropriate legislative action, went further to consider if the practice of polygamy was constitutional or appropriate to Papua New Guinea.

The case concerned a woman who had murdered another woman because she was involved with her husband. It was however not clear if the victim was the appellant's second wife or lover. The National Court found her guilty of murder and sentenced her to 9 years' imprisonment. She appealed against the severity of the sentence arguing also that the lower court had erred in not taking into account inter alia the provocation of the husband taking on a second wife or having a lover. On the issue of provocation, the Supreme Court held that, even if the lower court had taken into account the circumstances of provocation, this was not reflected in the sentence. Taking into account the law on sentencing and circumstances, the remaining imprisonment period of 6 years and 11 months was suspended on condition that she kept the peace and was of good behavior for this period.

On the issue of the constitutionality of polygamy, the Supreme Court concluded that, in applying Sch 2.1 of the Constitution and relevant statutory provisions applying to the recognition and enforcement of custom generally:[17]

> '... we have no difficulty in arriving at the conclusion that the custom of polygamy is an inappropriate and unacceptable custom in our country because it does not apply universally and that it is repugnant to the general principles of humanity.'

This outcome is seriously objectionable both on procedural and substantive grounds. There was absolutely no justification at all for the Supreme Court to make this determination. It provided no legal or constitutional reasons for reaching this conclusion. The court did not indicate what these general principles of humanity are that it was referring to nor did it explain how Sch 2.1 and s 3 of the Customs Recognition Act Ch 19 which provide for the notion of repugnancy to the general principles of humanity render polygamy unsuitable, inappropriate, repugnant to the principles of humanity or otherwise unconstitutional. Moreover, it is settled law that it is not a requirement for a custom to be universally observed before it can be recognised and enforced by the courts. It seems obvious therefore that the court was influenced by the problems caused by polygamy and the sufferings by existing wives than by the existence of any constitutional or statutory provision prohibiting polygamy.

---

16 *Kumbamong v State* (SC1017 (29 September 2008)).

17 At 13.

The substantive 'legal' issue for determination concerned the severity of the sentence, not whether the custom of polygamy was unconstitutional or otherwise inappropriate to the circumstances of the country. This kind of judicial excitement is characteristic of many judicial decisions. It is tantamount to unintended judicial activism against polygamy in favour of a lobby for monogamy. The consequence of many such platitudes of social and moral concerns in court decisions is that many are of little 'precedent' value. In the present case, since the issue of the constitutionality of the practice of polygamy was not part of the substantive issue of the appeal, no legal arguments were necessary and therefore not presented to justify the Court proceeding to make 'final' determinations on a matter that demands full and proper legal arguments. Courts have a general duty to provide reasons for their decisions. To provide reasons is a function of due process and therefore of justice. This is neither clear nor apparent in reaching the conclusion it did. Reference to constitutional and statutory provisions which were not argued do not constitute reason. The author argues that the Supreme Court in this matter acted both outside and beyond the mandate provided to it by the appeal. Courts are foremost courts of law and not necessarily of justice and clearly not of morals.

V POLYGAMY, CULTURAL RIGHTS AND THE UNDERLYING LAW

The present generation has a duty to prepare the next generation to continue building this country using the foundation provided by our diversity. This cannot happen if we continue to allow this country to be used as a plantation for foreign and inappropriate values and standards presented as universally applicable models to measure our worth or if we begin by dismantling the cultural blocks that give us our identity and unity in diversity.

Papua New Guinea must not surrender its diverse cultural heritage in exchange for counterfeit values and standards that are presented as having universally applicable qualities. The intellectual community must therefore show maturity and independence of thought and analysis in commenting on matters of important cultural relevance. It must not confuse advocacy, activism, and lobbying with objective intellectual inquiry. Seeking to have polygynous polygamy outlawed, legislated against, or declared unconstitutional is too simplistic an approach. Failing to carefully and patiently develop appropriate rules and principles of the underlying law as tools for nation-building is tantamount to intellectual laziness, impatience and social irresponsibility. The extensive anthropological research over many years into the cultures and traditions of the country's societies remains to be translated into a body of 'conversations' to develop an autochthonous jurisprudence for the underlying law. Yet every year, this country sends delegations to New York and other international headquarters to bring back more international cargo of prefabricated solutions, recipes and formulas presented as requirements for our development.

The plurality of 'legal conditions' and mosaic cultures in our communities provides us with the greatest opportunity and the platform on which to build a truly 'rainbow' country. The Constitution already provides the framework within which citizens can 'grow' this country to truly reflect our journeys from the past. The diversity of our pasts is important. It marks the beginning of our present in the same way that our present marks the beginning of our future. Many successful citizens are offspring of polygynous polygamy and will look back on their family experiences with varying degrees of fondness or frustration. It is also possible that, without this background, many would not have developed the personal attributes that have made them as successful as they have been for themselves, their families, and for Papua New Guinea.

Some also argue that the present social and economic realities make polygyny an inappropriate facility. We have yet to be told what these realities are. In any case, what might be reality for some might not be the reality for others and might indeed be a deception for scores of others even within single communities. Are the arguments against polygyny for these reasons defendable? Victims of family crises do not want to know what the arguments against polygamy are. What they are demanding is a response to the realities of the crises confronting them. There are increasing numbers of women victims of family and relationship breakdowns whose economic realities are driving them to seriously consider or attempt polygyny as a solution (often with dire consequences).

Many have little choice but to use their bodies for prostitution on a full- or part-time basis just to survive and provide for their children. Why drive them into such moral depravity when the country can easily protect them from trading their dignity for subsistence by providing the necessary legal environment to enable them to safely marry polygynously? Many others of course simply abandon the polygyny idea altogether out of fear of the criminal threats and violence they can expect from competitor first wives and to avoid attracting the associated 'husband stealer' or 'pamuk' label, and may continue living by resorting to whatever means they can afford. In the end, economically vulnerable women have to choose between two necessary evils: marry polygynously or suffer the inequities and indignities precipitated by the realities of their economic vulnerability.

The author argues that the social and economic costs that individuals and families will bear and the need to protect them far outweigh the benefits that may be gained from the human rights agenda and if polygynous polygamy is outlawed or abolished. Many in the unregulated sphere who make ends meet already know that the human rights agenda does not put food on the table. That belongs to the unreal world. Ultimately, therefore, what is required is for policy-makers, legislators, and other leaders to explore other options which might be better suited to mitigating some of these hardships.

This is a national challenge for which national strategies must be considered to mitigate these hardships and protect citizens. To this end, polygamy can be considered as one of those strategies by making it available generally to any citizen who may wish to make this choice and not restricting it only to members of communities whose customs embrace polygamy. Exploring for options as to what type of legal environment might be suitable for this country will require a separate discussion.

An objective discussion of polygamy is not possible without first rejecting bias and personal experience. If one already has a bad relationship experience, it is likely to weaken one's ability to maintain objectivity. Unmarried people are also handicapped. Activists and lobbyists are dangerous to any objective discussion of matters impacting on people's traditions and cultures. No individual, group, or profession has a monopoly on views regarding important cultural issues but it is the human right of every person to be different, but not discriminated against, because of their cultures. Polygynous polygamy is about human rights, culture and society. Culture is also an important matter for human rights and justice.

The UN human rights system has neglected, if not failed, cultural rights for years. Its 'achievements' reflect, on the whole, the interests and values of dominant cultures which are also more active in, and engage more effectively with, the UN human rights system than members of subordinate groups. The marginalisation of subordinate groups and their cultural rights is seen by some as a form of 'cultural imperialism'. Moreover, the UN human rights system's emphasis on the individual rather than the collective dimension further weaken, erode and will ultimately see the demise of important cultural material that make peoples and societies unique.[18]

The cost of implementing the UN system of values and standards is a very important matter that has also to be considered for a developing country such as Papua New Guinea. Can the cost of implementing a human rights agenda, for instance, be justified when such expenditure seriously weakens the state's ability to deliver on services so critical to the well-being and advancement of its people such as in the health and education sectors? Is the UN human rights system which emphasises the interests of the individual more than those of the group appropriate to Papua New Guinea? Would it be justified and hence be defendable? Should the cost that must necessarily accompany implementing the UN system of human rights not be redirected instead to other areas of greater need so that the country develops for the benefit of the majority of the people?

There is also a growing sense of impatience and widespread frustration with the increasing annual expenditure and allocation of resources on implementing the human rights agenda in this country. Why should so much more effort and resources be directed to protecting the rights of individuals and the opponents of peaceful coexistence than on the realisation of the rights of the majority to promotion of social and economic advancement and well-being, medical

---

[18] P Hunt 'Reflections on International Human Rights Law and Cultural Rights' in M Wilson and P Hunt *Culture, Rights, and Cultural Rights: Perspectives from the South Pacific* (Huia Publishers, Wellington, 2000) 28–29.

services, education, and other social services and utilities? The recent introduction of the death penalty and the reintroduction of corporal punishment represent the clearest translation of the people's frustrations regarding these matters. They also indicate the country's resolve to make the bold shifts required to relate the UN agenda to the country's requirements and challenges and to implement the wider human rights concerns incrementally and over time. They also represent a political desire to search for solutions to the serious social and economic challenges facing her people from within, instead of being dictated to by the international community as to what these solutions are or ought to be.

VI CONCLUSIONS

This chapter has been as much in defence of polygamy as a form of marriage as it has been to expose the inherent weaknesses of the arguments against polygamy. It has been argued that the existing constitutional framework regarding citizens' basic freedoms and human rights allows polygynous polygamy to coexist with monogamous marriage. Indirectly as well, it has been about providing information to enable people to make choices they want and know the likely implications of the choices they make. Religious freedom allows people to make choices between whether to enter into matrimony or live outside wedlock. If they choose the former, they must further choose the form of matrimony, whether statutory, customary, monogamous or polygamous. This is perfectly constitutional. It is non-constitutional to say that Papua New Guinea is a Christian country and unconstitutional to impose the views of one religious group upon others especially if those views and beliefs are arguably wrong and without biblical or cultural basis.

It has also been an attempt to respond to some of the concerns and assumptions about Biblical polygamy that have been presented as truths. It has not been about seeking the support or sympathy of people. The argument for polygamy stands alone and on its own. It should be allowed to defend itself. Far from asking for sympathy, it is a demand that people accept polygamy as a form of marriage. Polygamy itself is not wrong. Its management is the problem because it is failing a lot of people. Polygamy is not inconsistent with underlying principles and values of human rights. The real and the biggest challenge to polygamy is the threat posed to it by the enemies of polygynous polygamy as a form of marriage in our cultures.

Polygamy must and can be understood and embraced within the broad framework of human rights. To denounce polygamy using only human rights criteria is a cop-out. People who condemn polygamy using only the human rights criterion have failed to show why polygamy cannot be embraced within a human rights context.

Those who denounce polygamy must also take some responsibility for the growing number of de facto unions involving married men and the consequential increase in the number of illegitimate offspring who may never inherit customary land and other property from their fathers. They must also take some blame for the growing incidence of violence in marriage, marriage breakdowns, and the increasing number of sexual sins being committed by married 'Christians' in our Christian country. Some have argued that polygamy is not in the best interests of children. Sometimes this is true, but not necessarily or always. However, polygynous polygamy is not about children's rights; it is only and all about a woman's right to choose a man willing to be her husband.

This country must be built on a majority voice, and responsible democracy. It must be based on the values of the majority of the people whose customs embrace polygamy, not on what international experts and their local facilitators want for themselves or for this country. Also implicit in the foregoing is the view that the practice of polygynous marriage should be rejected by people and by society only through the natural process of social change rather than by legal processes or interventions. Society generally everywhere has rejected polyandrous polygamy as a form of marriage. Likewise, polygynous polygamy should remain an option for any man and a woman of marriageable age willing to enter into such a marriage until it is overtaken by social change or the need for it no longer exists.

POLAND

SEPARATION OF ASSETS WITH EQUALISATION OF ACCRUED GAINS (ACCRUALS): A MARITAL PROPERTY REGIME FOR THE MODERN FAMILY?

*Anna Stępień-Sporek and Margaret Ryznar**

Résumé

La séparation de biens avec un partage des acquêts est un des régimes matrimoniaux adoptés en 2005, mais ce n'est pas le régime de prédilection en Pologne car les contrats de mariage n'y sont pas très populaires et qu'il y a un manque d'information à ce sujet dans les médias. Ce chapitre présente les grandes lignes de ce régime et suggère quelques nécessaires réformes. Il fait également état de l'utilité de ce régime tant dans l'Union européenne que dans des pays comme les États-Unis.

I INTRODUCTION

Separation of assets with equalisation of accrued gains[1] is one of the marital property regimes introduced to the Family and Guardianship Code[2] in Poland in 2005.[3] Regulation of the regime was initially limited because lawmakers intended to observe the regime's adoption by couples before implementing

* Stępien-Sporek, Assistant Professor of Law, University of Gdańsk (Poland); Ryznar, Associate Professor of Law, Indiana University Robert H McKinney School of Law (USA).

1 There are different translations of the name of this regime, which in Polish is termed 'rozdzielność majątkowa z wyrównaniem dorobków'. For example, a translation previously used is 'separate property with compensation for possessions gained' (see N Faulkner *Kodeks rodzinny i opiekuńczy. The Family and Guardianship Code* (CH Beck, 2010). However, in our opinion, a literal translation shows the most important characteristics of this regime. See also Anna Stępień-Sporek, 'Sharing of Accruals as the Best Solution for Marriage?' in B Verschraegen (ed) *Family Finances*, (Jan Sramek Verlag, 2009) 369–379.

2 Act of 25 February 1964 (Dz U no 9, item 59 as amended), hereinafter 'the Family Code' or KRO.

3 It was introduced by the act of 17 June 2004 on amendment of the Family and Guardianship Code (Dz U no 162, item 1691).

further regulations. However, although the regime has been in force for almost a decade and has certain advantages,[4] it is still not very popular among couples.[5]

The reasons for this regime's lack of popularity are two-fold. First, marital property agreements are not generally popular, although their number continues to increase. Secondly, there is a lack of information in the media: there have not been any social campaigns aimed at popularising the regime and scholars have not written much about it. Spouses considering this regime are alone in their choice and do not have enough assistance on either the doctrinal or jurisdictional details. Problematically, the consequences of the regime may turn out differently than the spouses would expect.

However, this marital property regime is important and popular across Europe, with similar regimes applied in different countries in the European Union.[6] For example, the French–German Agreement of 2010[7] has introduced an optional marital property regime based on participation in accrued gains[8] and all members of the European Union have been invited to join this agreement. The Principles of European Family Law Regarding Property Relations Between Spouses also stipulates participation in acquisitions[9] as one of the default regimes (a regime applied when spouses have not agreed otherwise). This regime is based on a separation of property during the marriage and a sharing of some assets upon the dissolution of the regime (principle 4:17).[10] Separation

---

4 See T Smyczyński 'Kierunki reformy Kodeksu rodzinnego i opiekuńczego' *Kwartalnik Prawa Prywatnego* no 2/1999, 314.

5 K Pietrzykowski in K Pietrzykowski (ed) *Kodeks rodzinny i opiekuńczy. Komentarz* (CH Beck, 2010) 509. There are neither official statistics regarding marital agreements of spouses nor a register of such agreements. Therefore, it is hard to give precise numbers.

6 K Boele-Woelki, F Ferrand, C González Beilfuss, M Jänterä-Jareborg, N Lowe, D Martiny and W Pintens *Principles of European Family Law Regarding Property Relations Between Spouses* (Cambridge, Antwerp, Portland, Intersentia, 2013) 140.

7 Agreement on the establishing of an optional matrimonial property regime/Abkommen zwischen der Bundesrepublik Deutschland und der Französischen Republik über den Güterstand der Wahl-Zugewinngemeinschaft/Accord entre la République fédérale d'Allemagne et la République Française instituant un régime matrimonial optionnel de la participation aux acquêts. For more information about the agreement see, eg, R Süß 'Der deutsche-französische Güterstand der Wahl-Zugewinngemeinschaft als erbrechtliches Gestaltungsmittel', *Zeitschrift für die Erbrechtspraxis* 2010; T Klippstein 'Der deutsch-französische Wahlgüterstand der Wahl-Zugewinngemeinschaft', GPR nr 4/2012; A Foetschl 'The Common Optional Matrimonial Regime of Germany and France. Epoch-Making in the Unification of Law', *Yearbook of Private International Law*, vol 11/2009.

8 In this regime, during marriage, each spouse has his or her own property and upon its dissolution a pecuniary claim arises. It is a claim regarding a share in the growth of the other spouse's property (participation in acquisitions). For more details, see C Gonzáles Beilfuss 'The Franco-German Treaty Instituting a Common Matrimonial Regime of Participation in the Acquisitions: How Could Catalonia Opt in?' in AL Verbeke, JM Scherpe, C Declerck, T Helms and P Senaeve (eds) *Confronting the Frontiers of Family and Succession Law* (Intersentia, 2012) 626.

9 Participation aux acquêts, Errungenschaftsbeteiligung.

10 K Boele-Woelki, F Ferrand, C González Beilfuss, M Jänterä-Jareborg, N Lowe, D Martiny and W Pintens *Principles of European Family Law Regarding Property Relations Between Spouses* (Intersentia, 2013) 142.

of assets with equalisation of accrued gains is rather different from the two above-mentioned regimes,[11] but the aims of the regimes are the same — to give one spouse a share in the other spouse's property. These international approaches prompt the consideration of the Polish regime of separation of property with equalisation of accrued gains, which can serve as a model not only for European lawyers, but also for American lawyers.

This chapter presents the regime of separation of assets with equalisation of accrued gains, suggesting a direction for necessary reform that could increase the regime's popularity. The chapter also endeavours to address the usefulness of the marital property regime for families in both the European Union (where efforts to harmonise marital property law were recently undertaken) and in other countries such as the United States. The latter shares to some extent the concept of the regime but may also be interested in alternatives to its two current regimes, particularly given that American couples, themselves, are free to agree to their own property arrangements by virtue of a premarital or marital agreement.[12]

II CONCEPT OF THE REGIME

Separation of property with equalisation of accrued gains (accruals) is a type of separation of property[13] and is a contractual regime adopted by spouses through a marital agreement before or during marriage. According to art 51^{2} KRO, the provisions on separation of property apply. During marriage, spouses

---

11 Separate property of each spouse is comprised of two parts: reserved property (*biens reserves, Vorbehaltsvermögen*) and acquisitions (*acquêts, Errungenschaft*). The latter is more important because a claim on participation regards this part of property. Acquisitions are all property that is not reserved property. Reserved property includes: (a) assets acquired before the commencement of the regime, (b) gifts, inheritances and bequests acquired during the regime, (c) assets substituting reserved property, (d) assets that are personal in nature, (e) assets exclusively acquired for a spouse's profession, (f) increase in value of the property included in (a) to (e) (principle 4:19). There is also a rebuttable presumption that assets are owned jointly by both spouses (principle 4:20). The reasons for its introduction are practical. In many cases, it is not possible to prove who is the owner of an asset (K Boele-Woelki, F Ferrand, C González Beilfuss, M Jänterä-Jareborg, N Lowe, D Martiny and W Pintens *Principles of European Family Law Regarding Property Relations Between Spouses* (Intersentia, 2013) 164).

12 In states with equitable distribution, the uncertainty of property outcomes in cases of divorce are similar to those in countries that recognise the separation of property with equalisation of accrued gains in that they are based on extensive judicial discretion and litigation. In determining a particular division under the equitable distribution approach, American courts consider several legislated factors, such as the length of marriage, the causes for the dissolution of the marriage, the age and health of the parties, and the amount and sources of income, as well as the vocational skills, liabilities, and needs of each party. Margaret Ryznar 'All's Fair in Love and War: But What About in Divorce? The Fairness of Property Division in American and English Big Money Divorce Cases' (2010) 86 *North Dakota Law Review* 115. In the minority community property states, each spouse has an interest in the community property, as opposed to separate spousal property holdings. Ira Mark Ellman 'O'Brien v. O'Brien: A Failed Reform, Unlikely Reformers' (2007) 27 *Pace Law Review* 949, 951.

13 T Sokołowski in T Sokołowski and H Dolecki (eds) *Kodeks rodzinny i opiekuńczy* (Wolters Kluwer, 2013) 346.

do not have common property and each spouse has his or her own property which is managed by that spouse. No action regarding this separate property requires the consent of the other spouse. The key issue in this regime comes after the dissolution of the regime: a spouse whose accrued gains are less than the accrued gains of the other spouse may claim for equalisation of gains by payment or transfer of rights (art 51^4 § 1 KRO).

The accruals are the increases in the value of the property of each spouse after concluding a marital agreement (art. 51^3 § 1 KRO).[14] The accrued gains are a book value and not specific assets. The amount of accruals is in money and the claim for equalisation of accruals is thus monetary. In order to establish the amount of accruals, spouses may prepare an inventory of property, but there is no legal obligation to do so. However, the lack of inventory can be problematic after a long-lasting marriage, and spouses may have difficulty proving their rights.

Although it seems clear what accruals are, there are some unclear areas on which opinion is divided, such as whether one should take into account the net value of property of each spouse or the gross value of property.[15] However, the separation of property with equalisation of accruals is similar to the community of property regime, which is based on gross value of property.[16] If the results of both regimes should be alike, the gross value of property should be decisive in distribution of property.

In their marital property agreement, spouses may decide how accrued gains are calculated, which is advisable given that the relevant regulation is unclear on the issue. If the spouses do not provide for it, according to art 513 § 2 KRO, the calculation of accrued gains does not take into account property acquired before concluding the marital agreement, or that referred to in art 33, points 2,[17] 5–7[18] and 9, and any assets purchased in exchange for them,[19] but will include the value of:

(a) donations made by either spouse, with the exception of donations to the common descendants of the spouse and minor donations normally made to other people;

---

14 For more details about the marital agreements in Poland, see M Ryznar and A Stępień-Sporek 'To Have and to Hold, for Richer or Richer: Premarital Agreements in the Comparative Context' (2009) *Chapman Law Review* 13.

15 Eg Elżbieta Skowrońska-Bocian claims that the gross value should be determinative (see *Małżeńskie ustroje majątkowe* (LexisNexis, 2008) 135). In her opinion, an opposing position could encourage spouses to overburden their property. An opposing opinion is presented by Tadeusz Smyczyński (*System Prawa Prywatnego, Prawo rodzinne i opiekuńcze*. Tom 11 (CH Beck, 2009) 465–466).

16 Eg decision of the Supreme Court of 15 April 2011, II CSK 430/10.

17 Property acquired by inheritance or donation.

18 Rights that cannot be transferred and may only be exercised by one person; items received as damages for bodily injury or triggering a health disorder, or as a compensation for harm suffered; debts concerning remuneration or other gainful activities.

19 The scope of accruals is similar to the scope of common property under the default regime of community of property (see art 31-33 KRO).

(b) services rendered personally by one spouse to the other spouse's property; and

(c) investment and expenditure on the property of one spouse from the estate of the other spouse.

There are many ambiguous areas of the regime. For example, the scope of accruals is not clear: it is doubtful whether the increase in the value of property acquired before the conclusion of the marital agreement is part of accrued gains. Spouses usually expect such a result,[20] but it seems that the entirety of property acquired before the beginning of the discussed regime is outside of accruals. Also undefined is how to calculate donations between spouses — whether they should be included in the property of the donor or the recipient. The next question regards the services rendered by one spouse. The Family and Guardianship Code does not definitively answer to whose property such services are added — to the property of the recipient spouse or the provider spouse. In this context, especially problematic are the services rendered by a spouse of an entrepreneur that cause damages. Furthermore, the regulation does not answer the question of whether services should be chargeable or not. Problems arise in drawing a line between services rendered as part of the spouse's duty to act for the good of the family pursuant to art 23 KRO and extraordinary services, which can be calculated as accruals.[21]

Accrued gains are calculated according to the state of the property at the time of the dissolution of the regime and according to the prices upon equalisation (art 51^3 § 3 KRO). The dissolution of the regime takes place upon the death of either spouse, divorce, annulment, legal separation,[22] entrance into a marital agreement that selects another regime, incapacitation,[23] and judgment on separation of property.[24] Situations wherein the regime ends by virtue of a judgment — particularly in cases of divorce, separation, or annulment — can be unfavorable to the spouse entitled to the claim on equalisation. The administration of each spouse's property is not limited and in cases of conflict between the spouses, it is probable that they will try to reduce their property, taking into account the moment that is relevant to the calculation of accruals. In the case of divorce, that moment is when the judgment is final. Thus, there are no measures to protect the entitled spouse from the other spouse's disloyal behaviour.

The claim on equalisation of accrued gains can be reduced for important reasons (art 51^4 § 2 KRO). Such reasons include, for example, situations wherein one spouse wrongfully does not use his or her abilities to earn money,

---

20 T Sokołowski in T Sokołowski and H Dolecki (eds) *Kodeks rodzinny i opiekuńczy* (Wolters Kluwer, 2013) 352.

21 M Nazar in J Ignatowicz and M Nazar *Prawo rodzinne* (LexisNexis, 2006) 190.

22 Art 54 KRO.

23 Art 53 KRO.

24 Art 52 KRO.

leaves his or her family, or spends his or her money on drugs and alcohol.[25] The wording of this provision is effective because regulations should not be too casuistic and indeterminate language is especially useful in the field of family law, where relationships between spouses differ and analyses of the individual circumstances of each case are essential.

Spouses can elect equalisation of accrued gains by agreement without a court. In their agreement, they decide on the sum that should be paid by the richer spouse or the rights that should be transferred to the entitled spouse. If the spouses cannot agree on the manner or the rate of compensation (equalisation), the court will decide (art 51^4 § 3 KRO). The court may decide only on the payment of money.[26]

A special rule is applied upon the death of either spouse. In such a case, the equalisation of accrued gains occurs between the heirs and the surviving spouse. Some representatives of this doctrine say that this rule can be applied only when the surviving spouse is not an heir.[27] However, it may be unfair that the situation of heirs would depend on whether the surviving spouse is an heir or not.

Pursuant to art 51^4 § 2 KRO, if the decedent had brought an action for divorce, annulment, or legal separation, the spouse's heirs may demand that the obligation of equalisation of accrued gains be reduced. This privilege is important but applies only if the relationship was deteriorated and the marriage was going to end.

The claim on equalisation of accrued gains is terminated after 10 years. This period starts when the marriage ends. Sometimes it is a few years after the end of the regime because marital property regimes can be changed during marriage by a marital property agreement. According to art 121 point 3 Civil Code,[28] a limitations period does not start and, if started, is suspended for claims made by one spouse against the other for the duration of the marriage.

In summation, separation of property with equalisation of accrued gains is an additional option for couples seeking a marital property regime in Poland. In the United States, each state has one of two default marital property regimes: community property, wherein marital property is held together by the spouses, and the common law system, wherein marital property may be held separately. The majority of American states have a common law system as the default regime, and upon divorce, the judge has significant discretion over the property

---

25 T Smyczyński in *System Prawa Prywatnego, Prawo rodzinne i opiekuńcze*. Tom 11 (CH Beck, 2009) 474.

26 M Nazar in J Ignatowicz and M Nazar *Prawo rodzinne* (LexisNexis, 2006) 190.

27 T Sokołowski in T Sokołowski and H Dolecki (eds), *Kodeks rodzinny i opiekuńczy* (Wolters Kluwer, 2013) 359.

28 Act of 23 April 1964 (Dz U no 16 item 93 as amended).

distribution no matter who holds legal title to the property.[29] In equitably dividing the property between the spouses, courts in common law states will consider factors such as the length of marriage, the causes for the dissolution of the marriage, the age and health of the parties, and the amount and sources of income, as well as the vocational skills, liabilities, and needs of each party.[30] Although courts often award half of the marital property to each spouse,[31] even a 95/5 split between the spouses may be considered equitable.[32] To avoid this default property regime, couples may contract by a premarital or marital agreement to employ a different marital property regime.[33] The various marital property regimes currently being explored in Poland and other European countries can offer couples in the United States new options in structuring their own property regimes by agreement.

III DIRECTION OF AMENDMENTS

Current regulation in Poland on separation of property with equalisation of accrued gains is not comprehensive, especially compared to that concerning the default regime of community property. On the one hand, it is logical that the most important rules on property relations are developed by most spouses themselves and, therefore, legislative provisions on contractual regime should not be developed. On the other hand, there remain many doubts on how to apply the regime and ensure the equalisation of accrued gains. This ambiguity discourages spouses from selecting the regime. Certainty is important, particularly in the property relations of spouses who want to be sure of the financial consequences of their regime. Therefore, at least some amendments to the current regulation should be considered.

---

29 D Kelly Weisberg and Susan Frelich Appleton *Modern Family Law* (5th edn, Wolters Kluwer, 2013) 230.

30 Margaret Ryznar, 'All's Fair in Love and War: But What About in Divorce? The Fairness of Property Division in American and English Big Money Divorce Cases' (2010) 86 *North Dakota Law Review* 115. In the minority community property states, each spouse has an interest in the community property, as opposed to separate spousal property holdings. Ira Mark Ellman 'O'Brien v. O'Brien: A Failed Reform, Unlikely Reformers' (2007) 27 *Pace Law Review* 949, 951.

31 For example, Indiana is a common law state that requires equitable distribution of marital property at divorce, but the Indiana Code provides that: 'The court shall presume that an equal division of the marital property between the parties is just and reasonable. However, this presumption may be rebutted by a party who presents relevant evidence.' Factors to rebut the presumption that an equal division would not be just and reasonable include: the contribution of each spouse to the acquisition of the property, the extent to which the property was acquired by each spouse before the marriage or through inheritance or gift, the economic circumstances of each spouse at the time the disposition of the property is to become effective, the conduct of the parties during the marriage as related to the disposition or dissipation of their property, and the earnings or earning ability of the parties as related to a final division of property and a final determination of the property rights of the parties. Indiana Code 31-15-7-5.

32 See, eg, *Bean v Bean*, 115 SW3d 388, 393 (Mo Ct App 2003).

33 Margaret Ryznar and Anna Stepien-Sporek 'To Have and to Hold, for Richer or Richer: Premarital Agreements in the Comparative Context' (2009) 13 *Chapman Law Review* 27.

One of the potentially problematic aspects of the separation of property with equalisation of accrued gains regime is the lack of necessary consent by the other spouse on property actions, particularly when they involve the family home and significant assets.[34] The Polish Family and Guardianship Code does not contain an extended regulation regarding protection of the family home. The only exception is art 28[1] KRO, stating that if one of the spouses has the right to a residence, then the other spouse is authorised to use the residence in order to meet the needs of the family. This provision is applicable to all marriages, regardless of which regime governs their property relations. However, it is insufficient to prevent a spouse from transferring the family home. For this reason, protection of the family home is guaranteed by both the French–German Agreement[35] and the Principles of European Family Law Regarding Property Relations Between Spouses.[36] It is true that introducing rules to protect the family home is a limitation of freedom on the administration of property by each spouse — a notable characteristic of regimes based on separation of property — but it is important to strike the proper balance between the rights of each spouse and the family as a whole. Particularly in cases of conflict between the spouses, it is essential to provide legal instruments that guarantee family members rights to occupy the home.

Calculation of accruals can be very complicated and the lack of an inventory of initial property can make it more difficult. Currently, spouses can prepare such an inventory, but it is not legally required. Introducing a legal obligation to complete such an inventory is an interesting proposal.[37] Marital property agreements in Poland are made by notarial deed,[38] and perhaps the notary public should prepare such an inventory at the time of making the agreement between spouses choosing separation of property with equalisation of accrued gains.

The equalisation of accrued gains can be made even decades after the selection of the regime. During all these years, spouses are free to enter into any legal transactions regarding their separate property. One consequence is that a spouse who is entitled to a claim on equalisation may not know the size of the other spouse's property. Therefore, it seems necessary to introduce an obligation of spouses to inform each other on this issue, at least regarding their most significant transactions.[39]

It is also advisable to follow the Principles of European Family Law Regarding Property Relations Between Spouses[40] and introduce a rule that the accrued

---

34 T Smyczyński in *System Prawa Prywatnego, Prawo rodzinne i opiekuńcze*. Tom 11 (CH Beck, 2009) 471.

35 See art 5.

36 See principles 4.5 and 4.6.

37 See T Smyczyński in *System Prawa Prywatnego, Prawo rodzinne i opiekuńcze*. Tom 11 (CH Beck, 2009) 472.

38 See art 47 § 1 KRO.

39 T Smyczyński in *System Prawa Prywatnego, Prawo rodzinne i opiekuńcze*. Tom 11 (CH Beck, 2009) 470.

40 See principle 4:25.

gains should be calculated from a different moment when the regime ends upon divorce, separation, or on the basis of another judgment. In such cases, the decisive moment should be the day the lawsuit is launched. The proceedings can last years, during which time spouses can solely administer their property without any limitation, which may result in potentially disloyal behaviour.

The last proposal is to introduce specific regulation on whether debts should be taken into account in calculating the accrued gains. Legal certainty requires the legislator to make a decision on this question. Given the functional similarities of the discussed regime to community of property, debts should not be taken into account as they are excluded in the distribution of common property in the default regime.[41]

IV USEFULNESS OF THE REGIME

Separation of assets with equalisation of accrued gains can be appealing because it combines the best characteristics of separation of property and community of property. During the marriage, spouses have a broad freedom in the management of their property, which enables them to be active on the market and undertake different commercial activities despite their riskiness and size. Meanwhile, the property of the other spouse is protected because the creditors of the active spouse do not have recourse against him or her. On the other hand, a spouse who wants to be less active in the field of commercial activity and spend more time in the domestic realm can share in the accrued gains of the other spouse. These general characteristics of the regime make it initially appealing.

Although this regime was considered as a default regime while Parliament was reforming marital property law in 2004,[42] legislators have abandoned this idea because Polish society is accustomed to community of property and it will not be easy to make any changes.[43] There is also no universal regime that is good for all families because arrangements of relationships can differ and spouses decide who cares for the children and the home and who engages in paid labour.

However, it is important to establish the common model of family in Poland and then answer the question of whether this regime is suitable for this model of family. In Poland and other European countries, women have become more active at the labour market.[44] At the same time, they continue to be active at home, often prioritising the family and devoting significant time to their

---

[41] See, eg, decision of the Supreme Court of 15 April 2010, II CSK 430/10 and decision of the Supreme Court of 5 December 1978, III CRN 194/78.

[42] The reform has been made by abovementioned act of 17 June 2004.

[43] T Smyczyński, *Reforma małżeńskiego prawa majątkowego*, Monitor Prawniczy no 18/2004, 827–828.

[44] See Główny Urząd Statystyczny. Kobiety i mężczyźni na rynku pracy 2012 (http://stat.gov.pl/cps/rde/xbcr/gus/f_kobiety_i_mezczyzni_na_rynku_pracy_2012.pdf).

children and home.[45] Although fathers are eager to spend more time with their children,[46] women still devote more time to housekeeping and children[47] and their incomes are often lower than the incomes of men. These factors suggest that separation of property, which guarantees the independence of each spouse, is not an ideal solution for these families if their chosen regime is to guarantee the lower-income or non-income spouse a share in the property acquired by the other spouse. The separation of property with equalisation of accruals regime and community of property are both this kind of regime, but the key difference is the moment at which a share in the property of the other spouse is acquired.

Specifically, the separation of property with equalisation of accruals guarantees a share in the other spouse's assets after dissolution of the regime, but it demands legal action by the entitled spouse. It may be difficult, however, for an inexperienced spouse to take the necessary legal steps. In such a situation, community of property may be more favorable for the spouse because it gives him or her a share in the property acquired by the other spouse from the moment of its acquisition. Each spouse is entitled to the property and spouses have equal rights to common property. Both regimes provide for non-monetary contributions of each spouse, but at different times.[48]

Thus, separation of property with equalisation of accruals may be a good solution for a marriage of two independent spouses with similar levels of education and activity in the market. In the traditional model of family, however, some practical obstacles may arise with the exercise of the rights of an entitled spouse. The existence of these factors has been noted by those considering replacing community of property with this regime as the default regime in Poland. When the model of the family changes and both spouses are active at work and at home, it may be time to consider a change in the default regime in Poland.

Couples in the United States can also learn from the experiences of Polish couples. As couples contract into their own property regimes in the United States, they should be aware of which property regime protects a lower-income or non-income spouse.[49] If they do not agree on a marital property regime and live in a common law state, they may experience extensive litigation on the

---

45 I Buber, *The influence of the distribution of household and childrearing tasks between men and women on childrearing intentions in Austria*, Max Planck Institute for Demographic Research. Working paper 2002, 10.

46 A Smith, *Working fathers in Europe learning and caring?* Centre for research on families and relationships, Research briefing 30, The University of Edinburgh, January 2007, 2–3.

47 SM Bianchi 'Maternal Employment and time with children: dramatic change or surprising continuity?' Demography nr 37/2000, 406–412.

48 B Rešetar 'Matrimonial Property in Europe: A Link between Sociology and Family Law', Electronic Journal of Comparative Law no 12/2008, 8.

49 A recent study suggests that the number of stay-at-home mothers in the United States is increasing for the first time in decades. D'Vera Cohn, Gretchen Livingston and Wendy Wang *After Decades of Decline, A Rise in Stay-at-Home Mothers*, Pew Research Social & Demographic Trends, 8 April 2014, available at www.pewsocialtrends.org/2014/04/08/after-decades-of-decline-a-rise-in-stay-at-home-mothers.

question of property division given the court's extensive discretion on this question.[50] Therefore, couples in the United States should also be aware of their property regime default and their options in reaching another arrangement by agreement.

V CONCLUSION

Separation of property with equalisation of accrued gains is a regime combining elements of separation of property and community of property, which may make it appealing.[51] Similarities between this regime and community property exist because both guarantee spouses a share in the acquisitions of the other spouse.[52]

The proposals summarised in this chapter can make separation of property with equalisation of accrued gains more attractive for spouses,[53] but they should nonetheless consider the model of their family. If it is a traditional model of family with a stay-at-home spouse and a breadwinner spouse, the couple may decide to select community of property, which provides an economically vulnerable spouse with legal title to the property. This can be beneficial for spouses not interested in litigation, which would be necessary under the regime of separation of property with equalisation of accrued gains.

Currently, separation of property with equalisation of accrued gains remains less desirable for spouses. Its regulation is not comprehensive and has at least a few gaps. Therefore, spouses who select the regime cannot be certain as to the regime's consequences. Their situation is analogous to the situation of spouses in American common law states with equitable property distribution, which may result in various outcomes given judicial discretion.[54] Both countries are representative of different legal cultures, but the experiences of each country can be helpful in planning legal reforms.

---

50 Margaret Ryznar 'All's Fair in Love and War: But What About in Divorce? The Fairness of Property Division in American and English Big Money Divorce Cases' (2010) 86 *North Dakota Law Review* 115. In the minority community property states, each spouse has an interest in the community property, as opposed to separate spousal property holdings. Ira Mark Ellman 'O'Brien v. O'Brien: A Failed Reform, Unlikely Reformers' (2007) 27 *Pace Law Review* 949, 951.

51 M Nazar in J Ignatowicz and M Nazar *Prawo rodzinne* (LexisNexis, 2006) 189.

52 T Sokołowski in T Sokołowski and H Dolecki (eds) *Kodeks rodzinny i opiekuńczy* (Wolters Kluwer, 2013) 346.

53 Currently, it is a relatively unchanging institution. Reform of the regime and a public campaign could be helpful in making the regime more appealing.

54 Margaret Ryznar 'All's Fair in Love and War: But What About in Divorce? The Fairness of Property Division in American and English Big Money Divorce Cases' (2010) 86 *North Dakota Law Review* 115.

PUERTO RICO

ELECTRONIC VISITATION, LESBIAN ADOPTION AND SUPPORT

Pedro F Silva-Ruiz[*]

Résumé

Ce texte sur les récents développements du droit familial portoricain couvre plusieurs sujets: (1) le droit d'accès virtuel ou informatique du parent non gardien dans le cadre des procédures de divorce; (2) l'adoption d'un enfant mineur par la femme qui cohabite avec la mère biologique; et (3) la réforme des lignes directrices en matière de fixation et de révision des ordonnances alimentaires.

This survey of the family law in Puerto Rico covers various topics: (1) virtual, computer visitations by the non-custodial parent in divorce proceedings; (2) the adoption of a minor by the woman cohabiting with the biological mother of the said minor; and (3) the revision of the Guides to establish and modify support decrees.

I ELECTRONIC VISITATION

The first topic is Law no 264 of 25 September 2012, known as the Law of Virtual – computer, internet, electronic or 'e' visitation, cybernetic visits or visitation – visitation of the non-custodial parent in divorce actions.[1] Internet visitations are no substitute for personal contact – person-to-person, face-to-face – between children and their parents. It is a complementary way to maintain relationships among parents and their children.

The stipulations for internet or electronic visitation can be general or very detailed ones. It is convenient that the stipulations cover who and how the internet services are to be paid or if a DSL line or greatest quality band-width is required.[2]

---

* Lawyer, Puerto Rico, Retired Professor of Law, Puerto Rico, member of various Academies.

1 See Pedro F Silva-Ruiz, 'Las visitas virtuales del progenitor no custodio en acciones de divorcio (Puerto Rico)' available at www.acaderc.org.ar/doctrina (accessed June 2014).

2 DSL – asymmetric digital subscriber line (ADLS). DLS service is delivered simultaneously with wire telephone services on the same telephone line (Wikipedia).

A judge could order virtual visitations, at the request of a non-custodial parent without the need for legislation, but as not all judges are up to date with available technological matters, it was preferable to legislate, so that this alternative is available to any party. According to the law, if a court orders the non-custodial person to pay out of his or her own pocket the cost for the equipment necessary to establish virtual or cybernetic visitation with the children, such cost cannot be considered in a petition for the modification of a support order.

II LESBIAN ADOPTION

The second topic is the adoption of a minor by a woman that cohabits with the biological mother of the minor.

Two woman living together since 1988 decided that the youngest one would procreate a child by artificial insemination. They contacted a man and contracted with him for the donation of his sperm. JMAV was born and was taken care of and raised by both women. They have doctoral degrees in the area of human behaviour and many years of experience working with minor children.

A petition for the adoption of JMAV was brought by the non-biological mother, AAR. It was asked that the filial relation between JMAV and the biological mother (CCV) be maintained. The biological mother consented to the adoption. As an adoption is only granted judicially, before the court the parties pleaded that the doctrine of Second Parent Adoption, as well as arts 137 and 138 of the Civil Code in force were applicable. The Second Parent Adoption is a legal procedure that allows a same-sex parent to adopt a partner's biological or adoptive child without terminating the legal rights of the first parent.

Both the courts of first and second (appellate) instance denied the petition, stating that arts 137 and 138 of the Civil Code did not allow it.

The case came before the Supreme Court.[3] It confirmed the decisions of the lower courts denying the adoption of JMAV by AAR, by a 5–4 vote. All sort of arguments are found in the various opinions rendered by the judges, including the dissidents as well as the ones in conformity. All the petitions for reconsiderations were denied.

On 6 March 2013 a Bill was introduced in the Senate of Puerto Rico to amend art 138 of the Civil Code. The Senate Commission studying the proposed Bill agreed to recommend it. It would allow the adoption that had been denied in the case *Ex Parte AAR*. It should be approved by the full Senate, then by the House of Representatives and signed into law by the Governor. It takes a matter of months. Then, AAR can adopt IMAV. The girl will then have two mothers as

---

[3] *Ex Parte AAR*, 2013 TSPR 16 (20 February 2013).

she always has. All parties – JVAV, the minor girl, CCV, the biological and legal mother and AAR, the non-biological mother, but legal mother – will be satisfied by the outcome.

III CHILD SUPPORT

The third topic I would like to bring to the attention of the reader is the revision of the Guides to Establish and Modify Support Decrees.[4]

According to art 8 of the Guides, the Guides 'must be revised at least every four (4) years to ensure that support decrees/orders resulting from their application be just and adequate'.[5] Economic inflation must be considered to determine the need for possible adjustments. Article 8 established a permanent commission for the revision of the Guides. More than a dozen persons will be named to the commission. This, it is suggested, is too many.

Neither the Department of the Family nor the Administration for Maintenance of Children has taken any steps to revise the Guides, notwithstanding the claim that they do so. They are in open violation of their own regulations (Guides).

Finally, the Commission for the revision and reform of the Civil Code, including the chapters on persons and family, has been dismantled and abolished.

---

4 'Las guías ...deberán ser revisadas por lo menos cada cuatro (4) años para asegurar que las pensiones alimentarias resultantes de su aplicación sean justas y adecuadas ...'.

5 'Guías para determinar y modificar las pensiones alimentarias en Puerto Rico', Reglamento 7135, efectivo el 24 de mayo de 2006 (Administración para el Sustento de Menores del Departamento de la Familia del ELA de Puerto Rico).

SOLOMON ISLANDS

FAILING TO ADOPT A NEW APPROACH: THE LAW OF ADOPTION IN SOLOMON ISLANDS

Jennifer Corrin and Eleanor Foote[*]

Résumé

Dans les îles Salomon, la (fréquente) lutte entre les normes concurrentes du droit de l'État et du droit coutumier est particulièrement aiguë dans le domaine du droit de la famille. Une difficulté supplémentaire s'ajoute avec le droit international, les demandes y ayant trait entrant souvent en conflit avec la culture locale. Le présent article examine la loi sur l'adoption dans les îles Salomon, à la fois historiquement et dans le cadre du régime actuel. Le système juridique dans lequel la loi sur l'adoption fonctionne est décrit, y compris le pluralisme juridique complexe composé du droit de l'État, des lois coutumières et du droit international. L'article examine la loi sur l'adoption, à la fois par rapport à la loi britannique sur l'adoption de 1958 (Adoption Act), qui s'appliquait auparavant aux Îles Salomon, et par rapport à la loi locale sur l'adoption rédigé en 2004, et met également cette loi en perspective par rapport à la jurisprudence existant en la matière. La législation est examinée au regard des exigences de la Convention sur les droits de l'enfant et la compatibilité entre la législation et l'adoption coutumière est discutée. Bien que la loi ait été réformée en 2004, il est soutenu que de nouveaux changements sont nécessaires, à la fois pour tenir compte de la Convention et pour clarifier les liens entre l'adoption en vertu du droit de l'État et l'adoption en vertu des lois coutumières.

I INTRODUCTION

Solomon Islands' legal system is one of complex legal pluralism. In the field of family law, the contest between the (often) competing norms of state law and customary laws is particularly acute. A further complexity arises from international law, the demands of which can conflict with local culture. Where

* Professor Jennifer Corrin is Director of the Centre for Public, International and Comparative Law in the TC Beirne School of Law at the University of Queensland and an Australian Research Council Future Fellow. Eleanor Foote is a BA/LLB student and a Summer Research Scholar at the University of Queensland.

children are involved, the welfare principle enshrined in state law and international law has come into conflict with the patriarchal and status-based norms of customary laws.

This chapter examines the law on adoption in Solomon Islands, both historically and under the current regime. The chapter commences with a brief overview of Solomon Islands, its people and its culture, to provide a context for the discussion of the approach to adoption. The legal system within which the law on adoption operates is outlined, including a discussion of both the colonial laws and the current complex pluralism comprised of state law, customary laws and international law. The chapter then looks in more detail at the law on adoption, both under the Adoption Act 1958 (UK),[1] and under the Adoption Act 2004 (SI), with reference to the relevant case-law. The relationship between the Acts and the more commonly used system of customary adoption is discussed. The legislation is also assessed against the requirements of the Convention on the Rights of the Child (CRC).[2] Although the law was reformed in 2004, it is argued that there is a need for further changes, both to take account of the CRC and to clarify the relationship between adoption under state law and adoption under customary laws. It is argued that the 2004 Act failed to take the opportunity to bring the law into line with international requirements or to take account of the customary laws and practice.

II BACKGROUND

Solomon Islands, as an archipelago in the South Pacific, is a challenging environment for legal reform. It consists of 992 islands of varying sizes, only two-thirds of which are inhabited. The country covers an area of approximately 28,330km^2, with an exclusive economic zone of 1,340,000km^2. It has a population of approximately 560,000, made up of 94.5% Melanesians, together with small numbers of Polynesians, Micronesians, Chinese and Europeans. Importantly, children under 15 years old represent 40.56% of the total population.[3] Only 20% of the population live in urban areas.

Solomon Islands is home to around 70 other living languages, including some which are spoken by as few as 75 people.[4] While English is the official language, Pijin is more commonly spoken. The country is predominantly

---

1 Adoption Act 1958 (UK) 6 & 7 Eliz 2, c 51 ('Adoption Act 1958').

2 United Nations Convention on the Rights of the Child, opened for signature 20 November 1989,1577 UNTS 3 (entered into force 2 September 1990) ('Convention on the Rights of the Child').

3 Solomon Islands National Statistical Office, *2009 Population and Housing Census: National Report (Volume 2)* (Ministry of Finance and Treasury, 2009) xxii. By comparison, in Australia that age group represents just 19% of the total population: Australian Bureau of Statistics, *3235.0 – Population by Age and Sex, Regions of Australia, 2012* (30 August 2013) Australian Bureau of Statistics: www.abs.gov.au/Ausstats/abs@.nsf/mf/3235.0.

4 M Paul Lewis, Gary F Simons and Charles D Fennig (eds) *Ethnologue: Languages of the World* (SIL International, Dallas, Texas, 17th edn, 2013).

Christian, made up of 45% Anglican, 18% Catholic and 12% Methodist or Protestant. Literacy stands at 76%, and more than 80% of the population rely on subsistence agriculture and fishing for survival. The average GDP/capita is AUD$2,116.46,[5] and more than one-third of the domestic budget is derived from overseas development assistance.[6]

Culture and tradition play an important role in Solomon Islands, particularly with respect to interpersonal relationships. Solomon Islanders have a strong allegiance to members of their extended family, which includes aunts, uncles, grandparents, cousins and other relatives.[7] Families and local communities provide a social support system. Children are valued highly as a source of labour and assistance and because they ensure the survival of the family line.[8] However, particularly in urban areas, the traditional way of life is being eroded due to societal changes, including the economic transition from subsistence living to a cash economy, exposure to external cultural influences and labour migration as Solomon Islanders move from their home environment in search of employment.[9] These changes have weakened family support networks and adherence to customary norms.

III THE LEGAL SYSTEM

Solomon Islands became a British Protectorate in 1893.[10] Customary laws, which had governed the conduct of Solomon Islanders prior to the arrival of foreigners, were not originally recognised as part of the state legal system, except to the extent that they were used as the basis for determining customary land issues.[11] However, customary laws were tolerated provided they were not 'repugnant to natural justice and humanity',[12] and, in 1942, Native Courts were 'constituted in accordance with the native law or customs of the area in which the court [was] to have jurisdiction'.[13] These courts applied 'the native law and custom prevailing in the area'[14] in minor civil and criminal matters involving indigenous Solomon Islanders.[15]

---

5 Department of Foreign Affairs and Trade, *Solomon Islands* (December 2013) Country and region fact sheets: www.dfat.gov.au/geo/fs/solo.pdf.

6 Katy LeRoy *Public Participation in Constitution-Making: the Pacific Islands* (Interpeace, 2011) 26–27.

7 Michael Kwa'iola *Living Tradition: a Changing Life in Solomon Islands* (University of Hawai'i Press, Honolulu, 1999) 27–30.

8 Michael Kwa'iola *Living Tradition: a Changing Life in Solomon Islands* (University of Hawai'i Press, Honolulu, 1999) 27–30.

9 Michael Kwa'iola *Living Tradition: a Changing Life in Solomon Islands* (University of Hawai'i Press, Honolulu, 1999) 132–134.

10 Pacific Order in Council 1893 (UK).

11 Land and Titles Ordinance 1968 (UK), s 219.

12 Native Courts Act [Cap 33] (SI), s 18.

13 Native Courts Act [Cap 33] (SI), s 3. See now Local Courts Act [Cap 19] (SI).

14 Native Courts Act [Cap 33] (SI), s 11. See now Local Courts Act [Cap 19] (SI).

15 Native Courts Ordinance, s 10.

At independence on 7 July 1978, Solomon Islands' new Constitution provided that United Kingdom statutes 'of general application' in force on 1 January 1961 would continue to apply.[16] As discussed below in relation to the Adoption Act 1958, the phrase 'of general application' was not defined in the Constitution, and has not been interpreted consistently by courts in Solomon Islands or elsewhere in the Pacific.[17] These foreign laws were intended to apply only until the newly formed Parliament introduced its own laws, tailored to the country's specific situation. However, a lack of resources and an inactive legislature meant that many outdated, unsuitable United Kingdom statutes, including the Adoption Act, were retained for many years post-independence.

As is common in small South Pacific countries, the independence Constitution of Solomon Islands explicitly recognises the importance of customary laws, which had survived the colonial era and continued to play a vital role in land and family law.[18]·The Constitution provides that customary laws shall have effect as part of the law of Solomon Islands,[19] and that particular regard should be paid by Parliament to the 'customs, values and aspirations of the people of Solomon Islands' when providing for the application of laws.[20] The relationship between customary laws and other sources of law is dealt within Sch 3, which provides that customary laws are superior to common law and equity, but inferior to the Constitution and Acts of Parliament.[21] The term 'Act of Parliament' in Sch 3 has been read as 'Act of Solomon Islands' Parliament', meaning that, in theory, the courts should apply customary laws even if they are inconsistent with an Act of the UK Parliament.[22] However, at least in the context of custody proceedings, the High Court of Solomon Islands has suggested that the two sources of law rank equally, and the choice will be determined on the basis of public policy, taking into account the circumstances of each particular case.[23]

It should also be noted that the preceding theoretical description of the hierarchy of laws belies the complexity of the legal system which operates in practice. Common law is often applied as a matter of course, whereas customary laws are only considered if they are raised (and proved) by the

---

16 Constitution of Solomon Islands 1978, s 76(1) (the Constitution is a schedule to Solomon Islands Independence Order 1978(UK)). English common law and equity was also retained in force: Constitution of Solomon Islands, s 76(2).

17 Jennifer Corrin 'Discarding Relics of the Past: Patriation of Laws in the South Pacific' (2008) 39 *Victoria University of Wellington Law Review* 635, 642.

18 Jennifer Corrin and Don Patterson *Introduction to South Pacific Law* (3rd edn, Palgrave MacMillan, South Yarra, Vic, 2011) 40.

19 Constitution of Solomon Islands, s 76.

20 Constitution of Solomon Islands, s 75.

21 Constitution of Solomon Islands, s 76(2)(1).

22 *R v Ngena* [1983] SILR 1; Jennifer Corrin and Don Patterson *Introduction to South Pacific Law* (3rd edn, Palgrave MacMillan, South Yarra, Vic, 2011) 47. The Court's decision in relation to custody disputes in particular have not reflected this interpretation: see the discussion of the customary laws on adoption at section IV(a) below.

23 *K v T* [1985-1986] SILR 49. This case involved a custody dispute, and accordingly is arguably of questionable relevance to the interpretation of the phrase outside this area of law.

parties.[24] Further, customary laws differ from place to place.[25] Using different language groups as a rough indication of the likelihood of diverse customary laws, there may be over 70 different bodies of customary laws.[26] Where parties to a case which comes before a state court come from different areas, the Customs Recognition Act 2000 makes provision for resolving any dispute as to the customary law which applies. However, this Act is not yet in force.[27]

International law also plays a role in Solomon Islands' legal system. The country is party to various international treaties and conventions, including the CRC. However, due to Solomon Islands' dualist system, these instruments do not have any direct legal effect unless they are incorporated in national legislation.[28] To date Solomon Islands has not passed any domestic legislation to implement its international obligations in relation to children. This flows from a lack of resources, weak enforcement mechanisms and limited external pressure from civil society organisations such as the Pacific Forum.[29] It may also reflect the fact that, as touched on above, international laws are often at odds with aspects of local culture, and this is discussed further below.

IV LAW ON ADOPTION

(a) Customary laws

Prior to Solomon Islands becoming a British Protectorate, arrangements regarding children were dealt with under customary laws. Those laws survived the colonial era and are still widespread throughout Solomon Islands. Whilst the term 'customary adoption' is used in this chapter to refer to the process by which children are passed into the care of someone other than their biological parents, there is no direct equivalent of adoption in customary law systems. In contrast to the Western concept of adoption, which involves creating a 'new' family and severing the adopted child's contact with their biological parents, customary adoption arrangements are more akin to fostering or child

---

[24] Jennifer Corrin 'Accommodating Legal Pluralism in Pacific Courts: Problems of Proof of Customary Law' (2010) 15 *International Journal of Evidence & Proof* 1, 2.

[25] Jennifer Corrin 'A Question of Identity: Complexities of State Law Pluralism in the South Pacific' (2010) 61 *Journal of Legal Pluralism* 145, 147.

[26] See also Customs Recognition Act 2000 (SI), s 10 (not yet in force).

[27] Customs Recognition Act 2000 (SI), s 10 provides that, in the case of a conflict of customary laws, the Court 'shall consider all the circumstances and may adopt the system that it is satisfied the justice of the case requires'.

[28] Jennifer Corrin 'Cultural Relativism vs. Universalism: The South Pacific Reality' in Arnold Rainier (ed) *The Universalism of Human Rights* (Springer, Dordrecht, 2012) 103, 107.

[29] Sue Farran 'Child Adoption: the Challenges Presented by the Plural Legal Systems of South Pacific Island States' (2009) 21 *Child and Family Quarterly* 462, 464.

guardianship.[30] Further, customary adoption is not necessarily a clear-cut, single event as occurs under state law, but may be a gradual process, extending over a number of years.[31]

Due to the lack of formalised written records, it is difficult to ascertain with accuracy the rates of customary adoption, but it has been suggested that most adoptions occur within traditional customary systems, particularly in rural areas.[32]

Although customary adoptions are widespread, the norms governing such adoptions vary between different communities.[33] For example, within the Bellonese clan, the primary purpose of customary adoption is to secure a male heir for the first son of a family. Within the Temotu clan, unborn children can form part of a marriage contract, with the offspring of the marriage being assigned to particular relatives at the time of betrothal.[34]

Despite this heterogeneity, it is possible to discern some general patterns. Customary adoptions typically occur within the extended family.[35] This reflects the cultural norms which emphasise extended family and the significant role of children. The norms of customary adoption also echo the prominence of kinship and community, and the importance of collective, rather than individual, responsibility.[36]

Customary adoption also operates within the context of the broader role that customary laws play in providing social support. For example, grandparents may adopt an orphaned child to ensure proper care.[37] A common situation is for parents who have many children to allow one or more of the children to be adopted by an extended family member who has few or no children.[38] Given

---

30 Kenneth Brown *Reconciling Customary and Received Law in Melanesia: the Post-Independence Experience in Solomon Islands and Vanuatu* (Charles Darwin University Press, NT, 2005) 143.

31 Sue Farran *Law and the Family in the South Pacific* (University of the South Pacific, Fiji, 2011) 54.

32 Dejo Olowu 'The Legal Regime of Child Adoption in the South Pacific and the Implications of International Regulatory Standards' (2007) 19 *Sri Lanka Journal of International Law* 109, 137; Anita Jowitt 'The Future of Law in the South Pacific' (2008) 12 *Journal of South Pacific Law* 43, 44.

33 Solomon Islands Government *Reports Submitted by State Parties under Article 44 of the Convention: Solomon Islands*, UN Doc CRC/C/51/Add.6 (12 July 2002), 54.

34 Solomon Islands Government *Reports Submitted by State Parties under Article 44 of the Convention: Solomon Islands*, UN Doc CRC/C/51/Add.6 (12 July 2002), 54. Cf *Igolo v Ita* (1983) SILR 56.

35 Solomon Islands Government *Reports Submitted by State Parties under Article 44 of the Convention: Solomon Islands*, UN Doc CRC/C/51/Add.6 (12 July 2002) 30.

36 Dejo Oluwu 'The Legal Regime of Child Adoption in the South Pacific and the Implications of International Regulatory Standards' (2007) 19 *Sri Lanka Journal of International Law* 109, 137.

37 Solomon Islands Government *Reports Submitted by State Parties under Article 44 of the Convention: Solomon Islands*, UN Doc CRC/C/51/Add.6 (12 July 2002), 54.

38 Jennifer Corrin and Don Patterson *Introduction to South Pacific Law* (3rd edn, Palgrave MacMillan, South Yarra, Vic, 2011) 201.

the close family ties between the birth parents and adoptive parents, both sets of parents remain involved with the child's upbringing.

In some cases, these customary norms conflict with state and international norms. For example, a marriage contract may stipulate that, upon the father's death, any children of the marriage will be cared for by the deceased father's relatives, rather than the biological mother.[39] The rights of adopted children within a family may differ from those of the biological children, particularly in relation to property.[40]

Arguably the most distinctive feature of customary adoption law is the lack of state intervention. Formal state law adoption, on the other hand, is assumed to be subject to the control and approval of the state (through the courts), and particularly in recent times often requires the investigation of the prospective adoptive parents by child social workers. Such an investigation in relation to a customary adoption is inconsistent with the traditional view of adoption as a private family affair, the purpose of which is to maintain intergroup cohesion.[41]

There is nothing to prevent customary adoptive parents subsequently making an application to adopt under state law.[42] However, as discussed further below, a customary adoption cannot provide a shortcut through the necessary state law formalities.[43]

(b) State law

Until 2008, when the Adoption Act 2004 came into force, Solomon Islands did not have its own statute governing adoption. This gap was initially filled by the Adoption Act 1958.[44] The 1958 Act was, until 2007, applied by the courts without any consideration of whether it fulfilled the constitutional requirements of being 'of general application' and appropriate to the circumstances of Solomon Islands.[45] As required by the Constitution,[46] the Act was incorporated into Solomon Islands law as it existed on 1 January 1961. In the United

---

39 Solomon Islands Government *Reports Submitted by State Parties under Article 44 of the Convention: Solomon Islands*, UN Doc CRC/C/51/Add.6 (12 July 2002), 54.

40 Sue Farran 'Child Adoption: the Challenges Presented by the Plural Legal Systems of South Pacific Island States' (2009) 21 *Child and Family Quarterly* 462, 473.

41 Kenneth Brown *Reconciling Customary and Received Law in Melanesia: the post-Independence Experience in Solomon Islands and Vanuatu* (Charles Darwin University Press, NT, 2005) 142.

42 Solomon Islands Government *Reports Submitted by State Parties under Article 44 of the Convention: Solomon Islands*, UN Doc CRC/C/51/Add.6 (12 July 2002), 54.

43 *Re Belo* (Unreported, High Court, Solomon Islands, Brown J, 12 December 2003) available via www.paclii.org at [2003] SBHC 84.

44 Jennifer Corrin and Don Patterson *Introduction to South Pacific Law* (3rd edn, Palgrave MacMillan, South Yarra, Vic, 2011) 200.

45 The Act was applied in at least four cases between independence and 2007: *Re V* [1985-6] SILR 252; *Re Okini Manu* (Unreported, High Court, Solomon Islands, Palmer J, 30 July 1999) available via www.paclii.org at [1999] SBHC 74; *Re Stickel* (Unreported, High Court, Solomon Islands, Kabui J, 31 August 2001) available via www.paclii.org at [2001] SBHC 138; *Re Belo* (Unreported, High Court, Solomon Islands, Brown J, 12 December 2003) available via

Kingdom[47] and elsewhere in the common law world[48] adoption legislation was reformed to reflect the prevailing notion of the centrality of the child's best interests in adoption proceedings.[49] However, reforms of the law on adoption in the United Kingdom did not form part of Solomon Islands law.[50]

Not only was the Adoption Act 1958 out of date in the common law world, but it was also out of step with customary norms. The Act was based on the assumption that state intervention into family affairs was justified. This assumption was symptomatic of the poor cultural fit which often plagues introduced law. The lack of popular acceptance of the law also led to bureaucratic inertia in implementing the law, which was not supported by the necessary local infrastructure.[51] In particular, there were no child welfare experts, but only one or two social workers who could be called on to prepare a report.[52]

Before making an order, the court was required to be satisfied that the adoption order would be for the welfare of the child.[53] However, the Act provided little guidance on how this was to be determined. The only factors specifically referred to were the health of the applicant, and the need to give due consideration to the wishes of the child, taking into account their age and degree of understanding of the proceedings.[54] In cases decided under the Act, the High Court commonly considered the ability of the applicants to provide for the needs and welfare of the child.[55] The court in some cases expressly referred to 'the best interests of the child' as the basis for making an order. For example, in *Re V*,[56] Ward CJ granted the adoption order on this basis. The views of the child were also taken into account in several cases. For example, in *Re Okini Manu*,[57] Palmer J did not expressly refer to the child's welfare, but he did consider the child's preference that the adoption order be granted.

---

www.paclii.org at [2003] SBHC 84. In each of these cases, the court referred to the requirements of the Act in reaching a decision to grant or refuse adoption orders.

46 Constitution of Solomon Islands, Sch 3.

47 Adoption and Children Act 2002 (UK) c 38, s 1(2).

48 See, eg, Adoption Act 2009 (Qld), s 6(1); Adoption Act, RSBC 1996, c 5, s 2.

49 Sue Farran 'Child Adoption: the Challenges Presented by the Plural Legal Systems of South Pacific Island States' (2009) 21 *Child and Family Quarterly* 462, 464.

50 Sue Farran 'Child Adoption: the Challenges Presented by the Plural Legal Systems of South Pacific Island States' (2009) 21 *Child and Family Quarterly* 462, 469.

51 Cf Jennifer Corrin and Lalotoa Mulitalo 'Adoption and "Vae Tama" in Samoa' in B Atkin (ed) *The International Survey of Family Law, 2011 Edition*, (Jordan Publishing Limited, 2011) 313.

52 Jennifer Corrin was a private practitioner in Solomon Islands from 1986 to 1996 and this information is based on her personal experience.

53 Adoption Act 1958, s 7(1).

54 Adoption Act 1958, s 7(2).

55 *Re Stickel* (Unreported, High Court, Solomon Islands, Kabui J, 31 August 2001) available via www.paclii.org at [2001] SBHC 138.

56 *Re V* [1985-6] SILR 252.

57 (Unreported, High Court, Solomon Islands, Palmer J, 30 July 1999) available via www.paclii.org at [1999] SBHC 74.

The Act also failed to make any provision for intercountry adoptions. This is perhaps not surprising, given that the Act required adoptive parents to be domiciled in Solomon Islands.[58] However, in practice the courts allowed intercountry adoptions, without safeguarding the adopted child's future welfare. For example, in *Re Stickel*[59] the Court granted the adoption order to a couple who were ordinarily resident in the United States and who planned to return to the United States following the proceeding, notwithstanding the requirement that they be domiciled in Solomon Islands.

The Adoption Act 1958 was drafted for use in the United Kingdom, and consequently made no reference to customary laws. Whilst the practice of customary adoption was recognised as a fact by the courts, it did not lead automatically to the subsequent grant of a formal adoption order. For example, in *Re Belo*[60] the court refused to make an order based only on the existence of a prior customary adoption of the child by the applicant, stating that this missed the point that under the 1958 Act the Court was obliged to consider factors impacting on the welfare of the child. In *R v Takabea*[61] the defendant had been adopted under Kiribati custom by a citizen of Solomon Islands, and he argued that on that basis he held Solomon Islands citizenship. The Court held that, in order for the adoption to be recognised, the defendant would need to commence proceedings for a formal adoption order under the Adoption Act 1958.

Despite at least four preceding decisions of the High Court applying the 1958 Act,[62] in 2007 Brown J refused to apply the Act on the basis that it was not an Act of general application. His Lordship stated in *Re Tiokobule Bero* that the Act was 'wholly irrelevant' to Solomon Islands and was applicable only to UK residents.[63] His Lordship based this conclusion primarily on the fact that the Act required reports and consents from authorities which only existed in the United Kingdom. Brown J stated that customary adoption was more appropriate for Solomon Islands and suggested that customary adoption could be recognised through a Certificate of Recognition of Adoption. His Lordship set out various criteria to be satisfied before the granting of the Certificate, including that the adoption must have taken place in accordance with the custom of the child and the adoptive parents. This procedure was not drawn

---

58 Adoption Act 1958, s 1.

59 *Re Stickel* (Unreported, High Court, Solomon Islands, Kabui J, 31 August 2001) available via www.paclii.org at [2001] SBHC 138.

60 (Unreported, High Court, Solomon Islands, Brown J, 12 December 2003) available via www.paclii.org at [2003] SBHC 84.

61 (Unreported, High Court, Solomon Islands, Palmer J, 23 December 1993) available via www.paclii.org at [1993] SBHC 81.

62 *Re V* [1985-6] SILR 252; *Re Okini Manu* (Unreported, High Court, Solomon Islands, Palmer J, 30 July 1999) available via www.paclii.org at [1999] SBHC 74; *Re Stickel* (Unreported, High Court, Solomon Islands, Kabui J, 31 August 2001) available via www.paclii.org at [2001] SBHC 138; *Re Belo* (Unreported, High Court, Solomon Islands, Brown J, 12 December 2003) available via www.paclii.org at [2003] SBHC 84.

63 *Re Tiokobule Bero* (Unreported, High Court, Solomon Islands, Brown J, 27 July 2007) available via www.paclii.org at [2007] SBHC 94.

from the Adoption Act 1958, which Brown J had held did not apply. Instead, His Lordship appears to have drawn on the law on adoption in Papua New Guinea.[64] In any event, these remarks were obiter, as it was ultimately held that there was not enough evidence before the court to make a decision on adoption. Apart from ignoring pre-existing case-law, this approach seems rather ironic in the light of the fact that in the earlier case of *Re Belo*,[65] discussed above, His Lordship raised no objection to an application made under the 1958 Act, but refused to make an adoption order on the basis that it was a court's 'duty to be satisfied in relation to particular matters' under the legislation.

Later the same year, in *Re Miria*,[66] Palmer CJ restored the status quo and held emphatically that the 1958 Act was an Act of general application. His Lordship applied the test used by the High Court in *R v Ngena*[67] to determine whether an Act was of general application. It was decisive that the Act applied to persons not normally resident in the UK, it was not inappropriate to local circumstances and it concerned matters which were of general relevance and not particular to the UK. In fact, it is arguable that, in the context of adoption, the second requirement is not fulfilled. As discussed above, the Adoption Act 1958 was not a good fit with local circumstances, while customary adoption, which is based on very different norms, was and is a widespread and well-accepted practice.

Due to the deficiencies of the UK Act, Solomon Islands' adoption law was obviously in need of reform. This prompted Solomon Islands Parliament to enact the Adoption Act 2004. This Act, which was not brought into force until 2008, requires separate analysis and is discussed in detail later in the chapter.

(c) International law

In 1995, Solomon Islands ratified the CRC. However, other international instruments, some relating to children's rights generally, and some with specific implications for adoption have not been ratified.[68] In particular, Solomon Islands is not a party to the Hague Convention on Protection of Children and

---

64 Section 54 of the Adoption of Children Act 1968 [Cap 275] provides that the Local Court may, on application by a party, grant a certificate that a customary adoption has been made or terminated.

65 (Unreported, High Court, Solomon Islands, Brown J, 12 December 2003) available via www.paclii.org at [2003] SBHC 84.

66 *Re Miria* (Unreported, High Court, Solomon Islands, Palmer CJ, 1 November 2007) available via www.paclii.org at [2007] SBHC 138. See also *Re Hain* (Unreported, High Court, Solomon Islands, Palmer CJ, 2 May 2008) available via www.paclii.org at [2008] SBHC 112.

67 [1983] SILR 1.

68 These include the Hague Convention on Jurisdiction, Applicable Law and Recognition of Decrees Relating to Adoptions 1965 ('Hague Convention I'), the United Nations Declaration on Social and Legal Principles Relating to Protection & Welfare of Children with Special Reference to Foster Placement and Adoption Nationally and Internationally 1986 ('UN Declaration 1986'), the Hague Convention on Protection of Children and Cooperation in Respect of Intercountry Adoption 1993 ('Hague Convention II') and the Convention on the Rights of the Child 1990 ('Convention on the Rights of the Child').

Cooperation in Respect of Intercountry Adoption 1993 ('Hague Convention II'), and thus has only limited international obligations in relation to intercountry adoption procedures. Neither is it a party to the United Nations Declaration on Social and Legal Principles Relating to Protection & Welfare of Children with Special Reference to Foster Placement and Adoption Nationally and Internationally 1986 ('UN Declaration 1986'), which regulates adoption agencies.

The CRC, which was adopted by the United Nations General Assembly in 1989, seeks to protect the human rights of children, including rights relevant to adoption proceedings. It has been ratified by almost every country around the world. It is incumbent on all state parties to incorporate children's human rights into all relevant legislation, including legislation governing adoption. The most important article is art 3, which provides that in all actions involving children, the best interests of the child shall be a primary consideration. More specifically, art 21 goes further than art 3 in relation to adoption proceedings. It provides that the system of adoption within a country must ensure that the best interests of the child are not just 'a' but 'the' paramount consideration. This has obvious ramifications for customary adoptions where the interests of the adopted child may be subordinated to the best interests of the family and/or community.[69] Article 21 also requires procedural safeguards; any adoption must be 'authorised only by competent authorities, in accordance with law and on the basis of all pertinent and reliable information'. Articles 7 and 12 are also relevant. The former provides that, as far as possible, a child has the express right to know and be cared for by their parents, while the latter provides that all children have the right to be heard in relation to matters concerning them. Neither state law nor customary laws in Solomon Islands appear to provide adequate scope for this to occur.

The CRC requires parties to submit regular progress reports.[70] Solomon Islands' first report to the Committee on the Rights of the Child, which is tasked with overseeing the implementation and interpretation of the Convention, was lodged in 2002.[71] The Committee responded in 2003 in its Concluding Observations.[72] The Committee highlighted the lack of specific legislation governing children's rights, and emphasised the need to bring domestic legislation and customary laws in line with the principles of the Convention.[73] The Committee also noted that the importance of the 'best interests of the child' principle was not reflected in the practices of decision-makers. The Committee recommended that further training be given

---

69 Sue Farran 'Children of the Pacific: Giving Effect to Article 3 UNCRC in Small Islands States' (2012) 20 *International Journal of Children's Rights* 199, 204.

70 Convention on the Rights of the Child, opened for signature 20 November 1989,1577 UNTS 3 (entered into force 2 September 1990) art 44.

71 Solomon Islands Government *Reports Submitted by State Parties under Article 44 of the* Convention*: Solomon Islands*, UN Doc CRC/C/51/Add.6 (12 July 2002).

72 Committee on the Rights of the Child *Concluding Observations: Solomon Islands*, 33rd sess, UN Doc CRC/C/15/Add.208 (2 July 2003).

73 Committee on the Rights of the Child *Concluding Observations: Solomon Islands*, 33rd sess, UN Doc CRC/C/15/Add.208 (2 July 2003) 2.

on the meaning and implementation of the best interest of the child. The Committee also expressed the view that there was a risk that informal (customary) adoption would lead to female children being used as de facto domestic workers, and recommended that Solomon Islands 'take all necessary measures to end the practice of informal adoption'.[74]

As highlighted by the Committee in its Concluding Observations, despite its ratification of the Convention, Solomon Islands has not made any domestic reforms to protect children's rights. The Constitution incorporates a Bill of Rights in Sch 1, based on an amalgamation of the Universal Declaration of Human Rights and ch II of the European Convention on Human Rights.[75] However, the Constitution contains no specific provisions on children's rights. A Child Rights Bill was drafted in 1993 by the National Advisory Committee on Children and sought to give binding effect to the Convention, but it is not currently before the Parliament for consideration.[76]

In the interim, the High Court of Solomon has stated, in the context of prosecution of a child for murder, that the Government of Solomon Islands has 'the responsibility indeed the obligation to enact legislation that will give effect to these conventions [including the CRC]'.[77] In the absence of such legislation, the court would 'do all within its powers to protect juveniles within the safeguards provided by the Constitution … and the Juvenile [Offenders] Act'.[78] On the other hand, in *K v R*,[79] the Court held the requirements of conventions including the CRC were 'already well reflected' in domestic legislation, making further legislation unnecessary.

More specifically, the Adoption Act 1958 did not provide protection for children involved in adoption proceedings to the extent required by the CRC. It did not explicitly provide for the best interests of the child to be the paramount consideration.[80] Nor did it expressly give the child a right to be heard, nor

---

74 Committee on the Rights of the Child *Concluding Observations: Solomon Islands,* 33rd sess, UN Doc CRC/C/15/Add.208 (2 July 2003) 8.It has been argued that the Committee has marginalised non-Western cultural values and practices, and viewed customary laws as inhibiting the full realisation of human rights: Sonia Harris-Short 'Listening to "the Other"? The *Convention on the Rights of the Child*' (2001) 2 *Melbourne Journal of International Law* 304, 334.

75 Solomon Islands' Government is currently carrying out a constitutional reform programme. The most recent draft of the new Constitution retains the rights provisions of the previous Constitution: Solomon Islands Constitutional Reform Program, 2011 Draft Federal Constitution of Solomon Islands: www.sicr.gov.sb/2011%20Draft%20Fed%20Const%20of%20SI.pdf, Ch III.

76 Jennifer Corrin *Report on the UN Convention on the Rights of the Child in Solomon Islands: Its Implementation in National Law* (unpublished 2014).

77 *R v K* (Unreported, High Court, Solomon Islands, Naqiolevu J, 12 July2005) available via www.paclii.org at [2005] SBHC 80.

78 [Cap 14].

79 (Unreported, High Court, Solomon Islands, Palmer CJ, 16 September 2005) available via www.paclii.org at [2005] SBHC 150.

80 As mentioned above, the only protection in the Adoption Act 1958 was that the granting of an adoption order 'be for the welfare of the child': s 7.

make the child's consent a prerequisite to the making of an adoption order, nor give the child a right to object to their adoption, regardless of age or understanding.[81] In the United Kingdom the law has been reformed to eliminate these deficiencies,[82] but these changes did not become part of the law of Solomon Islands. While local reforms might have been expected to bring the law into line with the CRC and developments in the United Kingdom, as discussed in the next section of this chapter, this was not the case.

(d) The Adoption Act 2004

In 2004, Solomon Islands' Parliament patriated adoption law by enacting the Adoption Act 2004, although the Act was not brought into force until 2008.[83] The reform of the law of adoption in Solomon Islands offered the opportunity to provide clarity on the relationship between customary adoption and formal adoption, and to bring the law into line with relevant international law.

However, to some extent, these two objectives were in conflict and state and customary adoptions present a classic example of the conundrum faced by Solomon Islands. Customary law, endorsed by the Constitution as a source of law, is founded on norms which are often patriarchal, status-based and which emphasise duties to the community. International law, on the other hand, is based on Western, liberal political tradition and promotes the rights of the individual (including, in the case of the CRC, the rights of the individual child). It has been argued that it is possible to integrate customary laws and international human rights law by identifying the underlying values that they share, such as respect for the inherent dignity of all persons.[84] However, in the area of child rights, it has been recognised that it is particularly difficult to identify such common ground. The fundamental principle of rights being granted to children as individuals is challenging to customary notions of parental authority and respect for elders,[85] and a culture where a child's welfare is placed in the wider context of family and community welfare.[86]

Unfortunately, the 2004 Act did not even try to achieve a balance between the two competing objectives. Nor did it choose between them. Which of these paths would be preferable is a complex question which this chapter does not attempt to answer. However, it is a vital question for Solomon Islands to address in its development as a nation. Instead, the reform of the law was

---

81 Jennifer Corrin *Report on the UN Convention on the Rights of the Child in Solomon Islands: Its Implementation in National Law* (unpublished 2014).

82 Adoption and Children Act 2002 (UK), s 1(2), (4)(a).

83 Attorney General 'Gazette Notice 145' in Solomon Islands, *Solomon Islands Gazette,* No 46, 5 May 2008. The Act commenced on 1 June 2008.

84 New Zealand Law Commission *Advancing the Implementation of Human Rights in the Pacific* (Study Paper 17, Law Commission, 2006) 11.

85 New Zealand Law Commission *Advancing the Implementation of Human Rights in the Pacific* (Study Paper 17, Law Commission, 2006) 11.

86 New Zealand Law Commission *Advancing the Implementation of Human Rights in the Pacific*, (Study Paper 17, Law Commission, 2006) 104.

limited to a new Act which exhibits all the same flaws as the Adoption Act 1958, which it replaces.[87] In fact, the provisions of the new Act were mainly copied from the 1958 Act. The only substantive changes that were made are as follows:

- the Act is explicitly stated not to apply to customary adoptions.[88] This means that the limited protections in the Act do not apply to the majority of adoptions in Solomon Islands;
- 'infants' are defined as children from 6 weeks[89]to 18 years;[90]
- the names of the adoptive parents are not required to be entered in the adoptive Adopted Children Register.[91]

Key features of the 2004 Act copied from the 1958 Act are:

- the adoptive parents must be 'domiciled' in Solomon Islands;[92]
- 3 months' notice of intention to apply for an adoption order must be given by both adoptive parents. During these 3 months, the child must reside with the adoptive parents for a period of bonding and care.[93] Where one or both of the adoptive parents is not ordinarily resident in Solomon Islands, the 3 months' notice may be given by one spouse only, and the 3 months of bonding may also be fulfilled by one spouse if the two spouses live together in Solomon Islands for at least one month of the 3;[94]
- when giving their consent, the biological parents may impose conditions as to the religion of the adoptive parents.[95] However, there is no provision for the biological parents to impose conditions as to the race or ethnicity of the adoptive parents. The biological parents have no right to know the identity of the adoptive parents;[96]

---

87 Adoption Act 2004 Constitution of Solomon Islands, s 76: [Acts of the Parliament of the United Kingdom] shall have effect 'until Parliament makes other provision'.

88 Adoption Act 2004, s 28.

89 Adoption Act 2004, s 5(1).

90 Adoption Act 2004, s 2, definition of 'infant'. The Adoption Act 1958 defined an infant as a child from 6 weeks (s 3) to 21 years (s 57).

91 This change may have been made in error. Schedule 1 of the Adoption Act 1958 sets out eight fields to be included in the entry in the Adopted Children Register: entry number, date and country of birth, name and surname of child, sex of child, name, surname, address and occupation of adoptive parents, date of adoption order, date of entry, and the signature of officer. The Solomon Islands Act includes an almost identical Sch 1, but the field for 'Name [etc] of adoptive parents' has been replaced by a field for 'Name and surname of officer deputed by Registrar General to attest the entry'.

92 Adoption Act 1958, s 1; Adoption Act 2004, s 3.

93 Adoption Act 1958, s 3; Adoption Act 2004, s 5.

94 Adoption Act 1958, s 12; Adoption Act 2004, s 12.

95 Adoption Act 1958, s 4; Adoption Act 2004, s 6.

96 The Court has discretion under certain circumstances to dispense with consent of the biological parents: Adoption Act 1958, s 5; Adoption Act 2004, s 7.

- non-resident adoptive parents may be granted a 'provisional adoption order', allowing them to remove the child from the jurisdiction in order to adopt the child under the law of another jurisdiction;[97]
- it is an offence to procure a child for adoption, to receive payment or to advertise for the adoption of a child.[98]

A particular area of concern relates to a child's right under s 7 of the CRC to know his or her parents. The Act, which is supplemented by Regulations introduced in May 2008,[99] provides for the establishment of an Adopted Children Register, to be maintained by the Registrar General.[100] Each entry must include an entry number, the date and country of birth, the name and surname of the child, the sex of the child, the name and surname of the officer making the entry, the date of the adoption order, the date of entry, and the signature of the registering officer.[101] However, the entry does not include the name of the adoptive parents or of the biological parents. The Registrar General must create an index of the Adopted Children Register, which is open for public inspection, and certified copies of entries may be obtained. The Registrar General must also keep a register that records the connection between the child's entry in the Register of Births and the corresponding entry in the Adopted Children Register. This register is only accessible through a High Court order.[102] Accordingly, a child may only discover the names of his or her birth parents by obtaining an order from the High Court. Given the geographic and economic obstacles which may limit a child's ability to access the High Court, the provisions may amount to a violation of the Convention.[103]

The Adoption Act 2004 is in stark contrast to, for example, the Adoptions Act 2002 of Marshall Islands, which goes much further to incorporate the CRC into domestic legislation. The Marshall Islands Act includes the principle that the best interests of the child are the 'controlling consideration' to be considered 'first and foremost' in making an adoption order,[104]and gives a detailed definition of the criteria to be considered in determining the best interests of the child. These include the child's safety, health and welfare, the child's physical and emotional needs, and the fostering of a strong personal identity.[105] In contrast, the Solomon Islands Act, like its predecessor, whilst incorporating the welfare principle,[106] falls short of spelling out that it is the paramount consideration. This is all the more surprising in the light of the fact that the Guardianship of Infants Act 1925 (UK),[107] which, like the Adoption

[97] Adoption Act 1958, s 53; Adoption Act 2004, s 26.
[98] Adoption Act 1958, s 50; Adoption Act 2004, s 23.
[99] Adoptions Regulations 2008 (SI).
[100] Adoption Regulations 2008 (SI), s 13; Adoption Act 2004, s 18.
[101] Adoption Act 2004, Sch 1.
[102] Adoption Act 2004, s 18(4) and (5).
[103] Article 7.
[104] Adoptions Act 2002, 26 MIRC 8, s 809.
[105] Adoptions Act 2002, 26 MIRC 8, s 825.
[106] Adoption Act 2004, s 9(1)(b).
[107] Guardianship of Infants Act 1925 (UK).

Act 1958, is applied as an Act of general application in Solomon Islands,[108] provides that in deciding questions of custody, the court must 'regard the welfare of the infant as the first and paramount consideration'.[109] Further, unlike the Adoptions Act 2002, the Solomon Islands' Adoption Act does not list the factors to be taken into account in determining 'welfare'. Relevant considerations in making this assessment are limited to the health of the applicants.[110]

The Adoption Act 2004 provides that the Court shall give 'due consideration' to the wishes of the infant, but does not give a child the right to object in adoption proceedings. In contrast, the Adoptions Act 2002 of Marshall Islands grants a child over 12 the power to decisively object to the adoption.[111] The child's views towards being adopted are listed under s 825 as a criteria to be considered in determining what is in the best interests of the child.

The other area where the Adoption Act 2004 falls short is in relation to intercountry adoptions. Indeed, s 12 of the Act in particular seems formulated to facilitate adoptions by non-residents.[112] Given that Solomon Islands is not a signatory to the Hague Convention governing intercountry adoptions,[113] domestic legislation safeguarding the welfare of the adopted child after removal from the jurisdiction of Solomon Islands is required.[114] Further, the diversity and richness of culture in Solomon Islands makes it particularly important to

---

108 See, eg, *Sukutaona v Houanihou* [1982] SILR 12; *In re B* [1983] SILR 223; *K v T* [1985-86] SILR 49; *Sasango v Beliga* [1987] SILR 91.

109 Guardianship of Infants Act, s 1.

110 Adoption Act 2004, s 9(2).

111 Adoptions Act 2002, 26 MIRC 8, s 819. Where the child is under 12, their objection is not decisive but the Court must determine whether adoption would be in the child's best interest.

112 Under the Adoption Act, the High Court may grant to non-resident adoptive parents a 'provisional adoption order', which allows the parents to remove the child from Solomon Islands for up to 2 years where the parents wish to adopt the child under the law of another jurisdiction.

113 Hague Conference on Private International Law *Status Table 28: Convention of 25 October 1980 on the Civil Aspects of International Child Abduction* (9 April 2014) HCCH Status Table: www.hcch.net/index_en.php?act=conventions.status&cid=24; Hague Conference on Private International Law, *Status Table 34: Convention of 19 October 1996 on Jurisdiction, Applicable Law, Recognition, Enforcement and Co-operation in Respect of Parental Responsibility and Measures for the Protection of Children* (3 December 2012) HCCH Status Table: www.hcch.net/index_en.php?act=conventions.status&cid=70.

114 In relation to intercountry adoptions, some commentators have argued that there is an urgent need for Solomon Islands to increase protections for children adopted by non-Solomon Islanders by ratifying the Hague Convention II. In an ideal world, this would have the benefit of universalising international adoption standards, and would facilitate information-sharing and other forms of collaboration between Solomon Islands and the 'destination' countries to which adopted children are transported: Dejo Olowu 'The Legal Regime of Child Adoptions in the South Pacific and the Implications of International Regulatory Standards' (2007) 19 *Sri Lanka Journal of International Law* 109, 142. However, it has also been argued that there is little to be gained by encouraging Solomon Islands to ratify further international treaties while problems with implementation persist. It would be more beneficial to ensure that wealthier countries which have ratified the Hague Conventions, and which are often the destination for intercountry adoptions, fulfil their responsibilities: Sue Farran 'South Pacific children: the Law on Adoption and Issues of Concern' (2009) 6 *New Zealand Family Law Journal* 330, 331.

also incorporate art 20 of the Convention, which refers to the importance of giving consideration in adoption proceedings to the child's ethnic, religious, cultural and linguistic background, into domestic law.[115]

Whilst the Act does not incorporate the CRC into domestic law, neither does it take account of customary adoptions. Rather, as stated above, it excludes them from the statutory scheme.[116] It is perhaps worth noting here that, whilst other Solomon Islands' legislation referring incidentally to adoption is usually silent on whether customary adoption is included in the term,[117] there is at least one Act in place in which it does recognise customary adoption for the purposes of that Act. Under the Wills, Probate and Administration Act,[118] children adopted under customary laws are included in the distribution of property upon intestacy. To the contrary, the Affiliation, Separation and Maintenance Act,[119] defines, 'parents' of an adopted child for the purposes of making maintenance orders as the adopted father and mother of the child, except where the child is 'adopted only in accordance with current customary usage', in which case an order may only be made against the natural parents 'unless that adoption has been registered with the Magistrate'.[120]

The need to expressly exclude customary adoptions from the Adoption Act 2004 could be taken as recognition of their validity, but it does not make it clear which rules will take precedence in relation to the legal consequences of adoption. Although the section does clarify to a limited extent, and in a negative fashion, the relationship between customary adoption and state law, it means that the few procedural and substantive protections that do exist under the Act do not apply to the majority of adoptions taking place in Solomon Islands.[121]

As mentioned above, the Committee has suggested that informal customary adoptions should be brought to an end. Whether customary adoptions should be allowed or, at least, fettered by the state in some way in all cases is a difficult question which Solomon Islands has yet to address. Given the high rate of customary adoptions and the social purposes that such arrangements fulfil, this is a complex question requiring extensive exploration and consultation. In the meantime, where formal recognition of an existing customary adoption by the state is required, for example for the purposes of obtaining a passport, the 2004 reforms could have introduced a clear process. In fact, a model for addressing such problems is readily available from Solomon Islands' near neighbour, in

115 Sue Farran 'Child Adoption: the Challenges Presented by the Plural Legal Systems of South Pacific Island States' (2009) 21 *Child and Family Quarterly* 462, 478.

116 Adoption Act 2004, s 28.

117 See, eg, Citizenship Act Cap 57, s 6, which refers to adoption 'under the provisions of any law', which would arguably but not definitively include customary law.

118 Cap 33 (SI), s 97.

119 Cap 1.

120 Section 21(6).

121 Solomon Islands Government 'Reports Submitted by State Parties under Article 44 of the *Convention*: Solomon Islands' CRC/C/51/Add.6, 12 July 2002, 30.

Papua New Guinea. The Adoption of Children Act (PNG)[122] provides for the recognition of customary adoptions for state law purposes. It provides for the issue of a certificate which constitutes conclusive proof of adoption, and gives customary rules precedence in relation to property rights and obligations.[123] However, whilst this model introduces certainty as to the consequences of customary adoptions and a process for state recognition, it does not incorporate any child welfare safeguards.

Angelo, in relation to his patriation work in Tokelau and Niue, divided foreign laws into three categories: those that were 'accessible and reasonably applicable' and could merely be re-enacted as local legislation; those that were relevant but were not properly adapted to local circumstances, which needed to be re-enacted as local legislation with substantial amendments; and those that were of no relevance in the local context, the applicability of which needed to be repealed.[124] The Adoption Act 1958 has been treated as belonging to the first category and has been replaced by a local law, the Adoption Act 2004. However, the patriation process consists mainly of replacement of the terms 'England' and the 'United Kingdom' with 'Solomon Islands' and removal of sections relating to Scotland, with substantive provisions largely remaining the same. The amendments fail to make even obvious cosmetic changes to update the legislation. For example the term 'infants' is used, as opposed to the more modern term of 'child' or 'minor'.[125]

Whilst patriation is an important assertion of sovereignty, laws modelled on overseas legislation which is alien or contradictory to customary legal norms will not necessarily result in 'ownership' of the legal system.[126] Certainly it could be argued that, given the developments in adoption best practices since 1958, it would have been preferable for the Adoption Act 1958 to have been placed in the second or third categories, with the new local law making substantial amendments to, for example, reflect the centrality of the child's best interests in adoption proceedings. Nevertheless, patriation of the law on adoption in Solomon Islands is nevertheless a positive development, reducing the post-independence reliance on foreign laws which is damaging to the coherence of many legal systems in the South Pacific.[127]

---

122 [Cap 275].

123 Adoption of Children Act 1968 (PNG), s 53.

124 See the summary of Angelo's approach to patriation and reference to his important work in Jennifer Corrin 'Discarding Relics of the Past: Patriation of Laws in the South Pacific' (2008) 39 *Victoria University of Wellington Law Review* 635, 637.

125 For example, 'child' is the term used by the CRC.

126 Jennifer Corrin Care 'Negotiating the Constitutional Conundrum: Balancing Cultural Identity with Principles of Gender Equality in Post-Colonial South Pacific Societies' (2006) 5 *Indigenous Law Journal* 51, 52; New Zealand Law Commission *Advancing the Implementation of Human Rights in the Pacific* (Study Paper 17, Law Commission, 2006) 11.

127 Jennifer Corrin 'Discarding Relics of the Past: Patriation of Laws in the South Pacific' (2008) 39 Victoria University of Wellington Law Review 635, 650.

(e) Case law

As mentioned above, the 2004 Act did not come into force until 1 June 2008.[128] Since that time it has been considered by the courts in at least seven cases.[129] Despite the fact that, as discussed above, the wording of the welfare provision in the Adoption Act 2004 is less emphatic than it might be, the High Court has considered the welfare principle in four of the seven cases coming before it.[130] Although the court has not in any case used the language of the Act (the 'welfare of the infant'), it has referred to the 'best interests' of the child,[131] the 'interests' of the child,[132] and the 'well-being' of the child.[133] In assessing welfare, the court has considered the health and finances of the adoptive parents,[134] their education level and employment,[135] and their ability to provide a secure home and good future for the child.[136]

The case-law also demonstrates the stark contrast between the consequences of customary adoption and the consequences of adoption under state law. For example, one of the grounds for granting the adoption order in *Re Armstrong*[137] was that the biological parents understood that the adoption order meant that they would no longer have 'care, control or responsibility' for

---

128 Attorney General 'Gazette Notice 145' in Solomon Islands, *Solomon Islands Gazette*, No 46, 15 May 2008.

129 *Marumaru v Wetara* (Unreported, High Court, Solomon Islands, Mwanesalua J, 28 July 2009) available via www.paclii.org at [2009] SBHC 28; *Re Rietveld* (Unreported, High Court, Solomon Islands, Mwanesalua J, 3 February 2012) available via www.paclii.org at [2012] SBHC 9; *Re Rabaua* (Unreported, High Court, Solomon Islands, Mwanesalua J, 27 July 2012) available via www.paclii.org at [2012] SBHC 77; *Re Wetara* (Unreported, High Court, Solomon Islands, Mwanesalua J, 21 November 2012) available via www.paclii.org at [2012] SBHC 130; *Re Armstrong* (Unreported, High Court, Solomon Islands, Mwanesalua J, 2 April 2012) available via www.paclii.org at[2012] SBHC 26;*Re Matautia* (Unreported, High Court, Solomon Islands, Mwanesalua J, 21 March 2013) available via www.paclii.org at [2013] SBHC 22; *Re Duinkerke* (Unreported, High Court, Solomon Islands, Mwanesalua J, 2 September 2011) available via www.paclii.org at [2011] SBHC 82.

130 *Re Rabaua* (Unreported, High Court, Solomon Islands, Mwanesalua J, 27 July 2012) available via www.paclii.org at [2012] SBHC 77.

131 *Re Armstrong* (Unreported, High Court, Solomon Islands, Mwanesalua J, 2 April 2012) available via www.paclii.org at [2012] SBHC 26; *Re Rabaua* (Unreported, High Court, Solomon Islands, Mwanesalua J, 27 July 2012) available via www.paclii.org at [2012] SBHC 77.

132 *Re Duinkerke* (Unreported, High Court, Solomon Islands, Mwanesalua J, 2 September 2011) available via www.paclii.org at [2011] SBHC 82.

133 *Re Matautia* (Unreported, High Court, Solomon Islands, Mwanesalua J, 21 March 2013) available via www.paclii.org at [2013] SBHC 22.

134 *Marumaru v Wetara* (Unreported, High Court, Solomon Islands, Mwanesalua J, 28 July 2009) available via www.paclii.org at [2009] SBHC 28; see also *Re Rietveld* (Unreported, High Court, Solomon Islands, Mwanesalua J, 3 February 2012) available via www.paclii.org at [2012] SBHC 9.

135 *Re Rabaua* (Unreported, High Court, Solomon Islands, Mwanesalua J, 27 July 2012) available via www.paclii.org at [2012] SBHC 77.

136 *Re Wetara* (Unreported, High Court, Solomon Islands, Mwanesalua J, 21 November 2012) available via www.paclii.org at [2012] SBHC 130.

137 *Re Armstrong* (Unreported, High Court, Solomon Islands, Mwanesalua J, 2 April 2012) available via www.paclii.org at [2012] SBHC 26.

the child. In *Re Matautia*,[138] the biological mother gave evidence that she had given her consent and that she understood that 'adoption would permanently deprive her of her rights as a parent'.

Whilst the courts have held that customary adoption alone is insufficient evidence to found an adoption order,[139] there has not yet been any discussion of whether customary adoptions are in a child's best interests. By analogy with custody cases, the approach taken is likely to depend on the facts of the case, and customary arrangements may be regarded as relevant to a determination of what is in a child's interest. As stated in *Sukutaona v Houanihou*,[140] 'regard for the custom background may well be an important factor in deciding where that interest lies in the sense that custom rules may well be designed to protect the children from an unsatisfactory family life'.[141]

V CONCLUSION

Solomon Islands' Government, as a signatory of the CRC, has an obligation to provide legal protection for children in its domestic law.[142] The changes to the law on adoption in 2004 provided an ideal opportunity to fulfil a portion of this obligation. Failure to take up this opportunity may be partly explained by the country's lack of resources, but may also stem from a lack of political will. In turn, this may be linked to recognition that international law and state law on family matters are often a poor cultural fit with customary norms.

Not only does the 2004 Act fail to bring adoption law into line with international law, but also it fails to clarify the inter-relationship between state law and customary laws. No process for state recognition of customary adoptions is provided. Moreover, the reforms sidestep the vital question of how Solomon Islands can achieve a balance between the competing norms of customary and international law and, if such a balance cannot be found, the question of which should prevail. The Act does patriate the law on adoption in Solomon Islands. However, it does not do so in a way that takes account of the country's pluralistic legal system, other than to exclude customary adoption from the operation of the Act. As discussed in this chapter, the new Act essentially mirrors all the flaws of the 1958 Act, with very few substantive changes.

---

138 *Re Matautia* (Unreported, High Court, Solomon Islands, Mwanesalua J, 21 March 2012) available via www.paclii.org at [2013] SBHC 22.

139 *Re Belo* (Unreported, High Court, Solomon Islands, Brown J, 12 December 2003) available via www.paclii.org at [2003] SBHC 84.

140 [1982] SILR 12. In reliance on the provision in the Guardianship of Infants Act 1925 (UK) that the court must 'regard the welfare of the infant as the first and paramount consideration', the courts rejected customary custody arrangements driven by principles of patriarchy, rather than by the child's best interests. See also *Re B* [1983] SILR 223;*K v T* [1985/86] SILR 49; *Sasango v Beliga* [1987] SILR 91.

141 Ibid.

142 Convention on the Rights of the Child, art 4.

There is a delicate balance to be drawn between protection of human rights, whether enshrined in the Constitution or derived from international instruments, and the promotion of indigenous culture and customary laws. It has been argued that the Committee on the Rights of the Child, which is tasked with overseeing the implementation and interpretation of the Convention, has consistently marginalised non-Western cultural values and practices and treated customary laws as an inhibition on full implementation of the CRC.[143] It is important that Solomon Islanders have a sense of 'ownership' of their legal system, which cannot be achieved if laws are seen as alien or contradictory to indigenous, widespread norms.[144] For this reason, creative solutions are required, including sui generis legislation rather than superficial changes to foreign Acts.[145]

To date it appears that Solomon Islands Law Reform Commission has not been involved in the reform of the law on adoption. The Commission has a mandate to ensure that the law is 'relevant, responsible, effective, equally accessible to all, and just'.[146] This is an area where, that mandate remains to be fulfilled.

---

143 Sonia Harris-Short 'Listening to 'the Other'? The Convention on the Rights of the Child' (2001) 2 *Melbourne Journal of International Law* 304, 334.

144 See more generally, Jennifer Corrin Care 'Negotiating the Constitutional Conundrum: Balancing Cultural Identity with Principles of Gender Equality in Post-Colonial South Pacific Societies' (2006) 5 *Indigenous Law Journal* 51, 52; New Zealand Law Commission *Advancing the Implementation of Human Rights in the Pacific* (Study Paper 17, Law Commission, 2006) 11.

145 Sue Farran 'Child Adoption: the Challenges Presented by the Plural Legal Systems of South Pacific Island States' (2009) 21 *Child and Family Quarterly* 462, 465.

146 Solomon Islands Law Reform Commission, *The Commission's Work* (2012),*What We Do*: www.lawreform.gov.sb/index.php/about-us/what-we-do.

SWITZERLAND

NEW RULES ON PARENTAL RESPONSIBILITY IN SWITZERLAND

Ingeborg Schwenzer and Tomie Keller[*]

Résumé

Les nouvelles règles de l'autorité parentale entreront en vigueur en Suisse le 1[er]juillet 2014. L'objectif de la réforme est d'ériger l'autorité parentale conjointe au rang deprincipe,indépendamment de la situation conjugale des parents. Il s'agit donc d'une part, de renforcer l'égalité de traitement entre hommes et femmes, et d'autre part,d'éliminer les discriminationsentre enfants nés hors mariage et enfants de parents divorcés ou séparés. Cependant, certaines distinctions résistent. Tandis que les parents mariés sont automatiquement investis de l'autorité parentale conjointe, les parents célibataires ou divorcés doivent remplir d'autres exigences. La réforme et les intentions du législateur constituent, malgré tout, une étape importante.

I INTRODUCTION[1]

On 1 July 2014 the new rules on parental responsibility entered into force in Switzerland.[2] The aim of the reform was to introduce joint parental responsibility as a general rule independent of the parents' marital status and therefore to enhance equal treatment of women and men and to eliminate discrimination of children born out of wedlock and children of divorced or separated parents.[3]

---

* Ingeborg Schwenzer, Prof Dr iur, LLM (UC Berkeley), Professor for Private Law, University of Basel, Switzerland.
Tomie Keller, Master of Law, Research and Teaching Assistant, University of Basel, Switzerland.

1 Abbreviations: AB (*Amtliches Bulltin*) = Official Bulletin which publishes verbatim reports of debates in the National Council and the Council of States (www.parlament.ch); BFS (*Bundesamt für Statistik*) = Statistics of the Swiss Federal Statistical Office; BGer (*Schweizerisches Bundesgericht*) = Swiss Federal Supreme Court; SR (*Systematische Sammlung des Bundesrechts*) = Swiss Classified Compilation of Federal Legislation.

2 Arts 133, 134 (2–4), 179(1), 270a, 275(2) and 296–311 Civil Code (CC), SR 210; cf Message of the Federal Council of 16 November 2011 on the Swiss CC (parental responsibility) (*Botschaft zu einer Änderung des Schweizerischen Zivilgesetzbuches (Elterliche Sorge)*), Bundesblatt 2011 9077 et seq, cited as Msg Parental Responsibility.

3 Msg Parental Responsibility, above n 2, 9078.

Until the reform of parental responsibility, Swiss law distinguished between married and unmarried parents with regard to the attribution of parental responsibility. If the parents of a child were married, parental responsibility vested in both of them and they exercised it jointly during marriage. If the parents of a child were not married, parental responsibility was primarily vested in the mother. In case of divorce parental responsibility had to be allocated to only one of the parents. It was not until the divorce reform in 2000[4] that under certain circumstances unmarried or divorced parents could be awarded joint parental responsibility.[5] Still, this situation contravened the European Convention on Human Rights (ECHR).[6] Therefore, the Swiss legislature has amended the rules on parental responsibility. This chapter gives an overview on the changes and the new rules on parental responsibility in Switzerland.

II GENERAL

Parental responsibility, which is still called parental care (*elterliche Sorge*)[7] in Switzerland, is linked to legal parentage.[8] A person who is not a legal parent of the child cannot exercise parental responsibility. He or she may only be appointed as a guardian for the child.

III MAIN PRINCIPLES (ART 296 CC)

The new rules first establish in art 296(1) CC that the main principle of parental responsibility is the welfare of the child. As every child has a right to have parents who both take responsibility for the child's education and upbringing, the Swiss legislature is of the opinion that joint parental responsibility generally best reflects the welfare of the child.[9] Accordingly, the reform introduced as a general rule in art 296(2) CC that parents of minor children are vested with joint parental responsibility. According to the Swiss

---

4 Arts 111–149 CC; cf Message of the Federal Council of 15 November 1995 on amendments to the Swiss CC (divorce law) (*Botschaft über die Änderung des Schweizerischen Zivilgesetzbuches (Personenstand, Eheschliessung, Scheidung, Kindesrecht, Verwandtenunterstützungspflicht, Heimstätten, Vormundschaft und Ehevermittlung)*), Bundesblatt 1996 I 1 et seq, cited as Msg Divorce.

5 Former arts 133(3), 298a(1) CC.

6 ECHR cases *Zaunegger v Germany* (2009) Application no 22028/04 and *Sporer v Austria* (2011) Application no 35637/03; cf Meier *L'autorité parentale conjointe – L'arrêt de la Cour EDH Zaunegger c. Allemagne – quels effets sur le droit suisse?, Zeitschrift für Kindes- und Erwachsenenschutz* (ZKE) (2010) 246 et seq.

7 The term parental care was only introduced by the divorce reform in 2000 (see above n 4) and replaced the term parental force (*elterliche Gewalt*).

8 Büchler/Vetterli *Ehe Partnerschaft Kinder – Eine Einführung in das Familienrecht der Schweiz*, Helbing Lichtenhahn Verlag (2011) 224; for the rules on parentage in Switzerland cf Büchler 'Parentage in Swiss Law' in Schwenzer (ed) *Tensions Between Legal, Biological and Social Conceptions of Parentage* (Intersentia, 2007) 343 et seq.

9 Msg Parental Responsibility, above n 2, 9092.

legislature this principle is applicable independently of whether the parents are married or not, separated or divorced.[10] Only in order to protect the child's interests is a deviation from joint parental responsibility justified.[11]

According to art 296(3) CC and as already stated in the former law,[12] minor parents or parents subject to a general deputyship (*umfassende Beistandschaft*) cannot hold parental responsibility. When the parents reach majority, parental responsibility is automatically allocated to them.[13] If the general deputyship is set aside, the child protection authority has to decide on the attribution of parental responsibility regarding the welfare of the child.[14]

IV MARRIED PARENTS

Marriage rates have been consistently around 42,000 marriages per year in Switzerland.[15] Around 80% of the children are born in marriage.[16] This high percentage is due to the fact that parents in Switzerland often marry when planning or expecting their first child.[17] Although there is no statistical data available with regard to this question,[18] it can be reasonably assumed that avoiding the effort and trouble of applying for joint parental responsibility as an unmarried couple was (amongst other things) motivation to marry when expecting a child.

With regard to married parents, the reform did not change the rules on allocation of parental responsibility. According to the general principle[19] in art 296(2) CC, both parents are vested with parental responsibility and they exercise it jointly during marriage. At the child's birth joint parental responsibility is allocated to the married parents. There are no further requirements.

---

10 Msg Parental Responsibility, above n 2, 9092.
11 Msg Parental Responsibility, above n 2, 9078.
12 Former Art 296(2) CC.
13 Art 296(3) 2nd sentence CC.
14 Art 296(3) 3rd sentence CC.
15 BFS, www.bfs.admin.ch/bfs/portal/en/index/themen/01/06/blank/key/05.html (accessed June 2014).
16 BFS, www.bfs.admin.ch/bfs/portal/en/index/themen/01/06/blank/key/02/03.html (accessed June 2014).
17 So called '*kinderorientierte Heirat*' (children-oriented marriage), cf Büchler/Vetterli, above n 8, 13.
18 Msg Parental Responsibility, above n 2, 9086.
19 There is no explicit article for married parents any more such as found in the former art 297(1) CC.

V DIVORCED PARENTS (ART 298 CC)

Over the past few years the divorce rate in Switzerland has been around 42%,[20] after a peak of 54% in 2010.[21] In many divorces minor children are affected, in 2012 all in all a total of 12,703 children.[22]

Until recently, parental responsibility generally had to be allocated to only one parent upon divorce. It was not until the divorce reform in the year 2000 that joint parental responsibility for divorced parents was made possible under restricted circumstances.[23] According to the former law the court could only award parental responsibility to both parents (provided this was in the child's best interests) if they jointly requested it and if they had concluded a valid agreement regulating their contributions to childcare and the division of child support.[24]

However, although joint parental responsibility after divorce was only possible under the aforementioned restrictions, numbers of divorcing parents applying for and granted joint parental responsibility were steadily growing. Whereas in 2000 just about 15% of the children affected by a divorce stayed under joint parental responsibility, a divorce did not affect joint parental responsibility for approximately 40% of minor children in 2010.[25]

The new law introduced joint parental responsibility for divorced parents as a rule. As stipulated under the main principle in art 296(2) CC, parental responsibility is vested in both parents. Hence, according to the new law a divorce of the parents of a child does generally not change the allocation of parental responsibility.[26]

Pursuant to the new art 133(1) CC the court has to decide about the questions of parental responsibility, custody, visitation rights or shares of childcare and child support. The court thereby has to have regard to all circumstances relevant for the welfare of the child.[27] It also has to consider a joint request submitted by the parents and, wherever feasible, the child's opinion.[28] However, as with regard to all child matters, the court is not bound by the parties' requests and is obligated to establish the facts ex officio.[29] The court has the

---

20 Cf for 2011, 2012 and 2013 BFS, www.bfs.admin.ch/bfs/portal/en/index/themen/01/06/blank/key/06.html (accessed.

21 BFS, www.bfs.admin.ch/bfs/portal/en/index/themen/01/06/blank/key/06.html (accessed June 2014).

22 BFS, www.bfs.admin.ch/bfs/portal/en/index/themen/01/06/blank/key/06/06.html (accessed June 2014).

23 Msg Divorce, above n 4, 125 et seq.

24 Former Art 133(3) CC.

25 Msg Parental Responsibility, above n 2, 9083.

26 Msg Parental Responsibility, above n 2, 9101.

27 Art 133(2) 1st sentence CC.

28 Art 133(2) 2nd sentence CC.

29 Art 296(1) and (3) *Zivilprozessordnung* (ZPO), SR 272 (Swiss Civil Procedure Code (CPC)); Msg Parental Responsibility, above n 2, 9103.

duty to assure whether or not the requirements for joint parental responsibility are fulfilled.[30] Hence, according to art 298(1) CC the court may award parental responsibility to only one parent in order to ensure the welfare of the child. The threshold to be considered by the court to withdraw parental responsibility of one parent corresponds to the threshold set in art 298b(2) CC to deny joint parental responsibility in the case of a joint declaration by unmarried parents.[31]

According to art 298(2) CC the court may, however, refrain from revoking parental responsibility and instead restrict its decision to questions concerning custody, visitation rights or the care of the child if there is no perspective that the parents will reach an agreement on those questions.[32] If neither the father nor the mother are to be considered to assume parental responsibility, the court has to request the child protection authority to provide a guardian for the child.[33]

VI UNMARRIED PARENTS

Over the last 10 years, the number of children born out of wedlock has almost doubled. Around 20% of births in Switzerland are outside marriage.[34] Before the reform, parental responsibility of a child born out of wedlock had been allocated to the mother by law.[35] If the parents pursued joint parental responsibility, they had to jointly request it at the child protection authority. This authority could only award parental responsibility to both parents if they had concluded a valid agreement regulating their shares of childcare and the division of maintenance costs provided this was in the child's best interests.[36]

Nevertheless, since the possibility of joint parental responsibility for unmarried parents had been introduced in Switzerland in the year 2000[37] the number of parents requesting and awarded joint parental responsibility had steadily been growing.[38] For example in the canton Zurich,[39] there was an increase of children born out of wedlock being under joint parental responsibility by way of the parent's request from 44% in 2000 to almost 68% in 2010.[40]

---

30 Msg Parental Responsibility, above n 2, 9103.
31 Msg Parental Responsibility, above n 2, 9103; for the threshold set in art 298b(2) see below section VI(a)(ii).
32 Art 298(2) CC.
33 Art 298(3) CC.
34 BFS, www.bfs.admin.ch/bfs/portal/en/index/themen/01/06/blank/key/02.html (accessed June 2014).
35 Former art 298(1) CC.
36 Former art 298a(1) CC.
37 Msg Divorce, above n 4, 162 et seq.
38 Msg Parental Responsibility, above n 2, 9085.
39 There is no nationwide statistical data available with regard to this question.
40 Msg Parental Responsibility, above n 2, 9086.

(a) Joint parental responsibility

The general principle of joint parental responsibility (art 296(2) CC) is also applicable to unmarried parents.[41] The new law distinguishes between the allocation of joint parental responsibility in the case of joint declaration, by decision of the child protection authority if one of the parents refuses joint parental responsibility, and by decision of the court in connection with a paternity suit.

(i) Joint declaration (art 298a CC)

If both parents pursue joint parental responsibility, pursuant to art 298a(1) CC two requirements have to be fulfilled. First, legal paternity has to be established between the child and the father, be it by acknowledgement of paternity (*Vaterschaftsanerkennung*)[42] or by court decree of paternity (*Vaterschaftsurteil*)[43] if (in the latter case) joint parental responsibility has not already been awarded by the court in connection with the paternity suit.[44] Secondly, the parents have to jointly declare their will to exercise parental responsibility together.

In the declaration the parents have to first confirm their willingness to be jointly responsible for their child[45] and, secondly, that they have discussed custody and visitation rights or shares of childcare as well as the division of child support.[46] Information with regard to the discussed solution itself (such as information and details about the shares of childcare and the division of child support) is not required.[47] The content of the declaration can no longer be reviewed by the child protection authority.[48] This clear deviation from the old law[49] has been intended by the legislature to demonstrate that any distrust of unmarried couples has been abolished.[50] The requirement of the declaration with regard to questions related to parental responsibility (art 298a(2) no 2 CC) was intended to make the parents aware of the fact that an agreement with regard to those questions has to be reached.[51]

According to art 298a(3) CC, the parents may seek advice from the child protection authority before making their declaration. If the declaration is made together with the acknowledgement of paternity, the civil registry office

---

41 Msg Parental Responsibility, above n 2, 9092.
42 Art 260 CC.
43 Art 261 CC.
44 Art 298c CC, see below section (VI)(a)(iii)).
45 Art 298a(2) no 1 CC.
46 Art 298a(2) no 2 CC.
47 Msg Parental Responsibility, above n 2, 9104.
48 Vote Sommaruga Simonetta, *Amtliches Bulltin* (AB) 2013, S 11 ('*Der Inhalt [der Erklärung] darf nicht überprüft werden*').
49 Cf former art 298a(1) CC, see above introduction of section VI.
50 Msg Parental Responsibility, above n 2, 9104.
51 Vote Sommaruga Simonetta, *Amtliches Bulltin* (AB) 2013, S 11 ('*Man will auf diese Weise den Eltern bewusstmachen, dass über diese Fragen eine Regelung gefunden werden sollte*').

(*Zivilstandsamt*) is the competent authority.[52] As the acknowledgement of paternity may be effected before the child's birth,[53] a declaration for joint parental responsibility before the child's birth is also possible.[54] A declaration after the birth of the child must be made at the child protection authority of the child's domicile.[55] Until the declaration the mother is vested with sole parental responsibility.[56]

The requirement of the declaration has been criticised in different respects. First, it has been discussed that no specification with regard to the content of the declaration is required.[57] The only requirement that has to be fulfilled is the confirmation by the parents that questions about custody, visitation rights or shares of childcare as well as child support have been discussed. Therefore, the declaration does not require any content and only the existence of a discussion about the questions related to parental responsibility has to be confirmed.[58]

Secondly, it has been criticised that such a declaration is required at all.[59] On the one hand, the Swiss legislature is convinced that the welfare of the child is (generally) best complied with by joint parental responsibility, as every child has the right to be educated and raised by both parents. On the other hand, with the joint declaration of unmarried parents a formal step is still required to achieve joint parental responsibility. Actually, in the preliminary draft of the reform of parental responsibility, the proposal had been made to automatically allocate joint parental responsibility to unmarried parents when the father recognises his child.[60] Unfortunately, under the new law, joint parental responsibility will still not automatically[61] be allocated to unmarried parents.

---

52 Art 298a(4) 1st sentence CC.

53 Art 11(2) *Zivilstandsverordnung* (ZStV), SR 211.112.2 (Regulation on Civil Status (RCS)); more than half of all recognitions of paternity in Switzerland are made prior to the child's birth, cf BFS, www.bfs.admin.ch/bfs/portal/en/index/themen/01/06/blank/key/10.html>.

54 Msg Parental Responsibility, above n 2, 9104.

55 Art 298a(4) CC.

56 Art 298a(5) CC.

57 Bucher 'Elterliche Sorge im schweizerischen und internationalen Kontext' in Rumo-Jungo/ Fountoulakis (eds) *Familien in Zeiten grenzüberschreitender Beziehungen*, 7 *Symposium zum Familienrecht* (2013) Universität Freiburg, 1, 17 et seq.

58 Bucher, above n 57, 1, 18.

59 Gloor/Schweighauser 'Die Reform des Rechts der elterlichen Sorge – eine Würdigung aus praktischer Sicht' *Die Praxis des Familienrechts* (FamPra.ch) (2014) 1, 4.

60 Preliminary draft (Vorentwurf) art 298(1) CC from January 2009: If the parents are not married, parental responsibility is vested in the father and the mother by law if the father has recognised the child.

61 Msg Parental Responsibility, above n 2, 9092; in the discussions after the publication of the preliminary draft (*Vernehmlassung*) the majority did not want parental responsibility to be automatically allocated to the recognised father of a child, cf. Rumo-Jungo 'Gemeinsame elterliche Sorge geschiedender und unverheirateter Eltern' in Jusletter 15 (Feburar 2010) 1, 3.

(ii) Decision of the Child Protection Authority (art 298b CC)

According to the former law, joint parental responsibility could only be awarded if the parents jointly requested it.[62] Accordingly, the parent vested with parental responsibility – mostly the mother – actually had a veto right if he or she did not want the other parent to be included in the parental responsibility.[63] It had therefore been criticised that parental responsibility should not be oriented towards the parents' interests but rather be allocated according to the welfare of the child.[64] Hence, the reform has introduced a possibility for the parent not vested with parental responsibility to apply for joint parental responsibility.

If one of the parents does not want to declare joint parental responsibility, the other parent has the possibility to request the child protection authority to decide upon the question of parental responsibility.[65] According to art 298b(2) CC the child protection authority will then award joint parental responsibility to both parents provided that the welfare of the child does not require sole parental responsibility of either the mother or the father. The request for joint parental responsibility will probably mostly be sought by the father not vested with parental responsibility[66] but can certainly also be made by the mother vested with sole parental responsibility in order to include the father in the parental responsibility.[67]

The threshold to be considered by the child protection authority for the denial of parental responsibility[68] has been discussed at length.[69] Article 298b(2) CC only states that sole parental responsibility should be awarded in order to ensure the welfare of the child. According to the Swiss legislature, parental responsibility should only be denied to one parent if the authority immediately had to revoke it afterwards due to reasons corresponding to those for the revocation of parental responsibility as a child protection measure in art 311 CC.[70]

According to art 311 CC parental responsibility must be withdrawn if the parents are unable to exercise it as required because of inexperience, illness,

---

62 Former art 298a(1) CC.

63 Rumo-Jungo, above n 61, 1, 3.

64 Büchler/Cantieni/Simoni 'Die Regelung der elterlichen Sorge nach Scheidung de lege ferenda' *Die Praxis des Familienrechts* (FamPra.ch) 2007, 207, 213; Rumo-Jungo, above n 61, 1, 4.

65 Art 298b(1) CC.

66 Art 298b(5) CC provides for the mother to be vested with sole parental responsibility until a declaration according to art 298a CC has been made, see below section VI(2).

67 Gloor/Schweighauser, above n 59, 1, 6.

68 Or in case of divorce, for the revocation of parental responsibility, art 298(1) CC (see above section V.).

69 Bucher, above n 57, 1, 10–11, 29; Gloor/Schweighauser, above n 59, 1, 6 et seq; Rüetschi 'Podiumsdiskussion vom 16. Februar 2012 in Basel, Aktuelle Reform des Rechts der Elterlichen Sorge und des Unterhalts nach Trennung und Scheidung' *Die Praxis des Familienrechts* (FamPra.ch) (2012), 627, 635.

70 Msg Parental Responsibility, above n 2, 9105.

disability, absence, violence[71] or other similar reasons.[72] Further, parental responsibility can also be revoked if the parents have not seriously cared for the child or have flagrantly violated their duties towards the child.[73] The reasons for withdrawal according to art 311 CC have to be severe and in practice revocation of parental responsibility due to art 311 CC only occurs in extreme cases.[74]

With the reference to art 311 CC, the legislature changed the threshold set by the Swiss Supreme Court.[75] Before the reform the threshold of art 311 CC did not have to be met in order to change joint parental responsibility to sole parental responsibility.[76] It has therefore been criticised that art 311 CC is not suitable to allocate parental responsibility in case of unmarried parents unwilling to declare joint parental responsibility.[77] Contrary to the Swiss legislature, during the debates of the Swiss parliament it had been clearly stated that further and not as severe reasons as listed in art 311 CC can also lead to a withdrawal of parental responsibility.[78] The threshold to be considered is yet to become clear.

Furthermore, pursuant to art 298b(3) CC the child protection authority may also decide on remaining disputed questions, such as childcare or visitation rights.[79] As already provided for in the former law, the court will remain the competent authority for child support claims.[80]

Finally, art 298b(4) CC regulates the case of a minor mother or of a mother subject to a general deputyship (*umfassende Beistandschaft*). Depending on the welfare of the child the child protection authority then assigns parental responsibility to the father or appoints a guardian for the child.

(iii) Decision of the court in connection with a paternity suit (art 298c CC)

In the case of a successful paternity suit, art 298c CC states that the court awards joint parental responsibility to the parents provided that the welfare of the child does not require allocating sole parental responsibility to the mother.

---

71 This reason has been introduced by the reform of parental responsibility in order to protect the child from domestic violence, Msg Parental Responsibility, above n 2, 9105, 9109.

72 Art 311(1) no 1 CC.

73 Art 311(1) no 2 CC.

74 Gloor/Schweighauser, above n 59, 1, 6.

75 Gloor/Schweighauser, above n 59, 1, 6.

76 BGer 5A_638/2010 from 10 November 2010, consideration 2.1.

77 Gloor/Schweighauser, above n 59, 1, 6; Rumo-Jungo, above n 60, 1, 7.

78 Gloor/Schweighauser, above n 59, 1, 7 and Bucher, above n 56, 1, 10–11, both with examples and further references.

79 Msg Parental Responsibility, above n 2, 9105.

80 Art 298b(3) last sentence CC.

The court has to respect the same threshold as the child protection authority has to have regard to in the case of denial of parental responsibility according to art 298b(2) CC.[81]

(b) Sole parental responsibility (art 298a(5) CC)

It was the legislature's intention that only exceptionally should sole parental responsibility be awarded.[82] Nevertheless, unmarried parents are still not automatically vested with joint parental responsibility.[83] As already elaborated, joint parental responsibility will only be awarded to unmarried parents if they jointly make a declaration, or if the child protection authority or the court decides in favour of joint parental responsibility. Article 298a(5) CC therefore provides for the unmarried mother to be vested with sole parental responsibility at the child's birth. Only if a declaration has been made prior to the child's birth will parental responsibility be allocated to both parents from the very beginning. Hence, in the case of unmarried parents, regularly still only the mother will be vested with parental responsibility (at least at first).

(c) Abolition of the welfare advocate (*Beistand*) (art 309 CC)

According to the former art 309(1) CC, if an unmarried woman gave birth to a child the child protection authority had to appoint a welfare advocate for this child.[84] The welfare advocate had the duty to determine the father of the child born out of wedlock and to advise and support the mother as circumstances required. This regulation has been abolished by the reform.[85] A welfare advocate for the child should only be appointed if necessary and the mere fact that the child is born out of wedlock does not constitute such a situation.[86] According to the legislature both the protection of the child as well as the right to know his or her origins are still ensured.[87]

VII CHANGE OF CIRCUMSTANCES (ARTS 134 AND 298D CC)

According to either art 134 or 298d CC parental responsibility for either divorced or unmarried parents may be reallocated in the case of substantial change in circumstances in order to ensure the welfare of the child. At the

[81] Msg Parental Responsibility, above n 2, 9106.

[82] Msg Parental Responsibility, above n 2, 9078, 9102.

[83] Msg Parental Responsibility, above n 2, 9092.

[84] According to art 50(1)(a) RCS (above n 53) every birth of a child born out of wedlock had to be registered at the child protection authority.

[85] The abolition of art 309 CC has been critised, cf Bucher, above n 57, 1, 16, 35 et seq; Häfeli, in: Podiumsdiskussion vom 16. Februar 2012 in Basel, above n 68, 627, 644; Reusser/Geiser, Sorge um die gemeinsame elterliche Sorge, Zeitschrift des bernischen Juristenverein (ZBJV) 2012, 758, 765 *et seq*.

[86] Msg Parental Responsibility, above n 2, 9095.

[87] Msg Parental Responsibility, above n 2, 9108.

request of one of the parents, the child or the child protection authority, the competent authority[88] then has to decide upon a new attribution of parental responsibility. The authority can restrict its decision to the rearrangement of custody, visitation rights or shares of childcare.[89]

VIII DEATH OF A PARENT (ART 297 CC)

No major changes occurred with regard to the situation where one of the parents dies. If the parents have exercised parental responsibility jointly, the surviving parent is automatically vested with sole parental responsibility.[90]

In case of death of the parent vested with sole parental responsibility, the child protection authority may either confer parental responsibility upon the surviving parent or appoint a guardian for the child.[91] The child protection authority thereby has to consider the welfare of the child and might further also take into account the reasons which led to sole parental responsibility in the first place.[92]

IX CONTENT OF PARENTAL RESPONSIBILITY

Parental responsibility encompasses the duty of upbringing and caring for a child as well as the power to represent the child in all dealings with third parties.[93] The reform on parental responsibility did introduce a new paragraph on the general rules of the content of parental responsibility as well as a new article on the competence of deciding the residence (*Aufenthaltsort*) of the child.

(a) Competence to solely decide (art 301(1bis) CC) in case of joint parental responsibility

In principle, joint parental responsibility requires the parents to regulate everything concerning the child together and neither of the parents has priority in the decision-making. Article 301(1bis) CC has been introduced to deal with the situation where the parents vested with joint parental responsibility, however, do not live together and de facto only one parent raises and educates the child (at the same time).[94]

---

88 Art 134(3) and (4) CC: the court or child protection authority in case of divorced parents; Art 298d CC: the child protection authority in case of unmarried parents.

89 Art. 298d(2) CC; Gloor/Schweighauser, above n 59, 1, 12.

90 Art 297(1) CC.

91 Art 297(2) CC.

92 Gloor/Schweighauser above n 59, 1, 5; Msg Parental Responsibility, above n 2, 9103.

93 Art 301 CC et seq.

94 Msg Parental Responsibility, above n 2, 9106.

The parent caring for the child may solely decide if the matter concerned is an everyday or urgent matter.[95] Such matter could for instance include questions of nutrition or clothing of the child, however, not decisions about a change of school or religion.[96] The legislature indeed deliberately chose not to stipulate in detail which matters it considers as an everyday or urgent matter and intended to let the practice and case-law define the range of what is of fundamental importance or not, or which matters are so urgent that it cannot be expected to wait before making a decision.[97]

Further, the parent taking care of the child may also decide solely if the other parent is not reachable with reasonable effort.[98] This could be the case if for example a parent is travelling without having left an address or phone number to be reached.[99]

(b) Determination of the residence (*Aufenthaltsort*) (art 301a CC)

According to the new art 301a CC, parental responsibility encompasses the right to determine the residence of the child. The residence (*Aufenthaltsort*) has to be distinguished from the domicile (*Wohnort*) of the child which is defined in art 25 CC. Before the reform, it was understood that the right to determine the residence of the child was subject to the right of custody.[100] The new art 301a CC had been highly controversial during the reform of parental responsibility,[101] mainly, because in the draft of this provision it was envisaged to regulate the change of residence not only of the child but also of the parents and, hence, contravening the right to freely choose one's domicile.[102]

Article 301a(2) CC regulates the case of the parents jointly exercising parental responsibility. In the case of one of the parents wanting to change the residence of the child, the other parent has to approve this change if either the new residence is abroad[103] or the change of residence significantly hinders the other parent from exercising his or her parental responsibility and visitation rights.[104] As stated in art 301(2)(a) CC the move to another country always requires the

---

95 Art 301(1bis) no 1 CC.

96 Msg Parental Responsibility, above n 2, 9106; Gloor/Schweighauser, above n 59, 1, 14 with further references and examples.

97 Msg Parental Responsibility, above n 2, 9106; Cantieni in: Podiumsdiskussion vom 16. Februar 2012 in Basel, above n 69, 627, 641, criticising the fact that the legislature has not clearly regulated which decisions have to be made by both parents and which not. See also the proposal for a more detailed system with regard to the competence to decide, Büchler/Cantieni/Simoni, above n 64, 207, 220 et seq.

98 Art 301(1bis) no 2 CC.

99 Msg Parental Responsibility, above n 2, 9106.

100 Gloor/Schweighauser, above n 59, 1, 17; Schwenzer in Honsell/Vogt/Geiser (eds) 'Basler Kommentar Zivilgesetzbuch I' 4th edition, (Helbing Lichtenhahn Verlag, 2010), Art 296 n 6.

101 Gloor/Schweighauser, above n 59, 1, 16; Reusser/Geiser, above n 85, 758 et seq.

102 Vote Sommaruga Simonetta, AB 2013, S 14.

103 Art 301a(2)(a) CC.

104 Art 301a(2)(b) CC.

consent of the other parent. This holds true independently of how far away the new location is. According to the legislature such a change leads to another jurisdiction which complicates the enforcement of any regulation on parental responsibility made in Switzerland and therefore justifies the requirement of the approval by the other parent.[105]

If the parents cannot reach an agreement on the child's residence, the court or child protection authority has to decide upon this question.[106] If one of the parents decides to move with the child to a contracting state of the Hague Convention of 25 October 1980 on the Civil Aspects of International Child Abduction or of the European Convention of 20 May 1980 on Recognition and Enforcement of Decisions concerning Custody of Children and on Restoration of Custody of Children without the consent of the other parent, he or she may initiate return procedures on the grounds of international child abduction.[107]

If only one parent is vested with parental responsibility, he or she must inform the other parent in due time about the change of residence of the child.[108] This duty to inform exists independently of where and how far away the new residence of the child is going to be.[109] Pursuant to and wanting to change his or her own domicile.

In any case, according to art 301a(5) CC the parents have to discuss adjustments with regard to the allocation of parental responsibility, custody, visitation rights and child support if necessary.[110] The parents thereby have to consider and ensure the welfare of the child. If no agreement can be reached the court or the child protection authority has to decide on those questions.

X TRANSITIONAL LAW (*ÜBERGANGSRECHT*) (ART 12(4) AND (5) FINT)[111]

The new rules on parental responsibility entered into force on 1 July 2014. They are, however, not only applicable to parents of children born after this date but also to those parents with children born prior to this date.

If only one of the parents is vested with parental responsibility the other parent may request joint parental responsibility within the first year after the new law entered into force.[112] For that matter the competent authority has to apply art 298b CC analogously.[113] In cases where parental responsibility had been

---

105 Msg Parental Responsibility, above n 2, 9108.
106 Art 301a(1) CC.
107 Msg Parental Responsibility, above n 2, 9108.
108 Art 301a(3) CC.
109 Gloor/Schweighauser, above n 59, 1, 17.
110 Vote Sommaruga Simonetta, AB 2013, S 14 ('*in allen Fällen*').
111 Final Title of the Swiss Code of Obligations (FinT) = Schlusstitel (SchlT).
112 Art 12(4) FinT.
113 Art 12(4) last sentence FinT.

allocated to only one parent due to a divorce, the parent not vested with parental responsibility may, however, only request joint parental responsibility if the divorce had been issued within 5 years of 1 July 2014. The Swiss legislature wanted to avoid reopening discussions about the allocation of parental responsibility which have stood the test of time.[114] Finally, divorced or unmarried parents can jointly apply for joint parental responsibility at any time.[115]

XI CONCLUSION

The principle of joint parental responsibility has been discussed in Switzerland for almost 40 years.[116] With this reform, the legislature introduced joint parental responsibility as a rule independent of the parents' marital status. However, distinctions on the allocation of parental responsibility remain. Whereas married parents are automatically vested with joint parental responsibility, unmarried or divorcing parents have to fulfill further requirements in order to be awarded joint parental responsibility. In any case, the changes introduced by the reform will lead to more children being under joint parental responsibility.

As with every reform, questions remain open and some consequences have yet to become clear. Nevertheless, the reform and the intentions of the legislature are a very welcome step towards diminishing discrimination of children born in marriage and out of wedlock and towards a family law oriented by the welfare of the child.

---

114 Msg Parental Responsibility, above n 2, 9110.

115 Gloor/Schweighauser, above n 59, 1, 23.

116 Report on the Preliminary Draft of the Revision of the Parental Responsibility (January 2009) (*Bericht zum Vorentwurf einer Teilrevision des Schweizerischen Zivilgesetzbuches (Elterliche Sorge) und des Schweizerischen Strafgesetzbuches* (art 220)), 4.

UNITED STATES

DEVELOPMENTS IN FAMILY LAW IN THE UNITED STATES OF AMERICA IN 2013

*Lynn D Wardle**

Résumé

Ce chapitre s'attache à d'importants développements intervenus aux Etats-Unis en 2013, principalement liés à plusieurs décisions hautement controversées relatives à la définition du mariage et des relations familiales alternatives. Ces cas n'impliquaient pas seulement la question des couples, mais également les relations entre parents et enfants. La tendance générale de ces décisions en 2013 s'oriente vers l'octroi, pour les relations familiales non-traditionnelle set les relations quasi-familiale, d'un statut familial légal et formel et d'une équivalence avec les couples mariés. Les hypothèses montraient que les formes et les relations familiales conventionnelle sont été, dans une certaine mesure, remodelées par un nombre important et croissant de relations familiales non-traditionnelle sou quasi-familiales. Les juridictions sont destinées à traiter les relations imparfaites, et les juges américains vont devoir s'occuper de plus en plus de telles relations dans un futur proche. L'ultime question subsistante est de savoir dans quelle mesure la reconnaissance de ces relations familiales extra-traditionnelles, ainsi que leur inclusion au sein des formes familiales connues des juges aux affaires familiales, vont altérer les relations et les droits traditionnels entre mari et femme d'une part, et parent et enfant d'autre part, ainsique les questions de responsabilité parentale.

I INTRODUCTION TO FAMILY LAW IN THE AMERICAN LEGAL SYSTEM

Several highly controversial decisions about the definition of marriage and of alternative family relationships dominated the developments in family law in the United States in 2013. Such doctrinal developments did not only concern adult relationships but involved parent–child relationships as well. The general trend in the decisions in 2013 was towards giving formal legal family status and marital equivalence to non-traditional family and quasi-family relations.

* Bruce C Hafen Professor of Law, J Reuben Clark Law School, Brigham Young University, Provo, UT 84602. The valuable research assistance of Roselyn Lewis and Zachary Ashby is gratefully acknowledged.

This chapter reviews 2013 family law developments in the United States in a family life-sequence. Thus, after this introduction, the recent developments (mostly case decisions) will be discussed in a before (creation), during (ongoing), and after (dissolution) sequence, with developments in the horizontal (spousal and quasi-spousal) family relations separated from developments in the vertical (parent–child and similar) family relations. Concluding reflections on the American family law developments in 2013 will complete this report.

To understand the significance of American family law decisions requires recognition that the judicial system in the United States of America has two quasi-independent (interdependent) parts: federal and state. Most family law cases are heard in and decided by state courts, and only a relatively few cases involving family law-related issues arise in the federal courts.[1] Most state courts have three levels: trial courts, intermediate courts of appeals and courts of last resort (usually called the state 'supreme court'). Federal courts generally abstain from adjudicating or dismiss claims that are primarily domestic relations in nature, especially when related proceedings are pending in state courts.

An example of the 'domestic relations' exception to federal court jurisdiction decided in 2013 is *Wallace v Wallace*.[2] In that case a man filed an identity theft tort claim in a diversity action in the federal court against his wife, after she filed for divorce. He claimed that during their marriage she had purloined his personal information and used it to obtain several credit cards in his name upon which she charged about $40,000 in purchases, resulting in his being sued for non-payment. The federal district court dismissed the suit under the domestic relations exception to federal court diversity jurisdiction. The US Court of Appeals for the Eighth Circuit affirmed holding that when a federal suit is 'inextricably intertwined' with a state domestic proceeding the federal court should decline to exercise jurisdiction when the federal suit 'involves a remedy which is essentially domestic' and its effect 'is to modify, nullify, or predetermine the domestic ruling of the state proceeding'.[3]

State courts hear a staggering number of cases each year. For example, in 2010 the total number of newly filed cases reported by state courts in the United States was approximately 18,200,000 cases.[4] That amounts to about 6,000 new state court cases filed for every 100,000 population, up about 20% since 2001.[5] In contrast to other categories of civil litigation, which recently have been declining,[6] it was reported in October 2012 that: 'Domestic Relations

---

1 Syracuse University, US Court System (2013), available at www2.maxwell.syr.edu/plegal/scales/court.html (accessed 18 February 2014).

2 736 F3d 764 (8th Cir 2013).

3 Ibid at 767.

4 National Center for State Courts, Court Statistics Project, Civil Caseloads Fell 3 Percent in 2010 (2013), available at www.courtstatistics.org/Civil/20121Civil.aspx (accessed 18 February 2014).

5 Ibid.

6 Ibid.

cases essentially have been on the rise since 2007'.[7] The National Center for State Courts reports that: 'Divorce drives Domestic Relations caseloads'.[8] The increase in divorce and other domestic relations cases may be related to the struggling US economy.[9] Additionally, most courts are unable to 'clear' as many domestic relations cases as are opened in a given year due to their complexity and duration, and that contributes to growing backlogs.[10]

II MARRIAGE LAW DEVELOPMENTS

Both federal and state courts rendered decisions, and state legislators enacted new laws, that significantly altered existing marriage concepts and doctrines. The legislatures in the states of Hawaii and Illinois enacted, and the governors of those states signed, legislation amending state marriage law to allow same-sex couples to marry. The Hawaii legislation also enabled parties to same-sex civil unions to convert such unions into marriages. The statutes in both states also purported to protect religious liberty by providing that clergy and religious organisations are free to decline to provide facilities or clergy to facilitate or celebrate marriages. The Hawaii legislation, the Marriage Equality Act 2013,[11] took effect in December. The efficacy of its provisions to protect rights of conscience remains to be seen.

In Illinois, the Religious Freedom and Marriage Fairness Act[12] will legalise same-sex marriage effective 1 June 2014. The Illinois law provides fewer explicit protections for religious liberty, which has been the source of controversy and threatened litigation. A major concern regarding both bills has been the collateral effects such as in teaching about marriage in public schools, and in employment in faith-based adoption agencies, hospitals, private schools, etc. Again, the protection of the rights of objectors to same-sex marriage to espouse their views is unclear.

The federal government took the lead in promoting the legalisation of same-sex marriage in 2013. Normally, state legislators establish the definitions, terms, conditions and legal rights and responsibilities of marriage for purposes of family law in the United States. Likewise, normally it is Congress that determines what marriages are recognised and how they are regulated in federal

---

7 National Center for State Courts, Court Statistics Project, Domestic Relations Caseloads on the Rise (2013), available at www.courtstatistics.org/Domestic-Relations/20121Domestic.aspx (accessed 18 February 2014).

8 National Center for State Courts, Court Statistics Project, Divorce Drives Domestic Relations Caseloads (2013), available at www.courtstatistics.org/Domestic-Relations/20124Domestic.aspx (last viewed 18 February 2014).

9 National Center for State Courts, Court Statistics Project, Domestic Relations Caseloads on the Rise (2013), available at www.courtstatistics.org/Domestic-Relations/20121Domestic.aspx (accessed 18 February 2014).

10 Clearance Rates Lag for Domestic Relations Cases (2013), available at www.courtstatistics.org/Domestic-Relations/20123Domestic.aspx (accessed 18 February 2014).

11 Haw Rev Stat Ann Div 3, Tit 31, Ch 572 Note.

12 750 Ill Comp Stat Ann 80/1 (LexisNexis 2013).

law. Thus, historically, Congress has recognised for purposes of federal law some marriages that were not recognised in the parties' state of domicile, and has refused to recognise some other marriages that were recognised or created by state laws.[13] In 2013 the administration of President Obama abandoned the domicile rule for purposes of federal tax recognition of same-sex marriage in favour of a place-of-celebration rule.[14] The effect of that change was to increase the number of same-sex marriages recognised by the federal government, and to create internal dissonance (federal law versus state law) within states that do not recognise same-sex marriage that might give such states an incentive to recognise same-sex marriages.

A number of judicial decisions dealt with same-sex marriage issues. In *United States v Windsor*,[15] the Supreme Court altered the traditional understanding of federalism in favour of a stronger version of deferential federalism, requiring the federal government to recognise all same-sex marriages that have been created in or recognised in any state. In 1996, Congress enacted the Defense of Marriage Act (DOMA),[16] one provision of which provided that, for purposes of federal laws, programmes and agencies, the term 'marriage' 'means only a legal union between one man and one woman'.[17] The specific purpose of DOMA was to not interfere with the states' freedom to define marriage however they wished (including to legalise same-sex marriage) for state domestic relations purposes, while protecting the traditional gender-integrating definition of marriage for purposes of federal law. In *Windsor*, a wealthy lesbian couple entered into a Canadian same-sex marriage that was recognised as lawful in New York, where they lived. When one of the women died, the other, Windsor, was unable to obtain the special federal tax treatment allowed married persons and faced a potential federal tax of over $300,000 on the $3million dollar estate she inherited. So she sued and the Supreme Court of the United States held that she was entitled to marital status recognition on two interrelated grounds. First, federalism principles supported requiring the federal government to recognise her state marital status, and, second, principles of due process and equal protection combined to support federal recognition of the 'equal liberty' of same-sex couples to marry, which New York (and at that time about a dozen other states) had recognised. Justice Kennedy wrote the opinion for the Court's 5–4 decision, and his opinion expressed enthusiasm for the legalisation of same-sex marriage as well as surprisingly pejorative disdain for opposition to same-sex marriage and for supporters of that policy.

A companion case, *Hollingsworth v Perry*,[18] involved a California state constitutional amendment approved by voters in 2000, which, like similar state

13 See Lynn D Wardle 'Involuntary Imports: Williams v. Lutwak, the Defense of Marriage Act, Federalism, and "Thick" and "Thin" Conceptions of Marriage' (2012) 81 Fordham L Rev 771.

14 IRS Revenue Ruling 2013-17, available at www.irs.gov/pub/irs-drop/rr-13-17.pdf (accessed 19 February 2014). See further below, n 48, and accompanying text.

15 570 US 12, 133 SCt 2675 (2013).

16 Pub L 104–199, 110 Stat 2419, enacted 21 September 1996.

17 1 USC § 7 (1996).

18 570 US 12, No 12 144 133 SCt 2652 (2013).

constitutional amendments in 30 other states, defined marriage as the union between one man and one woman. The lower federal courts held that the parties had standing under California law to challenge the amendment and that the state amendment was unconstitutional. However, the Supreme Court of the United States, by a 5–4 vote, ruled that the sponsors of the state amendment lacked standing to appeal the dubious federal lower court rulings that invalidated the amendment.[19] The effect of the procedural ruling was to leave intact the lower court decisions invalidating the state marriage amendment. For the four dissenting justices, Justice Anthony Kennedy (from California) argued that the Court should defer to California in determining whether parties have standing to challenge the California amendment. In that respect, the *Perry* decision seems inconsistent with a 2004 US Supreme Court decision in *Elk Grove Unified School District v Newdow*,[20] where the Court held that a non-custodial father lacked standing to challenge a school's mandatory pledge-of-allegiance recitation requirement because, under state law, only the custodial parent had the right to litigate on behalf of the child.

Three state court decisions about other aspects of marriage law in 2013 deserve mention. Together they suggest a state court concern to protect the stability of marriage and the family support obligations thereof.

In *In re Estate of Laubenheimer*,[21] a woman executed a will leaving her estate to her husband, with the proviso that it would go to his three children from a prior marriage if he died before she did. He died in 2001 after they had been married for 30 years. Thereafter, she began to live with Joseph McLeod. She suffered a stroke in 2007 and was found incapable of making her own health care decisions. McLeod removed her from the nursing home in 2008, and then married her. After she died, he filed a claim to her estate as her husband and his stepdaughter contested the marriage. Distinguishing the declaring of a marriage to be void ab initio from annulling a voidable marriage, the court held that the marriage was void ab initio because of incapacity to contract marriage, and not protected by a provision of Wisconsin's law providing that a marriage cannot be annulled after the death of one of the parties.

In *Kelley v Cooper*,[22] the Georgia Court of Appeals held that the 'meretricious relationship' defence did not apply to preclude recovery of damages for a claimed breach of promise to marry. Even though the parties were living together without marriage, since the claim was for failure to perform a promise (which may have induced the plaintiff to engage in the premarital cohabitation) the traditional defence was deemed inappropriate.

In *In re Marriage of Facter*,[23] an intermediate court of appeals in California invalidated per se a premarital agreement provision which waived entirely the

---

19 Ibid.
20 542 US 1 (2004).
21 350 Wis2d 182, 833 NW2d 735, 2013 WI 76.
22 No A13A0982, 2013 Ga App LEXIS 979 (Ga Ct App 22 November 2013).
23 212 Cal App 4th 967, 152 CalRptr3d 79 (2013).

man's child support obligation; invalidated as unconscionable in the circumstances a provision which severely limited his alimony obligation (he had $3 million in assets and earned about $600,000 annually when the agreement was signed). However, the court ruled severable and enforceable a provision in the prenuptial contract which waived the wife's interest in the community property he generated. California is one of ten community property states; the other 40 states and the District of Columbia follow common law (title) property regimes.

In *Zulpo v Blann*,[24] the Arkansas Court of Appeals held that a deceased man did not stand in loco parentis to his stepchildren and that the stepchildren were not entitled to a share of the proceeds from a wrongful death settlement obtained in an action filed by their mother. The two boys were teenagers when their divorced mother and the stepfather married in 1974. Their father was awarded custody in the divorce and both boys lived with, and were supported by, him until they each turned 18. They claimed to have developed a good relationship with their stepfather after they were 18, and that they recognized him as their stepfather and he recognized them as his stepsons, such that they had an interest in the proceeds recovered for his wrongful death. The relationship that developed after majority was deemed irrelevant to the in loco parentis claim.

As 2013 wound to a close, two courts ordered the legalisation of same-sex marriage in two states, and another struck down a law prohibiting polygamous cohabitation. In *Brown v Buhman*,[25] a federal district court in Utah ruled that the Utah law violated the Free Exercise Clause, violated Due Process, and was void for vagueness. The state law provided that: '(1) A person is guilty of bigamy when, knowing he has a husband or wife or knowing the other person has a husband or wife, the person purports to marry another person or cohabits with another person.' After state officials threatened to prosecute them for bigamy, Kody Brown and his wives, the stars of a reality TV show, 'Sister Wives', sued the state arguing that the part of the statute that makes it a crime for a legally married person to 'cohabit' with a third party was unconstitutional, at least as applied to persons engaging in religiously motivated polygamous cohabitation. The court held the statute was subject to strict scrutiny under the Free Exercise Clause of the First Amendment, applicable to the states through the Fourteenth Amendment. Relying heavily upon a dissenting opinion in a case decided by the Utah Supreme Court, the federal court found:[26]

> 'the cohabitation prong of the Statute unconstitutional on numerous grounds and str[uck] it. As a result, and to save the Statute, the court adopt[ed] the interpretation of "marry" and "purports to marry," and the resulting narrowing construction of the Statute, offered by the dissent in State of Utah v. Holm, 2006 UT 31, ¶¶ 131–53, 137 P.3d 726, 758–66, thus allowing the Statute to remain in

---

24 2013 Ark App 750, 2013 WL 6712532.
25 947 FSupp2d 1170 (D Utah 2013).
26 Ibid at 1234.

> force as prohibiting bigamy in the literal sense – the fraudulent or otherwise impermissible possession of two purportedly valid marriage licenses for the purpose of entering into more than one purportedly legal marriage.'

On 19 December 2013, the New Mexico Supreme Court ruled in *Griego v Oliver*[27] that the state's dual-gender marriage rule violated the equal protection guarantee under the state constitution. The court ruled that same-sex couples who sought to marry were similarly situated to opposite-sex couples who sought to marry, that '[s]ame-gender couples are as capable of responsible procreation as are opposite-gender couples'.[28] The court held that:[29]

> 'Excluding same-gender couples from civil marriage prevents children of same-gender couples from enjoying the security that flows from the rights, protections, and responsibilities that accompany civil marriage. There is no substantial relationship between New Mexico's marriage laws and the purported governmental interest of responsible child-rearing. There is nothing rational about a law that penalizes children by depriving them of state and federal benefits because the government disapproves of their parents' sexual orientation.'

The conclusion seems to beg the question about gender and parenting. Despite many overlapping abilities, it is undeniable that men and women differ in profound and profoundly important ways and that both men and women make special, uniquely beneficial contributions to children in parenting. A child that has two 'moms' is deprived of a dad, and a child with two dads still needs a 'mom'. It seems to defy experience, reality and logic to insist that gender is entirely fungible in parenting.

On 20 December 2013, a federal district court ordered the state of Utah to allow same-sex couples to marry in *Kitchen v Herbert*.[30] In a long opinion, the federal court held that Utah's historic, traditional dual-gender marriage requirement violated both federal due process and equal protection principles. Since the sources upon which the court's ruling were based are applicable in all states, the implications of the decision for the potential eventual national legalisation of same-sex marriage are not insignificant. The ruling has been appealed, and has been stayed pending appeal, so the litigation is far from final.[31] However, before a stay was entered (the trial court refused the usual practice and declined to stay his ruling), over one thousand same-sex couples had become married in one of the most conservative, religious, strongly opposed-to-same-sex-marriage states in America.

When the year 2013 ended same-sex marriage was legal in 16 of the 50 American states – less than one-third of the states – plus in the District of

---

27 316 P3d 865 (NM 2013).

28 Ibid at 887.

29 Ibid at 888.

30 961 F.Supp.2d 1181, 2013 WL 6697874 (D Utah, 20 December 2013).

31 The federal district court in Utah declined to stay its order pending appeal, as did a panel of the Tenth Circuit Court of Appeals, so the Supreme Court ordered a stay of the order legalising same-sex marriage in Utah pending the appeal.

Columbia.[32] However, seven of those states had legalised same-sex marriage in 2013. The states and dates of legalisation of same-sex marriage are: Massachusetts (2004), Connecticut (2008), Iowa (2009), Vermont (2009), New Hampshire (2010), New York (2011), Maine (2012), Maryland (2012), Washington (2012), Delaware (2013), California (2013), Minnesota (2013), Rhode Island (2013), New Jersey (2013 de facto), Hawaii (2013) and New Mexico (2013). Additionally the District of Columbia (2010) has legalised same-sex marriage. Moreover, as noted above, a judicial decision ordering same-sex marriage was entered in Utah, but stayed pending appeal. Further, lawmakers in Illinois voted in 2013 to legalise same-sex marriage in legislation to become effective in June 2014. Also, 5 of the 566 US Indian tribes have legalised same-sex marriage: the Coquille, Suquamish, Odawa Tribes, Santa Ysabel and Pokagon Band of Potawatomi Tribe.[33] So while the strong majority of American states still do not allow or recognise same-sex marriage, 2013 was a banner year for advocates of same-sex marriage.

III PARENTAGE CASES

Most of the law of parentage was created to facilitate the determination of fathers who procreate by natural biological intercourse. Recently, the use of new artificial reproductive technology and increasing social acceptance of new forms of adult intimate relations have opened up more complicated parental relationship issues, several of which were addressed by state courts in 2013.

Appellate courts in several states cleared the way for lesbian partners to have co-parental rights. For example, in *DMT v TMH*,[34] the Florida Supreme Court held that the state's assisted reproduction statute which terminated parental rights of all gamete or pre-embryo donors (except a commissioning couple or father who has executed a preplanned adoption agreement) was unconstitutional as violative of both due process and equal protection doctrines. Likewise, in *In re ARL*,[35] a Colorado intermediate appeals court held that a child born during a lesbian relationship 'may have two mothers under the UPA [Uniform Parentage Act] – a biological mother and a presumed mother'.[36] The court held that the mother's partner may be recognised as a child's other mother if she can demonstrate presumptive parenthood under the UPA. In *Gartner v Iowa Dep't*

---

32 Voters approved same-sex marriage in three states in 2012 (ME, MD and WA). In at least six of the states where SSM now is legal it was the result of judicial decree or initiative (MA, IA, CA, CN, NJ, NM and possibly VT). A trial court in New Jersey ruled that it was unconstitutional for the state to not permit same-sex marriage; the state supreme court denied a stay pending appeal on grounds that the state was unlikely to prevail on appeal, and then the Governor withdrew the state's appeal.

33 See 'Legal Status of Same-Sex Marriage and Unions in the USA and World', available at BYU Law School, Marriage & Family Law Research Project, at www.law2.byu.edu/site/marriage-family/home (accessed 21 February 2014).

34 129 So3d 320 (Fla 2013).

35 318 P3d 581, No 13CA0342, 2013 Colo App LEXIS 1879 (Colo Ct.App 2013).

36 Ibid at *1.

Pub H,[37] the Supreme Court of Iowa (one of 16 US states that has legalised same-sex marriage) held that the state's presumption of parentage statute, which expressly referred to a mother, father and husband, did not require the state to list the spouse of the birthing parent as the second parent on the birth certificate of the child born to the other spouse during a lesbian marriage; and that the statute violated equal protection under the Iowa Constitution as applied to a married lesbian couple to whom a child is born during the marriage. Since the Iowa Supreme Court was one of the first to mandate the legalisation of same-sex marriage in a state, the ruling of that court in this case was not unexpected.

In *LF v Breit*,[38] the Virginia Supreme Court held that a state assisted reproduction statute which prohibited a sperm donor from ever establishing his parental rights violated the statutes' express purpose, and also violated constitutional due process. A man and woman who had lived together as an unmarried couple for several years desired to have a child together. Finding that they could not conceive naturally, they conceived a child through in vitro fertilisation with assistance from a fertility doctor. The child was born while they lived together and they signed an agreement giving the mother custody and the father visitation. The father was named on the birth certificate and the child was given a hyphenated surname including the father's name, and after the couple separated he continued to support and visit the child until the mother unilaterally terminated contact. The Virginia Supreme Court held that the contractual and constitutional rights of the biological father overrode the assisted reproductive technology (ART) law, the Status of Children of Assisted Conception,[39] which provided, in the relevant part, that '[a] donor is not the parent of a child conceived through assisted conception, unless the donor is the husband of the gestational mother'.[40] So the statutory purpose of establishing a uniform and predictable method for non-marital fathers to obtain parental rights was subordinated to the wish for a fair outcome in the particular case.

On the other hand, in *Columbia v Lawton*,[41] the Vermont Supreme Court held that it could not hear a parentage action regarding a child in the face of an existing final judgment of parentage regarding the child. JB was born while the mother was in a non-marital relationship with her father, who acknowledged parentage and claimed the child as his own, and who was ordered to pay child support. A month after the court issued the order, Columbia filed a parentage action claiming that he had a sexual relationship with the mother and she had told him he was the father. The court found that Columbia lacked standing under the Vermont statute that denied further parentage actions once a parentage order had been issued (in this case as part of the child support action). On appeal, the Vermont Supreme Court affirmed, holding that the statute was unambiguous in denying further parentage actions once a court

---

37 830 NW2d 335 (Iowa 2013).
38 285 Va 163, 736 SE2d 711 (Va 2013).
39 Va Code, tit 20, ch 9, §§ 20-156, et seq.
40 Va Code § 158(A)(3).
41 71 A3d 1218 (Vt 2013).

order had been issued. This outcome furthered the best interests of the child, the family, and the state's interest in continuing and stable child support. As Columbia had made no contributions to the mother or child until after the earlier parentage determination, he lacked the right to open and relitigate the paternity issue.

In *Engelking v Engelking*,[42] the Indiana Court of Appeals affirmed that children born as a result of ART during a marriage were children of the marriage for whom the ex-husband could be ordered to pay child support. When the husband had learned that his vasectomy could not be reversed, he encouraged his wife to conceive a child by artificial insemination from a sperm donor, assisted his wife to acquire artificial insemination paraphernalia, and helped select the sperm donor. The court affirmed that the children were lawfully the husband's children under Indiana law.

In *Whelan v CG (In the Interest of CN)*,[43] the North Dakota Supreme Court held that a juvenile court correctly ordered a father to pay child support while also terminating his parental rights. Termination of parental rights under the Juvenile Court Act does not necessarily terminate the duty of a parent to support the child, the court noted. The father was serving a 30-year prison sentence for sexual abuse of a half-sibling when this child was born.

IV ONGOING SPOUSAL AND QUASI-SPOUSAL RELATIONS

In *In re Fonberg*,[44] a committee of judges in the US Court of Appeals for the Ninth Circuit held that denying health benefits to the same-sex partner of a former federal court law clerk violated the US District Court for the District of Oregon's Employment Dispute Resolution Plan and the US Constitution. The court rejected the Office of Personnel Management's argument that *US v Windsor* protected same-sex spousal benefits only and not other forms of same-sex relationships besides marriage.

A marriage between a man and a woman that was valid when entered into does not automatically become void when one of the parties has his or her birth certificate amended to indicate a change of gender, the Indiana Court of Appeals held in *In re Marriage of Davis*.[45] When her husband changed his gender and name to female the wife filed a petition for dissolution. The trial court dismissed the petition on the ground that the marriage automatically was voided by the husband's sex change. Indiana law provides that '[a] marriage between persons of the same gender is void'.[46] However, because the effect of the lower court ruling would permit a spouse to effectively abandon his own

42 982 NE2d 326 (Ind Ct App 2013).
43 2013 ND 205, 839 NW2d 841.
44 736 F3d 901 (9th Cir 2013).
45 1 NE3d 184 (Ind Ct App 2013).
46 Ind Code § 31-11-1-1 (1997).

child, the Court of Appeals reversed and remanded, interpreting the quoted language to be applicable solely at the time of marriage.

In *People v Trzeciak*,[47] the Illinois Supreme Court held that the state marital-privilege statute does not prevent a woman from testifying at a murder trial that her abusive husband once beat her, tied her up and threatened to kill both her and the murder victim. The court held that the defendant's physical acts 'were not nonverbal conduct intended to convey a message', and his verbal threats were not protected by the marital privilege because they were not manifestations of the special trust and affection of the marital relationship that the statute was intended to shield.

The Internal Revenue Service of the United States issued a formal ruling, *Revenue Ruling 2013-17*, declaring that for federal tax purposes the terms 'spouse', 'husband and wife', 'husband' and 'wife' would include persons in same-sex marriages.[48] The ruling also announced that new definitions would apply even if the parties were domiciled in a state that did not recognise same-sex marriage. The latter part of the ruling changes long-settled federal practice to defer to and apply the law of the parties' domicile regarding marriage validity, and adopts a new rule designed to give maximum recognition to same-sex marriages, even evasive marriages that would not be recognised in the couple's domicile. The new rule's purposes clearly include expansion of federal recognition of same-sex marriage and encouraging states to recognize same-sex marriage.

V ONGOING PARENT–CHILD RELATIONS

In the 'Ongoing parent–child relations' category, the theme of notable decisions was wrestling with whether to protect the boundary of legally recognised parental relationships. Cases involving the Hague Convention on the Civil Aspects of International Child Abduction were also significant.

In *Zulpo v Blann*,[49] an Arkansas appellate court affirmed that the two stepchildren of a deceased man were not entitled to a share of his estate. They had been teenagers when their mother married him in 1974, and they continued to reside with their biological father until they turned 18, so their stepfather did not stand in loco parentis to them. His relationship with them after they became adults (turned 18) could not create in loco parentis status.

In *Bower v EgyptAir Airlines Co*,[50] a father was unsuccessful in suing an airline that had flown his two abducted children to Egypt. The US Court of Appeals for the Second Circuit affirmed a district court ruling that an airline (EgyptAir)

---

47 5 NE2d 141, 2013 Il 114491 (Ill 2013).
48 IRS Revenue Ruling 2013-17, available at www.irs.gov/pub/irs-drop/rr-13-17.pdf (accessed 19 February 2014).
49 2013 Ark App 750 (2013).
50 731 F3d 85 (1st Cir 2013).

was not liable to the American father of the abducted children for allowing his Egyptian ex-wife to abduct their two children and fly them to Egypt because the airline had no actual knowledge that the mother planned to abduct the children, and it had no duty to investigate.

In *Yaman v Yaman*,[51] the US Court of Appeals for the First Circuit denied a petition for return of a child under the Hague Convention on the Civil Aspects of International Child Abduction. After a mother accused the father of abusing their daughters, he filed for divorce in Turkey and was awarded full custody of the children. Thereafter, the mother abducted the daughters going to Greece, then Andorra, and finally to New Hampshire where they lived for over 2 years when the father found them and filed his petition for return. The federal trial court denied his petition and accepted the mother's claim that the daughters were 'well settled' under the Hague Abduction Convention because they had been in the jurisdiction for over a year before the petition for return was filed, and should not be removed. The father responded that, because the mother had made it impossible for him to locate them, the one-year limit on filing under the Hague Convention should be tolled to prevent the 'well-settled' defence. Affirming the district court ruling that it did not have the authority to toll the one-year period the federal appeals court reasoned that the language and history of the treaty clearly set a firm one-year limit on petitions for return.

US courts are split about tolling the time for the 'well-settled' defence. The Supreme Court of the United States has pending a case, *Lozano v Alvarez*, No 12-820 (pending since 2013) in which that same issue is raised. The case was argued in February 2014 and a decision by the Supreme Court is expected before July 2014.

In *In re Custody of AFJ*,[52] the Washington state Supreme Court held that a foster parent could become a de facto parent and affirmed awarding her custody of her partner's biological child. One of the women in an on-again-off-again lesbian relationship became pregnant and had a child. While she was suffering from substance abuse and addiction, her occasional lesbian partner, who was the foster parent of the child, sought and was awarded custody. The top state court affirmed and held that a person's status as a foster parent does not preclude her recognition also as a de facto parent.

VI DISSOLUTION OF MARRIAGE AND ITS LEGAL CONSEQUENCES

Upon divorce, many smoldering disputes between the disaffected married parties often erupt into litigation and sometimes the cases are filed in different courts. Sometimes considerations of federalism and deferential federal court

---

51 730 F3d 1 (1st Cir 2013).
52 314 P3d 373 (Wash 2013).

respect for state courts' domestic relations jurisdiction requires abstention or dismissal of claims filed in the federal court.

For example, in *Wallace v Wallace*,[53] the US Court of Appeals for the Eighth Circuit affirmed a federal district court's dismissal of a man's suit against his divorcing wife for identity theft, holding that a federal suit that is 'inextricably intertwined' with a state domestic proceeding should not be heard by the federal court. That illustrates the federal court's 'domestic relations exception' to federal court diversity jurisdiction. In other words, even though the statutory requirements for federal court jurisdiction are satisfied (complete diversity and amount-in-controversy satisfied), the federal court will properly decline to adjudicate the case if the 'federal suit is "inextricably intertwined" with a state domestic proceeding, thereby depriving the federal court of subject matter jurisdiction, where the requested federal remedy overlaps the remedy at issue in the state proceeding'.[54]

Money can exacerbate the contention in divorce and increase the litigation. This is illustrated by the decision of the District of Columbia Court of Appeals in *Araya v Keleta*.[55] There, a couple divorced after less than 5 years of marriage. At the time of marriage, the husband, a cosmetic surgeon, owned the row house the couple used as their marital home, and during the marriage he later acquired an adjoining row house and combined the two units into one house. The couple had three children and the appellate court affirmed the award of sole physical custody to the wife, citing the husband's pattern of domestic violence against the wife. It affirmed the trial court's order that husband pay monthly child support of $3,128 and rehabilitative alimony of $6,000 per month for 24 months to the wife, even though the husband contested the income calculations upon which those awards were based. ('[T]he court imputed to him a net income of at least $283,484 (instead of his reported earned income of $100,000, his salary from his medical practice'.)[56] Even though the husband held title to both properties in his name, the trial court in the District of Columbia awarded the family home to the wife. The DC Court of Appeals (the court of last resort in the jurisdiction) upheld the property award even though the home consisted in part of the husband's separate property and was part (later-acquired) marital property (arguably). While the court would not adopt the rule that a home used as a family residence is automatically thereby transformed into marital property, it would allow the fact that the home is used for family living to be considered in determining whether separate property has been transformed into marital property. The appellate court agreed that '[r]eal estate acquired following marriage is . . . marital property which must be equitably distributed upon a final decree of divorce, regardless of whether that property is titled jointly or individually or by the parties in another form'.[57] The court found that neither of the properties

---

[53] 736 F3d 764 (8th Cir 2013); see above n 2, and accompanying text.
[54] Ibid at 767.
[55] 65 A3d 40 (DC 2013).
[56] Ibid at 47.
[57] Ibid at 49.

was the husband's separate property because during the marriage he had substantially renovated the first and had purchased the second, and he failed to establish that the funds used for those expenditures were solely his separate funds. Moreover:[58]

> '[b]ecause the court found that the wife "contributed substantially to the marriage" by bearing and raising the children and freeing the husband to build his practice and pursue his business ventures, and because the court distributed most of the other marital realty (eleven parcels) to the husband, we cannot say that the court abused its discretion in awarding the S Street property to the wife.'

The DC courts generally have applied 'the so-called "inception of title approach", ... articulated as the principle that "property acquired prior to the marriage is the sole and separate property of the spouse who originally owned it and must be assigned to that spouse upon divorce"'.[59] Property held initially as separate property may be transformed into marital property if the other spouse's contributions to the marriage are so substantial that the nature of the property is thereby effectively transformed from separate into marital.[60] Consideration of cases from other states led the DC court:[61]

> 'to conclude that where a spouse's separate property has been combined or blended with marital property in such a way that (1) the two items of property came to be used as one property and (2) one or both properties would be destroyed or damaged or left with a gaping deficiency or defect if the properties were separated, the Darling rule permits the trial court to treat the separate property as "transformed" and the combined or blended property as marital property that is subject to equitable distribution.'

The DC Court of Appeals also affirmed the award of nearly $81,000 in attorney's fees for wife's attorney in *Araya*. The evidence in the record that, during most of the marriage and at the time of divorce 'the wife was unemployed, had no income, and had hospital and credit card debt that she was unable to pay', was sufficient to establish her need for attorney's fees to be paid by her husband.[62]

> 'Properly, the fee award was based on "the actual services performed by the attorney", ... and on an assessment of counsel's skill and experience, the reasonableness of his rates over 14 months of representation, the successful result obtained, the husband's financial ability to pay the award, and the wife's lack of financial ability to do so'.[63]

Thus, the appellate court could 'discern in the attorney's fee award to the wife no legal error and no abuse of the court's broad discretion'.[64]

---

58 Ibid at 53.
59 Ibid.
60 Ibid at 53-55.
61 Ibid at 56.
62 Ibid at 57–59.
63 Ibid at 59.
64 Ibid.

In *In re Marriage of Burwell*,[65] the California intermediate appellate court resolved a dispute over insurance between the first and second wives of a deceased man. During the time that Gary and Becky were married, Gary purchased a term life insurance policy. When Becky filed for divorce in 2004, the court ordered that no beneficiaries would be changed on any insurance policies, and a keep-the-status-quo judgment was entered in 2005. Gary failed to disclose this particular insurance policy in the divorce proceedings. They finally agreed to property division in 2008. In 2008, Gary changed the insurance policy beneficiary from Becky to his new wife, Cynthia. Gary committed suicide 2 years later and Becky filed a civil action to prevent payment of the $1 million life insurance policy to Cynthia, Gary's widow. The trial court found that the insurance policy should have been divided in the divorce and ordered half of the proceeds distributed to Becky. The appellate court remanded, stating that the status of the property depended on how the final insurance term was paid for and the record was insufficient to make that determination. If the final policy payment came out of funds from Gary and Becky's marital estate, it was their community property and Becky would get half of it. If the payment came out of Gary's separate funds, it was his separate property. If it was paid for out of the marital estate of Gary and his second wife, it was their marital property and Becky would not be entitled to any of it.[66]

Several divorce-related cases in 2013 concerned bankruptcy. That is quite normal for, as the night follows the day, so bankruptcy seems to follows divorce. In *Taylor v Taylor (In re Taylor)*,[67] for example, a divorced woman filed for Chapter 7 bankruptcy and sought to discharge a judgment against her for $50,660 that she owed to her ex-husband for overpayment of spousal support. However, while agreeing that the debt was not in the nature of a non-dischargeable domestic support obligation (DSO), the US Court of Appeals for the Tenth Circuit held the debt was non-dischargeable under Bankruptcy Code, s 523(a)(15) because she incurred the debt 'in connection with a separation agreement'.

In *Steele v Heard*,[68] the parties divorced in 1994, and Heard was ordered to pay Steele a portion of his retirement payments when he received them. Heard began to receive his retirement benefits in 2006, but made no payments to Steele. Five years later, Steele petitioned the Illinois state court for a Qualified Domestic Relations Order (QDRO) dividing Heard's pension. Before the hearing on the claim for the QDRO, Heard filed for Chapter 13 bankruptcy protection in the federal bankruptcy court in Alabama. The federal bankruptcy court ruled that the pension division was not DSO, and Steele had no vested

---

65 221 CalApp4th 1, 164 CalRptr3d 702 (2013).
66 Ibid at 15–17
67 737 F3d 670 (10th Cir 2013).
68 487 BR 302 (Bankr, SD Ala 2013).

interest in the pension. Rather, the court order indicated that the pension division was a property division and a dischargeable debt. The district court affirmed, concluding:[69]

> 'In sum, the centerpiece of Steele's appeal is her contention that her property rights in the Pension Settlement vested [when] the September 1994 Judgment was entered, such that the Pension Settlement is her sole, separate property and outside Heard's bankruptcy estate. For this argument to succeed, Steele must demonstrate that Illinois law would find her property right in the Pension Benefit to be vested, sole and separate. She has not done so. The Brown case which she characterizes as "the leading case for [her] position" cites no Illinois authority embracing that legal principle. The Illinois Constitution has an anti-alienation provision that generally forbids diminution or impairment of a public employee's contractual relationship with a pension plan. While the Illinois legislature has created an exception to that anti-alienation provision that allows pension benefit division pursuant to a QILDRO, Heard's refusal to execute a consent form renders the availability of a QILDRO highly problematic here, particularly with Steele identifying no authority to the Bankruptcy Court or in her principal brief on appeal that might support a conclusion that the consent requirement is satisfied. Although Steele champions a "majority rule" from other jurisdictions, she does not offer any legal support to advance the notion that either Illinois has adopted the majority rule, or that the majority rule is any more persuasive than the "minority rule".'

In *In re Fitch*,[70] the federal bankruptcy court held that the money a bankruptcy debtor-husband still owed to his wife was part of a domestic support obligation and was a priority debt. The couple had filed for Chapter 13 bankruptcy while married into which the wife paid $122,000, but they separated before completion of the proceeding. When the wife filed for divorce, the court ordered the husband to repay the wife $700 per month for his share of their $65,000 outstanding tax debt and for his $40,000 child support arrearage. The husband later filed for Chapter 7 bankruptcy individually. The wife filed a claim that the debt he still owed her was part of a non-dischargeable DSO and was a priority debt upon which she relied to make ends meet. The bankruptcy court agreed that it was a DSO and a priority debt. It found that (1) the wife needed the payment for her support; (2) the payment was direct to the spouse; and (3) although it was not contingent on death, remarriage, or Social Security it was not infinite because it had a specific termination date.

Not surprisingly, some divorce-related claims decided in 2013 involved the break-up of same-sex relationships. To illustrate, in *Dee v Rakower*,[71] a woman filed a claim for breach of contract/partnership/joint venture and for equitable claims against her former same-sex partner, alleging that they had orally agreed that the plaintiff would share in the partner's earnings and pension in exchange for quitting her full-time job in order to care for their children. The parties had lived together for 18 years and were raising two children when they broke up. The New York intermediate appellate court held that the claims for breach of

---

69 Ibid at 316-317.
70 No 12-21191, 2013 WL 305217, (Bankr, ED Ky 2013).
71 976 NYS2d 470 (NY App Div 2d Dept 2013).

contract/partnership/joint venture should not have been dismissed for failure to state a claim because allegedly they had been supported by consideration:[72]

> 'The fact that the alleged agreement was made by an unmarried couple living together does not render it unenforceable. "New York courts have long accepted the concept that an express agreement between unmarried persons living together is as enforceable as though they were not living together, provided only that illicit sexual relations were not 'part of the consideration of the contract'".'

However, her equitable claims for constructive trust were properly dismissed:[73]

> 'Unlike divorcing married couples who can rely upon the equitable distribution law ... to fashion a formula for the court to calculate a coverture value of a spouse's pension, we find that the allegation of an equitable right to share the defendant's pension on an equal basis is insufficient to support a cause of action to impose a constructive trust.'

Thus, even in this day of tolerance of many non-traditional relationships, and even in a state that recognised same-sex marriages (New York), the law privileges marriage in some ways that are dissimilar to the treatment of other adult intimate relationships.

VII PARENT–CHILD RELATIONS AFTER DISSOLUTION OR BREAK-UP

In *Chafin v Chafin*,[74] the Supreme Court of the United States interpreted provisions of the Hague Convention on the Civil Aspects of International Child Abduction, and the federal implementing statute, the International Child Abduction Remedies Act (ICARA).[75] The father was American and the mother, his ex-wife, was Scottish. They had married in Scotland in 2004 and had one child. They both agreed that Scotland was the child's habitual residence until February 2010, when the mother brought the child to Alabama where the father lived. She overstayed her visa when the father took the child's passport away. He filed for divorce in Alabama. The mother filed a petition for return of the child under the Hague Abduction Convention in a federal district court which ordered the child be returned to Scotland. The child was immediately returned to Scotland while the father appealed. The Eleventh Circuit dismissed his appeal as moot because the child had already been removed from the jurisdiction to Scotland. The Supreme Court held that, because of the pending appeal, the dispute was 'still very much alive' and 'ongoing' even though the child and her mother were no longer within the jurisdiction.[76] If removal of the child pending appeal mooted cases under the Convention and ICARA, it would

---

[72] Ibid at 475.
[73] Ibid at 477.
[74] No 11-1347 133 SCt 1017 (2013).
[75] 42 USC §§ 11601–11611 (2005).
[76] Chafin, 133 SCt at 1123-1124.

lead to more stays, more appeals, and longer delays before children could be returned.[77] It also might give more incentive to such child-snatching behaviour.

Another significant Hague Abduction Convention case was decided by the Ninth Circuit Court of Appeals. In *Valenzuela v Michel*,[78] the court affirmed that parents who had a 'shuttle custody' (dual habitual residence) arrangement under which their Mexican-born children split their time between living in the father's home in the US and the mother's home in Mexico shared an intent to abandon Mexico as the children's sole habitual residence. Thus, the father's retention of them in the US, their habitual residence, was not wrongful under the Hague child abduction convention and he was not required to return them to the mother in Mexico.

A US District Court in Massachusetts ruled that a father's retention of his daughter in the United States after retrieving her from Colombia – where she had lived with the mother for 2 years – was not wrongful under the Hague Abduction Convention because the US was the daughter's country of habitual residence. In *Londono v Gonzalez*,[79] the court relied upon finding that the parties planned for the mother to reside in the US which showed their shared intent that the US was to be the child's habitual residence.

A woman did not have standing to seek visitation with the child adopted by her former same-sex partner during their relationship, the Tennessee Court of Appeals ruled in *In re Hayden C G-J*.[80] The partner lacked standing because she did not fit any definition of 'parent' under state law. The court reaffirmed its prior ruling in *In re Thompson*,[81] that women who have no biological or legal relationship with the children of their former lesbian partners lack standing to seek visitation. The court noted that this principle was accepted by the legislature and settled because, since the ruling in *Thompson*, '[t]hirteen legislative sessions have come and gone with no change as to this aspect of the law'.[82]

In *Moix v Moix*,[83] the Arkansas Supreme Court, perhaps seeking to appear to be progressive, and with three justices strongly dissenting, reversed and remanded a lower court ruling that granted the non-custodial father's motion to increase his visitation with a minor child, but, citing the public policy against romantic cohabitation, prohibited his long-term, same-sex domestic partner from being present during any overnight visitation with the child. The majority found that, in the absence of a finding of harm to the child, the lower court erred in ruling that such a provision was mandatory. The court confirmed that the best interest of the child standard governs whether an unmarried parent's

77 Ibid at 1127.
78 736 F3d 1173 (9th Cir 2013).
79 Civil Action No 13-11106 FDS 2013 WL 6093782 (D Mass 18 November 2013).
80 2013 WL 6040348 (Tenn Ct App 2013).
81 11 SW3d 913 (Tenn Ct App 1999).
82 Ibid at *4.
83 2013 Ark 478, 2013 WL 6118520 (2013).

visitation order should contain a provision prohibiting the parent from cohabiting with a partner during the child's overnight stays. However, the state's public policy against a parent's romantic extramarital cohabitation in post-dissolution child custody and visitation matters did not state a blanket rule. The majority declared:[84]

> 'In the present case, the circuit court found from the evidence presented that appellant and his partner are in a long-term, committed romantic relationship and that "Mr. Cornelius poses no threat to the health, safety, or welfare of the minor child." The court further found that, "[o]ther than the prohibition of unmarried cohabitation with a romantic partner in the presence of the minor child, there are no other factors that would militate against overnight visitation." However, because the circuit court also stated that the mandatory application of our public policy against unmarried cohabitation required it to include a non-cohabitation provision, it made no finding on whether such a provision was in the best interest of R.M. Therefore, we reverse and remand for the circuit court to make this determination.'

In *In re NC*,[85] a grandmother living in Wyoming took in her two granddaughters who had been living in Texas with her daughter, their mother, and where they had been abused by their mother's boyfriend. The grandmother sought judicial assistance to protect them from the mother's boyfriend who had bitten the girls. The mother reconciled with the boyfriend in Texas. The Wyoming state child protection officials filed a juvenile neglect petition in the state court and gave notice to the mother. The mother's attorney informed the court that a termination of parental rights case has already been filed in Texas. The district court proceeded with the juvenile petition, holding that it had jurisdiction in Wyoming. After the district court found the mother to be negligent and the boyfriend abusive, the mother challenged the district court's jurisdiction. The court then awarded permanent custody to the grandmother. On appeal, the Wyoming Supreme Court held the district court erred in not following the Uniform Child Custody Jurisdiction and Enforcement Act (UCCJEA). Under the Act, Texas was the proper state to exercise jurisdiction because it was the children's home state and Texas had not deferred to the Wyoming court's jurisdiction. While the child abuse was sufficient to allow the Wyoming court to exercise emergency jurisdiction, the trial court had erred in exceeding the exigencies of the emergency. It lacked jurisdiction to award permanent custody.

VIII CONCLUSION

The cases reviewed above illustrate that conventional family forms and relationships are being pressed upon and, to some extent, reshaped by a wide variety and growing number of non-traditional family and quasi-family relationships in the United States. And as these 2013 cases also illustrate, many

---

84 Ibid at *7.
85 294 P3d 866 (Wyo 2013).

of those alternative family forms appear to be less stable, less-enduring, and more dysfunctional than traditional husband–father or parent–child family relations.

Of course, courts exist to deal with less-than-ideal relationships. They exist because human relationship problems of all forms and varieties exist and those problems must be resolved. Generally they are best resolved in legal proceedings (rather than, for example, self-help, or might-make-right actions, or parochial community dynamics). Thus, it appears that for the foreseeable future, American courts will have more, and more varied, opportunities to address disputes arising out of new forms of family and quasi-family relationships.

The unanswered and ultimate question is to what extent legal recognition of such alternative-to-traditional-family relationships, and inclusion of them within family forms dealt with by family courts, will detrimentally alter traditional husband–wife and parent–child relationships, rights and family responsibilities. It is not unreasonable to ask how much deviation from traditional family structures, relations and conduct American family law can accommodate before the core purposes of family law – to protect and promote the kinds of relationships that experience, history, and research have shown provide the best environment for nurturing families and for strengthening and supporting societies – are irreparably damaged? Or will those who make, interpret and administer American family laws begin to resist and curb the current trend toward disintegrative integration into 'family law' (unbounded expansion of what constitutes a 'family' relationship treated as such in the law), which may undermine the purposes of the family and of legal protection for family relationships? To find the answer to those questions we must look ahead to 2014 and beyond.

ZIMBABWE

THE CONSTITUTION OF ZIMBABWE 2013 – A CONSTITUTIONAL CURATE'S EGG

F Banda[*]

Résumé

La Constitution de 2013 est l'événement récent le plus important dans le droit zimbabwéen. Comme la loi suprême, ses dispositions auront un impactsignificatif, si ce n'est en pratique, au moins sur l'application du droit de la famille par les tribunaux. Les garanties constitutionnelles d'égalité et de non-discrimination, notamment entre les sexes etau sein du couple, vont défier les lois discriminatoires qui existent à l'égard des femmes. Les coutumes et la culture sont assujetties à la non-discrimination et à l'égalité, ce qui est un grand pas vers la fin des discriminations qui ontnotamment conduit au refus d'accorder aux femmes les mêmes droits successoraux que les hommes. La révision des lois sur la citoyenneté et l'élimination de la discrimination envers les femmes mariées sont également bienvenues. On regrettera, en revanche, que la visionstrictement hétérosexuelle de la famille et du mariage dans la Constitution, conduise à nier les droits des personnes homosexuelles.

I INTRODUCTION

After the rejection of one state-approved draft Constitution in 2000 led to widespread human rights violations, Zimbabweans were circumspect about rejecting the next draft that was put before them in a referendum held in 2013.[1] The new Constitution, promulgated in May 2013, replaced the much amended 1979 Constitution.[2] It draws heavily on constitutions from other African countries, which, in turn, relied for their drafting on international and regional human rights treaties.[3] This chapter examines the new Constitution focusing on provisions covering discrimination and family including the rights of children.

---

* Fareda Banda, Professor of Law, School of Oriental and African Studies, University of London.

1 International Bar Association *Report of Zimbabwe Mission 2001* (IBA, 2001) 13.

2 Constitution of Zimbabwe Amendment (No 20) Act 2013.

3 One can see inspiration from the 2010 Kenyan Constitution, the 1996 South African Constitution and the 1995 Ugandan Constitution amongst others. Constitution of Kenya, 2010; Constitution of the Republic of South Africa Act 108 of 1996; Constitution of Uganda of 22 September 1995.

II CONSTITUTION

The original 1979 Constitution had been handed down as part of the post-colonial political settlement. The focus was on establishing peace and protecting the interests of minorities while securing confidence for inward investment following a civil war. With this in mind, the two key provisions were those entrenching a 20% parliamentary seat allocation for the former minority rulers, and outlawing nationalisation of land by providing that the state could only acquire land on a willing seller–willing buyer basis. Issues pertaining to family law were neglected. Indeed taking its cue from the indirect rule era, the Constitution ring-fenced customary law from constitutional scrutiny. The situation for African women was exacerbated by the omission of sex from the listed prohibited grounds of discrimination. The outcome of this customary protection and sex exemption was gender-based discrimination, best exemplified by the case of *Magaya v Magaya*[4] which privileged the inheritance rights of brothers over those of a sister who had actually undertaken the day-to-day care of her deceased father. While sex had eventually been added to the Constitution as a prohibited ground, the ring-fencing of customary law had continued leading the United Nations Committee on the Elimination of all Forms of Discrimination to recommend repeal of the provision.[5]

The millennium did not start well for Zimbabwe. There was widespread political violence. As a compromise measure following a contested election, the three opposing political parties entered into a Global Political Agreement (GPA) which was signed on 15 September 2008. A part of this Agreement was the requirement that a new constitution be drafted to replace the 19 times amended 1979 Constitution. Article VI of the GPA set out a broad framework to be followed in the Constitution-making process. A Parliamentary Constitution Select Committee (COPAC) comprising members from all three political parties was appointed. The Committee was assisted by three draftspersons and 17 technical experts. 17 themes were identified for coverage in the new Constitution. These themes, which included citizenship, human rights including those of women, youth and the disabled and issues of gender, were to be fleshed out by Thematic Committees. Civil society took an active interest in the constitutional drafting process and participated extensively in the Thematic Committees. Stakeholder meetings were held with interested members of the public and there was widespread publicity given to the constitution drafting process.[6] A referendum was held in 2013 resulting in a resounding vote approving the draft Constitution.

In terms of family law and the rights of women, the 2013 Constitution has much to recommend it. However, there are still contentious provisions, not least those relating to land and the state's ability to compulsorily acquire land paying compensation only for 'improvements'. Britain, the former colonial

---

4 *Magaya v Magaya* 1999 (1) ZLR 100.

5 CEDAW CO Zimbabwe CEDAW/C/ZWE/CO/2-5 (2012) paras 13 and 14(a). (The Committee is also called CEDAW or the Women's Committee.)

6 COPAC *Milestones Towards a New Constitution in Zimbabwe* (COPAC, 2012).

power, is encouraged to pay compensation for land.[7] Appeals are not permitted. The usurpation of judicial review, carried forth from previous constitutions, is also to be regretted.[8] The justification given is the righting of historical wrongs of unlawful colonial dispossession of land. However, one cannot right an injustice by perpetrating another. Failure to guarantee the protection of *all* human rights, including to the peaceful enjoyment of property properly and lawfully acquired, undermines the enjoyment of even those human rights that are guaranteed without reservation. This chapter will now move to focus on sex, gender and family.

Part one of the Constitution provides that there is a duty on the part of both the state and non-state actors to respect the Constitution, thus reinforcing the vertical and horizontal application of all the rights and freedoms enshrined.[9] This is particularly important because many of the violations of rights in family law are as a result of private actors rather than state breach. However, it is of course also true to say that the failure of a state to have clear legislation guaranteeing the compatibility of family law and human rights principles has been a source of many problems that have arisen in Zimbabwe and indeed globally.[10] Part one of the Constitution also provides that the interpretation of the Constitution must take account of all the international treaties and conventions to which Zimbabwe is a state party.[11] Zimbabwe operates on the dualist model requiring domestic incorporation of international treaties signed before they can take force. However, the inclusion of this provision in the Constitution makes it clear that there is a commitment to principles of equality found in international and regional human rights documents.

The principles of equality and non-discrimination are enshrined in part two of the Constitution which lays out a range of rights that are protected, while part three provides an elaboration of some of those rights. Section 56 guarantees equal protection and benefits of the law to all persons. Echoing the Covenant on Economic, Social and Cultural Rights, equality between the sexes is reinforced in s 56(2).[12] The list of prohibited grounds of discrimination is

---

7 Constitution 2013, s 72.

8 It was successfully challenged before the Southern Africa Development Community Tribunal (SADCT) Tribunal in the case of *Mike Campbell (Pvt) Ltd and Others v Republic of Zimbabwe* (2/2007) [2008] SADCT 2 (28 November 2008). After a protest from the Zimbabwean government the Tribunal was held to have been improperly constituted. G Naldi '*Mike Campbell (Pvt) Ltd et al v The Republic of Zimbabwe*: Zimbabwe's Land Reform Programme Held in Breach of the SADC Treaty' (2009) 53(2) Journal of African Law 305.

9 Constitution 2013, s 45. This provision meets the recommendations made by the CEDAW Committee to the Zimbabwean Government in its concluding observations. See CEDAW CO Zimbabwe CEDAW/C/ZWE/CO/2-5 (2012) para 14(b).

10 See M Freeman 'Article 16' in M Freeman, C Chinkin and B Rudolph *The UN Convention on the Elimination of all Forms of Discrimination: A Commentary* (Oxford University Press, 2012) 409; CEDAW General Recommendation 21 on Equality in Marriage and Family Relations, UN Doc HRI/GEN/1/Rev.9 (Vol II).

11 Constitution 2013, s 46(c).

12 International Covenant on Economic, Social and Cultural Rights, 1966, 993 UNTS 3, art 3. See also CESCR General Comment 16 on 'Article 3: the Equal Rights of men and women to the enjoyment of economic, social and cultural rights' in UN Doc E/C.12/2005/3, 13 May 2005

lengthy and includes both sex and gender as well as the new grounds of custom, culture, marital status, pregnancy or whether a person is born in or out of wedlock.[13] This is the most far-reaching provision introduced into the new Constitution. Specifically, it is important that there is not any special provision made for the exemption of customary law from scrutiny where discrimination is alleged. The inclusion of custom and culture as grounds on which one cannot discriminate raise interesting questions about how contestations between groups each claiming prohibited grounds discrimination will be resolved. Can a group that does not recognise the right of women to inherit equally with male relatives claim custom and culture as protective shields from charges of discrimination on grounds of sex and gender? The answer would seem to tilt towards the privileging of sex and gender. This is in part because s 56(5) proscribes unfair discrimination which requires any claim for exemption to prove that it is 'fair, reasonable, and justifiable in a democratic society based on openness, justice, human dignity, equality and freedom'. Clearly denying a group of people the right to inherit simply because of their sex is irrational and violates women's dignity. This interpretation finds support in s 80 on the rights of women. Section 80(3) provides that:

> 'All laws, customs, traditions and cultural practices that infringe the rights of women conferred by this Constitution are void to the extent of the infringement.'

The right of all persons to have their human dignity in both public and private life is guaranteed in s 51. The provision on women's dignity in art 3 of the African Protocol on Women's Rights 2003 is reiterated in section 80(1). Dignity and equality are interlinked, not least in s 16(1) of the Constitution. The right to dignity is, with the rights to life and to be free from torture and to be protected from slavery, regarded as non-derogable, including in times of emergency.[14]

Rights, including those pertaining to family law issues are covered in part two of chapter four on the declaration of rights, with some provisions being further elaborated in part three. Marriage is one example of double scrutiny being dealt with in s 26 (part two) and s 78 (part three) of the Constitution.

III MARRIAGE

In keeping with standard human rights provisions on family, ss 26(a) and 78(2) of the Constitution require consent of the parties to marriage noting that a person cannot be compelled to marry against their will.[15] Reflecting art 16(1)(c) of CEDAW, s 26 also calls for there to be 'equality of rights and obligations of

---

and CESCR General Comment 20 on 'Non-discrimination in economic, social and cultural rights (art.2 para.2)' UN Doc E/C.12/GC/20, 2 July 2009.

13 Constitution 2013, s 56(3).

14 Constitution 2013, s 86(3)(b).

15 International Covenant on Civil and Political Rights, 1966, 999 UNTS 171, (ICCPR) art 23; CEDAW, art 16(1)(b).

spouses during the marriage and at its dissolution'. This is particularly important when one considers gendered inequalities of bargaining power between spouses. The Constitution also provides for 'the necessary protection of the spouse and any children' when the marriage is ended by either death or divorce. What are the spouse and children being protected from? Is it the property-grabbing that occurs when a man dies and his relatives come and take all of the family property? Is it the inequitable distribution of marital property on divorce which undervalues the contribution made by the wife notwithstanding that, in civil marriages, the Matrimonial Causes Act calls for consideration to be given to domestic contribution?[16]

Although short, s 78 on marriage throws up many issues. It starts by noting that any person over 18 can marry.[17] This is in keeping with art 21 of the African Charter on the Rights and Welfare of the Child and art 6(b) of the African Protocol on Women's Rights, both of which also set 18 as the minimum age for marriage.[18] The aim is to prevent early and child marriage with the objective of keeping children, especially girls, in school for longer. It also reinforces the rights of the child to be 'protected from economic and sexual exploitation' and to have their interests treated as paramount.[19] While laudable, the challenge remaining is enforcement and also transforming cultural attitudes. In customary law it was the attainment of puberty and not chronological age that was used as the standard to determine whether a girl or woman was deemed to be 'ready for marriage'. The Marriage Act which governed civil marriage provided 16 as the minimum age.[20] Given Zimbabwe's parlous economic situation, there are few opportunities for good quality education or paid employment opportunities making early marriage, especially for women, the only viable career option. Parents are loath to keep unmarried daughters for fear that they will be 'spoiled' (impregnated) outside marriage, reducing the bridewealth that a family can seek from a prospective bridegroom. Indeed if the man decides to deny responsibility it is entirely possible that the woman's parents will be faced with an extra mouth to feed. There is no provision for state assistance or welfare in Zimbabwe. The problem of early and child marriage is not unique to Zimbabwe.[21] At least three states have entered reservations to the African Protocol provision setting 18 as the minimum age. Moreover, the data show that early and child marriages especially involving girls are prevalent in parts of the continent. Using data

---

16 Matrimonial Causes Act (Cap 5:13), s 7(3)(e).

17 Constitution 2013, s 78(a).

18 African Charter on the Rights and Welfare of the Child, 1990 OAU CAB/LEG/24.9/49, art 21(2). See also Convention on the Elimination of all Forms of Discrimination, 1979, 1249 UNTS 13, art 16(2). CRC General Comment No.4 on 'Adolescent health and development in the context of the Convention on the Rights of the Child' CRC/GC/2003/4, 1 July 2003.

19 Constitution 2013, s 81(1)(e) and (2).

20 Marriage Act (Cap 5:11).

21 See UNICEF 'Child Protection from Violence, exploitation and abuse: Child Marriage' updated 21 December 2012 at: www.unicef.org/protection/57929_58008.html (accessed 12 April 2014).

generated by UNICEF, the International Centre for Research on Women shows that 15 out of the 20 countries with the highest prevalence of marriage before the age of 18 are African.[22]

Section 78(1) reinforces s 26(b) outlawing the pledging into marriage of girls.[23] The pledging issue is linked to a cultural practice of the family of a person who has killed another, 'giving' a (virgin) daughter to the family of the murder victim, as compensation for the loss of a family member. The practice is known as *kuripa ngozi*. The daughter becomes a wife to the new family and is expected to bear at least one child to replace the deceased. It has been illegal for many years, but continues, albeit in ever-decreasing numbers. Clearly there are both consent and child rights issues.[24] Equally problematic, but also declining, is the practice of *kuzvarira* which involves a daughter being given to the husband of a sister or another family member who has not been able to have children, for the purpose of giving birth on their behalf.[25]

In keeping with state-sponsored homophobia, s 78(3) of the Constitution provides: 'Persons of the same sex are prohibited from marrying each other.' Given that Zimbabwe has, like many other African states, retained colonial laws banning same-sex relations, this provision is not altogether surprising. However, there is a particular virulence to the hatred shown to people who manifest same-sex orientation. In large part, this is as a direct result of frequent, unedifying and hateful rhetoric spewed out by the country's President at every, and even the most inopportune moments (funeral orations). It is also the result of an intolerant, judgmental strain of Christian teaching that has, as in many other states, been exacerbated by foreign preachers. Nevertheless, it remains worth noting that the status of lesbian and gay people was debated during the constitutional drafting process. This is progress of sorts. The idea of including sexual orientation as a prohibited ground for discrimination following the example set by South Africa in its Constitution was mooted.[26] However, even the 'liberal, human rights keen' opposition leader and Prime Minister in a coalition government was said to be reluctant to recognise the inclusion of the rights of same-sex people in the Constitution.[27] It is ironic that the opposition did not show any appetite to stand up for the rights of same-sex couples, when

---

22 International Centre for Research on Women 'Child Marriage Facts and Figures' (2013) at www.icrw.org/child-marriage-facts-and-figures.

23 See also CEDAW, art 16(2).

24 The Committee on the Rights of the Child identified this practice as an area of concern in its concluding observations to the Zimbabwean report in 1996. CRC CO Zimbabwe CRC/C15.Add.55 (1996) para 13.

25 R Hanzi *Sexual abuse and exploitation of the girl child through cultural practices in Zimbabwe: a human rights perspective*, unpublished thesis (LLM (Human Rights and Democratisation in Africa)) University of Pretoria, 2006. Available at: http://repository.up.ac.za/handle/2263/1214.

26 Constitution of the Republic of South Africa 108 of 1996.

27 Pink News 'Zimbabwean Prime Minister Morgan Tsvangirai accused of hate speech by gay rights groups' at: www.pinknews.co.uk/2013/03/08/zimbabwean-pm-morgan-tsvangirai-accused-of-hate-speech-by-gay-rights-group, 8 March 2013. See also, BBC News 'Zimbabwe's PM Morgan Tsvangirai in gay rights U-turn' at: www.bbc.co.uk/news/world-africa-15431142, 24 October 2011.

one considers the mutual experience of state harassment and victimisation of the two groups. It is of course possible that a constitutional challenge on grounds of gender-based discrimination can still be brought by those who feel unfairly treated because of their sexual or gender identity. The success or failure of such an action will be dependent on how the courts choose to construct 'gender'. There is an unfortunate tendency to conflate sex and gender whereby the two terms are used interchangeably and as synonyms. Preferable is a view of gender that moves beyond sex binaries to take on board the pluralities of human sexuality and gender identity.[28]

The Constitution is silent about the effect of legal pluralism on family law. Specifically, the marriage provisions are silent on the issue of polygyny which is recognised as forming part of customary law. What does it mean for men and women to have the same rights to enter marriage and within marriage when men can enter into marriage with more than one wife? Is polygyny a breach of equality which should be abolished as recommended by the CEDAW to the Zimbabwean Government? Is the abolition of polygyny an abstract assertion of formal equality which ignores the socio-economic context of women's inequality?[29] Similarly, is the Committee's recommendation that *lobolo* (bridewealth) be prohibited as unrealistic in a society in which it is entrenched and considered a part of the marital contract?[30] Would, as the CEDAW asserts, the promulgation of a unified family code lead to the elimination of discrimination against women?[31] Does unity mean uniformity, or, does respect for cultural and religious difference necessitate the recognition of different family forms and norms? Can marital pluralism continue to exist with the proviso that equality is to be the governing foundation of all marriage and family laws?

IV PROTECTION FROM VIOLENCE

In keeping with international trends to pass legislation on violence against women in the domestic sphere, the Zimbabwe Government enacted a comprehensive Domestic Violence Act 2006 which sits alongside the Sexual

---

28 F Banda 'Gender Discrimination and the Right to Family Life' in J Eekelaar and R George (eds) *Routledge Handbook of Family law and Policy* (Routledge, 2014) 297. See also Report of the Special Rapporteur on the promotion and protection of human rights and fundamental freedoms while countering terrorism, UN Doc A/64/211, 3 August 2009, paras 20–22.

29 Contrast the Protocol to the African Charter on Human and Peoples' Rights on the Rights of Women, art 6(c) which notes a preference for monogamy, but acknowledges the existence of polygyny and requires the promotion of the rights of women in these marriages.

30 See, for example, the unsuccessful constitutional challenge on bridewealth alleging sex and gender discrimination in the Ugandan case of *Mifumi(U) Ltd & 12 Others v Attorney General, Kenneth Kakuru* [2010] UGCC 2. Discussed in JD Mujuzi 'Bride Wealth (Price) and Women's Marriage – Related Rights in Uganda: A Historical Constitutional Perspective and Current Developments'(2010) 24 (3) Int J Law Policy Family 414. The majority was not persuaded.

31 CEDAW Zimbabwe CEDAW/C/ZWE/CO/2-5 (2012) paras 21, 37, 38.

Offences Act 2003 which outlawed marital rape.[32] While acknowledging these developments, the CEDAW urged the Zimbabwean Government to take a due diligence approach ensuring that victims had redress and protection and that perpetrators were prosecuted and punished. Further, the state was urged to ensure that judges, prosecutors and police received training to facilitate proper implementation of the Act. The Committee also urged a roll out and proper funding of domestic violence shelters particularly in the rural areas. The Committee recommended that the state should encourage women to report violence as a way of de-stigmatising it. Moreover, the state was urged to address violence perpetrated against lesbian, bisexual and transgender women by enacting legislation to protect this group and by running sensitisation campaigns aimed at changing public attitudes.[33] The government was given 2 years to submit a follow-up report to the Committee on action taken in light of recommendations made.[34]

One action that the Zimbabwean Government can report having undertaken is the inclusion of the prohibition of violence in the new Constitution. Section 52 on personal security provides that everyone has a right to have their dignity respected and that this includes the right to 'freedom from all forms of violence from public or private sources'.[35] The challenge, as identified by UNICEF, is in attitudinal change. Both men and women appear to think that there are circumstances where a husband is justified in beating his wife. These include the failure of the woman to fulfil her gender ascribed roles including arguing, refusing sex, neglecting the children or going out without permission.[36] The economic situation leading to high unemployment has no doubt exacerbated the problem of domestic violence. Although Victim Friendly Police Units have been set up, they also suffer from resource shortages.

In line with developments in international human rights law, there is greater understanding of the importance of focusing on specific groups experiencing discrimination because of a protected characteristic. The Zimbabwean Constitution includes the elderly (defined as over the age of 70), persons with disabilities and children.[37] For all three groups, the focus is on the provision of socio-economic assistance in order to facilitate the (progressive) realisation of their rights.[38] The Constitution requires the state to put in place measures to enable persons with disabilities to 'live with their families'.[39] As a right to

---

32 The Domestic Violence Act was discussed by F Banda'Recent Developments in Zimbabwe' in B Atkin (ed) *International Survey of Family Law, 2007 Edition* (Jordans Publishing Ltd, 2007) 333–351.

33 CEDAW CO Zimbabwe CEDAW/C/ZWE/CO/2-5 (2012) paras 23 and 24.

34 Ibid para.44.

35 Constitution 2013, s 52(a).

36 UNICEF, *A Situation Analysis on the Status of Women's and Children's Rights in Zimbabwe, 2005–2010: A Call for Reducing Disparities and Improving Equity* (UNICEF, 2010) 22.

37 Constitution 2013, ss 21 and 82 (elderly), ss 22 and 83 (persons with disabilities), ss 19 and 81 (children).

38 Constitution 2013, s 19(2); s 21(2); s 22(2).

39 Constitution 2013, s 83(b). Cf UN Convention on the Rights of Persons with Disabilities, 2006 United Nations, *Treaty Series*, vol 2515, 3.

housing and an enforceable guarantee of employment is not included within the package of rights, it is difficult to see how this right can be realised. Similarly, access to justice for redress is not included. The many negative stories about the mis-direction of state funds by the government indicate that it is failing to meet its minimum core obligations to take targeted, concrete steps to ensure the realisation of the rights guaranteed within the Constitution.[40]

V CHILDREN

In keeping with its ratification of the African Charter on the Rights and Welfare of the Child, the Zimbabwean constitution seeks to place the interests of the child, as a paramount consideration.[41] While retaining the standard 18 as the age at which childhood ends, it is not clear what the position is on when a child's life begins. The provision on the right to life calls for an Act of Parliament 'to protect the rights of the unborn child', thus implying that life begins at conception. However, there is scope for a different reading because it goes on to say, 'the Act must provide that pregnancy may be terminated only in accordance with that law'.[42] Does this mean that abortion is still permissible under certain conditions? The Termination of Pregnancy Act 1977 which is still in force permits it when the life of the woman is endangered, the child may suffer a permanent physical or mental defect, or the foetus was conceived as a result of rape or incest.[43] These exemptions are in keeping with art 14(2)(i) of the African Protocol on the Rights of Women in Africa which Zimbabwe has ratified without reservations.[44] A discussion of the legality of abortion services is in many ways rhetorical as evidence shows that a collapsing health system and the complex procedure for obtaining abortion has made it a paper entitlement. The reality is a high rate of illegal abortion particularly within the 15–24 year age group.[45]

Section 81(1)(a) of the Constitution provides that children have the right to equal treatment before the law which includes the right to be heard. Again, the child's right to express their opinions subject to evolving capacity is enshrined in both the CRC and the ACRWC.[46] Just as both the CRC and the ACRWC make provision for parental guidance and reinforce the child's responsibility to

---

40 Africa Confidential 'ZANU-PF's Gem of a Campaign' (2012) 53(2) *Africa Confidential*, 16 November 2012. See also CESCR General Comment 3, The Nature of States Parties Obligations, UN Doc E/1991/23.

41 Constitution 2013, ss 81(2) and 19(1). African Charter on the Rights and Welfare of the Child, CAB/LEG/24.9/49 (1990), art 4. See also United Nations Convention on the Rights of the Child, A/RES/44/25 (1989, art 3.

42 Constitution 2013, s 48(3).

43 Termination of Pregnancy Act (Cap 15:10).

44 Protocol to the African Charter on Human and Peoples' Rights on the Rights of Women, 200, OAU AHG/Res.240.

45 IRIN, 'Zimbabwe: Abortion figures underscore need for more reproductive health education' 30 March 2005 available at: www.irinnews.org/report/53659/zimbabwe-abortion-figures-underscore-need-for-more-reproductive-health-education.

46 CRC 1989, art 12; ACRWC 1990, arts 7 and 9.

respect her parents, so too the Constitution makes the rights of a minor to enjoy freedom of conscience, subject to parental control with parents having the right 'to determine, in accordance with their beliefs, the moral and religious upbringing of their children provided they do not prejudice the rights to which their children are entitled under this Constitution'.[47] Those entitlements are elaborated in ss 19 and 81 and include the child's right to family or parental care or to appropriate care when taken from the family environment, the right to be protected from 'economic and sexual exploitation, from child labour and from maltreatment, neglect or any form of abuse'.[48] The child is also entitled to health care, education, food and shelter.[49] Some practical issues arise with respect to the enjoyment by children of their rights.[50] If, as both human rights and the Constitution provide, children do have the right to express their views, why should the Constitution seek to prevent them from determining their own religious views, including making a decision to renounce or not practise the faith of their parents? Religion has been mis-used to deny children their voice, and for girl children, to compel them to enter into early and forced marriage. In Zimbabwe sects such as the Apostolic Faith require early marriage to ensure purity. This is clearly a breach of the rights of the girl child. The situation is exacerbated by the fact that the Customary Marriages Act does not specify a minimum age for marriage.[51] Moreover, as UNICEF notes, the economic crisis has resulted in a rolling back of state provision for children. The ongoing impact of the HIV crisis, which has resulted in many children being orphaned, coupled with the poor economy has resulted in children being taken on by relatives who may have very little to offer.[52] Where relatives are unable to cope, the children can find themselves in child-headed households lacking legal capacity and agency to advocate for themselves with state agencies.[53] UNICEF notes:[54]

> 'As the coping strategies of families and communities have become increasingly taxed, children have become more and more vulnerable to violence, exploitation and abuse in schools, communities, across borders and within their own homes with little recourse to justice services.'

The antipathy of the Zimbabwean Government to inter-country adoption means this avenue is closed leaving the Committee on the Rights of the Child to

---

47 CRC 1989, arts 5 and 29(c); ACRWC 1990, arts 20 and 31. Constitution 2013, s 60(3).

48 Constitution 2013, s 81(1)(d) and (e); s 19(2)(a)–(d), (3)(a) and (b).

49 Constitution 2013, s 81(1)(f).

50 In its concluding observations to the 1996 report submitted by Zimbabwe, the CRC expressed concern that: 'insufficient attention has been paid to the principle of the best interests of the child both in legislation and practice, as well as to the respect for the views of the child in school, social and family life. In this regard, it is noted that, as recognized by the State party, the civil rights and freedoms of the child are to be exercised subject to parental consent or discipline, thus raising doubts as to the compatibility of this practice with the Convention, notably articles 5 and 12.' CRC CO Zimbabwe CRC/C/15.Add.55 (1996) para 16. See also para 30.

51 Customary Marriages Act (Cap 5:07).

52 UNICEF (2010), above n 36, 25.

53 CRC CO Zimbabwe CRC/C/15.Add. 55 (1996) para 17.

54 UNICEF (2010) x, 25.

recommend that Zimbabwe consider ratifying the Hague Convention for the Protection of Children and Cooperation in respect of Inter-Country Adoption of 1993.[55] Even when parents and guardians are alive, they are unable to provide for their children resulting in many children entering institutional care or worse, going on the streets.

Furthermore, UNICEF notes that, compared to neighbouring countries, Zimbabwe's social welfare and protection services are under-resourced leaving vulnerable children without the requisite protection.[56] This is clearly a breach of the state's constitutionally enshrined duty to ensure that children who are not living with their families, and indeed those who are, receive appropriate care. Faith organisations end up accommodating many children who do not have parents or family able to look after them. The setting up of Victim Friendly Courts to work alongside Victim Friendly Police Units, both with well-trained staff, is welcome, but, again, UNICEF identifies resource shortage as an issue of concern.[57] Additionally, the organisation identifies the non-incorporation of the CRC into national law as an area of concern. More than that, the failure of the Zimbabwean Government to submit regular and timely reports to the CRC indicates a lack of commitment to upholding the rights of the children of Zimbabwe. It is again disappointing that the government has misdirected the use of resources meaning that children's rights to education, health, shelter and protection are neglected.

A major change wrought by the 2013 Constitution has been an overhaul of the citizenship rules removing the sex discrimination embedded in the old law. Chapter three of the Constitution focuses on citizenship. There are three ways of acquiring citizenship: birth, descent or registration.[58] To become a citizen by birth, one needs to have a parent who is a citizen or a grandparent who is a citizen by birth or descent.[59] If born outside the country, then the child will acquire citizenship if either of their parents was a Zimbabwean citizen and ordinarily resident or working for the state or an international organisation.[60] The innovation is that the Constitution does not distinguish between mothers and fathers. Section 81 on children's rights provides that a child who is born in Zimbabwe, or who is born outside Zimbabwe and is a Zimbabwean citizen by descent, is entitled to the 'prompt provision of a birth certificate'.[61]

A major change is art 40 providing that neither marriage nor divorce should result in the loss of citizenship. While this is in keeping with many international provisions including the UN Convention on the Nationality of Married Women 1957, art 9(1) of CEDAW and art 6(g) of the African Protocol on Women's

55 CRC CO Zimbabwe CRC/C/15. Add.55 (1996) para 29.
56 UNICEF (2010) 24.
57 UNICEF (2010) 24 and 25.
58 Constitution 2013, s 35(1).
59 Constitution 2013, s 36(1)(a) and (b).
60 Constitution 2013, s 36(2).
61 Constitution 2013, s 81(1)(c)(i) and (ii).

Rights,[62] it marks a sea change for Zimbabwe. Previously a woman would lose her citizenship if she married a foreigner. Any children born within the marriage would also be barred from acquiring Zimbabwean citizenship by descent. Even those born in Zimbabwe would still be excluded from citizenship. By way of contrast, the foreign wife of a Zimbabwean citizen could acquire citizenship by marriage and their children would automatically acquire Zimbabwean citizenship, by descent if born outside the country and by birth if within. Several constitutional challenges were brought highlighting the discriminatory impact of the previous citizenship arrangements. Women's rights to family life and freedom of movement were negatively impacted because they could not bring their husbands to live with them in Zimbabwe. There was no rational reason for distinguishing between children born to Zimbabwean mothers and those born to Zimbabwean fathers. Indeed, the discrimination against married women made marriage unattractive and encouraged the birth of children outside marriage as a means to evade the irrational citizenship laws.[63]

As a child born in Zimbabwe of a Zimbabwean mother and Malawian father, I can attest to the denial of my rights to citizenship by both birth and descent. Applying for what would have been my third Zimbabwean passport in 2004, I was required first to acquire Zimbabwean citizenship by registration and forced to renounce the Malawian citizenship that I had never taken out. Citizenship by registration has been retained for those who do not fit into the birth or descent categories, or who, like me, were living outside the country when the 2013 Constitution was promulgated. This is because s 43 provides for the restoration of citizenship to those people who had lost it (because they could not prove a Zimbabwean male link). It now allows anyone whose parent is, or was, a citizen of the Southern African Development Community at its inception in 1992 to claim Zimbabwean citizenship, *provided* they were resident in the country on the date of promulgation.[64] Not being so resident, I am still not able to claim citizenship by birth or descent. Ironically, my two daughters who were neither born nor have ever lived in Zimbabwe and who have a foreign Scottish father will be allowed to acquire citizenship by descent both because 'either their parent or grandparent was a Zimbabwean citizen by birth or descent' (so my mother), or if 'either of their parents was a Zimbabwean citizen by registration' (me). All that is required is that I register their births in Zimbabwe.[65]

Section 38 lists the categories of persons entitled to apply to be registered as citizens. This includes anyone who has been married to a Zimbabwean citizen for 5 years. While the sex neutral drafting is welcome, the provisions on marriage are clearly aimed at those in heterosexual marriages. This heteronormativity leaves those in same-sex relationships without any protection. In the same way that heterosexual women's rights were previously

---

62 Convention on the Nationality of Married Women 1957, 309 UNTS 65.

63 See, for example, *Rattigan and Others v Chief Immigration Officer and Others* 1994 (2) ZLR 54 (SC); *Salem v Chief Immigration Officer* 1994(2) ZLR 287 (SC).

64 Constitution 2013, s 43(2)(a) and (b).

65 Constitution 2013, s 37(a) and (b).

violated, so too those who are in same-sex relationships, where one party is not a Zimbabwean citizen cannot enjoy their right to family life because their relationship is not and cannot legally be recognised.

A person who has lived lawfully in Zimbabwe for 10 years is entitled to apply for registration as a citizen. Finally, a child who is not Zimbabwean citizen but who has been adopted by a Zimbabwean citizen is entitled to citizenship by registration. This is a positive development. However, it calls into question the inter-country adoption ban currently in place. Also positive is the recognition that a person can adopt a child on their own rather than as part of a couple. Given the open borders with its neighbours, Zimbabwe has found itself hosting children whose parents are unknown. It is therefore a positive development that sees the granting of citizenship to a child found in Zimbabwe, who appears to be less than 15 years old and whose parents are unknown.[66]

VI CONCLUSION

The 2013 Constitution is the most significant development in Zimbabwean law. As the supreme law of the country, its provisions will have a significant impact on family law in the courts, if not in practice. Specifically, the constitutional guarantees of equality and non-discrimination including on grounds of sex, gender and marital status will do much to challenge laws that discriminate against women. The explicit specification that customs and culture made subject to the non-discrimination and equality provisions is a huge step ending as it does the historically legitimated discrimination which led to women being denied the same rights to inherit as male relatives. Also to be welcomed is the review of citizenship laws and the removal of discrimination, especially against married women. Problematic, and to be regretted, is the constitutional enshrining of a narrow heterosexist view of family and marriage which denies the existence of and rights of those of same-sex orientation.

---

[66] Constitution 2013, s 36(3).